S0-ADT-321

Paul Cassell

Pam Palmer

SAMS
Teach Yourself

Microsoft®
Access 2000

in 21 Days

SAMS

A Division of Macmillan Computer Publishing
201 West 103rd St., Indianapolis, Indiana, 46290 USA

Sams Teach Yourself Microsoft® Access 2000 in 21 Days

Copyright© 1999 by Sams Publishing

All rights reserved. No part of this book shall be reproduced, stored in a retrieval system, or transmitted by any means, electronic, mechanical, photocopying, recording, or otherwise, without written permission from the publisher. No patent liability is assumed with respect to the use of the information contained herein. Although every precaution has been taken in the preparation of this book, the publisher and author assume no responsibility for errors or omissions. Neither is any liability assumed for damages resulting from the use of the information contained herein.

International Standard Book Number: 0-672-31292-1

Library of Congress Catalog Card Number: 98-85913

Printed in the United States of America

First Printing: May 1999

01   00   4   3   2

Trademarks

All terms mentioned in this book that are known to be trademarks or service marks have been appropriately capitalized. Sams Publishing cannot attest to the accuracy of this information. Use of a term in this book should not be regarded as affecting the validity of any trademark or service mark.

Microsoft is a registered trademark of Microsoft Corporation.

Warning and Disclaimer

Every effort has been made to make this book as complete and as accurate as possible, but no warranty or fitness is implied. The information provided is on an "as is" basis. The authors and the publisher shall have neither liability nor responsibility to any person or entity with respect to any loss or damages arising from the information contained in this book or from the use of the CD-ROM or programs accompanying it.

EXECUTIVE EDITOR
Rosemarie Graham

ACQUISITIONS EDITOR
Rosemarie Graham

DEVELOPMENT EDITORS
Kitty Jarrett
Marla Reece-Hall

MANAGING EDITOR
Jodi Jensen

PROJECT EDITOR
Tonya Simpson

COPY EDITOR
Mike Henry

INDEXER
Mary Gammons

PROOFREADERS
Mona Brown
Betsy Deeter-Smith

TECHNICAL EDITOR
Dallas Releford

SOFTWARE DEVELOPMENT SPECIALIST
Andrea Duvall

TEAM COORDINATOR
Carol Ackerman

INTERIOR DESIGN
Gary Adair

COVER DESIGN
Karen Ruggles

LAYOUT TECHNICIANS
Ayanna Lacey
Heather Miller
Amy Parker

Overview

Contents

About the Authors

Paul Cassel started using computers by converting accounting systems to automated ones back in the mainframe days of yore. When minis such as the DEC PDP series made computing more accessible, he moved to that platform. His first PC database experience came in the early days of personal computing with dBASE II and the BASIC language on the first IBM PCs. His experience with Access goes back to the first version. He has been recognized by Microsoft with several MVPs for Access, Windows, and Visual Basic and by Borland (Inprise) as a TeamB member.

He has taught computers and computing concepts to students at the University of New Mexico. He has written over a dozen books, published hundreds of articles, and has his own hour-long weekly computer radio show, ComputerScene on the Air. His database consulting business is based in New Mexico and includes the Department of the Navy, University Hospital, University of New Mexico, New Mexico Tech, AMREP, Lovelace Health Systems, the New Mexico State Bar, the State of New Mexico Finance Division, the Zuni Nation, and the Jicarilla Apache Nation, plus many others, as his clientele.

He resides in New Mexico with his daughter, Tirilee.

Pamela Palmer is an independent consultant specializing in the development of applications using Visual Basic, Access, and Visual Basic for Applications. Pamela has more than 15 years' experience in the computer industry. She contributed to Que's *Using Visual Basic for Applications 5*, *Using Word 97*, *Using Excel 97*, *Using Project 98*, *Using Outlook 97*, and *Using Visual Basic 3*, as well as co-authoring two other books on Visual Basic 5 and 6. Although the majority of her time is spent developing applications, she divides the rest of her time between writing and editing and providing training to users and developers. She can be reached at ppalmer@compuserve.com.

Dedications

This book is dedicated to my daughter, Tirilee, who has shown both strength of character and patience well beyond her five years in allowing me the quiet time I needed to write it.

—Paul Cassel

This book is dedicated to my husband, David, and my children, Christopher and Katie, for being patient and supportive with the effort for this book. It is also dedicated to our new daughter, Deanna, who waited until the first draft was completed to arrive.

—Pam Palmer

Acknowledgments

All books are collaborative efforts, but this, my first Access book with a co-author from the planning stage onward, was more so than others were. It's also the best book I've been involved with writing. This is clearly due to the help of my co-author Pam Palmer, whose expertise and writing skills helped create a much better book than I could have done alone.

Marla Reece-Hall and Kitty Jarrett shared the development editing chores. A development editor is a creature unknown to most readers, but she's a very important part of the writing cycle. In short, the "DE" acts like a super reader catching the structural omissions and errors we authors commit. Because our goal for this book was to include every fundamental needed by a person to become an Access developer, Marla and Kitty's jobs were considerably more intense than for most books.

Thanks also goes to Dallas Releford for checking the technical accuracy of our material and Tonya Simpson and Mike Henry for allowing us to keep our author voices and correcting our grammatical mistakes.

I wish to thank the executives at Macmillan, especially Rosemarie Graham, whose collective support allowed us to write a truly comprehensive book. We, the authors, trashed deadlines, whined about everything, and demanded resources, and all the while the folks at Macmillan accepted this in the name of making this book as good as it can be.

Finally, I have to thank my daughter, Tirilee, who, at five years old, spent many hours quietly reading so Daddy could finish writing one chapter or another. If it weren't for her self-containment and patience, I couldn't have gotten this book written.

—Paul Cassel

I would like to thank Rosemarie Graham and Paul Cassel for the opportunity to work on this book. I would also like to thank the editing team for providing careful consideration and great feedback on the material.

—Pam Palmer

Tell Us What You Think!

As the reader of this book, *you* are our most important critic and commentator. We value your opinion and want to know what we're doing right, what we could do better, what areas you'd like to see us publish in, and any other words of wisdom you're willing to pass our way.

As an Associate Publisher for Sams Publishing, I welcome your comments. You can fax, email, or write me directly to let me know what you did or didn't like about this book—as well as what we can do to make our books stronger.

Please note that I cannot help you with technical problems related to the topic of this book, and that due to the high volume of mail I receive, I might not be able to reply to every message.

When you write, please be sure to include this book's title and author as well as your name and phone or fax number. I will carefully review your comments and share them with the authors and editors who worked on the book.

Fax: 317-581-4770

Email: `office_sams@mcp.com`

Mail: Michael Stephens
          Associate Publisher
          Sams Publishing
          201 West 103rd Street
          Indianapolis, IN 46290 USA

Introduction

Behind This Book

The book you hold is the culmination of many years' work. This is the sixth edition of a book originally written for Access 1.0 back in the early 1990s; however, it contains no previously published material. It is 100 percent written specifically for the needs of today's Access developer or user. It is also written specifically for Access 2000.

The previous editions play an important part in this book through reader feedback and writing experience. The original author, Paul Cassel, conceived of the idea that to learn a database product, a reader needn't be forced to construct a database to practice upon. To put it another way, the most important part of learning a database product such as Access is learning the fundamentals of how to do tasks—not the repetitive chores of data object construction.

For example, after a reader has learned to manipulate form objects, there is no need to require the reader to manipulate hundreds of those objects before moving on to the next fundamental. Other books published at the same time the previous editions of this book were published required just this—the reader had to laboriously construct some database object and then the book would explain what the reader had created.

The concept of fundamental learning without tedium was a success. Various individuals, institutions including large, medium, and small corporations, and colleges (as a text book) have adopted editions of this book. It has sold internationally in English and in other language translations, among which are German, Korean, Polish, French, and Portuguese.

This success in diverse settings created a substantial feedback loop allowing subsequent editions to build on what readers thought useful and to revise what they thought unclear or not as helpful. In a real way, the book you're holding, the sixth edition, even though 100 percent new, is the end result of many years writing and the aggregate synthesis of hundreds of thousands of readers' insights.

This edition adds Pam Palmer as a co-author while Paul Cassel remains on board. Pam's extensive experience as a database specialist in Access extends the experiential scope of this work. Together, Pam and Paul literally have a lifetime of experience working with databases, and both have extensive specific experience with not only Access, but also all Microsoft professional products. No other book on the market combines such experience and so many years of reader feedback.

Who Should Buy This Book

This book is about Microsoft Access 2000. It will teach you every principle you will need to succeed using Access as an individual, a corporate guru, or as an independent developer.

Access isn't a trivial product. To cover all the territory required, we have concentrated on the product and database concepts exclusively. This book, then, is for the person who is comfortable using a computer and has some familiarity with any modern Microsoft Windows product such as Windows 95, Windows 98, Windows NT 4 (any version), or Windows 2000 (any version).

You don't need specific database or Access experience to use this book successfully as a self-teaching tool or as a classroom text book. If you do have some familiarity with either Access or another database product, you'll likely be able to skim some of the topics. Due to the scope of this book, all but the most advanced Access 2000 developer will get value from this book. Even fairly accomplished working developers familiar with Access 2000 will benefit from the chapters on SQL, VBA, and developer concepts.

If you have a good knowledge of previous Access versions, this book will get you up to speed on the new areas in Access 2000. Make no mistake about it; this Access isn't just a re-release of a previous version with a new name stuck on. There are new features as well as new ways to do old things. Even advanced developers familiar with older Access versions will find much worthwhile material in this edition.

WEEK 1

At a Glance

The best way to learn how to use Access 2000 is sequentially. This first week, you'll start off by learning some theory of database application, and then move right on to actually using Access. The theoretical material can be somewhat difficult to fully understand at first. You shouldn't have any problems with Access, however. Don't be overly concerned if the theory at the beginning of the book isn't completely clear. For many people, the theory becomes clear after they learn the practice.

1

2

3

4

5

6

7

DAY 1

Understanding Relational Database Concepts

Before using a relational database such as Microsoft Access 2000, you must understand the concept behind the product. Although the wizards and other built-in aids will allow you to just wade right in, the bigger your picture, the better your chances of success, especially when it comes to advanced topics. Today you will learn the following:

- What is data and what is information
- Transforming data into information
- The nature of a relational database
- The theory and practice behind structuring a database
- Key fields
- Linking fields for data retrieval
- The types of relationships
- Normalization and the normal forms
- Hardware considerations

- Repair and maintenance of databases
- Access's life mission

Data Isn't Information

The purpose of a database system such as Microsoft Access is to change data into information. Many people use those two terms interchangeably, but there is a world of difference between the two if you consider information as being the same as knowledge. Data is a collection of facts. Information is that data organized or presented in such a way as to be useful for decision making.

Look at Figure 1.1. This shows actual voter registration data for a particular county shown in Access. It includes voters' names, addresses, registration information such as political party, and also the voting records for each person registered. It doesn't, of course, show who voters voted for (that's unavailable as data), but it does show whether and how the voters voted for each election cycle. A voter can vote by mail-in ballot, early voting, or at the polls.

FIGURE 1.1

County clerk records showing voter information and voting behavior is data.

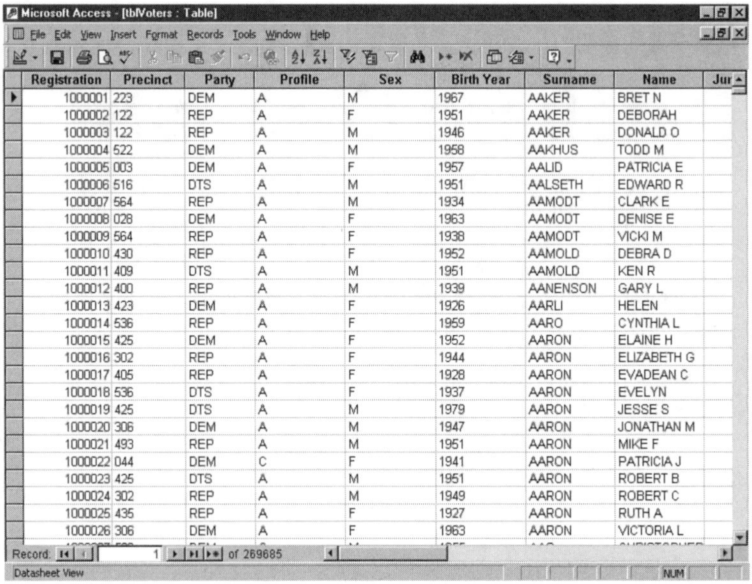

Registration	Precinct	Party	Profile	Sex	Birth Year	Surname	Name	Jur
1000001	223	DEM	A	M	1967	AAKER	BRET N	
1000002	122	REP	A	F	1951	AAKER	DEBORAH	
1000003	122	REP	A	M	1946	AAKER	DONALD O	
1000004	522	DEM	A	M	1958	AAKHUS	TODD M	
1000005	003	DEM	A	F	1957	AALID	PATRICIA E	
1000006	516	DTS	A	M	1951	AALSETH	EDWARD R	
1000007	564	REP	A	M	1934	AAMODT	CLARK E	
1000008	028	DEM	A	F	1963	AAMODT	DENISE E	
1000009	564	REP	A	F	1938	AAMODT	VICKI M	
1000010	430	REP	A	F	1952	AAMOLD	DEBRA D	
1000011	409	DTS	A	M	1951	AAMOLD	KEN R	
1000012	400	REP	A	M	1939	AANENSON	GARY L	
1000013	423	DEM	A	F	1926	AARLI	HELEN	
1000014	536	REP	A	F	1959	AARO	CYNTHIA L	
1000015	425	DEM	A	F	1952	AARON	ELAINE H	
1000016	302	REP	A	F	1944	AARON	ELIZABETH G	
1000017	405	REP	A	F	1928	AARON	EVADEAN C	
1000018	536	DTS	A	F	1937	AARON	EVELYN	
1000019	425	DTS	A	M	1979	AARON	JESSE S	
1000020	306	DEM	A	M	1947	AARON	JONATHAN M	
1000021	493	REP	A	M	1951	AARON	MIKE F	
1000022	044	DEM	C	F	1941	AARON	PATRICIA J	
1000023	425	DTS	A	M	1951	AARON	ROBERT B	
1000024	302	REP	A	M	1949	AARON	ROBERT C	
1000025	435	REP	A	F	1927	AARON	RUTH A	
1000026	306	DEM	A	F	1963	AARON	VICTORIA L	

Record: 1 of 269685

NEW TERM Figure 1.1 is a table with a mass of data—hundreds of thousands of people each with over 60 data points. In other words, there are millions of items to look at and correlate. In the real world of databases, this isn't a terribly large *dataset* (or any set of data), but it still is too large for the human mind to gain insight from.

Changing Data into Information

Now let's take that data and organize it into information. Suppose that in the 1998 congressional race the Democratic candidate lost by 3,216 votes. Using the Count() function built into Access, the database user notes that Republican voters mailed in 5,423 more ballots than the Democratic voters. This is information. Using it, the Democrats can see that if their candidate had emphasized mail-in balloting more (perhaps by mailing out applications for such ballots), he might have won.

Note

> This chapter skips over the technicalities of how to perform most operations such as using the Count() function. You'll see how to do this and perform other exercises in subsequent days. However, it's not too early to tell you that getting such a count of mail-in votes for a particular party from a dataset of this size takes only a few seconds after you know how to use Access. You'll consider such feats child's play after you've finished this book.

Of course, you must approach even such information using your own common sense or specific knowledge of the task at hand. Knowing that Republicans mailed in more ballots than Democrats did implies more mail-in votes for the Republican candidate, but that's inferred information. In reality, nobody can know whether this is the case, because all you really know is that those mail-in ballots came from registered Republicans. The votes themselves might have been for the Democratic or Green candidate.

A world of information is possible from any proper dataset. Suppose the Democratic candidate won by those 3,216 votes, but you see that Republicans outvoted (in all modes) Democrats by 7,987 voters. This is rather irrefutable information that the Democrats fielded a candidate attractive to Republicans, or that the Republican candidate wasn't what Republicans wanted in a congressman, or both.

Getting Complex

I've used the voter registration and voting record example because it is simple, but large in scope. Manually counting the Democratic and Republican mail-in ballots is possible even with a dataset of 270,000 voters, as in this example. Using Access for such tasks speeds things up quite a bit, but barely scratches the surface of this program's power.

Suppose instead of voter records, you have a database of shopper behavior. This shows each shopper's visit cataloged by day, date, time, weather conditions, and purchases tracked by those shopper "discount" cards issued by most large grocery stores today. Using date data, you assemble the dataset in Table 1.1 for purchases of a particular laundry detergent.

TABLE 1.1　PURCHASES BY DATE

Date	Packages of Detergent Purchased
2/3/98	23
2/4/98	90
2/5/98	20
2/6/98	25
2/7/98	15
2/8/98	87
2/9/98	12
2/10/98	10
2/11/98	97
2/12/98	101
2/13/98	9

Looking at this so-called information in Table 1.1 gives you no hint as to why on some days this detergent sells like crazy, but on most days it sells roughly the same number of boxes per day.

Recasting the data to correlate boxes sold to a different criterion as shown in Table 1.2 creates useful information.

TABLE 1.2　PURCHASES BY WEATHER CONDITIONS

Weather Condition	Packages of Detergent Purchased
Sunny	23
Rain	90
Pt. Cloudy	20
Pt. Cloudy	25
Sunny	15
Snow	87
Sunny	12
Sunny	10
Rain, Fog	97
Rain	101
Sunny	9

A quick glance at this table will give you all the knowledge you need to understand the buying patterns of your customers when it comes to this detergent. The key was to try different correlations until you found one that clicked.

The Key to the Transformation

The way to transform data into information is to organize that data in such a way that you can view it in a useful form. The two preceding examples—the number of voters voting in a particular way and the correlation between weather and sales—show you this transformation.

Access itself won't do the entire job for you, even though help in that aspect has been a major design goal of Microsoft for many years. You must structure your database in such a way as to make the transformation possible.

The key here is to keep foremost in your mind what form the information you hope to derive will take. In other words, when creating a database structure, think about how you'll extract information from the dataset. This is clearly the most difficult task for a person new to databases.

 Caution Failure to properly structure your database will always lead to suboptimal database performance. It often leads to useless collections of data.

Not Fun, but Necessary

Using Access is a lot of fun. Learning how to use Access, how to extract (select) data from large data collections, create forms and reports, and program in macros or VBA are likewise a lot of fun. There is a huge temptation to jump right to this interesting and seemingly immediately rewarding aspect of Access, and skip over the boring structural theory later in this lesson.

Try not to succumb to this temptation. You can be an expert in the mechanics of Access, but if you lack the know-how to structure your data properly, the mechanics won't do you much good when it comes time to transform your data into information.

Unfortunately from a learning perspective, understanding database theory in a vacuum isn't easy. The best approach is to read over the following material, keeping in mind those concepts that don't click right off, but not laboring over trying to get it all.

After you have an overview of structure, proceed to the rest of the book. This will teach you enough about Access to elevate you to the level of developer—albeit one with little field experience. At that point, be sure to return to the sections that follow and you'll find they make a lot more sense when added to your mechanical understanding of Access, the program.

> **Tip**
>
> Master carpenters have a saying, "Measure twice, cut once." Master database developers have a similar saying, "Plan long, work short." The mechanics of making most database projects should be undertaken only after a thorough planning stage. If, project after project, you find yourself having to revise your structure from what you planned, you must plan more.

The Nature of Access Data

NEW TERM   Access is a *relational database*. Some purists claim that few if any databases today are truly relational because they fail one theoretical test or another. The best thing to do if you run into one of these zealots is to agree that Access (as well as most other products) isn't fully and truly relational, and then to continue using it (or those products) to get your work done.

The father of the relational model is named E.F. Codd. I'll be the first to agree that Access doesn't fully meet all the rules Codd proposed for the relational model, but it does meet the spirit of that model. Here is a list, not of all the relational rules, but of the idea behind the relational model:

NEW TERM   • All data is stored in tables or two-dimensional grids. The columns of that grid are called *fields*. The rows are called *records*. Look at Figure 1.1. The columns Registration, Precinct, Party, and so on are all fields. The rows contain the data corresponding to the fields.

NEW TERM   • Each record in a table has a *primary key* to positively identify it. The primary key for a record is a datum unique to that table. In Figure 1.1, the Registration field is the primary key. No two records in this table have the same value for their Registration field. In addition, Access orders (sorts) the table according to the primary field. You can see this sorting in the ascending order of primary field values within this table.

NEW TERM   • Data within a database is broken into small, but logically consistent parts. Each of these parts has its own table. The breaking up of data into these parts is called *normalization*. For example, a database of student registration (for a college, let's say) will contain a table with the students' personal information. Another table will contain data relating to the students' classes, another table will contain class data such as class time and place. Each table will have logically consistent contents. For example, no table will contain class instructor data and student scholarship data because those two datasets aren't logically connected.

- Data can be assembled from various tables by linking those tables by fields containing identical data. For example, the student personal table will contain the student ID (the primary key, because it's a unique value for each student). The table containing student classes taken will contain this student ID for each record. This will enable the database engine to link the students with their classes without error.

You can see these concepts in action in the following section by looking at the figures as you read the text. If you're somewhat adept at Access at this point, you can see the objects shown in these figures contained within the sample data in the Day 1 folder in the database relational model.

Note

Don't be concerned if you don't understand the mechanics of how to view and manipulate the database objects shown in the following figures. The purpose of this section is to illustrate the points given above. In a few days, you'll be able to do the operations shown here with ease.

Figure 1.2 shows the Relationships window. This window currently contains two tables. The table tblStudentPersonal contains data such as the student's ID number (Social Security number), name, and address. The other table contains data about what classes the student is now or has been signed up for in the past. Note the link on the StudentID field. This allows the database manager to associate the students with their classes.

Note

All the data in these examples has been simplified from actual data that might be used in a real college or university. The benefit of the simplification is that it makes it easier to grasp concepts than if you were drowned in extraneous data.

Figure 1.3 shows the data from the tblStudentPersonal table. A real-world example would contain more data, such as the phone numbers for these fictitious students. Note the StudentID numbers for each student here.

 Figure 1.4 shows the classes a student has currently signed up for or has taken in the past. Again, this is overly simplified for the sake of illustration. A real-world database

would also have a table with class details (such as student personal details) linked to this table as well. This table has been left out of this series for clarity's sake.

FIGURE 1.2

You can view the Relationships window by choosing Tools, Relationships from the main Access menu.

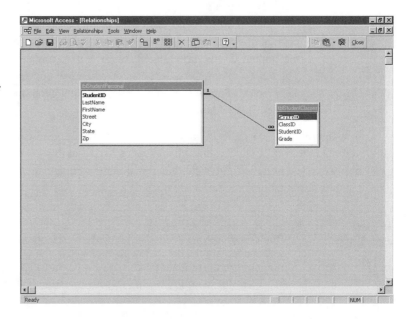

FIGURE 1.3

tblStudentPersonal contains data from the home life of the students.

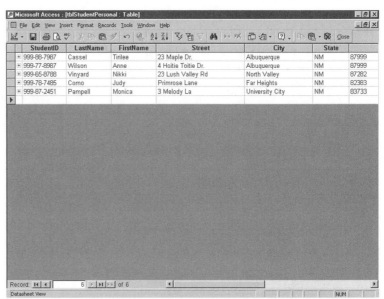

FIGURE 1.4

This table, taken from a simplified example of a registration database, contains data about students and their classes.

SignupID	ClassID	StudentID	Grade
1	Eng101	999778987	B+
2	Spa220	999872451	In Process
3	Eng101	999872451	A
4	Eng101	999887987	In Process
5	Mth201	999658788	C
6	Eng400	999787485	In Process
7	Egg120	999778987	In Process
(AutoNumber)			In Process

> **Note**
>
> A Social Security number is a universal identification number used in the United States of America to positively identify its citizens and non-citizen workers. Assignment of such an identity number is mandatory at a citizen's birth.

Figure 1.5 shows how Access has grouped the classes with the proper students.

FIGURE 1.5

The Access JET engine (the heart of the database system) keeps track of students and their classes.

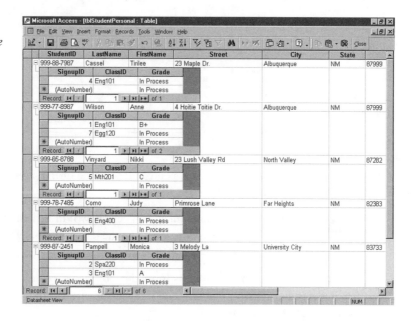

The display in Figure 1.5 isn't very clear, nor is it easy to use. However, by creating a query with two tables, shown being designed in Figure 1.6 and then running in Figure 1.7, you can put together the students and their classes in a synthesized two-dimensional grid.

FIGURE 1.6

First you design a query using the two tables in this limited dataset.

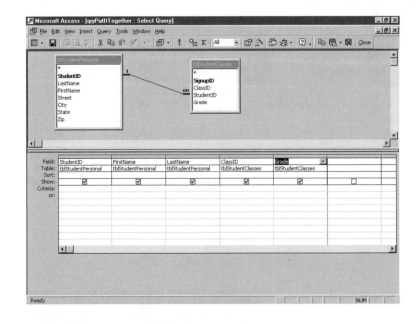

FIGURE 1.7

Then you can see the data from two tables put together in a cogent and easy-to-use manner.

StudentID	FirstName	LastName	ClassID	Grade
999-65-8788	Nikki	Vinyard	Mth201	C
999-77-8987	Anne	Wilson	Eng101	B+
999-77-8987	Anne	Wilson	Egg120	In Process
999-78-7485	Judy	Como	Eng400	In Process
999-87-2451	Monica	Pampell	Spa220	In Process
999-87-2451	Monica	Pampell	Eng101	A
999-88-7987	Tirilee	Cassel	Eng101	In Process

 If you have today's database open, you can look at the query shown in Figures 1.6 and 1.7. The query name is qryPutItTogether.

NEW TERM Access has the data linked and can show it in various modes. Figure 1.8 is a *form*. The fields on the left show the data from the personal table, whereas the box to the right shows the classes this student has completed or is taking.

If you know how to open an Access form, this object is saved under the name frmStudents and Classes. The left- and right-facing arrows at the lower part of the form move through the records.

NEW TERM A *report* is a form designed for output only—especially to a printer. You can output reports as Web pages or even as generic files if you so choose. Figure 1.9 shows the data from Figures 1.5 through 1.8 in a report.

FIGURE 1.8

An Access form showing student personal data and classes. The presentation is much clearer than the same data shown in Figure 1.5, but the data is the same.

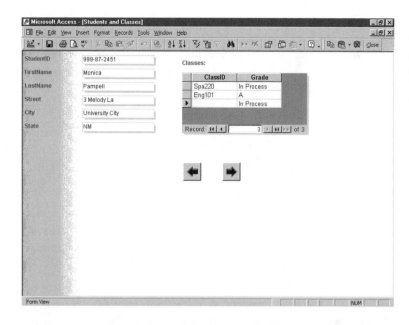

FIGURE 1.9

Reports formerly were headed mostly for the printer. Today many find their way onto the Internet or an intranet.

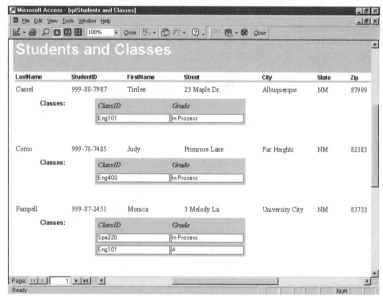

The Theory of Database Structure

Many people believe that structuring real-world data for a relational database is an art form more than an exercise in science. Perhaps a better way to state this is that database design is an art based on a science. For example, keep in mind that there might be practical considerations that will make you create a database structure that's less than optimal. Knowing when that is the right way to go is the art form. Knowing what the optimal structure is remains the science.

Here, in summary form, are your goals for structuring your data:

- Create a dataset optimized for selection and retrieval of data as information.
- Make data entry easy and economical. This means making sure any datum appears only once in your database. For example, if you have a student's address in a table, you shouldn't have that address anywhere else, but be able to link to that data (through common fields) whenever you need it.
- Have the data structured in a logical form so the database documents (explains) itself by its very structure. This also means that alterations to the database or the data are simple to carry out.

Do	Don't
DO plan your structure including, for complex projects, feasibility of concept studies.	DON'T jump right in. A rule of thumb is that the more complex the output required, the longer the time you should spend planning.

The tables in your database represent groups of real-world objects either tangible or abstract. For example, a table might hold inventory data (tangible) or addresses (abstractions). The fields in tables (columns in the grid) determine what type of data the table holds, while the rows (records) give values to the fields. Figure 1.10 shows a table from the Microsoft-supplied database, Northwind.

The Last Name field in Figure 1.10 tells the user that this field contains last names for the employees of this company. The name Davolio, the first value in Figure 1.10, tells the user that this is the specific value for one record.

FIGURE 1.10

Fields or columns define the type of data, whereas rows or records give specific values to fields.

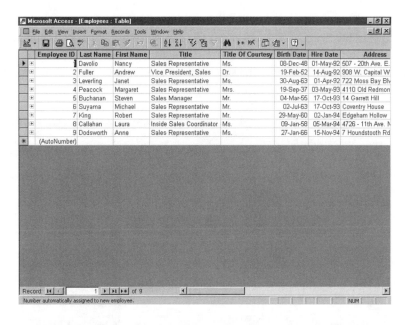

FIGURE 1.11

The foreign key EmployeeID appears in Orders to link this table to Employees.

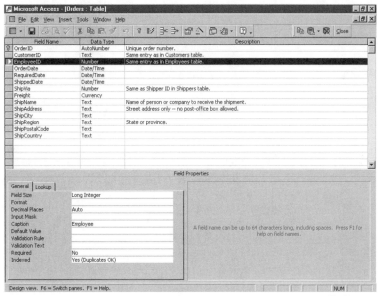

The primary key for this table is EmployeeID (shown as Employee ID in this figure). This field will also appear in other tables as a link value. The inclusion of this field in the Orders table allows this database to track the orders with the employees who took the order. Figure 1.11 shows the Orders table in Design view with the row showing the EmployeeID field highlighted.

FIGURE 1.12

Data entry people didn't have to type the employee's name when taking an order, the link did the grunt work for them.

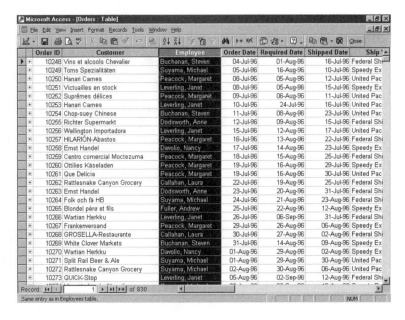

NEW TERM   *Foreign key* is the name of a primary key field of one table when included as a linking field in another table. Here, EmployeeID from Employees (a table) appears in Orders (another table) as a foreign key. Figure 1.12 shows that the inclusion of this field allows the display of the employee name in the Orders table. Remember, the data entry people didn't have to enter the employee's name to achieve this, only the EmployeeID number—it was done by way of a pull-down combo box.

Figure 1.13 shows the form used by data entry people to enter order information. The links in this database mean that once entered, data need never be entered again. The combo box shown here links to the Employees table through the inclusion of the foreign key field EmployeeID shown in Figure 1.11.

FIGURE 1.13

After the tables are linked, forms based on those tables can benefit from those links.

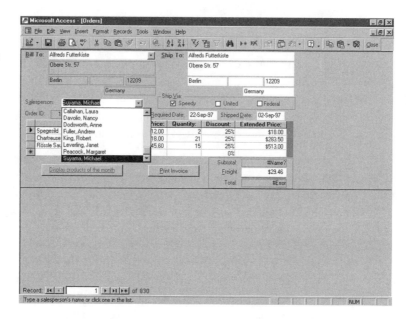

Note

Again, don't worry that the mechanics of how a database designer created the objects shown in these figures aren't apparent to you at this point. After a few more days, doing chores such as table design, field linking, and form design will be easy for you. For now, concentrate on the idea of database structuring.

The Practice of Database Structure

Deciding what to use for a primary key and how to "break up" or normalize your real-world data are primary skills for a database designer. Don't expect to get them right at first—nobody does. Instead, do the best you can using the guidelines given in this section. When things go wrong (as they will) downstream in your database projects, reflect how the structure could be made better to avoid the problems you have encountered. Over time you'll find yourself making fewer and fewer mistakes, and those will be easily correctable.

Choosing the Primary Key

Access has a built-in primary key generator called the AutoNumber type field. This will generate either unique sequential or random numbers for use as a primary key. Although this works, and Microsoft seems to encourage this practice, database purists sneer at including any non-data values in a table.

NEW TERM Don't be afraid to use the generator even if it means a slight increase in your table sizes. However, don't automatically figure that this is the only way to choose a primary key or even the optimal one. Your first approach should be to examine your table data to see whether you can find a natural primary key. A *natural primary key* is a field or fields that exists as data, but is also unique, so can serve as such keys.

The use of a Social Security number (SSN) in a student personal table is an example of natural data that's useful for a primary key. Access will also allow the use of several fields used in aggregate to form a composite primary key. For example, the composite of a date of birth field and a home phone number field can serve as a primary key because there is little likelihood that two students will have the same date of birth and home phone number. Neither field by itself is suitable for a primary key because is it is possible for two students to have the same date of birth or the same home phone number (sisters). This scheme will fail, however, in the case of twin sisters attending your school at the same time. If you want to avoid such cases, you'll need to add more fields to your composite key (first name) until you've achieved uniqueness again. Here you can see the advantage of using the AutoNumber facility in Access. There is no chance you will end up having to restructure your data if an unanticipated event ruins the uniqueness of your primary key.

Although you shouldn't be afraid of creating an artificial field in tables for use as a primary key, use real data whenever possible. Keep in mind that a natural field or fields for a primary key is suitable if it meets the following criteria:

- Assured uniqueness for any table
- No subset of the primary key also meets the first requirement

In other words, make it unique and simple.

Do	Don't
DO use unique data that occurs naturally in your dataset as a primary key.	DON'T compromise the unique quality of your primary key fields. If necessary, use Access's AutoNumber data type for a field if that's the only assured way to find a unique identifier for every record.

Relationship Types

When structuring your data, keep in mind the different type of relationships that can occur between tables. The following list uses a hospital database as the example. The tables are

- Patients
- Procedures
- Providers (doctors)
- Beds

NEW TERM Of course, in a real-world hospital database there would be more tables than these. The *relationships* are

- *One to many*—Patients to Procedures. One patient can have many procedures performed during his stay at the hospital.
- *Many to many*—Patients to Providers. One doctor can have many patients; one patient can also have many doctors.
- *One to one*—Patients to Beds. One patient can have only one bed and one bed can have only one patient.

You will need to keep these relationship types in mind when designing your tables. For now, just remember there are these three relationship types.

> **Note**
>
> Relational theory is replete with its own often confusing jargon, using terms such as domain, tuple, entity integrity, and constructor. Whenever possible I'll avoid using such jargon in this chapter, and instead use either common terms (such as "row" instead of the technically correct "tuple") or discuss concepts descriptively rather than by relying on jargon.

Getting to Normalization

NEW TERM The terms *normal* and *normalization* when used in a database context don't refer to behavioral, chemical, or biological normals, but stem from the mathematical concept of being perpendicular to a plane. Relational theory has its roots in set theory, but has been extended well beyond the types of unions postulated in that theory. This basis in mathematics is the reason for some of the unusual jargon, including the often-confusing terms normal and normalization, which refer to proper table structure rather than an alteration from an abnormal state to one more common (normal). Because no alternative word conveys the same concept as normal, and the use of this word is widespread even among novices, I've not tried to avoid its use.

The structure data in tables, or the contents of tables, can be described as being in various *normal forms*. Ideally you will construct your tables, and by extension your relationships, in the first, second, or third normal forms that are described later today. In practice, you might violate normalization rules for some of your tables, although purists will sneer at such practice.

Well, we can't live our lives or base our database practices on the often impractical ideas of theorists, so let's move on to learn about the three normal forms with a note about the fourth. Keep in mind that all higher normal forms are supersets of lower forms.

NEW TERM The *first normal form* is the so-called *atomic* form because there is no possibility of splitting it further. Consider a table of department personnel shown in Figure 1.14.

FIGURE 1.14

The first normal form prevents multiple entries in one row, such as these entries in the People column.

DepartmentID	Supervisor	People
1	3	Carroll, Smith, Jones, Wells
2	4	Usural, McMillan, Fancy
3	9	Malarky, Fina, Pena, Blanca
4	1	Peel, Em, Wheeler

The table shown in Figure 1.14 presents problems in data selection and manipulation, especially as the number of employees grows. Although Access can handle such violations fairly gracefully when departments hold three or four people, it will fall apart fast when the numbers get into the hundreds, thousands, or even higher.

The correct way to structure the data you see in Figure 1.14 is to have a row for each distinct value in the People field. In most systems, there will also be another table with People data implying the way to create this table is to link from the People field to the source table. This would place a foreign key in the People field, although by using an SQL statement you can view the people's names rather than the primary field value (such as SSN) in this table. Generally speaking, even if you use a foreign key in a table, you will want to display a more user-friendly value than that key.

As a preview of things to come, the SQL statement to retrieve and then display sorted data from a source table called tblEmployees as a usual name is

```
SELECT DISTINCTROW tblEmployees.EmployeeID,
➡[LastName] & ", " & [FirstName] AS Name FROM tblEmployees
➡ORDER BY Employees.LastName, Employees.FirstName;
```

Figure 1.15 shows the results of restructuring the data from this table into the first normal form.

FIGURE 1.15

The Supervisor field also has an underlying SQL statement displaying the name of the supervisor from the Departments table, rather than the foreign key linking to the primary key field of that table.

NonDataIDFiel	Supervisor	People
1	Smith	John Carroll
2	Smith	Susie Smith
3	Smith	Sam Jones
4	Gonzalez	Jose Pena
5	Gonzalez	Rosa Blanca
(AutoNumber)		

Note that there is no need for both the supervisor and the department information. The inclusion of a foreign key as data for the Supervisor field can let this table display any and all information from the table holding departmental information.

NEW TERM The *second normal form* is the first normal form plus the criterion that all non-primary key fields must be dependent on the entire value in the primary key field. The word "entire" is important to include due to cases in which a primary key is made up of more than one field.

Figure 1.16 shows a table meeting the requirements of the second normal form. The two fields, PurchaseOrder and LineNumber, form a composite primary key for this table. The two non-key fields derive all their identity from this composite key, but are useless as information without the entire key.

FIGURE 1.16

The non-key fields in this table depend on the entire primary key. Thus this table meets the requirements of the second normal form.

PurchaseOrder	LineNumber	Quantity	ItemID
1	1	4	8
1	2	9	90
1	3	2	9
2	1	1	34
2	2	23	95
0	0	0	0

NEW TERM The *third normal form* calls for all non-key fields to be mutually independent of each other. Remember they still must be dependent on the entire primary key because this is a superset of the second normal form. Mutual independence means simply that the values of the non-key fields can't vary depending on the contents of another field.

For example, suppose you have a table with price and quantity information. If you add a third field that calculates the total cost by multiplying the price times the quantity, you would violate the rules for the third normal form because this field would be dependent upon the values in two other non-key fields. You can use a query, a form, or a report to do this calculation if such a calculation is needed for your project.

In some instances, you might want to violate this or other normalization rules. Asking a query to do this calculation will take some time, which your users might find irksome. In a case like this, you can calculate the total cost and place that value in a table in violation of the math rules, but to the benefit of your users.

Overall, keep in mind that normalization is just common sense applied to the database problem. If your application works well and meets the needs of your users, its structure is right even if it violates some theoretical mathematical model.

Do	Don't
DO include a primary key for every table.	DON'T worry overly that your tables meet the criteria set for a particular normal form.

Access' Mission

Access was originally conceived by Microsoft as a defensive product. At that time, common knowledge said that Microsoft led in every office software category other than databases, so the Redmond giant decided it needed to address that type of software. When introduced, the leading database products were both MS-DOS based. The dominant but waning dBASE line was being supplanted by the MS-DOS version of Borland's Paradox, with a version of Paradox for Windows close over the horizon. The two programs, dBASE and Paradox, owned the personal computer database territory.

Access differed from both these products in several ways, but perhaps the most important differences were its closer adherence to the relational model than either competitor did (or does), and its use of BASIC (Access BASIC then) rather than the PAL language of Paradox. When Paradox for Windows arrived, it relied on the technically excellent OPAL (Object PAL) language. However, OPAL's C-like syntax and obscure keywords condemned it to seasoned developers only. Access' BASIC was accessible to all users from advanced novices on up. BASIC was and remains Bill Gates' favorite language for this reason—accessibility to the non-advanced market.

Microsoft Extends Access

Microsoft extended Access for version 2.0 into both directions, making it much easier to use and capable of serious data handling. The next version of Access, 95, saw the concurrent creation of the Upgrade Kit allowing Access applications to be migrated to SQL Server applications with very little work or fuss.

This kit is vital even though few Access users know of its existence and fewer will ever use it. Prior to the kit, users had to size their applications before they chose a program to host it. The choice came down to a modestly capable but relatively easy to use database program such as Paradox or dBASE. The alternative was to use a highly capable, but expensive and difficult to use package such as Oracle or SQL Server.

If your Paradox data outgrew the program's capacity, you had to redo the entire package using a more capable program. However, the kit let you use Access with a clear mind. If your data outgrew Access, you could easily migrate up to SQL Server, which for the vast majority of applications can't be outgrown.

Partly due to its ease of use, partly due to the popularity of Microsoft Office of which it's a part, and partly due to the upgrade kit, by the time Access 95 hit the streets it had eclipsed both dBASE and Paradox in all their forms to become the leading database product for personal computers. It remains so today.

Hardware Requirements

Unlike Word or Excel, which for the most part reach diminishing performance returns well shy of the Pentium II, Access will continue to improve in performance as you feed it better equipment. It will run on the minimums specified by Microsoft, but it won't sparkle.

While a faster processor will boost Access' speed, more RAM and a faster disk will better serve most systems. Access uses temporary files to a great extent when it runs short of RAM, so the further you can extend that point and the faster you can read and write those temporary files, the better will Access perform.

SCSI disks are, as of this writing, the fastest, but also run hotter and cost more than UIDE disks, which are catching SCSI in performance. If you have a fast UIDE disk you won't see much performance increase by moving to a SCSI setup. If you're building a system from scratch or have a punky IDE disk, SCSI will reward your extra expense.

The minimum RAM for decent Access performance will depend on your operating system. Figure 32MB for Windows 98 and 64MB for Windows NT or Windows 2000 (and its successors). These are the minimums. Windows 98 runs much better at 64MB, whereas Windows NT and 2000 really start to shine at 128MB. Increasing beyond these numbers will yield some benefit, but unless you run many tasks at the same time you run Access, you won't see drastic performance improvements.

Don't refuse a faster processor because that's not the area of greatest sensitivity. Rather, if you currently have a 200MHz Pentium with 32MB RAM and Windows NT, you would be better off moving to 128MB RAM rather than moving to a 450MHz Pentium Xeon with the same 32MB RAM. Better still, get that Xeon but also get the 128MB RAM. Even better yet, get a computer with two Xeons for even faster performance. Keep in mind that a dual-processor Windows NT machine won't be improved with Access as much as with other applications (such a rendering program) that are heavily processor dependent.

Maintaining Access Databases

You've probably heard it before—it's not *if* you'll lose data, but *when*. Computers aren't infallible, power fails, and parts—especially disk drives—go bad. The only defense is to back up your data.

A full discussion of backup devices is beyond the intended scope of this book. The two fundamental methods are some sort of network backup—either through your LAN or by subscription over the Internet—and backup to removable media such as tape, removable hard disk, or writable CDs. Pick a method and use it.

Repairing in Place

Access files are somewhat more susceptible to corruption due to power failure than other non-database programs, such as Word. Although you should be always able to restore your files from a backup, sometimes that isn't possible or desirable. For example, you might have done quite a bit of data entry after your last backup. In such a case, you would prefer not to restore from backup, which would require repeated data entry.

Access 2000 does have a facility that will repair many instances of damage to a database. You can find this in the main Access menu under Tools, Database Utilities. Compact and repair are now one operation.

Figure 1.17 shows the menu selections for compacting and repairing a database.

If you have a database open and choose Tools, Database Utilities, Compact and Repair Access will operate on the open database. If you have no database open it will prompt you for a file to work on. This latter method is how you'd attempt a fix on a file you can't open.

FIGURE 1.17

Compact and repair are a single operation under Access 2000.

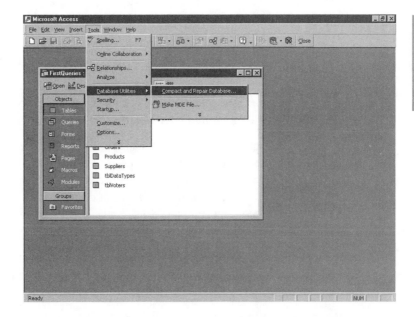

Access has a quirk that forces the occasional compaction of a database. Although Access will dynamically expand to accommodate additional database objects and data, it won't dynamically compress itself as objects or data are removed. You must do this either programmatically or manually.

The repair and compact operation are as foolproof as Microsoft can make them, but nothing is truly 100% reliable. Unless you like playing with fire, back up your old databases before doing the repair and compaction routine. If you do a compaction/repair on a non-open database, Access will prompt you for a name for the output. This is a form of backup, but because it's not to an external source such as a CDR disk, it's not as foolproof as a real backup.

Tip

In some cases, the repair facility will fail to fix a corrupted database. Occasionally, you can work around this failure by creating a new database container and then importing the objects from the old corrupted database container into the new one. If they import all right, they'll almost always run properly. You can find the import facility in the main Access menu under File, Get External Data, Import.

Summary

Few people care about data. The point of a data manager such as Access is to allow you to turn data into information. Data are entries in a table. Information is what that data means. For example, a list of voters' behavior in a particular election is data. That Republicans out voted Democrats in mail-in balloting is information. You manipulate and extract (select) data to turn it into information.

Altering poorly structured data into information is difficult or even impossible. The relational model was created to simplify this conversion. This model specifies that all data reside in tables, or two-dimensional grids. You decompose data masses into logically related groups that can be re-linked using fields of common data. Although the entire relational theory is large and complex, using a relational database such as Access is more a matter of common sense than mathematical precision.

Access was originally conceived to fill a missing piece in Microsoft's Office suite. Because of its ease of use and sizability, it has grown to be the dominant data manager for personal computers.

Although you must keep your data, including your databases, backed up, Access is capable of repairing some types of damage. Because Access will expand to accommodate expanded data, but not contract when data is deleted, Microsoft supplies a compaction utility to meet this need.

Q&A

Q I'm still unclear about relational theory and its application. Do you have any suggestions?

A There are many books on relational theory, but most of them are either dense or superficial. I won't discourage you from trying this route, but eventually you'll have to get down to actually using the Access product. Use is what will teach you what works and what doesn't—and that's the acid test of whether your database structure is right or wrong.

Q What's wrong with including data twice in a database?

A There is nothing wrong about doing this, but you lose some efficiency and your database increases somewhat in size. In many cases, your users will demand that you do this. Don't adhere to arbitrary rules to the detriment of your users' reasonable demands.

Q How important is it to include a primary key in every table?

A This is one rule you can't violate. You can't be sure Access is doing a proper and complete selection of data in a table lacking a primary key. Don't leave the console without one.

Q How often should I compact?

A There is no rule about this. It depends on your usage frequency. Some heavily used databases are backed up and then compacted daily. Moderately used ones can get away with a compaction every week or even less often. Just make sure to back up when it will take you longer to replace data than it takes to do the backup.

Workshop

The Workshop helps you solidify the skills you learned in this lesson. Answers to the quiz questions appear in Appendix A, "Answers."

Quiz

1. What's it called when a primary key field appears as a link field in another table?

2. Would you classify the following statement as data or information: "In the last election, Republicans outvoted Democrats 5 to 3."

3. Would you agree with the following statement: "Because Access is a relational database, there is no need to back up its files."

4. Will Access dynamically shrink files to reflect deleted data?

DAY 2

From Idea to Project

Taking a few minutes to familiarize yourself with the parts of Access and how it's organized will let you concentrate on learning the product. Today's lesson will help you become familiar with the following:

- The Access user interface
- The objects bar
- Groups
- The types of Access objects
- Opening and closing objects
- Access object views
- The Database Wizard
- Access's global options

The Access User Interface

Access 2000 has a new user interface designed to be not only easier for the beginner to navigate through, but also to make the life of the Access expert simpler. The concept of the user interface stems from two metaphors, the bar and tab interface common to all Microsoft Office applications, plus the object collection concept from object-oriented programming. The original object metaphor is purely abstract, whereas the translation into Access user interface is concrete.

Like so many concepts in small computers, gaining familiarity with Access' interface is best done by a hands-on approach, so let's get started. Launch Access by choosing it from the Start, Programs menu entry. In some administrative (network) installs, Access will be part of a group under Programs, in which case you'll need to locate where Access is to launch it. For most people, Access will be an entry directly under Start, Programs. Upon launching, Access will offer you several choices. See Figure 2.1 for a typical screen after launching Access.

FIGURE 2.1

Access launches, offering you three choices: create a new database, use an existing one, or start a blank database.

If this is the first time you've launched Access, you won't have any entries in the list box at the bottom of the dialog box. From top to bottom the three post-launch options are

- Create a New Database Using a Blank Access Database—This will create a new container (explained in the following text), ready for you to populate with your database objects.

- Create a New Database Using Access Database Wizards, Pages, and Projects—This will also create a new database, but by use of a wizard or two to give you a quick start.

- Open an Existing File—This will allow you to choose from a list or browse for an existing database to open.

In addition, you can click the Cancel button to open Access with no database loaded. Because setup will register Microsoft Access 2000 with your operating system, you can also launch Access with a database loaded by double-clicking on the database (files with .mdb or .mde extensions) from the Explorer.

For this, a first tour of Access, locate the Northwind sample database supplied with Office. Highlight it, and then click Open or double-click on its entry in the list box. If you need to browse for it, highlight More Files and click OK. That action will open up a standard File Open browsing dialog box.

Note | Northwind is part of most installs, but it might not be present on your machine. If not, you can still get a good idea of the Access user interface by the screens within the following section, or you can run Office setup again to install it.

Navigating the Database View Window

After you've opened Northwind, your screen should resemble Figure 2.2. This is called the Database view and you'll become very familiar with its functions and features as you work with Access. This window contains all the objects in your database and toolbars for manipulation of these objects, and provides starting points for working with a database.

FIGURE 2.2

The Database view holds a collection of all database objects within your project.

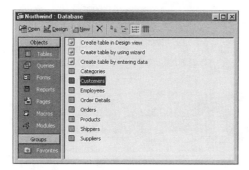

The new window on your screen is also an object in the Microsoft hierarchy of objects, a fact that you'll want to remember when you start working with objects in VBA or macro code. For now, though, we'll refer to this window as the Database View window for the object Northwind: Database, which appears in the title bar. This window is divided into three main parts, shown in Figure 2.3:

- The toolbar with actions and view selections;
- The left pane, which lists the types, or *classes,* of available objects within all Access databases, such as tables and forms;

- The right pane, which shows a listing of the individual objects within the selected class on the left pane.

One new feature here is the Group class option on the left pane, which you'll learn more about in the "Groups" section, later in this lesson. As you can see by clicking through the various objects in the left pane, the Northwind database has several objects as a part of its application.

The new object, the one that says Northwind: Database in its title bar, is the Database view or database container, as it's sometimes called because it contains various objects that make up a database system. It displays all the items or objects within your project collected by classification. The series of buttons on the left side of the container allows you to choose from different types of objects, such as tables or reports. Click on the Forms entry (or any entry other than the one currently selected) and the right pane will reflect all the database objects so as to show the one class selected within the Database view. Figure 2.3 shows the Database view for a simple database.

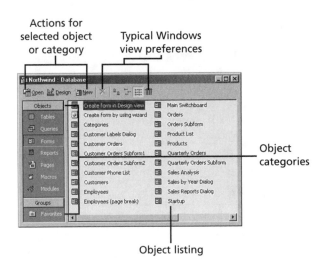

FIGURE 2.3

Choosing different objects will change the display within the Database view. Compare the Forms selection here with the Tables selection in Figure 2.2.

Actions for selected object or category

Typical Windows view preferences

Object categories

Object listing

> **Note**
>
> In keeping with the Windows look and feel, the Access Database view window has its own toolbar between the title bar and the split panes. The icons on the buttons indicate they will perform an action rather than select an object.

You'll see a set of icons telling you what actions on the toolbar you can perform on the objects listed in the Database view panes. The first eight entries, from left to right, allow you to do the following:

- Open—Launch an object in its native mode, such as for data entry. Access uses the term *view* for different object modes.
- Design—Launch an object in such a way as to allow you to edit its structure rather than its data.
- New—Create a new object of the type highlighted within the Object list.
- Delete—Delete the highlighted object. This functions only for objects created by a user or developer, not for the objects that appear in a new database.
- Large icons—Display the database objects in large icon view. Analogous to the same view in Windows Explorer or My Computer.
- Small icons—Display the database objects in small icon view. Analogous to the same view in Windows Explorer or My Computer.
- List—Display the database objects in list view. Analogous to the same view in Windows Explorer or My Computer.
- Details—Display the database objects in Details view. Analogous to the same view in Windows Explorer or My Computer.

Right-clicking is alive and well in Microsoft Access 2000. Right-click on any true object (as opposed to an action within the Database view) and you'll see a context (or shortcut) menu containing all the actions within the Database view as well as a few more. True to its name, the context menu for each class of objects will vary. Figure 2.4 shows the context menu for form type objects.

FIGURE 2.4

The context menu is a superset of the Database view actions. The specific actions within a context menu will vary depending on the class of object.

Tip   You can also right-click on the Objects entries to see shortcuts to Access
facilities such as the VBA editor or the database startup dialog box.

Groups

Note the Groups entry within the context menu for Figure 2.4. This is a new feature for
Microsoft Access 2000. As mentioned earlier, the right pane reflects only the list of
objects under the category or classification that you select on the left pane. However, you
can now create groups of objects, allowing a mixed bag of objects within one group or
collection to appear at the same time. Prior to this version of Access, there was no simple
way to collect and display different categories of objects (such as forms and reports)
within one "button" of the Database view. Now you can. To create a new group, right-
click in the Groups area and choose New Group from the context menu. To follow this
example, create a new group called Tirilee Traders.

Now that you have a multiple–category-capable group, you can add objects to it by right-
clicking on the object you want to add, choosing Add to Group from the context menu,
and then specifying the group from the submenu. Figure 2.5 shows a form being added
to the Tirilee Traders group.

FIGURE 2.5

*You can use the context
menu for an object to
add it to a group. The
same context menu will
also allow you to cre-
ate a new group.*

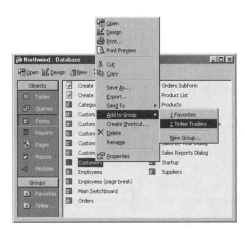

Figure 2.6 shows the new group, Tirilee Traders, with a mixed classification of objects
within it. You can tell that the objects are heterogeneous by their differing icons. I've
changed the view from List to Large Icons to make the point clearer.

FIGURE 2.6

The new Microsoft Access 2000 groups can hold diverse objects.

2

 Tip

You can also use drag and drop to drag and then drop an object from its object classification (such as Queries) to a multiclass group.

 Tip

If your database has few objects, create an All Objects group and then copy all the objects into that group. This will save you and your users many mouse clicks.

Views, Opening, and Closing Objects

NEW TERM Access uses the term *view* to refer to different object modes. The two main views used throughout Access are Normal view (just called view) and Design view. Normal view is the mode you use to interact with the object and its data (if relevant). Design view is the mode you use to change the characteristics, or design, of an object.

If you double-click on an object within the right pane, it will open in Normal view. Normal view isn't a standard Microsoft term. I use it to mean the common way for an object to open. For example, normal view for a form is any data entry or data viewing mode.

If you have Northwind, try opening the Employees form by selecting (clicking on) the Forms entry in the left pane and then double-clicking on the Employees entry in the right pane. Figure 2.7 shows the resulting form opened for data entry.

FIGURE 2.7

The Normal view, or the default mode, for an Access object is the view ready for data entry, viewing, or editing.

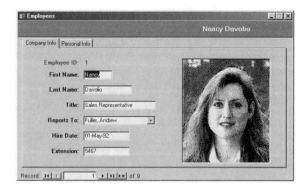

You could have also highlighted the Employees form, and then clicked the Open button on the toolbar of the Database view to open Employees in this view. To close an object, click on the Close button in the upper-right corner of its window, or choose File, Close from the main menu when the object is selected (active). Remember your "right" to right-click if you prefer manipulating objects that way.

To see an object in Design view, highlight it and then choose Design from the toolbar of the Database view. Figure 2.8 shows the Employees form opened in Design view. The views available in the Database container are analogous to those in My Computer or Windows Explorer.

FIGURE 2.8

Design view is the mode you use to manipulate the object's design rather than the underlying data.

The View button toggles views

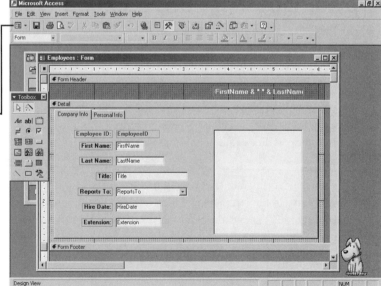

You can also dynamically switch views by clicking the View button in the main Access toolbar. The View button is on the far left on the toolbar shown in Figure 2.8. Try switching back and forth from Design to Normal view using the View toolbar button until you get a feel for it. This is an important switch that you'll use quite a bit when designing certain Access objects—especially forms.

When you're ready, close the Employees form. If Access prompts you to save or discard changes, that means you made some modification to the form. Don't save any changes now.

Just Like Everyday Windows

A window containing an Access object such as the Employees form acts just like any Microsoft Windows window. You can maximize it, minimize it, move it around, stretch, and shrink it just like any usual window. The only restriction is that, other than a Page object, all Access objects must remain within the main Access program's container.

Try opening Employees again in Normal view. Maximize it and then minimize it. When in windowed mode, move it around. Grab a corner or other border with your mouse cursor and try shrinking, and then stretching, it in all directions until you have a good feel for how things work within Access. You can likewise shrink, maximize, minimize, and manipulate the Database view window. Closing this window will, however, close the database.

Global Options

Microsoft Access 2000 has several options allowing you to customize the way it looks and acts. This customization means, that to the extent Microsoft has foreseen, you can make Access behave in the way most comfortable and convenient to you.

To see the Options dialog box, choose Tools, Options from the main Access menu. Figure 2.9 shows the resulting dialog box.

Many entries on these tabs refer to advanced topics best left until later in the book when you're more familiar with this product. However, there are several entries of interest to users of any level. Table 2.1 is a short list of these entries, the tabs they appear on, and a short explanation of what they can do for you.

FIGURE 2.9

The Options dialog box for Microsoft Access 2000 sports the familiar tabbed look.

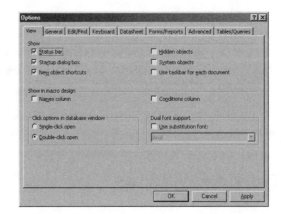

TABLE 2.1 SOME OF THE OPTIONS YOU CAN CHOOSE IN ACCESS

Entry	Tab	Description
Click Options in Database Window	View	Single or double-click to open objects
Default Database Folder	General	Where Access stores files by default
Confirm	Edit/Find	Confirm major actions (leave on for now)
Use Taskbar for Each Object	View	Does the taskbar have an entry for every Access object open or only one entry for Access itself (MDI or SDI)?
Fonts and Formatting	Datasheet	Various entries for the default appearance of Access grids (datasheets)

The entry causing the most confusion for users in general, and for those who are used to any previous version of Access, is Use Taskbar for Each Object. This is the Single Document Interface (SDI) standard, which has replaced the Multiple Document Interface (MDI) previously standard on all relevant Microsoft Office applications. However, Access, unlike other Office applications, gives you the option of MDI or SDI in the 2000 version.

With SDI active, every open object within your database has its own entry on the taskbar. With MDI active, only the Access program and the currently active object have an entry on the taskbar. It might seem that SDI is the way to go because it places all objects in easy reach—true. The downside of SDI is that many open objects mean a cluttered taskbar.

Add a few other applications, especially adamantly SDI applications such as Word or Notepad to a Windows session, and you can end up with a miserably cluttered taskbar. Figure 2.10 shows Access in SDI with several open objects, plus Word with several open documents, and one other application, PaintShop Pro. The taskbar is so cluttered that it is almost useless.

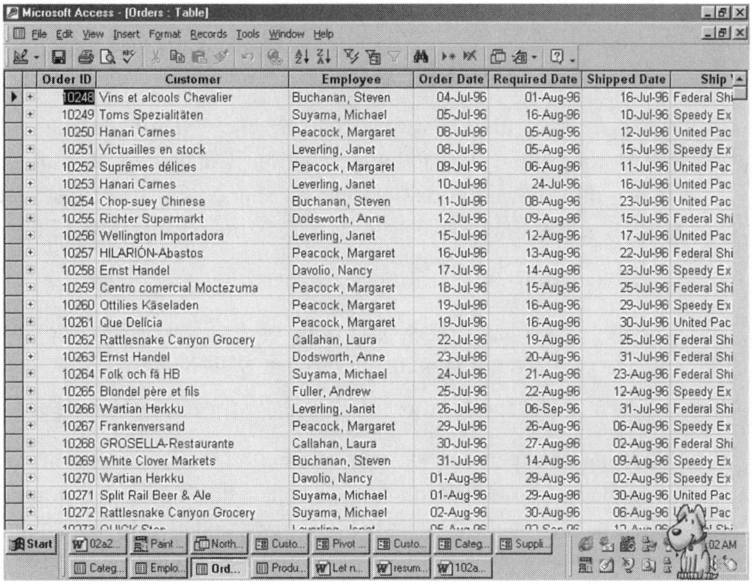

Microsoft Access - [Orders : Table]

Order ID	Customer	Employee	Order Date	Required Date	Shipped Date	Ship
10248	Vins et alcools Chevalier	Buchanan, Steven	04-Jul-96	01-Aug-96	16-Jul-96	Federal Shi
10249	Toms Spezialitäten	Suyama, Michael	05-Jul-96	16-Aug-96	10-Jul-96	Speedy Ex
10250	Hanari Carnes	Peacock, Margaret	08-Jul-96	05-Aug-96	12-Jul-96	United Pac
10251	Victuailles en stock	Leverling, Janet	08-Jul-96	05-Aug-96	15-Jul-96	Speedy Ex
10252	Suprêmes délices	Peacock, Margaret	09-Jul-96	06-Aug-96	11-Jul-96	United Pac
10253	Hanari Carnes	Leverling, Janet	10-Jul-96	24-Jul-96	16-Jul-96	United Pac
10254	Chop-suey Chinese	Buchanan, Steven	11-Jul-96	08-Aug-96	23-Jul-96	United Pac
10255	Richter Supermarkt	Dodsworth, Anne	12-Jul-96	09-Aug-96	15-Jul-96	Federal Shi
10256	Wellington Importadora	Leverling, Janet	15-Jul-96	12-Aug-96	17-Jul-96	United Pac
10257	HILARIÓN-Abastos	Peacock, Margaret	16-Jul-96	13-Aug-96	22-Jul-96	Federal Shi
10258	Ernst Handel	Davolio, Nancy	17-Jul-96	14-Aug-96	23-Jul-96	Speedy Ex
10259	Centro comercial Moctezuma	Peacock, Margaret	18-Jul-96	15-Aug-96	25-Jul-96	Federal Shi
10260	Ottilies Käseladen	Peacock, Margaret	19-Jul-96	16-Aug-96	29-Jul-96	Speedy Ex
10261	Que Delícia	Peacock, Margaret	19-Jul-96	16-Aug-96	30-Jul-96	United Pac
10262	Rattlesnake Canyon Grocery	Callahan, Laura	22-Jul-96	19-Aug-96	25-Jul-96	Federal Shi
10263	Ernst Handel	Dodsworth, Anne	23-Jul-96	20-Aug-96	31-Jul-96	Federal Shi
10264	Folk och fä HB	Suyama, Michael	24-Jul-96	21-Aug-96	23-Aug-96	Federal Shi
10265	Blondel père et fils	Fuller, Andrew	25-Jul-96	22-Aug-96	12-Aug-96	Speedy Ex
10266	Wartian Herkku	Leverling, Janet	26-Jul-96	06-Sep-96	31-Jul-96	Federal Shi
10267	Frankenversand	Peacock, Margaret	29-Jul-96	26-Aug-96	06-Aug-96	Speedy Ex
10268	GROSELLA-Restaurante	Callahan, Laura	30-Jul-96	27-Aug-96	02-Aug-96	Federal Shi
10269	White Clover Markets	Buchanan, Steven	31-Jul-96	14-Aug-96	09-Aug-96	Speedy Ex
10270	Wartian Herkku	Davolio, Nancy	01-Aug-96	29-Aug-96	02-Aug-96	Speedy Ex
10271	Split Rail Beer & Ale	Suyama, Michael	01-Aug-96	29-Aug-96	30-Aug-96	United Pac
10272	Rattlesnake Canyon Grocery	Suyama, Michael	02-Aug-96	30-Aug-96	06-Aug-96	Pac

FIGURE 2.10

The SDI interface isn't terribly useful if your application or work habits require many Office documents open simultaneously.

Figure 2.11 shows the same computer with the same documents, objects, and applications open, but with Access in MDI mode. Note how much less cluttered the taskbar is.

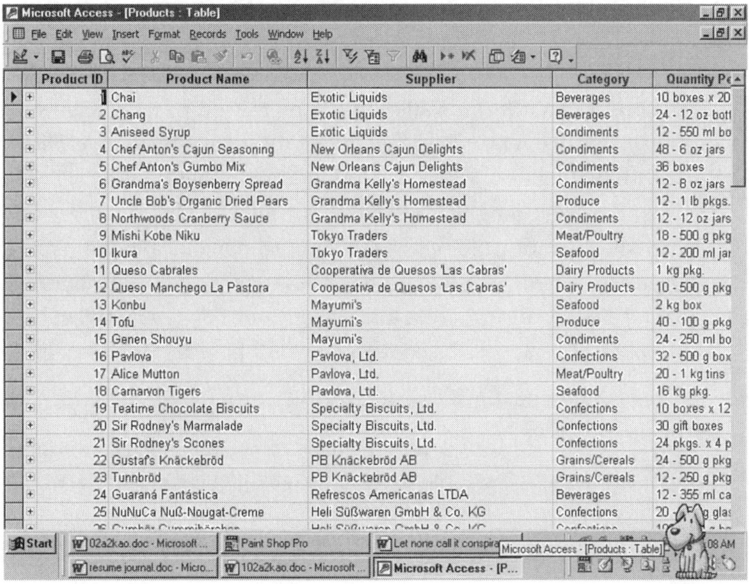

Microsoft Access - [Products : Table]

Product ID	Product Name	Supplier	Category	Quantity Pe
1	Chai	Exotic Liquids	Beverages	10 boxes x 20
2	Chang	Exotic Liquids	Beverages	24 - 12 oz bott
3	Aniseed Syrup	Exotic Liquids	Condiments	12 - 550 ml bo
4	Chef Anton's Cajun Seasoning	New Orleans Cajun Delights	Condiments	48 - 6 oz jars
5	Chef Anton's Gumbo Mix	New Orleans Cajun Delights	Condiments	36 boxes
6	Grandma's Boysenberry Spread	Grandma Kelly's Homestead	Condiments	12 - 8 oz jars
7	Uncle Bob's Organic Dried Pears	Grandma Kelly's Homestead	Produce	12 - 1 lb pkgs.
8	Northwoods Cranberry Sauce	Grandma Kelly's Homestead	Condiments	12 - 12 oz jars
9	Mishi Kobe Niku	Tokyo Traders	Meat/Poultry	18 - 500 g pkg
10	Ikura	Tokyo Traders	Seafood	12 - 200 ml jar
11	Queso Cabrales	Cooperativa de Quesos 'Las Cabras'	Dairy Products	1 kg pkg.
12	Queso Manchego La Pastora	Cooperativa de Quesos 'Las Cabras'	Dairy Products	10 - 500 g pkg
13	Konbu	Mayumi's	Seafood	2 kg box
14	Tofu	Mayumi's	Produce	40 - 100 g pkg
15	Genen Shouyu	Mayumi's	Condiments	24 - 250 ml bo
16	Pavlova	Pavlova, Ltd.	Confections	32 - 500 g box
17	Alice Mutton	Pavlova, Ltd.	Meat/Poultry	20 - 1 kg tins
18	Carnarvon Tigers	Pavlova, Ltd.	Seafood	16 kg pkg.
19	Teatime Chocolate Biscuits	Specialty Biscuits, Ltd.	Confections	10 boxes x 12
20	Sir Rodney's Marmalade	Specialty Biscuits, Ltd.	Confections	30 gift boxes
21	Sir Rodney's Scones	Specialty Biscuits, Ltd.	Confections	24 pkgs. x 4 p
22	Gustaf's Knäckebröd	PB Knäckebröd AB	Grains/Cereals	24 - 500 g pkg
23	Tunnbröd	PB Knäckebröd AB	Grains/Cereals	12 - 250 g pkg
24	Guaraná Fantástica	Refrescos Americanas LTDA	Beverages	12 - 355 ml ca
25	NuNuCa Nuß-Nougat-Creme	Heli Süßwaren GmbH & Co. KG	Confections	20 g glas

FIGURE 2.11

MDI is the way to go with Access if you have many database objects open or if you use other applications along with Access.

> **Tip**
>
> After switching Access from SDI to MDI or back again, be sure to close then open it to see your changes.

The Parts of Access

NEW TERM It's time to get a little technical here. A *database* is an orderly collection of data for presentation and manipulation. The data itself is all stored in *tables*, which are two-dimensional grids (matrices). Other database objects, such as forms and reports, present, select, filter, or otherwise modify the presentation of the data within tables.

To graduate to being a real Access expert, you need to master only two general skills:

- An expert has at least a working or descriptive knowledge of all the tools within Access and perhaps its big brother, SQL Server.
- An expert applies those tools ideally for each given task.

Becoming an expert sounds easy, doesn't it? Well, in theory it is, but as in many things, the fundamentals are simple but the details don't quite fall in place so easily. If they did, there would be nothing but Access experts, and clearly that situation doesn't exist. However, nothing about learning Access is overly difficult if taken in small bites.

  The first part of learning Access is to gain a working familiarity with the nature of the objects within the Database view. To proceed, launch Access if necessary and then open the database Start.mdb located on the CD-ROM that accompanies this book in the Day2 folder.

Tables

If necessary, click the Tables choice on the left of the Database view to make the table objects visible. Open the table object tblFriends by double-clicking it or clicking Open with it highlighted. Your screen should resemble Figure 2.12. The prefix tbl is a shorthand flag indicating that an object is a table. Although this is obvious when looking at the collection of table options, it's not so obvious at other places within Access. For example, if you were in a group, would you rather try to figure out whether that icon is a table, a query, or just see a three-letter prefix for each object positively identifying it? Also, in some areas of Access, you won't have an icon to help you.

> **Note**
>
> This book uses the most common naming convention derived from an early convention by Greg Reddick and Stan Lyszynski as modified by Lyszynski and the Kwery Corporation.

FIGURE 2.12

Fields go up and down, records go across in rows. Keep that in mind and you'll never get your fields crossed with your records.

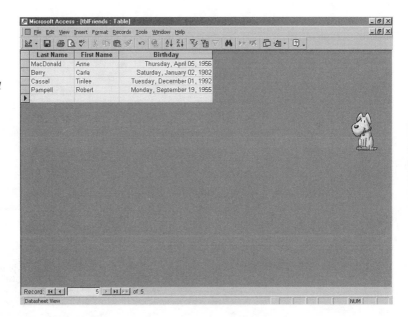

NEW TERM   This table has only a few entries. It holds the first name, last name, and birthday for a few people now, but of course it can be expanded to hold millions of names if necessary. The headings across the top of the grid are *field names*. The rows are *records*. The concept of which are the fields and which are the records is vital to understanding and using Access or any other database product.

- *Fields* hold similar data such as text, numbers, or dates. Fields classify data according to its data type. Each field in Figure 2.12 holds text classified by Last Name, First Name, or Birthday.

- *Records* classify data in the sense of a data picture of the table's purpose. In Figure 2.12, each record holds all the pertinent data for a particular person.

Click the View button at the far left of the toolbar to move into Design view. Figure 2.13 shows this view for this table. Remember, Design view is the view in which you modify the actual design of an object. It excludes all data information.

You can get a pretty good idea of how to design a table based on examination of Figure 2.13. The Design view is again a grid, but one with fixed columns. The first column is the field name that, also by default, appears as a table heading, the second column is the data type where you tell Access what kind of data it's going to store in that field, and the third column holds comments.

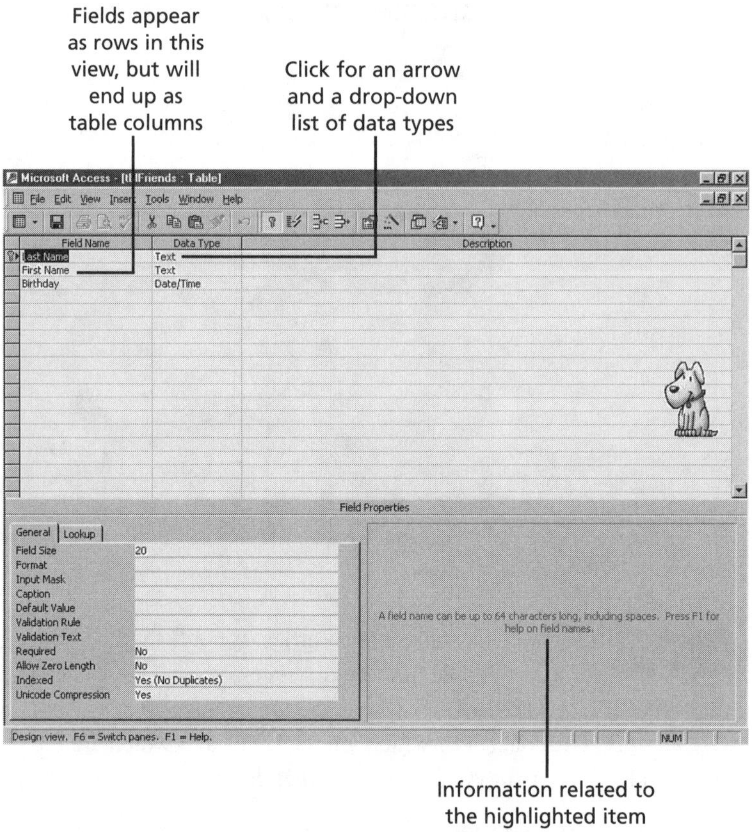

Fields appear
as rows in this
view, but will
end up as
table columns

Click for an arrow
and a drop-down
list of data types

Figure 2.13

*The Design view of an
object allows you to
examine or edit its
properties.*

Information related to
the highlighted item

The Design view is context sensitive. Click on the Birthday field and watch how the bottom portion of the grid (the Table Properties) changes to reflect the properties associated with a date/time field as opposed to a text field (Last Name).

Soon all these table properties will become second nature to you, but before proceeding there, let's move on to finish our tour of Access' objects. The next stop is queries.

Queries

Although tables hold all data, clearly the heart of Access is its query system. Using queries, you can select, order, present, filter, modify, and otherwise party it up with your data. Access has two basic ways to create queries, by directly entering SQL statements (difficult for beginners) or using the query by example grid. By the time you're finished with the 21 days, you'll have gained expertise in both systems.

To see a query in action, close the table object tblFriends if it's still open. Click on the Queries button and open the query qryFilteredFriends. Your screen should resemble Figure 2.14.

Note

To open a query in this context means to run it against existing data.

FIGURE 2.14

A query allows you to select, order, and otherwise present or modify your data.

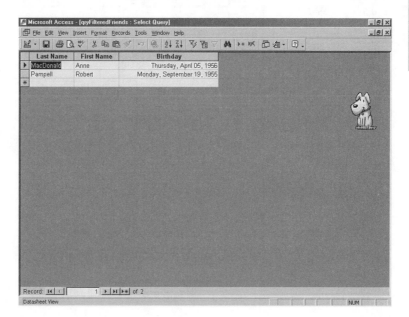

NEW TERM This query filters the table tblFriends to present only people who have birthdays before January 1, 1980. Keep in mind that doing this doesn't, by itself, affect the data in the underlying table. This is called a *select query* because it selects data according to your criteria. Also keep in mind that unless you take measures to prevent it, all select queries in Access are live. If you modify the data pulled up in your query (shown in Figure 2.14), these changes will affect the data in the underlying table. The select query itself doesn't do the modifications, but any editing will.

There are other types of queries besides the select query, known as *action queries*, which will change data in the underlying table. These are more complex queries and you'll learn about them on Day 15. For now, though, just be aware that "selecting" doesn't alter the data.

NEW TERM To see the magic behind the query, click the View button to move to Design view. Again you'll see a grid, this time the *query by example grid.*

Tables used as the
query's source

FIGURE 2.15

The query by example grid uses a visual metaphor to construct queries.

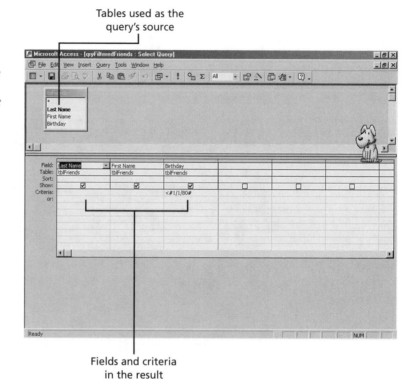

Fields and criteria
in the result

Again, you can probably figure out how the query works by simple examination of its upper and lower panes. The upper pane represents the fields in the linked (bound) table, tblFriends. This is the source for the query's data. In this case, all the fields from tblFriends are included in qryFilteredFriends, but they don't all need to be. You can also use more than one table in a query to combine data from more than one table, as you'll see later in Day 4, "Using Queries for Data Retrieval." Feel free to peek ahead to see how this looks.

The key to filtering or selecting within this query is the following statement in the criteria line under the Birthday field:

`<#1/1/80#`

This restricts the display of records to those that have a value less than (or, in other words that are before) January 1, 1980.

The other important view of a query is the SQL (Structured Query Language) behind it. Pull down the combo box view button at the far left of the toolbar and choose SQL View from the drop-down list. Your screen should resemble Figure 2.16.

FIGURE 2.16

The particulars of SQL are complex, but the language itself is plain English, which makes it fairly easy to get an idea of what's going on even if you have never seen it before.

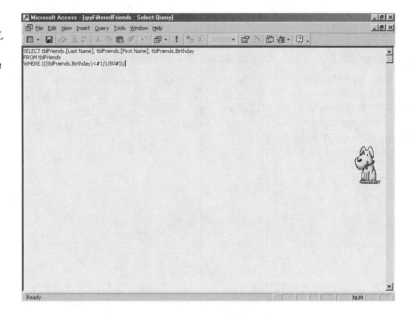

Again, even if you've never seen SQL before, you should be able to get an idea of how it works by examining the statement in Figure 2.16 and seeing the results in the Query view.

See how easy this can be? SQL is one of the most complex topics in Access and you already have an idea of how it works. You'll learn more about SQL on Day 14, "Understanding SQL." However, next on the tour of Access is forms—the fun part of database design.

Forms

Forms display data for viewing, editing, or entering. In addition, you can use form tools to help in data entry, data validation, or other related duties. Most people find that entering or editing data within forms is a lot easier than using the grid format of a query or table.

 In short, like queries, there is a lot of depth in forms, but also like queries, getting started with forms is fairly easy. Day 2 has a form called frmFriends, based on the object tblFriends. This is a simple form created by a wizard. It took about a minute to make because the special formatting is part of the designs supplied by Microsoft with Access 2000.

To see this form in action, close any open objects, click on the Forms entry in the Database view, and double-click on the object frmFriends. The form will open in Normal (or data) view. Your screen should resemble Figure 2.17.

FIGURE 2.17

This simple but attractive form bound to the tblFriends table took about a minute to make from start to finish, courtesy of a wizard.

Navigation
buttons

Number of records
in the table

Record on the form

This form shows the first entry in the table, the one for Carla Berry. The table has Last Name as its key field (a design mistake we'll get to later), so it orders its records by that field. Because Carla's last name is first alphabetically, it appears as the first record.

Take a look at the bottom of your screen, the status bar. You'll see the word Record and a box with the number 1 in it. That tells you that the record shown is first, and farther to the right you can see that there are four records total. Click the VCR-like control—the one with the wedge pointed to the right. That will move you one record at a time through the records until you're at the last record. You can jump forward and backward using the buttons with lines on them. The button with a star on it will jump you to a new record— the expressway to data entry.

Pull down the View button on the toolbar and choose Datasheet View from the pull-down list. That will change your screen to look similar to the underlying table. Figure 2.18 shows this view.

FIGURE 2.18

The Datasheet view is a form, too.

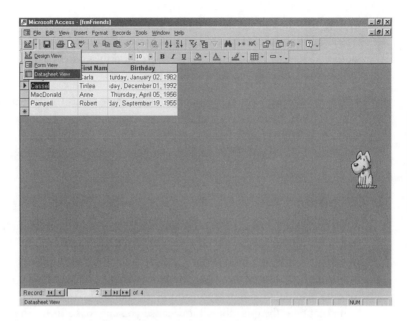

Finally, click the View button to go to Design view. The result will be the form design grid shown in Figure 2.19. Although this grid is a bit more complex than the grids you've seen before, you should be able to get a general idea of how the form is constructed.

FIGURE 2.19

The form design view is more complex than some of the grids in Access, but the actual use of the grid is, paradoxically, easier.

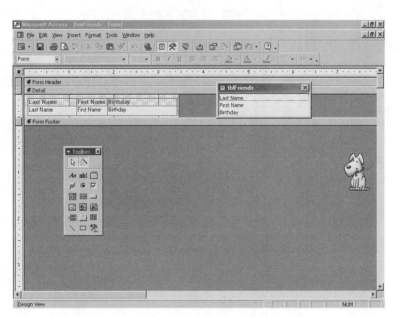

New Term   Again, as in the query design grid, there's a box (window really) showing the available fields for this form based on the table it's bound to (tblFriends). The *toolbox* (a toolbar that floats by default) toward the center of the screen holds the tools (or controls) you can use to construct your forms.

New Term   The *Detail section* of the form holds three fields (or controls) for data and three labels to tell users what the fields represent. Try switching back and forth between the Design and Form views to see how the controls and their labels make the transition. When you're finished, close the form and discard changes if you've made any; it's time reports took the center stage.

Reports

Novices to Access tend to be a bit confused about why there are both forms and reports within the product because you can print forms and show reports on your screen. The simple answer is that reports are forms optimized for printing whereas forms are, well, forms optimized for screen use. The more complex answer is that forms have facilities for data manipulation and reports don't, thus bringing issues such as database security to bear. That begs the question a bit because you can make forms that won't tolerate any data manipulation. So let's just leave it that forms are optimized for screens, whereas reports are optimized for the printer.

 Open the report rptFriends by choosing the Reports section in the Database view and double-clicking on that object. Your screen should resemble Figure 2.20.

FIGURE 2.20

To put it simply, a report is a form optimized for the printer, but as you can see it works all right on the screen, too.

Last Name	First Name	Birthday	
MacDonald	Anne		Thursday, April 05,
Last Name	First Name	Birthday	
Berry	Carla		Saturday, January 02,
Last Name	First Name	Birthday	
Cassel	Tirilee		Tuesday, December 01, 1992
Last Name	First Name	Birthday	
Pampell	Robert		Monday, September 19, 1955

When you open a report by double-clicking or by choosing Open from the action buttons in the Database view, Access will put you in Print Preview view. This shows the report as it should print out from your printer. Like the form, the report can scroll though records using the VCR-like buttons at the bottom of the screen. Because all the records from tblFriends easily fit on one screen, this facility isn't relevant to this report.

Click the now-familiar View button on the toolbar to switch to Design view for this report. Your screen should resemble Figure 2.21.

FIGURE 2.21

The report design grid is very similar to the form design grid. That's by design (ahem), not accident.

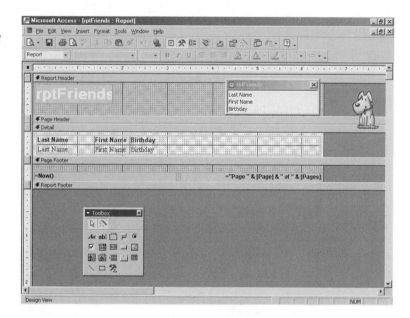

This should look familiar to you by now. The report design grid is very similar to the form design grid. There is a toolbox, a list of available fields, a Detail section, and two header sections that are active in the report where they weren't in the form. However, they're present in both forms and reports, although the entire business of headers and footers is a bit more complex in reports than forms.

Again, you have field controls in the Detail section, in which the actual data will appear when the report runs or prints. There are field labels, and some more labels in the header and footer sections. By switching between Design and Print Preview views, you can gain a good idea of how all the design features work in the actual report.

One of the greatest things about Access is its skills transferability. Just about anything you learn about designing forms is applicable to reports. The characteristic is commutative.

Pages

Starting with the previous version of Office 97, Microsoft got serious—some would say frantic—about the Internet. Suddenly every application was at least somewhat Internet enabled. Access was no exception. Through it you could save objects as HTML objects for display or even live manipulation on the Web.

Creation of static or dynamic objects for use on the Web is easier with the more powerful Dynamic Access Pages feature in Access 2000. This is an entirely new component of Access. Unlike other objects, Dynamic Access Pages exist outside the database container (the .mdb file).

The beauty and power of a Dynamic Access Page is that through it you can display (or edit) data contained within an Access database through the Web. Think of a Dynamic Access Page as the link between Access data and a person on the Internet or an intranet. Although most Dynamic Access Pages display Access data, they can also display data contained within an Excel spreadsheet or both.

Figure 2.22 shows a Dynamic Access Page in Design view. This Dynamic Access Page was created by a wizard and is based on the Employees table from the sample database Northwind.

FIGURE 2.22

The Page Design view is similar to other graphical objects such as forms or reports.

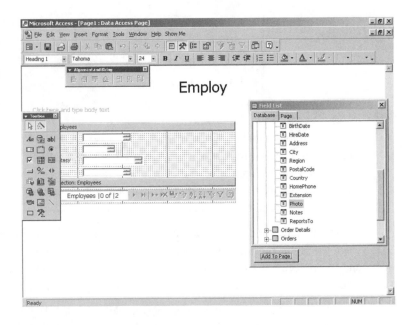

After a few edits, the final Dynamic Access Page is ready for display, as you can see in Figure 2.23.

FIGURE 2.23

After completion, the Dynamic Access Page is ready for display not only in Access, but in any network, including the Internet.

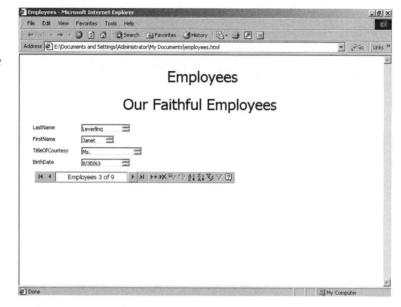

Note that the Dynamic Access Page shown in Figure 2.23 is displayed in a browser (Internet Explorer 5) but shows data from inside the Northwind database. The page has dynamic links to the database itself. Edits made to the data shown in Figure 2.23 will affect the data contained in Northwind.

Macros

NEW TERM The *macro* language within Access is a simple way to program Access for foreseeable events or to automate tasks. Close any open objects in the Day 2 database, click the Macros section in the Database view, and open the macro mcrMessage either by clicking the Open button or double-clicking the entry. Your screen should resemble Figure 2.24.

Click OK to clear the message box. If necessary, highlight the macro named mcrMessage in the Database view and click the design button to see the macro's design. Your screen should resemble Figure 2.25.

Once again, you should be able to examine the macro design grid and get a good idea of how this macro operates. The Action column should be self-explanatory—this macro's action is to display a message box (msgbox). Pay special attention to the Action Arguments section, where you'll see entries for both the title bar and the message itself.

If you want to see the macro in action so you can observe the transition from the design elements to the running elements, click the Run button on the toolbar. This has an exclamation point for an icon. When you're satisfied you have this macro figured out, close it and discard changes.

FIGURE 2.24

The macro design grid is yet another grid resembling the table design grid, but vastly different in use.

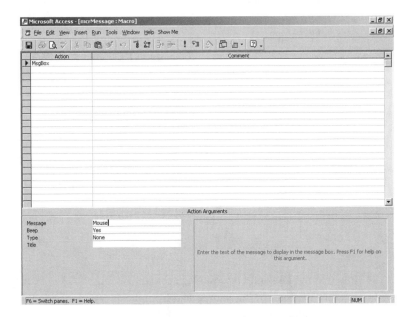

Click to run
the macro

FIGURE 2.25

The chief characteristic of this simple macro is the macro action specified in the left column. In this case, when the macro is run, it will display a message box.

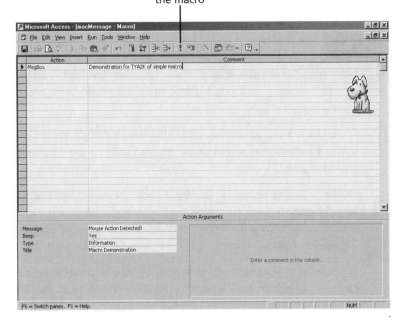

"Well," you might wonder, "that was interesting, but useless." So let's continue with the macro demonstration by showing an admittedly trivial, but good for demonstration purposes, macro activation upon an event.

NEW TERM   *Events* are actions that occur with or to an object. For example, a mouse moving over a button on a form is an event. Microsoft takes care to name events in such away to make them easy to associate with the real world. For example, the event for the mouse cursor moving over an object might be labeled MouseOver.

Return to the Forms section of the Database view and open the form frmMacroDemo in Form view. Move your mouse all around the form, being sure to avoid the red rectangle labeled Mouse Corral. When you're satisfied that nothing's strange, pass your mouse cursor over the Mouse Corral. Your screen should resemble Figure 2.26.

FIGURE 2.26

A macro's power comes when it springs into action due to some event or occurrence within your program.

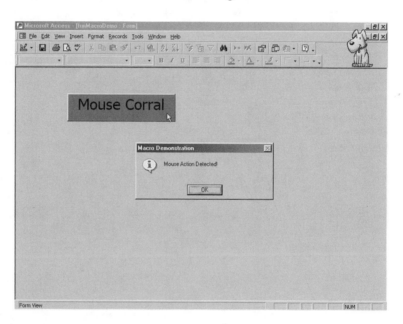

Obviously this is a rather silly example of what you can use macros for, but I think you'll understand the principle, so let's move on to modules.

Modules

NEW TERM   *Modules* are VBA (Visual Basic for Applications) code—real computer programming. The extent of VBA programming is enormous and often needed for externally distributed Access projects. The enormousness (but not enormity) of VBA tends to discourage some otherwise adept Access users, but it need not be that way. Although the potential for VBA is huge, just like anything else, taking it in small bites will surely be within the reach of anybody who cares to take the time.

This example of a VBA module is overly simple to demonstrate that VBA as a topic doesn't have to overwhelm even the most novice user.

Follow along here or, if you feel like jumping in, you can follow the steps using your own copy of Access.

Close all database objects, discarding changes. Click on the Modules section of the Database view. Double-click on the module modDemo. Your screen should resemble Figure 2.27.

Return to the
standard
Access view   Click to run
a module

FIGURE 2.27

*The module design
area is considerably
different in look,
behavior, and use than
any other Access
design facility.*

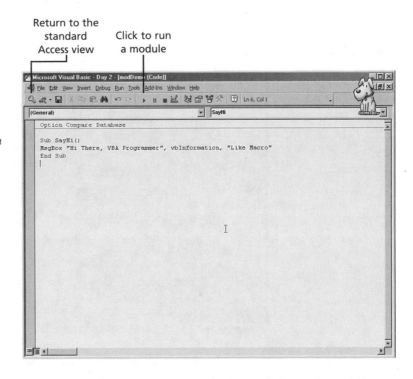

Click the Run button on the toolbar. That's the one close to the middle with the right-pointing wedge; or, if you prefer, click F5 (Run). Access will prompt you about which module to run, but because you have only one choice, just click Run. Your screen should resemble Figure 2.28.

By examining the code in Figure 2.27, you should have a pretty good idea of how this routine works. To return from the screen in Figure 2.27 to the standard Access screen, click the View Microsoft Access button on the toolbar. That's the one at the far left in

Figure 2.27. It has a key for an icon. Day 13, "Introducing VBA," has a complete introduction to VBA.

FIGURE 2.28

*A VBA module can call
macros and macro-like
actions or do non-
macro duty.*

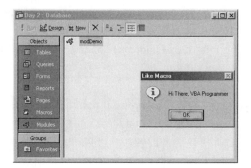

2

Well, that's it for your fast tour of the various Access objects. Close all objects and
Access itself because the next sections don't use the Day 2 database.

Analysis of Your Project

Bluntly put, the success of any database project depends on the quality of its planning.
Access is much more forgiving of poor data design than other database systems, but even
it can't make a good project out of no planning.

You, as the developer, will need to find a planning method that suits you best, but most
people do at least roughly similar tasks. Because the point of a database system is data
organization (or information), you must pay attention to the output. In fact, it's a fairly
common practice to design the database system around what it needs to output. Here is
one way a certain developer goes about looking at a project. You can use this list and
modify it to suit your tastes and needs.

1. Determine the purpose of the project—What will come out of it? What level of
   users will have to manipulate the data? How much flexibility do they need?

2. Determine the workflow and see how it will integrate into the organization—Will
   the organization modify its behavior, forms, and other data-related objects for this
   project, or does the project need to conform to systems already in place? What is
   the level of the expertise available to you within the company (useful if you're an
   external person)? What time is available for this project?

3. What data is available to you?—Is what you need already structured in another
   computer system, or will you need to have your people enter the data from scratch?
   Can this system save time or steps in another area of the organization?

4. Conceptualize the data for use within the system—Think of your data not in human terms, but computer ones. For a relational database such as Access, this boils down to normalizing your data or breaking it into a table system with data linked by key fields and no duplication (or as little as possible) between tables (normalization). That is, if you have a person's address anywhere in a database table, you should not have that address repeated anywhere. Instead, think of a structure in which you can link the address to any other data (such as name) you want to display.

5. Prototype the system—This is an optional part, useful for large projects in which a do-over will cost you dearly. Create a model of your proposed system and test it with live data. If you're working externally in any aspect, show it to users and approvers to get their input. The latter step can be a disaster if you lose control of the input sessions, but is very useful if there is any doubt that the people you will be depending upon to make use of this system are at all reluctant to use it. Reluctant users can destroy any database system.

Don't Be a Slave to Convention

When reviewing currently used systems, don't try to duplicate them utterly. A well-designed paper system (or a mainframe one) isn't necessarily a good template for a modern database system. Always keep in mind the parts of Access and its particular capabilities and strengths.

For example, a paper system can't have a pull-down text box (combo box), whereas Access can. A paper system can't validate entry; Access can. A paper system can't automatically call up information based on partly entered data; Access can.

Although you can automate and improve a paper or mainframe system by simply duplicating it using Access, you won't be using the program to its fullest. You've got the most capable and up-to-date database program in existence, so use it like it should be used.

Don't Worry Yet

If you've considered actually putting these steps into action using a database problem you currently face and despaired, don't worry. Putting these fundamentals into action requires a good working knowledge of Access. That's something you'll gain in the next 19 days or so.

The point is to keep on hand the following information:

- Knowledge of your data source
- Your informational output

- User characteristics
- Current workflow
- Your workers' task mutability—will they adjust to the system or must the system come to them?
- The parts of Access
- The restructuring or viewing of your data in relational form rather than human form

Trying to visualize putting all these elements into action at this point is asking too much of yourself. After you've finished this book, come back to this section and it will all be much clearer.

Do	Don't
DO learn and use reference material including database theory.	**DON'T** slavishly adhere to convention when it threatens to hurt your work. Be creative.

Getting Help—The Office Assistant

Microsoft has had a goal, often called "accessibility," for Office applications such as Access. This differs from the Accessibility Options in Windows—special aids for users with unusual needs. However it's thematically similar.

It's fairly easy for Microsoft or another company to pack a program with features, but two things prevent users from availing themselves of those features.

- The users can't find them.
- The users can't figure out how to use them after they are found.

Microsoft has decided the best way to aid users is to pump up the online help facility. This has several advantages for users and Microsoft itself.

- Users will call for Microsoft support less often.
- Users will get better use from the product, and presumably talk up the wonders of the program to their friends, family, and coworkers.
- Microsoft can have a less-guilty conscience about eliminating just about all written documentation, thus forcing users to buy third-party instruction manuals such as this one.

The first iteration of the Office Assistant (OA) showed up in Office 97—the infamous or famous paper clip. Some users thought it cute and loved this iteration, but too many considered it patronizing or even an interference with their work.

Microsoft has vastly improved the OA for Office 2000. The dog you see wandering about in the Start database objects is named Rocky—one of the newer OAs. He's supposed to understand natural English (or whatever language you speak) questions; however, he occasionally fails to get your point.

The configuration of the OA is straightforward. Open Access. You won't need an active database to try the elements in this section.

Right-click on Rocky or whatever assistant you have active. Choose Options from the context menu. If you have no assistant available, choose the menu selections Help, Show the Office Assistant. If this isn't available, you'll need to install the OA using Office setup.

Figure 2.29 shows the Options dialog box with the Options tab active.

FIGURE 2.29

The options for the Office Assistant allow you to choose the OA you want to talk to, and also its (his?) behavior.

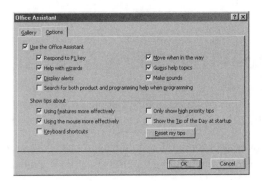

The Gallery tab allows you to choose from a selection of Office Assistants. The dog shown in Figure 2.29 and throughout this chapter is called Rocky. Microsoft promises to issue new OA's from time to time and distribute them for free through its Web site.

Real Experts Shun Help—Ha!

If you ever get a chance to visit an Access convention where the heavyweight Access programmers hang out, ask a few whether they use the help facility in Access. They will universally tell you that they do. There is no shame in not wanting to memorize thousands of properties, keywords, functions, and the other folderol you need to develop an Access application. Why should you bother?

Microsoft has also included many examples you can copy and paste directly into your application from the help facility. These are guaranteed to run flawlessly (bug free), so why not paste them in and then modify them to your specific needs? There is no reason not to!

The Ways of Help

To see the help facilities in action you'll need to open a database, so if you want to follow along, open Start.mdb. Click on Rocky or your OA, and choose See a Complete List of Help Topics. Locate the Show icon at the top of the resulting screen and click it. Your screen should resemble Figure 2.30.

FIGURE 2.30

A complete list of help topics includes the help text itself, an index, a table of contents, and a natural language find engine.

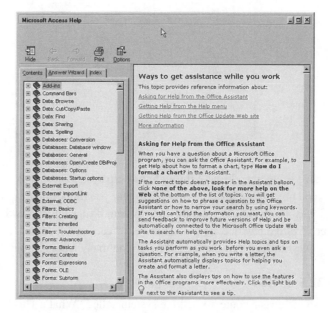

From here you can find topics by browsing through the table of contents (Contents), by using the Answer Wizard (identical to asking the OA directly), or by entering what you hope is a keyword in the Index section.

Figure 2.31 shows a real help page about forms. The underlined entries in the text screen at the right are links to other topics. These work identically, and are really identical in all important aspects, to the links on a Web page. If you want to drill down deeper in any area summarized in the page shown, just click on it.

FIGURE 2.31

The format of the Office help system is identical to Web pages. You can drill down (using hypertext) by clicking on any link.

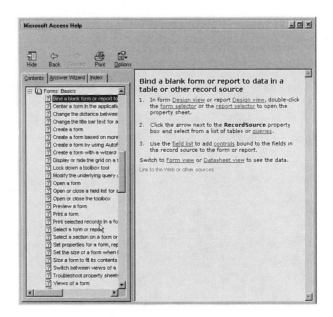

If you have some time, browse through the help system now looking at the organization of the contents. Locate a word within help that you think might be a keyword and enter it in the Index section to see what the help system brings up. Try asking Rocky or the Answer Wizard a few questions such as "How can I get a date on Saturday night?" (a famous question asked of the wizard by all too many Access programmers).

What's This?

Help also includes a context-sensitive system called "What's This?". To use this facility, locate a dialog box with a question mark for an icon in its title bar, click on it, then click on objects in the dialog box. If a context subject exists, Access will bring up a short cheat sheet–type balloon help with a hint as to what goes in the dialog box or what an object is.

Here's an example. From the main menu, choose Tools, Security, Set Database Password. Click on the question mark icon next to the Close icon in the title bar of the resulting dialog box. The cursor changes to a pointer with a question mark attached. Click on the Password field. Your screen should resemble Figure 2.32.

FIGURE 2.32

Context-sensitive help can also call up the main help facility. Here if you click the tiny button with the right-pointing chevron, Access will launch its full help facility.

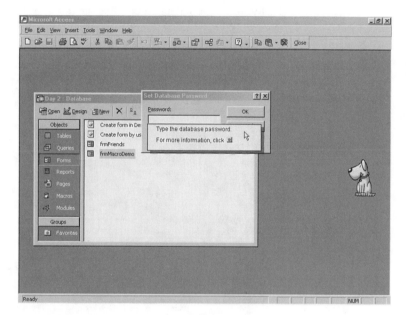

This ToolTip-like help has a button in it that will bring up a lot more information about this topic. Don't, at this point, actually add a password to your database or you risk locking yourself out. Day 20, "Understanding Access Security," addresses security issues.

You can also call up context help by pressing Shift+F1. Try this: Return to the Database view (Database view) itself. Press Shift+F1 and click on the title bar of the database window. In this way, you can call upon context help for objects that don't have the question mark icon.

Toolbars

If you're familiar with using toolbars in any Office application, you have a good working knowledge of how to use them in Access. Access does allow you to link certain toolbars to objects, but that's an advanced topic to be covered in Day 16, "Advanced Form

Concepts." That day also covers how to place custom macros and other user-defined objects on a standard or custom toolbar. This section only covers use of toolbars in the standard Office way.

To add a button to a toolbar, right-click on any toolbar and choose Customize from the context menu. That will bring up a dialog box like the one shown in Figure 2.33.

FIGURE 2.33

The toolbars in Access are fully customizable.

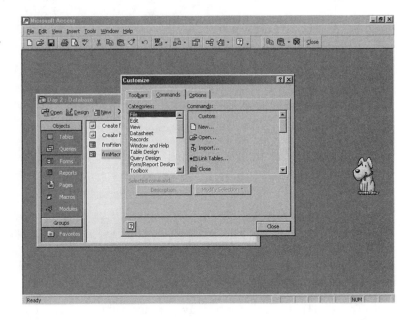

To add any command to a toolbar, locate it using the left and right panes of the dialog box, and then drag it to the toolbar, dropping it where you want it to reside. To remove a button from a toolbar with the Customize dialog box showing, just drag it off the toolbar and drop it anywhere on the desktop. To remove a button without the Customize dialog box, press the Alt key while dragging it off the toolbar.

Try this: With the Start database open, scroll the left pane (Categories) of the dialog box until you can highlight the All Macros entry. This will bring up the macMessage macro in the Commands (right) pane. Drag this macro to any toolbar, dropping it in a convenient place. Close the dialog box by clicking on OK. Now click on the new button you just added. Your screen should resemble Figure 2.34.

When you're finished, you can remove this button by pressing Alt and dragging it off the toolbar.

Figure 2.34

Adding user-defined buttons to a toolbar isn't too difficult. Note the mouse cursor hovering over the new button added to the toolbar. This button now triggers the macro.

You can dock your toolbars at any edge of the screen or let them float around your display. Most people find floating toolbars to be annoying and leave them docked, but that is your call. To move or resize a toolbar, grab it by its handle (the raised portion at the left of a toolbar) and drag. If the cursor is in the shape of a cross, you can move the toolbar. A double-arrow cursor is the icon for sliding and resizing. A little experimentation with these toolbars is all you need to get a feel for them.

The menu bar is a type of toolbar, too, and like the usual-looking toolbars, you can float it around. Figure 2.35 shows Access with all the standard bars and one optional bar afloat. You can also dock them in any order you want. For example, Figure 2.36 shows one toolbar docked on the left, the menu bar docked on the right, and the clipboard toolbar docked on top. This arrangement isn't terribly practical, but it shows what you can do with toolbars.

Figure 2.35

You can float all or some toolbars. It's a matter of taste.

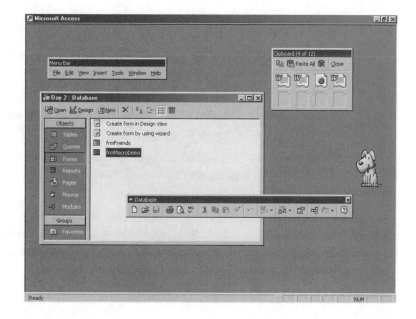

FIGURE 2.36

*Toolbars can dock at
the sides, bottom or
top of a screen.*

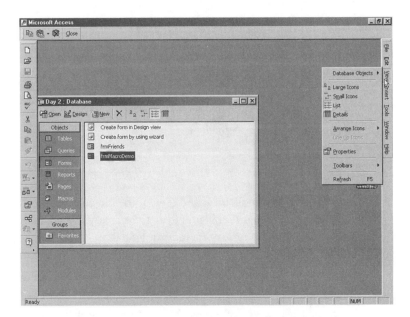

Using the Database Wizard to Create an Application

Access comes with several predefined databases you can create by using a wizard. For the most part, there is little you can do during the wizard process to affect the output other than choosing the inclusion or exclusion of certain optional fields.

The chief value of the new database wizard is to create templates for later modification by you using Design view for the various objects you want to customize. A secondary value to those new to Access is that you can examine the output of the wizard to see how it assembles various applications.

To see the wizard in action, with Access open, choose File, New, and then choose the Databases tab. Your screen should resemble Figure 2.37.

To launch the new database wizard, choose any entry shown in this tab and then click OK. Access will walk you through the wizard, where your chief options will be the formats used in display objects.

If you feel adventurous, this is a good time to run through a few of the wizards and then examine the output to see how the various objects in Access fit together. The best aspect of these wizard-generated databases is that you can always erase them and re-create them identically. This allows you unlimited experimentation without any consequences.

FIGURE 2.37

The Databases tab has several options for wizard-generated pre-defined databases.

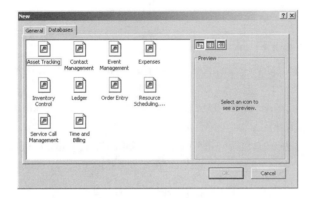

2

Summary

To use Access, or to even plan an Access project, you need a good working familiarity with the Access user interface and the objects that make up a project. Today's lesson gave you a good foundation in these areas.

The primary display in Access is the Database view. This is where you can see all the objects within your database, either classified by type or clustered within a heterogeneous group. The Database view has an object bar allowing views of other types of objects and a toolbar (below the title bar) allowing you to take actions on the selected objects.

There are seven types of Access objects grouped within the Database view: tables, queries, forms, reports, pages, macros, and modules. Tables hold data. The other objects either display or manipulate that data.

You analyze and apply a project by examining your Access skills, Access' capacities, your users' needs, and your users' facilities. The successful developer finds the ideal synthesis for these often competing aspects of a project.

Real Access developers use help almost constantly. You can use the table of contents, the Answer Wizard, or muck through the index. Help can be context sensitive, and will contain a wealth of examples for you to adapt to your needs.

The Database Wizard quickly and easily creates canned applications. If your needs are close to what a wizard outputs, you're likely a candidate for modifying a wizard-generated application rather than making one from scratch.

Q&A

Q Why can't I store data in a query?

A Queries query either another query or a table. They can't be the original store for data.

Q Why not just enter data directly in a table and skip all the form bother?

A You can if you want to, but most users find forms easier for data entry. Also, forms have extended facilities for data entry not directly available in tables. Few, if any, good Access developers ask users to add data directly into tables.

Q Can I print a form?

A Yes, but the results aren't generally satisfactory because form controls aren't optimized for printing.

Q Can I use color in reports? The example today was all grayscale.

A Yes, but keep in mind that if your users don't have color printers, using color can have unpredictable results.

Q Why does the query date criteria have number signs (#) around it?

A That's Access' way to signal that the enclosed string is a date. In most cases, Access will autoformat that for you when you just enter a date as a query criteria.

Workshop

The Workshop helps you solidify the skills you learned in this lesson. Answers to the quiz questions appear in Appendix A, "Answers."

Quiz

1. What Access object is optimized for display of data on a screen? A printer?

2. Will double-clicking on a form in Database view open it in Design view?

3. Can you run a macro from the macro design view?

4. What language does a module use?

5. Where does Access store data?

6. Are the columns in a table the fields or the records?

7. Is the type of data in a record always uniform (of the same data type)?

Exercises

1. Open the Start database.

2. Change the user interface from SDI to MDI, or to MDI if it is already SDI.

3. Close all dialog boxes.

4. Open tblFriends in Design view.

5. Add a field named Telephone with the data type left at default text.

6. Switch to Table view, and add a few phone numbers to the existing data.

2

DAY 3

Exploring the Data Foundations—The Table

The past two days have mired you down in theory. Today starts the real hands-on use of Access, which, for most people, is a lot easier than abstract discussion. I think you'll also find that using Access is just plain fun. So let's get started. Today, you will learn the following:

- The nature of a table
- Creating a table
- Table properties
- Editing table properties

The Nature of a Table

Yesterday you saw the way a table looks in Data and Design views. Today you'll learn how to create a table. You'll also gain an understanding of the theory behind various table elements and how to apply that theory to your projects.

Remember that a table is the fundamental element in a relational database. It is the place where the system stores all data. The other objects of a database system manipulate or present the data, all of which is stored in these tables. The irony of a table's position in a database system is that although it's the simplest object to create or modify, it's also the most important in the sense that if the table structure is wrong, the database system can't be right.

The most important element in table design is making sure that the table's fields are suitable for the intended data. For example, if you define an address field as being able to hold only 20 characters, you will be in deep trouble when people start entering real addresses in that field. You can change much of a table's design after the fact, but some changes will cause ripple problems (downstream trouble) if the table is linked to other tables, or if you have other database objects expecting a certain data structure.

The moral of the story is to plan three times and do once.

Examining a Table

Locate and open the Tables.mdb database on your CD-ROM. Click the Tables entry in the object bar, and then open in Datasheet view (double-click on) the tblAllTypes object. Your screen should resemble Figure 3.1.

FIGURE 3.1

A table is a simple structure, but it holds the key to the success of your database.

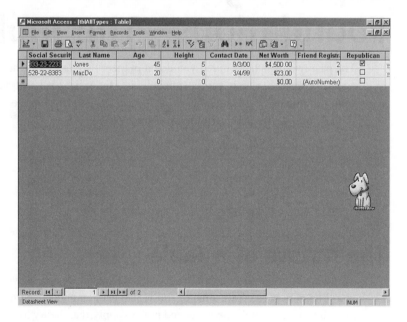

This table has various field types (data types) and is a trivial example, but should give you a feel for the nature of a table and the types of data it holds.

Click in the Social Security Number field. Note that Access creates a template for a Social Security number. That template is called an input mask. Enter a Social Security number. Now click on the Last Name field and try entering the last name Gonzalez. You can't because the field size for this field has been defined too small to be useful for a Last Name field. This is a rather obvious error, but one of the types you as a developer must watch out for.

Continue to enter data, observing from entries that have come before what type of data you suppose the field should hold. The final field, Sound, contains a sound file (.wav) that you can play if you have a sound-enabled computer, but don't worry about entering new sounds in this field. Try entering apparently wrong data such as 3/4 in the Contact Date field. The table won't accept data that's inappropriate. You won't need to (or can't) enter a number in the Friend Registration Number because that will auto-increment when you're finished with the record.

When you're finished experimenting, switch to Design view by clicking the view button at the far left of the toolbar. Your screen should resemble Figure 3.2.

FIGURE 3.2

Here is a table that contains a sample of various data types.

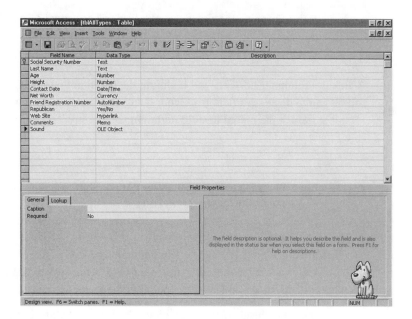

When designing your tables you must focus on the following main issues:

- What will be the key field for the table?
- What data type will you use for each field?
- What properties for each field do you need to set?
- How does this table fit into your entire data structure scheme?

Use the `tblAllFields` object in Design view to explore the various elements of this elementary table's design. Pull down combo boxes; examine how the Properties section changes as you click different fields (having different data types). Click the Last Name field entry, and examine the Field Size property, noting that it's too small to accommodate most of the world's last names (remember the problem you had when you tried to enter Gonzalez?).

Return to Datasheet view for this table, discarding any changes you might have made in Design view. Place your cursor between any two columns until the cursor changes to a bar with opposite-facing arrows. Click and drag, noting how you can change the visible size of a field.

Note   Changing the visible size of a field will not alter its Field Size property.

Click the column head. This will highlight the column. Pressing Delete at this point will allow you to delete this field from your database. Click to the right of the Social Security Number field at the record level to highlight an entire record. Your screen should resemble Figure 3.3.

Tip   Using the usual Explorer keys Ctrl and Shift, you can make multiple selections of fields or records.

Again, pressing Delete will delete any highlighted records. Keep in mind that although this works for a few records, an action query is a better way to delete records from a live database, as discussed on Day 15, "Examining Special Query Uses."

Click any column head, keeping the mouse button pressed, and then drag the column to the right or left. This will change the column order display, but it won't affect the order of fields in Design view.

FIGURE 3.3

Using a record selector, you can highlight a record or a series of records.

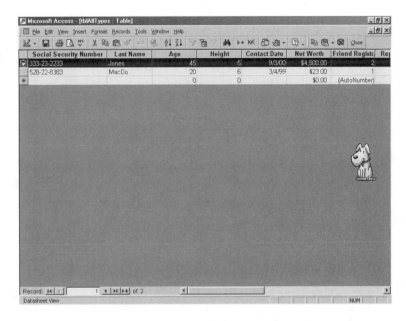

Finally, click between two rows on the far left of the table—in the record selector area. Your cursor will change to a double arrow with a bar. Drag up or down to change the width of all records.

Note

All rows (records) in a table must be the same width. You can't resize rows individually.

Finally, click the Format entry in the main menu bar. Note the entries that are available to you for this table. Microsoft has made some changes to Access to make it work somewhat like Excel for tables and queries (when feasible), so you get the Excel-like entries for hiding and freezing columns (fields).

Keep in mind that it should be a very rare or even non-existent event that users even see a table, much less make data entries to it or edit its layout (change column or row order or widths). Microsoft added these table facilities apparently to make Excel experts feel more at home. An adept Access developer will have his or her data entry done all through forms or automated by macros or VBA.

> **Tip**
>
> Using the same technique as record selection, you can alter (drag) the field order in Design view. This will alter the order of fields in Table (Data) view. Conversely, altering the order of fields in Table view will not alter their order in the design grid.

Creating Your First Table

By now you probably have enough experience in tables and their views to have a good idea of how to create the critters, but follow along with this section because you'll likely pick up a few interesting details.

There are three ways to make a table. They are

- Use the design view grid
- Use data entry to create a table by example
- Use a wizard

Table Design Basics

The design grid is the way almost all (maybe all) experienced Access developers create their tables. This grid is the only way to have the fine control of your fields' properties that you must have in any but the most elementary Access applications.

Somewhat perversely, Microsoft tries to get you to use the sample entry (shown following) for tables by automatically launching that method when you define a new blank database. This likely stems from some user focus groups, but it's truly baffling for most Access users.

Here are the steps to creating a table using the design grid:

1. From the Database view, click New and then choose Design View from the resulting dialog box, and click OK.
2. Enter a field name in the first row of the Field Name column.
3. Press Enter or Tab to move to the Data Type field.
4. Enter a data type for this field. Access will scroll using the first letter of the data type. You can also pull down the combo box, and choose the data type from a list.
5. Alter the Field Properties section of the table design grid as needed.
6. Add a comment in the Description column if desired.

The following are the various data types and their uses:

- Text—Alphanumeric data up to 255 characters. Access uses dynamic storage, so specifying a field fewer than 255 characters will not affect disk storage needs, but it can have an effect on auto-generated objects (such as forms) based on the field.

- Number—Various kinds of numbers from byte (0–255) to decimal. Use the Number type only for fields that must have computational operations on them; otherwise, use Text. You specify what kind of Number data types your field will hold by altering the Field Size property. Figure 3.4 shows the combo box for the Number data type with its selections exposed.

FIGURE 3.4

The Number data type uses the Field Size property to specify the type of numbers your field will receive.

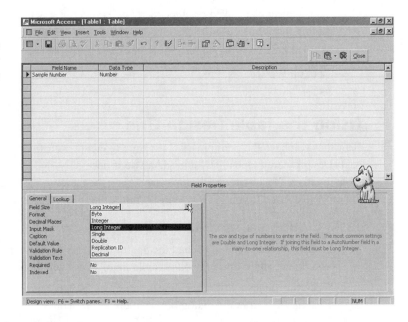

Tip

Use the least-precise Number data type you can to preserve database size and to optimize Access' performance.

- Date/Time—Really a Number data type too because Access stores dates as sequential numbers. Used to store dates or times.

- Currency—Another variant of the Number data type. This is optimized (it's very precise) for currency calculations and it formats using a currency sign.

> A Number data type entry can't start with a zero, so use Text for any fields (such as Social Security number) in which there exists the possibility of a leading zero or zeros.

- AutoNumber—A field that either sequentially or randomly assigns a number to each record without any user input.
- Yes/No—A very compact data type that is either on or off (yes or no). Good for check box type fields such as Application Received?.
- OLE Object—A linked or embedded OLE object of any type. Normally used for adding items such as music, sound, or pictures to a table.
- Hyperlink—A URL such as a Web site address or an email address.
- Lookup Wizard—Not really a data type, but a way to link a source to a field within a table.

Using the Table Design Grid

Now that you have the preliminaries, it's time to create your first table using the design grid (Design view). Open the Tables database if necessary, and open the tblEmployees table in either Table view or Design view. That's the table you'll be creating in this and the other task lists. If you get lost, consult this table to see where you went wrong.

Task: Creating a Table Using Design View

1. Launch Access and either load the Tables database or start a new blank database. If you do the latter, close the blank table that Access will auto-launch.
2. Click the Tables entry in the object bar. Click New to start a new table. Choose Design View from the dialog box, and click OK. That will launch the design grid. You can also choose Create Table in Design View from the Database view.
3. Enter the field name Employee ID in the first row of the Field Name column. Press Enter to enter the Data Type field. Your screen should resemble Figure 3.5.
4. Click the Key Field icon (the one with the key on it) in the toolbar. The Employee ID field will be the field used to link the tables within this database. Click in the Field Size field in the Field Properties section of the grid. Edit the value to read 6, the size of an employee number in this company.

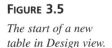

FIGURE 3.5

The start of a new table in Design view.

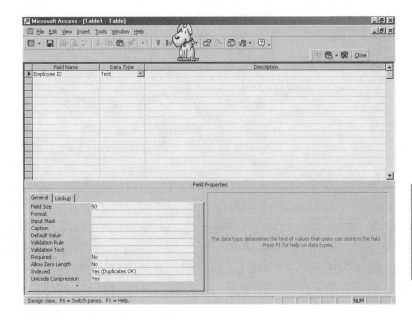

5. Click in the second row of the Field Name column and enter Last Name. Keep the Data Type as Text, but edit the Field Size property to 20.

6. Enter Field Names for first name and middle name, changing the Field Size to 15 for both, but keeping the Data Type as Text.

7. Enter the Field Name Vested and change the Data Type to Yes/No.

8. Enter a Field Name for vestment date and change the Data Type to Date/Time. Also change the Format property to Medium Date.

9. Choose File, Save or click the Save icon on the toolbar. If you're in a new database, use the name tblEmployees for a table name. If you're using the Tables database, choose another name to prevent overwriting the existing table.

10. Click the View button to switch to Table view. Your screen should resemble Figure 3.6.

FIGURE 3.6

Your new table in Datasheet view is ready to receive data about your company's employees.

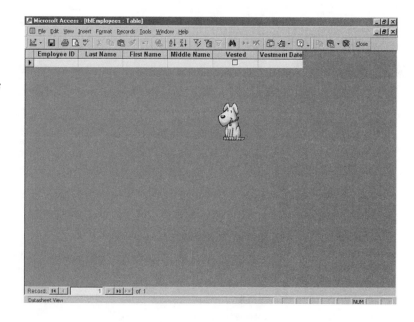

Note

Note that Access automatically knew to use a check box for the field you designated as Yes/No.

Although there are more details, such as many other field properties you need to gain familiarity with, that's how to create a table using the Design view.

Using the Datasheet View to Make a Table

Microsoft added this facility against some objections from the database community. It's not that using this method necessarily ends up in a bad way, but it really saves nothing over using the Design view method and can lead to sloppy designs in all but the most elementary databases. It's your call if you like using this method. To see this table finished, open the table tblByDatasheet from the Tables database. Here is the method in all its glory.

Task: Using the Datasheet View to Create a New Table

▼ TASK

1. Launch Access and either load the Tables database or start a new blank database. If you do the latter, Access will launch a blank table for your use. Skip to step 3 if this is the case.

▼   2. Click the New button or choose Create Table by entering data from the Database view. If you clicked the New button, choose Datasheet view from the dialog box and click OK. Your screen should resemble Figure 3.7.

FIGURE 3.7

You can use the Datasheet view to define certain data types on-the-fly.

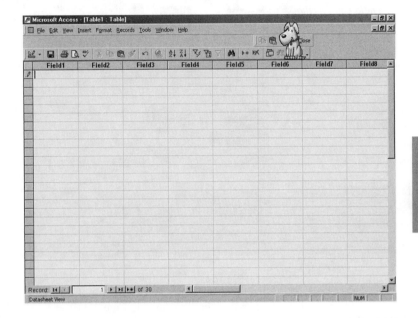

3. Enter 000234 for the first field in the first row.

4. Right-click on the first column header (now labeled Field1) and choose Rename from the context menu. That will place the column header in edit mode. Enter the field name Employee ID for this field.

5. Enter some name data of your own choosing (why not use your name?) for each of the next three fields, editing the field names to Last Name, First Name, and Middle Name, respectively.

6. Move to the next column, enter Yes, and edit the column header to Vested.

7. Move to the next column, enter a date such as 2/3/99, and edit the field name to Vestment Date. Your screen should resemble Figure 3.8.

8. Click the Save icon in the toolbar (the one with the diskette icon) and name the table tblByDatasheet if you're in a new database. If you're in Tables, choose a
▼   unique name to prevent overwriting the existing table.

FIGURE 3.8

Creating a table using the data entry method can be quite tedious for any but the smallest tables.

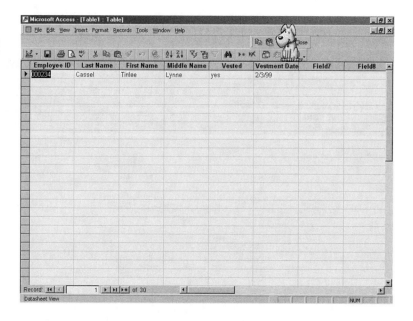

9. Click the View button to switch to Design view, refusing the offer to create a primary key. Your screen should resemble Figure 3.9.

NEW TERM   A *primary key* is a field holding values that are unique over the entire table. Each record in a table must have a primary key to absolutely identify it.

FIGURE 3.9

The datasheet entry method does a respectable job of guessing the correct data types for your fields.

Note that Access did a good job of guessing the right data types for the fields based on the data you entered in the first record. You want the Text type for Employee ID, and there's no control over the Field Size property except in Design view.

To see a limit of the Datasheet view method, switch back to Table (or Data) view and note that the leading zeros have disappeared from the Employee ID field. This is because a Number data type field can't have leading zeros. From here, you can fine-tune this table to meet the exact criteria you did when you created the same table in Design view.

It's your call if you think that this method saved time or was simpler than the all–Design view method.

The Table Wizard

The Table Wizard is somewhat misnamed. Other wizards allow you to create objects more or less of your own choosing. The Table Wizard only allows you to pick and choose from predefined tables and fields, yet it still can be a time saver. Remember, you can use Design view to edit any fields or field properties created in any table, including those done by a wizard.

That said, take a look at the table from the Tables database called tblService Records. This is the table you'll be creating using the wizard. When you're finished reviewing the outcome of this experiment, it's time to actually do the work.

Task: Using the Table Wizard to Create a New Table

1. Launch Access and either load the Tables database or start a new blank database. If you do the latter, Access will launch a blank table for your use. Close this table.

2. For something new, double-click on the Database view entry Create Table by Using Wizard. Your screen should resemble Figure 3.10.

3. Click the Personal option button in the left center section of the dialog box.

4. Scroll down the Sample Tables list box until you find the table Service Records. Click on it to highlight it.

5. Click the single right-facing caret to move the current field from the sample table to the table you're creating. Use the double-caret button to move all fields. Similarly, you can remove a field or all fields from your table by clicking the single or double left-facing carets, respectively. For this table, include all the fields from the sample table into your table. Click the Next button to move on.

6. To maintain our naming conventions, rename the table tblService Records. Allow the wizard to set the primary key for you. Click Next.

FIGURE 3.10

The Table Wizard is really a picker of predefined tables and fields within those tables.

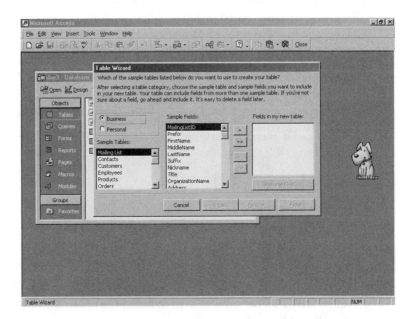

7. The next screen is rather interesting because Access will try to establish a relationship with existing tables by examining all the primary keys. Because the other tables currently existing in Day 3 don't have anything to do with tblService Records, Access correctly guesses that no relationships should exist. Your screen should resemble Figure 3.11.

8. Click Next, and then Finish to see the table in Datasheet view. There is no need to manually save the table. The wizard does that for you.

FIGURE 3.11

The Table Wizard is a trouper in that it even tries to establish relationships with existing tables. In this case, no relationship is possible and it recognizes the fact.

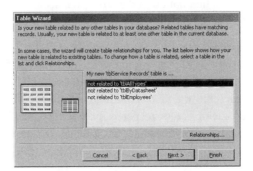

Analyzing the Wizard's Table

The wizard didn't do a very good job of making a table. Although the general table is all right, you should be able to do better and you will be able to before you've finished this book. Let's look at some of the design flaws in this table.

Flat Model Instead of Relational

With the table in Data (or Table) view, scroll over to the Parts Replaced field. That's a normal text field. As you likely know, most repair jobs require more than one part to be replaced, so how would a data entry person handle this field? Let's say a person wanted to determine the cost of this job by linking the parts to his or her cost? There's no way to do this. The following are the two ways:

- Put a bunch of parts in one field as shown in Figure 3.12. That the field is of data type Memo implies that this is the designer's intent.

FIGURE 3.12

This table violates one of the primary rules of relational database design. How could a data entry person handle one field for many entries?

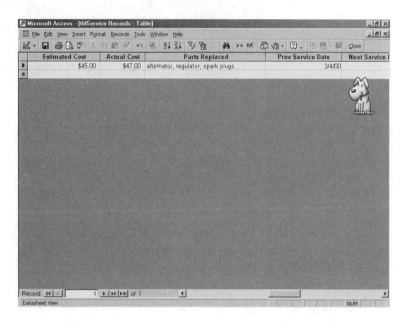

- Put each part in a duplicate record, as shown in Figure 3.13.

FIGURE 3.13

The solution of a new record for each part is worse than the preceding multiple entry solution. What a waste of time and effort, not to mention the confusion about whether these are a single service or more than one incident.

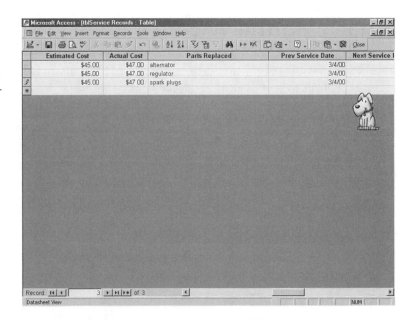

We'll correct this structure in just a moment to show the correct way to structure this type of data.

Possible Wrong Field Types

Switch to Design view for the Service Record table. The Description field is Text data type of 255 characters long. There is also a Problem Description field of Memo data type. There are no comments to tell you, the programmer, or the user what the difference in these fields is, or whether the 255 characters in Problem Description is sufficient.

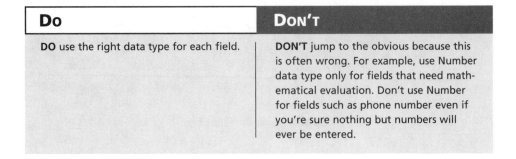

Do	Don't
DO use the right data type for each field.	DON'T jump to the obvious because this is often wrong. For example, use Number data type only for fields that need mathematical evaluation. Don't use Number for fields such as phone number even if you're sure nothing but numbers will ever be entered.

Equally worrisome is the AutoNumber data type for the ServiceRecordID field. This is all right if you want to allow Access to uniquely generate an ID for each job, but what if the service orders are pre-printed or your user wants to use a custom code for each service record?

The AutoNumber data type is useful for generating index numbers when you're sure that you won't need to edit or specify the values for this field other than the starting number, but it isn't ideal for all uses.

Linking Fields—The Heart of the Relationship

The really serious problem with tblServiceRecords as it stands is the bunching of parts within a single field. Open the Tables database in the Day3 folder, if necessary; close any open objects to clear the deck, and get ready to work.

Click the Tables entry in the Object bar and locate the two tables, tblServiceIncident and tblPartsUsed. These are the two tables you'll be linking.

The purpose of this task is to have one record for the service incident, and a way to not only record all the parts for this job, but to cost it as well. The solution is to put the service incident details in one record and the parts in many records. The reasoning will become clearer as you work through this task. You can then further link up the parts-used information to cost information for those parts.

Some of the presentation in the rest of this section will be a bit beyond where you've gone, but try not to worry about it. Concentrate on the idea of the link, and how it makes the one-to-many relationship of having many parts to a single service job much clearer and more useful than lumping all the parts into one Memo field.

Task: Using the Table Wizard to Create a New Table

1. Open the two tables tblServiceIncident and tblPartsUsed in Design view either at the same time or separately. Note that there is a field called ServiceRecordID in both tables. This will be the link field.

 Note Linked fields must be of the same data type. AutoNumber by increment— the data type in tblServiceIncident—uses Long Integers for incrementing, so the link field in tblPartsUsed is Number with a field size of Long Integer.

2. Choose Tools, Relationships from the main Access menu. Your screen should resemble Figure 3.14.

FIGURE 3.14

The Relationships window is where you link tables using their common fields.

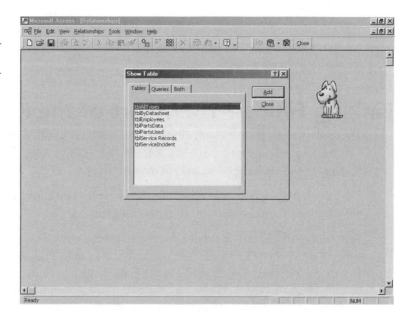

3. Locate the two tables tblServiceIncident and tblPartsUsed. Click on each and click the Add button to move them from the Show Table dialog box to the Relationship window. If you want to, adjust the size of the field list boxes to show more fields or to show all the fields. Your screen should resemble Figure 3.15.

4. This link will be one-to-many, meaning that there might be many parts for any single service incident. Also, you should enforce relational integrity. That means that you can't assign a part to a job that doesn't exist. In other words, a matching record must exist in tblServiceIncident before you can attribute a part to it in tblPartsUsed.

5. Click on the ServiceRecordID field in tblServiceIncident and drag your cursor to the ServiceRecordID in tblPartsUsed. Release the mouse button. When you're finished, your screen should resemble Figure 3.16.

6. You might have noticed that Access guessed and created a cursor to the effect that this is a one-to-many relationship. Check the Enforce Referential Integrity box and the two other check boxes in the dialog box that become enabled. Your screen should resemble Figure 3.17.

FIGURE 3.15

These tables are ready to have a link defined for their one-to-many relationship.

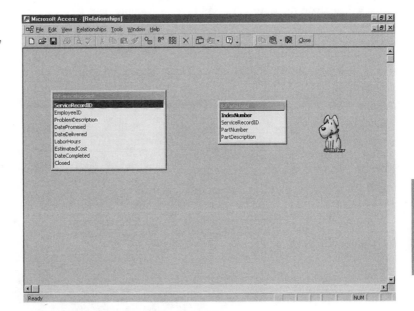

FIGURE 3.16

The simple drag method establishes the link.

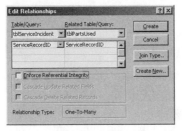

FIGURE 3.17

The link is established with integrity enforced. Don't worry about the join types at this point. You'll learn about this in Day 11.

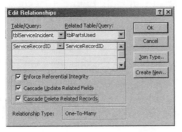

7. Click Create New to close the dialog box, and notice that Access graphically shows you the new link (and that it's one-to-many) in the Relationships window. Close the Relationships window by choosing File, Close from the main menu.

The idea of the link field is to make sure that the items in tblPartsUsed will match up correctly to the right job listed in tblServiceIncident.

Currently there are two records in the tblServiceIncident table. There are several parts in tblPartsUsed for each of these jobs. Open both tables to examine the entries. Figure 3.18 shows these two tables with their entries as of this point.

FIGURE 3.18

Each part used is linked to the job it's been used for by the common link field ServiceRecordID.

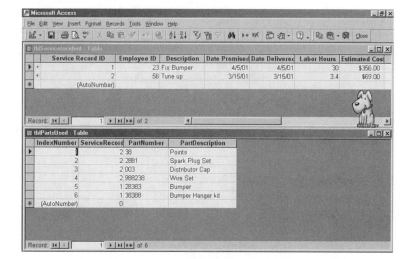

Shortcut to Data Entry

Access does include a way to add linked records to the many table quite easily, but remember it's not really a good idea to do so. Still, because it's there, it's worth knowing about. Open the tblServiceIncident table. Note the new feature—a plus sign at the extreme left of each record. Click on the plus sign. That will open up a new table-like window in which you can add parts to any job. Figure 3.19 shows the parts window opened for job number 2.

This is one of those things that appears somewhat confusing in a screen shot. By all means, open tblStudentIncident and click on the plus sign yourself to see how this facility works. Most experts believe that the best way to do data entry in a one-to-many relationship is through a form with a subform. You can get a preview of that topic by looking ahead to Day 16, "Advanced Form Concepts."

FIGURE 3.19

Access has a table-level entry facility to enter items to the many side of a one-to-many relationship.

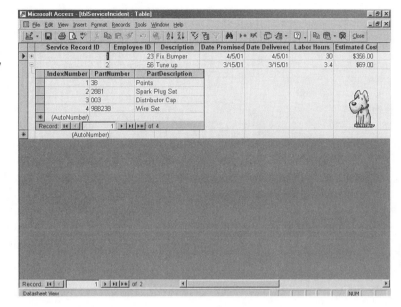

The Outcome of a Relationship

At this point, you might think that this is a lot of work compared to including all the parts in one memo field like the original table did. Here's where you must jump ahead a bit so you can see the reason for all this foundation work.

 There is another table in the database Tables called tblPartsData. This table contains cost and supplier information about each part this auto repair facility stocks or orders. If you examine that table's data or structure and tblPartsUsed, you'll note a slight violation of proper normalization because the part description is repeated in each table. I left things that way to make some earlier steps clearer for you, but in an actual application, I wouldn't have had this data duplicated.

Figure 3.20 shows a query in which the information in the two tables, tblServiceIncident and tblPartsUsed, is linked up again. You can see that due to the link between the fields, the query is able to match up the parts used with the job where the parts were used.

FIGURE 3.20

The link field lets Access match the parts used with the jobs they were used in. Note this query includes data from both tables.

Service Record ID	Employee ID	Description	Labor Hours	PartNumber	PartDescription
1	23	Fix Bumper	30	28383	Bumper
1	23	Fix Bumper	30	38388	Bumper Hanger kit
2	56	Tune up	3.4	38	Points
2	56	Tune up	3.4	2881	Spark Plug Set
2	56	Tune up	3.4	003	Distributor Cap
2	56	Tune up	3.4	988238	Wire Set
(AutoNumber)					

The query shown in Figure 3.20 is part of the Tables database and has the name qryBasicMatchUp. If you want to run this query, click on the Queries entry in the object bar and double-click on its entry. Open this query in Design view to see how it is constructed.

The Best Is Yet to Come

That's fine, but you might still be wondering, "Why bother?" If you listed all the parts in one huge Memo field, they would also be matched up with the right job.

 Now it's time for the relationship trump—the matchup you can't do using the Memo field method of including many items in a single field in a table. Figure 3.21 shows another query, this time including cost information from the table tblPartsData. This query is called qryCosting and is also part of your sample data. Open it in Design view to see how it works if you want a peek ahead on query construction.

FIGURE 3.21

At last, all the extra work pays off. The cost information is yours without any additional work.

Service Record ID	Description	Date Promised	Estimated Cost	PartDescription	PartNumber	Cost
2	Tune up	3/15/01	$69.00	Points	38	$2.00
2	Tune up	3/15/01	$69.00	Spark Plug Set	2881	$23.00
2	Tune up	3/15/01	$69.00	Distributor Cap	003	$9.40
2	Tune up	3/15/01	$69.00	Wire Set	988238	$6.78
1	Fix Bumper	4/5/01	$356.00	Bumper	28383	$129.00
1	Fix Bumper	4/5/01	$356.00	Bumper Hanger kit	38388	$4.56
(AutoNumber)						

Yes, you could have manually entered all the cost information in the original table, but why bother? This way, after you've created the relational structure, Access will automatically look up linked information for you.

Note

One of the main purposes of a relational database is having the database look up related data rather than requiring that data entry personnel enter it redundantly.

Not Convinced?

If you're not convinced yet, open the query qryTotalCost in Query view by double-clicking on it. Your screen should resemble Figure 3.22.

FIGURE 3.22

Computer programs love to add things up. Here Access gathers up all cost data for each job and sums that data, matching the sum to the job.

By all means, look at the magic behind this query by switching to Design view for it. Although the workings of this query might not be superficially obvious, you should have a good idea of how it's operating.

There is no reasonable way to duplicate the costing and summation data you've seen in these past two queries by piling data into Memo fields. More importantly, having data normalized like this allows for easy lookups, faster data entry, and assured data integrity. The latter simply means that you can't enter a part for a job that doesn't yet exist. You must create a job first, and then you can add parts to it. Otherwise, you can end up with "data orphans" in your system.

More importantly, referential integrity means you must assign a part to a job. Therefore, you're assured that you'll bill all the parts when you bill the jobs. That doesn't necessarily mean the right part is attached to the right job, but that's another topic.

Some of what you saw in this section is a bit too complex to go into right now (such as how that query did its totaling magic) because the information so far is likely quite a bit of a load for you at this point. Day 11 builds on the foundation laid today.

If you remain skeptical that the referential model isn't the best for the vast majority of data tasks, how about just suspending your disbelief for a few days? Give it a while and you'll see why it's worth the bother to create a correct relational structure for your database projects. After a short while, you'll see that using a flat model would be less than satisfactory for most of what you will need to do using Access.

Seeing It Yourself

Grasping the concept of linking and relationships between tables is vital to the successful use of Access and similar products. The following task will use the objects you're now familiar with to show how this concept works in daily use.

Task: Adding Data to a Linked Table and Then Seeing the Result

1. Open the Tables database, if necessary. Open the tblServiceIncident table in Datasheet view (double-click on it in the Database view).

2. Click the plus sign to the far left of the first record in the table. This will open a window containing the linked table tblPartsUsed. Your screen should resemble Figure 3.23.

FIGURE 3.23

Clicking on the plus sign (expand view) will open a window to the linked table.

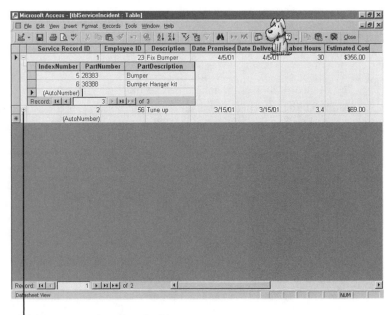

Click here to see the related table

3. Enter a few part numbers and descriptions of your own choosing to simulate entering actual parts for this service order. Keep in mind what you've entered.

4. Click in the same area, to the left of the first record, on the sign that's now a minus. The window will close.

5. Click on the plus sign to the left of the second record to open a window for that record. Again, enter some data in the window distinct from the data you entered in step 3. Close the table.

6. Click on the Queries entry in the Database view.

7. Run the query qryBasicMatchUp by double-clicking on it. Note that the parts you entered for record 1 are now linked to that record, and those you entered for record

2 are now linked to that one. Those are the essentials of a relational database. Your screen should resemble Figure 3.24.

FIGURE 3.24

You can see how Access links the records correctly by running this simple query.

Service Record ID	Employee ID	Description	Labor Hours	PartNumber	PartDescription
1	23	Fix Bumper	30	28383	Bumper
1	23	Fix Bumper	30	38388	Bumper Hanger kit
1	23	Fix Bumper	30	1234	Record 1 linked to
2	56	Tune up	3.4	38	Points
2	56	Tune up	3.4	2881	Spark Plug Set
2	56	Tune up	3.4	003	Distributor Cap
2	56	Tune up	3.4	988238	Wire Set
2	56	Tune up	3.4	5678	Record 2 linked to
(AutoNumber)					

Table and Field Properties

You've seen demonstrated only a few table properties as of now. This section will start your tour of a few additional table properties, plus some overall table settings.

Task: A Beginner's Guide to Field Properties

1. If necessary, open the Tables database and the tblEmployees table in Design view. Your screen should resemble Figure 3.25.

FIGURE 3.25

The tblEmployees table object will act as a test bed to learn about some additional properties available to the developer in Access tables.

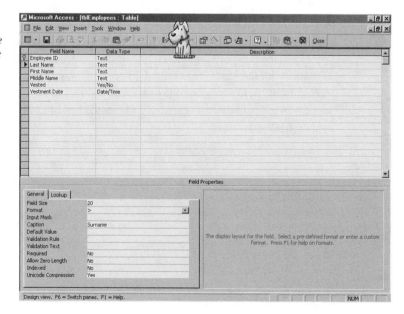

3

▼

Note

This task uses the tblEmployees, but any table will suffice for these demonstrations.

2. Click on the Last Name field to bring up the context-sensitive Field Properties list box.

3. Edit (or enter) Surname for the Caption property. The Caption property controls the label a field has, not only for the table, but for any objects (such as forms) derived or bound to the table. If the Caption property is blank, the field will use the field name for a Caption property. Switch to Datasheet view, saving changes when prompted. Figure 3.26 shows the results of the Caption property.

FIGURE 3.26

The caption or header for this field now overrides the default field name for a caption.

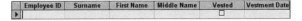

4. Note that the field name is now Surname, reflecting your entry in the Caption property.

5. Use of the Format property is a huge topic in detail, but the concept is simple. The idea is to alter the format or appearance of data. For example, you might want a data field to display in capital letters. To do this, enter a > for the Format property. Try that with the Last Name field. Change to Datasheet view, enter some lowercase letters in the field captioned Surname, and then leave the field. The entry will appear in capital letters. Figure 3.27 shows the use of the Format property to display a field in all caps.

▼

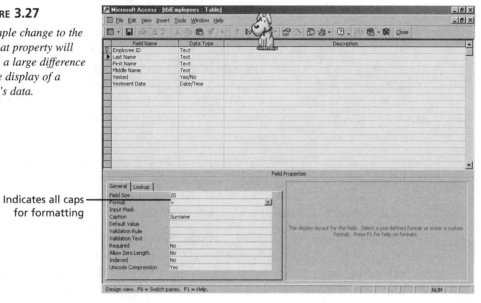

FIGURE 3.27

A simple change to the Format property will make a large difference in the display of a table's data.

Indicates all caps for formatting

Note

The data stored in the table with a Format property of > is in its original form—upper- or lowercase. The Format property changed only the way the data is displayed in the table.

The help system is a good reference for other format properties. Table 3.1 gives a few examples to get you going.

TABLE 3.1 A FEW SAMPLE FORMATS

Format	Enter	Displayed in Table
>	tirilee	TIRILEE
<	Tirilee	tirilee
@@@-@@@@	5558976	555-8976
@;"Empty"		Empty (displays the word Empty until you enter data)

Indexing and More on Key Fields

The key field (primary key) is the unique identifier for a record. All tables, without exception, should have a key field identified. For example, you can't generally use a Last Name field as a key field because most databases will have, or at least can have, more than one entry for any last name. The authors of this book, Palmer and Cassel, have fairly common names. If you used last names as a key field, you could only have one Palmer and one Cassel in the entire table—surely not a good design concept. Last Name won't work for a primary key, but the authors' Social Security numbers are unique to them, so that would work.

If possible, use natural keys—keys that are part of the data anyway. A good example of this is the previously mentioned Social Security number. Everybody's is unique and you might have that as part of the data anyway. If you're creating an auto service application, license plate (tag) numbers should work as a primary field.

If nothing works naturally, you can resort to using Access' AutoNumber facility to generate artificial (not part of the data) primary keys. A primary key not only uniquely identifies a record (you can have only one example in any table), but also speeds many Access operations. Don't leave the console without one.

Indexes (indices, really) order data within a database. An index with entries that can't be duplicated in that field within a table is a primary key, but you can also have secondary indexes. Figure 3.28 shows the tblEmployees in Design view. Examine the Field Properties for the Indexed property. The entry reads Yes (No Duplicates) for the definition of a primary key.

Click the pull-down tab for the Index property, and you'll note you can set this property to No, for no index, or Yes (Duplicates OK). The latter will order the table or at least keep a series of pointers to data for any field with that property.

Index any field you expect to search on, but except in the case of the primary key for a table, don't make the index exclude duplicates. Doing so might end up problematic if you need two identical entries in a field. For example, if you will know that you'll be searching employees under last name, index the field, but don't exclude duplicates or you'll only be able to include one last name per table.

You can sort (reorder) and filter data in tables although most developers prefer doing so within queries. The next section shows how you can do these feats while staying within tables.

FIGURE 3.28

The EmployeeID field is the primary key for this table.

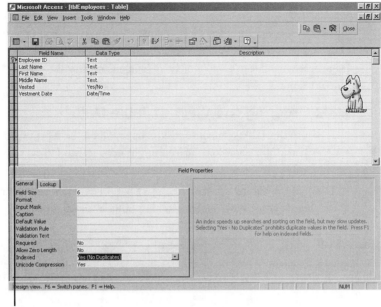

Primary Key

Sorting and Filtering in Tables

Database design purists cringe when hearing that people manipulate the views of a table. They complain that other database objects, especially forms and queries, are for that duty. Well, cringe causing or not, people seem to like playing around in Table or Datasheet view rather than creating additional objects for that purpose. There's really no reason not to use tables for viewing your data, other than that the data in tables should be normalized (fragmented) into less-than-useful chunks. A query will usually reassemble data into a more useful form, but if your needs can be met by viewing, ordering, or filtering data directly in tables, there's no reason not to do so.

Note

Edits made in a query will be reflected in the underlying tables. For example, edits made in the query shown in Figure 3.24 will be reflected in the respective tables underlying this two-table query.

Sorting

To *sort* a table or other datasheet is database talk to order it in a determined fashion. Ordering records alphabetically is an "alpha sort" in database lingo. Sorting a table in Datasheet view doesn't really alter its indexes, merely the display of the table. Here's how it's done.

Task: Ordering the View of Table Data

1. Close the Tables database, if it is open. Open the Northwind database. Northwind is part of the sample data. You might need to run Office setup again to install Northwind if it's not on your disk.

2. Click the Tables entry in the object bar. Locate the Customers table and open it in Datasheet view by double-clicking on it. Your screen should resemble Figure 3.29.

FIGURE 3.29

When opened, a table will order itself according to its primary key, which is the Customer ID for this table.

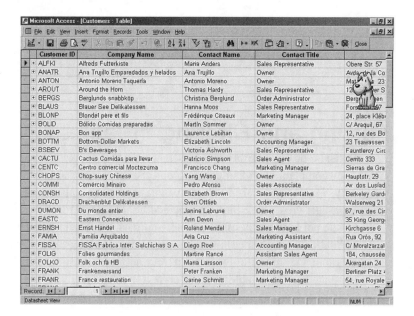

3. Click anywhere in the Contact Name column (field). This will cause your next action to act on that field.

4. Click the Sort Descending toolbar button. Figure 3.30 shows this button (the cursor is on it). Note the change in the table's order.

5. Click in the Contact Title field. Click on the Sort Ascending button to re-sort the table. This will bring all the accounting managers to the fore.

3

FIGURE 3.30

Changing the sort order changes the display of data, but not the order of the data within the table.)

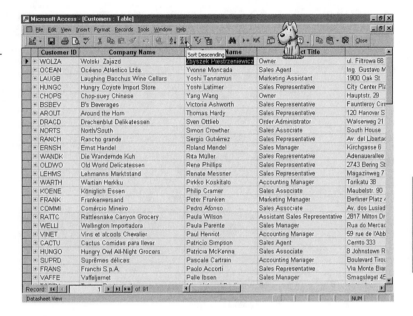

> **Note**
>
> The skills you gained today in filtering and sorting in tables are fully transferable to other objects such as queries and forms.

That's all there is to changing the sort order. To make sure you return the table or tables to their pre-sort condition, close them and discard layout changes, and then re-open. In this simple table, you can also sort ascending on the primary key, Customer ID, to achieve the same result.

Filtering

Filtering means to filter out all but the data you let pass your criteria or criterion. Access makes this operation as simple as sorting.

Task: Filtering

1. Open the Northwind table Customers again if you closed it after the last task. Locate a record within the Contact Title column with the entry Owner.

2. Click the Filter by Selection button on the toolbar. Figure 3.31 shows this button and how your screen should look after clicking.

FIGURE 3.31

Filter by selection takes a look at the current selection and filters according to it.

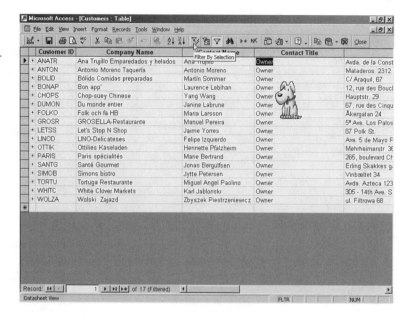

3. Click the Remove Filter button (two to the right of the Filter by Selection button) to remove the filter. Click the same button again to reapply the filter.

4. Click the Remove Filter button to remove any filter by selection. Click the Filter by Form button. This button is between the Filter by Selection and Apply/Remove Filter buttons. Your screen should resemble Figure 3.32.

5. Note the pull-down buttons. Pull down the combo box for Contact Title and choose Accounting Manager. Click the Apply Filter button (the one with the funnel as an icon). This will apply the filter as before. You can filter on more than one field using this method. After applying the filter your screen should resemble Figure 3.33.

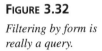

FIGURE 3.32

Filtering by form is really a query.

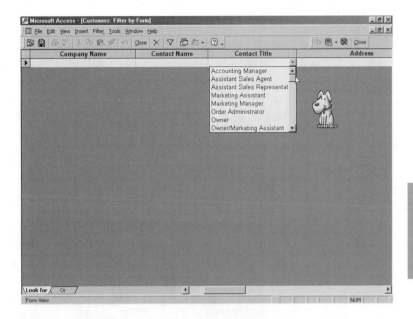

FIGURE 3.33

Filtering by form allows more than one field filter.

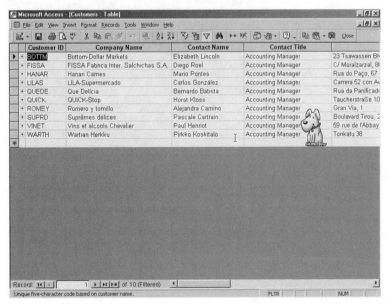

You can use Filter by Form to save and recall filters. Here's the trick in a task.

Task: Saving and Recalling Filters

1. Open the Customers table in Datasheet view.

2. Click the Filter by Form button. Choose the Contact Title field by clicking in it, and choose "Owner" from the drop-down list. Click the Save as Query button in the toolbar. Enter `qryFilterDemo` as a save name. Your screen should resemble Figure 3.34.

FIGURE 3.34

You can save a Filter by Form as a query.

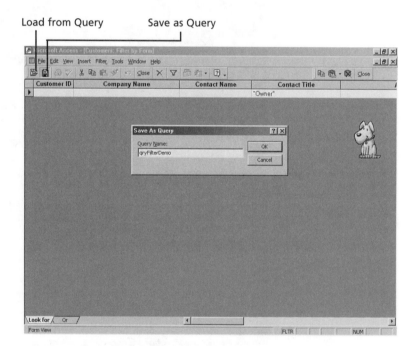

3. Click OK to exit this dialog box.

4. Click the Close button on the toolbar to close the Filter by Form screen. Close the table by choosing File, Close; discard layout changes, if so offered.

5. Open the table again. Click the Filter by Form button. Click the Load from Query button (far left). Your screen should resemble Figure 3.35.

6. Click OK to load the filter. Click the Apply Filter button and you'll have your table filtered as before.

FIGURE 3.35

You can recall saved filters using this dialog box.

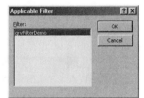

Finding Data

There's one more trick with tables to cover today, but it's an easy one to grasp—finding data within tables. Like the other skills, filtering and sorting, this skill is transferable to other database objects such as forms and queries.

3

Task: Saving and Recalling Filters

▼TASK

1. Open the Northwind database if necessary. Open the Customers table in Datasheet view.

2. Click in the Company Name field. Click the Find button on the toolbar (the button with the binoculars icon). Click the More button to expose all of the dialog box. Your screen should resemble Figure 3.36.

FIGURE 3.36

The Find dialog box is a quick route to locate data.

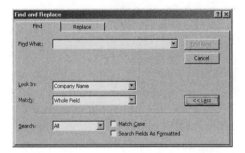

3. Enter Li in the Find What text box. Pull down the Match combo box and choose Start of Field. Click Find Next. Access goes out and finds the first entry in the Company Name field that starts with the two letters Li.

4. Pull down the other combo boxes in this dialog box to gain familiarity with other capabilities of Access' find facility. When you're finished, close everything.

▲

Find Cautions

Many users love the Find dialog box and use it regularly, but a few cautions are worth
mentioning, as well as some tips. Here they are.

Do	Don't
DO perform search and replace operations with caution. This can be helpful, but very dangerous. For example, if you learn that LINO-Delicateses is now LONO Delicateses and decide to search on LI and replace it with LO, allowing a Replace All will change LINO-Delicateses to LONO-Delocateses unless you tighten the search criteria. Use with care!	**DON'T** apply a find to an entire table (as opposed to a single field) because this can take a long time.
DO carefully check all options on the Find dialog box to make sure you know where you're looking for your hits.	**DON'T** apply a find to an unindexed field unless you have plenty of time; it will take longer than on an indexed field. If you plan to search regularly within a field, index it in table design view.

Note   You can use an action query to change table data. You'll encounter these
specialized advanced queries on Day 15.

Summary

Tables store all data within a relational database such as Access. Access offers three
ways to make a table: Design view, by entry example, and by a wizard. Each field within
a table must have a specific data type conforming to the type of data it's to hold. Each
field also has an array of developer-set options called field properties. The properties for
each field depend upon the data type.

Primary fields act as unique identifiers for a record within a table. Although you should
try to use actual data as a key, using artificial data such as an incrementing AutoNumber
field is much better than no key (which should never occur). By linking fields between
tables, which is the essence of a relational database, you can later construct various
views of data from more than one table.

Although other database objects such as forms or queries might do the job better (to
some people's view), you can filter, sort, and find data within tables.

Q&A

Q If I set a primary key field in my one table, should I also use that field as a primary key in my many table?

A No. This will make your link useless because you will potentially need many entries using the data from the one side in the many side. For example, say you have a list of employees with the Social Security number (SSN) as a primary key in a table called tblEmployees. You also have a table called tblFixedAssets in which each asset is assigned to an employee. The link is the SSN. Because any employee can have many assets, you can't have SSN as the primary key in tblFixedAssets. Instead, include SSN as a field in tblFixedAssets to link on, but use another unique field (such as asset number) for tblFixedAssets' primary key.

Q Why do I need a primary key for every table?

A Access enforces uniqueness for primary fields. Telling Access that a field is the primary key is the only way to be completely sure you have a unique identifier for every record in that table.

Q I want to have more than one sort for a table, but every time I change a table's field order I lose my old sort. How can I have more than one sort for a table?

A You can order or sort tables using a simple query. Each query can have its own sort order, so the answer is to use a series of queries, not sorts within tables. You can copy tables and sort them all, but that's a real waste of disk space.

Q Will the * wildcard work in Access' Find dialog box?

A Yes. For example, *c* will find any field with the letter *c* in it. But you really don't need this because you can also search in Any Part of Field, which covers the same territory.

Workshop

The Workshop helps you solidify the skills you learned in this lesson. Answers to the quiz questions appear in Appendix A, "Answers."

Quiz

1. Can a primary key field have two records with identical values for the primary key field?

2. Can the value of a primary key appear elsewhere (another field) in a record?

3. How often should identical data appear in a properly designed database?

4. If you create two tables you intend to have a one-to-many relationship, how do you create that relationship?

5. Will the letter Z appear first or last after applying a Sort (Descending) on a field containing all the letters of the alphabet?

Exercises

1. Open the Customers table in the Northwind database. Click in the Contact Title field.

2. Click the Filter by Form button on the toolbar. Enter a filter criterion to show only those records that begin with the letter A. Hint, use the criterion A*.

3. Apply the filter. Remove the filter.

4. If you saved the filter in the "Filtering," task click on Queries in the object bar.

5. Locate the query qryFilterDemo. Note that the object you saved as a filter is now a query (your first query!).

6. Double-click on this object to launch the query.

7. Did the result meet your expectations?

DAY 4

Using Queries for Data Retrieval

Tables hold data, and queries form the foundation of a system to change data into information. Today you'll learn the fundamentals of the query, including the following:

- The query in Access
- Using design view to create a query
- Using the Query Wizard
- Simple query criteria
- Using AND and OR in queries
- Multitable queries
- Creating links in queries
- An introduction to expressions

The Query in Access

Many developers call queries the heart of Access. Although tables store all data, it's the queries from which the vast majority of objects derive their data. Queries allow much more flexibility when selecting or manipulating data than the tables do.

A vital thing to remember whenever working with queries is that Access queries are live. Changes made to data in a Query Datasheet view are reflected in the underlying table, just as if you made those changes (or edits) directly in the table. This includes multitable queries, where changes made to any part of the query will be reflected in the underlying tables. You can even add new data to tables through queries.

> **Tip**   Although you can edit or add data to tables directly through queries, most applications work better if the developer uses forms for those changes.

A First Query

If you've been working your way through this book sequentially, you should already have a good idea of what the query design grid and the SQL view look like. You should also have a fair idea of how to construct a query. The next task covers some familiar ground, but within the task are details glossed over in previous sections, so at least take some time to review this task even if you think you've got a grasp on simple query construction.

There are three ways to create a query:

- Using the Design view
- Using a wizard
- Directly entering SQL commands using the SQL view

This chapter covers only the first two because the third method requires some understanding of SQL commands. SQL stands for Structured Query Language. SQL in and of itself is an intermediate-level topic, and is covered starting on Day 14, "Understanding SQL." Because you would need an understanding of that language before doing much in SQL view, this book will largely skip that topic for now.

Task: Creating a Query Using the Design View

1. Launch Access and open the FirstQueries.mdb database located in the Day4 folder on your CD-ROM. This database contains several tables from the Northwind database.

Note

This chapter uses some Northwind data, but doesn't work in that database itself for two reasons. Using a separate database allows the book to focus on the subject matter, and working outside Northwind prevents that database from being clogged up with practice database objects.

2. Click on the Queries entry in the objects bar. Click on the New entry in the Database view toolbar. Your screen should resemble Figure 4.1.

FIGURE 4.1

Starting a new query from the Database view.

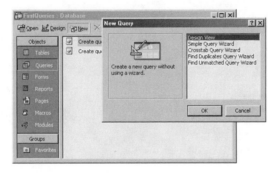

4

3. Click OK to accept the default of starting a query in Design view.
4. Click on the Customers table, and then click the Add button to add this table to the query.

Tip

You can also drag and drop objects from the Show Table dialog box to the design grid.

5. Click Close to close the Show Table dialog box.

> **Tip**
>
> As the tabs in the Show Table dialog box indicate, you can include tables, queries, or both in any particular query. That is, you can query a query—an important technique, as you'll later learn.

6. Adjust the size of the Field list box and the grid to suit your taste, as shown in Figure 4.2.

FIGURE 4.2

You can alter the aspect ratio of the query design grid to suit specific tasks or tastes.

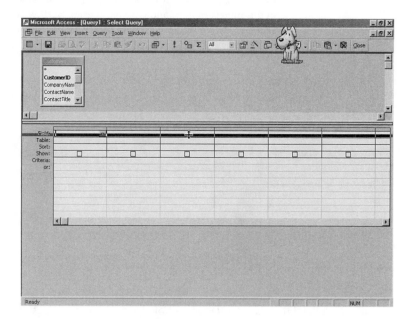

7. Click and drag the first four fields (one at a time) from the Field list box and drop them in the first four columns, respectively. Figure 4.3 shows this operation in progress for the last column.

8. Click on the next field down—the Address. Then press Ctrl and click the next field, City. This will highlight both fields. Drag them to the grid and drop them to the right of the Contact Title field. You can drag and drop as many fields as you want to by using the Shift or Ctrl selection method, which works identically here as in the Explorer.

9. Click in the next column to the right of the City field. This will bring up a pull-down caret (combo box). Pull down that combo box and choose Region from the drop-down list. Figure 4.4 shows this technique of adding a field to a query.

Dragging a field from a table to the grid

FIGURE 4.3

Dragging a field from the Field list box to the grid includes that field in the query.

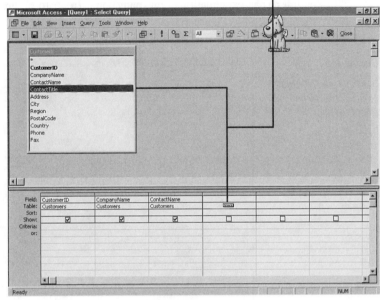

Click to run the query

FIGURE 4.4

You can drag and drop to include fields in a query or choose from a pull down list.

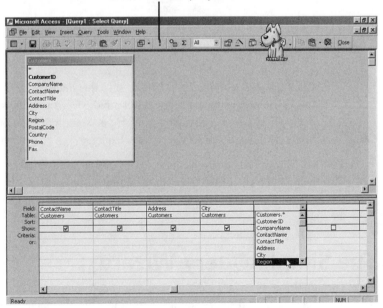

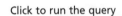

4

▼   10. Click the Run button on the toolbar to see how the query is coming along. The Run
button has an exclamation point (bang) on it (refer to Figure 4.4). Your screen
should resemble Figure 4.5.

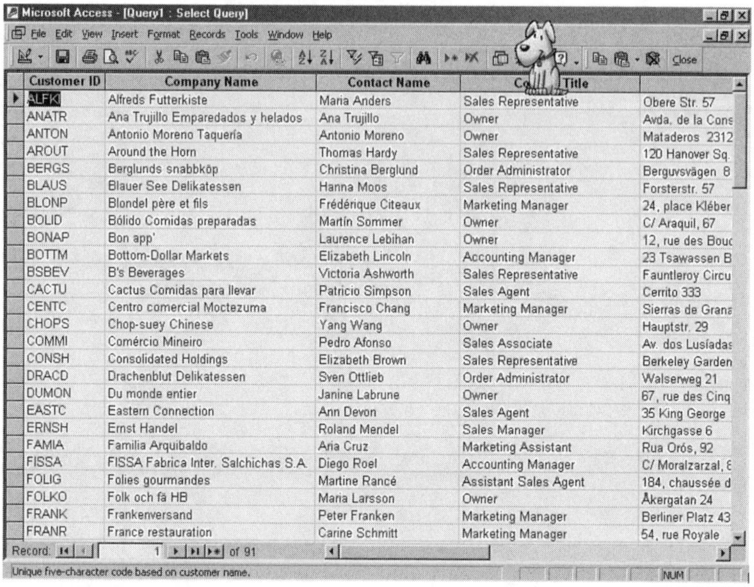

FIGURE 4.5

At this point the query only selects all records from the included fields.

11. Click the disk icon on the toolbar to save this query as qrySelectCustomers1, or
just qrySelectCustomers if you don't mind overwriting the sample query. Close the
query (File, Close) and take a break if you want to. If you prefer, leave it open—
▲   you'll be using it again later in this chapter.

That's it. You've just constructed a query by dragging fields from the list box labeled
Customers (the name of the table) to the query design grid. At this point the query is a
subset of the Customers table in the sense that it contains all records, but only some of
the fields.

The Simple Query Wizard

The simple query wizard can save some time constructing queries like the one done in
the preceding task. It's very similar (almost identical to, actually) the Table Wizard you

saw in Day 3, "Exploring the Data Foundations—The Table." Here's a tour of this wizard.

Task: Creating a Query Using the Simple Query Wizard

1. If necessary, launch Access and open the FirstQueries.mdb database located in the Day4 folder.

2. Click on the Queries entry in the objects bar. Double-click on the Create Query by Wizard entry in the Queries section of the Database view. You could have also clicked the New button on the toolbar and chosen Simple Query Wizard from the dialog box. In either case, Access will respond with the dialog box shown in Figure 4.6.

FIGURE 4.6

The simple query opening dialog box is familiar territory to anyone familiar with the Table Design Wizard.

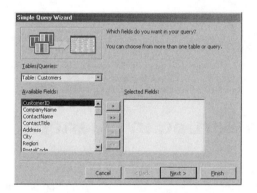

3. The wizard will default to the Customers table. You can pull down the combo box labeled Tables/Queries to see other objects you can query.

4. Add the Customer ID through Region fields to the query by clicking several times on the right-pointing caret button.

> You can use the double-right-arrow button to add all the fields to or remove all the fields from the query at one time.

5. Click Next to move on.

6. Name the query qryWizardQuery1 and click Finish. This will run the query. Your screen should resemble Figure 4.7.

FIGURE 4.7

FIGURE 4.7

There's no difference between the wizard-generated query and the one you did manu-ally using the Design view.

Filtering and Sorting in Queries

You can use the same techniques you used with tables to filter and sort data within queries when you're in a Datasheet view. However, queries are capable of storing such settings by using the query design grid (or SQL view) to create variations on a query.

Task: Quick Filtering and Sorting in Queries

1. Launch Access and open the database called FirstQueries.mdb located in the Day4 folder. Locate the query qrySelectCustomers. Double-click on it to open it in Datasheet view. Your screen should resemble Figure 4.5.

2. Click in the Contact Name field. Click the Sort Ascending button in the toolbar. As you saw in the Table Datasheet view, Access will sort the current field in alphabeti-cal order. Click in the Customer ID field and click Sort Ascending again to return the datasheet to its original view.

> **Caution**
>
> You can't undo a sort in Datasheet view, but the changes aren't saved by default when you close the query. A shortcut to returning a datasheet to its former sort order is to close the table, discard layout changes, and then re-open it.

▼ 3. Try clicking in various fields and then clicking the Sort Ascending or Sort Descending buttons.

4. Locate the first entry of Order Administrator in the Contact Title field and click in it. Click the Filter by Example button on the toolbar. Your screen should resemble Figure 4.8.

FIGURE 4.8

You can filter by example in a query as you can in a table.

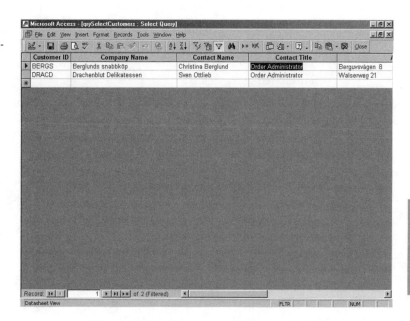

 Tip

You can filter by form from a query-generated datasheet, but you'll find it more flexible to do so using the Design view of the query.

5. Remove the filter by clicking on the Remove Filter button on the toolbar. Close the ▲ query, discarding layout changes.

Query Criteria

Using criteria in queries to select only certain records is perhaps the most called-on use for queries. This facility is very similar to filtering in Datasheet view. In fact, there's only a small difference for most queries.

Task: Creating a Query Using the Design View

1. Launch Access and open the FirstQueries.mdb database located in the Day4 folder. This database contains several tables from the Northwind database. Locate and open in Design view either the query qrySelectCustomers or qrySelectCustomers1, depending upon whether you want to use the sample query or one of your own.

2. Note the check boxes in the Show row of the query design grid. These control whether an included field displays in the query. Because all the fields are currently checked, all will display. Very shortly you'll see the importance of an included non-displayed query field.

3. Enter Du monde entier in the Criteria row under the CompanyName column. Tab out of the column. Access will add quotes to your entry. This indicates that the limit of this criterion is the string between the quote marks. Your screen should resemble Figure 4.9.

FIGURE 4.9

Access will make almost always correct guesses about adding delimiters to query criteria.

4. Click the Run button to view the query's output.

5. Note that the query is now limited to those companies bearing the name "Du monde entier"—or one single company.

6. Return to Design view for this query. Locate the ContactTitle column and enter Sales Agent in the second row of the criteria area. Your screen should resemble Figure 4.10.

7. Run the query. Your screen should resemble Figure 4.11.

8. The next query type worth examining is the AND criteria query. This query demands validity in both columns (fields) for any returned record. Return the query to Design view.

> **Tip**
>
> OR queries are inclusive. AND queries are exclusive. This is somewhat different from natural speech, in which we might say, "I want the records for

> those customers living in Chicago and Denver." The human will return customers who live in either place. The computer will only return those who live in both places.

FIGURE 4.10

Entering a criterion on two rows creates an OR criteria that will return records matching either criterion.

FIGURE 4.11

An OR query will return records meeting either of the entries on the Criteria row.

9. Cut or delete the entry for Sales Agent and then move it to the first row. Your screen should resemble Figure 4.12.

FIGURE 4.12

You construct an AND criteria by including the example on the same row.

10. Run the query. You should get a null return because there are no records in which the Company Name is "Du monde entier" and the Contact Title is Sales Agent.

11. Return to Design view. Remove the "Du monde entier" criteria. Click to the right of the quote marks in the column Contact Title and enter a space followed by the word or and the string "Owner". Your screen should resemble Figure 4.13. Be sure to include the quote marks when entering the second string, but not the OR keyword.

4

FIGURE 4.13

Using OR in a column will select either criterion from a field.

12. Run the query. Note that you'll get returns for any record in which the Contact Title meets either of your criteria. Note at the bottom of the screen that a total of 22 records are returned.

13. Return to Design view. Uncheck the Show check box for the Contact Title field. Run the query again. Your screen should resemble Figure 4.14.

FIGURE 4.14

Access returns the same 22 records even without the display of the Criteria field.

Customer ID	Company Name	Contact Name	Address	
ANATR	Ana Trujillo Emparedados y helados	Ana Trujillo	Avda. de la Constitución 2222	Méx
ANTON	Antonio Moreno Taquería	Antonio Moreno	Mataderos 2312	Méx
BOLID	Bólido Comidas preparadas	Martín Sommer	C/ Araquil, 67	Mac
BONAP	Bon app'	Laurence Lebihan	12, rue des Bouchers	Mar
CACTU	Cactus Comidas para llevar	Patricio Simpson	Cerrito 333	Bue
CHOPS	Chop-suey Chinese	Yang Wang	Hauptstr. 29	Ben
DUMON	Du monde entier	Janine Labrune	67, rue des Cinquante Otages	Nan
EASTC	Eastern Connection	Ann Devon	35 King George	Lon
FOLKO	Folk och fä HB	Maria Larsson	Åkergatan 24	Brä
GROSR	GROSELLA-Restaurante	Manuel Pereira	5ª Ave. Los Palos Grandes	Cara
LETSS	Let's Stop N Shop	Jaime Yorres	87 Polk St.	San
LINOD	LINO-Delicateses	Felipe Izquierdo	Ave. 5 de Mayo Porlamar	I. de
MAISD	Maison Dewey	Catherine Dewey	Rue Joseph-Bens 532	Bru
OCEAN	Océano Atlántico Ltda.	Yvonne Moncada	Ing. Gustavo Moncada 8585	Bue
OTTIK	Ottilies Käseladen	Henriette Pfalzheim	Mehrheimerstr. 369	Köln
PARIS	Paris spécialités	Marie Bertrand	265, boulevard Charonne	Pari
SANTG	Santé Gourmet	Jonas Bergulfsen	Erling Skakkes gate 78	Stav
SIMOB	Simons bistro	Jytte Petersen	Vinbæltet 34	Køb
TORTU	Tortuga Restaurante	Miguel Angel Paolino	Avda. Azteca 123	Méx
VICTE	Victuailles en stock	Mary Saveley	2, rue du Commerce	Lyo
WHITC	White Clover Markets	Karl Jablonski	305 - 14th Ave. S.	Sea
WOLZA	Wolski Zajazd	Zbyszek Piestrzeniewicz	ul. Filtrowa 68	War

Record: 1 of 22

Unique five-character code based on customer name.

Tip

A field must be included in a query to have criteria entered for it, but it doesn't have to show in the query's output.

Quick Query Facts

There are a bevy of query tricks and shortcuts that experienced Access users learn over time. Here are a few of the more common to give you a boost toward becoming fast and easy with Access 2000.

- To include all fields in a query, drag the asterisk from the field list box to any column in the query design grid.

- To include all fields of a table or query in a query and also specify fields for criteria, drag the asterisk to the first column, and the fields to which you want to add criteria into the right columns. Add your criteria, but then uncheck the Show check box for the added fields.

- To remove a field from the query, highlight its column by clicking on the header, and then click the Delete key to remove it.

- To remove a field from the query, switch to SQL view and delete the field from the query in that view. SQL view is reflected in Design view and vice versa.

- To add another table or field to a query, click the Show Table button in the toolbar. Doing this will open the Show Table list box.

- You can move or resize columns in a query's Datasheet view just as you can in a table's Datasheet view.

- You can widen or narrow rows in a query's Datasheet view just as you can in a table's Datasheet view.

- You can widen or narrow columns in the query design grid if you need more room to display long criterion or expressions (expressions will be discussed soon).

- You can shrink the width of a field to zero in design grid to allow for other column's display without affecting the display of the query in Datasheet view.

4

- You can move a column in the query design grid just like you can move a column in Datasheet view. Moving a column in the Design view will change the column's place in the Datasheet view. Moving a column in the Datasheet view will not change that column's location in the Design view.

- Pull down the Sort row in any column to change the default order of a query (the default order is the sort created by the primary key).

- You can sort on multiple fields in the Design view. Sort priority is from left to right. To give a sort a higher priority, move the column to the left of other sorted columns. You can always move the column back to the right in Datasheet view without affecting the sort priority.

- You can filter and sort in Datasheet view queries that have sorts and criteria entered for them.

That's a good list to get you going in simple queries. The next topic is inclusion of more than one table or query in a query.

Multitable Queries

The normalization process splits data into logical, but smaller, "chunks." The point of this split is to increase efficiency, especially optimizing data entry chores and storage space requirements. However, there must be a way to reconstruct this split data or the efficiently stored data won't be very useful. The primary tool for data reconstruction in an Access database is the query.

The following task shows how to use data from two different linked tables to construct a datasheet containing elements from both tables. You can use the technique for queries using more than two tables. The only important element to remember is that for the rows to make logical sense, there must exist a logical link. In the case of this task, the link is the SupplierID field.

Before starting, take a look at Figure 4.15. This is the FirstQueries database with the Tools, Relationships window opened. Note the two tables used for this task and their pre-existing link.

To preview the result of this task, open the query named qryFirstLink in Datasheet view (or run it).

FIGURE 4.15

A multitable query doesn't require an existing link between tables, but it saves a step.

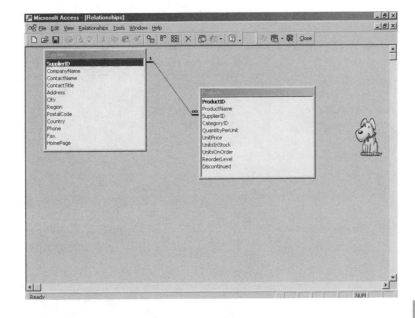

Task: Creating a Query Using the Design View

4

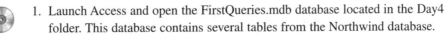

1. Launch Access and open the FirstQueries.mdb database located in the Day4 folder. This database contains several tables from the Northwind database.

2. Click the Queries entry in the object bar. Click New to start a new query. Choose the Design view. Add the Products table and Suppliers table to the query design grid. Your screen should resemble Figure 4.16.

3. Note that the Suppliers table has information about parts suppliers, whereas the Products table includes information about the products of the suppliers. Because any supplier can vend many products, but each product can have only one supplier, the relationship is one-to-many.

4. Drag and drop the CompanyName field from Suppliers to the first column in the grid, and the ProductName field from Products to the second column. Your screen should resemble Figure 4.17.

▼

FIGURE 4.16

Use the Show Table dialog box to add objects to a query. This begins a multitable query, like a single-table query.

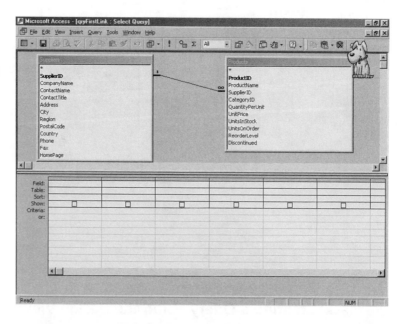

FIGURE 4.17

Access will link field data from more than one table even if the link field doesn't exist in the query grid or output.

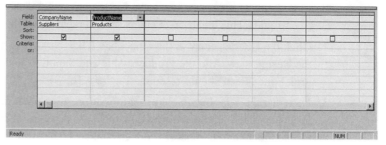

5. Save the query using a name of your choice other than the name the sample data uses, qryFirstLink. If you use that name, you'll overwrite the sample data.

6. Click the Run button or choose Datasheet view to see the results of this query. Your screen should resemble Figure 4.18.

Tip

You don't need to have a link established in Tools, Relationships. You can include two or more tables in the query design grid and drag and drop the link there. Creating a link in Tools, Relationships will create a link in the query design grid, but creating a link in the query design grid will not create a link in Tools, Relationships.

▼

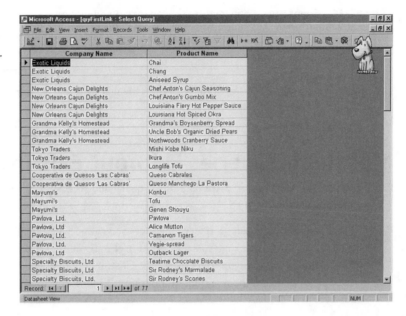

FIGURE 4.18

You've matched up all the products with their suppliers. In this simple step you've constructed a new Datasheet view from related tables.

You can enter additional fields if you want to, and the data will remain in synchronization due to the link field of SupplierID. To see how this worked, return to Design view for this query and choose the SQL view. Figure 4.19 shows this view.

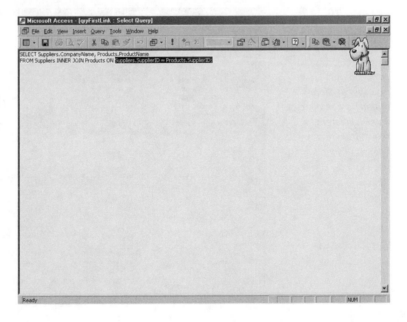

FIGURE 4.19

The SQL view reveals all. In this case, you can see that Access included the SupplierID link behind the scenes to keep the data records in proper synchronization.

This is the complete SQL statement from the query:

```
SELECT Suppliers.CompanyName, Products.ProductName
FROM Suppliers AS Suppliers INNER JOIN Products AS Products ON
➥Suppliers.SupplierID = Products.SupplierID;
```

Note | The SQL keyword ON specifies the link field for two or more tables.

Multitable Queries Without Existing Links

You can always throw in extra data into a query and Access won't really mind, but there's no reason to do so.

Your sample data includes a query called qrySenseless. Open that query in Design view to see that it's the same query as the useful qryFirstLink, but with the Customers table added. There is no logical link between the Customers table and either the Products table or Suppliers table, so the resulting output doesn't make any sense—thus the name of this query.

Switch to Datasheet view or run the query and you'll see that Access, a bit at sea as to how it should proceed given its illogical query, just repeats the same customer for each record. Figure 4.20 documents Access' distress.

FIGURE 4.20

Adding unrelated data to a query just confuses the issue. Access carries on like a trouper, but there's nothing it can do to make a meaningful return from this query's design.

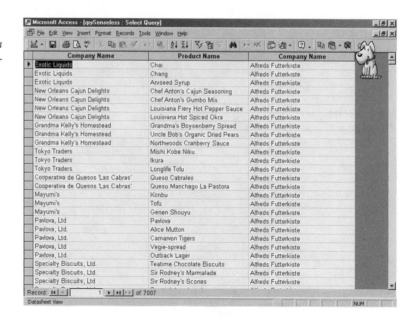

Actually, there is a link between these three tables, but it exists only as a path through two other tables, Orders and Order Details. The following task uses those two tables to create a five-table query, linking up the currently uncoordinated data shown in Figure 4.20.

Task: Manually Creating a Query

1. This task will make sense only in context. If you aren't familiar with the material in this chapter starting with the heading "Multitable Queries," take a minute to look it over now.

2. Launch the query qrySensible in the Queries group in Design view. Your screen should resemble Figure 4.21.

FIGURE 4.21

You can link fields working through various tables without including all those tables in the query results.

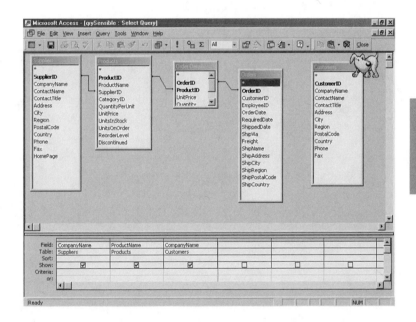

3. Note the two CustomerID fields in the Customers and Orders tables. To create a link between the two tables, click in either table at the CustomerID field and drag to the CustomerID field in the other table, dropping the link when you get to the second table. This will establish a link using the common field CustomerID.

4. Change your view to Datasheet view or choose Run from the toolbar buttons.

5. Now the query returns a list of products sold, the company vending the product, and the company that has bought the product.

| Note | The Orders and Order Details tables contain information about customer orders. |

6. Return to Design view for this query. Pull down the Sort combo box for the CompanyName field in the Customers table. Choose Ascending. Switch again to Datasheet view. You now have a list of all products purchased, sorted by customer instead of product. Your screen should resemble Figure 4.22. Close the query, saving or discarding changes as you prefer.

FIGURE 4.22

The query can be sorted on any field just like a single table query.

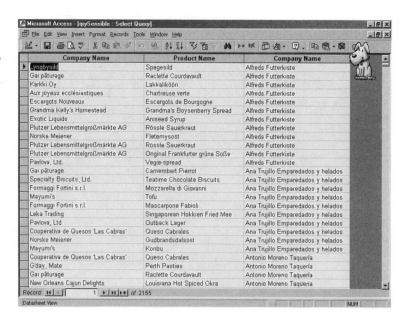

This task has little business value, but it does demonstrate how you can get to anywhere in a database as long as you can find a series of links to network into a logical construction.

Intermediate Criteria

The criteria examples so far today have been simple query by examples with the addition of the OR and AND, inclusive or exclusive. Criteria by example means using something like "Cassel" or "Palmer" on the Criteria row to return specific records.

A simple criteria example is only the very beginning of how you can select records using a query. Here are a few often-used criteria examples.

Wildcards and Like

The following examples use the table, tblVoters, included as one of the objects in the database FirstQueries. This table is a real list of registered voters minus the voting record section. The key field is the Registration number. This table has roughly 270,000 records in it. As such, it's a good one on which to practice your querying techniques.

The Like keyword combined with the wildcard asterisk character returns closely matching records. The Like keyword alone returns records Access' engine believes come close to your example.

The sample database contains a query, qryVoters, that's simply the table tblVoters included with all fields and, at this point, no criteria or sorts. To see how the wildcard and Like keyword behave, proceed to the following task.

Task: Exploring More Complex Criteria

1. Open the qryVoters query in Design view. Your screen should resemble Figure 4.23.

4

FIGURE **4.23**

Without any criteria, this query will return almost 300,000 records. That's about to change.

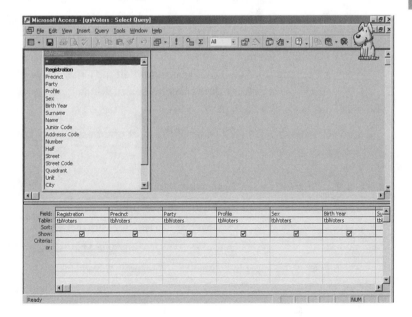

▼   2. Add the criteria `Like A*` in the Criteria row in the Surname column. Access will add quote marks around the `A*`. Tab or click out of the column. Switch to Datasheet view or run the query.

3. Access will filter out all records except those having surnames starting with the letter A. Return to Design view.

4. Edit the criteria to read `Like "[A-D]*"`. Be sure to include the quote marks as shown. Run the query again. This time Access will return all records in which the surname starts with an A, B, C, or D. Access understood the expression `[A-D]` as inclusive of the letters of the Roman alphabet in between A and D (in the English version of Access, anyway).

5. Return to Design view. Edit the criteria to read `Like "*av*"`. Again switch to Datasheet view. This time Access will return any records in which the surname has the letters *a* and *v* sequentially within it.

6. Return to Design view for this query. Edit the criteria to read `Like "ave?"`. Run the query. As you can see, the `?` wildcard works like it does on the command line—it replaces a single character. In this case, the query will return all records in which the surname starts with *ave* and has one more letter (or number, for that matter).

7. Return to Design view. Remove all criteria from the Surname field. Edit the Criteria row of the Birth Year column to read `Between 1950 and 1960`. Run the query. Access selects records for voters born in 1950 through 1960, inclusive.

8. Return to Design view. Edit the Birth Year criteria to read `>1960`. Run the query. Access selects records for voters born in 1960 or later.

9. One more example, and then it's on to other things. Return to Design view, remove all criteria from the Birth Year field. Edit the Criteria row of Surname to read `Not`
▲   `Like "A*"`. Run the query. Access selects for any record where the surname does not start with the letter A.

Table 4.1 shows a list with some of the most often-used query criteria expressions and what they return.

TABLE 4.1 QUERY CRITERIA EXPRESSIONS

Expression	Returns
`Between #12/1/98# and #2/3/99#`	Dates from 12/1/98 and 2/3/99, inclusive
`In ("Mary", "Louise", "Annie")`	Records with Mary, Louise, or Annie
`" "` (quotes with a space in between)	Records with a blank
`IsNull`	Records with no entry (null field)

Expression	Returns
`Like "Cas?le"`	*Cas* then any character followed by *le*
`Like "*s"`	Ends in *s* (case insensitive)
`Like "v*"`	Starts with *v* (case insensitive)
`<1000`	Less than 1000
`1000`	Equal to 1000
`Like "[A-C]??"`	Starts with *A* through *C* and has three characters
`????`	Any four characters
`Len([Surname])`	Any surname of four characters `=Val(4)`
`Right([Surname],2) = "is"`	Any surname ending in the letters *is*
`Left([Surname],4) = "Cass"`	Surnames starting with *Cass*

Summary

You can create a query using either the Design view or a wizard. In many cases, the add fields facility of the wizard can save you a lot of time compared to using the design grid exclusively. Although you can also create queries using SQL natively, that's an advanced topic, which is covered on Day 14, "Understanding SQL."

This chapter covered select queries that are subsets of fields, records, or both, of other queries or tables. After you've included the fields you want in your query, you can add criteria to the design grid (or the SQL view) to narrow down the selection of your query. You can add criteria for any field included in a query, even if that field doesn't show (or return) when the query is run.

You can do all the datasheet layout manipulation in a query that you can in a table's datasheet. Changes in field order in the Datasheet view won't change the Design view, but changes in field order in the Design view will change the datasheet's layout.

You can sort on fields in the design grid. The sorting priority is left to right. You can also filter and sort in Datasheet view just as you can with a table's Datasheet view.

Adding criteria to different rows in different columns creates an OR query selecting records based on either criterion. Entering criteria on the same row for two or more columns creates an AND query requiring both criteria to be satisfied for a record return.

Using built-in Access functions and expressions, you can construct sophisticated query selections spanning dates, times, or alphanumeric strings.

4

Q&A

Q **Can I use the OR and AND selections in a filter?**

A Yes. Entering two field criteria in a filter by form will create an AND query. Using the OR keyword in a field will create an OR criterion.

Q **Will sorting in Datasheet view take precedence over the design-designated sort order?**

A Yes, it will. The last sort order holds reign.

Q **Can I use the greater than or less than signs for dates?**

A Yes. >#12/31/99# will return records in which the date is at least the year 2000.

Q **How can I prevent a user from editing records in a query?**

A Here is a simple, brute-force method. In Design view, right-click in the gray area where field list boxes go, away from any list box. Locate the Recordset Type property and change it from the default Dynaset to Snapshot.

Q **Can I limit the number of records a query returns based on values relative to the dataset?**

A You can edit the Top Values box on the toolbar to a specific number of records or a percentage. Altering the sort will alter the order to the top or bottom values returned.

Workshop

The Workshop helps you solidify the skills you learned in this lesson. Answers to the quiz questions appear in Appendix A, "Answers."

Quiz

1. How can you filter for data by example in a datasheet?
2. What will the criterion >100 return?
3. What will the criteria "Cassel" AND "Palmer" yield in the Surname field of qryVoters?
4. You've set two sorts in the Design view of a query. Which field is the primary sort?
5. What does the SQL keyword ON mean?
6. Can you select by one table's fields but show another table's fields in a query?

Exercises

1. Locate qryDataTypes in the FirstQueries database. This is a small query based on the tblDateTypes table. It has only a few records consisting of differing data type fields.

2. Open the query in Design view to familiarize yourself with its structure. Switch to Datasheet view to see that at this point it returns all the records in tblDataTypes. While in Datasheet view, examine the Memo field (data type Memo and named Memo). Figure 4.24 shows this table in Datasheet view.

FIGURE 4.24

qryDataTypes is a good criteria practice query.

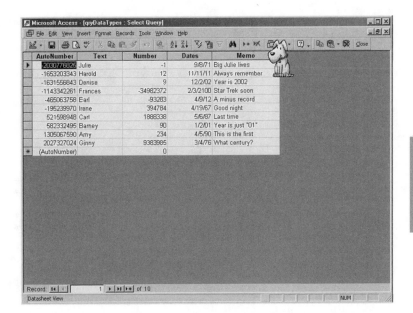

3. Return to Design view. Enter a criterion for the Memo field you think should return at least one record. Run the query. Did you get your expected return?

4. Return to Design view. Enter a sort order for the Memo field. Run the query. Did Access run as you expected?

5. Assume you wanted to find only records after the year 2000 in this query. Do you think the criterion >2000 or >#1/1/2000# would work to meet this goal within the Dates field? Would both work?

6. Close the qryDataTypes query and open qryVoters in Datasheet view. Click the Filter by Form button. Enter Like "A*" or Like "b*" in the Surname field. Apply the filter. Did it work as you expected it would?

7. Try some other likely filter expressions to see how they work.

8. Click the Filter by Form button again to return to the form. Add the filters "1970" in Birth Year and "M" in Sex. Apply the filter. Is this an AND or an OR filter?

9. Return to the Filter by Form form by clicking on the appropriate button. Note the Or tab in the lower-left corner of your screen. You can see this tab in Figure 4.25.

FIGURE 4.25

There is an OR criteria possibility within Filter by Form, too.

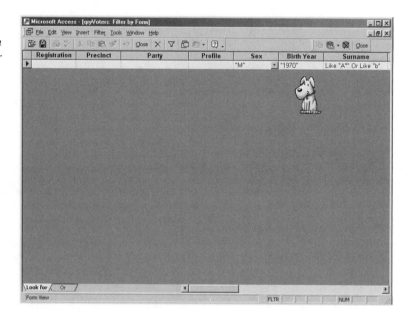

10. Click on the Or tab and enter 1969 for a additional criterion in Birth Year. Apply the filter. Did things work as you anticipated?

11. Pull down the View button and choose SQL view. Is your criteria part of the actual query itself?

12. Construct a criterion for Surname that will return only those records in which the birth year is before 1940 and the surname ends in the letter *s*.

VIEW FROM THE BEND OF THE ROAD BEACH
Edgartown, Massachusetts

KEDRON DESIGN ™

Sherborn, MA

© 1988
Anne Bell Robb

DAY 5

Creating Simple Forms for Data Access

When people think of a database, they tend to think of forms to fill in or view information. Forms not only provide a venue for these things, but their design can facilitate data entry and data validation. Today you'll learn about the following:

- The purpose of forms in a database
- The AutoForm Wizard
- Making a form with the General Form Wizard
- How to use the Form Design view
- Control and record source
- Customizing a form's tab order
- Form control naming conventions
- Bound and unbound forms and controls
- Option frames

- Filtering, sorting, and finding in forms
- Programming a command button using a wizard
- Form design properties

The Purpose of Forms in a Database

Developers use forms for data entry, editing, and viewing. The two reasons for using forms in your database application are

- Most people prefer and are used to seeing data in a form. Thus a form can increase people's comfort level with a computer application.
- Forms have facilities for data filtering, automation, and validation beyond that possible using tables or queries alone.

Forms consist of a blank work area, the form itself, and various controls existing on the form. Form controls can display fields for editing or consist of tools for varying kinds of automation.

Note

This chapter jumps around seemingly from topic to topic to cover a lot of territory. It will all come together for you when you actually design forms having some complexity.

 NEW TERM A form can be either bound or unbound. A *bound* form is linked to an underlying table or query and derives its data from and writes to that object. An *unbound* form neither gets data from nor writes to any object. The Record Source property of a form controls what object, if any, is bound to a form.

Within a form, controls can also be either bound or unbound. In a manner similar to a bound form, a bound control reads from or writes to a field within a bound object. Many forms mix bound and unbound controls. The property of a control that determines its bound or unbound condition is the Control Source property.

 The discussion so far has been rather abstract and because of this it might, at this point, seem a bit more abstruse than it really is. To get an idea of how all these concepts work together, open the SimpleForms database located in the Day5 folder of your CD.

Control and Record Source Properties

Examine the tblSales table by opening it in both Design view and Datasheet view. This is a very simple table having only two fields—one for a sale number (primary key field) and one for a sale amount.

Click on the Forms entry in the object bar and locate the form called frmFirstDemo. Double-click on this object to open it in Form view. Figure 5.1 shows this form.

FIGURE 5.1

This form has two bound controls and one unbound control.

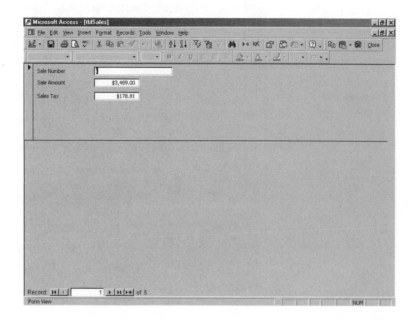

This form is bound to the tblSales table you saw earlier. From the top, the first field or control shows the primary key field, or Sale Number. The second control displays the Sale Amount field from the table. The third control is unbound from any underlying object. It calculates the sales tax (5.125% of the Sale Amount) for any sale.

To see how all these items work together, click the View button to move to Design view for this form. If the Properties list box isn't open, click the Properties button on the toolbar or choose View, Properties from the main menu. Make sure the current object is the form itself. If it is, the word Form will appear both in the formatting toolbar and the title bar for the Properties list box itself. Figure 5.2 shows the form opened in Design view with the form itself as the current object.

Also make sure the Field List list box is open. In Figure 5.2, it's the box with the title bar displaying tblSales. Click the Data tab in the Properties list box. Note the Record Source property is tblSales indicating that this form is bound to that table.

Click in the data display part of the first field, Sale Number. The properties in the Properties list box change from properties for a form to properties for a text box control—the type of control this form uses for the Sale Number field. If necessary, click on the Data tab and note the Control Source is set to Sale Number—the field in the table that's bound to this control.

5

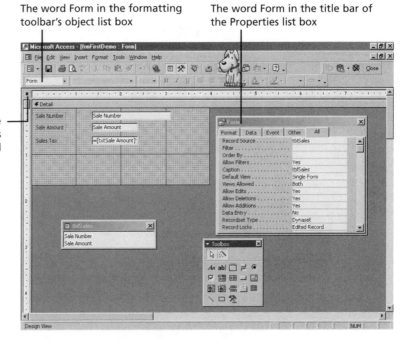

The word Form in the formatting
toolbar's object list box

The word Form in the title bar of
the Properties list box

FIGURE 5.2

*Three indicators show
the form is the current
object.*

The black square, the
Form Selector, shows
the form is selected

Click in the data area of the next field, Sale Amount. Again click on the Data tab of the
Properties list box, and note that the Control Source for this control is the Sale Amount
field in the bound table.

So far, things are likely unfolding about as you would expect they would have to. Now
things get interesting. Click in the Sales Tax field—where the sales tax itself appears
when you're in Form view. Again note the Control Source property in the Data (and All)
tab. It's

```
=[txtSale Amount]*0.05125
```

This time the Control Source doesn't point to a field within the bound table, but refers to
another control and a math formula.

Note

The brackets [] around the field txtSale Amount indicate to Access that the
enclosed name is a control.

The other important property you should gain early familiarity with is the Name property. Click in the All tab. Note the Name property for the bottom field is txtTax. Click in
the middle field and note the Name property for that control is txtSale Amount.

Note

> All controls in an Access form must have a name. Access will assign a name
> to a new control using its own algorithm. It's up to you as an Access devel-
> oper to use a cogent naming convention for your forms' controls.

All controls on a form, bound or unbound, must have a Name property. Using a logical
naming convention for form objects is vitally important for efficient use of Access. The
program doesn't care what naming convention you use, if any, but you should care. Take
a look at the Name property for each of the controls in the `frmFirstDemo` object. Note
that each name starts out with the three letters `txt`, followed by a name indicating the
function of the control.

This is a rather standard naming convention. The `txt` part of the names refers to the
nature of the controls—text boxes. If, for example, the controls were combo boxes, the
three-letter prefix would be `cbo`. The following part of the name is a mnemonic of some
sort to indicate the function of the control to the programmer.

Back in the early days of personal computers, programmers had to (or preferred to) use
short names for program objects. So you would get statements such as

```
A = 1
B = .05125
C = 2990
```

This works, but remembering exactly what the objects A, B, and C stand for isn't easy
when a programmer got to working deep down in the program. Instead, look at the following descriptive naming technique:

```
Periods = 30
InterestRate = .05125
PresentValue = 129950
```

This leaves no doubt as to what these values stand for.

Similarly, using a naming convention for all Access objects leaves little doubt about what
an object does, now or in the future. If you showed the object named `TxtTaxesDue` to any
programmer familiar with Access or modern naming conventions, he would be able to
make a good guess that this object is a text box that holds values stating the tax due. Try
it yourself. First, Table 5.1 shows the naming convention for some of the objects found
on a typical form.

5

TABLE 5.1   FORM OBJECT NAMING CONVENTIONS

Convention	Object
txt	Text box
cbo	Combo box
lbl	Label
ocx	Custom control
cmd	Command button
chk	Check box
img	Image
opt	Option button
fra	Option button frame (group)
tgl	Toggle button
lst	List box

Now take a look at Table 5.2. This shows named objects and their functions. Does this system make sense to you?

TABLE 5.2   TYPICAL USES OF NAMING CONVENTIONS

Convention	Object
txtTotalSales	Text box displaying total sales
cboSelectCustomer	Combo box to choose customers from a list
lblKafeeTraders	Label for the form called Kafee Traders
cmdClose	Command button to close form
chkSalesTaxExempt	Check box for tax-exempt customers
optUPS	Option button to select UPS as shipper
tglShowProduct	Toggle button to show a graphic of the selected product
lstProductsAvailable	List box to show available products

Feel free to use a system such as this, or another of your choosing, for your database objects.

Note

Unlike earlier systems, Access' object names can contain spaces, but most database developers are used to and prefer to use mixed-case to delimit words within a name.

Creating a First Form

There are two fundamental ways to create a form using Access. The first is using Form Design view, the second a bevy of wizards including the super-simple AutoForm. Unless your form needs are quite simple, you'll want to enhance the output of a form wizard through Design view.

This first task creates a two-field form using the wizard and then modifies the form controls.

Task: Using the AutoForm Wizard

1. Launch Access and open the SimpleForms database. Click the Tables entry in the object bar. Locate the tblSales table. Click on that object, but don't open it.

2. Locate the New Object button on the toolbar. That's the button that has an icon that looks something like a lightning strike.

3. Click the button to pull it down (it's a combo box). Locate the AutoForm entry (it should be first) and click on it. Access will create a form using this table as a record source. Your screen should resemble Figure 5.3.

FIGURE 5.3

The AutoForm isn't terribly artistic, but it's quite functional.

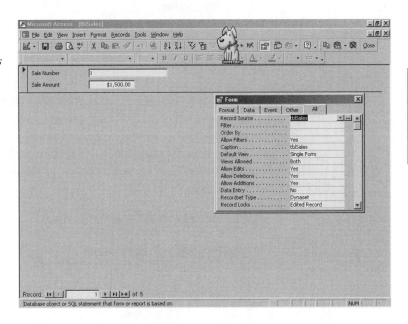

4. Save this form by choosing File, Save As from the main menu; give it the name frmFirstForm.

5. Close the form. Click on the Forms entry in the object bar (if necessary), and note that your new form is now part of the form objects in Access.

You can also use the Form Design Wizard to create a form. This is a bit more flexible than AutoForm. Here's how it works.

Task: Using the Form Wizard

1. Launch Access and open the SimpleForms database. Click the Forms entry in the object bar. Click New to start a new form. Choose the Form Wizard entry from the resulting list box. Note that you can also trigger the AutoForm wizards from this list box. Pull down the combo box toward the bottom of this dialog box and choose tblSales from the list. Your screen should resemble Figure 5.4.

FIGURE 5.4

The start new form process asks whether you want to use a wizard and what the record source for the form should be.

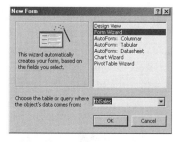

2. Click OK to start the wizard in earnest. The first screen you'll see should be familiar if you've been through a table or query wizard—the field selector list boxes. Because there are only two fields here, include them both for the new form. Click Next to move on. Leave the form as columnar, but you might want to return to this wizard later to see the output of the other types of form. Access' wizard does show a graphic representing what the other forms will look like. To see this graphic, click other option buttons. Return the option buttons to default (columnar) and click Next. Your screen should resemble Figure 5.5.

FIGURE 5.5

The Form Wizard lets you create a sharp look for your new form.

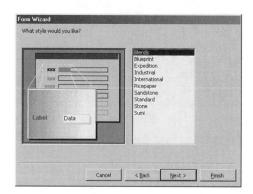

▼   3. Leave the form style selection at the default. Click Next.

4. Use the next screen to name the form frmStandardWizard. Click Finish.

5. Access will create the new form and open it in Form view. Your screen should resemble Figure 5.6.

FIGURE 5.6

In this case, the finished form is identical to the AutoForm, but has the style indicated in Figure 5.5 applied to it.

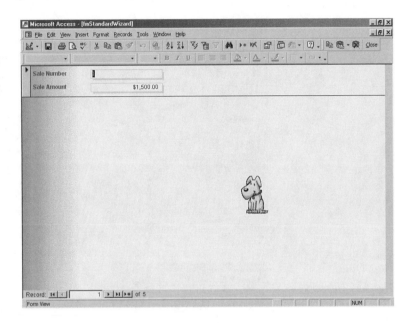

▲

Form Design View

There's nothing wrong with these kinds of forms for the simple two-field bound table. Look at Figure 5.7. This is an AutoForm Wizard output based on the table Household Inventory from the Inventory database—part of the sample data that comes with Access. You can find this form supplied with the SimpleForms database as frmHouseholdAutoForm.

The next task modifies the wizard-generated form from Figure 5.7.

Task: Using the Form Design View

1. Launch Access and open the SimpleForms database. Click the Forms entry in the object bar. Locate the frmHouseholdAutoForm form. Right-click on this entry. Choose Copy from the context menu. Right-click in the Forms area away from any entry and choose Paste from the context menu. Access will bring up a Paste As dialog box allowing you to enter a new name for this object. Enter frmHouseholdItems for a new name. Your screen should resemble Figure 5.8. Click OK to exit the dialog box.

▼

FIGURE 5.7

The form wizards lack imagination when applied to even a moderately complex object.

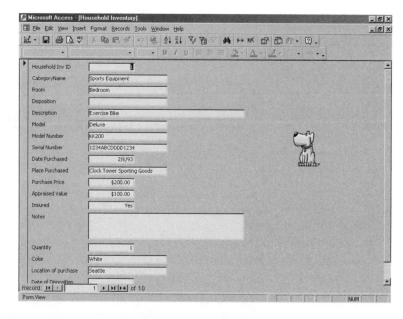

FIGURE 5.8

The Paste command in the Database view is really a Paste As command.

Tip

Step number 1 uses the Copy, Paste technique to show you how it works. You could also have opened the form and used the Save As command from the File menu to create a copy of the object sporting a different name.

2. If necessary, click on the new form to highlight it. Click the Design button in the Database view toolbar. This will open the new form in Design view. Your screen should resemble Figure 5.9.

3. Depending on the state of your Form Design view, you might not see all the objects shown in Figure 5.9—or you might have more. To view or hide any object in the form design grid, either click on its entry in the main toolbar (the buttons are toggles) or select/deselect its entry in the View submenu of the main menu. Figure 5.9 shows the field list box (similar to the field list boxes in the query design grid) and the toolbox for form design. The toolbox contains an array of controls for use on forms.

▼

FIGURE 5.9

The Form Design view is quite a bit different from the previous design views for queries and tables.

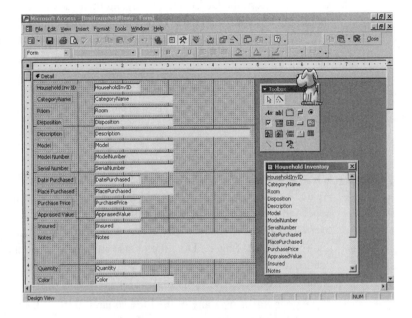

4. The form design grid uses a drag and drop approach for most of its layout chores. To move a field, click on it. This will surround the field with some boxes and lines indicating the field has the highlight. Figure 5.10 shows the Description field highlighted.

5

FIGURE 5.10

Access gives a strong visual clue to which field or fields are highlighted.

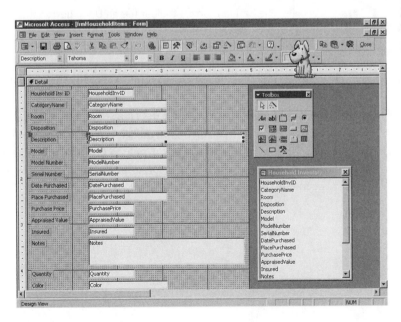

▼

5. Click away from the Description field, and then back in it, but don't release the mouse button. Your cursor will change to look like a hand. Move the mouse and you'll drag the field. Release the mouse button to drop the field in its new location. Note the field and its label moved in synchronization.

Tip

The hand cursor in Form Design view indicates you can move a form control.

---

6. Press Ctrl+Z (Undo) to snap the field back to its former position.

7. Again, if necessary, click in the field to highlight it. Locate the larger squares at the upper-left corners of the field data part and the label. Move your cursor to hover over either of those squares. The cursor will change to a hand with an upraised finger. (No, not that finger!) Drag the mouse and you'll move the field or label independent of the other. Drop the object you're moving and click Undo again to replace the objects.

8. Move your cursor over any of the little squares at the sides of either the data area or the label of the highlighted control. The cursor changes to a double-ended arrow. Click and drag to increase or decrease the size of the field. Drop the resized field and then click Undo to restore the field to its original size.

Tip

The standard Access toolbar has an Undo button that works identically to the Ctrl+Z command.

---

9. If necessary, click on the Description field to highlight it. Click the Del button to delete the field from this form.

10. Make sure the field list box for the Household Inventory table is visible. If it's not, choose the Field List entry from the View menu in the main menu bar. Locate the Description field in the list box. Click on this field and drag it to the form design grid, dropping it where the old Description field existed. Figure 5.11 shows this operation in process.

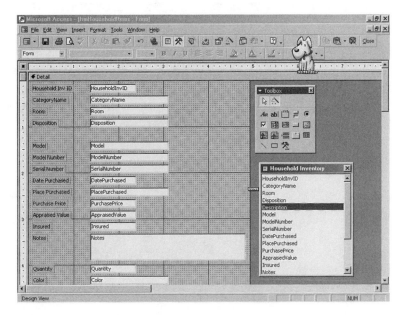

FIGURE 5.11

Adding fields to a form is a simple matter of dragging and dropping.

11. The type of control Access uses for a field depends upon the current tool selected from the toolbox or the default field—text box. Again, delete the Description field from the form design grid. Locate the combo box control within the toolbox and click on it to select it as the control you want to use for the next field placement. If the magic wand (wizard) button in the toolbox appears pressed, click on it to give it a raised look. Click on and again drag the Description field from the field list box to the design grid. Access will add the field, but this time it will use a combo box control to display it. Figure 5.12 shows this procedure finished except for the final location of the control.

5

Tip

The More Controls button in the toolbox will open a list of many more controls, some of which are useful for form design. The exact number and type of controls opened depend upon your computer's setup.

FIGURE 5.12

Access can use various toolbox controls to display a field.

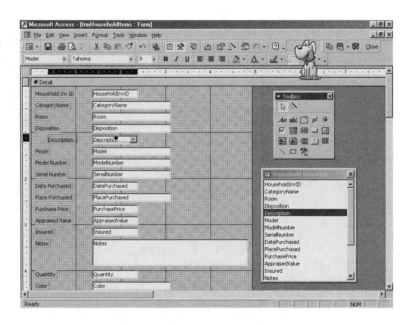

▲ 12. Close the form, discarding changes.

Some form controls make sense for displaying field data, and some don't. For example, the standard toolbox contains both command and toggle buttons, neither of which can display data, but instead find use as objects to control the flow of a program. Table 5.3 contains the most-used form controls and their prevalent uses.

TABLE 5.3 OFTEN-USED FORM CONTROLS

Control Name	Common Use
Text box	Contains text or numbers. Can be bound, unbound, or containing a calculation (expression).
Label	Name of form, name of field, instructions for data entry.
List box	List of values or entries. Usually bound, but can be filled programmatically, too.
Combo box	Familiar pull-down box. Actually a combination of a text box and a list box.
Check box	The square box useful for Yes/No data type fields or form choices.
Option button	Another Yes/No control often used in frames or option groups.
Option group	A group of option buttons or check boxes in which only one in a group can be selected.
Unbound object	Display an object (such as an image) that remains the same as records change.

Control Name	Common Use
Bound object	Display objects that should change for each record. For example, pictures of employees will change as the record changes.
Tab control	Create tabbed forms that have the look of Office 2000's option dialog boxes.
Subform	Create forms that are controlled by (or bound to) other forms. Most often used to create detail listings such as order details for customers.
Line	Create lines to visually delineate form elements.
Rectangle	Create squares and rectangles to delineate form elements.

Most of these controls are self-explanatory, but some people have trouble with the idea of option buttons or check boxes within a group until they use the control. If you have any doubt about the use of an option group, glance through the next section. If you're sure about its use, skip ahead.

Option Group

 An option group will permit only one control at a time to be set. Open the frmOptionGroup form in Form view. This form is part of the sample data located in the Forms section of the SimpleForms database. Figure 5.13 shows this form open.

FIGURE 5.13

This form has a set of option buttons in and out of an option group.

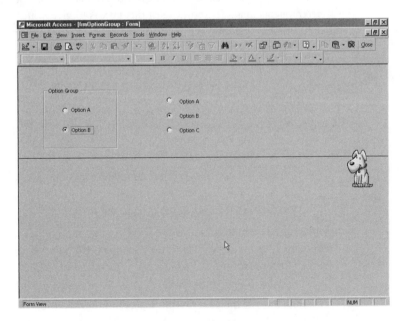

5

Try to get both option buttons within the group to be "on" at the same time. You can't. Now try to do the same with the three buttons on the right—the ones outside a group. Although this example used option buttons for the demonstration, it could have used check boxes with the same result. Use an option group or frame when a record must have one choice selected, but can't have more than one.

Tip

> Most users expect to see option buttons, not check boxes, in a group. This has become a Windows convention. As a developer, you will have better results following this and other conventions.

Form Control Alignment

You might have noted that the background of the form design grid does in fact look like graph paper or a grid. This isn't just for decoration, but is an enormously helpful aid in form design. You can set Access to snap controls (auto align) to this grid, to automatically align or space controls, and you can also adjust this grid to whatever fineness you need for your design work.

Open the frmGridAlign form (part of your sample data) in either view. This is a simple, unbound form with three text box controls scattered around it. These are the controls you'll need for this task. The purpose of this task is to give you the skills you'll need to create orderly looking forms and reports.

Note

> Most of the skills learned in form design are directly transferable to report design.

Task: Form Grid and Alignment

1. Launch Access and open the SimpleForms database. Click the Forms entry in the object bar. Launch the frmGridAlign form in Form view. Note the three text box controls scattered around the form.

2. Click the View button to move to Design view for this form. Make sure the Properties list box is visible. If not, choose it from the toolbar or from the View menu. Also make sure the form itself is the currently selected object. If it is, the word Form will appear in the title bar of the Properties list box.

3. Note the look of the grid (graph paper) in the background of the form design area. Click the All or Format tab in the Properties list box. Scroll down until you locate

▼ the Grid X and Grid Y properties. Note that both are set at 24. This is the number of lines per inch the grid exhibits. Alter the properties for both X and Y to 5. Your screen should resemble Figure 5.14.

FIGURE 5.14

The two Grid properties control the granularity of the design grid.

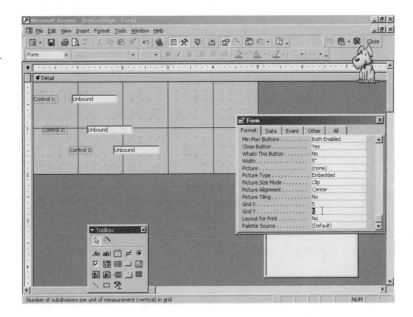

4. Move any control around. Note you can only drop it where the grid is. With the grid set to such a coarse granularity, you're severely limited to where you can place controls.

5. Open the Format menu. Locate the Snap to Grid entry and click on it to deselect this option. Again, try moving a control around the form. You can drop it anywhere. Re-activate Snap to Grid.

> **Tip**
> Activating Snap to Grid won't snap to grid objects currently off the grid until you move them.

NEW TERM

6. Click anywhere on the form away from the three text box controls. Drag a box around the three controls. Release the mouse. This is called a *marquee selection*—the marquee is the rubber band–like rectangle you saw during the drag operation. Figure 5.15 shows the marquee selection in process.

▼

FIGURE 5.15

The marquee selection is one of several ways to select several form objects at the same time.

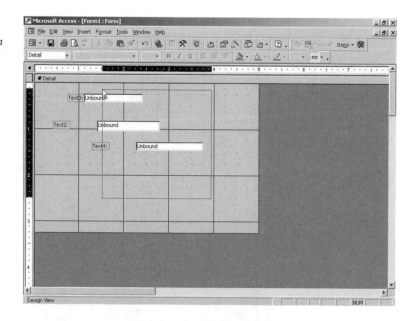

7. Drop down the Format menu. Locate the Align entry and move your mouse cursor down to that entry. Note the flyout menu has several alignment options. Try aligning these controls left and right, top and bottom to get a feel for what the effect of these choices will be.

 Tip

Shift+click will allow multiple selections of form objects.

8. Again examine the Format menu and locate the entries for Horizontal Spacing and Vertical Spacing. Experiment with the submenu entries for both these entries to see what effect they can have.

9. Separate (if necessary) any overlapping controls to give them some spread again. Highlight all three using either the Shift or the marquee method. Choose the Format menu's Group entry. This will place a rectangle around all three controls. A grouped set of controls can act in Design view as a linked set of controls. Click away from the group, and then click again in the group area on any of the grouped controls. Try moving one control of the group. Now click on the black square at the upper-left of the group rectangle. Drag the square to drag the group. Figure 5.16 shows a group.

FIGURE 5.16

You can move or otherwise modify grouped controls in concert.

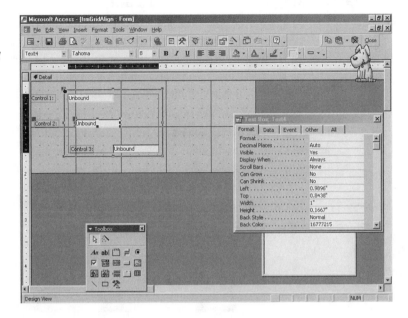

10. You can also change the entire size of the form. Move your cursor to the extreme bottom-right corner of the form. When at the corner, your cursor will change to look like an oval with four arrows pointing out of it. Drag to increase or decrease the size of the form in both directions. You can also change the vertical or horizontal size of the form by click-dragging on the right or bottom edge of the form design screen.

11. Close the form, saving or discarding changes as you see fit. If you want to preserve the original form and the modified one, choose File, Save As from the menu to save your modified form under a new name.

Form Headers and Footers

A form header is an area at the top of the form that remains the same no matter what record the form's Detail area displays. The form's footer is the same, but is at the form's lower edge. Form headers and footers are useful for displaying form titles or other data you want to persist from record to record. There are two classes of headers and footers. Form headers and footers persist for all records; page headers and footers persist for a particular form page.

5

Task: Taking a Look at Form Headers and Footers

1. Launch Access and open the SimpleForms database. Click the Forms entry in the object bar. Locate the frmHeaderFooter form and open it in Form view. Click the forward and back buttons at the bottom of the form to move through the records. This is a simple form based on some of the fields in the Household Inventory table, which also is in this database.

2. Note how the label in the Header section remains no matter what record is displayed in the Detail section of the form. Also note the same thing for the forward and back buttons in the Footer section.

3. Switch to Design view. Note the construction of this form shown in Figure 5.17.

FIGURE 5.17

The Form Header section of this form holds a label control that remains static no matter what is displayed in the Detail section.

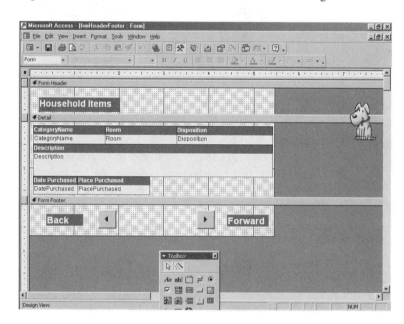

4. You can use headers and footers not only for labels, but also for navigation controls (such as the forward and back buttons), totals or subtotals. Close the form discarding or saving changes as you prefer.

Other Form Format Properties

Forms default to certain properties that almost always aren't all needed at the same time on the same form. These are shown in Table 5.4.

TABLE 5.4 DEFAULT FORM CONTROLS

Property Name	Usage
Default View	Form or datasheet (forms can display in the datasheet format too).
Scroll Bars	Horizontal, vertical, or both.
Record Selectors	Selects entire record in datasheet view. No use in Form view.
Navigation Buttons	Move one record forward or backward, or to end or beginning of records.
Control Box	This is the box to the extreme left of the title bar in standard Windows applications. Opens the Control menu.
Min Max Buttons	The minimize and maximize buttons in a standard Windows application.
Close Button	Close the application (or form in this case).
What's This Button	Context-sensitive help.

To see some of these properties in action, open the frmHeaderFooter form in Form view. If it's not visible, click the Properties button in the toolbar or choose it from the View menu. Your screen should resemble Figure 5.18.

FIGURE 5.18

You can auto-preview your form's look by manipulating its properties in Form view.

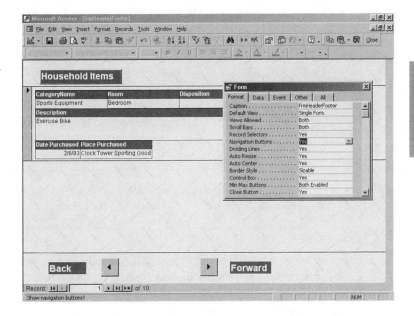

5

Click in the Record Selectors property and enter No, or pull down the combo box and choose No from the list.

| **Tip** | You can toggle many properties by double-clicking on them. |

Access will remove the gray bar to the left of the Form Detail section. As you can see, removal of this element doesn't detract at all from the usefulness of the form. A record selector is useful in a datasheet, but not a form. Similarly, change or toggle the other properties listed in Table 5.4. Watch the form as you do, noting what element each property controls. Some properties, such as the close, minimize, and maximize buttons, will require you to switch from Form to Design and back to Form view for the changes to take effect. If in doubt, toggle your view.

Tab Order

When in any Windows standard dialog box or form, you'll notice that there is a standard order for cursor movement. In other words, when you leave a field or object in Windows, your cursor doesn't randomly move to another object, but rather the programmer or program (by default) determines the cursor progression order for the available objects.

Like so many things, this is easier seen than explained. Open the SimpleForms database if necessary. Locate the frmTabOrder form by clicking on the Forms entry in the object bar and finding it in the list of available forms for this database. Double-click on this form to open it in Form view. This is a simple form bound to the Household Inventory table from the sample data Inventory database supplied with Office 2000.

| **Note** | An object is said to have the focus when an object can accept input, or in other words, has the "attention" of the cursor. |

Note that the cursor starts out in the primary key field for this table, the HouseholdInvID field. Press the Tab key to move to the next field in the tab order. The cursor jumps to the CategoryName field. This makes sense logically for data entry, but it's distracting to see the cursor moving in a disorderly fashion around the form.

Note Access assigns the tab order for a form based on the order in which you placed objects into the form's bands or areas. In this case, the CategoryName field was placed on the Form Detail area immediately after the HouseholdInvID field, causing their tab orders to be 2 and 1, respectively.

To get a feel for how annoying a disoriented tab order can be, click the New Record button on the toolbar (to the right of the Find button). This will bring up a blank record for your data entry. Tab out of the HouseholdInvID field because it auto increments. Enter a category name and then press Enter. Enter a room name or number and then press Enter (or Tab) again. Note the Stop (close form) command button now has the focus. This surely isn't a sensible way to design a form! If you press Enter to move to the next field, you'll end up closing the form.

Even leaving the Stop button out of it, having the cursor jump all over the form is distracting. The next task assigns a planned tab order to these fields and prevents an accidental closing of the form.

Task: Learning Tab Order and Tab Stop Properties

1. Launch Access and open the SimpleForms database. Click the Forms entry in the object bar. Locate the frmTabOrder form and open it in Design view. If you have the form open in Form view by following along in the introduction of this section, switch to Design view now.

2. Drop down the View menu and choose Tab Order from the menu. This will open the Tab Order dialog box. Your screen should resemble Figure 5.19.

3. The Tab Order dialog box has two ways to change the tab order of a form's controls. You can click on the Auto Order button to order the controls from left to right and top to bottom, or you can click on the gray square to the left of each control's name then drag and drop the control to a new place in the order.

4. Using either method, alter the tab order so the fields are ordered from left to right and top to bottom. The order of the fields in the Tab Order list box should end up as

1 Model

2 Category Name

3 Room

4 HouseholdInvID

5 ModelNumber

6 cmdExit

5

FIGURE 5.19

The Tab Order dialog box shows the current tab order for the object in each section of a form.

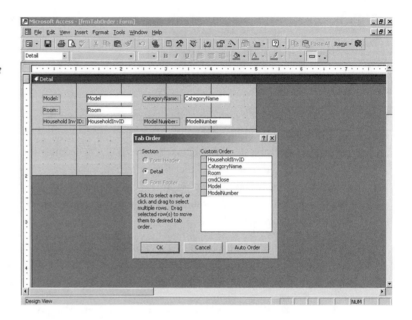

> **Note**
>
> The field names for the controls differ from the labels associated with those fields because the field names and the Caption property for those fields vary. Open the Household Inventory table in Design view to see the two labels.

5. Return to Form view. Again click the New record button in the toolbar and enter a new record. Although the current field order is less logical (to some ways of thinking), the data entry person will find the order of the field progression predictable, and therefore not worrisome as it was before.

6. A problem still exists. There is no need to give the focus to the Stop (close form) button for each record entered in this form. In fact, it's a bad idea because the data entry person might erroneously close the form and therefore lose time relocating and opening it. To fix this, return to Design view for this form.

7. Click on the Stop (close form) button to highlight it. Open the Properties list box, if necessary, by clicking on its entry in the toolbar. Click the Other or All tab and locate the Tab Stop property. Edit it to No (or double-click on it; that will toggle it to No). Your screen should resemble Figure 5.20.

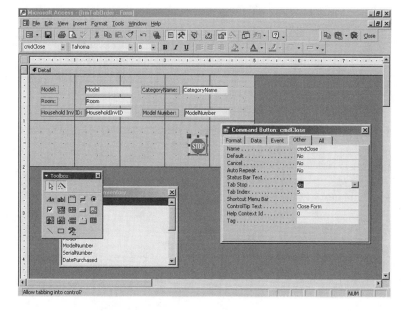

FIGURE 5.20

The Tab Stop property enables or disables the object's capability to accept focus from the tab order.

8. Save the changes you made to the form by clicking the Save button in the toolbar. Return to Form view and tab through the fields. Note that the cursor never lands on the Stop button. However, if you need to, you can click on the Stop (close form) button using a mouse click. This avoids the possibility of an accidental form closure, removes the extra Tab keystroke for every record entry, but preserves the use of the Stop button when it's needed.

9. There's a further improvement you can make to this form. The HouseholdInvID field is an auto increment field, so it requires no user entry at any time. In fact, there's no reason for this field to ever have focus because users can't edit values within this field or make entries here.

10. Return to Design view. Click in the HouseholdInvID field. Locate the Enabled property in the Data (or All) tab. Toggle this value from Yes to No.

Tip

Setting the Enabled property to No prevents the control from getting the focus, and therefore prevents the user from editing data values. Setting the Locked property to Yes allows focus but prevents data editing.

▼ 11. Return to Form view. Again click the New Record button to enter a new record for
       your household possessions. Note that this time not only does the cursor skip over
       the Stop button, it also skips over the auto increment field (HouseholdInvID).
       Compare how easy data entry is in the form now that you've set a proper tab order
       and tab stops compared to when you started with this form. The Enabled property
       is the property that controls "graying out" in Access applications, as you can see in
       Figure 5.21.

FIGURE 5.21

*Setting the Enabled
property to No grays
out a control in Access
and in Windows.*

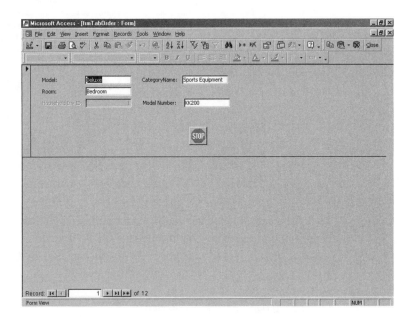

▲

Finding, Filtering, and Sorting in Forms

This is the easiest and simplest section you can imagine. Filtering by form, filtering by
example, and sorting data within forms are identical to doing these procedures in a
datasheet, whether that datasheet is a query or a table.

Remember, a bound form doesn't represent different data than a table or query, but only
a different presentation of that data. All the skills you learned on Day 3, "Exploring the
Data Foundations—The Table," are directly transferable without any changes to use in
forms.

If you have any doubts about your ability here, review the earlier material on Day 3 and
Day 4, "Using Queries for Data Retrieval," about filtering, finding, and sorting data in
datasheets, and then try the same procedures from the Form view. You'll note no differences whatsoever. Similarly, much of the skill set you picked up today will be transferable to reports, coming tomorrow.

Summary

Forms present data in a way most people find easier to edit or view than simple datasheets. You can create forms using the AutoForm Wizard, the regular Form Wizard, or using Design view. You can always modify the wizard-generated forms using Design view. Many developers let the wizard make a simple form and then modify the layout using Design view.

Forms have up to five bands. These are Form Header, Page Header, Detail, Page Footer, and Form Footer. You can add controls, either bound or unbound, to any of these bands. To add a bound control to a band, click on the field name in the field name list box, and drag it to the band on the form where you want it to appear. To add a non-default (non-text box) control to a form, click in the toolbox on the control type and on the field in the list box, and then click on the form where you want the control to reside.

Forms are heavily equipped with properties to control their function and appearance. Today's lesson covered some of the appearance and tab order properties, but there are many more to come. For example, you can alter the entire tab order of a form using the Tab Order dialog box, remove a control from the tab order by setting the Tab Stop property to No, and remove a control's capability to get the focus by setting the Enabled property to No.

Q&A

Q How does an Access form determine where its pages start and end?

A File, Page Setup determines this by whatever page size you enter. In the U.S. standard setup, this size is 8.5×11 inches. There is also a Page Break tool within the toolbox to set page breaks outside the Page Size property.

Q I've seen datasheets using only horizontal lines. How was that done?

A Here's one way. Open the frmTabOrder form in Datasheet view by highlighting and double-clicking on it in the Database view. Then choose Datasheet view from the View button on the toolbar. Locate the Gridlines button in the Formatting (datasheet) toolbar. If necessary, right-click on any toolbar and open the Formatting (datasheet) toolbar. Locate the Gridlines (horizontal only) entry and choose it. Your screen should resemble Figure 5.22.

5

Select the gridlines you want to display
from the drop-down options

FIGURE 5.22

*You have control over
the gridlines in a
datasheet.*

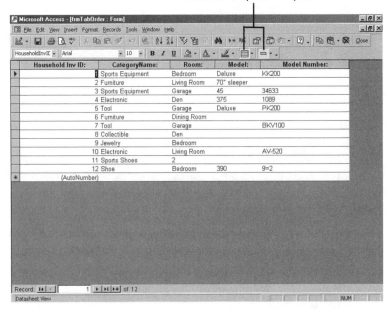

Q Are there global properties I can set for all controls on a form?

A Yes. Select the form itself using the Form Selector and then open the Properties list box to the Data tab. Note you can set the form to edit or not all records as well as several other related properties.

Q Can I set several properties at the same time for related controls?

A Yes, you can select several controls using Shift+click or marquee. The Properties list box will display Multiple Selection in its title bar. Any common properties will appear in the various tabs. Setting any property will set that property for all selected controls.

Q I am trying to set the color of a form, but can't find any property that sounds right for the form. Is there a way to do this?

A You set color for each band, not the form. For example, click in the Detail band away from any object, and then choose the Format tab from the Properties list box. Locate the Background color property. Click the ellipsis button that appears when that property has focus. Choose your color from the displayed palette.

Q Can I copy a control and paste it elsewhere on the form?

A The Clipboard works the same in Form Design view as elsewhere in Windows. You can copy, cut, and paste any object.

Workshop

The Workshop helps you solidify the skills you learned in this lesson. Answers to the quiz questions appear in Appendix A, "Answers."

Quiz

1. What allows the dragging of a control separate from its label?

2. How do you remove a control from a form?

3. How can you alter a control's size on a form?

4. Will a form header appear for all records on a form?

5. Can two option buttons in an option frame both be set to Yes?

6. How does filtering by form differ in a datasheet and a form?

Exercises

1. In the Forms section of the Database view, choose New. Choose the Form Wizard to create a form bound to the tblSales table. Include both fields in this new form. Save the form using a name of your choosing or use this example's choice: frmWorkshop. That form is part of your sample data. If you have trouble following along with this exercise, consult that form. Accept all the wizard's defaults for this form.

2. Switch to Design view. If the form footer isn't visible, choose (or toggle it) from the View menu. Enlarge the form footer to be the length of the form, but about one inch (2.5 cm) deep. Your screen should resemble Figure 5.23.

3. Make sure the toolbox is visible. If it is not, make it so using the View menu or the toolbar. Make sure the Control Wizards button is selected in the toolbox's toolbar. That's the button with the magic wand on it.

4. Locate the command button control in the toolbox. Click on it. Click in the form footer area of the form toward the right of the footer area. This will place a button on the form and launch a wizard. Your screen should resemble Figure 5.24.

5. Choose Form Operations and Close Form from the two list boxes shown in Figure 5.24. Click Next.

5

FIGURE 5.23

You are about to add a new control to a wizard form.

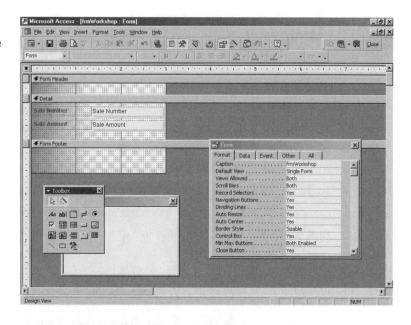

FIGURE 5.24

Some controls can trigger wizards. A command button is one of these.

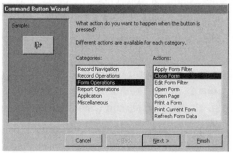

Tip

This is a good place to pause and study the other operations a command button wizard can do.

6. Choose the Stop Sign from the next screen. Click Next.

7. Name the command button cmdExit. Click Finish. Your screen should resemble Figure 5.25.

FIGURE 5.25

You've just created and programmed a command button to close this form.

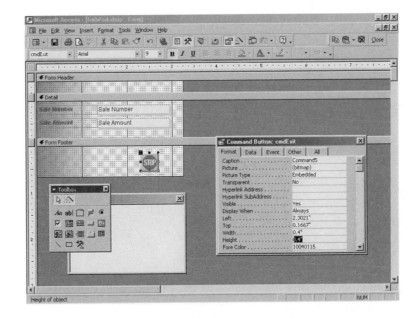

8. Save the form. Change to Form view. Try your new button to see whether it works as you expected it to. It should.

9. Return to Design view. Remove the new command button from the tab order but allow it to have focus. Return to Form view.

10. Test the tab order to see whether it includes your command button. It shouldn't. Return to Design view. Open the Tab Order dialog box from the View menu. Does the footer section include the cmdExit object in its list?

11. Close the form, saving changes if you choose to.

5

DAY **6**

Generating Basic Reports

Reports have traditionally been printed versions of database products. Today with many users online, database reports aren't just printed, but often displayed onscreen either through a LAN or the Internet. Today you'll learn the basics of creating such reports:

- The use of reports within Access
- The AutoReport Wizard
- The Standard Report Wizard
- Using the Report Design view
- Grouping within a report
- Summing in a group
- Keeping a report running sum
- Subtotaling on reports
- Sorting in one or multiple levels within a report
- Viewing one or more pages of a report
- Report bands

- Manipulating group properties to your advantage
- Making mailing labels
- Cutting, Copying, and Pasting Controls on Reports

Reports in Access

Reports differ from forms in their use within Access chiefly by being weighted to perform well with output devices, such as a Web page or a printer, whereas forms work best onscreen. The Web has changed this slightly; reports do duty as display-only pages, and forms do double-duty as display and edit or entry Web pages. For example, if you wanted to display your company's earnings over the Web, you would most likely choose a report. If you wanted to take customer orders, your first choice would have to be a form.

> **Tip**
>
> Forms can display or accept user input such as edits. Reports are read-only objects.

Access does blur the line somewhat between reports and forms. For example, there's a Form Wizard for a pivot table form (cross tab). This is a display device requiring no user input. Similarly, forms can contain graphics or the entire form can be a graphic—again a non-input or edit use for a form.

Today's lesson covers the report basics. Because there are many similarities between form design and report design, this chapter skips lightly over some basics assuming that you learned them in Day 5, "Creating Simple Forms for Data Access." This will prevent a lot of repetition if you are reading this book sequentially. If you're not familiar with yesterday's material on forms, this is a good time to at least skim over that chapter.

The AutoReport Wizard

The AutoReport Wizard behaves identically to the AutoForm Wizard, although obviously the output is a report, not a form. Here's how it works.

Task: Taking the AutoReport Wizard for a Spin

1. Launch Access and open the Basic Reports database. This database is on the CD in the Day 6 folder. Click the Queries entry in the object bar. Locate the qryVoterAddresses table. Click on that object, but don't open it.

2. Locate the New Object button on the toolbar. That's the button that has something that looks like an icon with a lightning strike.

3. Click the button to pull it down (it's a combo box). Locate the AutoReport entry and click on it. Access will create a report using this query as a record source. Your screen should resemble Figure 6.1.

4. Save this report by choosing File, Save As from the main menu. Name the report rptVoters if you want to overwrite the sample objects, or give it a name of your own choosing if you don't want to overwrite the sample.

FIGURE 6.1

The AutoReport is an example of a barely functional object. It does the job, but nothing more.

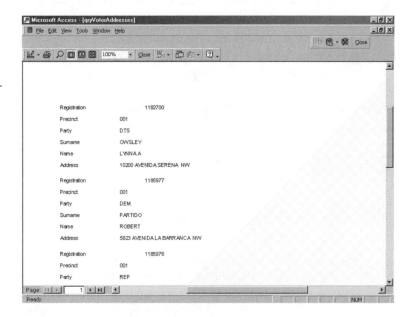

5. Close the report. Click on the Reports entry in the object bar (if necessary) and note that your new form is now part of the report objects in Access.

Note

> The reports in this chapter are based on a table of real voter data. DTS for party affiliation means the voter "did not state" party.

6

That's all there is to the AutoReport Wizard. If you want to open this report in Design view, you'll see how simple it is.

Report Wizard

The AutoReport is a wizard without options. There is also a general-purpose report wizard that's quite capable. The following task runs through a wizard session. Note that the facilities offered within this wizard will make your report designing chores easier, no matter what your level of expertise within Access.

Task: Trying Out the General Report Wizard

1. Launch Access and open the Basic Reports database. This database is part of the CD in the Day 6 folder. Click the Reports entry in the object bar.

2. Locate the New button on the Database view toolbar. That's the button that has something that looks like a book with a star. Click that button to start a new report.

3. Choose Report Wizard from the main list box. Pull down the combo box at the bottom of the dialog box and choose the query qryVoterAddresses for this report. Your screen should resemble Figure 6.2.

FIGURE 6.2

When you start the Report Wizard, you begin by binding it to a table or query.

4. Click OK to start the actual wizard process. The first dialog box is the familiar one in which you specify the fields to include in the report. Choose them all. Click Next. The subsequent dialog box enables you to specify what fields to group on, if any. Choose the Precinct field. Your screen should resemble Figure 6.3. Click Next.

FIGURE 6.3

The full Report Wizard includes the capability to group on one or more fields.

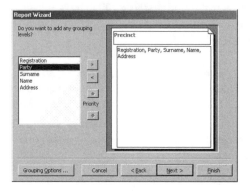

Note   The meaning of a group within a report will become clear when this report is finished and you preview it.

5. Don't specify any sort order at this point. Although you will most likely want a sort order in your report of this nature, the purpose of this task is to demonstrate the Report Wizard's nature. Sorting will only slow down previewing this report. Click Next.

6. Choose Outline 1 for your report's layout. Leave all other fields at their defaults. Your screen should resemble Figure 6.4. Click Next to move on.

FIGURE 6.4

The wizard offers layouts suitable for almost any style of report.

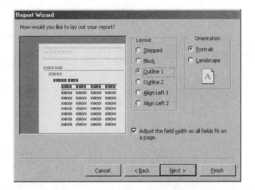

7. This example uses Soft Gray as the style for the report. Use it or one you prefer. I used Soft Gray because it reproduces well in a grayscale book. Click Next.

8. Name the report rptFullWizard if you want to overwrite the sample report supplied on the CD. If you want to preserve both reports, give yours a unique name. Click Finish to preview your report. A report preview is a screen view of how your report will look on the Web (approximately) or from a printer. Figure 6.5 shows this report in Preview view.

6

FIGURE 6.5

Print Preview is a screen rendition of how a report will look when printed.

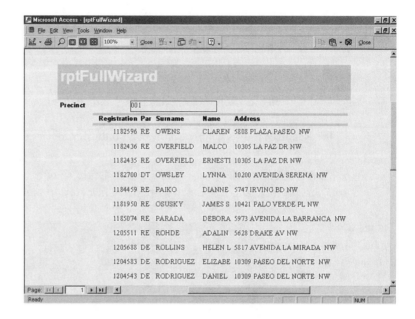

Report Preview Details

This report groups voters under their precinct number and then lists them in the order of their registration number. The registration number is the primary key for the tblVoters table. That is the table qryVoterAddresses uses. Because there are no specified sort orders in either the query or the report, Access preserves this order (but within the groups) for this report.

To see more than one report page at a time, locate the Two Pages or Multiple Pages buttons on the report toolbar. Click on the Multiple Pages button and choose the 1×3 selection in the first row to the extreme right. Your screen should resemble Figure 6.6. Depending on your monitor size and screen resolution, you might not have much detail in these multiple page views.

To see a page in detail from the multipage view, click on the page with the cursor/magnifying glass. Doing so will zoom you to the page.

By examining this report, you can see the result of a report group. Remember you grouped according to Precinct number. This sorts the precincts in ascending order (starting with 001) and groups every record belonging in that group under it sorted, in this case, by its default sort order (primary key field).

FIGURE 6.6

*You can see more than
one page at a time.*

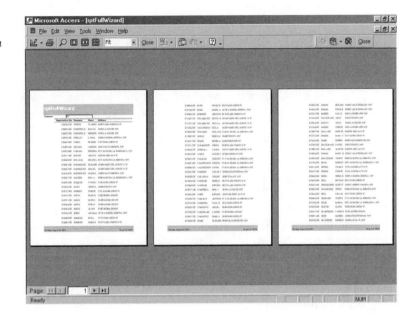

FIGURE 6.6

Similar uses of groups are

- To group employees under department number or supervisor
- To group customers under zip code or area code
- To group sales under salesmen
- To group customers under sales territory

I'm sure you can think up some other specific uses for groups in reports depending upon your specific needs.

Note

This report will seem to open very slowly on some machines. This is due to the need for Access to group the records. Grouping in a large dataset like the tblVoters requires a lot of processing power and disk read and write.

6

This report isn't perfect or even acceptable at this stage. Here are the major problems with this wizard-generated report.

- The Party field can display only two characters. Although for the most part you can make out what party each voter has an affiliation with, the report looks sloppy because of this limitation.

- The Name field is too short to display all the letters in the first name. This might not be correctable due to the need to fit the entire report on a single 8.5×11-inch page.
- The header for this report is the same as the report name in the Database view. This name (with convention) makes sense for developers to see in the Database and other developer views, but makes for a poor header in a report for public display.

The next section addresses these issues.

The Report Design View

The Report Design view is similar, but not identical to the Form Design view. All the skills learned in one view are fully transferable to the other. If you're unfamiliar with the Form Design view fundamentals covered on Day 5, this is a good time to review that material.

Without further ado, it's time to jump in to fix those elements of the Report Wizard that need addressing.

Task: Using Report Design View

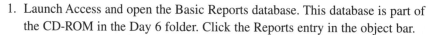

1. Launch Access and open the Basic Reports database. This database is part of the CD-ROM in the Day 6 folder. Click the Reports entry in the object bar.

2. Locate the report called rptFullWizard, which is part of the sample data. If the report is currently open in Print Preview, click the View button to switch to Design view. If you're at the Database view, highlight the report and click the Design button on the Database view toolbar. This will launch the report in Design view. Your screen should resemble Figure 6.7.

3. Take a moment to look at this report in Design view. Although it's a bit more complex than the forms yesterday, you should have a good idea of what's going on. The only completely new concepts are within the Page Footer band. You'll note two fields in that band one containing the function NOW(), on the left, and the objects Page and Pages on the right. The function NOW() will place the current system date or time on a form, report, or other object. The Page and Pages keywords will display the current and total pages in a report or form respectively. The NOW() function will put the current system date and time on the page footer of the report, and the expression on the left will display which page this is and how many pages are in the entire report. Figure 6.8 shows the bottom of the first page of this report in Print Preview. Note that there are over 10,000 pages in the entire report, so don't try to print it unless you're ready for a long print run.

FIGURE 6.7

The Report Design view looks similar to Form Design view.

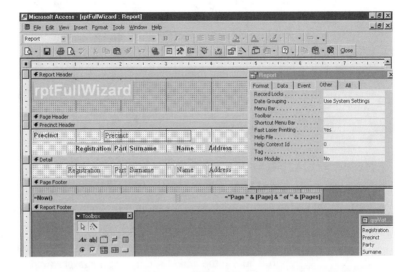

FIGURE 6.8

The built-in Access function NOW(), *and the* Page *and* Pages *keywords find good use in footers or headers for reports and forms.*

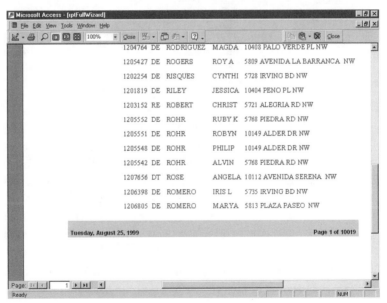

4. The first thing to correct in this report is the field length for the two short fields. Right now, the report goes to the right edge of the page, so you can't just stretch these fields or you'll end up beyond the margins of this report. Doing so will cause

Access to print a left and right part of each page, making this report over 20,000 pages long. Worse, with each logical page spread over two physical pages, the report will lose cohesion. Here are the strategies you can follow to address the field shortfall:

- Choose File, Page Setup to alter the size of the paper setup size. Stretch the right page side, stretch the two short fields, and then print to the wider paper.

- Choose File, Page Setup and reduce the margins of the page, thus giving you more room on the page, and then widen the right side of the report and stretch the fields.

- Choose File, Page Setup, and then change the report from portrait to landscape layout.

- Reduce the Address field and put the increase in the Party and Name fields. This will work, but might truncate the addresses.

- Move all the fields within the group to the left to reduce the indent of the report, and use the added room to make larger fields.

5. This task uses the last strategy because it's the best approach in this case, but might not be in all. The important concept here is not to disturb the relative position of the fields and their labels as you move them. The key to doing this is the multiple selection.

6. Click and drag to select all the fields and labels that must be moved left. Look carefully at Figure 6.9 to see which fields should be selected. You can use either marquee select or the Shift+click method to choose multiple fields and labels.

7. Drag the group of controls to the left about 0.5 inch (1 cm). When you're finished, click away from the highlighted group to deselect it. Now select the Address field and label and drag them back to the right margin. Be careful not to drag it beyond the current right margin. Then select the gray line just above the field labels and extend it to cover the new span of the fields and their labels. Your screen should resemble Figure 6.10. You can restore the field positions if they get out of synch, but that's an extra step.

8. The next step will require a fine touch. You might also need to cycle between Design and Preview view to adjust the fields to the optimal width. Here's what must be done.

- Widen the Name field and label the same amount and then move them right until they abut the Address field. You should use as much space as available for the Name field, except for one character space reserved for widening the Party field (next step).

▼   • Widen the Party field and label to accommodate the necessary three charac-
             ters for party affiliation. When you're finished, your screen should resemble
             Figure 6.11.

FIGURE 6.9

*Either marquee or
Shift+click will select
multiple controls on a
report or form.*

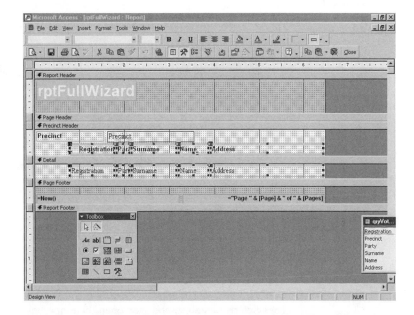

FIGURE 6.10

*Make sure when drag-
ging to move the field
and its label at the
same time to preserve
their relative positions.*

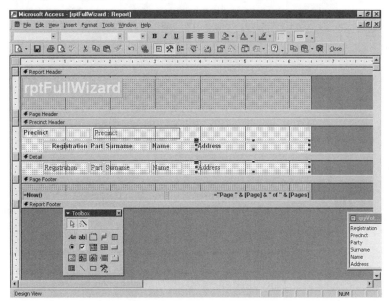

▼

FIGURE 6.11

You'll need to adjust control widths to accommodate anticipated field contents.

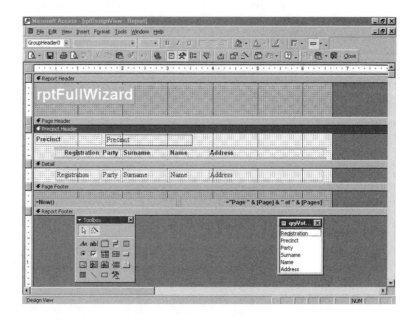

Tip

Here's an easy way to adjust the position and size of report objects such as lines. Select the object, and then open the Properties list box. Click the Format tab and note the position and size properties. Adjusting these numbers is much easier than dragging these objects to the size and place you wish them.

9. Save this report, optionally using a new name (File, Save As). This example used the name rptDesignView for the save name. The example also replaced the double gray lines (the ones above and below the field labels) of the wizard with single double-width lines.

Tip

If you find it tedious to switch between Design and Preview views, press F11 to open the Database view, choose Queries from the object bar, and then open the query qryVoterAddresses in Design view. Add the criteria "001" to the Precinct field. This will drastically reduce the size of the dataset and consequently speed up the generation of the report.

10. Switch your view to Print Preview by clicking on that selection on the View button of the toolbar. Your screen should resemble Figure 6.12.

FIGURE 6.12

When run, this report now has more room for the Name field and displays the full party label.

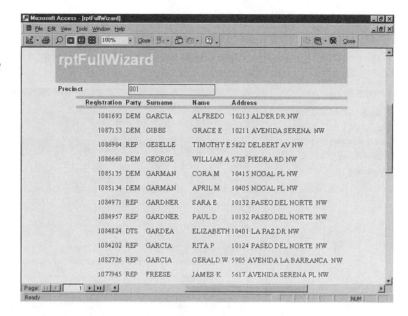

11. Return to Design view. Adjust any fields that need adjustment. Click on the label in the Report Header band. Open the Properties list box if necessary.

12. Locate the Format tab in the Properties list box and click on it. Locate the Caption property and edit it to read Voters by Precinct. Your screen should resemble Figure 6.13.

FIGURE 6.13

You can edit a label either directly in the label box or from the Properties list box.

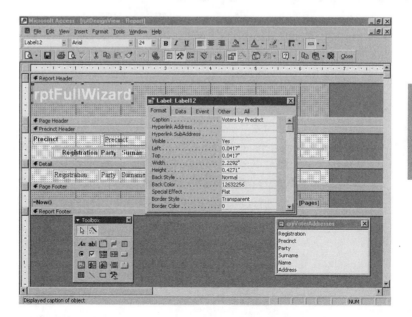

6

▼   13. Tab (or press Enter) out of the Caption field. The new caption will appear in the
        label. You'll need to widen the label to accommodate the new caption. Switch back
        to Print Preview. Your screen should resemble Figure 6.14.

FIGURE 6.14

*The report now displays
the fields properly and
has a more reasonable
report header name
(caption).*

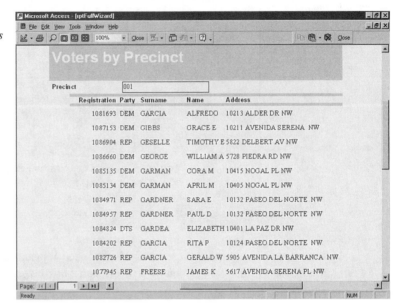

Grouping in Reports

The wizard took care of grouping all the voters within their precincts, but you could have
easily done this yourself. Manually creating a group consists of three steps.

1. Open the Sorting and Grouping dialog box to specify the field to group on and a
   sort order for that field.

2. Set the properties for the group.

3. Make any header or footer entries for the group.

As usual, these steps are fairly easy to grasp after seeing them in an example. To see how
a grouping works, locate the rptDesignView report in the sample data. You might have
saved this report under a name of your own choosing. Use either your report or the one
that's part of the sample data. Open it in Design view. Click on the Sorting and Grouping
button on the toolbar. Your screen should resemble Figure 6.15.

FIGURE 6.15

The Sorting and Grouping dialog box has two columns and a very important section for group properties.

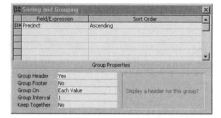

Note that you can enter (or select by pulling down the combo box) a field or an expression to group on. That's the left column. The right column lets you specify whether you want to sort the groups in ascending (lowest first) or descending order.

Note

You must specify a sort order for groups. Access will not permit you to use a random order for report groups.

The Group

Click in the Field/Expression column. Pull down the combo box and choose Party for a group criterion. Return to Print Preview. Because you have not changed the header information (precinct), you'll find you have grouped by party for each precinct. Figure 6.16 shows the results of using Party for a group.

FIGURE 6.16

If you really wanted to change the group to Party instead of Precinct, you should also change the header or footer information. However, this example serves well as a grouping demonstration.

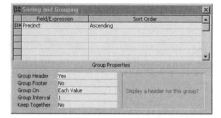

Return to Design view and likewise return the group criterion to Precinct.

Properties

It's vital you understand and set the group properties correctly to get the results you want. Here are the properties, along with an explanation of what each does.

- Group Header—Does the group get a header band for itself? If you say yes, you'll have a place to enter a label or labels telling your users what each group represents. Access will group just fine without a header, but the results might not be obvious to your users.

- Group Footer—Like a header, a footer is useful for delimiting and labeling groups. Footers also serve for holding expressions that subtotal or otherwise display summary information about a group. To give you an idea how handy this facility is, try the task that follows this list.

- Group On—Selects the criterion to start a new group. In other words, what breaks a grouping?

- Group Interval—Selects the number of characters Access should examine to decide whether a string is a group. Suppose you have data entries such as "Ford Explorer", "Ford Ranger", and "Ford Expedition". You would want Access to go beyond the word "Ford" to decide when a group starts.

- Keep Together—Whether Access should keep groups together on a page. In many cases this is impossible.

Task: Counting Voters by Precinct

1. Open the rptDesignView report in Design view. Choose File, Save As and give the report a distinct name. This example uses rptGroupFooter.

2. Open the Sorting and Group dialog box. Click in the Precinct entry in the Field/Expression column. Locate the Report Footer property. Double-click on that property to toggle it to Yes. Close the Sorting and Grouping dialog box by clicking on its entry in the toolbar (toggle).

3. Locate the Text Box tool in the toolbox. Click on it. Click anywhere to the right of the group footer to insert an unbound text box in the Report Footer band. Open the Properties list box (if necessary) and enter

```
=Count([Precinct])
```

▼   for a Control Source for this text box. Edit the label for this text box by clicking on
         it and editing its Caption property to something like

         Precinct Count:

         or another entry of your preference. Your screen should resemble Figure 6.17.

FIGURE 6.17

*This group footer
includes a function to
count voters within
precincts and report
the results in the Group
Footer band.*

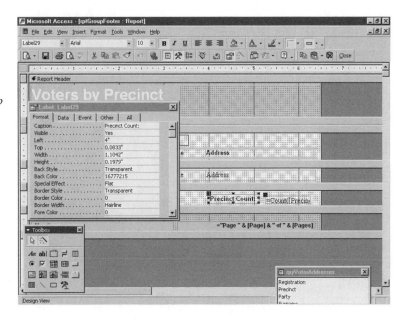

┌───┐
│   Tip   This task is moving along quickly. If you feel a bit lost, open the   │
│   rptGroupFooter report and examine the Sorting and Grouping dialog box,   │
│   along with the two new entries in the Group Footer band.   │
└───┘

4. Return to Print Preview. Move to the end of the report (the query has been limited
   to only precinct 001) by clicking the last record VCR button at the bottom of the
   screen. After the last entry, you'll see an entry with your label and a count of the
   voters in this precinct. Your screen should resemble Figure 6.18.

5. Close this report, optionally saving changes. If you want to see the counting function better presented, open the qryVoterAddresses query in Design view, remove
   the criterion for the Precinct field, and then rerun the report in Print Preview. Scroll
▼   through the report, noting how many voters exist in each precinct.

6

FIGURE 6.18

At the end of each group, Access will give you a count of the members of the group.

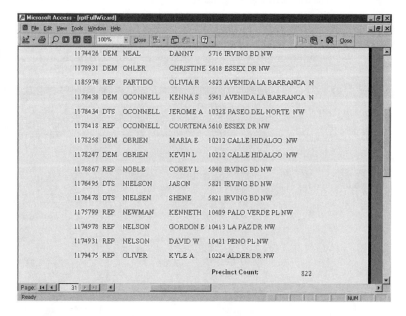

> **Note**
>
> The expression in the unbound text box is based on a built-in function of Access, Count(). The entire expression, =Count([Precinct]) tells Access to place the count (number of) of occurrences for Precinct in the Group Footer band. Access assumes you want to count the number of occurrences in each group. Had you placed the expression in a text box in the Page Footer band, you would have gotten a count of entries on each page. If you had placed the expression in a text box in the report footer or header, Access would have returned a count of all the occurrences in the entire report.

Mailing Labels

Access 2000 has a built-in wizard for making mailing labels. Essentially, this wizard creates a label layout using the fields within the table or query you want to use, and then formats the report to a page size that fits a particular label or sheet of labels. Unlike other report wizards, the Label Wizard turns out a report that requires no modification.

The following task takes you through the Label Wizard.

Task: Using the Label Wizard

1. Launch Access if necessary. Click on the Reports entry in the object bar of the Database view. Click New to start a new report. Choose the Label Wizard for a

▼   report wizard and the qryAddressesWithCity query for a query to bind the report
to. Your screen should resemble Figure 6.19.

FIGURE 6.19

The Label Wizard
requires a bound
table or query before
it can run.

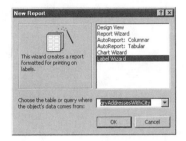

> You might want to examine this query and its bound table in both views
> before proceeding. The query has one field created by an expression, and
> another non-displayed field limits the query's return to a single precinct. The
> reason for limiting the query's selection is to make the query and the report
> run faster.

2. Click OK to start the wizard proper. The first dialog box requires you to specify a
   label by number and vendor or by size. The combo box at the bottom right lets you
   select a vendor. The large list box at the center enables you to choose from the vendor's selection. If your vendor or label isn't listed, choose the closest based on layout and size. This example uses a Herma 8007. Click Next to move on.

3. The next dialog box allows you to specify a font and its characteristics. Unless you
   have a good reason not to, leave this information at default settings because they
   work well for labels.

4. Click Next to move to the only tricky part of the Label Wizard. Here you must lay
   out the label itself. Don't just move all fields to be included in the label over
   because that will put them all on one line. You must specify which fields you want
   on the label (in this case, all of them) and where they go. To move a field from the
   Available Fields list to the label, highlight it and then click the Move (caret) button.
   To move to a new line in the label, press Enter. You enter punctuation such as
   spaces or commas by literally entering those characters using your keyboard.
   Figure 6.20 shows a finished label. Note there is no separate field for State because
   this field has been included in the City field. Although this is improper database
▼ design, it makes no difference in this context.

▼

FIGURE 6.20

*The Label Wizard asks
you to not only include
fields, but to lay them
out as you want to see
them in the finished
label.*

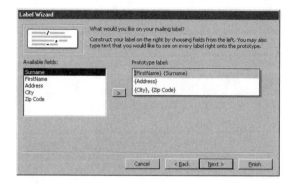

5. After your label looks similar to Figure 6.20, click Next to move on. In the next
   dialog box, choose to sort on Surname. Click Next.

6. Give the report the name rptVoterAddressLabels, or one of your own choosing if
   you don't want to overwrite the sample data. Click Finish to see your label. Your
   screen should resemble Figure 6.21.

FIGURE 6.21

*The current mailing
label will work fine
although it's not aes-
thetically perfect.*

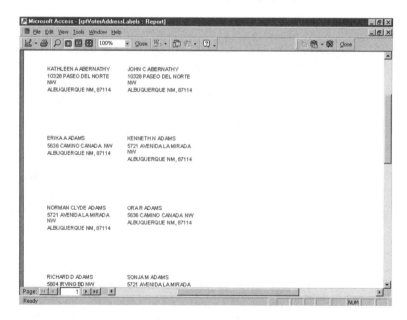

7. Switch to Design view for this report. Note all the fields are expressions that
   include the TRIM() function. That's a built-in function of Access that, as its name
   implies, trims the extra whitespace out of fields included in expressions. To see

▼

▼
▲
how TRIM() works, remove it from the first text box in the report and return to Print Preview, noting how the inclusion of extraneous whitespace in the Name field adversely affects the look of your labels.

Expression Details Explained

Take a look at the expressions used for the fields in the mailing label report. The first field is a text box control with the Control Source

```
=Trim([FirstName]&" "&[Surname])
```

The equal sign (=) tells Access that what follows is an expression.

The TRIM() function removes extra whitespace. Take a FirstName field that has 15 characters in it. Without TRIM(), the name Kathleen Arnold would appear like this:

```
Kathleen       Arnold
```

The name Moe Green would appear

```
Moe            Green
```

And the name Shelbyville Nathan would appear

```
Shelbyville    Nathan
```

Obviously, to make a good-looking report you want only a single space between the first and the last names. TRIM() removes all extra whitespace from a field, so the preceding fields appear as

```
Kathleen Arnold
Moe Green
Shelbyville Nathan
```

The next character is the ampersand. It concatenates the FirstName field to the next character, a space (" "). The double quotes mean the next character is a literal; in this case, it is a space. The next character is an ampersand concatenating the space with the Surname field.

6

Page Layout Settings

Critical to the success of any report is the page layout setting for that report. Launch Access, load the Report Basics database, click the Reports entry in the object bar, and then click the rptVoters report part of the sample data. Click the entry File, Page Setup from the main menu. Review the three tabs for page layout, noting the type of data each holds. The entries are self-explanatory.

Close the Page Layout dialog box by clicking either OK or Cancel. Highlight the rptVoterAddressLabels report, which is also part of the sample data. Again open the File, Page Setup dialog box. The critical part of this setup is in the Columns tab.

> **Note**
>
> You can't choose another report for the Page Setup dialog box while the dialog box is open because the box is modal. *Modal* means that it grabs the entire attention of the application, or even the system, preventing the focus from going anywhere else. The Print Setup dialog box is application modal. As long as it's open, nothing else in Access will accept the focus.

Click that tab and note the precise settings for the two columns that make up the report. Similarly, the Access Labels Wizard has assigned precise margin data for this report. The combination of the two makes for a label report that will hit the labels sheet after sheet without lag or creep.

> **Note**
>
> Newcomers to Access will often try to format a page the size of a label and print the report to that size page, figuring that by defining a page as having the dimensions of a label they will center the data on the label. Although this does work after a fashion, it means that you'll end up with one label per page rather than the desired multiple labels for each page (8.5×11-inches in the U.S.).

> **Tip**
>
> If your Access reports shoot out extra pages, either blank or with a few characters on them, you've created a report that's bigger than the net size of the page. The net size of a page is the actual page size less the sum of the opposing margins. A page that is 8.5 inches wide with 1-inch margins left and right has a 6.5-inch maximum print area. Print Preview will show you whether you'll be seeing extra pages. Always run Print Preview for a few pages (at least) before committing a report to a printer.

Sums, Subtotals, and Running Sums

Many reports will require you to sum or subtotal a field or fields. Naturally you can only sum on some sort of numeric field, such as those formatted as Number or Currency data types. There are several ways to sum in a report:

- Sum for a band such a page or group

- Sum for an entire report

- Keep a running sum of bands or groups

The key function to summing in Access is the SUM( ) function. Here's how to use that function, as well as how to do the various summing chores.

Task: Using Sum Functions in Reports

1. Launch Access if necessary. Click on the Reports entry in the object bar of the Database view. Locate the rptSumming report and open it in Print Preview. Your screen should resemble Figure 6.22.

FIGURE 6.22

The basic report complete with groups, but without any summing function yet.

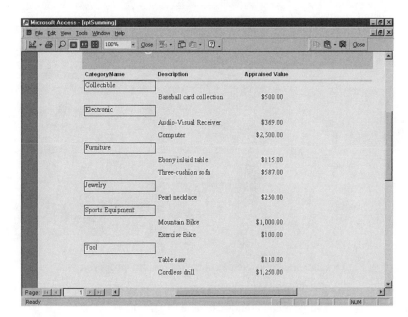

2. Switch to Design view for this report. Save it using a different name than it currently has. This example uses the name rptAllSums, but you should use a different name if you don't want to overwrite the sample data.

3. Open the Sorting and Grouping dialog box by clicking on its entry in the toolbar. Locate the Group Footer property and toggle it to Yes. Toggle the Grouping and Sorting dialog box to Closed.

4. Click on the Text box control in the toolbox. If the toolbox isn't visible, drop down the View menu and toggle it to Visible. Click in the CategoryName footer band to insert an unbound text box control there. Your screen should resemble Figure 6.23.

6

5. Open the Properties list box if necessary. Click on the Data tab and click in the Control Source property. Press Shift+F2 to open the zoom box for this property.

> **Tip**
>
> You can open a Zoom box for many areas in Access including any property list box and the query design grid.

FIGURE 6.23

This unbound control will have a summing function as part of its Control Source.

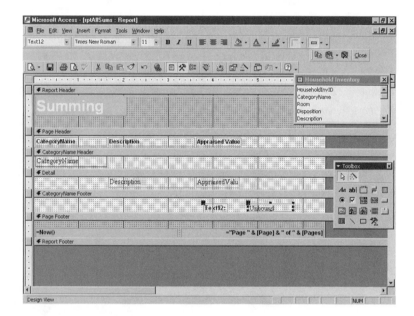

6. Enter the following expression for this property:

```
=Sum([AppraisedValue])
```

Your screen should resemble Figure 6.24.

FIGURE 6.24

Entering an expression using the Zoom box is a lot easier on the eyes than squinting at the Properties list box.

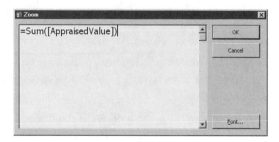

Tip

Clicking the Font button in the Zoom box will allow you to specify a font and font size for your Zoom box.

7. Click OK to close the Zoom box. Click the label area of the unbound text box. Click the Format tab of the Properties list box. Locate the property Caption and edit that to read

   `Group Sum`

   or anything you prefer. Switch to Print Preview and note that you now have a sum for every group on the report. Your screen should resemble Figure 6.25.

FIGURE 6.25

Getting a subtotal for every group or category is as simple as adding a function to the band.

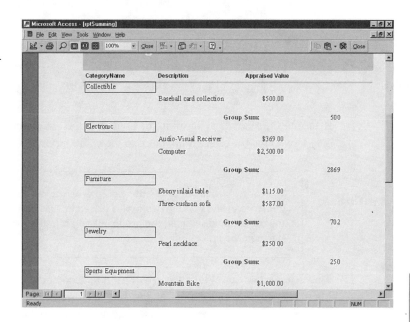

8. Return to Design view. Click on the unbound text control and locate the Format tab in the Properties list box. Locate the Format entry, pull down the combo box, locate the Currency entry, and choose it. Return to Print Preview.

9. Return to Design view. Marquee select the unbound text control from the previous steps and press ^C to copy it to the Clipboard. Click in the Report Footer band and press ^V to paste this control to that band. Your screen should resemble Figure 6.26.

FIGURE 6.26

The footer now has a field ready to display a sum for the entire report.

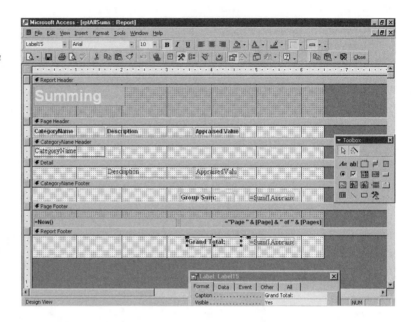

10. Return to Print Preview. Scroll to the bottom of the screen and note that you not only have sums for each group, but also the entire report.

Note

> The controls summed differently because Access will sum across the span or influence of the band the control is placed in. Placing the SUM() function in the group band summed the group. Placing it in the Report Footer band summed the report.

11. This gets a bit tricky. Widen the group band to accommodate another control. Marquee highlight the Group Sum text box and its label. Choose Edit, Copy from the menu. Choose Edit, Paste from the menu to paste a new copy of the old control into the same band. Your screen should resemble Figure 6.27. Edit the label to read

    Running Sum

12. Click on the data part of the control (as opposed to the label). Locate the Running Sum property in the Data tab. Change the value from No to Over All.

13. Return to Print Preview. You now have a report that sums for every group (subtotal), keeps a running sum for all groups, and gives you a grand total for the entire report. Your screen should resemble Figure 6.28. The report shown here doesn't

▼ have its controls finely aligned yet. That's a simple task after you're sure the report is working as you intend it to.

FIGURE 6.27

A simple property change will alter this control from a dupli-cate of an existing one into a running sum control.

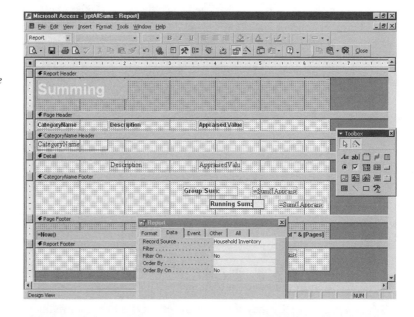

FIGURE 6.28

The report is now replete with sums of all sorts or, to put it anoth-er way, all sorts of sums.

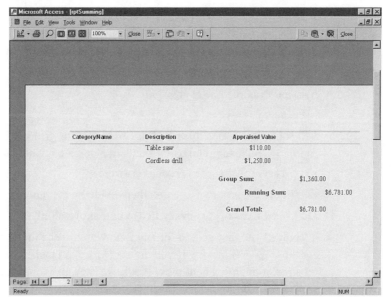

▲

6

Summary

Reports are to printers what forms are to screens. That's a bit of a simplification, but it does make the point of what each specializes in. The chief operational difference between a report and a form is that a report has no way to edit or enter data and a form does.

The skills you learn in report design or form design are almost 100 percent transferable to the other. Each object has an adjustable design grid, controls that can be bound or unbound, a toolbox, and the critical Properties list box for controls and other objects compromising the report. Additionally, both objects are constructed of bands.

You can use built-in (or user-defined) functions in unbound controls in reports, similar to how you can use them in forms. The function, when applicable, will operate differently depending on the band within which it is located. For example, a control with the COUNT() function in a group band will count occurrences over the group.

Q&A

Q If a report has one page, will there be any difference between the SUM() function in the Page and Report bands?

A Technically they'll behave differently, but in practice, they'll return the same values.

Q Can I sum within the Detail band?

A Sure. Your results will be the sum of the objects contained within that band.

Q Can I subtract, multiply, and divide in an expression?

A Yes. For example, the expression

```
=[SalesPrice]-[Cost]
```

will subtract the value of SalesPrice from Cost or give you the gross margin. Similarly, you can group using standard algebraic notation.

```
=([SalesPrice]-[Cost])/Count([Widgets])
```

will figure the gross margin and then divide by the number of widgets.

Q Do I need to use [] for every field in an expression?

A Technically no, but you do for any field with a space in the Name (Control Name for those old VB hands). If you do use [] for field names, Access will never make an error; it might without those brackets. They also immediately identify a field from a function to the developer. Use them always.

Q Can I use color in reports?

A Sure, and there are a few Microsoft-supplied styles in the wizard that use color.

Q Can I include pictures in a report?

A Yes. There are bound and unbound image controls available for reports just as there are for forms.

Workshop

The Workshop helps you solidify the skills you learned in this lesson. Answers to the quiz questions appear in Appendix A, "Answers."

Quiz

1. How can you customize which fields the AutoReport Wizard includes in a report?
2. Is there any difference between binding a report to a query versus a table?
3. What does the Keep Together property of a group do?
4. What does the [Pages] return in the report header?
5. What does the whitespace between the double quotes in the following expression do?

   ```
   =[Name]&" "&[LastName]
   ```

Exercises

1. Open the rptAllSums report in Design view.
2. Widen the Pager Footer band to accommodate a new field.
3. Copy the control along with its label that yields the sum of each group (not the running sum).
4. Paste that control into the Page Footer band. Edit the label to be sensible for a page summation rather than a group summation.
5. Switch to Print Preview. Is the control working as you expected?
6. Return to Design view.
7. Paste the control into the Report Header band. Edit the label accordingly.
8. Return to Print Preview. Is the value in the header the same as the footer?
9. Close the report, optionally saving changes.

6

DAY 7

Automating Your Access App: A Macro Primer

Macros are, without a doubt, the most often-used programming aspect of Access. The clear reason for this is that you don't need any programming lessons and you don't need to know obscure keywords or symbols to succeed in Access macros. This looseness is the macro language's best part, but it also makes macros somewhat controversial among some advanced developers. From my point of view, this controversy is silly. If macros posed any serious problems when implemented, Microsoft wouldn't use it in its own demonstration programs. Today you will learn the following:

- What macros are in Access
- The proper use of macros
- The macro controversy and why you should ignore it
- The macro design grid
- Creating a simple macro

- Associating macros with events
- Testing and debugging macros
- Creating a macro that runs only in certain conditions
- Creating a family of related macros
- Advanced macro concepts

Macros and Access

Macros, in the form of recorded and then played-back keystrokes, acted like a simple programming language in the first hit program for the IBM style PC—Lotus 1-2-3, back in the dark days of DOS version 1. Later, advanced users of 1-2-3 started using commands along with recorded keystrokes to write rudimentary programs for that three-in-one program.

"Real" computer programmers, those who used Turbo Pascal or BASICA, despised macro programmers for invading their turf with this "fake" programming system. Yet the popularity of 1-2-3's macro language and the ease with which untrained personnel could get results, assured the widespread use of this system, not only in 1-2-3, but also in other successor spreadsheets such as Excel.

Now, almost 20 years later, little has changed. Access includes both a macro language that incorporates commands and a keystroke player. It also sports a BASIC programming language, VBA (Visual Basic for Applications). Programmers of the BASIC persuasion, usually sporting either a lot of self-training or formal education in computers, look down on macros as well as those who use them. However, the popularity of macros, their ease of use, and their utility hasn't been lost on either Microsoft or the millions of people who automate their applications using this system.

In a bit of irony, there are certain things that only macros, and not pure VBA, will do. The existence of these tasks, marked by the VBA keyword DOCMD, remains a sore point for the VBA-only cadres.

And the Point Is?

The reason I've gone into this long introduction about macros is that many users will encounter anti-macro attitudes during their careers. Although in theory the arguments made against macros (such as their lack of any error traps) are valid, what's equally valid is that there are tens of millions of applications running macros with no difficulties whatsoever.

Keep in mind the following points about macros and VBA:

- Use macros sparingly and only when there isn't a way to do the task in VBA. Also, be reasonably sure the blind running method of macros won't harm your application.
- Most developers find that VBA-launched macros via the DOCMD keyword are easier to debug than macros created using the macro design view.
- Don't use macros if you believe there is a reasonable chance that they might put your application in an error condition.

Do	Don't
DO use the Sendkeys macro command when nothing else will do.	**DON'T** forget to free allocated memory with the free() function. If you don't free the memory, and the pointer to it goes out of scope, the memory will be unavailable during the execution of the rest of the program.**Don't** forget that this command blindly sends keystrokes to the computer. In some instances, this can cause quite a bit of troubles. If your users are having mysterious problems in the vicinity of a Sendkeys macro, try disabling that macro first to see if this is the problem.

Note

The concepts of keyword, event, error trap, and others used in this chapter might not be clear to you at this point. Just try to get a general sense of things today, and come back to this section later after learning about macros today and VBA in subsequent chapters. By then it will all make sense if it doesn't now.

Note

Microsoft has tried to address both Access developers who like macros, and those who fear macros due to their lack of error traps, by creating an on-error event that can trigger a macro or VBA code.

7

Elements of a Macro

Back in Day 2, "From Idea to Project," you saw how a simple macro could react to a
mouse cursor moving over an area of the screen (the mouse corral). The four elements of
a macro, one of which is optional, are

- The event—The reason the macro "fires" or trips. Some event examples are a form
  control gaining or losing focus, a mouse cursor moving over an area, a keystroke,
  or a form load.
- The action—What the macro roughly does. Some actions are load object, close
  object, requery, launch another application, or delete object.
- The action arguments (properties)—What specifics the action applies to. For example, when you use Access to create a macro that opens the frmDataEntry form, the
  action is to open a form, whereas the property of that action is the frmDataEntry
  form.
- Conditions—You can program your macros to fire (or run) only when certain conditions exist (such as a field having a specific value). The conditional capability of
  macros is considerably less developed than in VBA, but is still useful, as you'll see
  later today.

The Macro Design Grid

To see the Macro design grid, click the Macro entry in the Database view toolbar, and
then click New to start a new macro. Similarly, if you have some macros already created,
you can see the design grid with a macro loaded by highlighting that macro and clicking
the Design button. The Macro Design view is similar to other design views you've seen
in previous days. Figure 7.1 shows this grid.

 Note

> The Conditions column doesn't appear in Figure 7.1. If you want to see it,
> click its toggle button in the toolbar. You'll also see a Macro Names toggle
> button in this toolbar. This toggles a column to group macros under a single
> macro name.

A Very Simple Macro

The following exercise results in a free-standing macro that displays a special type of
dialog box called a message box. Windows uses various styles of message boxes to display messages upon the occurrence of certain events.

The point of this task is to familiarize you with the Action and Action Arguments areas
of the Macro Design view.

FIGURE 7.1

The Macro Design view is a grid with a context-sensitive Action Arguments list section at its bottom.

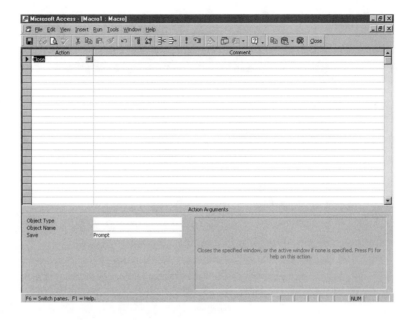

Task: The Message Box Macro

1. Launch Access and open the Macro Primer database. This database is part of the CD-ROM in the Day 7 folder. Click the Macros entry in the object bar. Click New in the Database view toolbar to start a new macro. Your screen should resemble Figure 7.1 but have no entry in the Action column yet.

2. Click in the Action column at the first row. This will change the row into a combo box. Pull down (expand) the combo box. Scroll down to find the action called MsgBox. Your screen should resemble Figure 7.2.

Tip

> When you click in the Action area, press the first letter of the action you want to use (in this case, *m*). Access will scroll to the first action that starts with *m*. This is the express train to finding actions on the list.

3. Locate the Message line in the Action Arguments section of the design grid. Enter `Overdrawn at the memory bank!` or any message of your preference. The specific message is unimportant.

4. Locate the Title line in Action Arguments and enter `Message from your RAM` or any other title for the message box you prefer. As with the message above, the specific wording is unimportant. Your screen should resemble Figure 7.3.

7

FIGURE 7.2

*The list of actions for
macros is part of a
combo box. You can
enter values directly or
pick them from a list.*

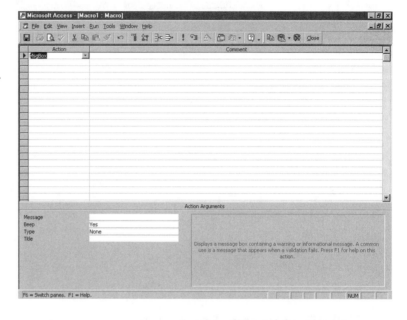

FIGURE 7.3

*You can customize
what your message will
be like using the Action
Arguments section of
the Macro Design view.*

5. Click the Run button on the toolbar. Access will prompt you to save this macro. Do
   so using the name mcrFirst. After saving, Access will display your new message
   box with your custom message and title. If your computer is sound enabled, you
   will also hear the default Windows sound. Your screen should resemble Figure 7.4.

FIGURE 7.4

*Creating a message
box with a custom mes-
sage takes only a few
seconds.*

Actions in a macro will execute sequentially from the top of the Design view to the bottom, unless a condition prevents them from occurring at all. To see this in action for
yourself, open the mcrFirst macro in Design view, and then add another message box
action along with a different title and message. Figure 7.5 shows the Design view of such
a macro.

FIGURE 7.5

Macros will execute actions sequentially from top to bottom unless a condition prevents execution of one or more actions.

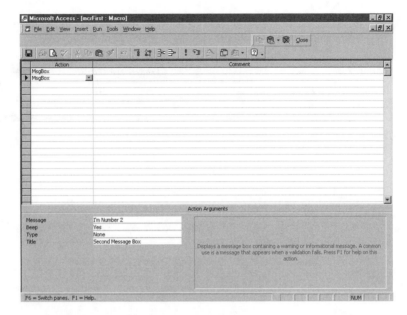

Run the macro. Access will prompt you to save the macro. Do so and the macro runs. As soon as you clear the first message box, the second one appears. Figure 7.6 shows the second macro action executing.

FIGURE 7.6

As soon as you clear the first action, the second executes.

Deleting Macro Actions

The next task isn't helped at all by having two macro actions, so it's time to remove the second. To do so, highlight the entire line where the action appears by clicking on the gray square that's the equivalent of the record selector. This is directly to the left of the Action entry. When you hit the right spot, the entire macro line will highlight.

Figure 7.7 shows the line highlighted with the cursor over the area you must click to make it so.

Press the Delete key to remove this line. You can also choose Delete from the Edit menu to remove a row.

If you wanted to insert a macro action in between two existing ones, highlight the lower one and then press the Insert key. You can also click in the row where you want a row to be inserted above and choose Insert, Rows from the main menu.

7

Shift+click and Ctrl+click work for multiple selections in the macro design grid as well. You can use these techniques to insert or delete multiple rows.

FIGURE 7.7

To delete or insert a line, you highlight a row in the Macro Design view.

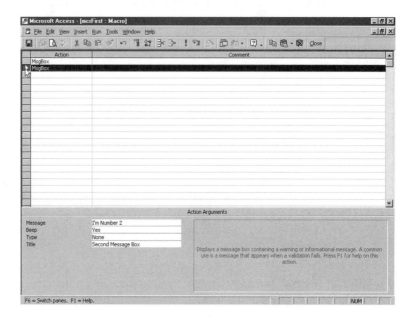

Macros and Events

The mcrFirst macro is interesting, but useless unless it conveys a worthwhile message. For a message box to do so, it must appear at a required or desired time.

Targeted events should trigger macro execution. A successful Access developer will not only do a good job designing macros (or VBA code), but also attaching those macros to the proper event. It will take a bit of thinking and experience before you reliably find the correct event for your macros and VBA code.

For example, take the two events for a text box, After Update and On Lost Focus. You might decide you want a macro to execute after a user makes an entry in a text box. Logically, you understand that after a user makes an entry, he'll move out of the field using Tab, Enter, or a mouse click. That causes the text box control to lose focus so you might attach the macro to the On Lost Focus event.

That wouldn't be right simply because a person can cause the loss of focus on a control without making any data entry or edits. The right event for execution after a user makes a data entry is After Update.

Tip

The key to knowing whether your macros are attached to the right event is testing. There are always unpredictable user actions that you as a developer must account for. Testing, using real people other than your own pre-dictable self, is the right way to make sure your application will work in the field as you envisioned it would when you designed it.

Using the example in this section, the On Lost Focus event would work just fine if you were sure that every time the user gave a field the focus, he would edit or update it and then move on. However, field testing will prove that is not the case with real-world people, so you must use the After Update event.

The following section gives you a few ideas of events and how they work with different form controls. The specifics in this section apply to reports as well as forms.

Tip

The Help system for Access is extremely useful for learning about events. In fact, most Access developers use Help extensively when designing their applications. To see a short note on any event, click in the event's line and look at the status bar. To see full help text on an event, click in its area in Properties and press F1.

Task: Associating Events and Macros

1. Launch Access and open the Macro Primer database. This database is part of the CD-ROM in the Day 7 folder. Click the Forms entry in the object bar. Note the location of the frmEventPractice form. This form has several controls ready for macro attachment. Each example will use the mcrFirst macro for a macro to attach or bind to an event.

2. Highlight the frmEventPractice form and click Design in the Database view toolbar to open the form in Design view. Your screen should resemble Figure 7.8.

3. Click on the command button labeled Click Me. If necessary, open the Properties list box by choosing it from the toolbar or the View menu.

4. Click on the Event tab in the Properties list box. Locate the On Click property. Click in the area to the right of the Event label. This will convert the line to a combo box. Pull down the combo box and choose mcrFirst from the list. Figure 7.9 shows what your Properties sheet should look like after you finish this operation.

7

FIGURE 7.8

*The sample data has a
form ready for some
macro practice.*

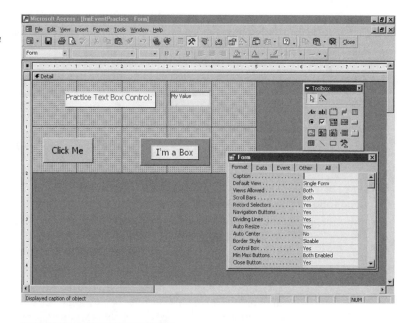

FIGURE 7.9

*To associate a macro
with a specific event,
you can choose it from
the drop-down list.*

5. Switch to Form view by clicking on the View button in the toolbar. Click on the Click Me button. Your screen should resemble Figure 7.10.

6. Clear the message box and return to Design view. Clear the On Click event from the command button's event listing. Click in the purple area of the rectangle labeled I'm a Box.

Tip

The I'm a Box control consists of a label control inserted over a rectangle control. Both have a 3D characteristic added and sport different colors. You can achieve the stacked effect for controls by, well, stacking them in this manner.

FIGURE 7.10

Now each time you click on the command button, the macro will fire.

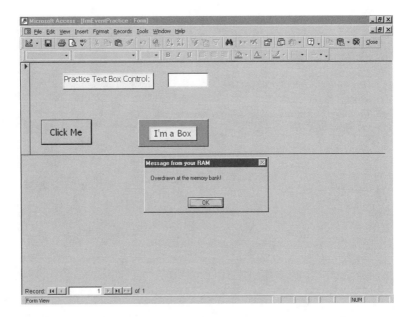

7. Locate the Mouse Move event in the Properties list box, pull down the combo box, and then choose mcrFirst from the list. Return to Form view. Move your mouse around, but not over the rectangle control. Move the mouse over this control. The macro will fire. Return to Design view.

8. Clear the Mouse Move event for the rectangle control. Click in the text box control. Add the macro to the On Got Focus event of the text box. Return to Form view. The macro executes immediately because the unbound text control is first in the tab order, so it gets the focus on form open. Clear the message box.

9. Click the command button. Nothing should happen if you've cleared the event from this control. Click back in the unbound text control. The macro again executes as the control regains the focus.

10. Return to Design view. Remove the macro from the On Got Focus event and add it to the After Update event. Return to Form view.

11. This time the macro doesn't fire on form open because there has been no update to the control. Click on the command button. Click in the text control. Add any entry (such as the letter *d*) to the control. Tab away from the text box. The macro fires, as you can see in Figure 7.11.

7

FIGURE 7.11

You can enter and exit this control indefinitely without the macro firing. However, if you do any updates to the control, the macro will fire upon the loss of focus.

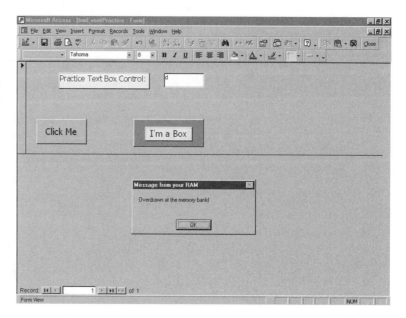

12. Experiment with other events. Feel free to add different controls to this form to practice with their events too. When you're finished, close the form discarding changes. If you want to preserve the modified form as a learning experience, you can always save it using a different name.

Commonly Used Macro Actions

The most common actions for macros are to open and close objects (usually forms or reports), to display message boxes, and to go to controls. In many cases, you'll want to couple these actions with conditions and group them under a name. Names come up in the following task. Conditions are discussed later today, so for now just keep in mind that these actions aren't generally the complete picture.

The following task shows you how to use macro names and create macros for opening and closing forms. You can use the same techniques to open and close any object (or do any macro action) within Access.

Task: Macro Names and Common Actions

1. Launch Access and open the Macro Primer database. This database is part of the CD-ROM in the Day 7 folder. Click the Macros entry in the object bar.

▼   Locate the mcrOpenAndClose macro, highlight it, and open it in Design view.
Your screen should resemble Figure 7.12.

2. Click in the Action column at the first row. This will change the row into a combo
box. Pull down (expand) the combo box. Scroll down to find the MsgBox action.
Your screen should resemble Figure 7.12.

FIGURE 7.12

*The Macro Name col-
umn allows for group-
ing sub-macros under
a single macro name
at the Database view.*

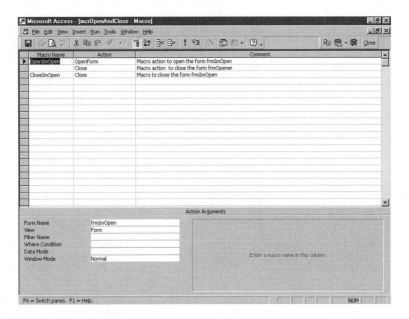

3. The first macro actions are under the macro name OpenImOpen. This macro name
has two actions. The first action opens the frmImOpen form. The second action
closes the frmOpener form. To see the actions and their Action Arguments, click in
the Action column and note the Action Arguments displayed along with the action.
For example, click in the first Close Action—the one grouped under the name
OpenImOpen. The Action Arguments for this action show that when this macro
fires, it will close the frmOpener form. Figure 7.13 shows the Action Arguments
for this action.

▼   4. Click in the Properties section. Pull down the combo boxes and note the entries
there.

7

Tip

When making macros to manipulate objects, first make the objects, and then make the macros. That way the objects will appear in the combo boxes for the macro design grid. Finally, assign the macros to the controls (if applicable).

FIGURE 7.13

This macro will first open a form, and then close another.

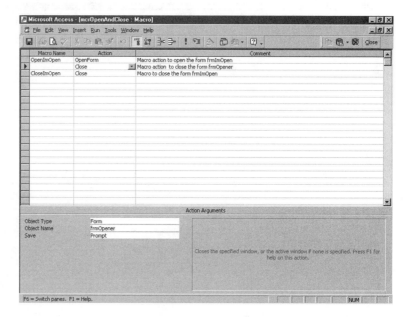

5. Close the mcrOpenAndClose macro. Click on the Forms entry and open the frmOpener form in Design view. This form has one command button. Click the button and note the entry in the On Click event. A macro that's part of a name appears with the name first, followed by the part of the macro you want to associate with the event. Figure 7.14 shows the On Click event for this command button. If necessary, return to the mcrOpenAndClose macro to see that this macro, when tripped by clicking on the command button, will first open the frmImOpen form and then close frmOpener.

6. Close the frmOpener form. Open the frmImOpen form in Design view. Click on the command button and examine its On Click event. It contains the mcrOpenAndClose.CloseImOpen macro. Again refer to this macro and you'll see that when you click on the macro button you will close the currently open form, frmImOpen.

7. Try putting it into action. Close the frmImOpen form. Back at the Database view, double-click on the frmOpener form. Your screen should resemble Figure 7.15.

FIGURE 7.14

A macro name group will appear with the Database view name first, and then a dot, and finally the macro name. This is a common Access naming convention that you'll soon grow familiar with.

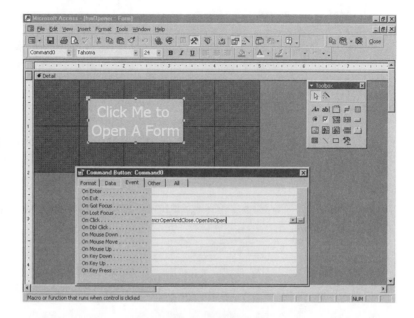

FIGURE 7.15

This form is the first in a trigger of three macro actions grouped under two macro names within one macro at the Database view level.

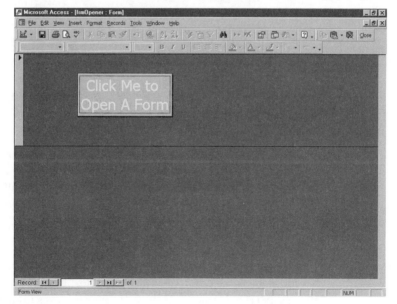

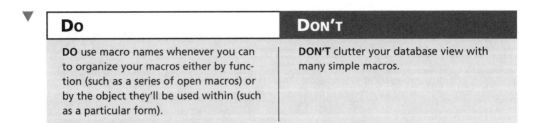

Do	**Don't**
DO use macro names whenever you can to organize your macros either by function (such as a series of open macros) or by the object they'll be used within (such as a particular form).	**DON'T** clutter your database view with many simple macros.

8. Click the command button labeled Click Me to Open a Form. This will first open another form, and then close this form. After the click, your screen should resemble Figure 7.16.

FIGURE 7.16

Clicking the first form closed it and then opened this one.

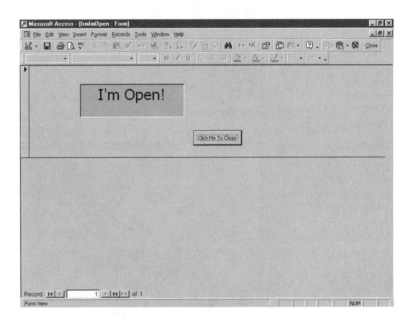

9. Click the command button on this form to close this form, too.

10. Open the mcrJumping macro. Note the action is GoToControl with the property (the control to go to) as txtThirdTextBox.

11. Open the frmJumper form in Form view. Tab through the three controls, noting that they are in linear tab order. Click in the first text box. Enter anything (such as the letter *d*). Tab away from the control. The cursor moves from the first control to the third, skipping the second.

▼ 12. The trick was to include the mcrJumping macro in the After Update event of the first control. When a person tabs through this form, the form preserves the tab order. When a person updates the first field, the mcrJumping macro fires, overrides the tab order (in a sense), and jumps to the third field. Figure 7.17 shows the Properties list box for the first control in the frmJumper form.

FIGURE 7.17

Although in reality the tab order remains, it has been apparently overridden by this macro.

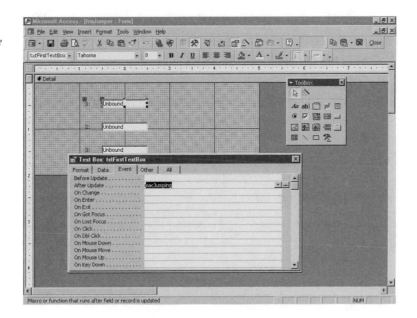

▲

Further Actions

Many additional macro actions are available to you using either the macro design grid or through VBA. Most, if not all, of the actions are self-explanatory by their names. Keep in mind that you have two excellent sources for information about macro actions, including examples for their use.

The first line of explanation is the status bar of the Macro design view. Pull down the Action combo box, choose an action, and you'll get a short explanation of how that action will operate. Additionally, the Action Arguments exposed contextually when you choose an action will give you a good hint as to what sort of objects or behaviors you can expect from that action.

Finally, there is online help. Microsoft has assembled an exhaustive reference type help for developers. Help won't teach you how to use Access, but it will work as a reference-type resource for details most, if not all, developers don't want to commit to memory.

7

Even the most accomplished developers don't want to memorize all the macro actions, much less the Action Arguments for each action. They use online help regularly. Now that you have a feel for how to create a macro and how to associate the macro action with its Action Arguments and an event, you're ready to explore the various actions and how they operate in a full Access project.

Only one topic remains: conditional macros. The next section covers that.

Conditional Macros

A conditional macro tests for a condition and fires when that condition is true. Truth in macros, as in all computer topics, doesn't refer to metaphysics or some obscure brand of anti-existentialism, but to the fundament of truth—whether a statement matches a condition.

To create a conditional macro, you need only add the step of constructing a conditional statement and associating it with a macro. Associating the macro with an event will also automatically associate the conditional statement to the event.

A conditional statement is an expression with a logical component that's either explicit or implicit. You've seen statements before in previous chapters. For example, the following is an expression:

```
Sum([Sales])
```

Add a logical conditional part like the following

```
Sum([Sales]) < 500
```

and what you're really saying is, "If total sales is less than 500."

The condition creates a program branch. A branch is an essential, perhaps *the* essential, element in computer programming. The computer tests for a condition and then executes one way if the condition is met, another if the condition isn't met. Failing to execute is a way of executing, just as not deciding an issue is a decision to accept the default situation.

The variety of conditional branching within the macro world is much less than in VBA. Although macros do a good job of firing this way if a condition is true and not firing (or firing a different way) if the condition is false or different, after your conditional needs grow slightly complex, you should investigate using VBA instead of macros.

This doesn't mean, as some VBA purists would have you believe, that using conditional macros is a bad idea, but like any shortcut, macros should be used only when fully appropriate.

> **Tip**
>
> Use VBA for branching if you, as a developer, believe there is any reasonable chance for an error condition to exist or develop over the course of the branch. Remember, you can trap and handle errors using VBA, but the errors trap you in the macro world.

The following task creates a conditional macro and uses it in a simple, but illustrative way as a check to make sure your users enter data in a required field. This is one way to make sure your users enter data. Another way is to make the field use the Required property in Table Design view.

However, this method has certain advantages that make it more desirable to you in some circumstances. It's also a good demonstration of a fairly complex macro with a conditional branch.

Task: The Conditional Macro

1. Launch Access and open the Macro Primer database. This database is on the CD-ROM in the Day 7 folder. Click the Forms entry in the object bar. Note the location of the frmMyTwoFields form. Open this form in Design view. Your screen should resemble Figure 7.18. Note it has two controls, both text boxes, along with their labels. One is txtName and the other is txtSurname. These controls are unbound, but the task would work the same were they bound to a table or report. Close the form after you're familiar with it.

> **Tip**
>
> You can keep this form open (active) and switch to the macro design grid by pressing F11 and choosing Macros from the object bar of the Database view. The reason this book closes and then opens views is to keep things simple and focused. You can either open and close like the book or differently if you choose. Your outcomes won't differ.

7

2. Click the Macros entry in the Database view object bar and choose New to start a new macro.

3. Choose as the first Action your old friend MsgBox. Enter for a Message property

   You need to enter a name

▼   For the Title property, enter

       `Empty Field Warning`

       Change the Type property to

       `Warning!`

4. Click on the Conditions button on the toolbar to expose the Conditions column (if
    necessary). Enter

    `IsNull([txtName])`

    on the same row as the message box action. Your screen should resemble
    Figure 7.19.

FIGURE 7.18

*This simple form
will be the test bed
for a conditional
macro.*

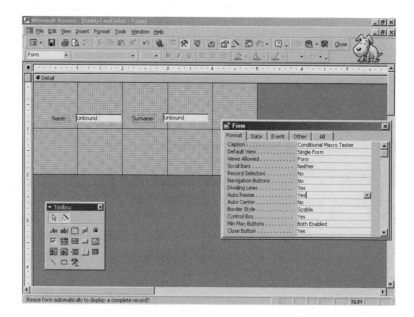

5. Save the macro, giving it the name mcrConditions or one of your own choosing if
    you don't want to overwrite the sample data.

> **Note**
>
> If you try running this macro, nothing will occur because the condition can't
> be met. Access will tell you it can't find the object you're testing to see
> whether it's Null.

6. Close the macro design grid. Open the frmMyTwoFields form in Design view.
    Associate the macro you just created with the On Lost Focus event of the txtName
▼   field. Your screen should resemble 7.20.

FIGURE 7.19

The completed conditional macro as of this point.

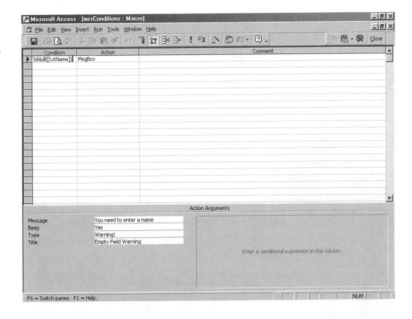

FIGURE 7.20

The stage is now set to test the new conditional macro.

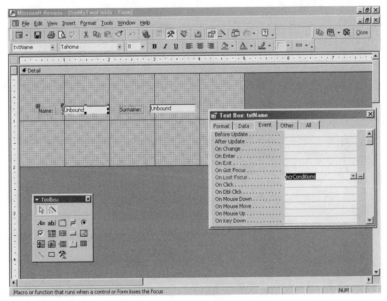

7. Switch to Form view. Enter some data in the Name field. Tab to the Surname field. Nothing should occur other than the cursor movement.

8. Click back into the Name field. Remove any entry in this field, thus making it null (empty or void). Tab away again. This time your message box will appear.

▼   9. However, there is a problem at this point from a developer view. The cursor remains in the Surname field after you clear the message box. The desirable action for this macro is to not only tell the user that there is a need for an entry in Name, but to also take him back there to make sure he does so. Close the form saving changes, or saving under a new name if you want to preserve the original form from the sample data.

10. Return to the mcrConditions macro in Design view. Click in the Conditions row below the existing condition and enter an ellipsis (...).

11. Enter an action, GoToControl, and enter a property to have the cursor skip to the control txtSurame. Repeat these two steps again, but add the txtName property as the second property.

12. The ellipsis will continue the condition to the next line and GoToControl will skip the cursor to the control specified in the Action Argument. Now when you leave the Name field null (empty), you'll see a message box advising you of your entry
▲   error and find the focus back in the Name field ready for data entry.

Summary

Macros are, in general, the most controversial section of Access. A significant number of Access "super experts" would have Microsoft eliminate macros from the program, thus forcing everybody into using VBA for programming chores.

These people make a good case in theory. Macros can't handle error conditions as VBA can, and their operation is similar to "close your eyes and fire." That's the theory. The fact is that the vast majority of Access developers use macros—often extensively—with good result. The truth is that you shouldn't be afraid to use macros. If you find that in some circumstances they lead your users into error conditions they can't easily recover from, modify your use of macros for those circumstances.

Also keep in mind that you can't stretch Access' programming possibilities to their utter extent using macros alone. As cool as macros are for doing simple chores like opening or closing forms, knowing macros isn't a substitute for learning VBA if you're determined to become a proficient Access developer.

You create a macro by opening the macro design grid, specifying a macro action, and filling in the Action Arguments. You can optionally specify a macro name to group macros under one name in the Database view. You can also specify conditions for the macro to execute.

The final step to create a macro is to associate an event (usually in a report or form) with a macro.

Tip

A macro named Autoexec at the Database view will fire automatically upon an application's startup. The name must be Autoexec (case insensitive), not mcrAutoexec.

Q&A

Q Can I call a macro from VBA or VBA from a macro?

A The DOCMD VBA statement is a call to a macro. The macro RunCode action can call a VBA sub or function. So, the answers are yes and yes.

Q Can a macro control the entries in a set of controls?

A The SetValue action, usually accompanied by a condition, can do this. Before using SetValue with conditional statements to examine and set a series of values, take a look at the `Select Case` statement for VBA.

Q Can I set an expression as a macro action?

A Yes. Precede the expression with the equal sign (=).

Q Why did you warn against the SendKeys action earlier in the chapter?

A SendKeys will blindly send keystrokes (interrupts) to the application. If an unanticipated object has or gains focus during this macro action, your results could be anywhere from odd to a disaster. Use with care.

Q Can I use macros to suppress spurious error message boxes?

A The SetWarnings macro action can do this. Set the action to SetWarnings and the Action Argument to No. Be sure to bracket your action by reactivating warnings later on when you want them to appear again.

Q How can I eliminate the flash and boom of a long series of macro actions executing?

A Set the macro action to Echo and the Echo On argument to No. You can also set text for the status bar to display while you're suppressing the macro flash display. Be sure to bracket the Echo statement when you want to show the macro display again.

Workshop

The following workshop introduces you to macro creation, attaching macros to events, and seeing an actual macro in use within a form. The answers to the Quiz are in Appendix A, "Answers."

7

Quiz

1. What constitutes properties for a macro action?

2. Will entries in the Macro Name column appear in the Database view?

3. Do you need to precede a condition with an equal sign?

4. What does the following condition mean?

   `[City]<>"New York"`

5. Is the following expression valid?

   `Between #4/5/98# and #4/5/99#`

Exercises

1. Open the frmMacroPractice form (in the Macro Primer database) in Form and Design views to familiarize yourself with it.

2. Start a new macro.

3. Create a macro action to go to a new record for this form. Hint: You will need to set the Action to GoToRecord, set the object type, the object name, and the Record to go to all in Action Arguments.

4. Save the macro using a name of your own choosing. The sample data saved this macro using the name mcrDay7.

5. Open the form frmMacroPractice in Design view.

6. Set this macro to fire when the form opens. You must make the form the object addressed, and locate the On Open event to do this.

7. Switch to Form view. The form should now open with a new record displayed, instead of record number 1 as it did in step 1.

8. Remove the macro from the event. Again switch to Form view. Note the effect of the macro.

9. Close the form, optionally saving changes.

WEEK 1

In Review

This week you've received an introduction to relational theory and how you can apply such theory to your benefit through the use of Access 2000. You've learned that Access, like other databases, stores all data in tables, and how to create and edit those tables. You've also seen the various fundamental parts of Access 2000 such as forms, reports, and queries. Day 7, "Automating Your Access App: A Macro Primer," introduced you to programming in the form of Access macros. You now have all the knowledge you need to use Access 2000 as a simple database manager, but there is much more to learn before you're a fully fledged Access developer

1

2

3

4

5

6

7

WEEK 2

At a Glance

This week has two major themes. The first builds upon the knowledge you gained in Week 1 by showing you how to expand your use of forms, tables, reports, and queries well beyond the basics. The second introduces new material in Visual Basic for Applications (VBA) and Structured Query Language (SQL). VBA is the programming language of Access 2000 and other Microsoft Office applications. Although you can use Access 2000 for simple applications without ever knowing one thing about VBA, any serious developer will need at least an intermediate-level mastery of this important topic. SQL is the standard language of relational databases. Its purpose is, as its name implies, querying tables or other queries. Access 2000 is built upon an SQL foundation, so knowing this language at least at a beginning level is quite important. Also, this language is the *lingua franca* of all relational databases, so learning it greatly increases your knowledge of how to use databases in general. People make their livings, and good livings at that, by just being SQL specialists.

8

9

10

11

12

13

14

DAY 8

Data Access Pages

Data Access Pages, or just Pages, are a new addition to Access 2000 with no direct precedents from previous versions of the program. This facility addresses the need for some people to place either dynamic or static information on the World Wide Web or a private Web such as an intranet. In this chapter you will learn about the following:

- Access' relation to the Web
- The nature of a Data Access Page
- Using a wizard to create a Page
- The two links of a Page
- Editing an existing Page
- When to use a Page and when not to use a Page

Access and the Web

In the mid-1990s, Microsoft found itself fearing for its life due to the triple related threats of Java, the Internet, and network computers (that is, light or thin clients). The company revised its overall strategy from one relying on heavy clients and its own online company (MSN) to one encompassing all the alleged benefits of the competition's triple threat. It succeeded in becoming not only a leading company of Internet technology, but in changing the face of Windows and Windows applications.

Microsoft's Office 2000 suite is almost equally at home on the Internet as on a stand-alone computer or a LAN/WAN. One of the chief features that makes this so is Access 2000's Data Access Pages, or Pages for short.

The Problem and the Problem Solved

A serious problem for Web developers is the display and possible interaction of database information (or just data) with users. Advanced Web developers use tools such as the Java or Common Gateway Interface (CGI) languages, but these facilities are well beyond the capabilities of most users who just want to get their jobs done without spending a lot of time to learn arcane skills.

Data Access Pages allow you to easily convert your database objects into a form that is usable on the Web. You can use Pages to provide simple display or even interaction.

Unlike other Access objects, Pages aren't only stored within the database container (the main .MDB file). This is functionally important because if it were so stored, people would need to have and run Access to use Pages (that is, they would have to open the container). Also keep in mind that Pages are more than just fancy formatted SGML (Standard General Markup Language) or HTML (Hypertext Markup Language) objects. They contain special mechanisms allowing them to function as a database object displayed on a LAN/WAN, extranet, the Internet, or an intranet.

Think of a Page as a form or report optimized for browser display over a network. Although that network is usually one of the TCP/IP types, there is no reason it can't be Novell's IPX or Microsoft's NetBEUI or some other protocol.

Note   You will need to install Office 2000's Internet Explorer 5 or later, or another browser with equivalent functionality, to display a Data Access Page. Internet Explorer 4, as well as its contemporaries, won't work.

Data Access Page Creation

You create a Page by using basically the same steps you use to create a report or a form. As you might guess, Access offers wizard creation and Design view facilities for Pages. As with reports and forms, each object on a Page is a control of some sort.

Pages are more like forms than like reports because you can enter data into them for inclusion in the bound database and database object. This discussion is beginning to sound more complex than it really is. So to get things grounded again, first take a look at the summary steps to Page creation, and then move on to review or follow along with a task showing how to create one of these objects.

The basic steps needed to create Data Access Page creation are

1. Using either Design view or a wizard, create a Data Access Page bound to an underlying object such as a table or query.

2. If you used a wizard, you can exit the wizard into Design view to edit the form.

3. Save the Page.

4. Test the Page within both the database container and the browser.

That last step is one you haven't used before in your work with Access. The following is a short task in which you will create a page using the wizard and then edit it by using Design view.

Task: Creating a Data Access Page by Using the Wizard

1. Open the DataAccessPages.mdb database. This is located in the Day 8 folder on your CD. This example uses the tblUsers table for an object to bind to the Page. If you want to examine this table, click the Tables entry in the database toolbar.

2. Click on the Pages entry in the database toolbar. Your screen should resemble Figure 8.1.

3. Double-click on the second entry, Create Data Access Page By Using the Page Wizard. This will launch the design process for a Page.

4. Pull down the combo box and select the tblUsers table to bind this Page to this table. You should see the dialog shown in Figure 8.2.

5. Add the two fields Name and Department to this Page. Click Next to move on.

6. Click Next until you get to the dialog box shown in Figure 8.3, which is where you enter a name for this database object. Name the Page anything you choose. This example uses the name FirstPage.

FIGURE 8.1

The database container has three default entries for Pages.

FIGURE 8.2

Binding a Page to a database object such as a table allows editing of that object's data through a browser.

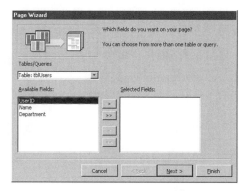

Note

If you use the name FirstPage in the same container as the sample data, you'll overwrite the sample data's Page object.

7. Make sure the Modify the Page's Design option button is selected. Click Finish to drop out of the wizard and into Design view for this Page. Your screen should resemble Figure 8.4. If you don't see either the Field List box or the toolbox, you can make them visible through using either toolbar buttons or the View menu.

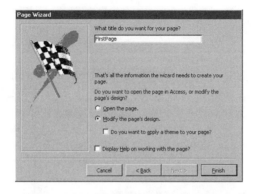

FIGURE 8.3

A Page, like any other Access object, needs a name; this name will also be used for the out-of-container page that Access will create upon saving this object.

FIGURE 8.4

The Page is functionally complete now, requiring only a bit of editing to make it fully complete.

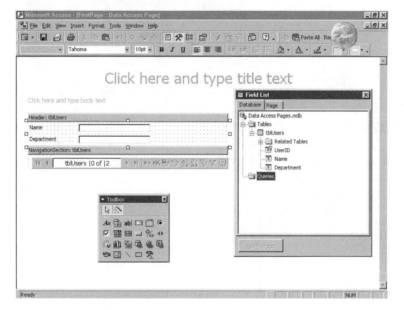

8. The wizard has left the phrase Click Here and Type... in two places: one for the title and one for the body text. Enter appropriate text in these two spots. Figure 8.5 shows the sample's entries. Use them or something of your own invention.

9. Click the View button to switch to Page view. Your screen should resemble Figure 8.6. You can enter or view data similarly to the way you would when using a form. You can also click the filter buttons to filter or sort just like in a form. So far, a Page shows you nothing special. That's coming next.

FIGURE 8.5

Access' wizard leaves placeholders for Page labels.

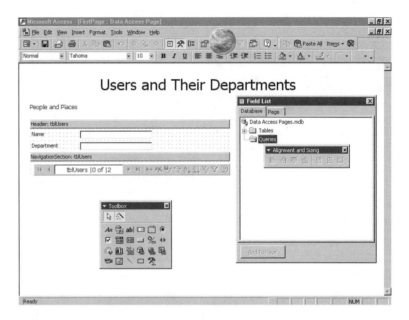

FIGURE 8.6

So far, the Page doesn't look unlike a form or do anything different than a form can do, but the next steps will show you how much different it really is.

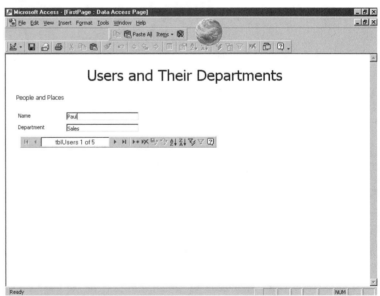

10. Locate the folder Access uses to store documents by default. This is usually c:\My Documents. To see which folder this is on your computer, choose Tools, Options, General and locate the text box with the label Default Database Folder

▼ shown in Figure 8.7. Now use the Explorer to navigate to that folder and locate an object with the save name of the Page, but with the extension .HTM. Figure 8.8 shows this object for the sample data.

FIGURE 8.7

The General tab shows where the default file save location is for your Access setup.

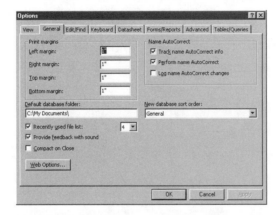

FIGURE 8.8

Access stores the external part of the Page in the default folder, giving it an HTML format and appropriate extension. This external file is the one highlighted in the left pane of Explorer.

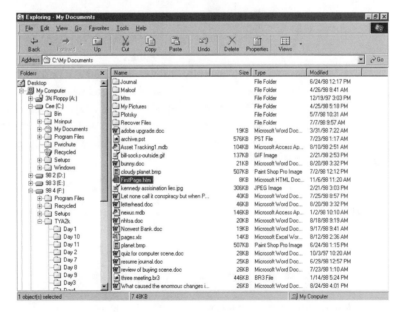

11. Double-click on the file with the .HTM extension—in this case, FirstPage.htm. Windows will load the page into the default browser, as you can see in Figure 8.9. You can browse, filter, and edit data through your browser just as you can through a form within your database container. You've just created a browser-friendly form that is hot-linked to your database. Congratulations.

FIGURE 8.9

Using a Page, your browser becomes an Access form viewer. You can edit data in this form just as you can by using a form within the Access database container.

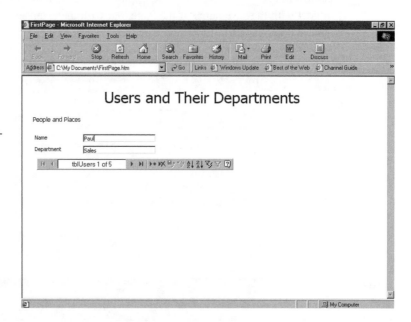

12. To assure yourself that this link works, shut down both Access and Internet Explorer (if they're open). Now use the Windows Explorer to locate the .HTM file you created, which is probably located in C:\My Documents, and launch it. Internet Explorer (or your default browser) will launch with the document loaded. The document will be able to access the data within the Access database (the .MDB file).

> **Note**
>
> The data displayed in the browser isn't located within the .HTM file, but rather within the host .MDB file.

The Need for Data Access Pages

Data Access Pages extend Access 2000 into the World Wide Web. You don't need to know anything about this facility to use Access as a database, even on an expert developer level. The only thing these Pages bring to the party is an ability to easily link a Web page to a database source.

That's the bad news. The good news is that for most people the Web is something to browse, not develop sophisticated data applications for. If your need is to develop display pages for the Web or an intranet complete with any and all links, hypertext, and multimedia, you don't need what Data Access Pages have. In fact, trying to create a multimedia presentation or just display Web page using Access is a needlessly difficult chore with no advantages.

You can fire up the very easy-to-use Microsoft Publisher 2000 or, if your needs are more sophisticated, you can use FrontPage 2000. Word 2000 is also a decent Web page design tool, but it is not nearly as easy as Publisher 2000 or as flexible as FrontPage 2000.

The elements in a Page include three classifications:

- Elements specific to the Web
- Elements specific to Access or other database products
- Miscellaneous elements not readily classifiable as either of the other two

The reason I mention these elements is that this book has taught nothing Web specific. Unless you've spent quite a bit of time reading Web references or have been a Webmaster, you probably don't know the jargon and objects of the Web. This lack will put you at a disadvantage when manually manipulating properties of these Pages.

Even the miscellaneous elements aren't necessarily easy to understand, and nothing you've seen previously in this book will prepare you for many of them. You should be able to figure out any Access-specific elements in Page design by now, however.

Do	Don't
DO use Data Access Pages to create a link to a database through a page.	**DON'T** struggle to create Web pages with Access unless they need a data link. Other tools within the Office 2000 suite do a better job of this.

Tip

Because Microsoft Access 2000 is an ODBC-compliant database, you can use FrontPage 2000 to connect to its .MDB files using the tools supplied within FrontPage and without using Data Access Pages. This is one of many examples in which Office 2000 applications allow you to work as you prefer.

The Design of Data Access Pages

Data Access Pages are similar to forms or reports, with the addition of linking information between the Page as displayed on the Web (in HTML form) and the database. A form (or table or query) can contain a hyperlink (often just called a link) to another file or Web page. For the purposes of discussion here, I'll call a link to another Web page or file a *hyperlink* and the link between a Page and the host application a *link*.

You can see how similar a Page is to a form or report by opening one in Design view.

Task: Examining a Page's Workings

1. Open the DataAccessPages.mdb database if it's not open already. Click the Pages entry in the Object bar of the Database view and click on the FirstPage entry. Click the Design button in the Database view toolbar. This will open the Data Access Page FirstPage in Design view. Your screen should resemble Figure 8.10.

> **Note**
>
> If you get an error message about Access not being able to find a link, click OK and browse or enter the location of the sample database in the dialog box that will automatically pop up. For more information on this link see the next task, "Establishing the Two-Page Links."

FIGURE 8.10

The similarity of a Page to a form becomes obvious when you view them in Design view.

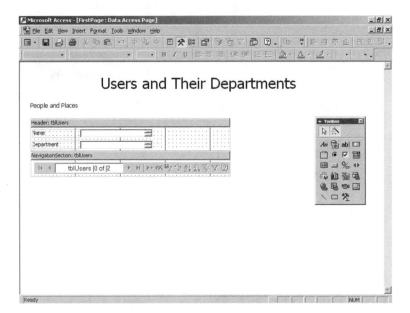

2. Open the Properties list box by choosing View, Properties from the main menu or by clicking its button on the toolbar. Browse through the various tabs and their entries, pulling down combo boxes if you find anything of interest. Here you will

▼   start to encounter properties exclusive to Pages and not found on either reports or
        forms. For example, many objects and object elements can be either auto or static.
        This controls whether the object appears fixed or not.

3. Microsoft has supplied good documentation to help you get an idea of what any
   property of a Page does. Enter `Data Access Pages Control Properties` at either
   the Office Assistant (OA) or in the Answer Wizard in standard help. Help will
   bring up a hyperlink page with all properties. Click on any hyperlink and you'll see
   a dedicated help page, shown in Figure 8.11, for that property and its parameters.
   You might want to keep the hyperlink page open for quick reference when you
   start to use Pages.

FIGURE 8.11

These hyperlinks will give you the information you need to set a Page's properties.

4. To get a feel for manual design of a Page, open the FieldList box by either choosing it from the View menu or clicking on its icon in the toolbar. Open the object
   list under the Tables entry by clicking on the plus sign.

5. Locate the Room field within the tblUsers object. Figure 8.12 shows the FieldList
   box with the field highlighted.

6. Drag the field from the FieldList box to the Page's body, dropping it in any location (other than an existing object). Adjust the control and its label to suit your
   sense of design. This example moved the label and the dropped control separately,
   so the label is above the control and to the right of the two previous field controls.
▼   Figure 8.13 shows the final adjustment of the label for this control.

FIGURE 8.12

To add a field to a Page, you need to locate it in the object hierarchy.

FIGURE 8.13

Just as on a form, you can move controls and their labels separately.

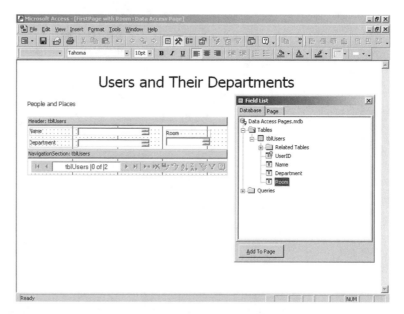

7. Switch to Page view by clicking on the toolbar button or using the View menu. You will see the new field now show up in your page. If you want this change to be permanent, you need to save the Page either on exiting or using the File menu. If you want to preserve both the original Page and the modified one, save the modified one using a different name through the File, Save As menu entry. The sample data has this modified Page saved under the name FirstPage with Room.

You can add any controls or elements to a Page that make sense. This is a good time to return to Design view for the Page you edited in the previous task. Open the Toolbox, using either the toolbar or the View menu, and examine the controls. Note that there are quite a few of them. Note also that there is a Control Wizard button.

Do	**Don't**
DO take some time to experiment with various controls for Pages. Most of these controls are obvious in usage, but some provide some interesting and unique characteristics in their properties you might find useful.	**DON'T** try to figure out the use of all these controls and control combinations without some assistance. Keep the wizard active and also keep online help open. After a few uses of any given control, you'll have figured it out, but you'll most likely wish to keep the wizard active anyway as it reduces Page design workload significantly.

 A good way to experiment with Pages is to use a simple table such as the tblUsers table, which is supplied as part of the sample data for today. Start a blank Page from the Database view by choosing New, and then Design View with the target table selected in the combo box. Try adding controls with the wizard active until you get a feel for how a Page works in Design view. Because you're already familiar with Form Design view, you will feel comfortable with Pages in a few minutes.

The following task steps you through two specialized Page features that Form Design view hasn't prepared you for.

Task: Establishing the Two-Page Links

1. Open the DataAccessPages.mdb database if it's not open already. Click the Pages entry in the Object bar of the Database view. Highlight the FirstPage entry and click the Design button in the Database View toolbar.

2. Open up the FieldList box either by using the View menu entry or clicking its entry in the toolbar. Right-click on the topmost entry on the Database tab, which will be the name of the open database. Choose the Connection entry from the context menu. This will bring up the dialog box you see in Figure 8.14. This dialog box is what you need if you change the location of the linked database.

3. Close this Page, discarding or saving changes as you see fit.

4. In Database view, double-click on the entry Edit Web Page That Already Exists. Browse for the Deleted.htm Web page, which is part of the sample data for today. Figure 8.15 shows the location of this file on one computer within My Documents on drive C:.

▼

FIGURE 8.14

Among other things, this dialog box controls security and the link between the database object and the HTML object.

FIGURE 8.15

You can create a database object Page by linking to the HTML output of a Page previously created using Access, in addition to creating the Page first and the HTML later.

5. Highlight the file, and then click the Open button. This will create the Page object Deleted in your database container. From here you can edit the HTML object, just like any other object. The Deleted object is a duplicate of the FirstPage object created specifically for this task. Save or discard the new database object as you see fit.

▲

That's a good beginning to the often-confusing world of Data Access Pages. The next section contains some practical working information about these objects.

Applied Data Access Pages

8

The "gee whiz" factor in Pages is high, which leads people to want to use them, but over-enthusiasm can be the road to permanent headaches. Pages are an add-on to Access to give the program the cachet of being *the* database for Web use. Keep in mind that Microsoft initially intended Pages to be useful for Intranet publications in which you, or at least your administrator, have great control over the server and users. This isn't always the case in the wild world of the international Internet.

Even within corporations, Pages shouldn't be the first line of data distribution because they add both complexity and overhead. For years past and for the foreseeable future, savvy developers have distributed Access databases with the ability to change object design to Windows users. The Premium version of Office 2000 contains tools for doing just that.

If your need for security is low, and your company is standardized on Office anyway, you can just have users run your .MDB directly from the LAN.

The only reason to use Pages is when the most practical way to view or edit data is through a Web browser. Before charging ahead to make a bunch of Pages for your users to see the data within a database, ask yourself whether there is a more conventional way to accomplish your task—such as a report or a report output to HTML.

Keep in mind that Pages and their links aren't as robust as other, more mature technologies. To alter an Access 2000–created HTML page, you can load it into a text editor, such as Notepad, or even a third-party Web page editor, but your results might damage the workings of that Page. Proceed with extreme caution, making sure you're well backed up if you choose to tread this path.

Do	Don't
DO edit any Data Access Pages you create using the tools supplied with Access 2000.	**DON'T** forget that in theory you should be able to create a Page using any text editor or Web page creation program and then link to the database, but in practice this road leads nowhere. If you want to create a Page linked to your database, do it within the Access program only.

Summary

Data Access Pages are a part of Access 2000 that allows you to provide a link through a Web browser to a database. The navigation bar on a Page allows users to move through records, filtering and sorting just as they could with the toolbar of a form.

You can begin creating most Pages by using a wizard, but you can manually create a Page using techniques similar to those used in form or report design. There are some specialized properties exclusive to Pages, and there are also some specialized controls. Online help has a dedicated section for these properties, and the control wizard option in the toolbox will help you with most controls.

Pages are objects of last resort. There are other methods to distribute your database objects that incur less overhead and rely on more mature technologies. There is nothing wrong with using Pages if there is no more practical way to let your users see your data, but don't use this feature in place of older, well-established ways such as allowing LAN users to share your database through the tools within the Office Premium Edition.

Q&A

Q How can I take an existing HTML page and link to an existing database?

A This is a lot of effort and the results probably won't work. You're much better off using Access to create a new Page bound to an existing database object, and then outputting to HTML. Back up the results, and then edit the HTML to include the features you want, using Copy and Paste to save time. Be prepared to scrap the entire project when you find out your edits somehow caused the original Page to malfunction.

Q How can I alter security for a Page?

A In the Field List box, right-click on the database name. Choose Connection from the context menu. Choose the Advanced tab, and you'll see the security entries.

Q Sometimes I open my Page in a browser and can't see any data. What's up?

A Probably the Page is encountering an open and stubborn database that's jealous of sharing data. Close the database in Access and refresh or reload the Page. That will probably do it. If not, open the Page in Access and make sure all the links are as they should be.

Q Can I link a Page to a parameter query?

A Yes, in theory, but in practice this will almost never work. Someone somewhere might have gotten it to work, but I haven't. Assign this one to sweet dreams that will come true some day, but not today.

Workshop

The Workshop helps you solidify the skills you learned in this lesson. Answers to the quiz questions appear in Appendix A, "Answers."

Quiz

1. A Data Access Page includes three linked objects. What are they?

2. Can you link a Page using a SQL Server data source?

3. How would you add a hotspot (click on to hyperlink) object to a Page?

Exercise

This exercise is very important to try if you want to gain more of an understanding of how pages work in detail. However, you only need to try it if you want to move beyond what the output of the Design Wizard can gain you.

1. Open DataAccessPages.mdb to Pages. Double-click on the entry `Create data access page in Design view`. This will bring up an unbound design grid.

2. Open the Field List dialog box. Expand the Tables entry. Locate the tblUsers table and click on it. Click the Add to Page button to add the fields from this table as controls on the Page. Your screen should resemble Figure 8.16.

FIGURE 8.16

You can bind a table to a Page within Design view of that Page.

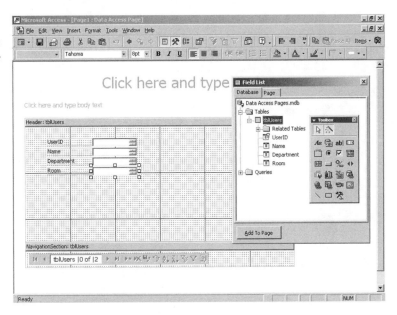

3. Manipulate the controls until you have a pleasing layout.

4. Add a hotspot image to the Page anywhere you please. Use any available bitmap for the image and any hyperlink you have readily available. If you want, you can hyperlink to one of the Pages made today, such as FirstPage.htm.

5. Edit the labels using text of your own choosing. Save the Page using names and a location of your choosing.

6. Choose File, Web Page Preview from the main menu. Try to use the Page—including the hotspot image—from within Internet Explorer. Congratulations, Web page designer!

DAY **9**

Refining Your Tables

Tables hold your data. Therefore, they are the heart of any database or information system. However, tables can do more than just contain data. They can ensure the held data is valid and formatted in any way you, the developer, choose. Today's lesson covers

- The need for data integrity
- The fundamental rule for data representation
- The data validation property
- Using expressions to ensure data integrity
- Using lookup tables for data validation
- The purpose of input masks
- Creating input masks with a wizard
- The symbols used for input masks
- Including OLE objects in tables
- Including hyperlink objects in tables
- Including hyperlinks outside the dataset
- Presenting table data in Web format
- Special considerations for editing hyperlink data

Tables and Data Integrity

You, as a developer, must control the quality of the data entered into your application. This applies not only to applications distributed to far-flung places, but also to applications you will use yourself.

 The reason to control data input is to be assured of data output. Take a look at Figure 9.1. This is a table that's part of your sample data in the Day 9 folder of the CD. The database name is Table Validation.

FIGURE 9.1

This tiny table is full of (often silly) examples of what can occur to a table's data if a developer doesn't take care in designing data input validation.

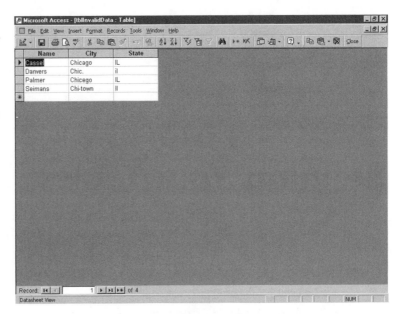

As you can see, there are several spellings and abbreviations for the city Chicago and the state Illinois. Most people familiar with the United States and looking at this table would understand that the entries Chicago, Chica., and Chi-town all refer to Chicago. However, the database isn't nearly as intelligent or experienced with U.S. cities and their abbreviations or hip names. Similarly, a person not familiar with U.S. cities and slang might guess that Chica. is an abbreviation for Chicago, but would likely miss Chi-town. In fact, a person familiar with U.S. cities might assume the word Chica is an error and that the entry is supposed to be the towns Chico or Chino, or even China.

It gets worse when you consider filters and queries as applied to multiple entries for the same data. A reasonable person might, when trying to select records in which Chicago is the city, use Chicago as the City field criterion. However, using that criterion on this table would miss all but one Chicago record. If you changed the criterion to one that selects all these records, such as `Like "Ch*"`, you would also select `China`, `Chico`, `Chirucuaha`, and so on.

The Rule

The rule for data entry is that any data must be represented in one and only one way in a database. It matters little if you choose to represent the city of Chicago as `Chica`, `Chi-town`, or `Chicago` just as long as you use one and stick to it. That way, when you select or filter using a criterion, you'll know for sure that not only have you selected for all the records matching that criterion, but that you haven't selected for records not meeting your criterion.

9

Note

> Remember that using the datasets you have been using (for the most part) in this book, you can visually examine the data to make sure that it's as you want it to be. However, in the real world of databases, your datasets will grow well beyond your ability to scan them for accuracy.

For example, suppose you're in charge of recordkeeping for a political party's fund-raising efforts. You have a database that has, among its tables, contributors along with their addresses. Your boss asks you to give him a list of all contributors from Chicago. You run a Select query using Chicago as a criterion. Your return is 10,348 records.

You likely aren't familiar enough with your data to know whether that's right. You must trust your database engine and your data so you know to an utter certainty that you do have 10,348 contributors who have addresses in Chicago. Hoping and guessing just won't do in this and other similar instances.

The first part of this chapter covers how you can design your tables to make sure they represent data uniformly.

Data Validation in Tables

You've already seen several expressions in use for queries, forms, and reports. Some data-validation techniques rely on expressions as well.

> **Tip**
>
> The easiest data-validation trick is to use a default value when you have a field, such as City, which can contain identical values. Users can override the default value of course, but having such values for often-repeated field values will not only create a validation for data entry, but will also save data input time.

The expressions for data validation look just like those expressions that might appear in a query as a criterion. For example, the expression `"CIA"` or `"AFL-CIO"` will only allow the values `"CIA"` or `"AFL-CIO"` to be entered in a field with that validation so defined.

The following task takes you through a sample data validation.

Task: Adding Data Validation to a Table

1. Start Access if necessary and locate the database Table Validation from the sample data. It is under the Day 9 folder on the CD. Locate the tblFirstValidation table, and open it in Design view.

2. This table was made using the Mailing List Table Wizard, but uses only a few of the available fields. Click on the OrganizationName field and locate the Validation Rule entry in the Field Properties list box. Enter CIA Or AFL-CIO for an entry. Your screen should resemble Figure 9.2.

FIGURE 9.2

The two properties for basic data validation in tables are Validation Rule and Validation Text.

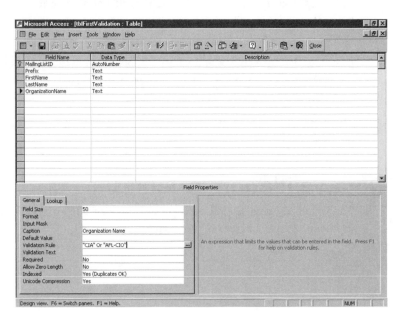

3. Save the table using a new name (File, Save As) if you don't want to overwrite the sample data. The finished version of this table is part of the sample data under the name tblFirstValidation-done. Switch to Table view after the save. Locate the field with the Caption Organization Name, and try entering any value such as FBI. Then tab out of the field. Your screen should resemble Figure 9.3.

FIGURE 9.3

Access has gained enough education through the validation process to reject this entry.

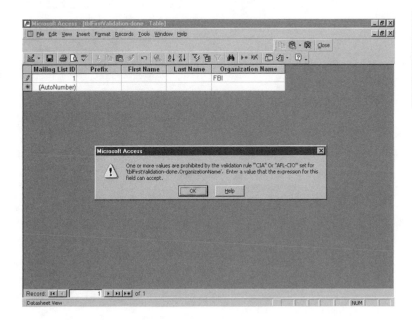

4. Click OK to clear the message box and try entering CIA for a value in the Organization Name field. Tab out again. This time the table will accept your entry because it meets the criterion for the Data Validation property.

5. Although the new validation entry does a fine job of requiring the user to enter one of the two values specified, the text of the error/warning message box isn't terribly informative, especially for beginners. Switch back to Design view.

6. Locate the Validation Text field under Field Properties. Enter Please enter AFL-CIO or CIA. as a property. Your screen should resemble Figure 9.4.

7. Save the table and return to Table view. Click in the Organization Name field and enter an invalid value, such as FBI.

8. Tab away from the field and now you'll see Rocky, or whatever other Office Assistant you use, delivering your custom message. Your screen should resemble Figure 9.5.

FIGURE 9.4

Now to enlist Rocky's help with data validation.

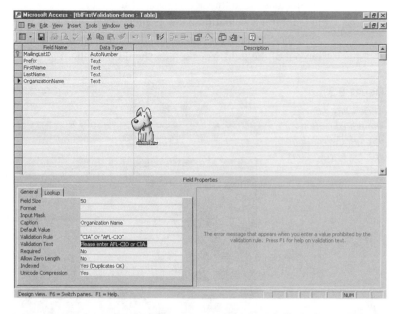

FIGURE 9.5

You can ask the Office Assistant for help in your data-validation messages.

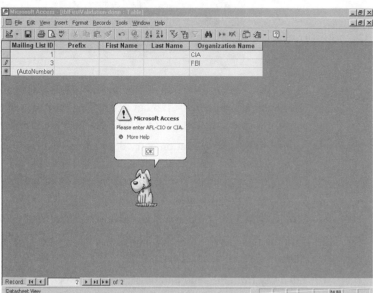

9. This technique works as long as you have only a few criteria and don't want users to be able to modify those criteria. When your needs grow more complex, you must use a lookup facility. That's coming right up.

Data Lookup in Tables

You can create combo boxes in your tables that will look up data from other tables. This can allow you, as a developer, to restrict your data entry to values existing in another table. There are several advantages to doing this. First, you can have your users (optionally) edit the looked-up table to alter its contents, thus letting users decide what is valid for entries. Second, you can list long (millions if necessary) values for lookups in which entering a long In or Or expression would be onerous.

Generally speaking, you shouldn't need to have a large table (in number of records) for data validation. However, you might be looking up from a large table when, for example, you want to enter records only in the many side of a relationship for which an entry already exists in the one side. Although you can force users to add records only in the many side where a one-side record already exists by enforcing referential integrity when establishing the link, if a user tries entering a non-existent, many-side record he'll only get an error message.

If you create a lookup system for record entry on the many side (such as orders for existing customers), you'll greatly speed up data entry in any system in which the data entry person hasn't memorized the values in the link fields (most systems are too big for memorization). Creating the lookup is quite simple; after you've seen the method for doing one, you know it for all.

This task is a simple variant of using a combo box in forms to look up data.

Task: Using a Lookup Table for Data Validation

1. Start Access if necessary and locate the Table Validation database in the sample data. It is in the Day 9 folder on the CD. Locate the tables tblLookUpValidation and tblCityLookUp. The first table is one in which a combo box will look to the second table for its data.

2. Open the tblLookUpValidation table in Design view. Your screen should resemble Figure 9.6.

3. Click in the City field. Note the Lookup tab behind the General tab.

4. Click on the Lookup tab to open that property sheet. Pull down the Display Control combo box (lots of combo boxes!) and choose Combo Box for the display control.

5. Locate the Row Source property. Pull down its combo box and place the tblCityLookUp table as the Row Source for this control. Change the Limit To List property to Yes. Your screen should resemble Figure 9.7.

FIGURE 9.6

This simple table structure will make the point of this task clearer than a complex table in which the trees might be lost due to the size of the forest.

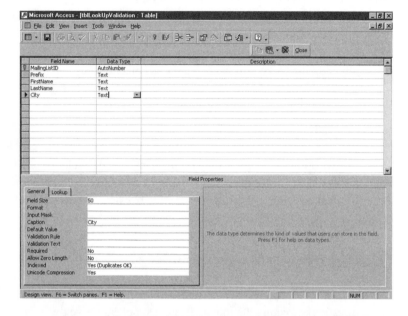

FIGURE 9.7

This Lookup tab set will limit the entries in one table's fields to the values in another table.

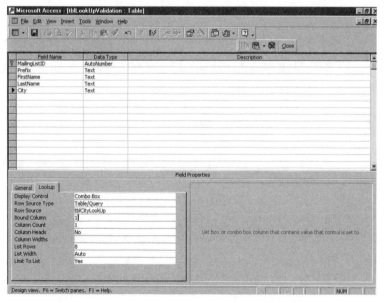

Tip Keep your eye on the rectangle to the right of the Field Properties list box to see pointers and tips about the property that currently has focus.

6. Save the table using a new name if you want to preserve the sample data in its original form. This example uses tblLookupFinished for a save name. Switch to Table view. Move to the City field and pull down the combo box that forms when the field has focus. Your screen should resemble Figure 9.8.

FIGURE 9.8

You're now limited to using the city names on this list. However, one entry seems to be spelled oddly.

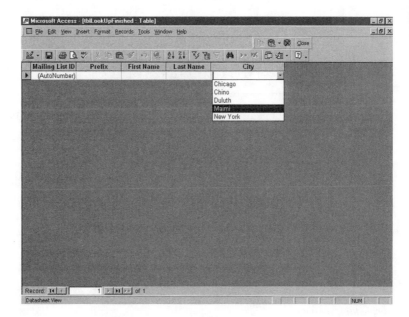

7. Well, this is a fine kettle of fish we're in. The entry for Miami is spelled *Maimi*, and we're limited to the entries on this list for the City field. The lesson to learn here is that if you use tight data validation, make sure your data is valid. In this case, during normal use, the users would enter Maimi for every entry in which the city was really Miami.

Tip If you find yourself with a set of bad data such as a city named Maimi instead of Miami, don't despair. You can fix the error using an Update query, as covered in Day 15, "Examining Special-Use Queries." You can also use Find and Replace to alter values in a table. If, due to audit considerations, you don't want to alter table data, you can link the values in tblCityLookUp to another table holding the correct values and use that link in your queries, forms, and reports.

Input Masks

An input mask is a template of how you want your data to appear or be entered into your project. For example, the date displayed as 12/12/01 has a template of ##/##/##, in which the character # holds the place for a number. Similarly, the common U.S. phone display of (302)555-8827 uses a template of (###)###-####, again using the # character as a placeholder for where numbers go.

Keeping this in mind, you can construct input masks to work alone or in conjunction with data validation expressions to further enforce validation or control display.

Tip

Input masks use wildcards as placeholders. This allows you to use them to specify the length or form of input without using the specific strings required in a data validation expression.

Like so many things in small computing, input masks are easy to understand after you've created one or two, as in the next task.

Task: Using Input Masks for Data Validation

1. Start Access if necessary and locate the Table Validation database in the sample data. It is under the Day 9 folder on the CD. Locate the tblMaskMe table and open it in Design view. Your screen should resemble Figure 9.9.

FIGURE 9.9

Here is another very simple table, perfect for practicing on.

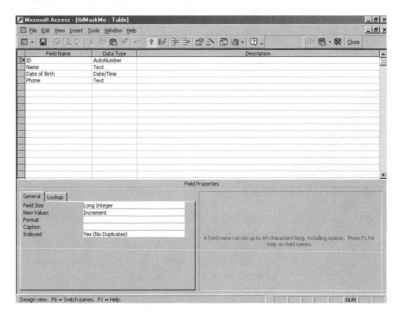

2. Switch to Table view. Enter a date for the Date of Birth field. Access will format the date to reflect the entry in the Format property for this field. This first mask will create a template for date entry in this field. Switch back to Design view.

3. Click in the Date of Birth field to bring up the properties for this field. Click in the Input Mask area of the Field Properties. You can manually enter a mask or use a wizard to build a mask for commonly masked field types. This task uses the wizard.

4. Click on the ellipsis (build) to launch the Input Mask Wizard. Your screen should resemble Figure 9.10. The first dialog box gives you a choice of various templates or masks to display the information in this field. Click on Short Date, and then in the Try It section below to see how your mask will work.

FIGURE 9.10

The Input Mask Wizard has several predefined masks for various data types. This is the predefined list for the Date/Time data type.

Access stores time and date data in the same numeric format. You can choose to display time, date, or both by changing the display characteristics. The Input Mask Wizard uses this universal date/time storage method to display time, date, or both.

5. Click Next to move on, leaving Short Date as the mask type. The next screen enables you to change the mask details, and to change the type of placeholder your mask will use to indicate to your users that the mask is looking for input. Pull down the Placeholder Character combo box and choose the # symbol for a placeholder. Your screen should resemble Figure 9.11. Click Next to move on.

FIGURE 9.11

You can customize the wizard process to make a mask of your own design.

6. That's it. Click Finish (as you could have done in the last dialog box) and you're finished. Access creates the input mask to your specification and places it in the Input Mask field property. The mask for this field is `99/99/00;0;#`.

7. Here's an explanation of this mask. The character *9* is a key character that will allow the user to enter either a number or a space. This will allow both the dates 12/12/12 and 1/1/12 to be entered. The last two zeros force the user to enter two numbers, preventing an entry such as 12/12/1. The zero after the semicolon tells Access to store the formatting characters (this time the slashes) with the data. The final character here is the placeholder.

8. Save the table, or Save As using a new name if you don't want to overwrite the sample table. This example uses the final save name as tblMaskMe-Finished. Switch to Table view. Try entering a date in the Date of Birth field. Try entering only one digit in the Year area and then tabbing away from the field. Access will prevent you from entering such a date in your table.

9. Return to Design view and enter an underscore for the last item in the mask. Save and return to Table view. Note how the look of the mask now differs. Return to Design view and replace the underscore with the number symbol again.

10. Click in the Phone field, and again click the build button in the Input Mask field of Field Properties to start another wizard. The Text data type field is quite flexible, and Access doesn't automatically know what type of data it's to deal with, so it offers you a list of various masks it has predefined suitable for a Text field. Choose Phone Number, which should be the default choice anyway. Click Next to move on.

11. Leave the next screen at default and click Next. Feel free to run through this wizard time and again to experiment with other options. When you get the dialog box asking you whether you want to store symbols with the data, choose not to. This dialog box with the proper option button chosen is shown in Figure 9.12.

FIGURE 9.12

This dialog box will permit you to include or exclude formatting characters from your dataset.

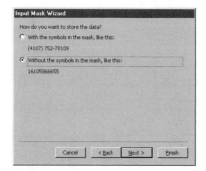

12. Click Finish to end the wizard process. This will leave you back at Design view. Note the mask reads !(999) 000-0000; ;_.

13. Note the empty space between the two semicolons. This indicates that the formatting characters will not be stored with the values entered in this field. Save the table and experiment with the Phone and Date of Birth field until you're satisfied about how they work. A complete table of input mask characters follows this task.

Table 9.1 gives a few examples of input masks and their results.

TABLE 9.1 INPUT MASK CHARACTERS

Character	Use in Mask
,	Thousands separator or other character as specified by the country format for Windows
/ :	Date and time delimiters or other characters depending upon the country format for Windows
\	Regard next character as literal
!	Fill from left to right (default is right to left)
"anystring"	Show the values in between the double quotes literally in mask
<	Display as lowercase
>	Display as uppercase
A	Force alphanumeric
a	Optional alphanumeric
&	Force any entry including whitespace
0	Force any number
9	Optional any number
#	Digit, space (default), or operand

TABLE 9.1 CONTINUED

Character	Use in Mask
L	Force alpha
?	Optional character
c	Optional character or space
.	Decimal delimiter or other character as specified by the country format for Windows

Do	Don't
DO create a data validation scheme for all your data and make it tight enough that no invalid data is possible.	**DON'T** forget to design your validation scheme with your users' convenience in mind. For example, using a lookup table to reduce the amount of data entry time will ensure valid data and ease the workload of your users.

Using OLE Objects and Hyperlinks in Tables

You can define a table field as having the data type OLE Object. An OLE object can be almost anything, from a sound to a movie clip to a still picture. The specific objects available to you will depend upon your computer's configuration.

Open the Table Validation database and locate the Employees table. This is a table imported from the Northwind database supplied with Access. Open Employees in Design view. Locate the Photo field and note that the data type is OLE Object.

Switch to Table view and scroll over to see the Photo field. Note that this field seems to have all the same entry: Paint.Picture. Right-clicking on this field will bring up a context menu with the entries Edit and Open, allowing you to open the picture in a bitmap editor if one is registered as part of your Windows environment.

Even if you don't have a bitmap editor, you can display the images by choosing AutoForm from the New Object button on the toolbar. Figure 9.13 shows the Employees table in Table view. Figure 9.14 shows the same table after the AutoForm Wizard creates a form for this table.

FIGURE 9.13

The contents of an OLE Object field might all appear the same because the contents aren't literals, but are descriptions of the type of object the field contains.

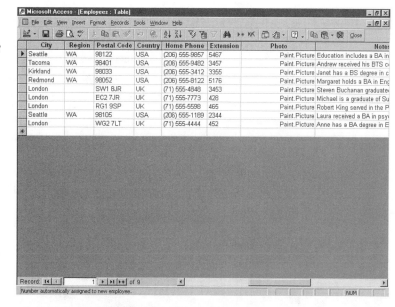

FIGURE 9.14

There's little to be gained by showing OLE objects in tables, but they make for great-looking forms. This AutoForm has been slightly modified to show the picture, along with the balance of the form controls.

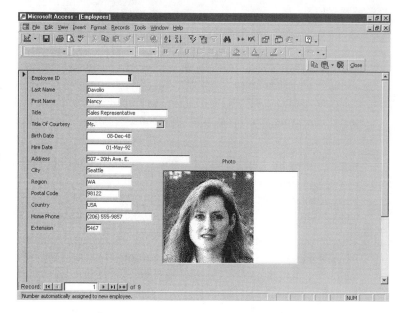

Inserting OLE Objects

To insert an OLE object into a field having the data type OLE Object choose Insert, Object menu. If you want to try this, you'll need an OLE object of some sort available to you. Although this example uses a picture, you could also use a sound, a movie clip, or any other object type your computer has registered.

To insert a new OLE object, click in the field where you want to place the object. In Access, that field must have the data type OLE Object. This example uses the Photo field in the Employees table. You can use this or the AutoForm as shown in Figure 9.14. This form is part of the sample data as frmShowOLEObject. Choose Insert, Object from the menu. This will bring up the critical dialog box shown in Figure 9.15.

FIGURE 9.15

This dialog box will show the types of OLE applications registered on your computer or allow you to browse for an existing object.

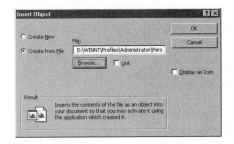

You can choose Create New for the object. If you choose this option, you'll go to the application registered for that OLE object type so you can start creating. After you're finished and exited, you'll have a chance to embed or link the new object to the table or form. This example uses an existing picture, so choose Create from File and browse for the file.

If you choose the Link check box, you won't embed the object in the table but rather will link to an existing object. Linked objects don't expand the database too much, but you must distribute the objects along with the application. Embedded objects, on the other hand, become part of the data but expand the database significantly.

After locating the object, click OK. Access will update the table with an indication that the new picture or other object is now part of your data. Figure 9.16 shows the updated table. Note that the object inserted (a picture) is registered in this workstation as a Paint Shop Pro image.

FIGURE 9.16

Browse and click OK to insert (embed) the new OLE object into the table.

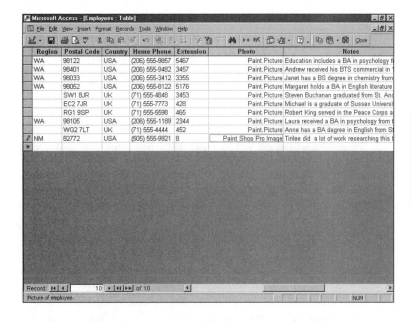

The updated table is saved as tblUpdatedEmployees and as part of the sample data. The form bound to this table is saved as frmUpdatedEmployees. Open the form to see the new object that's now part of this dataset. Figure 9.17 shows the new form with the object on display.

FIGURE 9.17

The picture of the vice president is now part of the dataset.

Note

To display this picture correctly, the Size Mode property was changed from the default of Clip to Zoom for this control.

Hyperlinks

Hyperlinks are jumps to other documents. Although the concept of hyperlinks predates it by quite a while, the World Wide Web, or just the Web, is the place most people first encounter it. You can include hyperlinks in Access forms, tables, and queries.

The basis for inserting a hyperlink in a table is to format the field as data type Hyperlink. Open the tblUpdatedEmployees table in Design view. This table is part of the sample data. Note the last field in the table is called Web Page. This field isn't part of the original Employees table. The data type is Hyperlink. Switch to Table view. Scroll to the Web Page field and click in it to give it focus.

You can enter a hyperlink either directly just like any other data, or you can click on the Insert Hyperlink button on the toolbar to access a dialog box to assist you with these insertions. By all means use the Insert Hyperlink for any insertions other than the most simple because the richness of the invoked dialog box acts almost like a wizard for link insertions.

 Tip

You can hyperlink to Internet Web pages, intranet pages, unpublished pages, and files.

Figure 9.18 shows this dialog box. If you are following along, your dialog box will have different contents.

FIGURE 9.18

This complex dialog box allows various settings for hyperlinks as data.

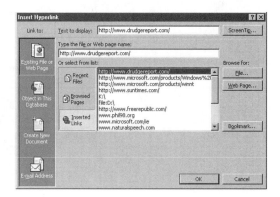

Note that this dialog box has its own object bar over on the left. You can include much more than just Web links in a form or table. Click on the Object in This Database button to bring up an Explorer-like tree view, allowing you to insert links to objects from the database.

 Tip You don't need to use the Insert menu to insert a hyperlink anywhere in Access. If you know the address, such as www.microsoft.com (a familiar one to many), you can just enter it directly.

Similarly, you can link to other files or drives on your computer or network.

The Hyperlink Edit Catch-22

After you've entered a hyperlink into a table, you will have a problem trying to edit it. Other kinds of data are easy to edit because they aren't hot (single-click) jumps. You can click in a non-hyperlink field with your mouse and edit away. If you click in a hyperlink field, you'll either end up jumping to the link site or you'll get an error message.

The trick to editing a hyperlink value is the Tab or Enter key. Click in the field preceding the hyperlink field (coming before in the tab order) and then press the Tab key. This will give focus to the hyperlink field.

Press either F2 to enter edit mode or Shift+F2 to enter zoom mode. Most people prefer Shift+F2 for this task. After entering either zoom or edit mode, you can edit the hyperlink. If you're in edit mode, leaving the field will restore the link facility. If you're in zoom mode, clicking OK will do so. Figure 9.19 shows the zoom mode method of editing a hyperlink field.

Free-Floating Hyperlinks

Starting in about 1996, Microsoft started running Internet amok. Office 2000, of which Access 2000 is a part, continues this trend to Internetworking everything.

In the preceding sections, you've seen how you can insert hyperlinks as field data for tables. You can also just create hyperlinks to drop on forms as free-floating objects or another type of form controls. This very short task takes you through the steps.

FIGURE 9.19

Trying to edit a hyper-link using the usual methods will only end in frustration. You must invoke either zoom or edit mode. Here is zoom mode.

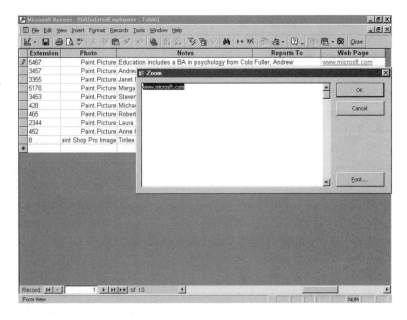

Task: Adding Hyperlinks to Database Objects

1. Launch Access and the Table Validation database, if necessary. Locate the frmHyperlinks form. This form is bound to tblUpdatedEmployees, but includes only three fields for simplicity.

2. Open the form in Design view. Choose the menu selections Insert, Hyperlink. Select a hyperlink of your own choosing or use www.microsoft.com as the example does. Enter Microsoft's Site in the Text to Display box. Click the Screen Tip button and enter Visit Microsoft. Your screen should resemble Figure 9.20.

FIGURE 9.20

The Insert Hyperlink dialog box offers a well-traveled computer many choices from History and Favorites, among other sites.

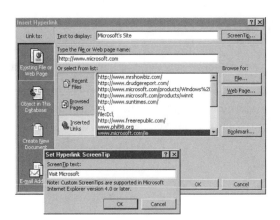

▼ 3. Click OK to move out of these dialog boxes. Access will drop a hyperlink some-
      where on your form. Drag this link to the right of the Photo field. Your screen
      should resemble Figure 9.21.

FIGURE 9.21

*Access will drop the
newly created hyper-
link somewhere on the
form, but because the
link isn't active in
Design view, you can
easily drag and drop it
to a location of your
choosing.*

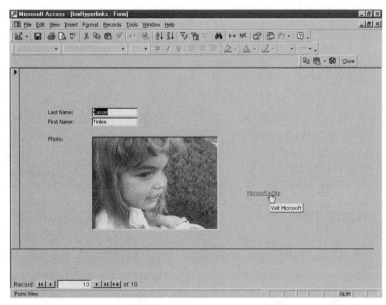

   4. Switch to Form view. Move your cursor over the newly created link. The cursor
      switches to the jump cursor. You'll also see your Screen Tip pop up. If you click
      this link (and are connected to the Internet), you'll jump to the main Microsoft site.

   5. Return to Design view. If necessary, click on the hyperlink field to give it focus.
      Open the Properties list box, if necessary. Click on the Format or All tab. Locate
      the two properties Hyperlink Address and Hyperlink SubAddress. Here is where
      you can manually enter the address for this link. A subaddress is a page at a site.
      Close the form, optionally saving changes. This finished form with the hyperlink is
▲   part of the sample data under the name frmHyperlinks-Finished.

Saving Tables as HTML

You can also save a table data as an HTML page for use at a Web site or for view by
those who don't have Access. Doing so is fairly simple. At the Database view, choose the
table you want to convert to HTML, click on it to highlight it, then choose File, Save As.
This will bring up the dialog box shown in Figure 9.22.

Figure 9.22

The Save As dialog box for tables allows the export of that table to a format readable by browsers.

Choose Data Access Page from the pull-down (combo box) list under the As label. Click OK and you'll get a standard Save dialog box. Choose a name for the save file, but be sure to leave the extension at its default.

Access will create not only the HTML page, but also an ASP control for browsing through the records in the table. At this point, anybody loading the page into a browser or other enabled application (such as Word) can browse through the records of the table so saved.

Summary

The lesson today built on the previous material about both tables and expressions. You, as a developer, need to control the quality of the data that can be added into your project. If some users enter the city Chicago as Chicago, while others use Chi or another variant, your queries and finds won't work as you expect them to. When you have real-world datasets containing thousands or millions of records, you can't expect to validate the quality of the queries by inspection.

You can control the quality of data (data validation) at the table level using several tools: validation rules, input masks, and lookup tables. Most developers use all of these tools, mixing and matching depending on the application.

The Millennium Bug

First in mainframe computers and then in the IBM-style PCs, programmers used two-digit date fields to store year information. This worked all right during the 20th century when you (and your computer) could assume the prefix 19 plus the two numbers in the field. For example, the date 1/4/98 was assumed to be January 4, 1998.

This scheme won't work now because we're looking at dates that might have prefixes of either 19 or 20 (2098 or 1998). By default, Access 2000 assumes any two-digit year date of 24 or before is prefixed 20 while 25 and over remain 19. Because there are still many folks alive who where born before 1925, this scheme won't work perfectly. In fact, relying on two-digit fields is a sure way to create disaster sooner or later.

Despite this, many other plans for the continued use of two-digit fields have been proposed because the switchover to four-digit year fields would take a lot of work. These ideas have all come and gone. The truth is that the only real solution is to use four-digit fields for the year section of Date/Time Date types.

Access 2000 contains an option to force four-digit date fields. Under Tools, Options click on the General tab. You'll see two check boxes shown in Figure 9.23 that will force such fields. Like Option Explicit in Visual Basic, this is one of those options that approach being mandatory.

FIGURE 9.23

Don't rely on two-digit year fields for your new databases. Access will prevent such entries if you let it.

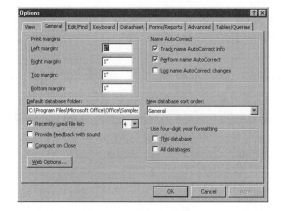

Don't rely on two-digit year fields for your new databases. Access will prevent such entries if you let it.

You can include hyperlinks as data by defining a table field as the Hyperlink data type. Similarly, you can include a hyperlink by dropping it anywhere on a form where it will act like an active label.

Access 2000 will save a table as a two-part HTML document. One contains the actual HTML; the other an ASP control for browsing through the records in the table. After it is so saved, anybody with a sufficiently up-to-date browser can view the table records.

Q&A

Q **What use is a free-floating hyperlink on a form?**

A One common use is to link to a help or reference facility that applies to the entire set of data represented in the form.

Q **Can I view a Data Access Page from within Access?**

A Yes. There is even a macro action, OpenDataAccessPage, to automate this for you.

Q **Do I need to include the equal sign as a prefix for data validation expressions?**

A No, just enter the expression.

Q **How can I order the items in a lookup to be different from the order of the primary key of the underlying table?**

A You can base your lookup not only on a table, but a query, too. Therefore, you can sort on any field in the query and then use the sorted query as a lookup source.

Q **Can I show more than one field in a lookup?**

A Yes. Just change the Column Count property from the default of 1 to however many columns you want to display. Also examine the Column Heads, Column Widths, and Bound Column properties for related information.

Workshop

The Workshop helps you solidify the skills you learned in this lesson. Answers to the quiz questions appear in Appendix A, "Answers."

Quiz

1. Can you display a hyperlink using a label or a different display text?
2. Will the expression In("Madrid","London") as a validation rule allow the entry of the city Belfast?
3. Do you need to use Access' built-in message boxes for validation violations?
4. What will the expression Not "Denver" do as a validation rule?

Exercises

1. Open the form frmHyperlinks.
2. Create a hyperlink to the site www.mrshowbiz.com to appear on the form anywhere. Have the link appear as Visit Mr. Showbiz on the form.
3. Close frmHyperlinks.

4. Create a table with two fields. The first is also the primary key of the data type AutoNumber with the New Values property set to Increment. The second field is OLE Object. Use names of your own choosing for the field names and captions.

5. Use the Insert, Object menu commands to insert some sound files in the second field.

6. Double-click on each field containing a sound file. Does the sound play all right? If the sound didn't play, did Windows give you a sensible message about why it didn't?

9

DAY **10**

Designing Customized Forms

Aesthetics vary, but most people can agree that when forms are functional they are attractive. This lesson covers ways to convert bare forms to ones users prefer to use and that, therefore, function better. This lesson covers the following topics:

- The practical side to attractive forms
- Changing colors in forms
- Altering form objects' formats
- Using a picture for a form background
- Including a static picture for decoration
- Using pictures on command buttons
- 3D and other object effects
- The most often used form format objects
- Modifying forms from form view

Making Attractive Forms

In a typical Access database project, users will interact with forms more than any other object. In fact, there are many Access databases in use in which the users see nothing but forms onscreen and reports from the printer. Happy users are the key ingredients to a successful application. One way to make users happy is to make the objects they interact with, forms for the most part, comfortable to use as well as attractive to view.

You've learned some of the elements available to you to dress up your forms, to give them added functionality, or both. Today's lesson goes into details somewhat glossed over earlier.

Using Colors in Forms

Access tends to default to gray, which is the dominant Windows color used for standard menus, toolbars, scrollbars, and status bars. There's nothing wrong with this color except it does tend to get a bit old after a while. You can use color (sparingly) to dress up forms and to make features stand out. For example, a gray command button doesn't jump out if it's on a gray background, but it does if it's on a blue background. This isn't too important if your target users are young or have good eyesight, but older users, or those with visual limitations, will greatly appreciate your efforts on their behalf.

 Note

> This book is limited to grayscale screenshots. Due to this, some of the color detail in the screens will be somewhat hard to discern, but you can see these changes by following along with the directions or viewing the sample data supplied on the CD-ROM.

Altering Object Color

There is no color property for the overall form. You must change form color by section. Launch Access if necessary. Open the Better Looking Forms database from the Day10 folder of your CD. Click the Forms entry in the object bar and then choose to make a new form through Design view.

Click in the Detail area to make it active. Open the Properties list box if necessary, and then click on the Format tab. Locate the Back Color property. Note that it's a long number. This is how Access stores color information about its objects, but it's not terribly user friendly.

Note The color number is a decimal representation of the bits set for whatever color depth is available on the computer. If an application uses an unavailable color, Windows makes an intelligent guess about what color to substitute.

Click in the area where you would enter a number and note the appearance of the Build button (an ellipsis). Click the button to bring up the standard Windows color picker dialog box. Your screen should resemble Figure 10.1.

FIGURE 10.1

The standard color picker dialog box for Windows will become familiar territory as you alter form object colors from their defaults.

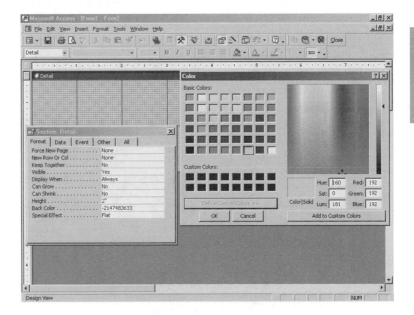

Choose another color. This example used a light blue. Click OK and the dialog box will close, the number will change in the Properties list box, and the form will appear in the new color.

Add a text box control to the form. Click on the label part of the control, and note that it too has a color assigned different from the form, but it appears to be the same color as the form. This is due to its Back Style property defaulting to Transparent. This property is directly above the Back Color property. Alter the Back Color property (this example uses red) using the Build button and then alter the Back Style to Normal. This will display the new color for the label.

The default text color is 0 or black. This doesn't show up too well with a red background, so locate the Fore Color property farther down the list, click the Build button, and alter the color to a bright yellow.

Note

The computer used today is set up to display in True Color, or about 17,000,000 colors (2^{24} colors). If you're set up for fewer colors, you won't have as wide a choice as you see in these screens.

Add another unbound text box control to the form. Again highlight the label part of the control; this time, pull down the Fill/Back Color button, and choose Red again. Doing this will not only add the color to the control, but will also switch the Back Style property to Normal. Now pull down the Font/Fore Color button and choose yellow. There's no difference in your result between the two methods. Which way you choose to work is up to you. When you're finished, your screen should resemble Figure 10.2.

FIGURE 10.2

Like so many features of Access and Windows, there are several ways to switch colors in form elements.

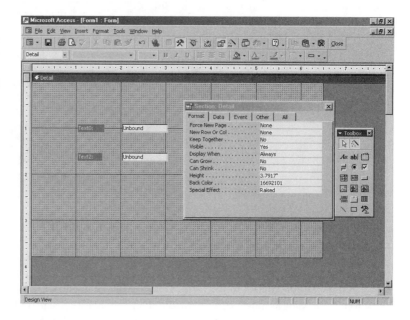

Form Object Pictures

Earlier you saw how the Form Wizard uses a graphic as a background for a form. You can duplicate this wizard facility and go it one better.

Click the form selection section of the form design grid. That's the gray square in the upper-left corner of the grid (right under the toolbar). Or you can pull down the object selection combo box in the form design toolbar and choose Form.

Locate the Picture property in the Properties list box. Click in the field and then either enter a filename and path for a picture (a bitmap) or click the Build button and browse for it. Figure 10.3 shows a picture embedded in a form as well as the properties list box showing the property that included the picture.

FIGURE 10.3

Although you can include a picture as a background for a form, doing so bears the risk of making the form less useful.

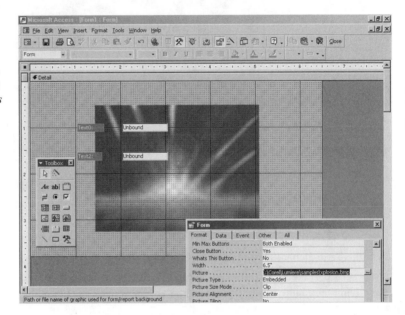

Although the picture in Figure 10.3 is attention getting, many might think it too busy for a working form. You can see the fields clearly, but reading their contents isn't nearly as easy as before. The field (or control) labels aren't nearly as well defined as without the picture.

Note the other picture properties such as Picture Type, Picture Size Mode, Picture Tiling, and Picture Alignment. These control whether the picture becomes part of the database (embedded) or is linked, how Access handles a picture that has a different size or aspect ratio than the form can handle, whether the picture appears once or as tiles, and how the picture relates to the form. Feel free to experiment with these properties to see how they interact. For example, by altering the Picture Size Mode from Clip to Stretch, you can stretch the picture to fill the entire form. This will distort the picture if the form has a different aspect ratio from the form. Figure 10.4 shows a stretched picture.

FIGURE 10.4

Changing one property can have a large effect on how a picture displays. This result is a bit lurid.

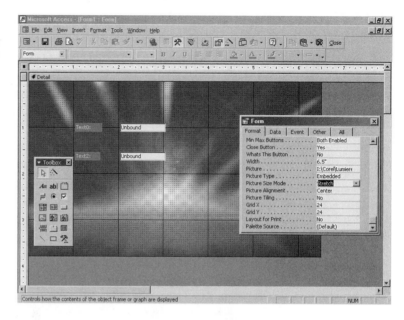

If you want to see this form, it's part of the sample data saved under the name frmLurid in the Better Looking Forms database.

Command Buttons

You can also add a picture to a command button. You saw this earlier when you used the wizard to create a command button to exit a form. Like form pictures, you can create a command button picture without the wizard.

The routine is identical to adding a picture to a form. Create the command button, locate the Picture property on the Format tab of the Properties list box, and finally, specify either a file and path for your bitmap or browse using the Build button. Figure 10.5 shows the Picture Builder dialog box where you can add pictures to command buttons.

Figure 10.6 shows a command button added to the form (the picture from the last section has been deleted) with a picture added to the button. In this case, the Build button will bring up a fairly complex dialog box, allowing you to browse for a file or choose from command button–type pictures supplied with Access. Figure 10.5 shows this dialog box.

There is no way you can include both a caption (or label) and a bitmap on a button, although many developers have requested such an ability. What you can do is include the label as part of a bitmap and use the bitmap or create a label for the command button.

If you want to see this form and button, it's part of the sample data under the name frmLuridButton.

FIGURE 10.5

Access comes with several bitmaps useful for icons on command buttons.

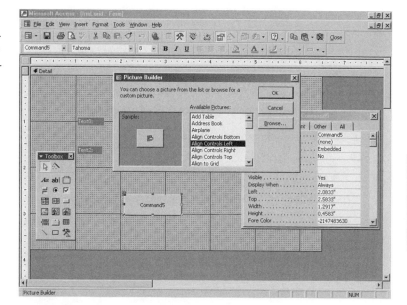

FIGURE 10.6

The flashy picture looks better on a command button, but leaves the reason why the button is there somewhat in doubt.

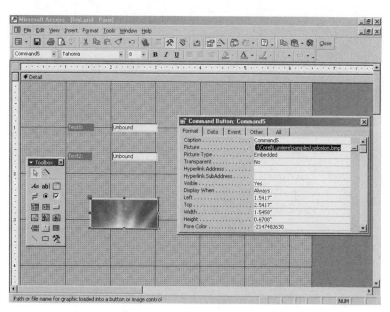

10

> **Tip**
>
> Open the frmLuridButton form in Form view. Click and hold on the command button to see the change in the bitmap when the button is pressed. Click and release the button several times to see the animation effect of this change. The bitmap change gives buttons equipped with pictures a strong visual clue when they're pressed. Keep this characteristic in mind if you create applications for visually impaired users.

3D Effects and Object Order

By using a combination of 3D effects, you can create some spectacular effects or just get an object to stand out. The following task is a quick tour that will give you a taste of what you can do.

Task: Adding Special Effects to a Form

1. Launch Access and open the frmRaiseLower form in Design view. The form is part of the sample data in the Better Looking Forms database.

2. Locate the rectangle tool in the toolbox. Click on it and draw a rectangle around the two form controls. If you lose view of the controls, locate the Back Style property in Properties and switch it from Normal to Transparent.

3. Locate the Line/Border button on the toolbar. Pull down the button to see its selections and choose a width of 4. Rectangles and lines are useful for highlighting form areas. The wider the border, the more attention the highlight gets. Locate the Line/Border color button and choose another color such as red.

4. You can also choose to use a 3D effect to highlight a form area. Locate the Special Effect button on the toolbar. Click on it to show its content and then choose Sunken for an effect. Applying a special effect to a form will remove the old border because the special effects are created by using special borders that give the illusion of depth.

5. You can add many rectangles, giving each a sunken or raised effect to give an even more startling look to your forms. Figure 10.7 shows three rectangles, all with a sunken effect. The cumulative effect is quite interesting.

6. You can also change the effect to shadowed, chiseled, or etched. Each will have a different look. Shadowed works well with most objects, whereas chiseled and etched look best when applied to a series of data type controls such as text or combo boxes. If you want to see this form, it's part of the sample data saved as frmRaiseLower-Done.

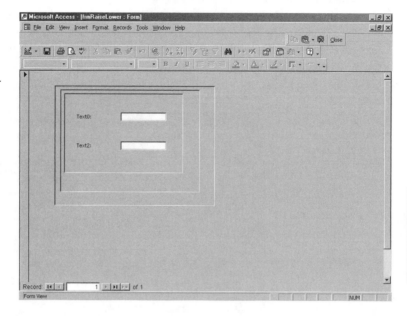

FIGURE 10.7

Successive sunken rectangles can create an interesting effect when either offset or concentric.

Tip Remember you can select multiple objects and "gang" set their matching characteristics. For example, if you select all three rectangles in frmRaiseLower, you can then set all of them to any effect at the same time.

Formats and System Tools

There are two active form views, Form and Datasheet. A Datasheet view looks for all the world like a table or query return. Most important, you can't have form objects such as command buttons appearing as a datasheet. On the other hand, Datasheet form views are terrific for browsing a dataset.

If necessary, open the Better Looking Forms database, locate the form frmEmployees, and open it in Form view. Your screen should resemble Figure 10.8.

Pull down the View button and switch to Datasheet view. Browsing for an employee is a lot faster in this view. Locate the employee named Steve Buchanan, employee number 5. Click anywhere in that record. Note the record selector at the extreme left of the screen shows a caret at the current record. Now switch back to Form view, using the View menu. Now the current record isn't Davolio, but Buchanan.

From Form view, click the first record button. That's the VCR-like button at the bottom of the screen to the left. This will jump you back to Davolio. Now click in the record number field at the bottom of the screen. This currently shows a number 1 because that's Davolio's record number in this dataset. Highlight the number 1 and enter the number 5. Press Enter and Access will jump you to record number 5. This jump to a record number feature is handy if you know the record number of the data you seek—a rather rare thing in Access.

FIGURE 10.8

The now familiar face of Nancy Davolio smiles at us from this simple form.

Tip

Click in the Notes field for any record. Note how this activates a scrollbar allowing you to scroll through the entire contents of this field.

Record selectors don't do too much in Form view. Alter the view for this form to Design view, open the Properties list box if necessary, and locate the Record Selectors property in the Format tab. If you don't see this property, make sure you have the form itself selected, and not an object within the form.

Change this property to No. Return to Form view. This gives you a much cleaner look without losing any functionality. Your screen should resemble Figure 10.9.

Switch back to Datasheet view. Note that the record selectors, now that you need them, reappear. There's no way to remove record selectors from Datasheet view. The other commonly used form formatting properties and their uses are in Table 10.1.

FIGURE 10.9

*Removing record
selectors from a form
gives the form a much
cleaner look without
sacrificing any func-
tion.*

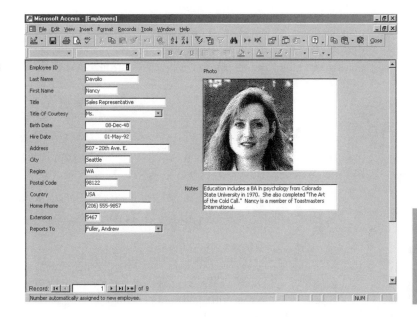

10

TABLE 10.1   COMMONLY USED FORM FORMATTING PROPERTIES

Property	Effect on Form
Caption	The text appears in the title bar when the form is open
Default View	The view when the form opens
Views Allowed	Views available to the user (Form, Datasheet, or both)
Scroll Bars	Types of scrollbars available to the form
Record Selectors	Include or exclude selectors in Form view
Navigation Buttons	Show or hide the VCR buttons at the bottom of the form
Control Box	Show or hide the control menu (the menu at the upper-left of the screen)
Min Max Buttons	Show or hide the minimize and maximize buttons (on the right of the screen)
Close Button	Show or hide the Close button
Auto Resize	Forces the form to size itself large enough to show a complete record, if possible

Although this isn't a comprehensive list, it does show the most commonly used form-for-
matting tools.

A great deal of user satisfaction comes from the aesthetic of an application. Removing
extraneous elements from your form, laying it out so the user can easily find information,
and including easy-to-use command buttons for often-used functions all are part of

making your users happy with your project. For example, if you have a Close Form command button (and you should) on your form, you don't need a Close button at the upper-right of your form. Removing this object not only makes your form cleaner looking, but gives your application a custom look different from other Windows programs, most of which sport such a button.

Adding Artwork

You can also add pictures or line drawings to forms. Figure 10.10 shows a variation of frmEmployees with these changes:

- The View, Form header menu selection chosen to open up the form header section.
- A label with the Caption property set to Watercolor Village Company was added to the header.
- The label was given a raised look and dark red for its text.
- An unbound object frame was added to the header portion.

- The file Watercolor Village.pcx (an original artwork by the authors that's part of the sample data) was added to the unbound object frame.
- Record selectors were deleted from the form.

If you want to see this form, it's part of the sample data under the name frmEmployeesWithPicture. If you want to try your hand at making this form, start with the frmEmployees form and follow the preceding steps. You will also need to move a few form controls to a new location if you want to show a full record on one screen. The latter consideration is dependent upon your screen resolution. The figure shown in 10.10 was shot at 800×600 and did require some control adjustments.

Try scrolling through the records in this database using the navigation buttons. Note that the header remains static while the records change.

Do	Don't
DO keep in mind the use of a form when designing it. Tab order is more important to most users than are pretty pictures, but pictures, lines, and rectangles can make a big difference to users, especially those who spend a lot of time in a form.	**DON'T** overdo color or expect that your idea of red, yellow, and purple is the universal aesthetic. Most users would prefer to use a form designed by Monet over one designed by Calder.

FIGURE 10.10

Adding a picture to a form header can increase the warmth of a form.

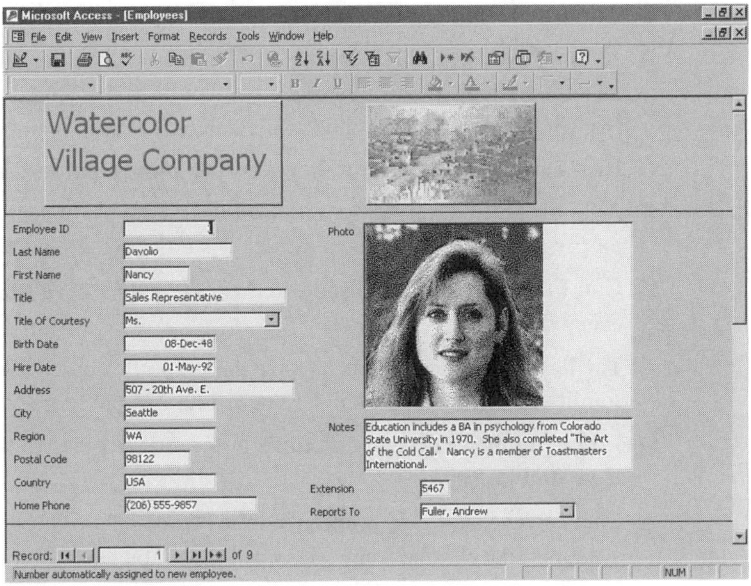

Summary

Aesthetics are important in forms, not only to make your applications pleasing, but also to help users navigate. In short, a pleasing form is a good form. Access provides many tools that you can use to spruce up your forms. You can add headers and footers as you've seen on past days. You can color the various parts of or objects within a form, add lines and rectangles, plus change the characteristics of any objects to make them seem indented, shadowed, raised, etched, or chiseled.

Access also contains a variety of options allowing you to change the functioning of a form. You can add or remove the minimize, maximize, control menu, record selectors, and similar objects on your forms. The only real caution when experimenting with form formatting is not to go overboard. It's very easy to make your forms look like a circus clown or a ransom note. A little formatting goes a long way in Access.

You can make a form much more attractive by adding a header label or a picture. Doing so will enlarge your database, but the price is often worth the gain in attractiveness. Like other formatting elements, use pictures and colors sparingly.

Q&A

Q How can I get my forms to open maximized?

A You can either maximize in Design view and then File, Save As the form, or you can create a small macro with the Action Maximize and then place it in the Form's On Open event.

Q Can I make my forms modal?

A Although you can, this is a powerful feature you should only use sparingly. Under the Other tab for the form's properties you'll find a Modal property. The default is No. Change to this to Yes and you've done the deed.

Q How can I restrict the Tab key's cursor movement to the current record?

A Alter the Cycle property for the form's property to Current Record. The Cycle property is on the Other tab.

Q Can I change lines from solid to dashed or do I need to add a new line for every dash?

A The line and rectangle objects have the property Border Style that controls the solidity of the line or rectangle. You'll find this property on the Format tab.

Q I'd like to make sure my pictures automatically size to fit the object frame. How do I do this?

A Change the Size Mode property on the Format tab to Stretch and they'll fill all the available space in the frame. This can distort pictures, however. Figure 10.11 shows Nancy Davolio's picture stretched to fit a frame. As you can see, the results aren't very attractive. You're usually better off including pictures of the same size and using a frame of the correct size, rather than altering this property to Stretch.

FIGURE 10.11

The Size Mode property affects how a bitmap will fit in its control. This example shows the use of Stretch for this property. As you can see, it doesn't work well with pictures of people.

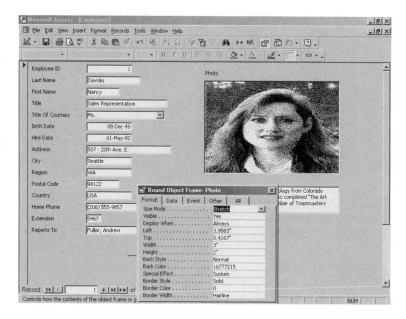

Workshop

The Workshop helps you solidify the skills you learned in this lesson. Answers to the quiz questions appear in Appendix A, "Answers."

Quiz

1. Can you alter one property to change background color for both the form footer and detail area?

2. Can you include a sunken rectangle object within a raised rectangle object?

3. Can you make some form design changes in Form view?

4. If you don't have as many colors to choose from for form color as you want, what can you do to increase your selection?

5. Can you change an identical property for several objects at the same time?

Exercises

1. Open the frmEmployeesWithPicture form in Design view.

2. Alter the bound object frame to a raised look.

3. Make sure the Allow Design Changes property for the form is set to All Views.

4. Switch to Form view. If the Properties list box isn't open, open it. If necessary, click on the bound object frame so Bound Object Frame appears in the title bar of the list box.

5. Alter the special effect (use the toolbar button) for this object to Raised and then Shadowed. Which property do you prefer?

6. Try to resize the bound object frame to be the exact size of the included picture. Can you?

7. Switch to Design view and resize the bound object frame to fit the table's pictures. Hint: Note the desired size of the photo to the watercolor picture in the unbound picture frame above it and use that as a guide to doing your resize chore.

8. Close the form, optionally saving changes.

DAY 11

Sorting Data with Queries and Joins

Back on Day 4, "Using Queries for Data Retrieval," you saw some of the power of select queries. Later, in Day 15, "Examining Special-Use Queries," you'll learn how easy it is to manipulate your data and the database itself using action queries. Today, you'll learn how to use expressions in queries, the meaning of joins, and some other highly useful, but often overlooked query capabilities. The following list shows the topics discussed today:

- Using expressions to create query fields
- The nature of the default or equi-join
- Left joins
- Right joins
- Self joins
- Theta joins
- Using ranges in query expressions

Today's lesson uses extensively the tables from the Microsoft-supplied sample database Northwind. These tables, as well as other database objects, are all part of your sample data stored in the folder Day 11 under the name Complex Queries.mdb.

Each feature or technique used today is fairly short in depth, so this day tends to jump around quite a bit from one seemingly unrelated topic to another. Although it's true that these subjects have little in common other than their use in queries, they do form a body of knowledge utterly vital to any serious Access developer.

Don't worry about memorizing each approach or method shown here in one exposure. Just get a feel for what you can do, and keep in mind that you can always come back here when you need a refresher on specifics. For example, it's important to know that you can perform date and time math in queries, but not important to memorize all the parameters of the expressions that do so.

 Tip

An expression is any combination of fields, controls, symbols, and operatives combined to achieve an outcome. The ones you see today to calculate totals, time, or other values work in forms and reports as well as queries, assuming the context is valid. Similarly, the expressions you saw as examples in days covering forms and reports will work in queries.

General Math in Queries

You've already seen how you can use Access functions such as Count() to do columnar calculations. You can use expressions to do various math calculations working across a query. For example, let's say you have a table (or query) with a column for price and another for percentage discount. You can easily create a third column showing the dollar value of the discount or the net cost to your customer. Here's how.

Note

This example uses very simple tables for clarity. Although the sample data is somewhat strained and not realistic in an actual operational scheme, the point is to show by example this aspect of Access queries and not to be a template for a real business.

Task: Using Expressions in Queries

 1. Launch Access and open the Complex Queries database. Start a new query using the Design view. Include the two tables, tblCustomerDiscounts and tblPrices. You might want to examine the Relationships window and the two tables in both

▼ Design and Table views before proceeding to get an idea of these tables' contents and their relationship.

2. Add CustomerName and Discount from tblCustomerDiscounts to the query design grid. Add the Price field from tblPrices to the grid, too. Your screen should resemble Figure 11.1.

FIGURE 11.1

This multitable query will be the start of this expression task.

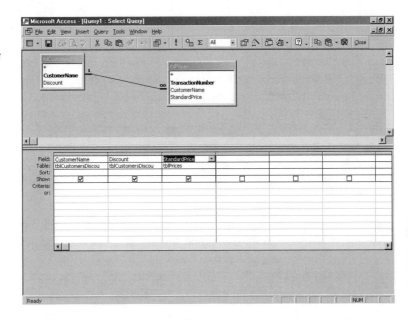

3. Switch to Query view to make sure your query works as you intend it should. Your screen should resemble Figure 11.2.

FIGURE 11.2

Here is your sanity check to make sure your query is functioning properly before moving on.

CustomerName	Discount	StandardPrice
▶ Noisy Noses	2.00%	$56.00
Pip Boys	12.00%	$1,239.00
Value Stores	0.02%	$234.00
Zoom Discounte	2.30%	$948.00
*		

4. Return to Design view. The first calculation to do is the discount amount. Click in the first empty column. Enter the expression

```
Dollar Discount: [Discount]*[StandardPrice]
```

5. This example uses the zoom window (Shift+F2) to enter the expression. You can

▼ see this operation in Figure 11.3.

11

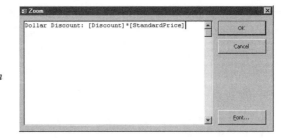

FIGURE 11.3

The query design grid is quite small, so the zoom box comes in handy to avoid typos in query expressions.

6. Switch to Query view. Access will use the string to the left of the expression's colon as a column header, and will place the requested calculation in the query return itself. Your screen should resemble Figure 11.4.

FIGURE 11.4

Access will use the label to the left of the expression colon as a column head.

CustomerName	Discount	StandardPrice	Dollar Discount
Noisy Noses	2.00%	$56.00	1.11999997496605
Pip Boys	12.00%	$1,239.00	148.679996676743
Value Stores	0.02%	$234.00	0.0467999988177326
Zoom Discounters	2.30%	$948.00	21.8040000423789

7. This column now has the right amount, but it is much too precise. Return to Design view, click in the expression column, and then open the Properties list box by clicking on the Properties button in the toolbar. Locate the Format property on the General tab. Pull down the combo box and enter the Currency entry for a value. Your screen should resemble Figure 11.5.

FIGURE 11.5

Query columns have properties, too.

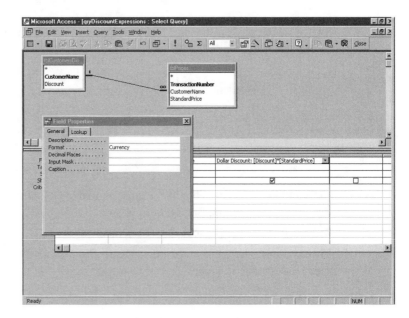

▼
8. Switch to Query view. The discount now appears appropriate to the values it holds. Return to Design view. In the next empty column enter

    `Net: [StandardPrice]-[Dollar Discount]`

9. Switch to Query view. Access now calculates the net amount based on the StandardPrice and the calculated discount amount. Your screen should resemble Figure 11.6.

FIGURE 11.6

Access can include an expression field in another expression.

CustomerName	Discount	StandardPrice	Dollar Discount	Net
Noisy Noses	2.00%	$56.00	$1.12	$54.88
Pip Boys	12.00%	$1,239.00	$148.68	$1,090.32
Value Stores	0.02%	$234.00	$0.05	$233.95
Zoom Discounters	2.30%	$948.00	$21.80	$926.20

▲
10. Save this query, giving it a name of your choosing. This example uses the name qryDiscountExpressions.

Date and Time Math in Queries

Very likely the most used math in queries is calculations of dates and times. Access, through built-in functions, can calculate not only time spans between two fields in a query, but also dynamically calculate time differentials between a field date and the current system date.

> **Note**
> Today's examples, as with the ones before, used Access' built-in functions exclusively. As a developer, you can also create your own functions by using VBA. You'll see how to do this starting in Day 13, "Introducing VBA," and continuing throughout the second half of this book.

Task: Seeing the Results of Date Math in Queries

1. Launch Access and open the Complex Queries database. Start a new query using the Design view. Include the Employees table.

2. Create the following expression and place it in the first column:

    `Name: [TitleOfCourtesy] & " " & [FirstName] & " " & [LastName]`

    This will give you a column with the label Name containing the courtesy title, plus the first and last names of all employees.

3. Switch to Query view to make sure your query is working as it should.

4. Return to Design view. This exercise will create an expression that will calculate the approximate age of the employee at hire date. It will use the two fields

▼

▼ containing the hire date and birth date as a basis for this calculation. Enter the following expression:

```
Age at Hire: DateDiff("yyyy",[BirthDate],[HireDate])
```

5. The `DateDiff()` function calculates the interval between two dates (or times) and returns the value in various forms. The `"yyyy"` parameter tells the function to return the interval in years. If you replace the parameter with `"m"`, your return will be in months. Switch to Query view. Your screen should resemble Figure 11.7.

FIGURE **11.7**

Access made quick work of a date calculation.

Name	Age at Hire
▶ Ms. Nancy Davolio	44
Dr. Andrew Fuller	40
Ms. Janet Leverling	29
Mrs. Margaret Peacock	56
Mr. Steven Buchanan	38
Mr. Michael Suyama	30
Mr. Robert King	34
Ms. Laura Callahan	36
Ms. Anne Dodsworth	28
∗	

6. Switch back to Design view. Access has built-in functions for the current system time. This expression will use one of these functions to calculate the approximate number of years the employee has been working for the company. Enter the following expression:

```
Seniority: DateDiff("yyyy", [HireDate], Date())
```

7. Return to Query view, and you'll see that the new field contains a value giving the approximate number of years an employee has been with the company. The number of years shown will depend upon your system date as returned by the `Date()` function.

 Note

The `DateDiff()` function is hardly perfect. In the preceding two examples it uses calculations based on the year only. A person who hasn't yet met his yearly anniversary still gets credit for the year as if he had. Although these examples serve well as approximates, if your date and time math needs are critical, such as calculating vesting, you'll either need to develop your own functions or create significantly more sophisticated expressions.

▲ 8. Save this query, giving it a name of your choosing. This example uses the name qryDateMath.

The two other significant built-in date functions are `DateAdd()` and `DatePart()`. The first calculates the value of adding time to a date or time. For example, `DateAdd("d", Date(),10)` will return the date 10 days from the current system date. If you enter the expression `DatePart("m",Date())`, Access will return the current system month.

Out of Order Sorting

Access will sort, or order, using fixed sort values. For example, depending upon whether the sort order is ascending or descending, Access will sort the following states like

```
California
Kansas
North Dakota
```

or

```
North Dakota
Kansas
California
```

There is no way you can convince Access, under usual circumstances, that the order you want is

```
Kansas
California
North Dakota
```

Similarly, you can't get Access, without some tricks, to sort in days of the week order, as the day names aren't alphabetically sequential. Figure 11.8 shows the results of applying such a trick.

11

FIGURE 11.8

By including a phantom field, you can sort in a way Access isn't naturally able to sort, but it requires extra storage space and data entry bother.

 Many Access developers get around this problem by adding a number field to a table, adding a number to any data, and then sorting on the number field but leaving it out of the query return. Figure 11.8 shows such a return sorted by date of week. This is the qryFalseData query that is part of your sample data. Figure 11.9 shows the construction of a query with a "phantom" or non-display field.

Although this technique will work, and is used quite often, it's inflexible. In addition, this technique not only adds extraneous data to a table, but it requires either an extra (but related) table or additional data entry.

You can also use the Switch() function, which is a superior way to solve this and similar dilemmas. Open the qryInvisibleSort query in Query view. Note the default sort order is the order of the AutoNumber field. The boss wants to sort this query in the following order:

```
Colorado
Kansas
North Dakota
California
Arizona
```

Note there is no way to do this by sorting, in either ascending or descending order, on any of the data fields available in this table or query.

To accomplish this seemingly impossible task, add the following expression to the first empty column:

```
Switch(Office="Colorado",1,Office="Kansas",2,Office="North Dakota",3,
➥Office="California",4,Office="Arizona",5)
```

Sort this column in ascending order. Your screen should resemble Figure 11.10.

Uncheck the check box to exclude the last field from the query return and switch to Query view. Your screen should resemble Figure 11.11.

FIGURE 11.9

The day order shown comes from an extra sorted field not included in the query return.

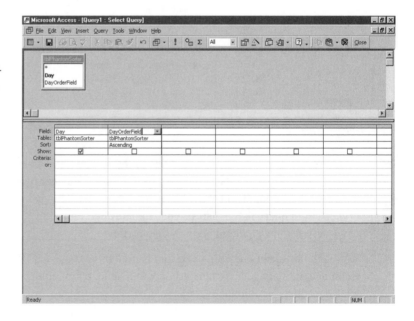

FIGURE 11.10

The Switch() *function examines a field and replaces found values with ones you specify.*

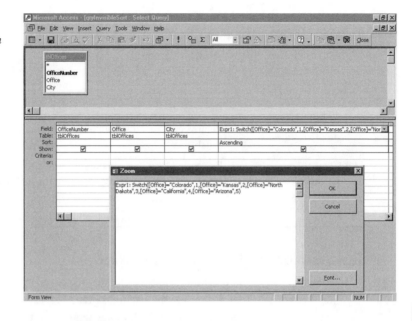

FIGURE 11.11

The query is now ordered in a manner impossible using only the data within either the query or the table itself.

OfficeNumber	Office	City
3	Colorado	Durango
4	Kansas	Fizro
5	North Dakota	Fargo
1	California	Burbank
2	Arizona	Sedona
(AutoNumber)		

11

Using an identical technique, you can order table data any way you want without including phantom fields to sort upon.

 The finished query shown in Figure 11.11 is part of your sample data for today, and is saved under the name qryInvisibleSort-Done.

Joins

When querying two or more tables, you'll note that Access indicates the linked or joined fields by a line. There are several different characteristics of this join. By far the most often used join is the one used by default (inner), but you should also gain familiarity with outer joins because they do come in handy during database development.

The Table 11.1 lists the three common joins used between two tables. The section after the table gives examples to illustrate the short explanations for these concepts. All explanations use specifics from the qryJoins query.

TABLE 11.1 JOIN TYPES

Join	Description
Inner	Returns only records from both sides where the join from both tables equal.
Left Outer	Returns all the records from tblJoinSuppliers whether or not there are any corresponding records from tblJoinProducts.
Right Outer	Returns all the records from tblJoinProducts whether or not there are any corresponding records from tblJoinProducts.

Task: Exploring the Three Join Types

1. Launch Access and open the Complex Queries database. Open the qryJoins query in Query view. Your screen should resemble Figure 11.12. This is an inner join in which there must be records from both tables (equal) for the query to return something in its selection.

FIGURE 11.12

An inner or equal join returns only records where there is correspondence in both tables.

SupplierID	Suppliers	Products
	Boxing Ring	Widges
1	Boxing Ring	Gigits
1	Boxing Ring	Slamming Sammmies
2	Ammo Dump	Whamos
(AutoNumber)		

2. Switch to Design view. Double-click on the line joining the two tables. This will bring up the Join Properties dialog box as shown in Figure 11.13. Click on the second option button for a left outer join, click OK to close the dialog box, and then return to Query view to see the results. Your screen should resemble Figure 11.14.

Note

In most situations, you would establish a link in Tools, Relationships between tables holding supplier and product information. You would also make sure, through referential integrity, that your users couldn't enter a product without a supplier. This example purposely leaves out this common (and usually required) link to demonstrate a right join.

FIGURE 11.13

The Join Properties dialog box enables you to change join types. It also gives an excellent description of the results of changing join types.

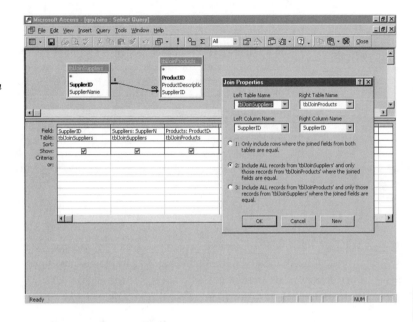

FIGURE 11.14

By switching the join type, the query now returns all suppliers even if there is no record of any of its products in the system. This is a left outer join.

SupplierID	Suppliers	Products
1	Boxing Ring	Widges
1	Boxing Ring	Gigits
1	Boxing Ring	Slamming Sammmies
2	Ammo Dump	Whamos
3	Soccer Kick	
4	Baseball Hit	
(AutoNumber)		

3. Switch to Design view. Again bring up the Join Properties list box, but this time switch to the third option by clicking the appropriate button. Close the dialog box and switch to Query view. Your screen should resemble Figure 11.15.

FIGURE 11.15

The right outer join will return all products even if no suppliers are associated with them.

SupplierID	Suppliers	Products
		No Supplier Mitts
1	Boxing Ring	Widges
1	Boxing Ring	Gigits
1	Boxing Ring	Slamming Sammmies
2	Ammo Dump	Whamos
(AutoNumber)		

4. Close the query, discarding changes.

> **Note**
>
> Some developers claim there are no such things as outer joins because the Access SQL statement for a left outer join can make do with just `left join`, while the statement for a right outer join can make do with just right join. Similarly, there are no inner joins because all common SQL dialects use the = sign, so they are really equi-joins or equal joins. However, when speaking descriptively, people use the term *outer* to indicate all the records from the left or right table should be returned. SQL is not standard across all implementations. Most SQL implementations use the full syntax for a right or left join, which does include the word *outer* as in `left outer`.

Self-Join

You can join a table to itself to select data from the single table in a way identical to that if the data were located in two tables. For example, assume you have a table with commission and salary data in it. You want to see the salaries that are higher than a certain commission value. A self-join is a way to do this.

To construct a *self-join*, add the same table twice to the query design grid. Access will add a "_1" to the second table you add. If you want, you can click the Properties button on the toolbar and give an alias to this second table. From there on, you can refer to this table by its alias. Figure 11.16 shows the Table Properties list box with an alias added.

FIGURE 11.16

You can give tables or queries included in queries a new working name through the Alias property.

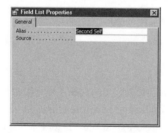

From here, what you do depends upon your goal. Most often, you'll drag to create a join on the two fields you want to join on, and then use either an expression as criteria in an expression field or construct a SQL statement using the WHERE keyword. For example, if you wanted to display records in which the salary was higher than the commission and your two table instances were aliased TableOne and TableTwo, your WHERE statement would look like the following:

```
WHERE TableOne.Salary < TableTwo.Commission;
```

You can also enter a criteria expression that would look like the following in the Commission field, if you prefer to enter expressions and let Access create the SQL statement:

```
>TableOne.Salary
```

 If you are confused, don't be alarmed. There is a query called qrySelfJoin that's part of the sample data for today. Open it in both the Design and Query views to get an idea of how it works. Experiment with the expression in the Commission field to see how editing this changes things. Try especially changing the lesser than symbol to a greater than symbol.

Although you won't hit the full discussion on SQL until Day 14, "Understanding SQL," the statement for this query is

```
SELECT tblSelfJoin.Name, [Second Self].Commission
FROM tblSelfJoin INNER JOIN tblSelfJoin AS [Second Self] ON tblSelfJoin.
➥ EmployeeNumber = [Second Self].EmployeeNumber
WHERE ((([Second Self].Commission)<[tblSelfJoin].[Salary]));
```

If you're feeling adventurous, try editing the statement to include more fields or the WHERE statement. Remember, as long as you don't save the query under the same name, you can't "ruin" it. Just close without saving and re-open to start afresh or restore from the CD. Figure 11.17 shows this query running, and Figure 11.18 shows the Design view.

FIGURE 11.17

This query returns only those records in which the commission is less than the salary. The single table acts as if its data is stored in two tables.

Name	Commission
Jones	$1,200.00
Buechlein	$3,400.00

11

FIGURE 11.18

The key to making this query work as desired is the dragged join between the two table instances (one aliased) and the expression in the Commission column shown here in the Zoom dialog box.

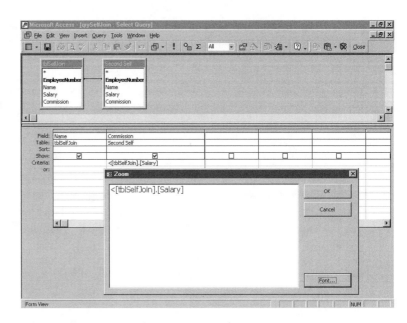

Inner to Theta Joins

NEW TERM An *inner*, or *equi-join*, is a specific case of the general case theta join. An equi-join returns records in which the linked fields are equal. This makes sense when joining text fields such as the name of a supplier.

NEW TERM *Theta joins* are more flexible, allowing the return where linked fields are not only equal, but greater than or lesser than. Although this doesn't have much use, if any, in true text data, it does when the data is numerical even if the data type for the field is set to Text. This includes not only data types of numbers and currency, but also dates and time.

The easiest way to create such joins is to edit the SQL statement for an equi-join to read another operator. To do this, perform the following steps:

1. Create the inner (equi-joined) query using whichever technique you prefer.
2. Switch to SQL view using the View button on the toolbar.
3. Locate the equal sign (=) and edit to <, >, <=, or >=.

Using Ranges in Queries

By adding a simple expression you can create queries that return a range of returns. The following task takes you through such a query.

Task: Creating a Query That Returns a Value Range

▼TASK

1. Launch Access and open the Complex Queries database. Start a new query using the Design view. Include the Products and Suppliers tables. Add the CompanyName field from Suppliers and the ProductName and UnitPrice fields from Products. Switch to Query view. Your screen should resemble Figure 11.19. Note that 77 records are returned.

FIGURE 11.19

It's always a good idea to see whether your query is working properly as you construct it. This avoids complex debugging if, in the end, you note the query's return is wrong or questionable.

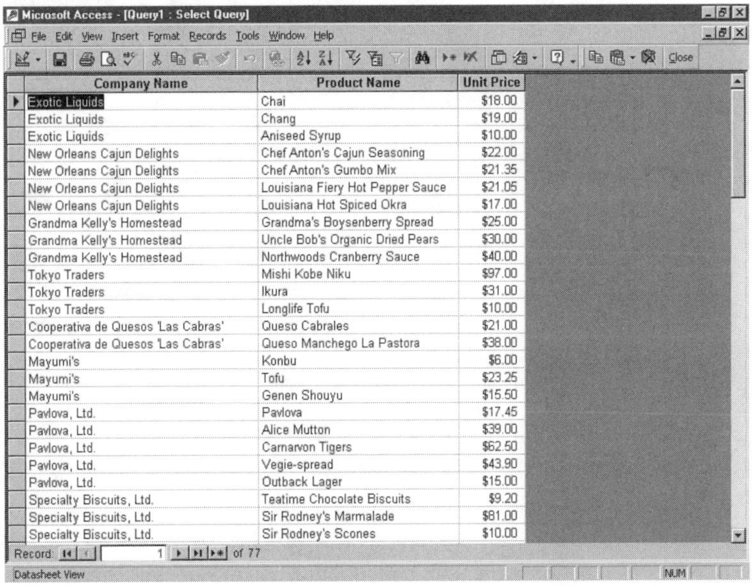

11

2. Return to Design view. Create the following expression in the criteria row of the UnitPrice column:

   ```
   Between 34 and 100
   ```

   Return to Query view. This time Access returns 29 records—only those in which the price is between $34.00 and $100.00, inclusive.

3. Return to Design view. Delete the criteria for UnitPrice. Enter the following expression in the criteria row of the CompanyName field:

   ```
   Between A* and C*
   ```

   This will restrict the return to those suppliers with a name starting with A, B, or C. Switch to Query view to see whether it works as you expect it to.

4. Return to Design view. Edit the expression in CompanyName to read

   ```
   Between E* and F*
   ```

▼

▼   Add a criterion on the second criteria row of UnitPrice of

           >100

           Your screen should resemble Figure 11.20.

FIGURE 11.20

Remember that criteria added on two different rows creates an OR criteria.

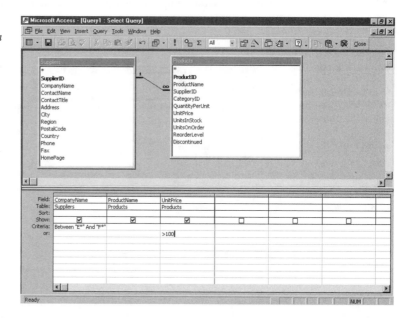

5. Return to Query view. Your return should be any record in which the supplier's company name begins with an *E* or an *F* or the UnitPrice is over $100.00. This is an example of using an OR criteria query with a range. Keep in mind that you can mix and match query types and expressions at will as long as you don't violate
▲   query logic.

Summary

Today's discussion dealt with query issues, which were, for the most part, considerably more complex than previous days. Don't feel bad if the entire material hasn't sunk in yet. Knowing how to construct something like a self-join isn't intuitive at all. The important thing is to know such constructs exist so when you need them, you'll at least know what to look up either in this text or in online help.

Besides various joins, you saw how to construct a new field in a query using an expression. You can also create new fields based on other expression fields. Finally, you saw how to construct ranges in queries and combine them with other criteria, which can be optionally ranged, too.

Q&A

Q Is it better to break data up so I never have to use a self-join?

A Doing so is possible, but you'll then run the risk of "over normalizing" your data. This is the process of breaking it into such small pieces that you inhibit the working of your database. For example, if you had salary and commission in two tables, you must have link fields and the links to relate back to the employee. In this and similar instances, the extra table isn't worth the effort.

Q Can I use dates in ranges?

A Yes. Doing so is identical to using any numerical data. For example, the following expression is perfectly valid to return records from April 5, 1990 to April 5, 1999, inclusive:

```
Between #4/5/90# and #4/5/99#
```

Q May I construct expressions with product and divisor operands?

A Yes. The product operand is an asterisk (*), the divisor operand is a slash (/). The exponentiation operand is a carat (Shift+6 or ^).

Q Can I query an existing query? What is the difference between doing this and querying a table?

A You can query an existing query just as you can a table. Operationally there is no difference. When run, Access will execute the queries sequentially. This does take some additional processing time.

11

Workshop

The Workshop helps you solidify the skills you learned in this lesson. Answers to the quiz questions appear in Appendix A, "Answers."

Quiz

1. How does Access store date and time information?

2. Must you use only built-in Access functions in queries?

3. What is the most commonly used built-in Access function for calculating date or time intervals?

4. What use is the Switch() function?

Exercises

1. Open up the query qrySelfJoin in Design view.

2. Alter either the expression or the SQL statement to return records in which the commission is less than the salary. Switch to Query view to see whether it worked as you expect.

3. Close the qrySelfJoin, discarding changes.

4. Create a new query using the Products and Suppliers tables. Have the query show the CompanyName, the ProductName, and the UnitPrice.

5. Create a criterion in which the only records returned were those in which the ProductName is in the range of the first letter starting with the letters R, S, T, U. Move to Query view to see whether it worked as you expect.

Extra credit for those who feel adventurous:

6. Remove the criterion from step 5. Create a criterion returning only those records in which the second letter of the CompanyName is the letter *e*. Hint: Use the Mid() function.

DAY 12

Developing Reports with Graphics and Expressions

Whether you like it or not, getting printed output from your database is not as simple as sending a printout to the printer. With the use of computers, readers' expectations are higher than ever. If you generate a simple printout, you are likely to get comments from everyone about its formatting. You will also get requests to see the data in another way or summarized. With Access 2000, you can add many of the formatting—desktop publishing—features suggested by your readers as well as use expressions to summarize the data.

Today's lesson covers the following topics:

- Examining complex reports
- Exploring the Report property sheet
- Adding images to reports
- Using expressions in reports
- Working with subreports
- Creating reports with multiple columns

To follow along with today's lesson, you'll need the sample database, Students.mdb, from the CD-ROM that accompanies this book. You'll find the database in \Day12\.

Students.mdb is based on the scenario that this database is used to manage the classes and student assignments for a high school. You must copy it to another location to allow you to save your work in this lesson.

Examining Complex Reports

In Day 6, "Generating Basic Reports," you had an opportunity to explore the Access reporting capability. You created reports from scratch, as well as used the Report Wizard to create more complex reports automatically. As you worked with the Report Wizard, you might have noticed that it added some additional formatting that created more professional reports. You might have also noticed areas that you might want to change for additional emphasis.

For example, some additional formatting was added by the Report Wizard in rptSchoolRoster (see Figure 12.1) to give you information about the report and when it was printed.

FIGURE 12.1

The Report Wizard added expressions to show the date the report was printed as well as page numbers in the footer.

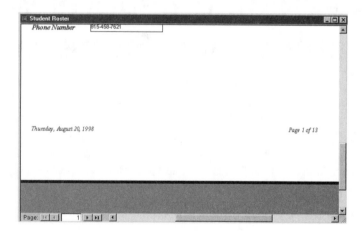

Expressions can be used to add information about the report. They can also be used to calculate information from the data and make the data look better.

One thing that you will notice about the data in rptSchoolRoster is that each field gets a spot of its own. This can increase the time it takes to read the information because there are more lines to read. You might want to modify the roster to display the information the way it is displayed for each mailing label in rptMailingLabels (see Figure 12.2).

FIGURE 12.2

The Labels Wizard uses unbound controls and expressions to concatenate the data to make it easier to read.

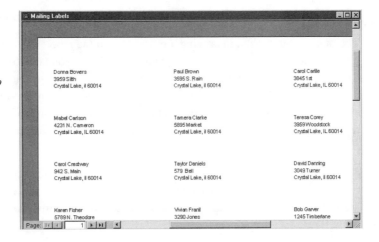

This approach reduces the space needed to display the data. It isn't perfect in the mailing labels because the state is in lowercase in many places. An expression can solve this problem as well.

The concatenation would allow you to condense the student roster and add some additional embellishment. You could add a graphic at the top, change the formatting of the text, and display the information in columns as shown in rptFinalRoster (see Figure 12.3).

FIGURE 12.3

The rptFinalRoster report shows some of the improvements that can be added.

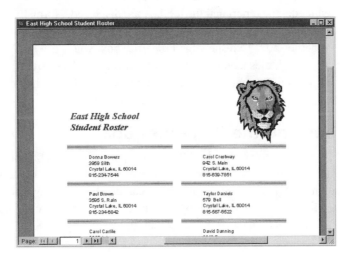

12

The rest of this lesson focuses on how to get reports with these formatting techniques. This lesson also demonstrates how to display graphics stored in a table and use charting. It also shows you how to display related information for a record in a subreport.

Exploring the Report Property Sheet

The place to start when improving a report is with the report and control properties. As a general rule, letting Access do as much as possible for you is a good idea. Most of the time, you will begin with the Report Wizard. It enables you to select the data source, add any grouping and sorting settings, select a layout and orientation, select a formatting style, and set the title for the report. This will save a lot of time when you are creating reports, but rarely is this the final version of the report that you are going to want to print.

After you let the Report Wizard set up the initial layout for the report, you can open the report in Design mode and make any necessary changes. For this part of the lesson, you are going to modify the rptStudentRoster report. To get started, complete the following steps.

Task: Opening a Report in Design Mode

1. Open the \Day12\Students.mdb file.
2. Select the Reports from the Objects list in the Database window.
3. Select rptStudentRoster and select the Design button.
4. Select File, Save As to open the Save As dialog to allow you to save the report with a new name, such as rptModifiedRoster, if you want.

You are now ready to begin making changes to the report. When you open a report in Design mode, the report and the toolbox are displayed. Normally, your first step is not to add controls from the toolbox, but you want to modify report properties. You must open the Properties box. To display the Properties box, you can select View, Properties or select the Properties icon from the Report Design toolbar. After the Property box is displayed, you might want to move it so that it is in the lower-right corner of your screen so you can see more of the report, as shown in Figure 12.4.

Examining the Properties Box

The Properties box is organized the same regardless of what object you are working with in Microsoft Access 2000. The Properties box displays a list of all the properties that can be set in Design mode. Some properties can be accessed only when the report is displayed in Print Preview. The Properties box has tabs representing the property categories, as well as a tab to view all the properties alphabetically.

Report Selector   Properties

FIGURE 12.4

The rptModifiedRoster report, shown in Design mode with the Properties box displayed.

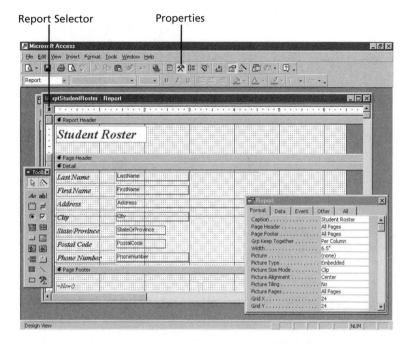

The first tab is the Format tab, which lists the properties that affect the format of the report as a whole. One of the first things you might want to change is the Caption property. It controls what text is displayed on the title bar of the report when you view the report in Print Preview. If you used the Report Wizard to create the report, the caption and the label in the Report Header will both display the text that was entered at the time you created the report. That text is also used to name the report.

If you are going to use the naming conventions recommended for Microsoft Access 2000 objects, this will present a dilemma. You can either enter the text you want to display in the Report Wizard and go back and rename the report in the Database window, or enter the name of the report and change the caption and the label in the report itself. If you want the title for the report to be East High School Student Roster, you must complete the following task.

Task: Changing the Report Caption

▼ TASK

1. Make sure the report is selected by clicking the Report Selection button.

2. In the Properties sheet, click in the Caption Property entry area at the beginning of the text box or press the Home key to move to the beginning of the property value.

▼

> After you have placed the cursor in the entry area for any property, you can use any of the standard keyboard navigation keys to move the cursor. You can use Home to get to the beginning of the entry area or End to move to the end of the entry area.

▲   3. Type East High School with a trailing space in front of Student Roster.

To change the caption for the label in the Report Header, follow this task.

Task: Changing the Title Label Caption Property

1. Click on the label to select it.
2. Click in the Caption Property entry area.
3. Type East High School and a space.

Notice that the label is no longer wide enough to display the text. You can modify the width of the label by dragging the right handle to the right until the text is displayed.

Tips for Adjusting Width

Another way you can adjust the width of an object is by using the Width property. Notice that as you drag the right handle of the label, the Width property adjusts to reflect the new dimensions.

With a report, the Width property works a little differently. If you click on the Report Selection button and take a look at the Width property, you will notice that it is set to 6.5 inches. If you are using standard 8.5×11-inch paper, there are two inches unaccounted for. The Width property for the report is only part of the settings.

If you select File, Page Setup, you will see that the missing two inches are actually represented as your left and right margins on the Margins tab. This means that you must be more careful when you adjust the width for the report. To illustrate the possible problem, adjust your report width in the following task.

Task: Experimenting with the Report Width

1. Close the Page Setup dialog, if it is still open.
2. Drag the right margin for the report to 7" on the ruler or type 7.0 for the Width property with the whole report selected.
▲   3. Click the View button on the toolbar to display the report in Print Preview.

The report will not automatically be displayed in Print Preview. An error message will be displayed (see Figure 12.5). This is just informing you that the Width property for the report and the page margins are greater that the width of the physical page.

FIGURE **12.5**

*The message box will
appear when you
attempt to preview a
report that exceeds the
page dimensions.*

After you click OK to continue the preview display, the first page of the report will be displayed and look fine. If you click the Two Page button on the toolbar, you can see the problem (see Figure 12.6). The larger Width property has forced the remainder to page 2. It creates a blank page with no information and without the page footer information.

FIGURE **12.6**

*When you click OK, it
will display the report
in Print Preview, but
with a blank second
page.*

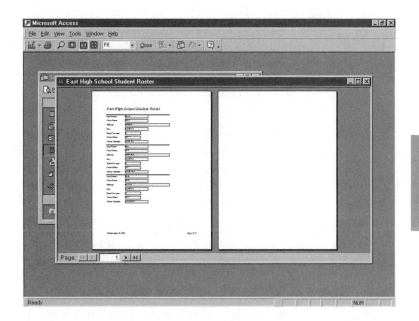

12

You must understand this problem because the Width property can be changed unintentionally. If you try to place a control too close to the right edge of the report so that it doesn't have room to be displayed, Microsoft Access 2000 will adjust the width for you. You might want to make a practice of checking the Width property after making any changes to the report.

To continue working with this report, you need to reset the Width property in the following task.

Task: Resetting the Report Width

1. Click the View button to return to the Design mode.

2. Click on the Width property for the report.

3. Change it back to 6.5.

Changing the Text Box's Border

Another change you might want to make to the appearance of this report is to remove the borders around the fields. This can be done with the Border Color property for the field text boxes. This can be most easily accomplished with the Line/Color drop-down list on the Formatting toolbar. You can select the text box and select transparent from the drop-down list to clean up the appearance of the text boxes.

> **Note**
>
> When you adjust properties in the Property sheet, you'll see that each property uses a space in its two-word name, such as Border Color. However, when you start manipulating object properties using VBA in Day 13, you'll use the names of properties without a space and in title caps, such as BorderColor.

Examining the Data Properties

The second category of properties is the Data category, shown on the Data tab. It allows you to control what data is displayed on the report. The first property on the Data tab is the one that you will work with the most. The Record Source property identifies where the data for the report is coming from.

When this report was created by the Report Wizard, it was based on tblStudents. You can base a report on a table, query, data definition, or create a SQL statement specifically for the report.

> **Tip**
>
> It is a good idea to avoid basing a report on a table if you are not going to use all the fields. This reduces the amount of time needed to generate the report because it will have to return less data.

If you have the query already defined, you can simply pick that from the drop-down list for this property or you can build a SQL statement by using the Build button next to the drop-down arrow. Because you already have the table selected, you will get a message when you click the Build button (see Figure 12.7). You do want to use tblStudents for the base of the query, so you can click Yes.

FIGURE 12.7

This message verifies that you want to use the selected table as the basis for the SQL statement.

After you select Yes, Access will display the SQL Statement: Query Builder window. It works just like the Query Design window. You can simply drag the fields that you want to use for the report down to the field table. When you have completed that step, you can click its Close button to return to your report. It will prompt you to save your settings. You will need to click the Yes button.

Now you will see the SQL statement displayed as the record source. This SQL statement was created based on your choices in the Query Builder. For more information about that SQL statement, please refer to Day 14, "Understanding SQL."

Introducing the Event and Other Properties

The other two categories store properties that affect the behavior of the report. The Event properties allow you to control how the report behaves as it is opened, previewed, and closed. You can add actions to these properties using macros or using Visual Basic for Applications (VBA) procedures. You had an opportunity to explore macros on Day 7, "Automating Your Access App: A Macro Primer." VBA is introduced on Day 13, "Introducing VBA," and further explored in Day 19, "Working with VBA."

The Other category stores many of the properties that are used as you create an Access application. You can add a custom menu or toolbar or add special help access. All of these are discussed later in this book. For now, you are going to continue embellishing your report with images.

12

Adding Images to Reports

Adding graphic images is one method for adding emphasis to your reports. They can be "attention getters" to draw the reader's eyes to your information. There are several methods for adding images to your reports:

- You can add an image that will print on every page of the report.
- You can add an image in a specific location in your report using the Image control.
- You can add images that have been stored in a table as an object.
- You can add a chart based on your data.

Adding a Repeating Image

The first method for adding graphics to your report is to add a graphic to the report itself. This can be done with the Picture property. For example, you want to add the school mascot to this report. You could add the image to the report itself by completing the following task.

Task: Setting the Report's Picture Property

1. Select the report with the Report Selection button.
2. Select the Picture property in the Properties box.
3. Click the Builder button to the right of the property to display the Insert Picture dialog.
4. Use the dialog to select a graphic file, such as the lion clip art file that ships with Microsoft Office 2000. It is in the \Program Files\Common Files\Microsoft Shared\ClipArt\cagcat50 folder. The file is an01124_.wmf.
5. Click OK to add the image to your report.

After you have completed these steps, you will see the graphic of the lion in the center of your report (see Figure 12.8). This is a great way to add graphics, but you must be aware of the graphic's placement in the report. As you can see, the graphic is actually placed behind the other controls. When you preview the report, the controls could hide part of the graphic if the data were long enough to fill the field.

You might want to use some of the other picture properties to control its placement and behavior. The Picture Type property allows you to determine whether the graphic becomes part of the database file or whether it represents a link to the original graphic. By default, this property is set to Embedded. This means that the graphic is a part of your database. This also means that the size of your database will include the size of the graphic, but it will preview and print faster.

FIGURE 12.8

The graphic is displayed in the center of the report.

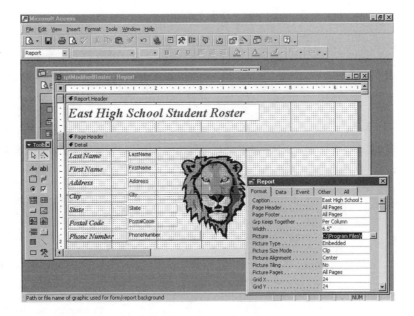

Linked is the other setting for the Picture Type property. This reduces the size of the database because the graphic remains an independent file. This also means that the report will preview and print slower because the graphic will have to be loaded each time you need the report. It also means that the directory where the graphic was loaded must be available on every machine that accesses the database and report.

The next property is Picture Size Mode. This determines how the graphic will be displayed. The default setting is Clip, which means that the graphic will be displayed in its original size. You can also select Stretch to enlarge the graphic to meet the dimensions, regardless of any distortion that might occur due to a mismatch of proportions between the report and the graphic. The other choice is to select Zoom. This will make the graphic as large as possible, but will preserve its aspect ratio.

The next property is the Picture Alignment property, which enables you to place the graphic in a specific location on the page. By default, it is placed in the center. You can change it to display the graphic in the Top Left, Top Right, Bottom Left, or Bottom Right. For the lion, it would be nice to get it out of the way of the data and place it in the top right. Notice that it appears to go behind the sections. It is placed on the page, regardless of any settings in the sections.

12

The Picture Tiling property enables you to cover the page with the graphic, and the Picture Pages property allows you to determine whether the graphic will print on all pages, the first page, or no pages. For the purposes of this report, you want to display it on the first page only, with the Report Header.

Setting a graphic image as part of the background is a great way to add emphasis to your report. Using the Picture property, you can use Windows Metafiles, enhanced metafiles, device independent bitmaps, bitmaps, icons, PC Paintbrush, JPEG, Windows bitmaps, Corel Draw, Encapsulated PostScript, GIF, Macintosh PICT, Portable Network Graphics, Targa, tagged image file format, and WordPerfect Graphics.

Do	Don't
DO consider your decision to use graphics carefully. Graphics will make your report preview and print slower because of the resources needed to display the report.	DON'T overdo it with graphics. You want to use graphic sparingly and when possible use only black-and-white graphics. This is especially true if you are sending it to a black-and-white printer where the color would be wasted anyway.

Using the Image Control

Another method for adding images to your report is to use the Image control. This allows you to add graphics to a specific location. For example, the Report Wizard added a line above the Last Name field to provide a visual separation between records. If you decide to make that separation more flashy, you could use one of the smaller clip art files for better emphasis.

To replace the line with a image, complete the following task.

Task: Adding Graphics with the Image Control

1. Select the line and press the Delete key.
2. Move the other controls down a little bit.
3. Select the Image control from the toolbox.
4. Click above the Last Name field to open the Insert Picture dialog.
5. Select a graphic to be displayed like the one of the divider clip art file that ships with Microsoft Office 2000. It is in the \Program Files\Common Files\Microsoft Shared\ClipArt\Themes1\Lines folder. The file is bd21348_.wmf.
6. Change the Size Mode to Stretch so you can resize the image to make it wider.

7. Make the width of the image 4.5".

8. Save and preview the report.

9. Close the report.

When you preview the report, you now have this more decorative border. Images can be placed anywhere on the report. When they are placed in the Detail section, they will be repeated with each record.

> **Tip**
>
> When you preview this report, notice that the image is above each record, but it doesn't follow the last record on the page. If you want to have it at the bottom of each page to maintain symmetry, you can copy the control and paste it in the page footer above the date and page number.

Adding Images from a Table

Microsoft Access 2000 also supports the integration of graphics for specific records. When you are creating your table definitions, you define the name, data type, and properties for each field. One of the data types is an OLE object.

Object Linking and Embedding (OLE) enables you to take advantage of data that was created in another application, such as Microsoft Word or Microsoft Excel. It can also be used to integrate graphics. With Microsoft Access 2000, you can insert a graphic or link to a graphic file on a record-by-record basis. In all cases, the application that created the object must be installed on the user's computer.

To give you an opportunity to try OLE object integration, the tblDepartment table has an OLE Object field for the department logo. This can be used to help identify it in the course catalog or department list. As mentioned earlier, OLE requires that the application used to create the objects must be installed on the user's computer.

>
>
> In the earlier examples, graphics from the Microsoft clip art collection were used. The clip art is supplied in the Windows metafile format. Microsoft Paint doesn't allow you to edit that format, so unless you have another graphics package installed that supports the WMF format, you couldn't work with the clip art as an OLE object.

 To facilitate this example, four clip art images from Macmillan's Imagine It! 111,000 Graphics have been added to the database on the CD as embedded objects (see Table 12.1).

TABLE 12.1 CLIP ART FILES

Department	Filename
English	1845536.pcx
Math	1845804.pcx
Science	1845802.pcx
Social Studies	1845504.pcx

When you work with OLE objects in Access, there are two controls in the toolbox. The Unbound Object Frame is for an object that will not be linked to data in a table, and the Bound Object Frame is for an object that is tied to data in a table. With the exception of one property setting, the process for adding these controls to a report is the same. To add a Bound Object Frame to a department list, complete the following task.

Task: Using the Object Frames

1. Open the rptDepartments report.
2. Select File, Save As, enter `rptModifiedDepartments` as the name, and click OK.
3. Click on the Bound Object Frame in the toolbox.
4. Point to approximately the 1.5" mark in the Detail section of the report and click. (Access will insert a very large frame with a label, as shown in Figure 12.9.)

FIGURE 12.9

This is the original size of the Bound Object Frame.

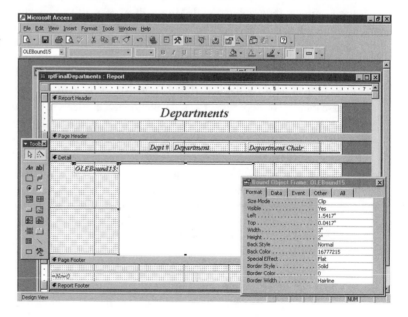

▼   5. Click on the label and press the Delete key.

   6. Select View, Properties or click the Properties button on the toolbar to open the Properties window.

   7. Set the Width and Height properties for the Image control to 1.25" and drag it to the left so that you can see the other controls.

   8. Resize the Detail section to eliminate the whitespace below the controls.

   9. Click on the Data tab and set the Record Source property to display the DepartmentLogo field.

   10. Click on the Format tab and set the Size Mode property to Zoom. This way, the OLE object will be displayed within the confines of the control, instead of only displaying the portion of the graphic that will fit in the space.

   11. Set the Border Style property to Transparent to remove the thin line around this object.

   12. Select the View button on the toolbar to display the report in Print Preview (see Figure 12.10).

FIGURE 12.10

The report now displays the graphic that is stored in tblDepartments.

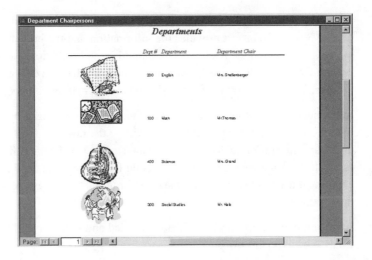

12

When you are working with the Bound OLE object, you must set the Record Source property as well as the Size Mode property. The other property settings were strictly for formatting purposes.

After you placed the control, you adjusted the size and placement of the control. In this example, you were using exact measurements for the size. In most cases, you will have to preview your report with the control to judge what size the control needs to be.

The Border Style property is set as a hairline border by default. This was removed in this example to minimize the fact that the graphics have different dimensions. Unfortunately, the object frames do not have the Picture Alignment property to allow you to adjust the placement of the graphic in the control.

> When you are planning to store graphics data in a table, whether it is to display a logo or a person's photograph, it is a good idea to keep the size consistent. It will make your reports look more professional.

Adding a Chart

Another graphic element that can be added to your reports is a chart. Many people have an easier time comparing numerical data when it is presented in a chart. With Microsoft Access 2000, you can create a chart of your data with the help of the Chart Wizard. Like all the wizards, the Chart Wizard will prompt you to select the information you want to chart, as well as to determine the characteristics of the chart.

As an example, consider a comparison of student counts. You can create a simple query like qryStudentCounts. It provides the information, but the burden of interpreting the information is up to the reader. A chart could provide additional assistance with interpreting the information. The good news is that the Chart Wizard makes this a painless process. The biggest job is to determine what information you need for your chart.

In the query, qryStudentCounts, the information is summarized by the query. When you want to chart data, you are better off providing the raw data for the Chart Wizard. In the query qryStudentCountChart, the raw data is provided. The first field uses an expression to add text for the Year field and the second field is the Year field itself. For more on the expression used as the first field, please refer to the "Using Expressions in Reports" section in this lesson.

After you have determined what data is needed and it is prepared, you are ready to let Chart Wizard do the work.

Task: Using the Chart Wizard

1. Select the reports from the Database window.
2. Select New to open the New dialog.
3. Select Chart Wizard from the list, and select qryStudentCountChart as the query to base the report on.
4. Click OK to start the Chart Wizard (see Figure 12.11).

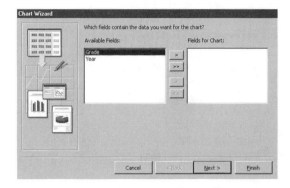

FIGURE 12.11

The Chart Wizard first must know what to chart.

5. Add both fields from the list to the chart and select Next to display the Chart Type selection (see Figure 12.12).

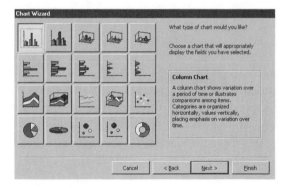

FIGURE 12.12

The Chart Wizard has 20 chart types available.

6. Select Pie Chart from the list of 20 types and select Next to adjust the data layout (see Figure 12.13).

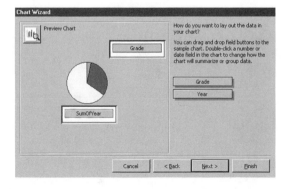

FIGURE 12.13

The Chart Wizard can summarize information using several expressions.

12

▼ 7. Double-click the field named SumOfYear to choose the summary type in the Summarize dialog (see Figure 12.14).

FIGURE 12.14

The Summarize dialog box enables you to select the expression to use.

8. Select Count from the Summarize dialog and click OK.

9. Select Next to add a title and additional elements (see Figure 12.15).

FIGURE 12.15

You can add a title and legend with the Chart Wizard.

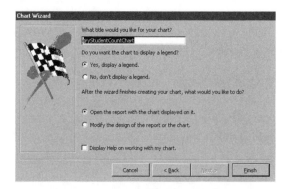

10. Enter Student Counts as the title for the report and click Finish to generate your chart (see Figure 12.16).

FIGURE 12.16

The Chart Wizard creates a chart using the data provided.

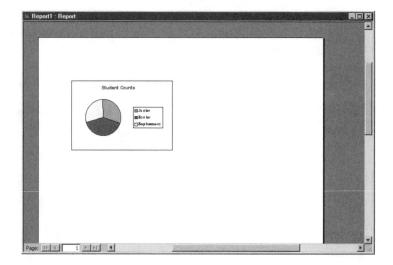

▼

▼
▲
11. Save the report as rptStudentCountChart and click the View button to switch to Design view.

The chart created might not exactly meet your expectations, but it does a lot of the work for you. Like with any wizard, you will want to customize the report from Design view.

The Chart Wizard creates a report without a data source with one object in the Detail section. It is an unbound object control. It is an OLE object linking to Microsoft Graph. You can make changes to the report, section, and control properties as well as make changes to the chart itself.

Modifying the Properties

Making changes to the report, section, and control properties is the same for this report as for any other. You might want to increase the Width property for the report, adjust the height of the Detail section, and adjust the size of the OLE control to make the chart larger. You might also want to remove the border from the control.

Notice that as you resize the control, the size of the pie chart doesn't change. As with any other graphic, you must set the Size Mode property to Zoom. This will size the chart to fill the space while maintaining the size ratio. The result will give you a chart that fills more of the page and doesn't look like a separate entity (see Figure 12.17).

FIGURE 12.17

The chart now looks like it is a part of the report.

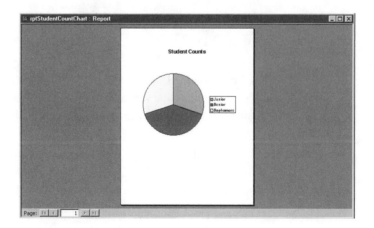

12

Modifying the Chart

When the report is ready to house the chart, you can focus on the characteristics of the chart itself. You might not like the chart placement, legend placement, or title. The chart is created with Microsoft Graph. Any changes to the chart will have to be made using its menus.

Task: Editing a Chart

1. Double-click on the chart to activate the chart and access Microsoft Graph.

2. Notice that a Datasheet window opens and that the menu and toolbar change (see Figure 12.18).

FIGURE 12.18

You now can edit the chart.

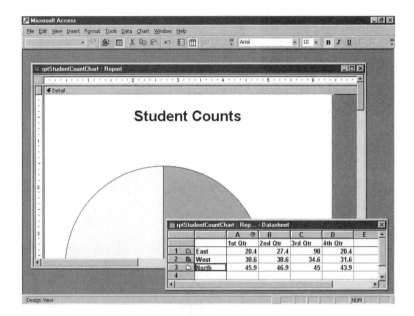

3. Click the Close button on the Datasheet window. Your data is being supplied by your database, so you will not be working with the Datasheet window most of the time. Don't let the text in the row headings bother you; it also will come from the table.

4. Click on the title to select it and notice the frame around the text (see Figure 12.19).

5. Double-click the work Counts to select it.

6. Type Enrollment and press Esc to deselect the title.

7. Double-click the legend to open the Format Legend dialog and select the Placement tab (see Figure 12.20).

8. Select Bottom from the placement list, and click OK.

9. Notice the legend is now below the pie chart and the pie chart is now centered.

10. Click the Report Selection button to return to the report.

▼ 11. Click the View button to see the results with your data (see Figure 12.21).

FIGURE 12.19

The title is selected to be moved or edited.

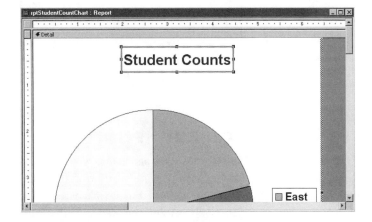

FIGURE 12.20

You can now change the placement of the legend.

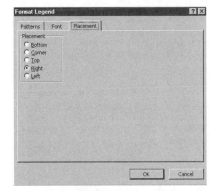

FIGURE 12.21

Now you can see the better format of the report.

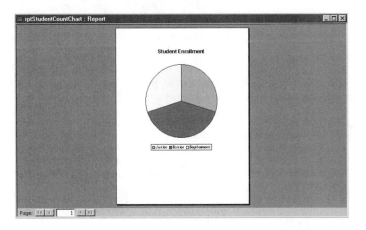

12

Creating charts with Microsoft Access using Microsoft Graph can be very easy. You also can modify them easily. In addition to modifying the title, legend, and chart placement, you can change the colors and labels for each data point and add highlighted text. Another benefit of Microsoft Graph is that it is used for charting with all the Microsoft applications. After you learn it, you can take advantage of it from word or Excel. Unfortunately, there isn't sufficient time in this lesson to explore all the features of Microsoft Graph.

Using Expressions in Reports

On Day 11, "Sorting Data with Queries and Joins," you got a chance to work with expressions to display derived data. When you are working with a database, you want to minimize the amount of data that is stored in the database. Using expressions allows you to minimize data storage as well as to prevent data integrity problems. When you store calculated information as a field, you also run the risk of having incorrect information stored in the table if the record is not updated correctly.

Expressions can assist you with these goals as well as give you flexibility as you work and display your data. Expressions can

- Perform mathematical operations
- Provide summary information, such as totals and averages
- Display information about an object
- Format information together, as with the concatenated fields in rptMailingLabels
- Change the appearance of information in a field
- Evaluate a field value to display other information or action

On Day 11 you got to see expressions in action. You got to see a simple calculation as well as using the Totals row to add summary calculations. You can also use expressions in your reports.

For reports, there are three types of expressions you will be working with. The first type is the simple expression that is a mathematical equation, and the second type uses built-in functions to provide a result. The third type is a custom function created with Visual Basic for Applications, which will be covered in Day 13, Day 18, "Examining VBA," and Day 19.

When you want to create an expression in your report, you must add a control to display the results of the expression. Regardless of whether you are adding a simple expression or a function, you must add a text box to store the results. This text box will not display field data because it's an unbound control.

After the text box is added to the report, you must build the expression. When you want to use an expression, you are going to set the Control Source property equal to your expression rather than a specific field. This is accomplished by typing the equal sign (=) followed by the expression.

Creating an Expression

To begin experimenting with expressions, you are going to create a simple calculation for the rpt1998Assignments report. If you open this report, it shows the scores and the total points, but there isn't a comparison of how the students did.

This can be accomplished with an expression, as illustrated in rptFinal1998Assignments. You must take the student's score, divided by the total points, multiplied by the percentage of the total grade:

```
=Score/MaximumPoints*PercentofGrade
```

Task: Adding a Comparison Expression

1. Open the rpt1998AssignmentPerformance report.
2. Select File, Save As.
3. Enter a new name like rptModified1998Assignments and click OK.
4. Click on the text box control in the toolbox.
5. Click to the right of the Score field in the Detail section.
6. Select the label and press the Delete key.
7. Click on the Label control in the Toolbox.
8. Click to the right of the Score label.
9. Enter Score % and press Enter.
10. Select the unbound text box next to Score.
11. Click the Property button from the toolbar to display the Property window.
12. Select the Data tab.
13. Select the Control Source property.
14. Enter the following expression and press the Enter key:

    ```
    =Score/MaximumPoints*PercentofGrade
    ```

> **Note**
>
> When you press the Enter key, Microsoft Access 2000 automatically places brackets around the field names.

> **Tip**
>
> When you create longer expressions, it will be difficult to see the expression. You can press Shift+F2 to open the Zoom window to see the entire expression at once, as shown in Figure 12.22.

FIGURE 12.22

The Zoom window gives you a complete view of your expression.

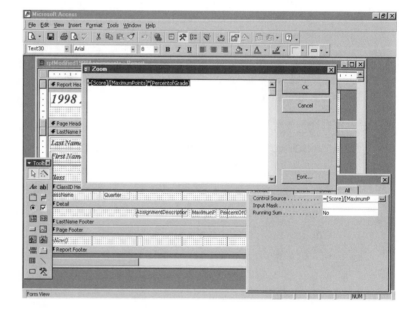

15. Select the Format tab.

16. Set the Format property to Percent.

17. Clean up any size and alignment problems between the label and text box.

18. Select the Save button on the toolbar to save your changes.

19. Select the View button on the toolbar to preview the report (see Figure 12.23).

20. Click the View button on the toolbar to return to Design mode.

FIGURE 12.23

The report now shows the percentage score.

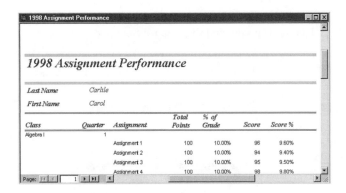

Using the Expression Builder

You have created a simple expression using values stored in three fields. When you create an expression by typing it in, the longer the expression the more likely you are to make a typing mistake, especially if you do not use the Zoom window. Another approach to creating expressions is to use the Expression Builder.

The Expression Builder is similar to a wizard. It is designed to assist you with creating expressions using your mouse. For example, in this assignment report, you created an expression to calculate the performance of the students on individual assignments, but you did not calculate their performance for the class.

This is accomplished with one of the built-in functions. Just as in Microsoft Excel, there are many functions to minimize the time spent creating expressions to perform common calculations.

On Day 11, you learned how to perform calculations in a query. One of those was the ability to summarize information about a field; for example, calculating a total. To add a score total to the assignment report, complete this task.

Task: Adding a Total Score

1. Drag the bottom border of the ClassID footer to make room for the text box and label to display the total.

2. Add a text box with attached label in the ClassID footer.

3. Align the label with the MaximumPoints and the text box with Score %.

4. Click the Properties button from the toolbar to display the Properties window if necessary. You might also need to move it so that you can see the footer.

▼ TASK

12

▼   5. Select the label and change its Caption property to Totals.

6. Select the new text box for the total.

7. Select the Data tab and the Control Source property.

8. Click the Builder button to the right of the drop-down arrow for this property. It will open the Expression Builder window, as shown in Figure 12.24.

FIGURE 12.24

The Expression Builder is designed to assist with expression construction.

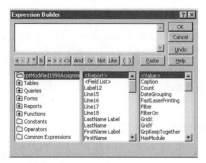

9. Double-click on Functions in the object folder list in the lower-left corner of the Expression Builder window.

10. Click on Built In Functions to display the function subfolder in the middle list and the expression components in the list on the right.

11. Click on SQL Aggregate in the subfolders list.

12. Double-click on Sum in the expression component list. It will place Sum(<<expr>> in the expression display.

13. Click on <<expr>> in the expression display to highlight it.

14. Click on rptModified1998Assignments from the object folder list.

15. Click on <Field List>.

16. Double-click on Score in the expression component list.

17. Double-click on MaximumPoints in the expression component list.

18. Click the multiplication symbol (*) or type an asterisk (*).

19. Double-click on PercentofGrade in the expression component list.

▼   20. Click OK to accept your expression.

▼ 21. Click the Format tab and change the Format property for this text box to Percent.

22. Save the report and preview the results (see Figure 12.25).

FIGURE 12.25

You can now see the student's total percentage for the class.

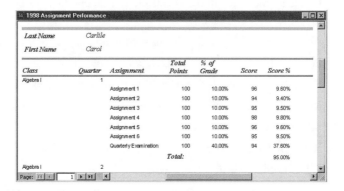

▲ 23. Close the report.

This allowed you to view the performance for the class while seeing individual assignment performances. Both of the expressions created to show percentage performances were created as text boxes on the report. You could have also created the first expression as part of the query, and then used the sum of that query field in the footer of this report.

Concatenating Fields with an Expression

NEW TERM   Earlier in the section, you examined some more complex reporting features. One technique used in the rptMailLabels report is the use of expressions to string text information and eliminate wasted space. It also makes the data easier to read. This technique is known as *concatenation* and it could really be helpful with the student roster.

When you want to concatenate fields, you are going to build an expression. It will start with an equal (=) sign. Then you will add the fields that need to be together. When you want to add a space or any other fixed character, the space or character must be placed in quotation marks. Everything is separated by the ampersand (&) to indicate that you want to concatenate the components.

In rptFinalRoster, the student information is not shown as individual fields. The information is displayed as it is in the mailing labels. To add this effect to the rptModifiedRoster, complete the following task.

12

Task: Concatenating Fields with Expressions

▲TASK

1. Open rptModifiedRoster in Design mode.

2. Delete all the fields in the Detail section except the Address and PhoneNumber fields. Delete their labels.

3. Add two text boxes to the Detail section and delete their labels.

4. Position the new text boxes above and below the Address field.

5. Select the three text boxes as well as the PhoneNumber text box.

6. Right-click on one of the text boxes to open the context-sensitive menu.

7. Select Align, Left.

8. Right-click on a text box and select Size, To Widest.

9. Select Format, Vertical Spacing, Make Equal.

10. Select Format, Vertical Spacing, Decrease or Format, Vertical Spacing, Increase if needed until it resembles Figure 12.26.

FIGURE 12.26

The text boxes are aligned and positioned similar to those in the mailing label.

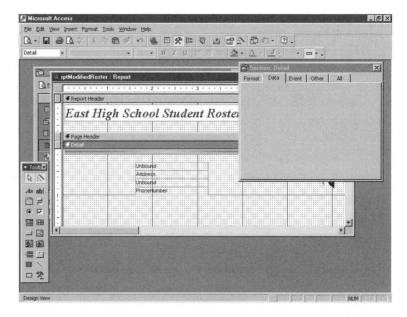

11. Click on the first text box.

12. Select the Data tab in the Properties window and select the Control Source property from the list.

▼ 13. Enter the following as the expression, making sure that there is a space between
        the quotation marks:

    =FirstName & " " & LastName

    14. Click on the second text box.

    15. Select the Data tab in the Properties window and select the Control Source proper-
        ty from the list.

    16. Enter the following as the expression, making sure that there is a space between
        both sets of quotation marks:

    =City & ", " & Ucase(State) & " " & PostalCode

Tip

When the state information is displayed in a text box by itself, you can use
the Format property to control the appearance of the text. You can display
the State field in uppercase by using the greater than (>) sign as the Format
property. When you are concatenating text fields, you will use the UCase
function. It accomplishes the same results.

    17. If you want, select all four text boxes and set the Font Size property to 10 point.

    18. Drag the bottom border for the Detail section to reduce the white space.

    19. Save the report and then preview it. It should resemble the report shown in Figure
        12.27.

FIGURE 12.27

*The student informa-
tion now takes up
much less room and is
easier to read.*

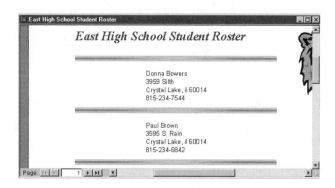

▲ 20. Close the report.

12

The report is easier to work with now. The data for each student takes up much less space. It is easier to read because it places the information in a format that many readers are used to. It will also reduce the size of the report. This will require less paper and printing resources as well as less time to print.

Evaluating Data with an Expression

In addition to calculating values and adjusting the way things appear, you can also use expressions to evaluate the contents of a field and display an answer. For example, you are going to generate a report to display those students who are eligible for the Current Events field trip.

The students must have a score percentage of 80% or above for the field trip. You could add that as a criterion for the query for this report, but then you would see only those students who qualify. You could also display all the students by score percentage in descending order. This would make it harder to locate a particular student than a report organizing them in alphabetical order.

With Access, you have three built-in functions that allow you to evaluate a value and display a value based on the result. In this case, the student is either eligible or ineligible. It is a Yes/No type of question. The IIF function is specifically designed for this type of evaluation. The syntax for this function is described in the following section.

The Syntax for IIF

The following is the syntax for the IIF function:

```
IIF( <<expr>>,<<truepart>>, <<falsepart>>
```

where *expr* is the expression to be tested, *truepart* is the value if the expression is true, and *falsepart* is the value if the expression is false.

To implement the IIF function, complete the following task.

Task: Creating the Eligibility Expression

1. Open the rptFieldTripEligibility report in Design mode.

2. Select File, Save As to open the Save As dialog.

3. Name the report rptModifiedFieldTripEligibility and click OK.

4. Select the txtEligible text box.

▼   5. Display the Properties window if necessary.

6. Select the Data tab and the Control Source property.

7. Click on the Expression Builder button next to the property drop-down.

8. Double-click functions in the object list to expand the list and select Built In Functions.

9. Select Program Flow from the subfolder list and double-click on IIF to add it to the expression display.

10. Click on <<*expr*>> to select it.

11. Click on rptModifiedFieldTripEligibility in the object list.

12. Click on <Field List> to display the fields in the expression component list, and double-click ScorePercent to add it as part of the expression.

13. Click on the greater-than (>) button or type >.

14. Click on the equal sign (=) or type =.

15. Type .8.

16. Click on the <<*truepart*>> argument and type "Yes".

17. Click on the <<*falsepart*>> and type "No" and click OK to accept the expression.

18. Save and preview the report (see Figure 12.28).

FIGURE 12.28

The IIF function allows you to represent numbers with words.

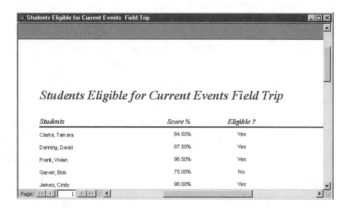

Students Eligible for Current Events Field Trip

Students	Score %	Eligible ?
Clarke, Tamera	84.50%	Yes
Denning, David	87.50%	Yes
Franl, Vivian	96.50%	Yes
Garver, Bob	75.00%	No
James, Cindy	98.00%	Yes

12

Now the report allows for a quicker assessment of the eligibility. It is now a matter of locating the student and reading Yes or No.

Note

In addition to the IIF function, you also have Choose and Switch. Choose allows you to input an index number and return a corresponding value from a set list. The Switch function allows you to evaluate expressions and based on the results, display a specific value.

 You can see an example of the Choose function in the rpt1999ReportCards report and an example of the Switch function in the rptFinal1998Assignments report to display a letter grade. For more information, please consult Microsoft Access' Help file.

Caution

All three program-flow functions will affect the performance of Access. You will want to use them sparingly. Using a Visual Basic for Applications procedure might be a better option. Visual Basic for Applications is discussed in later lessons.

Working with Subreports

Another tool you have to work with when designing reports is the subreport. With the assignment performance report, you used a query to combine information from more than one table to create a report. A subreport is another method for combining data.

 In the Students database, the tblStudentsAndClasses table has a field for grades. To show the benefit of using a subreport, you are going to work from the premise that the Grade field is populated only after the completion of the quarter. It is not used to generate report cards. The reason subreports are so useful for report cards is the data must be combined, but part of the data must be summarized before being combined.

With the rptFinal1998Assignments report, the report was based on a query that combines the data from five tables. It summarizes the information for a student for each of her classes and each assignment for each class. The total grade percentage and a letter grade were added to the report in the group footer using expressions for each class.

For a report card, you do not want to see the assignment performance—all you are interested in seeing is the letter grade. In this case, the data must be summarized before it is integrated with the student's information.

When you want to create a report using a subreport, you need to

- Create the subreport.
- Create the main report.
- Integrate the subreport with the main report.

Creating a Subreport

With the report card report, the subreport is the portion of the report that will display the grades. The first step is to create a query that summarizes the assignment performance. For this subreport, the query, qry1999SecondQuarterGrades, is already created. To create the subreport based on this query, it is easiest to let the Report Wizard do most of the work.

The results are stored in srpt1999SecondQtrGrades. Although you let the Report Wizard do most of the work, you are not finished with this report. Because it will be integrated in the report card, it will not display exactly the same as a standalone report.

The first change is to the report header and footer. The report header and footer will print on the report when it is a subreport, but you probably do not want as large a title on the report as you would on a standalone report. In many cases, this title can be deleted.

The second difference is that the page headers and footers will not be displayed when it is integrated. This poses a problem because the page header has the labels for the columns. These will need to be moved to the report header. After the column headings are moved, you can turn off the display of the page header and footer.

The last necessary change is to adjust the columns to make room for a letter grade at the right of the report. To prepare this report to be used as a subreport, complete the following task.

Task: Modifying the Subreport

1. Open srpt1999SecondQtrGrades in Design mode and save it as srpt1999SecondQtrGradesModified.

2. Delete the label in the report header.

3. Point in the vertical ruler next to the page header and drag straight down to select all the controls in the page header.

4. Point to one of those controls, drag it up to the top of the report header, and release the mouse button to move it to the report header.

5. Drag the bottom border of the report header up to make it smaller.

6. Select View, Page Header/Footer and select Yes to turn off the display of those sections.

7. Select the Department Name label and change it to Department.

8. Select the Class Name label and change it to Class.

9. Select the ScorePercent label and change it to Score.

10. Select DepartmentName and its label and set their width to .9".

▼ 11. Select SectionNumber and its label and drag them over to the left so that they are next to DepartmentName.

12. Select ClassName and its label, set the Width to .9", and drag them over so that they are next to SectionNumber.

13. Select Instructor and its label, set the Width to 1.2", and drag them over next to ClassName.

14. Select the ScorePercent and its label, set the Width to .5", and drag them over next to Instructor.

15. Select the ScorePercent text box and set the Format property to Percent.

16. Select the line and set its width to 5.5".

17. Add a new text box to the Detail section and delete its label.

18. Set the Control Source property of the new text box to

```
=Switch(ScorePercent<.6, "F",ScorePercent>=.6 and ScorePercent<.7,
➥"D", ScorePercent>=.7 and ScorePercent<.8,"C",
➥ScorePercent>=.8 and ScorePercent<.9,"B",ScorePercent>.9,"A")
```

Note | Here is another example of the Switch function to evaluate a field and display a value.

19. Add a label above the new text box and change its caption to Grade.

20. Set the Report's Width to 5.5".

▲ 21. Save the subreport and close it. It should now resemble the one named srpt1999SecondQtrGradesFinal.

Creating the Main Report

After you have created the subreport, you must create the layout for the main report before you integrate the subreport. You can create the report from a blank report or again rely on the Report Wizard. For the main portion of the report card, arrange the report so that it resembles rpt1999SecondQtrGrades, as shown in Figure 12.29.

The key element is to arrange the report, keeping in mind that you will need to plan for the location of the subreport. Additional design considerations include maintaining a standard look and feel to the main report and the subreport. It will appear more like one report instead of two. In this case, the use of the Corporate style when answering questions in the Report Wizard got these reports off on the right foot.

FIGURE 12.29

The report is designed to fit two report cards per page and there is an open space for the subreport.

In most cases, the subreport will not be the last item that you will add to the report. It will be added as you add other objects to the report. You are not required to save the integration of the subreport until all of your other design work is complete.

Note

Notice the Trim function was used to get rid of excess space with the name and address information. The Choose function is also illustrated in this report. It is used to modify the display of the numeric year into the text representation of the high-school years.

Integrating the Subreport

When you are ready to integrate the subreport, two methods can be used. You can use the Subform/Subreport tool from the toolbox to use the Subform/Subreport Wizard, or you can drag an existing subreport from the Database window to a location on your report.

The process for integrating a subreport is two-fold. The first step is to place the subreport in your main report. After it is in place, you must establish whether it is linked to the data in the main form. After these two steps are complete, you can adjust any formatting properties as needed.

12

Task: Inserting a Subreport

1. Open the rpt1999SecondQtrGrades report and save it as rpt1999SecondQtrGradesModified.

2. Click the Toolbox button from the toolbar to display the toolbox if necessary.

3. Click on the Subform/Subreport tool in the toolbox.

4. Click under the blue line below the City, State and PostalCode information. This will place the control and launch the Subreport Wizard (see Figure 12.30).

FIGURE 12.30

The wizard first prompts for the source of the subreport.

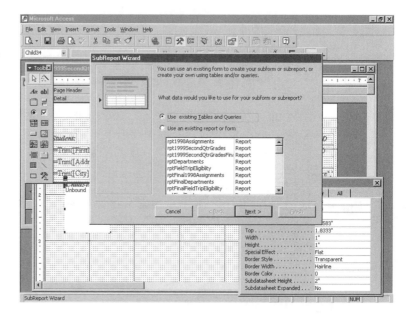

5. Select the srpt1999SecondQtrgradesModified report from the list and click Next. You can use a report that already exists or use a table or a query (see Figure 12.31).

6. Select Choose From a List and select the first choice for establishing a link, and then click Next.

7. Click Finish because you are not going to use the label for the subreport.

FIGURE 12.31

The wizard asks which field will be linked to the main report.

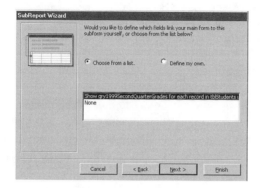

The wizard places the subreport on your main form. It also creates an attached label. The subreport itself is very short. The last page of the wizard asks about linking. You can have a report with several unrelated subreports just to control the display, or you can use the approach demonstrated here.

The only information to be displayed in the subreport is the information for the record displayed on the main form. If you are using this approach, the wizard sets two of the data properties for the subreport. The Link Child Fields and the Link Master Fields identify the fields in each recordset to be used to filter the data on the subreport. In this case, the StudentID field is used.

After the wizard has completed its work, you will need to work with its appearance and positioning to get the results that you want. There are some tricks to make this easier. The first thing to remember is that if your subreport has a Report Header section, you can normally delete the attached label.

The second thing that will make positioning and sizing your subreport is to remember its original dimensions. For example, this subreport was 5.5" wide. Your main report is 6.5" wide. This means that the Width property for the subreport should be 5.5" and the Left property should be .5" to center it between the margins of the main report.

12

Note

When you are working with a subreport or subform, you must be very careful what you click on to select the control. With Microsoft Access 2000, Microsoft enhanced the subform/subreport behavior. You can now see the contents of the subform/subreport as you work. This means that you must be careful where you click to select what you want to work with. You must be sure that you have clicked on the edge to select the subreport. You will

know that it is correct because the Property window will show
SubForm/Subreport: *name* in the title bar and there will be handles around
the control. If you are having trouble with this, do not forget that you can
select the subreport from the Object list on the Formatting toolbar.

The last formatting change you must make to this subreport is to set the Height property.
This setting is not as easy as the Left and Width properties. If you are displaying only a
fixed set of information, you can use the Height property from your subreport. This
approach won't work as well when the subreport is a tabular report. In that case, you
might have to try out several settings. For this sample database, you have only four classes per student so space is not much of an issue. If you use a setting of 2.1", you can
accommodate more classes as needed. It also balances out the section to use two report
cards per page.

Creating Reports with Multiple Columns

The last report feature for this lesson is the ability to create a report that has more than
one column. There is a lot of wasted space in the rptModifiedRoster report you worked
on earlier in this lesson. Displaying this report in two columns would save paper and
printing supplies.

Setting up a report to print more than one column is a little trickier than it might seem.
There are two steps. The first is to adjust the Page Setup for the report, and the second is
to make any formatting changes needed to support this new layout.

In the following task you will finish the student roster.

Task: Setting Up a Two-Column Report

1. Open the rptModifiedRoster report.
2. Select File, Page Setup.
3. Select the Column tab.
4. Set the Number of Columns to 2.
5. Set the Width to 3.125 and make sure the Same as Detail check box is not selected
   for Column Size.

Note

The most crucial step of this process is to complete step 5. By making sure that the Same as Detail check box is not selected, you can separate the treatment of the data from that of the report and page headers. That means you can leave the width of the report at 6.5" and build full report and page headers, but it also means that you must keep in mind your column width. Even though the space is displayed in the Detail and any group headers and footer sections, you can only place information in the narrower column width space.

6. Select Down, and then Across for the Column Layout.

7. Select the View button to view the preview of this report. It will display with two columns, but it still isn't perfect.

8. Select the View button on the toolbar to get back to the Design mode.

9. Select all the student information fields and set the left property to .6".

10. Select the border Image controls and set their width to 3.125" (see Figure 12.32).

FIGURE 12.32

The preview of this report when finished will display the image displayed in both columns.

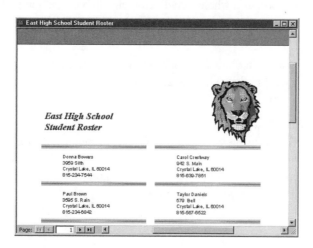

12

11. Select the image in the page footer, copy it to the Clipboard, and then paste it into the page footer. This will provide a matching image for the second column because the page footer is not displayed in columns.

12. Move the new image to the right edge of the report above even with the original.

▼   13. Drag the report header's bottom border down so that you can see the entire lion in
         the header and the lion isn't being partially covered with the second column. It will
         have a height of approximately 2".

     14. If you want, size the East High School Student Roster label to display it on two
▲   lines and move it to the bottom of the report header.

Summary

Today's lesson introduced some of the methods for enhancing the appearance of your
reports. In today's environment, more is expected of database reporting because of the
public's access to word processing tools. Their expectations are much higher than with
the older database formats.

In this lesson, you examined some of the tools that can be used to enhance your reports.
You can work with the report properties to change the behavior and appearance of the
report. This can include adjusting the width to allow for less or greater white space
around your report.

You also got to explore how graphics can be integrated into your report. You can add an
image to the report as a whole, or add an image in one location with the Image control.
You can also add images based on the data in your tables. You also have the ability to
add charts to your reports.

Another way to get more out of your reports is to use expressions. Expressions can be
used throughout Microsoft Access 2000, but with reports you can create calculations and
really change the way your data appears.

You also learned two other methods for creating special reporting effects. You can create
a combined report using subreports, as well as display the data in columns. If you are
interested in some more formatting techniques, Day 17, "Developing Professional-
Quality Reports," covers some additional formatting techniques, as well as introduces the
process for publishing your reports to the Web.

Q&A

Q When is the report's Picture Tiling property useful?

A If you are using a graphic designed to serve as a watermark, you might set the
      Picture Tiling property so that the graphic covers the page.

Q What if I do not want to display fields together, but I need to display only a portion of a text field?

A With Microsoft Access 2000, there are 31 functions for manipulating strings. If you need a portion of a field, you can use `Left`, `Right`, or `Mid` depending on where the information is located.

Q What is the disadvantage of using subreports?

A Depending on the amount of information displayed for each linked record, it could slow down the preview and print speed.

Workshop

The Workshop helps you solidify the skills you learned in this lesson. Answers to the quiz questions appear in Appendix A, "Answers."

Quiz

1. What is the best way to display a graphic in a fixed location on a report?

2. What does the Size Mode property control for an Image control?

3. Which built-in function should be used if you need to evaluate the contents of a field with several possibilities and display a value based on the results?

4. Why is the Same as Detail check box on the Columns tab of the Page Setup so important when you are going to create a report with multiple columns?

Exercises

1. With an expression, modify the rptMailingLabels report to always display the state in uppercase regardless of how it was entered into the record. Hint: You must use the `UCase` function.

2. Modify the rptModified1998Assignments report to display the student's name as one field. Hint: You must use concatenation.

3. Condense and format the rptModifiedFieldTripEligibility as a two-column report. Hint: Setting columns is a part of page setup.

12

DAY 13

Introducing VBA

On Day 7, "Automating Your Access App: A Macro Primer," you were introduced to the Access 2000 macros. They provide a simple method for automating tasks you perform regularly. As you begin automating tasks with macros, you will discover some limitations. Access 2000 has Visual Basic for Applications to overcome these obstacles.

Today's lesson covers the following topics:

- Understanding VBA
- Exploring uses for VBA
- Introducing the VBA wizards
- Examining the structure of VBA
- Exploring the Visual Basic Editor
- Introducing language elements

To assist with the completion of today's lesson, a sample database, Sales.mdb, is located on the CD-ROM that accompanies this book. It is located in \Day13\.

Sales.mdb is based on the scenario that this database manages the customers and inventory for a specialty gifts company. It will need to be copied to another location to allow you to save your work in this lesson.

Understanding VBA

As you have been working with Access 2000, you have been learning many new ways to make your work easier and take much less time. You have learned that you can use queries to combine information; create forms to make viewing, entering, and editing data easier; use reports to create professional printed output; and create macros to automate processes you use regularly.

NEW TERM There are two levels of automation when you are working with Access 2000. The first level is the Access macros. They are a quick way to accomplish simple automation. The second level is *Visual Basic for Applications* (VBA). VBA is a shared programming language for all the Microsoft Office applications.

Access 2000 provides both macros and VBA because macros have limited uses. Access 2000 is designed to make it easy for the new user to get started working with databases, as well as to provide a full-featured development environment for database developers. VBA provides the development power, and also makes it easy to automate all the Microsoft applications.

When Microsoft Office was introduced, each application had a separate method for automating your work. If you were working in Microsoft Word, you would have created macros using Word Basic. If you were in Excel, you would have automated using the Excel Macro language. In Access, you could have used macros or Access Basic. The problem with this approach is that if you learned how to automate your work in one application, automating in one of the others was a whole new learning process. Visual Basic for Applications was introduced to make it easier to transition from one product to another and to add flexibility.

Visual Basic for Applications is a core language that has a group of programming tools regardless of which package you are using. The process is the same for creating automation as well as basic language elements. As you switch from automating in one package to another, all you must learn are the elements unique to the application. For example, in Access, you must learn about manipulating forms and reports; in Microsoft Excel, you must learn how to work with workbooks, worksheets, and cells.

Exploring Uses for VBA

At this point, you might be asking yourself, "Why do I need to use Visual Basic for Applications? I think macros can do everything I need." There are several reasons why you might want to start using VBA:

- VBA code will execute faster than a macro.
- VBA allows more user interaction.
- VBA is generated by the Control Wizards.
- VBA allows you to work with a core language to make it easier to automate using other Microsoft applications.
- VBA allows greater flexibility as you develop your automation and ease of maintenance.

When you begin developing in Access 2000, you are trying to get the data organized and get your forms and reports to look and perform effectively. You are not thinking about automation. As time goes on, you will want this process to happen automatically. You might also want someone else to have access to the data without interrupting your schedule. That is when you start thinking about automation.

If you choose to use macros to automate your work, you might find that it is not as effective as it could be. The first issue is speed. VBA code will run faster than a macro. If you have a macro to open a form, you might not notice a significant difference. If you have a form that allows you to enter a criteria to open that form, you might notice a difference.

The second benefit is interaction with your process. Macros enable you to do some condition testing, but it is very limited. With a complete core language, VBA can accommodate multiple layers of condition testing. You also have more powerful tools to communicate with the user, whether that user is you or someone else.

The third benefit is that there are Control Wizards to assist you with automation. These will use VBA. VBA also enables you to interact with other Microsoft applications.

The last reason to consider VBA is its flexibility. You have more control over your processes and it is easier to modify and maintain as your process changes. VBA also gives you access to a wide variety of third-party tools that have been developed to work with Visual Basic for Applications and Visual Studio.

You can create a sophisticated application with VBA. It can walk you or someone else through the process of working with your data. It can help them locate the correct report or form. It can prompt them through an import or export process. It can assist them with

13

working with a subset of data without developing special queries every time. It can help you develop custom menus and toolbars. It can automate merging information with Microsoft Word or analyzing data in Excel. You can also create custom help with the Help window or with the Office Assistant.

The best news is that if you use VBA, it is the core language for Microsoft Office, as well as being a part of Visual Basic. That means as your needs grow, you will not have to learn a whole new method for accomplishing what you need. VBA can keep up with your application's growth.

Before you can begin creating an automated application, you must learn some fundamentals. The rest of this lesson is designed to give you a start with VBA. Day 18, "Examining VBA," and Day 19, "Working with VBA," build on this introduction to give you the basics in VBA development. Day 21, "Developer Considerations," talks about some of the issues that you must consider if you are creating an application for others to use, including the creation of a help system. The first step is to get used to creating VBA code.

Introducing the Control Wizards

The easiest way to get started using Visual Basic for Applications is to let Access 2000 do most of the work. In many cases, you can take advantage of a Control Wizard when you want to add VBA to one of your forms or reports.

NEW TERM *Control Wizards* are tools that automate the setup for specific controls. One of the most common controls to use for VBA is the command button. If you have the Control Wizards activated as you create the command button, the wizard will prompt you to create the VBA behind the scenes.

 The database for this lesson, Sales.mdb, is a database to store information about the clients, orders, products, and suppliers of a small gift company. To start working with VBA, you are going to add a command button on a form to open a report based on the information currently displayed on the form, all automated with VBA.

Task: Adding a Command Button

1. Launch Access and open the Sales.mdb database file.
2. Click the Forms tab in the Database window.
3. Open the frmSuppliers form.
4. Notice that it is simple to view, enter, and edit information about the suppliers.
5. Click the View button on the toolbar to display the form in Design mode.

6. Click the Toolbox button on the toolbar to display the toolbox as needed.

7. Make sure the Control Wizards button on the toolbox is selected, as shown in Figure 13.1.

8. Click the Command button from the Toolbox (see Figure 13.1).

Control Wizards button

FIGURE 13.1

The Control Wizards button activates a wizard and the Command button is one to create VBA code.

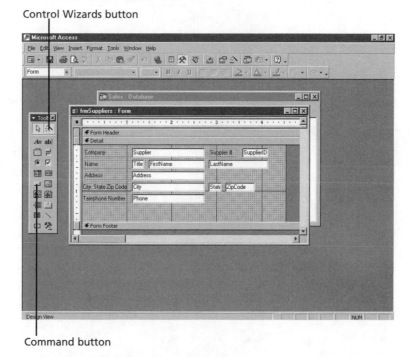

Command button

9. Click in the lower-right corner of the form's Detail section. The Command Button Wizard will launch (see Figure 13.2).

10. Select Report Operations from the Categories list.

11. Select Preview Report from the Actions list and select Next to display the list of reports (see Figure 13.3).

12. Select the rptProductsfromSupplier report and select Next to select the display of the button (see Figure 13.4).

13. Click the Text: option button, enter Preview Products Report, and select Next to enter the name for the command button (see Figure 13.5).

14. Enter cmdProductReport as the name and select Finish to create the command button (see Figure 13.6).

13

FIGURE 13.2

The Command Button Wizard enables you to create VBA by making selections from action lists.

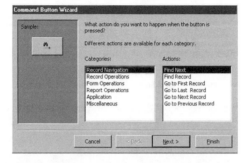

FIGURE 13.3

This gives you an opportunity to select an action from a list.

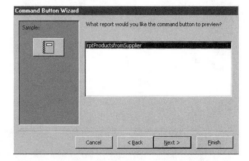

FIGURE 13.4

This lets you determine whether a text title or an icon will be displayed on the button.

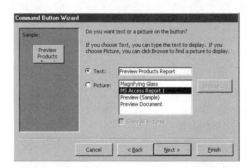

FIGURE 13.5

When you are going to be adding VBA to objects, complying with the naming conventions is helpful.

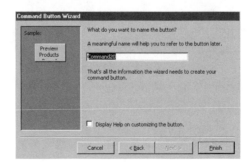

FIGURE 13.6

The command button is now placed on the form with the VBA code generated.

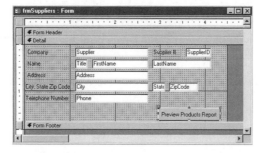

15. Save the form as frmSuppliersModified.

16. Click the View button from the toolbar to display the form in Form view. Notice you are looking at the first record.

17. Click the Preview Products Report button to display the custom report in Print Preview (see Figure 13.7).

FIGURE 13.7

The report opens modified.

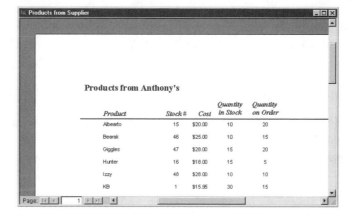

18. Close the report, move to the next record, and repeat step 17.

19. Notice that the report now displays the products for that supplier.

▲ 20. Close the report and click the View button on the toolbar to return to Design mode.

The Command Button Control Wizard created the button as well as the VBA code that previews the report. Now you are going behind the scenes to see what the Control Wizard created for you.

13

Examining the Structure of VBA

The Command Button Control Wizard created everything needed to perform the selected task. Now you are going to examine how Visual Basic for Applications fits into Access 2000.

When you add automation with VBA, you are creating a procedure. Procedures are stored in modules. When you create forms and reports, they do not have any Visual Basic for Applications in them. They are referred to as *light* forms and reports. When you need to add programming to a form or a report, you create a code module to store the code associated with that object. Each of these objects are explained further, later in this lesson.

Understanding Modules

NEW TERM   When you are creating VBA, it will be stored in a *code module*. All the modules act as container objects for your VBA procedures. The first two types, *form modules* and *report modules*, are very similar in structure and behavior. These modules are created when you add code to an object on a form or report.

There are three ways to create a form or report module. You can use the Command Button Control Wizard to generate code. You can select an object and set one of its event properties to create an event procedure (see Figure 13.8), or you can select the Code button on the toolbar. All these steps will automatically create the module. They will also automatically set the form or report's Has Module property to Yes.

A form or report module is like the other types of modules in the respect that it stores functions and subprocedures that can be executed by the user. It is different in the respect that it also stores event procedures. They provide a way to respond to actions of a user.

NEW TERM   The third type of module is a *standard module*. This type of module is not connected to another Microsoft Access object. It is designed to store procedures that you want to access from more than one object in your application. These used to be called global modules because they were accessible from anywhere in your application.

The standard module is stored under the Modules tab in the Database window. Many Microsoft Access developers use standard modules for procedures that they use in many applications. Because they are represented as a standalone object, they can be imported into other applications. The standard module is explored further in Day 21, "Developer Considerations."

The Code button

FIGURE 13.8

Adding a module to a form or report is automatic.

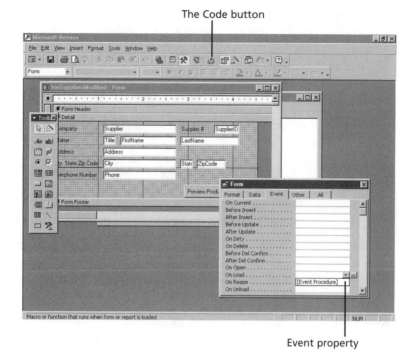

Event property

NEW TERM   The last type of module is a *class module*. This module is a special type that was added for developers. A class module is a code module that allows a developer to create his own custom objects to use in processing. This is for advanced development and is not a topic in this book.

Understanding Procedures

NEW TERM   Regardless of how the module is created, you are creating it to store procedures. *Procedures* are groups of code statements that will execute as a group when called upon in your application. As with modules, there are four types of procedures.

NEW TERM   The first type of procedure is an *event procedure*. That is what you have just created with the Control Wizard. As you work with in any application in Windows, whether it is Windows 95, Windows 98, or Windows NT, you are kicking off system events. When you move the mouse, touch a key, or open a window, these are all system events.

13

When you begin automating your work in Access, you often want code to execute in response to a user action. In the case of the frmSuppliers form, you want the code to execute when the user clicks on the Preview Products Report command button. You created an event procedure.

If you look at the Events tab in the Properties window for the command button, you will see that the On Click property now shows [Event Procedure] next to it. For the command button, you will see that there are 12 event properties. You could add code to each of these events.

New Term The second type of procedure you are likely to create is a *function*. In earlier lessons, you looked at using built-in functions to create fields in a query or to display information in a form or report. If there isn't a built-in function to perform a specific action, you can create your own custom function.

The key characteristic is that the function can return a value. It can be called from other procedures, used as a field source in a query, or used as the Control Source property for an object on a form or report.

New Term The third type of procedure is called a *sub procedure*. A sub procedure contains code that can be executed like the other two, but you will find that you will create these types of procedures less than event procedures and functions.

They are used less because of their limitations. Event procedures are automatically executed when an event is triggered for an object. Functions can be executed several different ways, but sub procedures cannot be so easily executed.

A sub procedure can be called only from another procedure. It cannot be automatically triggered or be used as a field or control source. It also cannot return a value. The value of a sub procedure is the fact that it can be used to isolate a block of code from other code. This is useful because it allows you to call on that code from several other procedures. This will be more valuable the longer you develop code. It can allow you to reuse the code as you create new objects or as you create new systems. For the professional developer, this is a valuable tool because larger tasks can be broken down and that can make maintaining them easier.

New Term The last type of procedure is a *property procedure*. This procedure is used only if you are creating class modules. In the previous section, class modules were introduced as a way to create your own custom objects. The property procedure is how you can add the characteristics of this new object. Again, this type of procedure is for developers and it is out of the scope of this book.

Now that you have an idea of some of the structure of Visual Basic for Applications, it is time to actually see what you have created and to get an idea of how code can be viewed and edited.

Exploring the Visual Basic Editor

When you create code, whether it is with the Control Wizard or by typing it into the module directly, it is entered as text. To assist you with the maintenance of your code, you have the Visual Basic Editor. This editor is universal across all the Office applications.

In the following discussion, you will see how to view the code you have created, as well as add code without using the Control Wizard. You will also see how to navigate in the Visual Basic Editor and edit your code.

Viewing Your Code

When you have used the Control Wizard to create a command button, the code is generated automatically. The Control Wizard sets the Has Module property under the Other tab in the Properties window, and sets the On Click event property to [Event Procedure] under the Events tab. If you click on the On Click property in the Properties window, the Build button will become visible to the right of the drop-down list (see Figure 13.9).

FIGURE 13.9

The Build button is displayed when you select an event property.

Viewing the code the Control Wizard created is as simple as clicking the Build button. It will launch the Visual Basic Editor for you and display the code for this object's event, as shown in Figure 13.10.

NEW TERM The *Visual Basic Editor* is a separate application, displaying in a separate window from your Access application. You will notice the title bar displays which file the code is from. When you add code to your Access application, you are creating a Visual Basic for Application project.

13

FIGURE 13.10

*The Visual Basic
Editor is a special
application to assist
with maintaining VBA
code.*

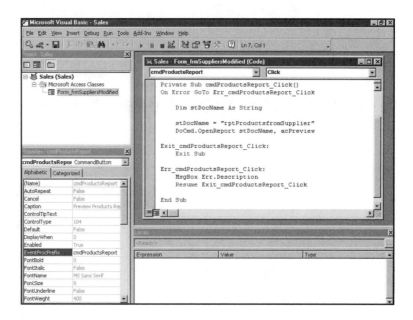

All the code for your application is stored with your database, but is accessible from this
window. To assist with the maintenance of your code, the Visual Basic Editor has a
collection of windows to allow you to manage various aspects of the project. Some of
these windows are currently in view and others are not shown until you need them. Some
of them float in the window and others are docked to the side of the window to keep
them in one place.

You are going to work with six windows in the Visual Basic Editor: the Project Explorer
window, the Properties window, the Code window, the Immediate window, the Locals
window, and the Watch window. All these windows assist you with creating and
maintaining your code.

Examining the Project Explorer Window

The Project Explorer window (see Figure 13.11) helps you manage your code. It lists all
the objects in your Access application that have code associated with them.

The Sales database at this point doesn't have any other objects that have code attached to
them, so this window doesn't have much to display. The objects are displayed in a folder
structure like the Windows Explorer. The top level is the name of your database. The
second level is Microsoft Access classes.

FIGURE 13.11

The Project Explorer displays all the objects in your database.

At this point, the only class displayed is the form class because you haven't added any other VBA code. Classes are types of objects like forms, reports, and modules.

The frmSuppliersModified form is displayed as the third level. Notice that in front of the form name is Form_. This indicates the object's class.

To view information about an object in the Project Explorer, you can simply click on it in the list. The Project Explorer has three buttons above the list. The first one opens the Code window, the second displays the object, and the third expands or collapses the folder list.

If you click on the View Object button, it will switch to the Access window for you. This is helpful if you need to add code for an object that doesn't currently have code attached to it.

Tip

You might find it cumbersome to have to click on the object and then click on the View Object button to get back to Access. The shortcut key to switch or toggle between Access and the Visual Basic Editor is Alt+F11.

The Code Window

The Code window (see Figure 13.12) is where your code will be displayed. This is the window where you can actually modify your code.

13

The title bar displays the name of your database as well as the class and object name. Under the title bar are two drop-down lists. The first list is the object list, which lists all the objects in this form. If you click on the Object list drop-down arrow, you will see the form, sections, and all the controls on this form.

FIGURE 13.12

You use the Code window to view and make changes to your code.

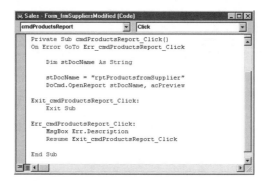

The second list is the procedure list. When you examined the Events tab in the Properties window for the command button, 12 event properties were shown. If you click on the drop-down window for the procedure list, you will see 12 events. Notice the Click is in bold. That is because it has code added to it.

On the right and bottom of the Code window are scrollbars. These work just like scrollbars in Word. They allow you to navigate to see more of the code. For example, if you click the up arrow of the vertical scrollbar a couple times, you will see a line above and a line of code above that. The line is a dividing line to separate procedures and the line of code is general instructions about this module. The contents of the Code window are discussed in the section, "Introducing Language Elements."

In the lower-left corner are two small buttons. The second one is currently selected. It allows you to see all the code in the module. This is called Full Module view. The first button restricts what you see by displaying only the procedure that is selected with the drop-down lists. This is called Procedure view.

On the left side of the window is a gray bar called the Breakpoint Selection bar. It assists you with testing your code, if you have trouble with a procedure. Testing your code is discussed later.

Editing code is similar to working in Microsoft Word. You will notice that you have a blinking insertion point. As you type, that is where the code will appear. If there is code to the right of the insertion point, it will scroll to the right. You can also take advantage of many of the same navigation keystrokes used in Word. A list is provided in Table 13.1.

TABLE 13.1 NAVIGATION KEYS

Keys	Action
Home	Move to the beginning of a line
End	Move to the end of a line

Keys	Action
Ctrl+Home	Move to the top of the current view
Ctrl+End	Move to the bottom of the current view
← or →	Move left or right one character
↑ or ↓	Move up or down one line
Ctrl+← or Ctrl+→	Move left or right one word
Ctrl+↑ or Ctrl+↓	Move to the top or bottom of a procedure

One difference between Microsoft Word and the Visual Basic Editor is that the Visual Basic Editor is stricter about how you enter your code than Microsoft Word is about how you enter the text in the document.

When you begin working with VBA, you must learn how the language works. In some respects, it is like learning a foreign language. You must learn the words used, and then you must learn how to construct a sentence. You must learn the grammar of the language.

Learning a programming language is the same. The words are your statements, functions, or commands that will accomplish the tasks you are trying to automate. The grammar of the language is called the syntax. Each statement, function, or command will have specific components that will perform the task.

As you take a look at the code displayed in the Code window, notice that some of the words are highlighted in blue. To make it easier to read the code, the Visual Basic Editor highlights the VBA keywords in blue.

NEW TERM As you type in your code, there is also a feature called *syntax checking* that acts like spell check in Microsoft Word. As you enter your code, syntax checking verifies that you have included all the necessary components to execute the specific task. In some cases, it will also give you some hints as to what is needed to complete the statement.

Examining the Properties Window

The next window is the Properties window, as shown in Figure 13.13. This window is a similar to the Properties window you are used to working with in Access, but it doesn't have as extensive a tab structure. You can view the properties in alphabetical order or categorized. When you first open the Visual Basic Editor to examine the code you have created, it will display the properties for the control you were working with, but with the Object drop-down list, you can select any control to view its properties.

13

FIGURE 13.13

The Properties window gives you a chance to see the property settings for the object that you are working with.

This window is helpful if you are going to change properties with code. You can see what the current setting for a control is as you write your code. You can also use this window to verify settings when you are testing your code.

Examining the Locals Window

The last window currently visible is the Locals window (see Figure 13.14). This window also assists you with locating problems with your code. As you create more sophisticated code, you will sometimes have problems or bugs crop up in your code. This occurs because of typing mistakes or design errors with the objects.

FIGURE 13.14

The Locals window enables you to view the current settings of your variables when you are testing your code.

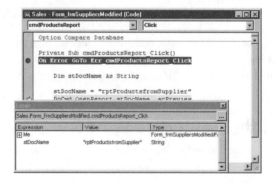

NEW TERM When these problems crop up, you will have to locate them and correct them. This process is known as *debugging*. The Locals window is one window that is available to assist you.

The Locals window displays the current settings for any objects and variables that are currently available when you are testing your code. It lists the expression, its value, and its type.

NEW TERM *Variables* are a special type of object to allow you to temporarily store information when you are running a procedure. They are discussed further in the next topic of this lesson. You will put this window to good use in the later lessons on VBA.

Examining the Watches Window and the Immediate Window

Two other windows will assist you when you are testing your work. When you first open the Visual Basic Editor, they are not displayed. You can turn them on as needed.

The first one is the Watches window (see Figure 13.15). To display the Watches window, you can select View, Watch Window. The Watches window is similar to the Locals window in the respect that it allows you to keep track of specific variables. As you are tracking down problems or debugging, you might want to halt the execution of your code.

FIGURE 13.15

The Watches window enables you to track a break in your code based on a setting.

This window works with one of the debugging features. You can set up the editor to watch when a variable becomes true or changes. This is a great asset when you want to track what is happening to settings in your code. This window lists the expression you are testing, its current value, what type of expression you are testing, and the context or location of the expression.

The last window is the Immediate window (see Figure 13.16). This window is also to assist you with debugging your code. This window allows you to test an expression dynamically, as well as set expressions to test specific problems that might crop up in your code.

To set a value to test, you can simply type in an expression. To test a value, you can use a question mark or Print statement followed by the name of the variable or setting. This works well with variable, constants, and properties.

13

FIGURE 13.16

The Immediate window enables you to interact with your code as it is running.

The Immediate window, the Watches window, and the Locals window do not have much use until you begin testing your code because they will display no valuable information until your code is running. You will get an opportunity to experiment with these tools later in this lesson. Before you begin debugging your code, you must have an introduction to some basic language elements.

Introducing Language Elements

You created your first VBA procedure using the Control Wizard. You let it build the code for you, but as your automation needs grow, the Control Wizard might not always do the job for you. That is when you must have a clear understanding of the language. In this topic, you will examine the code generated by the Control Wizard and learn the elements that went into that code.

Examining the Control Wizard's Results

Before you begin looking at the code that was generated, be sure you are using the Full Module view and that you are at the top of the module. If you are not sure whether you are at the top of the module, press Ctrl+Home to get to the top. This module contains the code in Listing 13.1.

LISTING 13.1   THE CODE GENERATED BY THE CONTROL WIZARD

```
Option Compare Database

Private Sub cmdProductsReport_Click()
On Error GoTo Err_cmdProductsReport_Click

    Dim stDocName As String

    stDocName = "rptProductsfromSupplier"
    DoCmd.OpenReport stDocName, acPreview

Exit_cmdProductsReport_Click:
    Exit Sub

Err_cmdProductsReport_Click:
```

```
MsgBox Err.Description
Resume Exit_cmdProductsReport_Click

End Sub
```

Note

> Before looking at the code itself, notice a couple of formatting techniques. Note that there are blank lines between some of the lines, and that some of the lines are indented. When you are writing a document in Microsoft Word, you frequently put a blank line or some whitespace in between paragraphs and offset some of the text. This makes the document easier to read. The same is true with your code.
>
> It is recommended that you skip a line to separate different actions in your code. It is also recommended that you indent lines of code to help you identify your procedures a little better.

Understanding Declarations and Options

ANALYSIS Now look at the code itself. The first line of code is the `Option Compare Database` line. This line of code is not part of your procedure; it is actually above your procedure.

If you look at the object list, you will notice that the object is (general) for every module you create. It is only surrounded by the parentheses to force it to the top of the object list. The Procedures list shows (Declarations).

NEW TERM The *general object* is a location to store declarations and procedures that must be used by more than one of the procedures in the module.

The *declarations section* is a location for you to declare any variables and constants that are needed in this module. It is also the location to set up some execution settings for the module. In this module, no variables or constants need to be shared, so there is only the `Option Compare Database` statement.

13

Note

> A statement is a Visual Basic keyword that represents an action that can be used in code.

The `Option Compare` statement is placed in every module to allow you to determine how text will be compared and sorted within your procedures. There are three settings for the `Option Compare` statement. You can compare text as `Binary`, `Text`, or `Database`.

`Option Compare Binary` will compare text based on its binary value. When characters are stored in memory, they are stored in a binary format. This means that an uppercase *A* has a different value than a lowercase *a*. This type of comparison is useful if you need to separate upper- and lowercase letters.

`Option Compare Text` compares the text value alone. This means that the upper- and lowercase letters will be treated alike. The last setting, `Option Compare Database`, is only available when you are using Access. It will use whatever the sort settings are for your database. This is similar to the `Text` setting. For the most part, you are not going to change this statement.

The other statement you are likely to see in the General Declaration section is `Option Explicit`. If you see the `Option Explicit` statement in a module, it means that before you can use a variable, you must declare it.

The general object is also where you would place any procedures or functions you need to use from several places in this module.

Using Procedures

After a line to separate the general declarations from the next procedure and a blank line, you have

```
Private Sub cmdProductsReport_Click()
```

This is the beginning of the procedure that was created. It is paired with the last line. For every procedure you create, there is an identifying line and an `End` statement. This procedure is an event procedure because the code is executed when the user clicks on the command button. An event procedure will follow a specific format or syntax.

```
Private Sub objectname_eventname([argumentlist])
    statements
    Exit Sub
    statements
End Sub
```

The first keyword for an event procedure is `Private`. This indicates that this event procedure can be used only by this form. The second keyword is `Sub`. It indicates that this is a sub procedure and will execute without returning a value.

The third word is the name of the object, followed by an underscore and the name of the event. In this case, this is the control name cmdProductReport and its click event. This is followed by a set of parentheses to hold any arguments. If information must be given to this procedure before it can execute, it is often delivered by an argument. In this case, the click event doesn't need any arguments to execute.

Under the procedure identification, you will place the code statements to execute. The last line will always be `End Sub` to indicate the end of the code to be executed. If you need to stop executing code within the procedure, you will use the `Exit Sub` statement.

In the earlier discussion about procedures, there were three other types: sub procedure, function, and property. These will not be generated by a wizard, you must create them from scratch. Also, they must be created with a specific syntax.

A general sub procedure is a procedure that will be called from another procedure. It is very similar to the event procedure.

```
[Private¦Public¦Friend] [Static] subprocedurename [(arglist)]
    [statements]
    [Exit Sub]
    [statements]
End Sub
```

The first keyword will be `Private`, `Public`, or `Friend`. This keyword will indicate where you can use the sub procedure. `Private` indicates that the procedure can be used only by other procedures in the module in which it is located. `Public` indicates that the procedure can be used throughout your database. `Friend` is new; it is only available in a class module, which is not a topic for this book.

The second keyword is `Static`. This word indicates whether any variables in the procedure will hold their values between calls to this procedure.

The name of the procedure is followed by the argument list inside parentheses. The rest of the lines are the same as those for the event procedures.

A function is very similar to a sub procedure. Its syntax varies in only a couple places:

```
[Public¦Private¦Friend] [Static] Function name [(argumentlist)] [As type]
    [statements]
    [name = expression]
    [Exit Function]
    [statements]
    [name = expression]
End Function
```

13

The first keyword will be `Public`, `Private`, or `Friend`. This will be followed by `Static`, if desired. The `Function` keyword is substituted for the `Sub` keyword, followed by the name of the function and the argument list.

Because the function returns a value, you can specify what type of value with the `As` keyword followed by the type of value to be returned.

The rest of the syntax is the same except for two differences. The Sub keyword is replaced with the Function keyword. The second difference is that within the code you must set the function name equal to a value because the function must return a value.

The last type of procedure is the Property procedure, which can be created only in a class module. The syntax will vary depending on what type of property procedure you are creating. It is again not a topic for this book.

Understanding Scope

NEW TERM   In the previous discussion of the syntax for procedures, the use of the Private and Public keywords was discussed. Their use indicates which procedures could have access to the code in a specific procedure. Access to execute code is normally referred to as the *scope* of the procedure.

Within your database, you can control what has access to your code. There are four levels of access to your code when you create your modules. These can provide access within your application, as well as from other applications.

The first level is the Public level. This level provides the widest possible access. Anything declared with the Public keyword is accessible from anywhere in your application, or from another application provided that application has the capability to access it. This is a wonderful capability, especially when you have more than one application or project that needs to share information.

If you need to have access from your application, but you do not necessarily want other applications or projects to have access to your code, you can restrict the access to your application or project by using another option. If you place the statement Option Private Module in the general declarations object, it can be used only within your project.

The third level is the module level. If you have variables, constants, or procedures that should only be accessed from a specific module, they should be declared with the Private keyword with the general object.

The last level is the local level and it is the most restrictive. If a variable or constant is needed only for a specific procedure, it is declared within that procedure.

The scope of a variable, constant, or procedure will also have an effect on the amount of memory needed. When something can be accessed at the local level, it will take up memory only while the procedure is executing unless the Static keyword is used. If something is declared using one of the other levels, it will remain in memory until it is unloaded. That means a module-level variable will be in memory until that object is closed. With the public level, everything remains in memory after it is initialized until the project is closed.

The key to declaring procedures, variables, and constants is to use the lowest level possible. If something is needed only for a procedure, make it a local declaration. If you need something throughout your application, but not outside your application, do not forget the Option Private Module statement in the general declarations.

Understanding Error Handling

Getting back to code, the next line in Listing 13.1 is the On Error statement. Earlier in this lesson, you were introduced to the windows in the Visual Basic Editor, and several of them were reserved for debugging. Debugging is the task of eliminating problems or bugs in your code to avoid operation failures when you are executing your code. You want to eliminate problems where you can in your code, but there are times it isn't possible. A good example is when you are trying to access something on a floppy disk and there isn't one in the drive. You can't solve this problem with debugging.

Unanticipated errors, like the floppy drive or a printer being out of paper, require some special attention. This is known as *error handling*.

The line On Error Goto Err_cmdProductsReport_Click sets up the error handling for this procedure. If anything goes wrong after this line, execute the code beginning with Err_cmdProductsReport_Click. That line is lower in the code:

```
Err_cmdProductsReport_Click:
    MsgBox Err.Description
    Resume Exit_cmdProductsReport_Click
```

NEW TERM   This line is what is called a *line label*. It is used in conjunction with a Goto to indicate where to pick up executing code. The code following the line label handles the error and then indicates what to do after the error is handled.

In this case, it uses the MsgBox statement to display a message about what went wrong. The next line indicates what should happen after the error is handled. After an error is handled, you can do one of two things. You can use the Resume keyword to continue execution at a particular place or you can exit the procedure.

Resume can be used by itself to continue execution with the line that caused the problem, or it can be combined with the Next keyword to continue with the line of code following the error. Resume can also be used with another line label to pick up the execution in another location entirely. That is the approach taken with the code generated by the Control Wizard:

```
Exit_cmdProductsReport_Click:
    Exit Sub
```

13

It resumes at the `Exit_cmdProductsReport_Click` line label. From there it uses the `Exit Sub` keywords to terminate the execution.

Error handling is needed to manage the circumstances that can't be handled with code. Examples of error handling will be shown in later lessons to give you a better idea of where you might need error handling. Some other techniques will also be demonstrated.

Using Variables

After a blank line, the next line in the procedure in Listing 13.1 declares a variable. That is followed by another blank line and the next line assigns the variable a value:

```
Dim stDocName As String

stDocName = "rptProductsfromSupplier"
```

In this procedure, the action you are trying to accomplish is the opening of a report. To accomplish this task, you must tell the application what report you are going to open. These lines of code accomplish this task.

NEW TERM   In several places in this lesson, the term *variable* has been used. A variable is a location in memory that has been assigned a name. It is often used to store data that will change over the execution of the code. Variables are used as a mechanism for transferring data from one location to another, populating arguments for procedures, statements, functions, and methods, and they are also great for storing data temporarily for evaluation.

In this case, the variable is used to store the name of the report you are opening. Realistically, this button opens only one report, so it wasn't necessary to create a variable. The benefit of the variable, in this case, is that the code is generic. It could be dropped into any procedure. The variable could be assigned a different report and it would work.

Declaring Variables

The first line of this code is the declaration statement for the variable. There are two ways to set up a variable. The first way is to declare the variable implicitly. To do that, you would set up a variable name in an expression without the declaration statement. The benefit is that this method is quick. There are several disadvantages. It is easier to make a typographical error later as you try to use the variable, and it doesn't allow you to determine the scope or type of data it will hold.

The second approach is to declare the variable explicitly. This is the approach used by the Control Wizard. The disadvantage of this approach is that it takes an additional line of code. The advantages far outweigh the disadvantage.

The first advantage is that you can indicate what type of data is stored in a variable. This can greatly reduce the amount of memory to store the variable. If the code did not include the Dim line, this variable would be an implicitly declared local variable of undefined dimensions.

When the size of a variable is not defined, Visual Basic for Applications assigns it as a Variant data type. This data type acts as a chameleon. It will evaluate any data coming into it and store that data in the most compact fashion. On the surface, this sounds like the most efficient way to do things. Unfortunately, there is some overhead associated with this data type.

To accomplish this, some additional space in memory must be reserved to allow that evaluation and to indicate how the data was stored. This translates to a variable that takes up a minimum of 16 bytes of space in memory. If you were only trying to store a number between 1 and 10, you would take 16 bytes to store 1 byte of data.

When you declare your variables, you must be aware of what procedures will need to access them. If you need a local variable that can be used only within the procedure it is declared in, you will use the syntax of the example in this procedure:

The Syntax for the Dim Statement

The following is the syntax for the Dim statement:

```
Dim variablename As typename
```

This syntax begins with the Dim keyword, which stands for dimension, and is a carryover from older versions of BASIC. Dim is followed by the name of the variable, the As keyword, and the particular type.

When naming variables, you must obey the naming rules. The variable name can be up to 255 characters. It can include letters or numbers. It must begin with a letter and it cannot be a Visual Basic keyword. You cannot have more than one variable with the same name within the same scope.

13

Note

Notice that the Control Wizard has named its variable with an st prefix. As with the controls, there are naming conventions for variables. For a string variable, you can use st or str. The other naming conventions are listed for you in the next section.

When you need a variable with a module or public scope and lifetime, you will not use the Dim statement. The Private or Public keyword will take its place:

Private *variablename* As *typename*

or

Public *variablename* As *typename*

The rest of the syntax remains the same. If you are following the naming conventions that have been outlined so far, you might also want to indicate the level of a variable in its name just like you indicate the type.

If you were going to have a module-level string variable for a last name, the name could be mstrLastName. If it were to be a public variable, it could be gstrLastName. It is a *g* rather than a *p* because public variables used to be referred to as global variables.

Visual Basic Data Types

As mentioned earlier, it is best to declare a variable with a type to conserve resources. It is very similar to assigned data types to your fields. The data types are summarized in Table 13.2.

TABLE 13.2 VISUAL BASIC DATA TYPES

Type	Storage	Range	Naming Convention Prefix
Byte	1 byte	0 to 255	b or byt
Boolean	2 bytes	True or False	f or bln
Integer	2 bytes	–32,768 to 32,767	i or int
Long	4 bytes	–2,147,483,648 to 2,147,483,647	l or lng
Single	4 bytes	–3.402823E38 to –1.401298E-45 for negative values; 1.401298E-45 to 3.402823E38 for positive values	sng
Double	8 bytes	–1.79769313486232E308 to 4.94065645841247E-324 for negative values; 4.94065645841247E-324 to 1.79769313486232E308 for positive values	d or dbl

Type	Storage	Range	Naming Convention Prefix
Currency	8 bytes	–922,337,203,685,477.5808 to 922,337,203,685,477.5807	c or cur
Decimal	14 bytes	+/-79,228,162,514,264,337,593,543,950,335 with no decimal point; +/-7.9228162514264337593543950335 with 28 places to the right of the decimal; smallest non-zero number is +/-0.0000000000000000000000000001	dec
Date	8 bytes	January 1, 100 to December 31, 9999	dt or dtm
Object	4 bytes	Any Object reference	o or obj
String (variable -length)	10 bytes + string length	0 to approximately 2 billion	s or str
String (fixed-length)	Length of string	1 to approximately 65,400	s or str
Variant (with numbers)	16 bytes	Any numeric value up to the range of a Double	v or var
Variant (with characters)	22 bytes + string length	Same range as for variable-length String	v or var
User-defined	Number required by elements	The range of each element is the same as the range of its data type	

Depending on the type of data you need to store, an explicit declaration can save you a lot of space in memory. The data types available match the field types pretty closely. There are a couple of differences. The first difference is that there is an Object data type. There are times when you must set a variable to represent an object. This requires some special handling and it has its own data type. This type is discussed in later lessons.

The second difference is that there isn't a Text data type. The Text data type is the equivalent to the String data type, but the String data type is more flexible. It can hold a lot more text. This is to accommodate the fact that you have a Memo field type.

13

The third difference is the inclusion of the Variant data type. This is the default data type and it accommodates data that can be stored in the other data types. It was included to account for the fact that sometimes you do not know what type of date you are going to store in a variable. This is especially true if you are going to exchange information with other applications.

The last data type is the user-defined type. This one is special because it enables you to create a combination data type. A user-defined data type enables you to declare a single variable with several components. It is like creating a temporary record template. The syntax combines elements of a variable declaration.

The Syntax for a Type Declaration

SYNTAX

The following is the syntax for declaring a type variable:

```
[Private ¦ Public] Type variablename
    componentname As type
    componentname  As type
End Type
```

You start with the `Public` or `Private` keyword. You cannot leave it off because it can be declared only in general declarations. It is never local. This is followed by the `Type` keyword and the name of the type. Each component of the type must be declared on a separate line. It resembles a variable declaration without a keyword. You will give the component a name followed by the `As` keyword and the type. After all the components have been declared, it is completed with the `End Type` keywords.

NEW TERM In addition to declaring a variable to store one value or declaring a type to store multiple variable components, you can also declare a variable to store multiple values of the same data type. This type of variable is known as an *array*. This is most useful when you are working with records directly. If you need to read through a group of records and get the same value from each record to perform a calculation, you could declare an array variable with a data type that matches the field. Read through the records and store each one in that array.

Setting up an array is very similar to defining any other variable. The syntax is

```
[Private¦Public] arrayname(NumberofElements) As Type
```

You must use either the `Private` or `Public` keyword to indicate its scope and lifetime. This is followed by the name of the array variable. Inside parentheses, you must indicate the number of elements that will be stored under this array name. This can be followed by the `As` keyword and one of the data types to cut down on the space needed in memory.

As you use the data stored in an array, you are going to refer to the array name with the index number of the element indicated in parentheses. There is a small trick to referencing the correct element. When you establish the number of elements in the declarations statement and then begin assigning values, the index numbering will begin with 0. That means the last element will have an index of less that the number of elements. If this is confusing for you, you can add the `Option Base 1` statement to your general declarations. This indicates that indexing will begin with 1.

The array capability in VBA is very powerful. In addition to changing the indexing, VBA also supports the creation and management of multidimension arrays with up to 60 dimensions, as well as dynamic arrays that allow you to redefine the number of elements in the last dimension of an array. For more information on these features, please refer to the Visual Basic Editor's Help.

Using Constants

The previous section introduced variables. These are named placeholders in memory for data that will be manipulated during the execution of your code. With Visual Basic for Applications, you also have another mechanism for storing data.

NEW TERM A *constant* is a named placeholder in memory for data as well, but it usually will not be modified during the execution of your code. The benefit of a constant is that it can make your code much more readable. If you saw an expression that had `curSubtotal = .0825*curOrderTotal`, you might have a hard time determining what the .0825 stood for in the calculation. If instead you saw `curSubtotal = curTAXRATE*curOrderTotal`, it would be much easier to read.

You will work with two types of constants. The first is a user-defined constant. It is similar to a variable in that you will declare it in your code. Examples of constants might include the tax rate, bonus rate, application name, company name, or department name.

The Syntax for Constant Declaration

SYNTAX

The following is the syntax for a constant declaration:

```
[Public | Private] Const constname [As type] = expression
```

The first word will be `Public` or `Private`, depending on the scope you want for the constant. It is followed by the `Const` keyword. Next is the name of the constant. You can indicate a data type with the `As type` combination. This is followed by the equal sign and the value you are assigning to the constant.

13

> **Note**
>
> Notice that in the preceding sample constant, curTAXRATE, the data type for the constant is given and the identifier is in uppercase. For variables, it is recommended that the identifier be in mixed case to make it easier to read. However, for constants, it is recommended that the identifier be in all uppercase to distinguish it from a variable.

The second type of constant you will be working with is a built-in constant. Many statements, functions, and methods in VBA require arguments with numeric settings. Instead of having to remember the numeric setting, they all have built-in constants to make your code more readable.

In the Control Wizard code, the mechanism for displaying the report is the OpenReport method. It has four arguments. One of those is how you want to view the report. Rather than remembering the setting is 2 to preview the report, the code has acPreview in place of the numeric setting.

You do not have to do anything to set up these constants. They are a part of the language. To help you identify them as built-in constants, they also use prefixes. If the statement, function, or method is part of the core VBA language, it will have a prefix of vb. If it is part of the Access extension of the language, it will have an ac prefix. The identifier will be in mixed case.

Understanding Methods

The last line of code that hasn't been discussed is the one that is actually previewing the report:

```
DoCmd.OpenReport stDocName, acPreview
```

New Term The way that you can preview or print reports automatically is with the OpenReport method. A *method* is a procedure that takes action on a specific object. In this case, the code is not as straightforward as it might be. You might think that the object is the report, but in this case the object is the DoCmd object.

On Day 7, "Automating Your Access App: A Macro Primer," you were exposed to the collection of macro actions that could automate your work. Many of those macro actions have a corresponding method to be used when you are automating with VBA. When you are using a method that has a corresponding macro action, the object, DoCmd, is a special one that runs those actions.

As you begin to work with Visual Basic for Applications, you will be working with many objects. These objects all have methods to perform actions.

The General Method Syntax

▼ SYNTAX

`object.method [arguments]`

The first step is to list the object you are working with. It can be `DoCmd` to access macro actions or a form. It can also be the `Screen` object to change the appearance of the screen as a whole or the printer object. This is followed by a period to separate it from the method.

The method name is next. It might or might not have any arguments. If it requires arguments to provide information about the action, the method name will be followed by a space and any arguments will be listed separated by commas.

In the case of the code generated by the Control Wizard, the `OpenReport` method is used to display the selected report in Preview. It does have some additional arguments:

`DoCmd.OpenReport reportname[, view][, filtername][, wherecondition]`

When you are working with a method, the first item will be the object. In this case, it is `DoCmd`. This is followed by a period and the name of the method. In this case, it is `OpenReport`. This is followed by a space and the arguments expected by the method, separated by commas. In the case of `OpenReport`, it is expecting up to four arguments.

The first argument is required. It is the name of the report, represented as a string. This means that you can use a string variable, which is what has been used in this code, or enclose the name of the report in quotation marks within the line.

The second argument is the view. This allows you to specify how you want the report displayed. You can display the report in Design mode, send it to the printer immediately, or preview the report. If you leave this argument blank, the report is sent to the printer as a default. You can specify which view you want with a built-in constant. You have `acViewDesign`, `acViewNormal`, or `acViewPreview`.

The third argument enables you to specify a filter to use to open the report. This argument is optional. If you want to filter the data, you indicate the name of a query to use as a filter.

The last argument, which is also optional, is the `wherecondition`. If you do not have a query to filter the data, you can indicate a string expression indicating your `WHERE` criteria. You would not include the `WHERE` keyword. For more information on `WHERE` clauses, please refer to Day 14, "Understanding SQL."

13

In the case of the generated code, only the first two arguments are specified. This report is not specifying a filter or a WHERE clause because the report that is opening is based on a query using a form for its criteria. For more information on using a form for a query criteria, please refer to Day 15, "Examining Special-Use Queries."

Using Objects

In the previous section, the DoCmd object was used to access the OpenReport method in the generated code. When you are working with Visual Basic for Applications, you are going to be manipulating objects.

NEW TERM   An *object* is a component of the application that can be manipulated with VBA. It has attributes or properties that can be accessed and set. An object has methods to take actions with or on it. It can also respond to events to which code can be added. In many cases, an application will have more than one instance of an object type. When this is possible, there will be a collection of all those types of objects.

Every Microsoft application has a collection of objects, and this is commonly referred to as the object model. Access actually has two object models you will work with: the Microsoft Access Object model and the Access Data Object model.

The Microsoft Access Object model is the one represented with this generated code. It allows you to manipulate Microsoft Access objects, such as forms and reports. The DoCmd object is a part of the Microsoft Access Object model. It allows access to the macro actions with VBA. More of the Microsoft Access Object model will be covered in later lessons in this book.

The Access Data Object model is the one that allows you to access the data directly. This is covered on Day 19.

Getting Help

This lesson has provided an introduction to the components of Visual Basic for Applications, but it has in no way covered all of the language components. As you develop in VBA, one key thing to remember is that help is available. You were introduced to using help with Access in earlier lessons.

You learned that you could click on an object and press F1 to get help. You can also do this with properties in the Properties window. You have full help support in the Visual Basic Editor as well.

The first way to access help is through the F1 key. If you are looking at this code and can't remember the purpose or all the arguments of the OpenReport method, help is a keystroke away.

All you must do is place the cursor in the word OpenReport and press F1. Help will open and display the OpenReport topic (see Figure 13.17). With the topics for VBA, there is a standard format. Help will first define the purpose of the language element.

FIGURE 13.17

The Help window will open with the topic already in view.

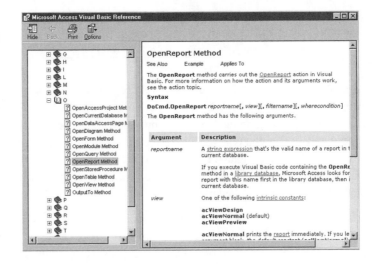

The second part will give the syntax for the command. The syntax will show the keywords in bold and the required arguments in regular text. Any optional arguments will be displayed in regular text with brackets around them.

Following the syntax, the syntax will be defined. The definition will tell you which arguments are required and optional. It will list the type of data that is expected. If an argument has built-in constants, they will be listed and their default settings will be indicated. If there are any common uses or restrictions, they will be listed after the syntax definition. In the case of OpenReport, you cannot exceed 32,768 characters in your *wherecondition* argument.

Another type of help is also available as you enter your code. As with other applications, the Visual Basic Editor has some user-defined options. One of those options is Auto Quick Info. This option provides information about what arguments are expected for statements, functions, and methods (see Figure 13.18).

13

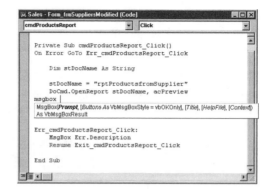

FIGURE 13.18

The Quick Info tips will display as you press the next key after typing the keyword.

Although you haven't entered any code yet, this could be one of your best learning tools. After you type the object, statement, function, or method keyword, you enter another character. Depending on the keyword, you follow the keyword with a space, period, or parentheses. When you type that character, the quick info is displayed. The item that is next on the list is highlighted in bold. As you enter the necessary elements, the bold will shift to the next expected element to assist you. This can be a valuable learning tool for mastering the syntax of the language.

Another valuable form of help is Auto Syntax Checking. Another one of the user options is to allow the Visual Basic Editor to complete a syntax check on your code as you enter it. If you mistype a keyword or use an incorrect data type, Auto Syntax Checking will display a message box as you press the Enter key for that line. Auto Syntax Checking will also change the color of a keyword if it is typed correctly when you press the Enter key. It acts as reinforcement that you are on the right track.

Summary

Today's lesson introduced some of the concepts and language elements for beginning to work with Visual Basic for Applications. You learned that Visual Basic for Applications was a shared development environment that allows you to automate your work in Access as well in other Microsoft applications. That is possible because all the Microsoft applications use the same core language features, and after you learn them you do not have to relearn them. If you want to automate your work in another package, you must learn only the application-specific language components.

To begin experimenting with VBA, you started by taking a look at what the Control Wizard could do for you. You created a procedure to preview a report.

After the code was created with the assistance from the Control Wizard, you took a look at what was created and how you view and edit it with the Visual Basic Editor. You took a tour of the Visual Basic Editor and learned about all its windows.

After you completed your tour, you looked at the VBA code that was generated. You learned that when code is added for a form, report, or control, a module is created for that form or report. You also learned that a module could be created separately from the database windows to store code that must be shared.

You also learned that when you add code to a form, report, or control, you are creating a procedure. You also learned that there are four types of procedures depending on what needs to be done.

This lesson also introduced some of the basic language elements. You learned some different methods to manage data. You also learned that with most of the code you will create, you are going to be affecting objects. You can set properties, use methods, and respond to user and system events for those objects.

You also learned that there is a lot of help available when you are creating your VBA code. You can get help with specific keywords with F1 and you will also get help through keyword prompting as you type.

Q&A

Q Why is a line of my code highlighted in a different color with a dot to the left?

A If you click in the gray bar to the left of a code line, you are using a debugging tool called a breakpoint. You are indicating that you want to temporarily stop the execution before that line is executed.

Q What if I do not see the Code window when I open the Visual Basic Editor?

A If the Code window isn't open, you can click on the module name in the Project Explorer and click the Code button.

Q What if I am entering a keyword and the Quick Info tip doesn't display as I type the next character?

A The display of Quick Info tips as well as Auto Syntax Checking are part of the user options. To turn them on or off, select Tools, Options from the Visual Basic Editor menu. After the Options dialog is displayed, select or deselect the options you want, and click OK.

13

Workshop

The Workshop helps you solidify the skills you learned in this lesson. Answers to the quiz questions appear in Appendix A, "Answers."

Quiz

1. Why should you assign a control a better name than the Control# that the control is assigned as it is created?

2. What is a module?

3. What is the most common type of procedure you will create?

4. Why are variables useful in your code?

Exercises

1. Modify the `cmdProductsReport_Click` event to send the report directly to the printer. Hint: Edit one of the `OpenReport` arguments.

2. Add a new button to frmSuppliersModified to close the form using the Control Wizard.

3. Use help to get information about the code generated for the new Close button.

DAY **14**

Understanding SQL

In Day 4, "Using Queries for Data Retrieval," you began to explore the benefits of working with a subset of your data. You explored how to limit the number of records with a criterion, how to sort the information, and how to combine information from more than one table. This lesson is going to build on that knowledge to get more out of your queries.

Today's lesson covers the following topics:

- What Is SQL?
- Understanding the Structure and Syntax of SQL
- Exploring the Simple SELECT Statement
- Using the WHERE Clause

To assist with the completion of today's lesson, a sample database, Gifts.mdb, is located on the CD-ROM that accompanies this book. It is located in \Day14\. The sample database is based on the same scenario in Day 13, "Introducing VBA." This database manages the customers and inventory for a specialty gifts company. You must copy it to another location to save your work in this lesson.

What Is SQL?

NEW TERM   Day 13 introduced you to Visual Basic for Applications (VBA). It is the primary
language you will use to provide automation for your database. *Structured Query
Language*, SQL, is another language provided with Microsoft Access. SQL is a language
that allows you to work with a subset of records stored in your database. Whether you
realize it or not, you have been working with SQL since Day 4.

That lesson introduced you to the Query object. A query that you create with the Query
By Example (QBE) window is a saved SQL statement. As you select the tables, select
the fields, create an expression, and establish a criterion and sort order, you are indicating the components of an SQL statement. The QBE window then translates this into
SQL.

SQL is very powerful. The simplest of its functions is to create a subset of your data. It
can also create a table, update your data, delete data, create a comparison of data, combine data, and allow you to select your information based on a prompt.

SQL is also not restricted to Microsoft Access. Most popular databases offer some form
of SQL. SQL was first developed by IBM in the 1970s to provide a method for managing data. As databases were introduced, each contained its own form of data management
language. As computers and databases were used more and more in business, there was a
general move to standardization. One of those moves involved database languages. The
American National Standards Organization (ANSI) released the first SQL standard in
1986. It was based on the IBM SQL releases.

Today, most databases take the ANSI standards and use them as the core of their SQL
languages. That makes it easier to manage data across databases. With all the databases
incorporating the core SQL, you will spend less time relearning, and more time learning,
the specialized features in a database. If you are migrating from another database, you
will find very few problems transitioning to the SQL provided with Microsoft Access.

Microsoft Access' QBE window also allows you to get a quick start in creating SQL.
When you use a query to select a subset of records, it can be used several ways in
Microsoft Access. It can be used as a standalone datasheet, it can be used as the record
source for a form or report, it can be used as a row source for a list, or it can be accessed
with VBA.

On Day 13, you learned about Visual Basic for Applications. You might be asking
yourself, "Why do I need two languages?" With VBA, you will develop two types of
operations.

The first type of operations was introduced in Day 13. You can manipulate Microsoft Access objects. You can open forms and reports, and change settings in those objects. You can create database objects or delete them if they are no longer needed.

The second type of operation you will work with is data manipulation. With VBA, you can work with the Access Data Object model (ADO). This enables you to manipulate a recordset. You can move through the records, search through the records, create a new record, update records, and delete records. The one characteristic shared by all of these operations is that you are going to be working with one record at a time. You might also find that you will use SQL to create a recordset to use with your VBA code so that you do not have to work with an entire table.

SQL works with the data a little differently. It doesn't work with each record separately. It treats the records as a group. When you set up your SQL statement, you are defining a subset of records. If you choose to create a new table with those records, update those records, or delete them, you are affecting the group as a whole. You are not working with individual records. This can dramatically increase the speed of an operation.

SQL is also capable of creating some special queries that cannot be accomplished with the QBE window. Microsoft Access is capable of working with data from an outside source. That source can be another personal database, or it can be a larger database application designed for more than one user, such as SQL Server. Some special SQL features are included to support that type of application. These are discussed on Day 15, "Examining Special-Use Queries."

The rest of this lesson focuses on introducing the fundamentals of the SQL language. It also goes into greater detail on how to set up a criterion for a query.

Understanding the Structure and Syntax of SQL

The place to begin the discussion is to take a look at the structure of SQL and examine some of the rules for creating an SQL statement. To begin, the following task creates a query with the QBE window.

Task: Viewing a Query in the QBE Window

1. Open the Gifts.mdb database.
2. Select the Query tab from the Database window to view the queries. Select the qryIllinoisClients query, and click the Design button to open the query in Design view, as shown in Figure 14.1.

14

FIGURE 14.1

Here is a simple query created in the Query by Example window.

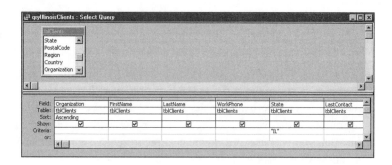

3. Notice that this is a simple query based on one table with six of the fifteen fields. This query is using the Sort row to sort, based on the organization name. This query also has a criterion for State to display only those clients in Illinois.

This is similar to queries you created in previous lessons. This is called a SELECT query. When you use the QBE window, you are setting up the components so that Microsoft Access can generate an SQL statement. To view the SQL statement, click on the View button's drop-down arrow to display the list (see Figure 14.2). You cannot just click the View button because that toggles, or switches, between Design and Datasheet views.

FIGURE 14.2

The View button has a drop-down list to let you get to the SQL view.

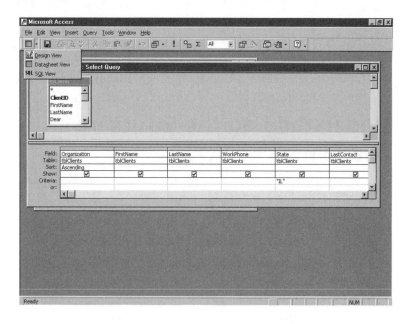

Select SQL View from the drop-down list. This will display the SQL statement that has been created, as shown in Figure 14.3.

Figure 14.3

The SQL statement to select the six fields with the sort and criteria specified in the QBE window.

When you display SQL view, the SQL statement is highlighted. To release the highlight, click anywhere in the window. When you create a query in the QBE window, it will generate the appropriate SQL statement:

```
SELECT tblClients.Organization, tblClients.FirstName,
➥tblClients.LastName,tblClients.WorkPhone,
➥tblClients.State, tblClients.LastContact FROM tblClients
➥WHERE (((tblClients.State)="IL")) ORDER BY tblClients.Organization;
```

This is all one statement, and it would all be shown on one line if it could. Unfortunately, the window is not large enough. The window does have a word wrap feature, so it will display the rest of the statement as a word processor displays the remaining text of a paragraph.

Note

Just like the QBE window isn't big enough to display the SQL statement on one line, neither is the page. In this lesson as well as some of the remaining lessons, when a line can't be displayed on one line, it will be split between lines.

When this is needed, the beginning of the statement will be printed and the additional split lines will have the line continuation icon ([ic:ccc]) displayed preceding the remainder of the line, as shown above. You should enter the SQL as one line, ignoring the line breaks and continuation icons.

As mentioned earlier, this is a SELECT statement. The syntax for the SELECT statement is covered in great detail later. Regardless of what type of SQL statement you are creating, there are several general structural and formatting features that you must include to make it correct, or might want to include to make the SQL statement more readable.

The first feature you will notice is the SQL keywords, which are displayed in uppercase. When you were examining the keywords in your VBA code, they were displayed in mixed case. The Visual Basic Editor also displayed them in a different color. With VBA, the keywords will be translated into mixed case regardless of how you type them.

14

When you want to create a query object, you could create a new query, switch to the SQL view, and begin typing SQL. The first thing you would notice is that it starts you off with SELECT;.

When you are in the SQL view in the query object, there is syntax checking similar to that of the Visual Basic Editor. It will not indicate any problems with your statement, nor correct any capitalization problems as you type. Instead, it waits until you select the Datasheet or Design view. It will correct the capitalization and locate any problems and notify you with a message box.

If you are working with SQL in VBA, it will not correct capitalization. It will notify you of a syntax problem when you run the procedure.

The second feature you will notice is the references to the fields. When you are working with queries, it is possible to include records from more than one table. When you enter a field in SQL, you will want to include its table by typing the table name followed by the field name separated by a period, like tblClients.Organization.

Earlier, you were introduced to the naming conventions for fields. Although it is possible to include spaces in a field or table name, you will find that working with those fields is more time-consuming because you must enclose any fields or table names with spaces in brackets. For example, suppose the clients are stored in Client Records and the last name of the contact was a field with a space. You would have to type [Client Records].[Last Name]. This is one area in which following the naming conventions will save some typing.

The third SQL feature is how the fields are separated. When you are referencing more than one field, you will separate them with commas. This is true whether you are indicating the fields to be displayed or used to sort the results.

The last universal feature of SQL is the semicolon at the end of a statement. When you are writing a sentence, you end the sentence with a period, question mark, or an exclamation mark. A SQL statement ends with a semicolon.

The rest of this lesson focuses on the most commonly used query, a SELECT statement. It also introduces how to get subsets of data using a criterion called the WHERE clause. Tomorrow's lesson introduces the more complex queries available with Microsoft Access SQL.

Exploring the Simple SELECT Statement

The place you will most likely start with SQL is creating a query to get a subset of the records. This is accomplished with a SELECT statement. It will not change the data in the underlying tables, it only retrieves a subset, or recordset to be viewed or used as a record source for a form or report. The SELECT statement has a specific syntax:

The Syntax of the SELECT Statement

▼ SYNTAX

▲

```
SELECT [predicate]
➥{*¦table.*¦[table.]field1 [AS alias1], [, [table.]field2]
➥FROM tableexpression [, ...] [IN externaldatabase]
➥[WHERE... ]
➥[GROUP BY... ]
➥[HAVING... ]
➥[ORDER BY... ]
➥[WITH OWNERACCESS OPTION]
```

Examining SELECT

When you are working with a basic query, the first component is the SELECT keyword. This indicates that you want to create a set or subset of records from your data. This is known as a recordset.

The next component is optional. You can indicate a predicate to help you specify how many of the records you want to return. This can be set to ALL, DISTINCT, DISTINCTROW, or TOP. If the predicate is not specified, it is ALL. ALL returns all the records defined by the statement. This is illustrated by the qryIllinoisClients query. It doesn't have a visible predicate.

DISTINCT enables you to eliminate duplicate records based on selected fields. If you have selected the Organization field and two records have the same organization name, only the first one found will be returned.

DISTINCTROW also enables you to eliminate duplicate records, but it is based on duplicate records, regardless of what fields are selected. If it finds duplicate records, it also will display only the first one.

TOP also eliminates records from the recordset, but it is not based on duplicate information. It enables you to display the top number of records by actual number or by percent. This is very helpful when you have a query working with numbers. You can set up your query to sort the records in ascending or descending order. The TOP component will eliminate those that do not meet the requirements.

The syntax supports either an exact number of records or a percent of the records. To support an exact number, you must use TOP *nn*. In qryTop10Prices, the syntax is

```
SELECT TOP 10 tblProducts.Product, tblProducts.Price FROM tblProducts
➥ORDER BY tblProducts.Price DESC;
```

14

This query produces the results shown in Figure 14.4. As you can see, it is not returning the requested 10 records—it is returning 11 records. When you are using the TOP *nn* component, it doesn't attempt to reconcile the records when more than one has the same value. It displays them through the matching value.

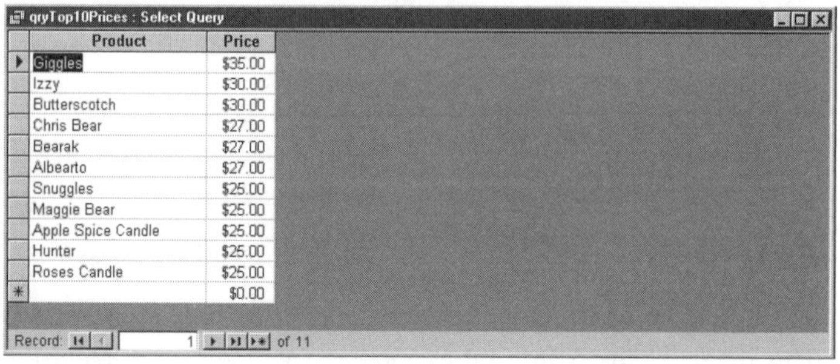

FIGURE 14.4

The SELECT *statement with a* TOP 10 *predicate returns 11 records.*

To use a percent, you would use TOP *nn* PERCENT. In qry25OldestContacts,the TOP 25 PERCENT predicate is used. The records are ordered by the LastContact field in ascending order. You are getting the oldest contacts first and you are picking off the top 25% of them. In this case, it also happens to be the number of records returned because there are only 100 clients.

Following the predicate, you will have a list of fields. This list of fields indicates which fields you want to display in the recordset. The fields in this list include the table or source query name. The structure is *tablename.fieldname*. These are separated by commas.

In the general syntax shown earlier, one field has the AS alias after it. As you have seen in the previous query lessons, it is not a requirement to use only fields. You can create expressions. When you create an expression using the QBE window, you indicate a name for the expression followed by the expression itself in the QBE window, as shown in Figure 14.5.

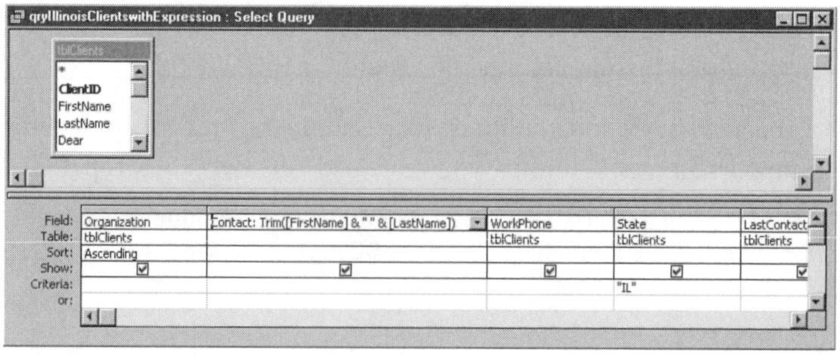

FIGURE 14.5

This query has an expression to combine FirstName and LastName.

This is translated into the AS alias component of the SELECT clause. The expression is the field, and it is followed by the AS keyword and the name you have given your expression. It is exactly opposite of what you see in the QBE window (see Figure 14.6).

FIGURE 14.6

The expression is followed first by AS and then the name of the expression in the SQL view.

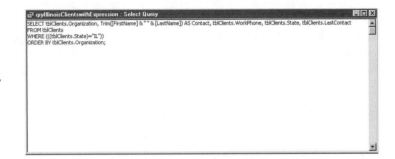

In qryIllinoisClientswithExpression, the TRIM function is used to concatenate the FirstName and LastName fields and reference it as Contact. It gives you a cleaner appearance of the name:

```
SELECT tblClients.Organization, Trim([FirstName] & " " & [LastName])
➡AS Contact, tblClients.WorkPhone, tblClients.State,
➡tblClients.LastContact FROM tblClients
➡WHERE (((tblClients.State)="IL")) ORDER BY tblClients.Organization;
```

After you have listed all your fields, you will need the FROM clause. Do not follow the last field with a comma.

Examining FROM

The second clause of the SELECT statement is the FROM clause. It indicates what tables or queries are acting as the source for the data. When you are setting up your SQL statement, you can retrieve data from any of the tables housed in your database, any queries you have built, or data from an outside source.

If you are basing your SQL statement on one table, the FROM clause is very straightforward. You use the FROM keyword followed by the name of the table or query you want to work with. With qryIllinoisClients and qryIllinoisClientswithExpression, the FROM clause just has tblClients.

When you want to combine information from more than one table or query, or access data from an outside source, the FROM clause will be combined with a join clause or an IN clause. Each of these is discussed separately.

14

Examining Joins

When you are combining information from more than one table, your `FROM` clause can indicate the relationship of the tables. This is accomplished with a join. If you have established relationships between your tables before you set up your queries, the query will pick up those relationships automatically when you are using the QBE window. If you are writing the SQL statement in the SQL view or with VBA, you will have to indicate the joins with the appropriate keywords. In Day 11, "Sorting Data with Queries and Joins," you learned that there are three different types of joins, each of which has its own keyword.

The first join, and the most common, is the `INNER JOIN`. An inner join is an equal join of the tables. It will create a recordset in which there are matching fields between the tables.

The syntax for a join is to list the tables involved in the join and indicate which fields represent the tie between the tables. An example of an inner join is shown in qryProductsbyCategory:

```
SELECT tblCategory.Category, tblProducts.Product,tblProducts.ProductID
➥FROM tblCategory INNER JOIN tblProducts
➥ON tblCategory.CategoryID = tblProducts.CategoryID;
```

When you have a join between two or more tables, the second part uses the `ON` keyword followed by an expression to indicate which fields represent the relationship between the tables. In the case of qryProductsbyCategory, the two fields are CategoryID from both tables. With this query, the CategoryID from tblCategory is the primary key for that table. There is a matching CategoryID field in tblProducts. This is often referred to as a foreign key. To increase your performance, it is best to have foreign keys in the table indexed.

In qryProductsOrderedbyClient, more than two tables are involved: tblClients, tblOrders, and tblOrderDetail. This requires more than one `INNER JOIN` clause. Each inner join has its own `ON` clause:

```
SELECT tblClients.Organization, tblOrders.OrderID,
tblOrderDetail.ProductID,
➥tblOrderDetail.QuantityOrdered FROM (tblClients INNER JOIN tblOrders
➥ON tblClients.ClientID=tblOrders.ClientID) INNER JOIN
➥tblOrderDetail ON tblOrders.OrderID=tblOrderDetail.OrderID;
```

In addition to `INNER JOIN`, you can also create outer joins. An `INNER JOIN` is a relationship equal between the tables. It will create a recordset containing only records in which the fields in both tables match. There are times when you want to set up a query that will find where there isn't a match, as well as where there is one. This is accomplished with an outer join. There are two types of outer joins, a left join and a right join. These are dependent on which table should display all of its records.

In qryClientOrders, you see an example of an outer join. This query lists all the clients, regardless of whether they have placed an order. The records listed do not represent a match between the tables. In Figure 14.7, you will see that some clients have a listing, but without a corresponding order number and date. You will also see some clients, such as TeleBasket, have more than one record shown. This is because there was more than one match in tblOrders.

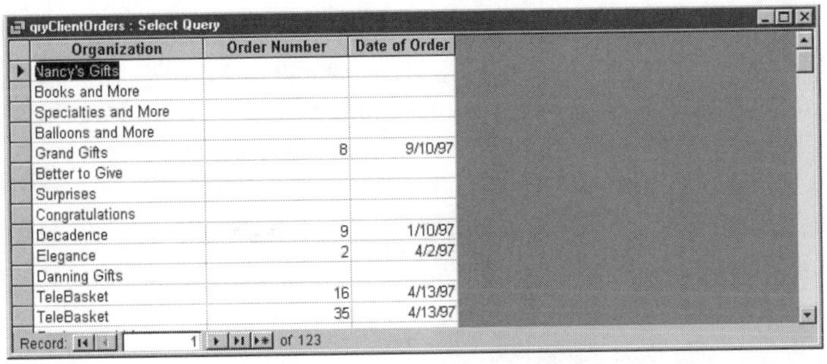

FIGURE 14.7

The recordset for qryClientOrders shows the unequal representation of tblOrders in this query.

When you examine the SQL statement, you will see that instead of the INNER JOIN keyword combination, it is a LEFT JOIN. The LEFT and RIGHT keywords are substituted for the INNER keyword, depending on which table you want to show all of the records:

```
SELECT tblClients.Organization, tblOrders.OrderID, tblOrders.OrderDate
➥FROM tblClients AS tblClients LEFT JOIN tblOrders AS tblOrders
➥ON tblClients.ClientID = tblOrders.ClientID;
```

In this case, tblClients is listed first, so this is a left join. If tblOrders had been listed first, this would have been a right join.

Examining IN

You use the IN keyword when the table supporting a query is coming from an outside source. This is used when you are storing the data in another PC database or a client/server database like SQL Server. The IN keyword is followed by the entire path of the database where the table is located.

The Syntax of the IN Clause

SYNTAX

```
FROM tablename IN pathanddatabase.databasetype
```

tablename is the name that the table is called in the other database. *pathanddatabase* is a formal system path and filename that identifies the database. In some cases, you will also specify the database type. Both of these items must be encased in quotations and they are not separated by commas.

14

Note

> If possible, it is better to create a link to the table than to use an IN clause. When a link is created, it doesn't have to be re-established every time the query is run.

Examining GROUP BY

The next clause that can be included in a SELECT statement is the GROUP BY clause. This clause will be included when you use a summary calculation like Sum or Count. If you open qryProductCountbyCategory in Design mode, you will see the Count function being used to count the number of products in each category (see Figure 14.8).

FIGURE 14.8

Count is selected in the Total row for ProductID, and Group By is visible for the other two fields.

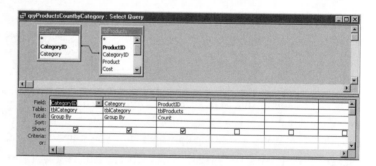

When a summary calculation is used in a query, you are indicating that you want to group the records by the previous fields and then perform the calculation on that one field. In the SQL view, this is translated into a GROUP BY clause:

```
SELECT tblCategory.CategoryID, tblCategory.Category,
➡Count(tblProducts.ProductID) AS CountOfProductID
➡ FROM tblCategory INNER JOIN tblProducts
➡ON tblCategory.CategoryID = tblProducts.CategoryID
➡GROUP BY tblCategory.CategoryID, tblCategory.Category;
```

In the field list for qryProductsCountbyCategory, the count is turned into an expression using the Count function. The CategoryID and Category have been added at the end of the query in the GROUP BY clause.

Examining HAVING

When you are using a GROUP BY to categorize your records in SQL, you might want to restrict which records are displayed. If you are using a GROUP BY clause, you will have a HAVING clause for your criteria. It is very similar to a WHERE clause.

In the qryProductsCountforCategory1 query, the query is only using the records for Category 1. You have created a criterion. When you examine the following SQL statement, note that there is now a HAVING clause after the GROUP BY clause with the criteria expression:

```
SELECT tblCategory.CategoryID, tblCategory.Category,
➥Count(tblProducts.ProductID) AS CountOfProductID
➥FROM tblCategory INNER JOIN tblProducts
➥ON tblCategory.CategoryID = tblProducts.CategoryID
➥GROUP BY tblCategory.CategoryID, tblCategory.Category
➥HAVING (((tblCategory.CategoryID)=1));
```

Examining WHERE

The WHERE clause is one of the clauses you are going to use most when setting up your queries. This allows you to narrow the scope of your query. It restricts which records are returned in the recordset. It follows the following syntax:

The Syntax of the WHERE clause

WHERE *expression*

Going back to look at the qryIllinoisClients query, it restricts the records returned by the query to those with IL in the State field. In the SQL statement, this is represented by the following:

```
WHERE (((tblClients.State) = "IL"))
```

The WHERE clause begins with the keyword, followed by any valid expression for the tables in the query. It will include at least one field with a test of value. It can include any of the operators available in Microsoft Access. The expression can also be a compound expression using AND or OR as a method for comparison.

Creating a valid expression requires knowledge of the data type for the field you are working with. In this case, State is a text field. Because it is a text field, the test value IL is surrounded by quotations. This is only for text fields.

The WHERE clause is one area in which you will spend a lot of time. It is the clause that allows you to restrict the records returned by a query. In the last topic of this lesson, "Using the WHERE Clause," you will explore some of the potential of the WHERE clause.

Examining ORDER BY

The next clause you might need in your SQL statement is the ORDER BY clause, which enables you to sort the query results. In qryIllinoisClients, the ORDER BY clause orders the records by the Organization field. The ORDER BY clause allows you to order the

14

records by one field or a group of fields. To specify more than one field, you separate the fields with commas. If you wanted to order the fields by last name and then by first name, the clause would appear as

```
ORDER BY tblClients.LastName, tblClients.FirstName
```

You can order the fields in ascending or descending order. In this query and in the preceding example, ascending order is set because it is the default sort order. If you want to specify descending order, add the DESC keyword after the field as shown in the following line:

```
ORDER BY tblClients.Organization DESC
```

Examining WITH OWNERACCESS OPTION

You don't use this clause unless you are using security to protect your database from modifications by other users. If you have a query that will make a modification to the database, such as making a table or appending records, you can prevent the user from executing the query with security. As a general rule, you want to prevent users from modifying the structure of your database. If you have a need for them to perform these types of actions, you can use the WITH OWNERACCESS OPTION to suspend the normal security restrictions for this one query with this option. Although this is available for the SELECT statement, it is more commonly needed with the special use queries covered in Day 15.

Using the WHERE Clause

When you are working with SELECT statements, you want to work with only a subset of the records stored in a table. This requires that you define a criterion to restrict which records are returned by the SQL statement. This is done with the WHERE clause.

In this lesson, the WHERE clause receives special attention because it can be a very powerful resource to assist you in narrowing down the scope of your recordsets. The proper use of a WHERE clause can make your SELECT statements more precise and increase their performance. You will have an opportunity to learn how to best use the following WHERE clause features:

- Work with the different field types
- Work with operators
- Use a wildcard
- Work with missing data
- Understand the restrictions

Entering SQL

This lesson has been focusing on the SQL language and what the SELECT statement looks like in the language. When you are creating your queries, you can enter the SQL directly into the SQL window; use the Query By Example window; or create an SQL statement in Visual Basic for Applications code, to support the where argument of the OpenReport method, for example.

When you are working with the SQL view, you will have to type in the WHERE keyword before you type your expression. With the QBE window and in VBA, you normally omit the WHERE keyword. In the following sections, you will see what you would enter and then view what is placed in the SQL statement to accomplish the objective.

Working with the Different Field Types

The preceding example of the WHERE clause selected only the records in which the State field was equal to IL for Illinois clients. It was stressed that it is important to know the field's data type for the field in your expression. It affects whether your query will display or generate an error when it is used.

Data types are important because they will influence what formatting must be placed around the test value for your expression. In the case of the State field, it is a text field. When you create an expression with a text field, you must surround the test value with quotation marks. If you use the QBE window and the Design view, it will place the quotations for you. If you want to create a client list for a particular state, do the following:

Task: Creating a WHERE Clause with QBE's Design View

1. Open the qryKansasClients query in Design view.
2. Click in the Criteria row in the State column.
3. Type KS and press Enter.

After you press Enter, the quotations are placed around the KS because it detected that you typed in text. If you wanted to enter the WHERE clause directly in the SQL View, you would perform the following steps.

Task: Creating a WHERE Clause with the QBE's SQL View

1. Open the qryKansasClients query in Design view.
2. Select SQL View from the View Button drop-down menu on the toolbar.
3. Click after FROM tblClients.
4. Enter a space and type WHERE tblClients.State = "KS" and follow it with a space.
5. Click the View button to view the recordset in the Datasheet view.

14

The last step will confirm that you have typed the WHERE clause correctly. If you are working with a text field in a WHERE clause, there is a difference between what you type in the SQL view and what you would type in VBA code. In VBA, you would set up a string variable and enter the entire SELECT statement inside quotations. This makes it very difficult to read when you must surround the test value with quotations as well. It means that you need triple quotations around it. In that case, you can substitute an apostrophe in place of the quotation inside the string. If you wanted to use the WHERE argument for OpenReport, it would look like this:

```
DoCmd.OpenReport "rptKansasClients", acPreview,,"tblClients.State = 'KS'"
```

If you are not working with text fields, the formatting is different. If you use a numeric field, you will not surround the test value with any formatting. This applies to all the numeric fields as well as the AutoNumber setting.

If you open qryProductsat25, you will see that it is looking for those products priced at $25. Here you could enter the number 25 as the criterion for the Price field (see Figure 14.9). When you press Enter to accept the number, the QBE window doesn't alter the criterion as it did with the text.

FIGURE 14.9

A numeric criterion will not receive any special formatting.

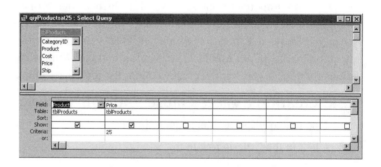

This makes the WHERE clause easier to create from scratch if you want. When you view the SELECT statement, it has created the WHERE clause with no formatting:

```
WHERE (((tblProducts.Price)=25))
```

The last data type you will be trying to select is the Date/Time type. For a date or time, you enter the value surrounded by the pound sign (#). To find out which clients were contacted on 5/5/98, you would do the following:

Task: Entering a WHERE Clause for a Date/Time Field

1. Open the qryMay5thClients query in Design view.

2. Click in the Criteria row in the LastContact column.

3. Type 5/5/98 and press Enter. As you press the Enter key, the pound signs are placed around the date just like the quotations around KS (see Figure 14.10).

FIGURE 14.10

A date criterion is sur-rounded by pound signs.

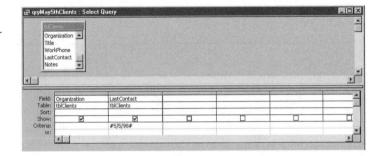

▲

When you view the SELECT statement in SQL view, it will also display the pound signs:

```
WHERE (((tblClients.LastContact) = #5/5/98#))
```

If you typed this in SQL view, it could be typed in after the FROM clause. You do not need to type the parentheses because Microsoft Access inserts them for you. If you were typing this in with VBA, the whole SELECT statement would still need to be surrounded with quotations.

Working with Operators

In the previous examples of the WHERE clause, you have been working with an equivalent expression. You were attempting to build recordsets that have a field that matches the test value exactly. When you work with the WHERE clause, you are not restricted to using only the equal sign to create your expression. Microsoft Access supports a wide range of operators. It offers a complete set of comparison operators. It also offers logical operators to combine expressions, as well as the Between operator to get a range of values.

Using a Comparison Operator

The comparison operators let you specify upper or lower bounds for a value and get any value meeting that criterion. . In addition to the equal sign (=), you can also perform comparisons for a range. You can use any of the operators listed in Table 14.1.

14

TABLE 14.1 MICROSOFT ACCESS COMPARISON OPERATORS

Operator	Description
=	Equal
<	Less than
<=	Less than or equal to
>	Greater than
>=	Greater than or equal to
<>	Not equal

As an example, suppose you want to see all products that cost more than $30. The 30 is the bound specified with the criterion. If you want to see all products that cost more than that amount, you could use the greater-than comparison. To set up this criterion in the QBE window, you cannot just enter the number 30. It will take a little more work, as detailed in the following task.

Task: Entering a Criterion with an Operator

1. Open the qrypPricesGreaterThan30 query in Design view.

2. Select the Criteria row for the Price field.

3. Type >30 and press Enter (see Figure 14.11).

FIGURE 14.11

The greater-than symbol must precede the value.

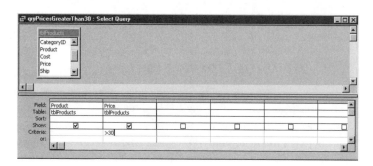

4. Click the View button to display the Datasheet view.

As you view the results, you will see that only one product has a price over $30. As you are creating this type of criteria, you must be very careful with the comparison operator you choose. If you look at qryPricesGreaterThanorEqual30, this query returns more records because it includes those equal to 30 as well as those greater than 30. The same is true using less-than versus less-than or equal.

The last comparison operator is the not equals comparison. There are times when you want to see all the records except those meeting the criteria. That is when you can combine the less-than and greater-than symbols without any space between them to create the comparison.

If you want to see all products except those from the stuffed animals category, the query would resemble qryNotStuffedAnimals (see Figure 14.12). In this case, notice that because CategoryID is a numeric field, you needed to know that stuffed animals has a CategoryID of 1.

FIGURE 14.12

If you want all records except those matching your test value, the not-equal operator is the one to use.

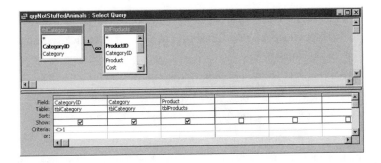

As you have been building the expression with the QBE window, you have been entering the operator and the test value only. With all of these operators, the SQL view will display a complete expression. It will take what you typed in and place it after the WHERE keyword and the name of the field used for the test.

Combining Expressions Using Logical Operators

Sometimes you must create a criterion that tests more than one expression. This requires that you create a combined expression, which you do with logical operators. The two most common logical operators that you will work with are AND and OR. The AND operator is designed to test multiple expressions and return only values that meet all the criteria. The OR operator is designed to test multiple conditions as well, but it requires only that one of the expressions be met. Working with logical operators is trickier in the QBE Design view. It involves keeping track of which line you are on.

If you are looking at the Design view for a query, you will notice that the Or row is below the Criteria row. When you are using logical operators and you want to create an AND comparison, all the criteria must be placed on the Criteria row. You will not want to place the expressions on the Or row.

14

For example, if you want to create a recordset containing clients who haven't been contacted since 1/1/98 who do not live in Illinois; this would be an AND comparison. The following task shows how you would create this query.

Task: Creating an AND Criterion

1. Open the qryANDComparison query in Design view.

2. Click the View button on the toolbar to display the recordset before the criteria. Notice that the 8th record of 100 is not one you want to see for this scenario.

3. Click the View button to return to the Design view.

4. Click in the Criteria row for State.

5. Type <>IL and press Enter. Access will automatically move to the Criteria row for LastContact.

6. Type <=1/1/98 and press Enter.

7. Click the View button to display the recordset in the Datasheet view. Notice that the record is gone and there are only 34 records in this recordset.

The key is that both of these entries stayed on the Criteria row. The SQL view provides a clearer look at the expression. It shows both test expressions combined with the AND keyword:

```
SELECT tblClients.Organization, tblClients.State, tblClients.LastContact
➥FROM tblClients WHERE
➥(((tblClients.State)<>"IL") AND ((tblClients.LastContact)<=#1/1/98#));
```

You create an AND expression using expressions from more than one field by using the approach illustrated in the preceding text. There are times when you must create a logical expression using more than one expression for a field. This requires a bit more typing. For example, suppose you need to see all the clients who have been contacted between 6/1/98 and 8/30/98. This requires the use of two expressions based on the same field. To see how to set up this query, open qryANDinSameField (see Figure 14.13).

FIGURE 14.13

When you need to get a range of values from one field, you must type the AND as you enter the test expressions.

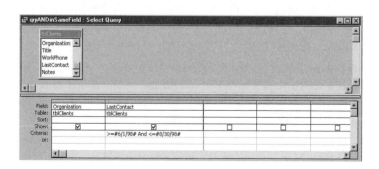

Here you are typing the right side of each expression with the AND keyword in between. When this is translated into SQL, it creates two complete expressions separated by the AND keyword:

```
WHERE (((tblClients.LastContact).=#6/1/98# AND
➥(tblClients.LastContact)<=#8/30/98#))
```

The second logical operator you will want to work with is the OR operator. This allows you to return a recordset that meets any one of multiple criteria. In the Design view for a query, you can simply place each test value on a separate line under the field to create the OR condition. For example, suppose you need a recordset containing only those clients in Illinois and Kansas. You could create the criterion by performing the steps in the following task.

Task: Creating an OR Criterion

1. Open the qryORComparison query in Design view.
2. Click in the Criteria row for the State field.
3. Type IL.
4. Click in the Or row for the State field.
5. Type KS and press Enter.
6. Click the View button on the toolbar to display the recordset. Notice that you are seeing clients in either Illinois or Kansas (see Figure 14.14).

FIGURE 14.14

Placing the two test values on separate rows for the State field created the OR condition.

Organization	FirstName	LastName	WorkPhone	State	LastContact
Avalon	Teresa	Jones	815-458-7852	IL	5/31/98
Better to Give	Gerry	Leverling	316-356-4321	KS	5/17/97
Clarrke's	Clarrke	Ramsey	316-356-9127	KS	7/9/98
Congratulations	Carol	Fuller	815-458-7621	IL	5/9/97
Grand Gifts	Steven	Peacock	815-555-2222	IL	9/10/97
Maple Tree	Mabel	Pierceson	815-458-1234	IL	11/5/98
Old Town Squa	Elizabeth	Trainer	316-606-1238	KS	3/15/97
Oliver Balloons	Truly	Oliver	815-458-9874	IL	11/1/97
Ross's	Ross	Fisher	316-606-3583	KS	2/5/98
Sensations	Cindy	Crane	815-458-9955	IL	4/24/97
Steve's	Steve	Darby	815-458-3322	IL	2/6/98

qryORComparison : Select Query

Record: 1 of 11

Again, when you examine the SQL code below, it has taken both of these test values and created complete expressions separated by the OR keyword. Both AND and OR can be combined with any of the other operators to create your expression for your query:

```
SELECT tblClients.Organization, tblClients.FirstName,
➥tblClients.LastName, tblClients.WorkPhone, tblClients.State,
➥tblClients.LastContact FROM tblClients WHERE
➥(((tblClients.State)="IL")) OR (((tblClients.State)="KS"))
➥ORDER BY tblClients.Organization;
```

14

It is also possible to combine the use of the AND and OR keyword in one test. For example, suppose you want to see all the clients in Illinois who have been contacted after 6/1/98 and you want to see all the clients who have been contacted after 1/1/98. This requires the use of both keywords. It also means that you must pay attention to which row you are on as you enter the criterion. To build this query, perform the following task.

Task: Creating an AND/OR Criterion

1. Open the qryANDORCombination query in Design view.

2. Click in the Criteria row under the State field.

3. Type IL and press Enter.

4. Type >=6/1/98.

5. Click in the Or row under the State field.

6. Type KS and press Enter.

7. Type >=1/1/98 and press Enter.

8. Select the View button from the toolbar to display the recordset. Notice that it picks up a record for a Kansas client for 2/5/98, but it doesn't have any records for Illinois that early in the year.

The following SQL illustrates nested expressions:

```
SELECT tblClients.Organization, tblClients.FirstName, tblClients.LastName,
➥tblClients.WorkPhone, tblClients.State, tblClients.LastContact
➥FROM tblClients WHERE (((tblClients.State)="IL")
➥AND ((tblClients.LastContact)>#6/1/98#))
➥OR (((tblClients.State)="KS") AND ((tblClients.LastContact)>=#1/1/98#))
➥ORDER BY tblClients.Organization;
```

The Illinois and the greater than 6/1/98 are combined with the AND, as are Kansas and the greater than 1/1/98. These two combinations are then combined with the OR keyword.

Using Between

In the discussion of the AND operator, you saw AND used with two expressions working on the same field to get a range of values. In that case, it was the clients who had been contacted between 6/1/98 and 8/30/98. An alternative to using this construction is to use the Between operator. This also allows you to specify a range. To create a query using the same range of contacts using the Between keyword, you would use the steps in the task that follows.

Task: Creating a BETWEEN Criterion

1. Open qryBetweenComparison in Design view.

2. Select the Criteria row for the LastContact field.

3. Type `Between 6/1/98 and 8/30/98` and press Enter.

▲ 4. Click the View button on the toolbar to display the recordset.

This query returns a recordset that contains the clients contacted between 6/1/98 and 8/30/98. The SQL generated also completes the expression like the other operators.

```
WHERE (((tblClients.LastContact) Between #6/1/98# and #8/30/98#))
```

This is not exactly the equivalent of the results of qryANDinSameField. It doesn't pick up the clients contacted on 6/1/98 and 8/30/98. In the discussion of that expression, it was noted that there was a difference between using greater-than and less-than and using greater-than or equal and less-than or equal.

The `Between` keyword is like omitting the equals comparison from both expressions. To resolve this, you would need to move the dates one day back and one day forward for the statement:

```
WHERE (((tblClients.LastContact) Between #5/31/98# and #9/1/98#))
```

Using a Wildcard

In the previous topics, you have been using different comparisons to bring back records that match a specific criterion. When you were working with a numeric value, you were even looking for a range of values. There are times, especially with text, when you do not know the entire test value you are trying to find. This is quite common when working with text fields. For example, you must locate a client, but you do not remember the name of the organization. You know it started with an *E*, but that is all you remember.

NEW TERM If you were in Microsoft Word, you would select Find and use a wildcard to search the document. A *wildcard* is a character that indicates missing information in the search string. The same technique can be used in Microsoft Access and even in queries. To set up a query to display the clients that begin with an *E,* perform the following task.

Task: Creating a Wildcard Criterion

1. Open the qryWildCard query in Design view.

2. Click in the Criteria row for the Organization field.

3. Type `E*` and press Enter.

4. Notice that the `E*` is changed to `Like "E*"`.

14

▼   5. Click the View button to display the recordset. Notice that all the organizations that begin with the letter *E* have been selected.

▲   6. Click the View button to return to the Design view.

When you want to use a wildcard to generate a recordset, use the Like operator. It allows a partial field comparison. The WHERE clause looks similar to the other expressions except for the operator:

```
WHERE (((tblClients.Organization) Like "E*"
```

The asterisk is the most common wildcard. It is a replacement for an unknown number of characters. The E* used in the preceding task indicates the first character must be an *E* and it can be followed with any number of any character.

Other wildcards are available. If you know what you are looking for, but you are unsure about a character, you can use the question mark. For example, qryWildCardQuestionMark used the question mark in its Like phrase to locate the Avalon organization. It indicates that you did not know the spelling of the word. You did not know what letter was in the third position.

There is also a pound sign wildcard, used when you are looking for a digit rather than any character in a position. In qryWildCardPoundSign, this is used to locate a client with a WorkPhone that begins with a 7#8* area code. The 8 is followed with an asterisk to indicate that any character is acceptable after the 8 in this field.

Working with Missing Data

Creating queries with multiple criteria and working with a wildcard to create a query when you are not exactly sure of what you are looking for are some of the powers of the WHERE clause. It can also assist you in creating recordsets in which there is information missing in a field. When data is being entered into a record, any numeric field begins with a Null setting. Any text memo or hyperlink begins with a Null value or an empty string. There are times when you want to look at only records with missing data in a field, and other times you want to work with those records that do not have missing information.

When you want to look at a field for missing information, you must enter Is Null as the criterion. The Is keyword indicates that you are looking for the state of a field. The Null keyword indicates what state you want are trying to look at. In qryMissingData, Is Null is set as the criterion for the Notes field. This is a memo for comments about a client. This returns a recordset with all but three of the records.

In most cases, you will probably want to look at only the records that have data in a particular field. In qryValidNotes, the `Is Null` is modified with the `Not` keyword. If you want only records with data in the Notes field, you place `Is Not Null` instead of `Is Null` as your criterion. This returns the three records with notes (see Figure 14.15).

FIGURE 14.15

The `Is Not Null` criterion enables you to look at only those records with data in the specified field.

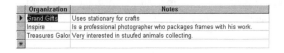

Organization	Notes
Grand Gifts	Uses stationary for crafts
Inspire	Is a professional photographer who packages frames with his work.
Treasures Galor	Very interested in stuffed animals collecting.

In this case, you might have been trying to locate an organization that was a professional photographer. The note is not in a searchable field because it is stored in a memo field. This means that you couldn't use `*photo*` as a criterion, but here you pull up only those organizations that you have created Notes for. The syntax for both of these is similar to the wildcard's `Like` syntax:

SYNTAX

The Syntax for the `Is Null` and `Is Not Null` Criteria

```
WHERE (((fieldname) Is Null))
```

and

```
WHERE (((fieldname) Is Not Null))
```

Understanding the Restrictions

When you begin creating more complex queries, you must be aware of the Microsoft Access restrictions concerning queries. There are restrictions involving the number of tables, relationships, characters, use of logical operators, and number of characters of the SQL statement as a whole. The first restriction involves the number of tables that can be used in a query. You can use up to 32 tables. With those tables, you can have up to 32 enforced relationships less any indexes and can include up to 255 fields.

You can use up to 255 characters to specify your sort order and you can use up to 1,024 characters for a criterion for one field. If you are using parameters, your parameter prompt can be no longer than 255 characters. Parameter queries are covered in greater detail on Day 15.

14

If you are using logical operators, you can have up to 40 combinations, as well as nest queries 50 levels deep. The recordset returned by a query can be up to 1GB. The biggest restriction is that the length of the entire SQL statement cannot exceed 64,000 characters.

In most cases, you will not hit these restrictions. The goal of SQL is to minimize the amount of data retrieved to speed up your performance. SQL provides many opportunities to streamline your view of the data.

Summary

Today's lesson introduced the basic concepts for working with Structured Query Language (SQL). SQL is designed to allow you to work with groups of records at one time. The basic SQL statement is the SELECT statement. It allows you to select a group of records to view and edit. You learned that it lets you reduce the number of fields shown in a recordset. It can also combine information from more than one table and enables you to manipulate the data for display. You can add expressions, group the records by a specific field, and create summary calculations. You can also sort the records based on a field or fields.

The most powerful feature of the SELECT statement is the capability to reduce the number of records returned in a recordset by using the WHERE clause. The WHERE clause allows you to create a test expression for a field or more than one field to locate matching records.

The WHERE clause can test data from any of the field data types as long as it has the right formatting. You can set up your expression using standard comparison operators. WHERE also supports the use of logical operators such as AND and OR. There is also a BETWEEN keyword to allow you to retrieve a range of values. The LIKE keyword allows you to retrieve records based on an incomplete test value using wildcards. The WHERE clause also lets you retrieve records that are missing data in a field or not missing data in a field. This is accomplished using the Is Null or Is Not Null test value.

The last thing covered in this lesson was an overview of the restrictions on using SQL in Microsoft Access. In most cases, these restrictions will not affect your work. As your queries become more complex, or if you are working with data from an outside source, knowing these restrictions can save you many hours of problems.

Q&A

Q What is an action query?

A The SELECT statement covered today is designed to create a recordset. An action query is similar to a SELECT query in that you can specify tables, fields, sort orders, and criteria. An action query is different because it does more than create a recordset; it can modify data. Action queries are covered in Day 15.

Q Is it necessary to type the table name and the field name in the SQL clause?

A The Design view will automatically place the table name in front of the field names in the SQL statement. If you are typing the SQL statement, you are not required to type the field names except when you are using more than one table.

When you are using more than one table and you are using one of the fields that are part of the relationship between tables, you will get an error message as you attempt to display the query because it cannot determine which field to display.

Q What happens if I forget to create a join or delete between tables when I am using more than one?

A The recordset will be significantly larger. If no join is indicated between tables, every record in the first table will be paired with every record in the second table. Instead of a subset of the data, you get a superset of data.

Workshop

The Workshop helps you solidify the skills you learned in this lesson. Answers to the quiz questions appear in Appendix A, "Answers."

Quiz

1. Why is SQL so valuable?

2. What is the key difference between building an expression in Design view and SQL view?

3. When you are setting up a criterion based on a date field, what formatting is needed?

4. What is the important thing to remember about using the Between operator?

14

Exercises

1. Create a query using tblClients listing Organization, FirstName, and LastName, and displaying only the clients whose last name begins with *M*.

2. Create a query using tblOrders and tblOrdersDetail, displaying only those orders from 1997.

3. Create a query using tblProducts displaying Product and Price. It should display only products whose price is between $10 and $15.

4. Create a query displaying the products in alphabetical order.

WEEK 2

In Review

Most people find the additional information on forms, reports, tables, and queries covered this week fairly easy to absorb. There are surely specific areas that haven't fully clicked yet, but the important thing is that you know certain features and abilities are in the product, even if you can't quickly and easily bring them to mind. A significant percentage of people, especially those who have had no programming background, find the VBA and SQL material to be quite a bit more difficult. If you're in this camp, you're with many folks. However, this information is well within almost everybody's reach. Move on to Week 3 now. From time to time while doing further work in Access 2000, even as a developer, return to these chapters for some review. After a few weeks on the job actually doing Access development, you'll see that these lessons weren't nearly as difficult as they might seem now.

8

9

10

11

12

13

14

WEEK 3

At a Glance

In the first two weeks, you began building the skills needed to develop a complete database application. You explored how to use the queries, forms, and reports to get more information from your tables. This third week focuses on polishing your Access 2000 skills. It begins with some additional study of SQL. Here you will see how to change the data in the tables with queries. Day 16, "Implementing Advanced Form Concepts," and Day 17, "Developing Professional-Quality Reports," will help you develop more professional forms and reports.

The remaining chapters focus on completing your database application. Day 18, "Examining VBA," and Day 19, "Working with VBA," will give you a chance to understand VBA a little better as well as see some possible uses. Day 20, "Understanding Access Security," introduces the Access security methods, and Day 21, "Developer Considerations," explores some of the concerns as you begin to let others use your database.

15

16

17

18

19

20

21

DAY **15**

Examining Special-Use Queries

In Day 4 and Day 14, you explored how to get more from your data by using SELECT queries. You learned how to get information from more than one table and also how to summarize data with queries.

This lesson focuses on special-use queries. A *special-use query* does more than create a recordset. Special-use queries can modify your data as well as assist with your data analysis. This lesson also presents two methods for getting criteria for a query from the user. Today, you will learn the following:

- Understanding Action Queries
- Using Crosstab Queries
- Understanding SQL-Specific Queries
- Examining Query Properties
- Creating Parameter Queries
- Getting Criteria from Forms

To follow along with today's lesson, you'll need the sample database, Action.mdb, from the CD-ROM that accompanies this book. You'll find the database in \Day15\. Action.mdb is based on the same scenario from Days 13, "Introducing VBA," and 14, "Understanding SQL": This database manages the customers and inventory for a special-ty gifts company. You will need to copy it to another location before you can save the work you do in this lesson.

Understanding Action Queries

On Day 14, you got an opportunity to learn the purpose and structure of SQL. You explored the simple SELECT statement and how to get the most of your WHERE clause. The SELECT statement is only the beginning of the SQL power. One benefit of SQL is its capability to work with more than one record at a time. You can not only create a record-set to be used for display or to support forms and reports, you can modify records with a query.

A query that affects the record contents is known as an *action query*. You can take advan-tage of four action query types:

- The Update query allows you to update records as a group instead of one at a time.
- The Append query lets you add records to an existing table.
- The Delete query eliminates records from a table as a group.
- The Make Table query creates a new table by using records from an existing table.

Using Update Queries

The first action query you will want to take advantage of is the Update query. The Update query allows you to set a query with any criteria that are needed to get the cor-rect recordset. You then can indicate how you want to change the field or fields.

Setting Up an Update Query

To illustrate how to set up an Update query, suppose your shipping costs increase by 2% for your stuffed animals because of the size of the package. You have all the information to set up an Update query. You know you are going to affect the tblProducts table. You are going to adjust the shipping cost for the products in Category 1, which is stuffed ani-mals, and you need to raise the shipping cost by 2% from where it is now.

First, you set up a Select query to test your selection criteria. This isn't required, but it will confirm that you are working with the correct records. It is like checking the car doors to make sure they're locked. You just locked them, but checking them makes you more comfortable. Then, you can turn it into an Update query.

Task: Setting Up an Update Query

1. Launch Microsoft Access and open the Action.mdb database.
2. Select the Query tab from the Database window.
3. Click the New button to open the New Query dialog box.
4. Select Design View to open the QBE window in Design view.
5. Select tblProducts from the Show Table dialog and click Add.
6. Select ProductID, CategoryID, Product, and Ship as the fields for this query.
7. Select the Criteria row for CategoryID.
8. Type 1 and press Enter.
9. Click the View button to display the Datasheet view with only the stuffed animals products (see Figure 15.1).

FIGURE 15.1

This is the simple Select query to make sure you are viewing the correct records.

Stock	Category	Product	Shipping
1	1	KB	$3.57
15	1	Albearto	$2.50
16	1	Hunter	$2.50
17	1	Maggie Bear	$1.50
18	1	Robbie	$1.50
19	1	George S. Bear	$1.50
45	1	Butterscotch	$4.00
46	1	Bearak	$3.00
47	1	Giggles	$4.00
48	1	Izzy	$3.00
49	1	Snuggles	$2.00
50	1	Chris Bear	$2.00
umber)	0		$0.00

Record: 1 of 12

10. Click the View button to return to the Design view.
11. Save the query as qryUpdateShippingCosts.

Now that the simple Select query is working, you are ready to turn it into an Update query. When you want to use a special-use query, you need to click the Query Type button on the toolbar to select the type of query you are going to need.

As you select the query type, the QBE window will adjust to display the action query options, and in some cases a dialog will be displayed. After you select the type, enter the options needed and then run the action query.

Task: Changing the Query into an Update Query

1. Click the drop-down arrow for the Query Type button on the toolbar or select Query from the menu.
2. Select Update Query from either menu.

▼ 3. Notice you now have a new row visible in the window. The Update To row is now ready for an expression (see Figure 15.2).

FIGURE 15.2

The Update To row is now available to enter the expression to update the field.

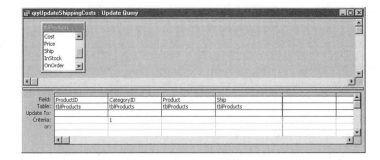

4. Click the Update To row under the Ship field.

5. Type `tblProducts.Ship*1.02` and press Enter.

6. Notice that Access saved you some typing by placing the brackets around the table
▲ and field names to indicate the data objects.

Running an Update Query

Now that the query is set up, you are ready to run the query. This is another part of the process that is different from a simple Select query. With a Select query, you are used to clicking the View button on the toolbar. This displays the query in the Datasheet view. Displaying the Update query in the Datasheet view provides a different view from when you viewed the query earlier. Click the View button and notice the changes (see Figure 15.3).

FIGURE 15.3

The Datasheet view of an Update query will display only the field to be updated for the selected records.

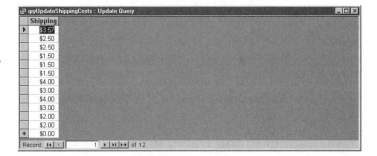

When you view the datasheet for an Update query, it will show you only the fields to be updated for the selected records. No other fields are displayed, not even the field for the criteria. This allows you to see the pre-update values. Click the View button to return to the Design view.

When you are building an Update query, you can omit any field that isn't used as criteria or isn't going to be updated. When you are sure that you are ready to update the records, click the Run button on the toolbar (see Figure 15.4).

FIGURE 15.4

The Run button will execute your action query, and in this case will update the records.

When you run an action query, you are modifying the data. Microsoft Access gives you plenty of warning before executing your query. After you click the Run button, Microsoft Access displays a message about how many records are going to be affected (see Figure 15.5).

FIGURE 15.5

Microsoft Access warns you that you are about to modify a specific number of records.

The reason Microsoft Access is so careful with this query is that an Update query cannot be reversed with the Undo command. You would have to create a new query to reverse the effects of the expression. If you are sure that you want to execute the query, click the Yes button in the message box.

Caution

All action queries warn you before executing because none of them can be reversed with the Edit, Undo command. You might want to take some precautionary steps before executing the action query. For example, you could back up the database. If your database is very large, you could make a copy of the table before running the query.

Depending on the size of the recordset, the execution of the query might take as little as a few seconds or up to several hours. With this recordset, it doesn't take long to update 12 records. Now if you click the View button to see the records, you can see that the Ship field values are all 2% higher than they were before you executed the query.

Now you can save the query and close it. When you are looking at the queries in the Database window, action queries are represented differently from Select queries. For example, qryUpdateShippingCosts has a small pencil with an exclamation icon next to it (see Figure 15.6).

FIGURE 15.6

An action query will have a different icon displayed in the Database window to distinguish it from the Select queries.

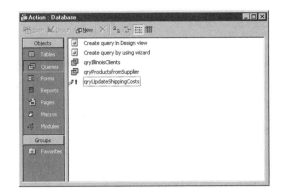

Using a Built-In Function with an Update Query

You can also use built-in functions to update fields with an Update query. If you look at the State field in the tblClients table, you will see that some of the entries are uppercase and some of them are lowercase. On Day 12, "Developing Reports with Graphics and Expressions," you looked at how to correct the display of the State field in a report with the UCase function. When this function is used as part of the Control Source property, you are changing the display and not the data itself. With an Update query, you could change the field itself and eliminate that formatting trick every time you create a report.

Task: Changing the Case in a Field

1. Click the New button to open the New Query dialog.
2. Select Design View and click OK to create the new query.
3. Add tblClients from the Show Table dialog and close it.
4. Select the State field.
5. Select the Update query from the Query Type drop-down list.
6. Select the Update To row for the State field.
7. Type UCase(tblClients.State) and press Enter.
8. Click the Run button on the toolbar.
9. Click Yes when prompted.
10. Save the query as qryUppercaseState and close it.

This Update query, unlike the first one, might be one that you want to run regularly. You do not have to open an action query in Design view to run it with the Run (exclamation) button.

Action queries will respond differently when they are opened from the Database window. If you double-click the qryUppercaseState query from the Database window, Microsoft Access will warn you with a message box that you are about to execute an action query (see Figure 15.7).

FIGURE 15.7

An action query does not display in the Datasheet view when opened from the Database window. It begins executing by displaying the warning.

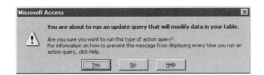

If you made a mistake in selecting the query, click No to halt the process. Otherwise, click Yes to execute the query. Access will then pick up the process, indicating how many rows will be affected.

Note

This query corrects the state's case status, but if someone were to enter data in between running this query and running a report that didn't use the UCase function, he could still have presentation problems.

On Day 16, "Advanced Form Concepts," you will see how you can use Access to correct data when it is incorrectly entered.

Examining the Update Query SQL Statement

When you are developing an action query like an Update query, the SQL statement is different from what you examined in Day 14. For example, the SQL generated for the qryUpdateShippingCosts query is very different from a Select query:

```
UPDATE tblProducts Set tblProducts.Ship = tblProducts.Ship*1.02
➥WHERE (((CategoryID)=1));
```

The SELECT keyword is not used because there are no fields to display. Instead, the UPDATE keyword indicates what table is being updated. This is followed by the SET keyword, which indicates what field or fields are changing, as well as a standard WHERE clause.

Using Append Queries

The Append query is designed to allow you to add records to a table from another table. You can even use it to add records from a table in another database.

Let's look at an example of using an Append query. Imagine that your company has recently picked up a new vendor, Stationary Options. Stationary Options has graciously sent us its product list in table format, and you have imported that table into your database. It is now time to merge it with the main product table.

Before you create the query, you might want to take a look at two things. First, open the tblSuppliers table and notice that the vendor has already been entered and automatically assigned a number.

Second, open the tblStationaryOptions table. Notice that there are 10 products. Also notice that the structure of this table isn't an exact match to the tblProducts table. It already has a stock number, which the tblProducts table assigns automatically, and it is missing the stock status. Assume that Stationary Options is shipping starting stock of 10 each. That means you must have the InStock field updated with a value of 10 for each record.

Tip

When you are bringing information into your database from an outside source, you are going to use the Access Import Wizard. With the wizard, you can indicate what table to import the data into. In some cases, it gives you an opportunity to determine what fields to import as well as what fields match the destination fields.

In the example used in this lesson, the data was imported into a separate table using the wizard. Then an append query is used to copy it to the tblProducts table. This approach works well when you have fields that don't exist in the outside source like the InStock field or you need to verify the data before adding it to the table. You can use an Append query and create the missing data as it is copied.

You might find that this approach works well when you are consolidating data from several sources. For example, you have several people who all do mailings to a certain group of people and each has a separate mailing list. The problem is that each mailing list is updated separately. If one person changes an address, the other lists don't reflect it. By importing each list in a separate table, you can use a Find Duplicates query to make sure that you don't get multiple records for one person as well as reconcile which one is correct before you import it into the main table.

For more information on importing, please refer to Day 21, "Developer Considerations." For additional information about the query wizards like the Find Duplicates wizard, please refer to Day 4, "Using Queries for Data Retrieval."

Creating an Append Query

The process of creating an Append query is similar to that of setting up an Update query. You will again start out like you are designing a Select query. The key is to set up the query by selecting the source of the data as the table to select.

15

Task: Setting Up an Append Query

▼TASK

1. Click the New button to open the New Query dialog.

2. Select Design View and click OK to create the new query.

3. Add tblStationaryOptions from the Show Table dialog, and close the dialog.

4. Select all the fields to add to this query. (Do not use the asterisk.)

5. Select Append Query from the Query Type drop-down list from the toolbar to display the Append dialog (see Figure 15.8).

FIGURE 15.8

The Append dialog is where you indicate the destination for the records from this table.

▲   6. Select tblProducts from the Table Name drop-down and click OK.

Notice the change to the Design view. It now has an Append To row. Notice that the Append To row contains the names of the corresponding field names in tblProducts (see Figure 15.9).

FIGURE 15.9

The Append To row is now visible and populated with the names of the fields from tblProducts.

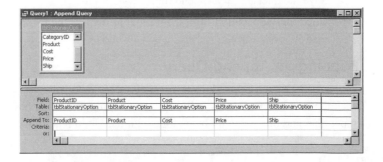

Microsoft Access tries to assist you as much as possible by filling in the field names that match. It isn't always perfect. For example, the names of the fields in this example match for ProductID, but the product ID for the vendor is not the ProductID in the Products table.

Caution

You must verify that Microsoft Access chose the correct fields for the append. It looks for matching field names only.

The vendor's product ID must be placed in a new field called SupplierOrderNumber. To re-assign it to that field, click the Append To drop-down arrow for the ProductID and select SupplierOrderNumber.

Another problem is the missing fields in the table. The vendor doesn't have CategoryID, SupplierID, or InStock fields in its table. The vendor is sending 10 items of each product. This means that you must create three expressions.

Task: Creating Expressions for Missing Data

1. Scroll over so that you can see three blank columns.
2. Click in the field of the first blank column.
3. Type `CategoryID:2` and Press Enter.
4. Type `SupplierID:12` and press Enter.
5. Type `InStock:10` and Press Enter.
6. Select the matching fields in the Append To row for each field.
7. Save the query as qryAppendStationaryOptions.
8. Click the View button from the toolbar to display the recordset to verify the information looks correct.

Running an Append Query

You can also run an Append query by clicking the Run button on the toolbar. When you click the Run button, Access will display a warning indicating how many records you are appending and that it cannot be undone with the Undo feature (see Figure 15.10).

FIGURE 15.10

Microsoft Access tries to prevent mistakes by warning you that your query is about to modify the data.

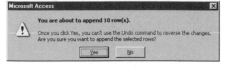

Microsoft Access

You are about to append 10 row(s).

Once you click Yes, you can't use the Undo command to reverse the changes. Are you sure you want to append the selected rows?

[Yes]   [No]

15

If you click Yes, Access adds the records at the bottom of the table. At the beginning of this section, you looked at the tblSuppliers table to see that the vendor had already been entered as a supplier. If you had entered a SupplierID that wasn't in the table, you would get another error message (see Figure 15.11). This message indicates that you cannot add records to the tblProducts table without a valid SupplierID because there is a relationship between tblProducts and tblSuppliers.

FIGURE 15.11

When you set up relationships to protect against integrity problems, the action queries follow the rules set up.

After the query has run, you can open the tblProducts table and see that the records have been added to the end of the table. Notice that the records have a ProductID assigned as the products were appended. The existing ID that came with the table has been placed in the new SupplyOrderNumber field (see Figure 15.12).

FIGURE 15.12

The appended records were automatically assigned an ID and the rest of their data was placed in the appropriate fields.

Stock	Category	Product	Cost	Price	Shipping	In Stock	On Order	Supplie	Order #
39	6	Congratulations Album	$7.00	$10.00	$1.00	15	15	6	
40	6	My Brother Book	$10.00	$15.00	$2.00	10	8	6	
41	6	Grandmother Book	$7.00	$10.00	$1.00	15	10	6	
42	6	Grandfather Book	$7.00	$10.00	$1.00	20	5	6	
43	6	Father Book	$7.00	$10.00	$1.00	5	10	6	
44	6	Mother Book	$7.00	$10.00	$1.00	10	10	6	
45	1	Butterscotch	$25.00	$30.00	$3.00	15	20	8	
46	1	Bearak	$25.00	$27.00	$2.50	10	15	1	
47	1	Giggles	$28.00	$35.00	$3.00	15	20	1	
48	1	Izzy	$28.00	$30.00	$2.50	10	10	1	
49	1	Snuggles	$20.00	$25.00	$1.50	15	20	8	
50	1	Chris Bear	$20.00	$27.00	$1.50	10	20	8	
62	2	Sunrise	$15.00	$20.00	$2.50	10	0	12	1
63	2	Daisies	$14.00	$20.00	$2.50	10	0	12	2
64	2	Gardener Walk	$15.00	$20.00	$2.50	10	0	12	3
65	2	Trumpets	$16.00	$21.00	$2.50	10	0	12	4
66	2	Ivy	$17.00	$22.00	$2.50	10	0	12	5
67	2	Gold Accents	$20.00	$25.00	$3.00	10	0	12	6
68	2	Silver Accents	$20.00	$25.00	$3.00	10	0	12	7
69	2	Red Ribbon	$18.00	$22.00	$3.00	10	0	12	8
70	2	Baby's Breath	$13.00	$19.00	$2.00	10	0	12	9
71	2	Teddies	$13.00	$19.00	$2.00	10	0	12	10

Record: 56 of 60

When you close the query, notice that it is also represented in the Database window with a different icon. It is differentiated from the other queries with a plus sign followed by an exclamation icon. It will also attempt to execute immediately as you attempt to open it or double-click on it.

Examining the Append Query SQL Statement

Again, the SQL statement is different from the SELECT statement. It doesn't use the SELECT clause as the first entry:

```
INSERT INTO target [IN externaldatabase] [(field1[, field2[, ...]])]
➥SELECT [source.]field1[, field2[, ...] FROM tableexpression
```

The INSERT INTO clause is first. This is followed by the target, which is the table in which to place the data. If the target is not located in the active database either as a resident table or a linked table, the target table is followed by the IN keyword and the path to the database. The fields to be used are placed in parentheses following the table name.

This is followed by the SELECT statement that selects the matching fields from the source table. It must include the field list as well as the FROM clause to indicate the source of the data. It can, if needed, contain the other clauses as well.

Using Delete Queries

The Append query enables you to insert a group of records into a table. The Delete query allows you to remove the records as easily. In the previous section, you added the records from the tblStationaryOptions table to the main products list by appending them to tblProducts. In this section, you will create a query to remove the same records.

Creating a Delete Query

As with the other queries, you must begin with a blank query, and then you will add the table and set up the criteria to select the records to delete. Like the Update query, you do not need to select all the fields. You will select only the fields used to set up the criteria.

Task: Creating a Delete Query

1. Click the New button from the Query tab in the Database window to open the New Query dialog.
2. Select Design View and click OK.
3. Select tblProducts from the Show Table dialog and click OK.
4. Select SupplierID as the first field.
5. Select Delete Query from the Query Type drop-down list from the toolbar.

6. Notice that the Design view changes, as shown in Figure 15.13.

▼ 7. Enter 12 as the criteria and press Enter.

8. Click the View button on the toolbar to see that you have only the last 10 records you just added.

9. Save the query as qryDeleteStationaryOptions.

FIGURE 15.13

The Design window has some different rows to set up the Delete query.

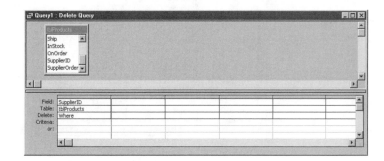

▲

Running a Delete Query

After the query is built, if you click the Run button, you get a message that you are about to delete the records (see Figure 15.14). This message allows you to confirm the operation because after you delete records with a delete query, you can't use Undo to get them back.

FIGURE 15.14

The Delete Query window displays a message box indicating that you are affecting the records and giving you a chance to cancel the process.

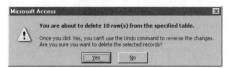

After you have deleted the records, you can open the tblProducts table to view the results, as shown in Figure 15.15. The records will be deleted. If you run the Append query again, the records will be returned, but they will have new ID numbers because once an AutoNumber field assigns a value, that value cannot be reused.

FIGURE 15.15

The table now shows that the records are gone.

		Stock	Category	Product	Cost	Price	Shipping	In Stock	On Order	Supplie	Order #	
	+	29	5	Vacation Album	$10.00	$14.00	$1.00	10	10	7		
	+	30	2	School Buses Stationa	$12.00	$17.00	$2.00	10	15	3		
	+	31	2	Cats Stationary	$10.00	$18.00	$2.00	15	5	3		
	+	32	2	Blue Mood Stationary	$11.00	$18.00	$2.00	10	15	3		
	+	33	2	Race Cars Stationary	$11.00	$18.00	$2.00	20	0	3		
	+	34	2	Hearts & Flowers Static	$11.00	$18.00	$2.00	10	15	3		
	+	35	2	Dogs Stationary	$11.00	$18.00	$2.00	5	15	3		
	+	36	2	Carnations Stationary	$15.00	$20.00	$2.00	20	10	3		
	+	37	6	Family Album	$7.00	$10.00	$1.00	10	10	6		
	+	38	6	My Sister Book	$7.00	$10.00	$1.00	10	10	6		
	+	39	6	Congratulations Album	$7.00	$10.00	$1.00	15	15	6		
	+	40	6	My Brother Book	$10.00	$15.00	$2.00	10	8	6		
	+	41	6	Grandmother Book	$7.00	$10.00	$1.00	15	10	6		
	+	42	6	Grandfather Book	$7.00	$10.00	$1.00	20	5	6		
	+	43	6	Father Book	$7.00	$10.00	$1.00	5	10	6		
	+	44	6	Mother Book	$7.00	$10.00	$1.00	10	10	6		
	+	45	1	Butterscotch	$25.00	$30.00	$3.00	15	20	8		
	+	46	1	Bearak	$25.00	$27.00	$2.50	10	15	1		
	+	47	1	Giggles	$28.00	$35.00	$3.00	15	20	1		
	+	48	1	Izzy	$28.00	$30.00	$2.50	10	10	1		
	+	49	1	Snuggles	$20.00	$25.00	$1.50	15	20	8		
▶	+	50	1	Chris Bear	$20.00	$27.00	$1.50	10	20	8		

Record: 50 of 50

If you attempt to run a Delete query that could remove records with related records in another table, Microsoft Access will protect you. If a product that is about to be deleted has been ordered, it has a relationship with a record in tblOrderDetails. Microsoft Access will indicate the problem in another message box, as shown in Figure 15.16. Click Yes to continue with the deletion of the other records or click No to cancel the process.

FIGURE 15.16

The Delete query will not remove records with related records by default.

Microsoft Access can't delete 1 record(s) in the delete query due to key violations and 0 record(s) due to lock violations.

Do you want to run this action query anyway?
To ignore the error(s) and run the query, click Yes.
For an explanation of the causes of the violations, click Help.

Yes   No   Help

When the Delete query closes, it is listed in the Database window. Its icon is the Delete symbol, a cross-out followed by an exclamation point. It also executes when you open it.

Examining the Delete Query SQL Statement

The SQL statement is different from the SELECT statement. It doesn't use the SELECT clause as the first entry:

```
DELETE [table.*] FROM table WHERE criteria
```

The DELETE clause is first, with the table name followed by period and an asterisk, to indicate that all the fields are to be deleted. The FROM clause indicates where the records are located. This is followed by a WHERE clause, which indicates what criteria are used to indicate what records are to be deleted.

Using Make Table Queries

The last of the action queries is the Make Table query. This query allows you to create a brand-new table consisting of the records specified from an existing table. That table can be within the active database or it can reside in another database. A possible use for a Make Table query in this sample database could be to create a table with the clients from one region for a sales rep.

Creating a Make Table Query

To create a Make Table query, the process is very similar to that for the other action queries. You start with a new query in Design view. You must add the tables and then turn it into a Make Table query with the Query Type drop-down list. Then you can set your fields and criteria.

Task: Creating a Make Table Query

1. Click the New button to display the New Query dialog.

2. Select Design View and click OK to open the query window.

3. Select tblClients from the Show Table dialog and select Close to close the dialog.

4. Click the ClientID field in the tblClients list and Shift+Click on Notes to select all the fields.

5. Drag the fields to the grid.

6. Scroll over to the Region field and select the Criteria row.

7. Type Midwest and press Enter.

8. Click the View button on the toolbar to view your recordset and notice that you have selected 43 of the 100 records.

9. Click the View button on the toolbar to return to Design view.

10. Select Make-Table Query from the Query Type drop-down list to display the Make Table dialog (see Figure 15.17).

FIGURE 15.17

The Make Table dialog is where you indicate a table name and the database if needed.

11. Type tblMidwestClients as the name for the table and click OK. You will leave this table in the same database.

 12. Save the query as qryMakeTableMidwestClients.

With the Make Table query, you might have noticed that the Design View window does not change. That is because all the information to make a new table is taken care of with the dialog.

Running a Make Table Query

Running a Make Table query is like running the other action queries. Click the Run button on the toolbar, and Microsoft Access warns you that you are about to paste 43 rows into a new table (see Figure 15.18). You can click Yes to continue or No to cancel the operation.

FIGURE 15.18

Microsoft Access always warns you before you run an action query that will affect records or the database structure.

After you click Yes to run the query, you will see the mouse pointer change to an hourglass while the query is processing and the table is created. If you decide to place the table in the active database, click the Table tab in the Database window and see the new table in the list (see Figure 15.19). If you open the table, you will find the records for the 43 clients that are in the Midwest region.

FIGURE 15.19

The Make Table query will create the table object and display it in the Database window.

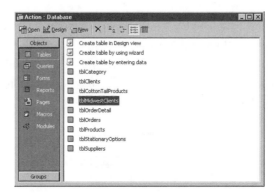

If you attempt to run a Make Table query after the table is created, Microsoft Access again protects you. It will display a message box indicating the existence of the table and ask you whether you want to delete it before you run the query (see Figure 15.20). You can click Yes to continue or No to halt the run of the query. It will then pick up with the message box indicating how many records are being pasted into the new table.

FIGURE 15.20

If the table already exists, Microsoft Access will ask whether you want to delete the table before you run the query.

As you close the Make Table query, you will see it listed in the Database window. The Make Table icon is a table with a starburst to indicate creation followed by an exclamation. It will also attempt to execute immediately as you attempt to open it or double-click on it.

Examining the Make Table SQL Statement

The Make Table query is like the rest of the queries you have looked at so far. The Design view generates the SQL for you. The syntax is

```
SELECT field1[, field2[, ...]] INTO newtable [IN externaldatabase]
➥FROM source
```

The first part is a standard selection of the fields that you want to use. The second part is what makes it a Make Table query. The INTO keyword indicates that you are creating a table. If it is in another database, the IN keyword will be followed with a path and name for the database. This is followed with the FROM clause for the SELECT statement to indicate the source of the records. If you have specified any WHERE or ORDER BY clauses, they will follow the FROM clause.

Using Crosstab Queries

Another type of special-use query is the Crosstab query. Many people use spreadsheets because their grid arrangement makes comparing data easy. When you switch to storing the data in tables, you lose some of the ability to create a quick comparison. You can create some comparisons using a standard Select query, but it might not be as easy to interpret as a spreadsheet of the same information. The Crosstab query allows you to summarize a field by using two of the other fields in the table and displaying the summary in a grid.

For example, in the tblClients table, where the date of the last contact is tracked with the LastContact field, you might want to compare the last contacts by month and year. You could create a query called qryContactsbyMonth.

If you open this query in Design view (see Figure 15.21), there are only three fields. The first field is an expression called LCYear. It uses the Year function to strip out the year component from the LastContact field. The second field is called LCMonth and uses the Month function to get the month. These are sorted in ascending order. The last field is the LastContact field, which is being summarized with the Count function.

FIGURE 15.21

This query summarizes the count of the LastContact field by month and then by year.

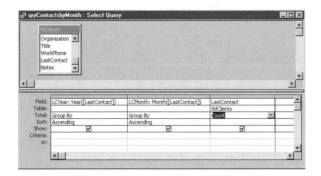

If you switch to Datasheet view (see Figure 15.22), you'll see the counts of contacts per month for each year. The problem is that if you had to compare the 1997 and 1998 figures using Datasheet view, you would spend a lot of time scrolling back and forth.

FIGURE 15.22

The Datasheet view reveals the summarized information, but comparing months for different years is tedious because there are many numbers in between the months.

LCYear	LCMonth	CountOfLastCo
1997	1	4
1997	2	3
1997	3	3
1997	4	6
1997	5	4
1997	6	1
1997	7	2
1997	8	3
1997	9	1
1997	11	3
1997	12	5
1998	1	4
1998	2	9
1998	3	4
1998	4	7

Record: 1 of 23

That is where the Crosstab query can help. It is designed to take table information and display it like a worksheet for easier comparison. The best news is that Microsoft Access has a Crosstab Query Wizard to assist with the creation of this type of query.

Note

Although it is possible to set up a Crosstab query in Design view, it isn't as straightforward as the other special-use queries. The Crosstab Query Wizard assists with this setup by providing a grid layout in which you can drag the needed fields to the appropriate locations on the grid.

Using the Crosstab Query Wizard

Creating a Crosstab query is easy because there is a Crosstab Query Wizard to create the query based on your responses to the wizard's questions. You can base a Crosstab query on a table if all the data you want to summarize exists in the table. You can also use a query as a source for a Crosstab query if you need to use expressions to get the data for your comparison.

Note | If you are going to use a Crosstab query to summarize data, you must have three fields in the recordset: a field to use as the row heading, one for the column heading, and one for the summary.

To get some practice with the Crosstab Query Wizard, you are going to create a comparison for the qryContactsbyMonthCTSource query. It is identical to qryContactsbyMonth except it doesn't summarize the data with the Count function.

Task: Using the Crosstab Query Wizard

1. Select the Query tab in the Database window.

2. Click the New button to open the New Query dialog.

3. Select Crosstab Query Wizard from the list and select OK.

4. Select the Queries option to display the Queries list in the recordset selection for the wizard, as shown in Figure 15.23.

FIGURE 15.23

The first screen of the wizard asks for the table or query to use as the base for the Crosstab query.

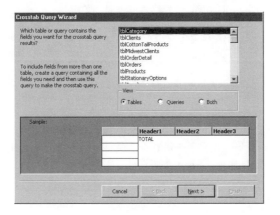

▼

▼ 5. Select qryContactsbyMonthCTSource and select Next to display the row heading selection screen (see Figure 15.24).

FIGURE 15.24

The second screen of the wizard is to establish the row source for this query.

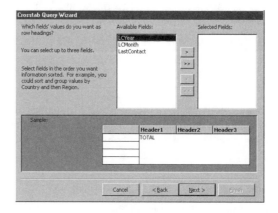

6. Select LCYear as the field to be used as a row heading, and click Next to display the next screen of the wizard (see Figure 15.25).

FIGURE 15.25

The third screen of the Crosstab Query Wizard is where you determine the columns for the Crosstab query.

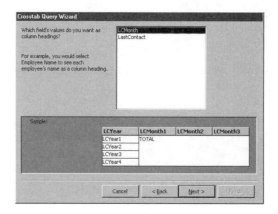

7. Notice that LCMonth was automatically selected as the field for the column headings because it was the second field in the source query. Select Next to display the comparison selection screen (see Figure 15.26).

▼

▼ 8. Notice that the wizard is automatically looking at the LastContact field and it has chosen to count the entries. You can choose any of the functions from the list and select Next to the final wizard screen.

9. Type qryContactsbyMonthCrosstab as the name, select View the query, and click Finish.

FIGURE 15.26

This wizard screen determines the compared field for the Crosstab query.

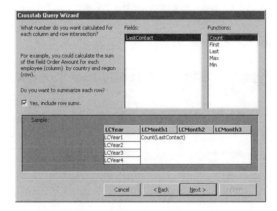

▲

After you have clicked Finish, the wizard will create the query and display it in Datasheet view (see Figure 15.27). This query lists the year, a total of all contacts, and then the count for each month.

FIGURE 15.27

The results give you a total of all contacts for the year as well as the month-to-month counts.

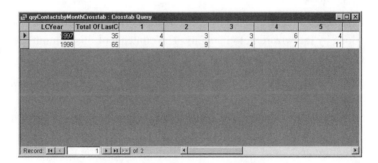

If you scroll over to the column labeled 10, you will notice that there is no data in this column for 1997. If there had been no data in 1998 for the column labeled 10, this column would have been omitted. This problem will be addressed later in this lesson.

Examining the Crosstab Query SQL Statement

The Crosstab query is one of the types on the Query Type list. You could have created this by starting with a standard Select query and selecting Crosstab Query from the menu. However, the wizard is nice because it helps you visualize what you want in the rows and columns.

When you are creating a Crosstab query or the wizard has created one for you, the Design view (see Figure 15.28) is changed to accommodate the special settings required for the Crosstab query.

FIGURE 15.28

The Total row has been activated to count the values.

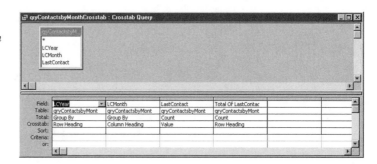

The first change you will see is the Total row. It is needed to summarize the data. Notice that the first three columns are identical to those that you saw in the original query, qryContactsbyMonth.

The second change you will notice is that a fourth column has been added. This was done by the wizard automatically. The contents of this column are identical to the count of the LastContact field only with a new name. This is to provide a total for each row.

What really makes the difference in this query is the Crosstab row. This Crosstab row is where you indicate the position of each element. You can indicate what should act as the row headings and what the column headings should be. You also indicate the element that will be summarized in the grid. That is where you will see the difference between the third and fourth columns. The third column is the value to be summarized, and the last column is summarizing the whole row with its designation as a row heading. These differences are translated into the SQL statement (see Figure 15.29).

A Crosstab query is a TRANSFORM statement. Its syntax is not a standard SELECT statement:

```
TRANSFORM aggfunction SELECT clause PIVOT pivotfield
➥[IN (value1[, value2[, ...]])]
```

FIGURE 15.29

The Crosstab query is a TRANSFORM statement.

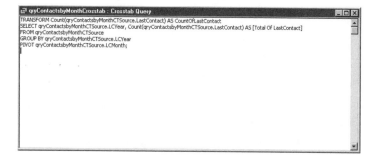

15

The TRANSFORM keyword indicates that you are going to create a Crosstab query. It is followed by the aggregate function that will summarize the data. In this case, it is the Count function of the LastContact field.

This is followed by the SELECT statement that will indicate the fields that are used for row headings. This is followed by the PIVOT clause to indicate the Column headings. The PIVOT clause can be followed with the IN keyword and a list of values to be used as column headings. That is one of the ways you can refine your Crosstab query.

Refining a Crosstab Query

When you create a Crosstab query, start by thinking about how you want to represent the data. You should think about what row and column headings you want displayed, what types of summary calculations you want to display, and how you want to order the columns.

Adjusting the Column and Row Headings

When you are creating any query, the columns pick up the names of the fields as the headings for columns. With Crosstab queries, this can be a problem because the row and column headings are the data in the field.

Take a look at the Datasheet view of the query. The column heading is showing LCYear, which is what it was named in the query, as is the case with Total of LastContact, which is the total count for the row. The actual rows are fine because you have used the Year function to strip out only the portion of the LastContact date you wanted. To fix the LCYear and Total of LastContact headings, you need to turn this into an expression by adding a name for the column.

Task: Fixing the Column Headings

1. View the query in Design view.

2. Click in front of LCYear in its column.

3. Type `Year:`.

4. Click in the Total of LastContact field after the word Total.

5. Type s and delete until you get to the colon.

6. Click the View button on the toolbar to view the new column headings for those two columns.

7. Click the View button on the toolbar to return to the Design view.

The rest of the columns look at the LCMonth data, which is using the Month function to get the number of the month. It is adequate, but it could be much better. Most people are used to seeing the months spelled out, or at least a 3-character abbreviation. In Day 12, you were introduced to the `Choose` function, which enables you to take an index value and display another value depending on the number. This is perfect for changing this heading.

Task: Adding the Choose Function for This Query

1. Select the LCMonth field name in its column.

2. Replace it with the following:

```
Month: Choose(Month([Lastcontact]),"January","February","March",
➥"April","May","June","July","August","September","October",
➥"November","December")
```

3. Press Enter.

4. Click the View button on the toolbar to view the new column headings (see Figure 15.30).

FIGURE 15.30

The names of the columns look better now.

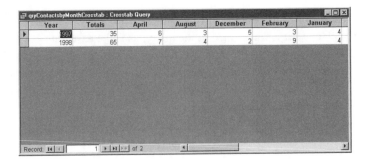

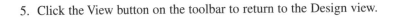

5. Click the View button on the toolbar to return to the Design view.

The column names are easier to read with the use of this function. There is still one problem with the way they appear. There are not in the correct order, but are in alphabetical order. We'll tackle that problem next.

Sorting the Column Headings

Even though the column names look good now, you still would like to see them in the expected, chronological order—January through December. To make this happen, you must adjust the sort order. This is done with one of the query properties. Queries, like the other objects in Microsoft Access, have properties. They can be viewed through the Properties window.

The Column Headings property can be used to adjust the sort order in a Crosstab query. You must type in the values in the order you want them to appear. They must be an exact match for the contents of the field, which is why you had to switch to the Choose function.

Task: Setting Up the Sort Order

1. Click on the gray background of the upper pane to select the query as a whole.

2. Click the Properties button on the toolbar to display the Properties window.

3. Select the Column Headings property.

4. Type the following:

```
"January","February","March","April","May","June","July",
➥"August","September","October","November","December"
```

5. Press Enter.

6. Click the View button on the toolbar to see the datasheet.

7. Notice the corrected order (see Figure 15.31).

FIGURE 15.31

The columns are now in chronological order.

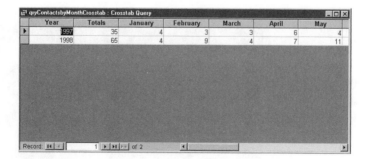

8. Click the View button again to return to Design view.

9. Close the Properties window.

Adding Summary Calculations

Another change you can make to the display of the Crosstab query is to add additional summary calculations. By default, it will give you a copy of the value calculation for the entire row.

You can use summary calculations in a Crosstab query as you would in a Select query. If you had a crosstab of the products by category and wanted an average price for a product, it would be quite easy to obtain because it is a numeric field. If the field's data type is a numeric field, you can set it up like any other summary calculation. But LastContact is a date field; this is a special circumstance requiring a special approach. Here you need to take the count, which is already calculated, and divide it by 12 because there are 12 months in a year.

Task: Adding the Average Number of Contacts

1. Click in the Field row for the empty column to the right of Totals.

2. Type `Average:Totals/12` and press Enter.

3. Select Row Heading from the Crosstab row for this column.

4. Click the View button from the toolbar to see the results and notice the new column after Totals.

5. Click the View button from the toolbar to return to Design view.

Moving Summary Row Columns

The new average is a nice addition to this query to help the reader get a feel for the performance of the contacts, but it still isn't quite right. In most cases, when you are designing a worksheet, the data is followed by the summary calculations. Here the summary calculations are displayed right after the row headings for year (see Figure 15.32). This is because technically they are row headings as well.

FIGURE 15.32

The summary calculations are listed before the data.

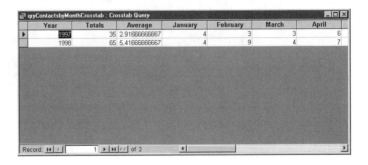

To adjust the arrangement, you need to be in the Datasheet view. You will move the columns just like you move columns around in any Datasheet view.

Task: Rearranging Columns in a Crosstab Query

1. Select the column headings for Totals and Average to highlight the columns.

2. Hold down the left mouse button and drag the columns to the end of the rows.

3. Release the mouse button to move the columns.

4. Notice that the summaries now appear after the column for December, as shown in Figure 15.33.

FIGURE 15.33

The summary calculations are listed after the data.

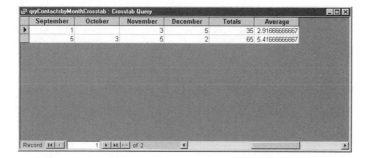

5. Click the View button's drop-down menu and select SQL View.

6. Notice that the change to the PIVOT statement and the addition of averages has become part of the SQL statement.

7. Notice that the sort order and this column arrangement are not part of the SQL statement.

8. Save the query and close it.

Understanding SQL-Specific Queries

In this lesson, you have been focusing on special-use queries to modify data as a group and to change the appearance of the data to make it easier for comparison. You can create action queries and Crosstab queries by using the Design view or writing the SQL directly. It is your choice. You can save a great deal of time by letting Microsoft Access do as much of the work as possible with the Design view, and you are less likely to make typing mistakes.

Three special-use queries are different from the ones you have already seen. They do not permit you to use the Design view to create them. With these queries, you have to write the SQL code:

- The Union query allows you to merge two or more tables into one recordset.
- The Pass-Through query is designed to enable you to take advantage of another database's SQL.
- The Data Definition query allows you to create database objects.

Note

The Design view is not available with the Union, Pass Through and Data Definition option because there isn't a way to display the structure in Design view.

Understanding Union Queries

The first of the SQL-specific queries is the Union query. The Union query is designed to allow you to take two tables with similar structure and display all the records from both as one list.

There are two methods for creating a Union query with Microsoft Access. One method can be used if the tables to be merged have a similar structure. That is, if the number of fields and the data types match for the tables in question, you can use this shorter approach: the TABLE...UNION...SELECT method. This requires far less typing than the second method. The syntax is

```
[TABLE] query1 UNION [ALL] [TABLE] query2
➥[UNION [ALL] [TABLE] queryn [ ... ]]
```

This method starts with the TABLE keyword to indicate that you want to work with the entire table. This is followed by the name of a table or query to be used. For any additional tables or queries, you will use the UNION ALL or UNION TABLE to indicate the entire table. This is followed with the name of the second or any other tables to be used.

This approach is illustrated with the qryOutsideProducts query. In this query, the product lists from two new vendors are merged into one recordset. The key to making this approach work is that there must be a matching number of fields with the same data types in the same order in each table or query. In this case, there are an exact match. The SQL statement is

```
TABLE tblStationaryOptions UNION TABLE tblCottonTailProducts;
```

You can still use this approach with tables that do not have matching structure, but you will have to create queries to get the structure and order to match one of the tables in the union. You can also use the approach of creating complete SELECT statements within the Union query.

When you do not have an exact match in structure between the tables, you can use the second Union query method, which involves combining SELECT statements with the UNION keyword. Here you list the fields you want and make sure that for each field in the order in each SELECT statement the data type matches. This is illustrated in the qryProductsandCottonTailProducts query (see Figure 15.34).

FIGURE 15.34

A Union query is created from two SELECT statements joined with the UNION keyword.

Here the fields are listed in each SELECT statement in matching order. It is not a requirement that the field names match as illustrated by ProductName and Product, but the data types must match. You can even indicate a WHERE clause or an ORDER BY clause. Notice that the ORDER BY clause uses the field name listed first for a field. In this case, it is ProductName.

Regardless of which type of Union query you create, it must be created in the SQL View. When you create a new query, you will not select a table from the Show Table dialog. You will close the dialog and then select Query, SQL Specific, Union. This will display the SQL View and you can begin typing. When you view the list of queries in the Database window, they are also differentiated with an icon—an icon with two joined circles.

Understanding Pass-Through Queries

The next type of query, which can be created only in the SQL view, is the Pass-Through query. Microsoft Access is very flexible as to where your data is located. You can store your data in the database where your query is stored, you can store it in another Access database, or you can store it in a database created with a product other than Access. It can also be stored locally on your machine or on a server.

The benefit of being able to access data in other databases is it allows you to work with larger databases, such as Microsoft FoxPro or Microsoft SQL Server, which have larger capacities to store data. An outside data source has its own version of SQL. It might have features that are not available in Microsoft Access. It might also allow you to run your queries faster because you will be using the resources of the host system rather than your own system.

When you create a Microsoft Access query using one of the tools covered in this lesson or the previous lesson, you are creating a SQL statement and saving it in compiled form for the best performance possible in Microsoft Access.

Pass-Through queries were added to Microsoft Access to allow you to take advantage of a client/server database system. With a Pass-Through query, you can take advantage of the SQL language of the host database. This means that you could create an error if you wrote your SQL and saved it as a regular Microsoft Access query because it would be compiled as it was saved.

Note

> When you want to create a Pass-Through query and not have it compile when it is saved, you need to create a new query, but not select a table or tables from the Show Table dialog. You close the dialog and select Query, SQL Specific, Pass-Through. This will prevent the query from compiling as it is saved.

An advantage of using a Pass-Through query is that you can use it to get access to the functions of the database where the data is stored. It also will run on the host system rather than tie up your system. This is useful especially for systems with heavy transaction processing. For example, a system that processes orders, maintains inventory, and controls shipping involves many transactions. New orders, vendor deliveries, and order shipments are all being added and maintained simultaneously.

The disadvantage of using a Pass-Through query is that if you are creating a query to produce a recordset for viewing, it returns a snapshot of the data. You will not be able to edit the data. If editing is your goal, you want to use a link to the table instead.

Understanding Data Definition Queries

The last type of query that must be created in the SQL View is the Data Definition query. In the section "Understanding Action Queries," you created a Make Table query by using another table's fields as a model for the table. A Data Definition query lets you create database table objects without a table to base them on.

The Data Definition queries enable you to create objects in a Microsoft Access and Fox Pro databases. You can create tables, alter the table structure, delete tables, and create new indexes with them.

As with other features, Microsoft Access provides several methods for accomplishing the same task. Data Definition queries are a part of Microsoft Access because in other databases they are part of the standard SQL language. This cuts down on the learning curve for those users who already know the Data Definition SQL.

Examining Query Properties

In the section "Using Crosstab Queries," you used a query property to set fixed column headings in a sorted order to improve the appearance of a Crosstab query. When you are creating a query, you'll want to use several properties, which are described in this section.

When you open any query in Design view, you can access two types of properties. There are properties for each field as well as the properties for the query as a whole. This section is designed to review some of the properties you have set as well as some of those you might find helpful.

Examining Field Properties

In the section "Using Crosstab Queries," you worked with the Column Headings property to put the column headings in specific order. You also added a column for average count per month. When you view the Datasheet view for this query, the one thing that probably annoys you about the average is the number of decimal places (see Figure 15.35). If you were in a form or report, you could use the Format property to correct that. You can do the same thing here.

FIGURE 15.35

This expression uses more decimal places than you need.

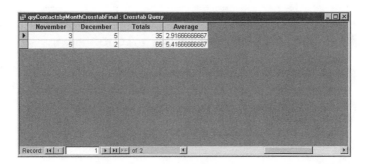

If you want to adjust a field property, select the field you want to change and open the Properties window. You then make any changes and press Enter.

Task: Fixing the Format of the Average

1. Open qryContactsbyMonthCrosstab in Design mode.
2. Click in the Average field.
3. Open the Properties window.
4. Select the Format property.
5. Select Fixed as the format and press Enter.
6. Enter 3 for the Decimal Places property if you want to override the default of 2.
7. Click the View button to display the results.
8. Close the query and save the changes.

You also have a Caption property, which you use to adjust the name displayed in the Datasheet view. You can also use the Description, Input Mask and Lookup properties, which you are used to working with in the table design. There are also properties for the query itself.

Examining the Query Properties

In Day 14, you experimented with creating queries that show the top number of values. This was done by including the TOP keyword in the SQL statement. When you are working with the Design view, you can accomplish the same task by using the Top property for the query. To see this property, you can look at either qry25OldestContacts or qryTop10Prices. The first one illustrates the use of a percentage and the second illustrates the use of a number of values.

> **Note**
>
> The query properties provide a mechanism for setting many of the options for the SQL statement without going to the SQL view.

Task: Viewing the Property in Action

1. Open qry25OldestContacts in Design view.
2. Click the gray background of the tables list pane to select the query as a whole.

3. Open the Properties window.

4. Look at 25% placed in the Top Values property (see Figure 15.36.

15

FIGURE 15.36

The Top Values property allows you to set the number of records to return with the Design view.

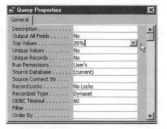

In addition to the properties you have taken advantage of, there are some additional ones you might want to use. At the top of the Properties window for the query is the Description property. It can be used to add information concerning the purpose of a query.

The second property listed is the Output All Fields property. As you add each field to the query, you have the opportunity to click the Show check box to determine whether the field is displayed. There might be a time when you want all the fields displayed. Rather than resetting those check boxes, you can set this property to Yes and it overrides the individual check boxes.

Under the Top Values properties, you have Unique Values and Unique Records properties. When you examined the SELECT statement, you learned that you could include a predicate ALL, DISTINCT, or DISTINCT ROW to indicate whether you wanted records that had all unique values in the chosen fields or completely unique records. These two properties let you select those without having to go to the SQL view.

The next property is Run Permissions. In Day 20, "Understanding Access Security," you will learn how to restrict a user's access through workgroup security. This will allow you to give a user more access to a query than is allowed with her user permissions by giving her the same access as the owner of the object.

Source Database and Source Connect Str are properties that are set when you are using linked tables. They direct the query where the source tables are located. ODBC Timeout is used to determine how long Microsoft Access will wait for the recordset to be returned when it is located in an ODBC database. The Max Records property allows you to restrict the number of records returned when you use an ODBC source so that you do not waste time waiting to create an extremely large recordset.

The Record Locks property gives you control of how the integrity of the data is protected in a multiple user system when someone starts editing. The first setting is No Locks. This means that more than one person could make changes to the record at a time. The one who saves last will have their changes in the table.

The second setting is All Records. This locks the entire underlying table while a user is editing one of the records. No one else can edit records while one person edits.

The last setting is Edited Record. This is the setting you will use most frequently. When a user begins editing a record, the page on which the record is located will be locked. A *page* is an area of the database where the record is stored. It is 4KB in size. Depending on the size of the records, the lock might affect more than one record. This would allow more than one person to edit different records simultaneously.

The Filter and Order By properties allow you to add a temporary filter for your query or a temporary sort order without disturbing your field settings.

Creating Parameter Queries

Another way to improve your queries is to allow the criteria to be set as the query is opened. This is known as creating a parameter query. In Day 14, the standard SQL statement was illustrated with the qryIllinoisClients query. This has a fixed criterion looking for State = "IL".

The problem is that tomorrow you might want to see Kansas clients instead. This would require you to change the criterion and save it with a new name. This is a perfect use for a parameter query. Letting you choose the state each time you run the query would save time.

Changing a fixed criterion to a parameter query is easy. When you want to a create a parameter, you enter a prompt, rather than the fixed criterion, inside brackets.

Task: Altering the Query to Make It Prompt for a State

1. Open the qryIllinoisClients query in Design view.

2. Save this query as qryStatePrompt.

▼ 3. Select *IL* and delete it.

4. Type [What State?] (see Figure 15.37) and press Enter.

FIGURE 15.37

The brackets indicate that this is a prompt for a parameter query rather than a criteria setting.

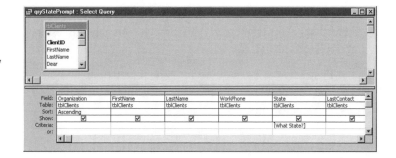

▲

Now when you run the query, it will not give you a selected state's clients. It will display a small dialog with the indicated prompt, as shown in Figure 15.38.

FIGURE 15.38

This is the prompt for a state abbreviation.

You can specify more than one parameter for a query. Set each one up as you did this one, inside brackets. When you try to display the Datasheet view, Access will prompt for each criterion, from left to right.

You can create a prompt using an operator, as with qryCostPriceComparison. You can either place the operator before the prompt or make it a part of the prompt (see Figure 15.39).

FIGURE 15.39

This query has two parameters, and it shows how to use operators with a parameter prompt.

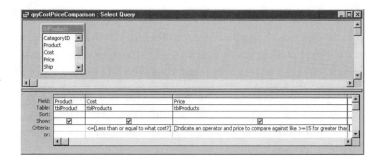

When this query is displayed in Datasheet view, the parameters prompt the user for the value. The first prompt is asking for a number and then using the less than or equal operator and the second prompts for both the price.

The benefit of using a parameter query is you define your criteria once and it will allow you to change the actual data every time you display the results of the query. There are three basic disadvantages:

- First, you must answer each prompt every time you run the query. For example, you can't use the state prompt query without specifying a state. This means that you can use this to see all states.

- Second, if you are using more than one prompt, you must work your way through all of them.

- Finally, if a typing error is made, the query will display no data. This can be quite irritating.

To combat the first two disadvantages, you can create a form to gather the information and then use that as the criteria for the query.

To combat the third disadvantage, you can use some special techniques on a form to minimize typographical errors. These techniques are covered in Day 16.

Getting Criteria for Queries from Forms

As mentioned earlier, an alternative to using a parameter query is to design a form to gather the criteria for a query. This approach eliminates the display of several parameter prompts and might make it easier to determine what information is being asked for. To use a form instead of a parameter query, you must complete two steps. You must create the form and then reference the controls on the form as the criteria for the query.

Creating a Form to Gather Criteria for a Query

The first step is to create a form to gather the criteria information. When you are creating a form to populate a query, you start off differently than you have in the forms you've created so far. You are not basing the form on a table or a query: It is unbound.

First, you add unbound controls for each criteria expression. Then you add a mechanism for opening the query to simplify the process of using the query. To give you an opportunity to walk through this process, take the qryCostPriceComparison query and change it so that it looks to a form for the criteria.

Task: Setting Up the Form

▼ TASK

1. Select the Form tab from the Database window.
2. Select New to display the New Form dialog.
3. Select Design View.
4. Do not select a table or query, and click OK.
5. Open the Properties window.
6. Set the form caption to Cost/Price Comparison.
7. Add a text box at the top of the form.
8. Change its name to txtCost.
9. Change its label caption to Compare a Cost less than or equal to: and press Enter.
10. Adjust the label's placement so that it can be read.
11. Add a second text box below the first.
12. Change its name to txtPrice.

Note

When you want to reference controls on a form from another object, such as a query, remembering what control you want can be tough. This is especially hard if you use the Name property defaults, such as Text1. Changing the Name property as you did in the preceding steps will make the name easier to remember or recognize when you're creating the reference to the control.

13. Change its label caption to Enter a price greater than or equal to: and press Enter.
14. Adjust the label's placement and dimensions so that it can be read.
15. Make sure the Control Wizard button is selected on the toolbar.
16. Click the Command button, and then click the bottom of the form.
17. Select Miscellaneous from the categories in the Command Button Wizard, select Run Query and click Next.
18. Select qryFormCriteria and click Next.
19. Select Text, type Open Query and click Next.

▼

20. Enter cmdOpen as the name and click Finish.

▼   21. Save the form as frmCostPriceComparison.

     22. Click the View button to display the Form view (see Figure 15.40).

FIGURE 15.40

*The finished form for
the criteria is ready for
input.*

     23. Enter 12 as the cost and 15 as the price.

▲   24. Leave the form open and select the Database window.

The form and its criteria are ready. You must change the query so that it will look at the
form for the needed information.

Setting Up the Query and Referencing Forms and Controls

To have a query look at a form for its criteria, you will have to reference the control that
holds the information. Naming the controls will make setting up the reference much easier. The new control name will make it easier to type in the reference or to locate in the
Expression Builder.

Task: Altering the Criteria

     1. Select the Query tab in the Database window.

     2. Select qryFormCriteria and select Design.

     3. Select the prompt inside the brackets after the <= operator for Cost and delete it.

     4. Click the Build button on the toolbar.

     5. Double-click on Forms in the Categories list.

     6. Double-click on Loaded Forms to expand the list.

     7. Click on frmCostPriceComparison.

     8. Double-click on txtCost in the sub categories list.

     9. Click OK.

▼   10. Select the entire criterion for Price.

▼ 11. Type >= and click the Build button on the toolbar.

12. Double-click on Forms in the Categories list.

13. Double-click on Loaded Forms to expand the list.

14. Click on frmCostPriceComparison.

15. Double-click on txtPrice in the sub categories list.

16. Click OK.

▲ 17. Save the query.

When you want to use a control on a form for part of a criterion or the entire criterion, you must reference that control. With Microsoft Access, you have the ability to reference any control on a form or report. The key is to indicate its full identifier.

When you look at what the Builder added to the criteria lines, you'll see that it is a bit more than the name of the control (see Figure 15.41). You have to also indicate what object the control is on. It's like finding someone in an office building. You need the address of the building, what floor they are on, and the suite number. In this case, you need the collection type of the object, the name of the form, and the name of the control.

FIGURE 15.41

The Expression Builder has added the object collection and its name in front of the control name.

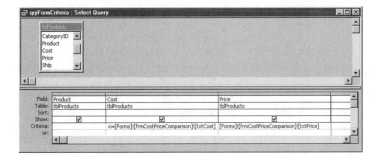

When you want to reference a control on an object, you need to use the proper syntax. The first part is collection type. In this case, it is Forms to indicate that the control is on a form. This is followed by an exclamation point. The second part is the name of the object, in this case, frmCostPriceComparison. This is also followed by an exclamation. Then you have the name of the control.

Now the criteria is in place. You left the form open with 12 as the cost and 15 as the price. You could click the View button to display the datasheet for the query, or you can close the query and click the Open Query button on the form. Either method will work. When you open this query, it looks at the contents of those controls for its criteria. There is less action on the screen than you have with the two parameter prompts, but it gets the same results.

Understanding the Issues with Using Form Entries

You have created a form for the criteria arguments, and therefore eliminated a lot of the action on the screen. But the form is still not perfect, and there is still room for problems.

The first problem that must be addressed is a typing error. What if you don't type a number? This would result in an error message. Using the Input Mask property will help to eliminate that problem by confining the entries to numbers.

The second issue arises when you do not want to use one of the criteria. Say you want a cost of less than $12 at any price. With this form, you cannot get that. If you leave the price blank, you will get an empty query. The answer to this problem is illustrated in Day 18, "Examining VBA."

Summary

Today's lesson expanded on the concepts introduced in Day 14. SQL offers a wide range of query types to assist you with managing your data. The first type of query introduced in this lesson is the action query. Action queries allow you to modify data and create new tables using SQL. You have an Update query to update data in fields for a table. You can create a new table using records from an existing table. You also have an Append query to add records from one data source to a table. You can delete records using a Delete query. Both of these need a little bit more concentration. When you have multiple tables in a database with relationships between them, these queries can run into problems.

Another type of special-use query is a Crosstab query. It gives you the benefit of a worksheet layout without sacrificing the optimum storage for your data. A Crosstab query makes it possible to do many things you might have taken the data to Excel to do.

There are also three special-use queries that can be created only in the SQL view. You can merge two tables together with a Union query, and take advantage of an outside database's native SQL with Pass-Through queries. You can also create and alter table definitions with a Data Definition query.

The last part of this lesson focused on making your queries more responsive to your changing criteria needs. You could create a query that would prompt you for the criteria values as it opened. This is known as a parameter query.

Another approach illustrated how to use a form to get a criteria value. This section only got you started taking advantage of this powerful capability. You will learn how to get more out of this feature in later lessons.

Q&A

15

Q Why might I get a Type Mismatch error when running an Update query?

A If you are populating a field with an expression with a different data type than the field you are updating.

Q Why do you exclude a field that is an AutoNumber field from a Make Table or an Append query?

A The AutoNumber field is automatically added to the record as the record is created in the table. If you attempt to place existing data in that field, Access will generate an error to warn you of the problem.

Workshop

The Workshop helps you solidify the skills you learned in this lesson. Answers to the quiz questions appear in Appendix A, "Answers."

Quiz

1. What is the most common mistake made when creating an append query?
2. What is the biggest disadvantage of a parameter query?
3. What is the biggest advantage of using a form to set the criteria in a query?

Exercises

1. Create a query to update the product prices for stationary by $.50. (Hint: You need to use an Update query.)
2. Create a parameter query to look for a city. (Hint: It will be similar to qryStatePrompt.)
3. Turn the query in step 2 into a query based on a form.

DAY 16

Implementing Advanced Form Concepts

In Day 5, "Creating Simple Forms for Data Access," and Day 10, "Designing Customized Forms," you explored how to use forms to make entering, editing, and viewing your data easier. This lesson focuses on some additional tools that can provide access to more than one table at a time, automate data entry, and provide quick access to other objects in your database. Today you will learn the following:

- Using multiple-table forms
- Constructing forms with subforms
- Using combo and list boxes
- Automating forms using control wizards
- Using SQL as form controls
- Creating custom menus and toolbars

To follow along with today's lesson, you'll need the sample database, School.mdb, from the CD that accompanies this book. You'll find the database in \Day16\.

School.mdb is based on the same scenario as Day 12, "Developing Reports with Graphics and Expressions." This database will assist with the tracking of departments, classes, students, and assignments. You will need to copy it to another location before you can save the work you do in this lesson.

Using Multiple-Table Forms

In previous lessons, you saw how valuable queries could be. They enable you to group related information from different tables into one view. Queries can be used by themselves or as a foundation for a form or report.

A benefit of using a query is that it displays related information from more than one table simultaneously. This eliminates a lot of cross checking of information from table to table, report to report, or form to form. When you base a report on a query, you take full advantage of this benefit. You can pull together information from more than one source for display. Because the purpose of a report is to view and print data only, this advantage creates no problems.

When you base a form on a query, you again have the benefit of viewing multiple-table data, but there is a possible disadvantage. When you attempt to edit the data, you might find you give too much or too little access to the fields in the underlying tables.

This means that the form might give the user access to edit a field that was displayed only to provide information regarding a record. Another possibility is that you will not be able to get a clear picture of the data because it is too segmented or provides information more than once. To get a better idea of the problems with basing a form on a query, you are going to create a form based on a query and use the form to update some records.

Creating a Form Based on a Query

Creating a form based on a query can be as simple as creating a form based on a table. You can start by creating a query and then taking advantage of the Form Wizard. To give you an opportunity to explore this approach, the qryDeptClasses is already built.

When you open the query in Design view (see Figure 16.1), you see that this query is using two tables. It is getting two fields from the tblDepartment tables and four fields from the tblClasses table. It is also using one expression to concatenate the word Year with the Year field.

FIGURE 16.1

qryDeptClasses takes advantage of several querying techniques.

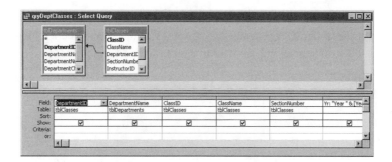

Tip

If you feel comfortable using the Form Wizard, you can open frmDepartmentandClasses in Design view.

After you close the query, you are ready to create your form. You can create a form from scratch using the Design mode or let the Form Wizard do the work for you.

Task: Using the Form Wizard to Create a Form

TASK

1. Select the Form tab in the Database window.

2. Select New to open the New Form dialog, and then select Form Wizard.

3. Click on the drop down arrow to choose the table or query. (see Figure 16.2).

FIGURE 16.2

The queries are listed with the tables in the New Form dialog.

4. Notice that the queries are listed, as are the reports. Select qryDeptClasses.

5. Click OK to open the wizard.

6. Select all the fields and click Next.

▼ 7. Select Columnar and click Next.

8. Select the Standard style and click Next.

9. Enter `Departments` and `Classes` as the Title and click Finish to allow the wizard to generate the form, which is shown in Figure 16.3.

FIGURE 16.3

The Form Wizard has built a form based on a query.

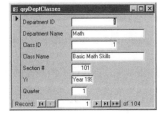

The resulting form looks like some of the other forms you have created, displaying the fields in text boxes. Aside from the title bar and the size of some of the text boxes, this form looks ready to use, but it has several problems.

Looking at the Problems

Look at the Department ID and Department Name fields. When you are on the Department ID field, you want to select a department, but you have to do so blindly. To complete the field, you would have to know what number is assigned to what department. You have the Department Name field, but it cannot help with the entry in the Department ID field. This field demonstrates the first problem you meet when basing a form on a query.

The second problem is the fact you can edit fields that are only for informational purposes like Department Name. In this case, the form is designed to enable you to maintain the classes. A class is a part of a department, but you do not want to make modifications to the department's name. If you type `Mathematics` and press Tab, you have changed the name of the department because this field is part of the tblDepartments table, not the tblClasses table. This affects all the classes in this department. This will be clearer when you move to the next record.

When you look at the next record, it is the second quarter of this class. When you changed the name of the department to Mathematics while viewing the first record, the department record in the tblDepartments table was changed. The department is not a name in the tblClasses table; it is stored as the department ID with a relationship with tblDepartments. The query retrieves the name in the query. If you are basing a form on a simple query with one relationship between the tables, you might have these two problems: You might have more editing power than you want and not enough help making choices.

Another problem occurs if you attempt to change the Class ID to a 2; you will not be able to modify it. If you look at the Status bar, you will see the message, `Control can't be edited, it's bound to an AutoNumber field 'ClassID'` (see Figure 16.4).Although this problem doesn't have anything to do with having the form based on a query, it must be dealt with.

FIGURE 16.4

The status bar indicates why it's not possible to change the field, but the user must look there to determine the problem.

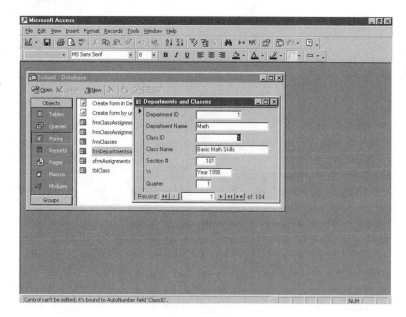

The third problem illustrated by this form concerns the Yr field. In the query, this is not a field from a table, it is an expression. In the form, there is no way to tell that it is an expression until you attempt to edit it.

If you attempt to type anything in this text box, nothing happens, except that again, you get a message on the status bar (see Figure 16.5): `Field 'Yr' is based on an expression and cannot be edited.`

The problem that certain fields cannot be edited is not related to the fact that the form is based on more than one table. It is a design issue involving the display of AutoNumber fields. Because the status bar is the only indication the problem exists, there is always the danger that the person trying to modify the data will not notice what is occurring. To clarify which fields can be edited, try setting one of the properties covered in Day 5, "Creating Simple Forms for Data Access." You can also use Visual Basic for Applications to add additional emphasis to messages informing the user if a field cannot be modified.

FIGURE 16.5

*The status bar is the
only indication that
you can't edit the field.*

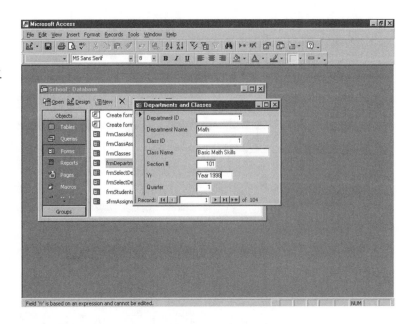

The next problem involves having too much information. If you take a look at the
qryClassAssignments query, you will see that it is based on four tables (see Figure 16.6).

FIGURE 16.6

*This query summarizes
data from tblClasses,
tblAssignments,
tblResults, and
tblStudents.*

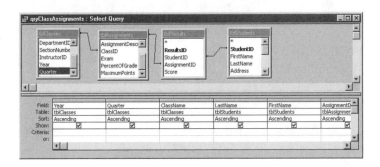

If you create a form using a columnar style, as in frmClassAssignments (see Figure
16.7), you end up having to view each class's assignments for each student. It is hard to
get a global picture of all the assignments for all the students in the class.

You might think that a solution is to switch to a tabular form with continuous records
(see Figure 16.8). This makes it better, but now you see lots of duplicate information.

FIGURE 16.7

Each assignment for each student is displayed separately.

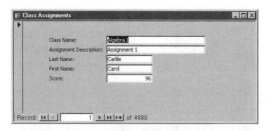

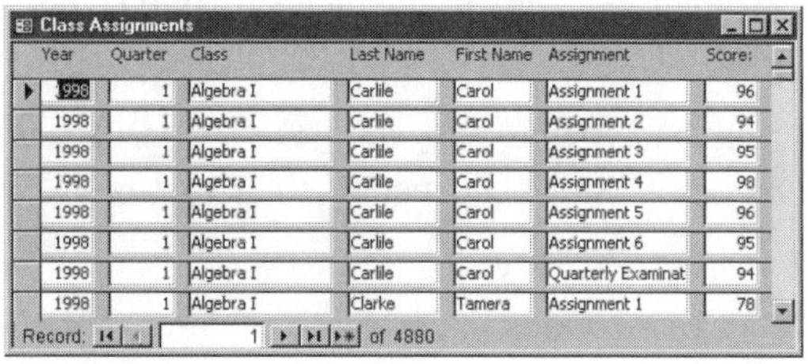

FIGURE 16.8

The tabular form enables you to see more data at a time, but it also repeats many of the fields that you only need to see once.

For each student in the system, you get to see all the information for each assignment. You get to see the year, quarter, class name, and student's name. This format can be difficult to read.

Examining Possible Solutions

The forms you have just looked at have three major problems. There are fields that cannot be edited, fields that you do not want to have edited, and too much duplicate information.

The first problem involves fields that can't be edited, like the AutoNumber field and expressions. Compounding this problem is that the appearance of the control doesn't give any clue that its contents cannot be changed. The key is to make the appearance match the field's behavior.

You could set the Enabled property to False to give a visual clue that it can't be edited as well as prevent it from being selected. If you don't want the field disabled on the form, you could use the Locked property to ensure that it wouldn't change and set the Tab Stop property to False, which would make it harder to get to the control. Another alternative is not to display the field at all.

You could also add some Visual Basic for Applications code to display a message box to stop the data entry and get the user's attention a little better. This will be covered later in Day 18, "Examining VBA."

The second problem is that some fields that can be changed are fields that you do not want to be changed. The Department Name field was an example of this. It is helpful for the user to be able to see the department name for the record, but the user should never be able to change the name of the department arbitrarily.

One approach is to lock all the data for a form so that no changes can be made. This will make the form read-only. You can do this by using the Recordset Type property for the form. By default this property is set to Dynaset. This creates a dynamic recordset. It enables you to make changes to any of the tables used to create the recordset, following the rules set up for the relationships between the tables.

You can set the Recordset Type property to Dynaset (Inconsistent Updates), which opens up the form even further. It allows the records to be updated without regard for the relationships.

Another solution to this problem is to protect the records from all changes. The Snapshot setting creates a static recordset; it is strictly for viewing purposes and cannot be updated. Complete the following task to try the Snapshot setting for the Recordset Type property.

Task: Changing the Recordset Property

1. Open frmDepartmentsandClasses in Design view.

2. Open the Properties window and select the Data tab.

3. Select the Recordset Type drop-down arrow to display the list. Select Snapshot from the list.

4. Click the View button on the toolbar to display the form in Form view.

5. Click on the Department Name field and type Math.

6. Notice that the status bar indicates The Recordset is not updateable. (See Figure 16.9.)

7. Close the form without saving the changes.

Unfortunately, this approach makes it impossible to change any of the fields or add new classes to the recordset. What you need is a way to update the fields that you want to change and safeguard data for fields that are providing information only.

In this case, you must select a department ID for the record, but you want to see the department name to make that choice. Later in this lesson, in the section "Using Combo and List Boxes," you will learn about two controls that can give you that option.

FIGURE 16.9

The recordset cannot be changed with the Recordset Type set to Snapshot.

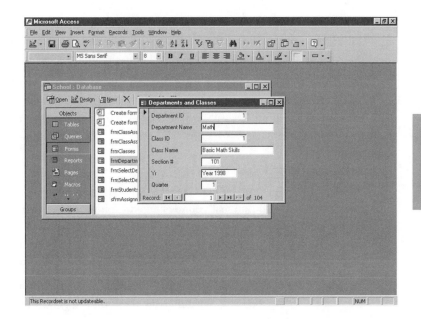

The last problem is that of duplicate data in the form. With frmClassAssignmentsTabular, you get to see more than one record at a time, but you see all the fields for each record. Most of the earlier fields are duplicates of the previous record.

What you need to do is create a form that summarizes your data for each class and assignment to display the information that you want to change, for example, student scores. In Day 12, "Developing Reports with Graphics and Expressions," you worked with subreports to show detail information related to a summary record. When you are working with reports, you can use a subreport. For forms, you can use a subform.

Constructing Forms with Subforms

NEW TERM A *subform* is a form that is embedded in another form to display records from another recordset related to the current record. It is a very nice method for displaying data from more than one recordset in one form.

When you want to use a subform, you will complete a process similar to the one you use to create a report with a subreport. You create the form that will be embedded as the subform, and then you create a main form to house the primary information. You embed the subform and set up its relationship to the main form.

If you want to add any expressions to summarize the data from the subform, you have to add text boxes to the main form and point to a control on the subform to get that information. All these steps are covered in detail in the following sections.

Although it is possible to have more than one subform and even to nest subforms, this section focuses on creating a single subform. You are going to create a form to display the class information. The subform will display the assignments for each class in a subform.

Designing a Subform

When you want to work with a subform, the first step is to design and build the form. In most cases, you will find that your design will follow a set pattern. It is quite common for the main form to be a columnar-based form with each record displayed separately. The subform is often a tabular form to allow you to see more than one of the records at a time and to minimize the amount of time navigating between records.

You can create the form using the Form Wizard or create the form from Design view. In most cases, letting the Form Wizard create the form is a good way to get started. For this example, you need to create a tabular form to display the assignment information.

Task: Creating the Subform

1. Select Forms in the Database window.
2. Select New to open the New Form dialog.
3. Select Form Wizard and select tblAssignments as the table.
4. Click OK to launch the Form Wizard.
5. Select AssignmentDescription, Exam, PercentofGrade, and MaximumPoints from the field list and select Next.

Note

One method to prevent users from attempting to edit fields that cannot be changed is not display those fields. AssignmentID was omitted from the list of fields you selected because it is an AutoNumber field. ClassID is needed as part of the recordset to establish the links between the subform and the main form, but you don't need to display it because its information will be in the main form.

6. Select the Tabular layout and click Next.

7. Select the Standard style and click Next.

8. Enter `sfrmAssignments` as the title and click Finish. The wizard generates the new form and displays it in Form view as shown in Figure 16.10.

FIGURE 16.10

The Form Wizard results need to be refined before you integrate the subform with the main form.

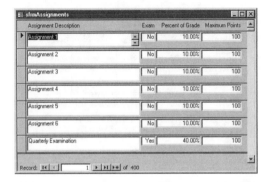

16

> **Note**
>
> When you named this form, you used the sfrm (for *subform*) prefix rather than the frm (for *form*) prefix for the name. That will help you distinguish between main forms and forms that are integrated as subforms.

The form you've created is tabular, and it needs some clean up. The Assignment Description field is so long that it has been allocated a second line. There is also too much space reserved for the Percent of Grade and Maximum Points fields. The key is not to use any more space than is necessary.

Task: Cleaning Up the Form

1. Click the View button on the toolbar to display the Design view.

2. Select all the fields.

3. Right-click on one of the fields and select Size, To Shortest.

4. Select the AssignmentDescription field and set its Scroll Bars property to None.

5. Change the height of the Detail section to reduce the amount of space between records.

6. Reduce the size of the Percent of Grade and Maximum Points labels and text boxes to remove some of the extra space in the text boxes.

7. Move the Maximum Points textbox and label to the left to reduce the space in between fields.

▼ 8. Reduce the Width of the Detail section to 5" approximately.

9. Reduce the size of the form window to display only the columns shown and approximately 5 lines.

10. Save your form and click the View button on the toolbar to view your revisions (see Figure 16.11).

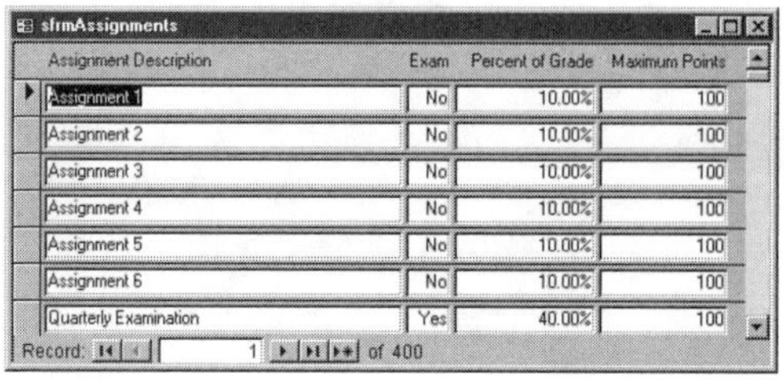

FIGURE 16.11

The finished subform takes up less space than the one created by the wizard.

Tip

If you remember how wide your subform is, it will save some time as you integrate the subform with the main form because you won't have to guess how wide to make the subform control on the main form.

Creating a Main Form

Now that the subform is created, you are ready to create the main form. Again, you can create it from scratch or by using the wizard. For this example, you can start by using the wizard.

Task: Creating a Form Based on the tblClasses Table

1. Select the Forms tab in the Database window.

2. Select New to open the New Form dialog.

3. Select Form Wizard.

4. Select tblClasses as the table and click OK.

5. Select all the fields and click Next.

6. Select a Columnar layout and click Next.

7. Select the Standard style and click Next.

▼ 8. Enter frmClasses as a title.

▼   9. Select Modify the Form's Design.

    10. Click Finish, and the Form Wizard generates a very simple columnar form (see Figure 16.12).

FIGURE 16.12

The wizard creates a very simple form, with all the fields in one column.

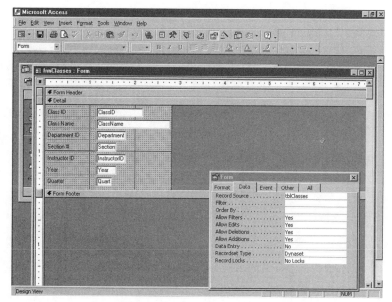

When you are going to incorporate a subform, you often need to reorganize the form to make it fit better with the subform. If you checked the width of the subform when you completed the changes, you found that it was approximately 5". Your main form will need to be at least that wide to accommodate the subform.

You might also want to organize the controls into a logical sequence for entry and set the Tab Stop property as well as adjust the Tab Order to minimize trouble with the fields that cannot be directly edited, such as ClassID.

Task: Getting the Main Form Ready for the Subform

1. Select the form.
2. Open the Properties window and select the Format tab.

3. Enter Classes and Assignments as the caption.

   4. Resize the form and move the controls around on the form to resemble the layout
       in Figure 16.13.

FIGURE 16.13

*The controls here are
organized in a more
user-friendly fashion.*

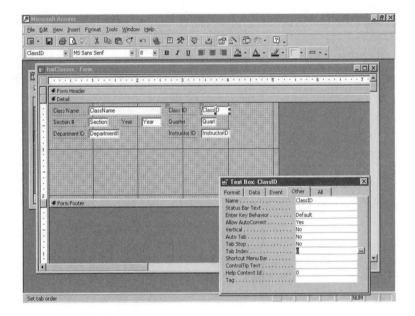

   5. Select the ClassID field.

   6. Select the Other tab in the Properties window.

   7. Set the Tab Stop property to No.

   8. Close the Properties window and save the form.

At this point, you have the form looking better, and you now have the space to add the
subform. You can use the Subform/Subreport control from the Toolbox as illustrated in
Day 12, "Developing Reports with Graphics and Expressions" or use the drag and drop
method to integrate the subform.

Task: Using Drag and Drop to Integrate the Subform

   1. Arrange the windows in Access so you can view the form and the Database win-
       dow simultaneously, as shown in Figure 16.14.

   2. Point to sfrmAssignments in the Database window and press the left mouse button.

▼ 3. Move the mouse pointer to below DepartmentID on the form and release the left mouse button.

4. Notice that the subform is now displayed below DepartmentID. You may also notice that the width of the form has increased to accommodate the size of the subform.

5. Click the View button from the toolbar to view the results.

6. Increase the height of the Detail Section and the subform so that you can see more than three assignments.

7. Click the View button from the toolbar to return to the Design view.

8. Select the sfrAssignments label, and set its Caption to Assignments.

9. Select the subform and set its Height property to 2.25".

10. Increase the size of the form window so that you can see the bottom of the subform control.

FIGURE 16.14

To use the drag and drop method for integration, you have to be able to see the Source object in the database window and the Destination location in the form.

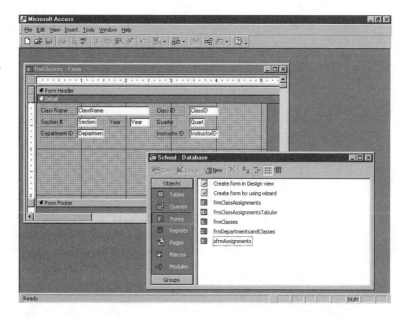

▼

▼ 11. Click the View button from the toolbar to display the Form view (see Figure 16.15).

12. Click the View button on the toolbar to return to the Design view.

FIGURE **16.15**

The subform is now in place for viewing the assignments for a class.

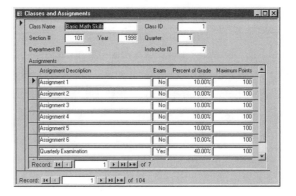

▲

NEW TERM When you are working with subforms or subreports, you need to create a connection between the main form or report and the subform or subreport. If you do not create a connection, you will see all the assignments in the table, regardless of what class is currently displayed in the main form. This is known as establishing *links*. The drag and drop method attempts to create these links as it places the subform in the form.

If you select the subform, open the Properties window, and select the Data tab. You will see two properties that identify the link between the subform and the main form. Because you are displaying related material, you have two fields that make up that relationship.

The Link Child Fields property is set to ClassID, which is the field in the subform that identifies the class for each assignment. The Link Master Fields property identifies the corresponding field in the tblClasses table, then identifies each class. In most cases, the Master field is the primary key for the table supporting the main form.

The steps for integrating subforms and subreports using drag and drop are relatively easy. You need to be careful that the Link Child Fields and Link Master Fields are pointing to the correct fields. Access does this for you, if you take the time to establish table relationships as you set up your table structures.

Understanding Navigation Concerns with a Form/Subform

When you look at this Classes and Assignments form in the Form view, it looks ready to use. There are few navigation issues that need to be cleared up.

When you first open the form, the active field is the Class Name field. Remember that you set the Tab Stop property to False for the Class ID field. It would have had the focus if you hadn't set that property, because Class ID was the first field placed on the form by the wizard.

You can click on a particular field to activate it; but that is definitely a slow method for changing information. Most people prefer to use their keyboard, moving from field to field by using the Tab key.

16

NEW TERM After you organize a form, it is a good idea to verify the forms *tab order*, which is the path the Tab key will take as the user moves from field to field. It is controlled by the Tab Index property. If you try to tab between fields in your Classes and Assignments form, you will notice that you are jumping in a haphazard order. Currently, the tab order is the order in which you placed the controls on the form. You move from Class Name to Department ID to Section, and so on, which isn't very user friendly.

Task: Setting the Tab Order

1. Click the View button to return to the Design view.
2. Select View, Tab Order to display the Tab Order dialog (see Figure 16.16).
3. Select AutoOrder and click OK.
4. Click the View button on the toolbar to switch to Form view.
5. Now press the Tab key to move from field to field.

FIGURE 16.16

The Tab Order dialog enables you to control the path through the form.

Now as you press the Tab key, you move through the fields on the form from left to right and top to bottom. Notice that you still skip over the Class ID field; this is because of the Tab Stop property setting.

After the Instructor ID field, it activates the subform. As you continue to tab, you will move from field to field and record to record inside of the subform. If you Tab while in the last field of the last record in the subform, you create a new record.

When you are working with a form that has a subform, you have to learn some new navigation keystrokes. Tab works fine to enter the subform from its preceding field, but you need a way to get back to the main form.

To navigate in a subform, there are three additional keystroke combinations you need. Shift+Tab will take you to the subform from a field that follows the subform in the tab order. Ctrl+Tab will take you out of the subform and to the next field in the main form if you are in the subform. Ctrl+Shift+Tab will take you to the previous field in the main form.

Using these keystrokes gives you a great deal of flexibility because you can create records in the subform before you move on to the next field. It can be a point of contention for touch typists and new users because of the number of keys used together to go in and out of the subform.

When navigating between the main form and subform, users can become confused about what record they are working with. If a user is in the subform and presses Ctrl+Tab, the Class Name field in the main form is activated. If the user looks at the record selector, he will also see that he is now looking at the next record. That happens because there are no controls after the subform on the form.

This can be confusing if the user is not expecting it to happen. If you want to provide a way to get back to the main form without moving to the next record, you can add an access key. You can add an access key for fast navigation by placing an ampersand (&) before a letter in the label of a field. The letter selected becomes the access key and displays as an underscored letter. When the user presses Alt with that letter he immediately moves to that field.

In this form, you could add an ampersand before the C in the Class Name label, which would enable the user to jump to that field rapidly.

Referencing Controls on a Subform

Sometimes when you're working with subforms, you need to reference information on the subform from a control on the main form. For example, you might want to make sure that the percentages of the assignments for a class add up to but do not exceed 100%. To do this, you would have to add a total for that field on the subform and then reference it from the main form.

With Access 2000, this process is now much easier than it has been with previous versions. Now you can edit your subform or subreport from the main form.

Task: Adding a Total for the Percent of Grade Field

◄ TASK

1. Click the View button on the toolbar to switch to the Design view.

2. Select the subform.

3. Select the Form Footer in the subform, and then point to its bottom border and drag down to display the form footer area.

4. Open the Toolbox and select the Text Box control.

5. Click in the Form Footer under the Percent of Grade field to create the control.

6. Change the label to Total %:.

7. Change the text box's Name property to txtTotalPercent.

8. Set the text box's Control Source property to =Sum([PercentofGrade]).

9. Set the text box's Format property to Percent.

10. Resize and position the text box as needed.

11. Click on the main form to release the subform.

12. Click on the subform.

13. Set the subform's Height property to 2.4".

▲

14. Save the form.

16

Now when you switch to the Form view, you have a total in the footer for the subform. The steps in this task create the control to summarize the data, but they do not perform a test to see whether the total matches 100%. This is done with VBA and is covered later in this lesson. When you get to that point, you will add code to this form to test the contents of this new text box. When you need to reference a control on a subform, you have to include information about the form and the subform. If you are referencing a control on a subform from another form, you have to include the full path to its location, including what form it is on. For instance, this new total would be referenced as

```
[Forms]![frmClasses]![sfrmAssignments].[Form]![txtTotalPercent]
```

[Forms] indicates what type of object you are referencing and is followed by an exclamation point, [frmClasses], which indicates the object, and another exclamation point. [sfrmAssignments] is the name of the object in the form, and is followed by a period. [Form] indicates that it is a form object. This is followed by an exclamation and the name of the control you are referencing.

Note

When referencing controls on the subform, you are using both the exclamation point and the period in the reference. You may wonder why you're using both.

The reference is composed of an object you want to access and its container, which is another object. The object and container are both identified with the type of object and an identifier, and they are separated by the exclamation point.

Given that you can nest objects inside multiple containers, each container needs to be identified with the type and identifier. To separate the different objects, the period is used.

If you are referencing a control on a subform from the main form, you can use the shorter form of the address. This skips the identification of the main form:

```
[sfrmAssignments].[Form]![txtTotalPercent]
```

If you do not specify the main form, Access will assume that the form exists within the object. Using this programming shortcut can save typing as well as processing time.

Using Combo and List Boxes

The other problem that arises for the form based on multiple tables is the difficulty of making a department choice using the Department ID field instead of a name. For example, you would have to know that 1 was the Math department ID in order to complete the form.

You can't solve this problem by including the Department Name field in the recordset. That actually creates another problem: It makes it possible for the user to change the department name while maintaining the classes table.

What you need is a way to display the name of the department and select a Department ID with one control. In the Toolbox, you have two controls that let you do just that: the Combo Box and the List Box control (see Figure 16.17).

FIGURE 16.17

The Combo box and List Box controls enable you to select values from a list.

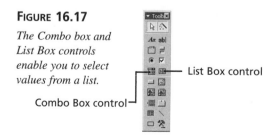

List Box control

Combo Box control

The Combo Box control allows you to provide a drop down list of possible choices for a field. The user can select from the list or begin typing the first character of a choice to move the list to that item. The combo box is very compact. It takes up the same amount of space vertically as a text box.

The List Box control is identical to the Combo Box control, except that it displays the complete list rather than having the user click on its drop down arrow to display the list. To really function best, it needs to be allotted the equivalent of three lines of space.

Both of these controls enable you to select from a list rather than remember a value for a field. When you set up the list, you can add values to the list by referring to a table, typing in a list, or using VBA.

To give you a chance to work with these two controls, you are going to replace the text boxes for Department ID and Instructor ID with a combo box and a list box. The Control Wizard will help you set up these controls.

Task: Adding a Combo Box

1. Select the Department ID text box and press the Delete key.

2. Make sure the Control Wizard button is selected in the Toolbox.

3. Select the Combo Box control in the Toolbox.

4. Click on the form where the DepartmentID field used to be to launch the Combo Box Wizard (see Figure 16.18).

FIGURE 16.18

The wizard needs to find out how you want to populate the list.

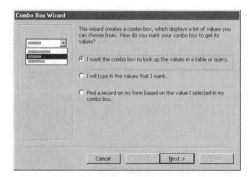

5. Select I Want the Combo Box to Look Up the Values in a Table or Query, and click Next to select a table or query (see Figure 16.19).

▼   6. Select tblDepartments from the list and click Next to select the fields for the list (see Figure 16.20).

7. Select DepartmentID and DepartmentName and click Next to view the contents of the list (see Figure 16.21).

FIGURE 16.19

The wizard needs to know what table or query to use.

FIGURE 16.20

The wizard needs to know what fields to use for the list.

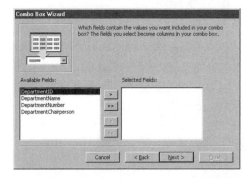

FIGURE 16.21

The wizard needs to find out how the list should be formatted.

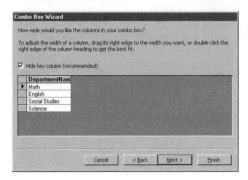

▼

▼ 8. Make sure the Hide Key Column check box is selected and click Next to determine what to do with the user's choice (see Figure 16.22).

FIGURE 16.22

The wizard needs to find out what to do with the selected value.

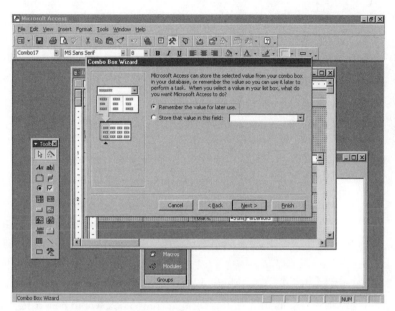

16

9. Select Store the Value in This Field and select DepartmentId from the list. Then click Next to set the label for this control (see Figure 16.23).

FIGURE 16.23

The wizard needs a label for the combo box.

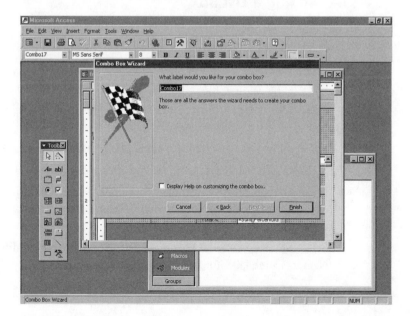

▼

▼   10. Enter Department as the text and select Finish to create the combo box.

11. Resize and position the label and combo box as needed.

12. Click the View button on the toolbar to switch to Form view.

13. Click the drop down arrow to display the list(see Figure 16.24).

FIGURE 16.24

The combo box elimi-nates the need for a reference card of val-ues or memorizing a list.

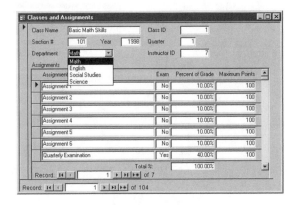

▲   14. Click the View button to return to the Design view.

With the orientation of this form, a combo box would be a better choice than a list box because there is very little space for the list box; however, to see the differences, you will add the list box. You need to replace the Instructor ID text box with a list box.

Task: Adding a List Box

1. Select the InstructorID text box and press the Delete key.

2. Make sure the Control Wizard button is selected in the Toolbox.

3. Select the List Box control in the Toolbox.

4. Click on the form to the right of Class ID to launch the List Box Wizard.

5. Select I Want the List Box to Look Up the Values in a Table or Query, and click Next to select a table or query.

6. Select tblInstructors from the list and click Next to select the fields for the list.

7. Select InstructorID and Instructor and click Next to view the contents of the list.

8. Make sure the Hide Key Column check box is selected, resize the column so you can read the longest name, and click Next to determine what to do with the user's choice.

9. Select Store the Value in This Field and select DepartmentId from the list. Click
▼   Next to set the label for this control.

10. Enter Instructor as the text and click Finish to create the combo box.

11. Resize and position the label and combo box as needed.

12. Click the View button on the toolbar to switch to Form view (see Figure 16.25).

FIGURE 16.25

The list box also displays values, but as a scrolling list rather than as a drop down.

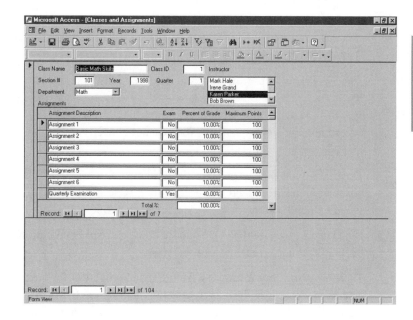

13. Select View, Tab Order to display the Tab Order dialog.

14. Select AutoOrder to fix the tab order.

15. Drag Combo17 above List19 and click OK.

16. Save the form.

Tip

If you set up the Look Up tab for fields such as DepartmentID and InstructorID as you create the table, the Form Wizard will insert the control selected on the Look Up tab.

To see this in action, create a new form by using the Form Wizard. Select tblClasseswithLookUp as the table.

Examining the Combo Box and List Box Properties

The Combo Box and List Box Wizards are designed to minimize your effort to set up these controls. They set up the control properties from the choices made.

The first question the wizards ask is whether you want the combo or list to get its information from a table or a query, a value list, or to look up values based on a field in this form. The wizard is getting information to set the Row Source Type property. It can be set to Table/Query or Value List, or you can set it up to look at a field list.

Another method for populating a combo or list box is to use VBA. If you are using this approach, you set the Row Source equal to a VBA function. This method is covered in Day 19, "Working with VBA."

The next screen of the wizard asks you what fields you need for the combo box or list box if you are basing it on a table or query. This is to set up the Row Source property. The wizard creates a SQL statement to populate the control. If you chose a value list instead of a table or a query, the Row Source property stores the list of values entered separated by semicolons.

The next screen enables you to look at the list of items. The Hide the Key Column check box determines what field in the supporting table will tie to the field in this table. It also sets the Bound column property to point to that field.

If you decide to store the value in a field, the Control Source property is set to point to the field that houses the data for this form.

There are also Limit to List and Auto Expand properties for the combo box. These enable you to restrict the user to selecting items from the list and automatically display the list when the control gets the focus. You also can control some of the formatting with these properties.

If you are displaying more than one column, you may want to include column headings by setting the Column Heads property to Yes. You can also control the column widths with the Column Width property. If you have more than one column, you separate each width with a semicolon. You can also use the List Rows property to control how many rows are displayed in a combo box when the list is dropped down.

Examining Combo and List Box Performance Considerations

The benefits of using a combo box or a list box are quite obvious. Instead of having to remember the numeric code that represents the department or instructor, users get to pick the department name or instructor name from a list. This minimizes the time it takes for them to complete the form.

A combo box can also minimize typing mistakes. For instance, if you have a State field, it might be beneficial to have that as a combo box with value list. Then the user cannot make a typing mistake such as il instead of IL. This will save formatting headaches with reporting.

Unfortunately, these benefits do not come without a performance price. Combo boxes and list boxes decrease the speed at which the form displays, as well as the speed of entry. Typing a number is faster than picking from a list and letting Access fill the field with the number.

To get the most benefit from these controls, you need to optimize their performance. The first trick to getting better performance is to create a query to use as the Row Source property. When the wizard sets the Row Source property, it is creating a SQL statement that looks at the entire table.

16

If you use the Build button to open the Build window. It behaves like the QBE window giving you an opportunity to create and save a query, and then use the saved query instead. When you save a query, it is a better performer because the query object is saved as a compiled SQL statement. This eliminates the compilation of the SQL statement as the combo box is initialized.

The construction of the table and query will also help. When you set up the Row Source property, you had a key field like Department ID. It is normally the primary key in the look up table. You can speed up the combo box or list box by having its corresponding foreign key in the table for the form indexed.

To increase the performance of these controls, try to keep any tables used by combo boxes and list boxes local. Try to avoid looking at linked data as a source. Looking at one table and minimizing the fields listed will also help.

Automating Forms by Using Control Wizards

In Day 13, "Introducing VBA," you got chance to begin exploring Visual Basic for Applications. You got to see one of the Control Wizards in action, generating the VBA code for you to display a report based on the active records in a form.

VBA can also be used to automate some of the common tasks of working with forms. In this section, you are again going to experiment with the Control Wizards to add automation. You are going to see how to add command buttons for automation and you will see how to use a combo box to locate a record in a form.

Adding Navigation with VBA

When you are working with a form, you have many different methods for navigating between records. The first method is to use the record selector. It not only displays what record is currently in view, but it has buttons to enable you to navigate and even create a new record.

With frmClasses, there are three potential problems with the record selector. The first involves new users. Many new users are intimidated by the record selectors. The navigation buttons are smaller than most buttons, and it may take users a while to recognize the buttons they need.

The second problem is that users cannot access the record selector from the keyboard as they can with the Tab key. The last problem is a presentation issue. As the user looks at the frmClasses form, the record selector for the frmClasses and the record selector for its subform are very close together. It might be easy to click on the wrong one.

Now another approach to navigation is to use the menus. All the record selector functions are located on the Edit, Go To menu. Again, this could pose a problem for new users. They have to locate these items and then remember where they found them.

The last possibility is to just use the keyboard. Moving to the next and previous records are simple keystrokes. Locating the keystrokes for moving to the first or last record may prove to be more challenging.

If you want to add command buttons for navigation, the Control Wizard can generate the code for you. To illustrate how to create command buttons for navigation, you're going to create a command button to move to the next record.

Task: Creating a Command Button to Move to the Next Record

1. Display frmClasses in Design View.
2. Scroll down in the Form window to view the Form Footer.
3. Drag the lower border of the Form Footer section to make room for the new button.
4. Open the Toolbox if needed, and make sure the Control Wizard button is selected.
5. Select the Command Button control.
6. Click in the Form Footer to launch the Command Button Wizard (see Figure 16.26).

FIGURE 16.26

The first step in the Command Button Wizard is to pick an action.

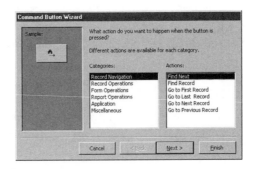

▼

▼   7. Select Go to Next Record from the Record Navigation category and select Next to
         determine the button appearance (see Figure 16.27).

FIGURE 16.27

The second step in the
Command Button
Wizard is to select the
appearance.

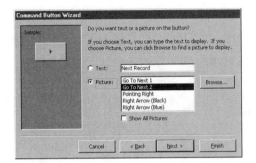

16

8. Select the Text option button and select Next to assign the Name property for the
    command button (see Figure 16.28).

FIGURE 16.28

The third step in the
Command Button
Wizard is to give the
control a name.

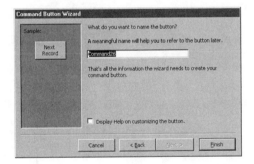

9. Enter cmdNext as the Name and click Finish to create this button.

10. Resize the window to make it taller.

11. Click the View button on the toolbar to display the form in Form view (see
    Figure 16.29).

12. Click on the Next Record button and notice that you are now looking at record 2.

▼   13. Click on the View button on the toolbar to return to Design view.

▼   14. Right-click on the Next Record button and select Build Event to display the gener-
         ated code in the Visual Basic Editor (see Figure 16.30).

FIGURE 16.29

*The button is now
available in the Form
Footer section.*

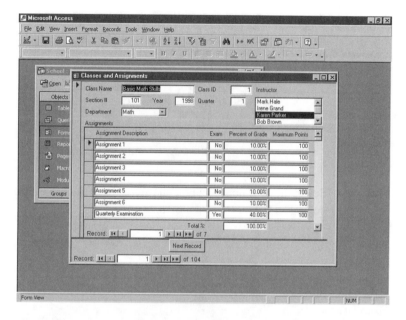

FIGURE 16.30

*The Command Button
Wizard has generated
the code to move to
the next record.*

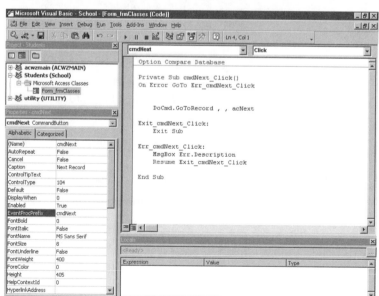

▲

The Command Button Wizard has created a button with the visual appearance that you selected and has added the VBA code to make it work. Here the Click event for the new button is created.

The first line is the On Error statement to set up error handling. (You were introduced to this when you created the button on Day 13.) The second line is the one that performs the navigation. It uses the DoCmd object with the GoToRecord method. This enables you to specify which record you want to move to. In this case, the acNext argument is used to move to the next record. This is followed by the remainder of the code needed for error handling. After examining the code, you can close the Visual Basic Editor.

To make your form even more usable, you could add command buttons for all the buttons on the record selectors. You could even add the ampersand to the captions to provide quick access keys.

16

> **Tip**
>
> The action to add a button to create a new record is in the Record Operations category of the Command Button Wizard.

Another feature you might want to add to your forms is the capability to have quick look up based on a field. The Combo Box Wizard can generate a combo box that uses VBA to accomplish this task.

Task: Adding a Combo Box to Locate Records with VBA

1. Point to the lower edge of the Form Header section and drag it down to make room for the new control.
2. Open the Toolbox as needed and verify the Control Wizard button is still selected.
3. Click the Combo Box control.
4. Click in the form header to launch the Combo Box Wizard.
5. Select Find a Record on My Form Based on the Value I Selected in My Combo Box and click Next.
6. Select ClassID, ClassName, Year, and Quarter as the fields to include and select Next.
7. Resize the columns as needed and click Next.
8. Enter Look Up Class as the label and click Finish.
9. Resize the control and label as needed.
10. Save the form.

▼   11. Click the View button on the toolbar to display the form in Form view.

     12. Click on the new combo's drop down arrow.

     13. Notice that you are viewing three fields instead of just one (see Figure 16.31). With classes, the name doesn't change, but the quarter and year do. You need these two fields to assist with identifying the correct class.

FIGURE 16.31

The combo box displays three fields.

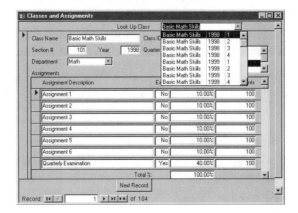

     14. Using the combo box's scrollbar, locate and select Algebra I for 1999, 1st quarter.

     15. Notice that the record is now active.

     16. Click the View button on the toolbar to switch back to the Design mode.

     17. Select the new combo box.

     18. Open the Properties window if needed and select the Event tab.

▲   19. Click on After Update and select the Build button to open the Visual Basic Editor.

The Combo Box Wizard has added the control and created the `Combo27_AfterUpdate` event for you. The `AfterUpdate` event is executed after the contents of the control are updated. To use a combo box to locate a record, you need three lines of code:

```
'Find the record that matches the control
Me.Recordsetclone,FindFirst "[ClassID] = " & Me![Combo27]
Me.Bookmark = Me.RecordsetClone.Bookmark
```

The first line assists with code maintenance; it is a comment. You can comment your code on a line by itself or on the same line after a statement. A comment must always be preceded by an apostrophe.

Do	**Don't**
DO add comments to your code. Whether you or someone else maintains the form, commenting makes the job of deciphering the purpose of your code easier. It is a good habit to develop.	**DON'T** rename this control without modifying the code. The Combo Box Wizard doesn't give you an opportunity to select a name during generation. If you rename this control, you will have to modify this event to match the new name.

16

When you have a form based on a table or a query, it is dependent on a recordset for its information. The form's `RecordsetClone` property enables you to work with a copy of that recordset with VBA.

When you are working with a recordset, you have the ability to locate records within the set. This is accomplished with the `Find` methods: `Find`, `FindFirst`, `FindLast`, `FindNext`, and `FindPrevious`. In this case, the second line of code uses the `FindFirst` method to locate that record.

The `Find` methods have one argument. It is an expression to test. It is a `WHERE` clause without the `WHERE` keyword. In this case, it is using the first field you selected for the combo box, the ClassID field.

The last line of code is the one that actually displays the matching record. When you are looking at a record in a recordset, you are on a particular record or at a location. This is tracked with the `Bookmark` property.

`Me.Bookmark` is the location the form is currently referencing.
`Me.RecordsetClone.Bookmark` is the location of the record that matches the combo box in the recordsetclone. This line takes the location in the recordsetclone and resets the form's bookmark to that location to display the record.

Caution

If you are using a text field as the look-up key, you may want to set the Allow AutoCorrect property for the look-up combo boxes to No. AutoCorrect can modify what the user types. It may add accents or a different spelling. If you do not turn off this setting, you have to edit this code to test for the apostrophe or other special characters.

Using SQL to Restrict a Form's Recordset

In the previous section, you began to explore ways to use VBA to automate some of your actions in a form. With the combo box, you got a chance to work with the FindFirst method which uses a WHERE clause to locate a record.

SQL can do more than locate a record for you in a form. When you open the frmClasses form, you are currently looking at 104 records. You have the look-up capability, but if you only wanted to work with the social studies classes, you have many records to wade through to get to the classes in social studies. You may want to restrict the type of records you see as you open the form.

One way of restricting the type of records displayed in a form is to create a selection form and use the choice made in that form to generate the WHERE argument for the OpenForm method.

If you open the form, frmSelectDepartments, in Design mode (see Figure 16.32); you will see the foundation for this example. This form has an option group to allow the user to select a department with an option button. The value for each button corresponds to its Department ID.

FIGURE 16.32

FrmSelectDepartments is designed to reduce the number of records in view in frmClasses.

This form also includes a command button to open the classes form. You can create this button by using the Command Button Wizard. If you right-click on the button and select Build Event, you can see the code that the wizard generates:

```
Private Sub cmdOpen_Click()
On Error GoTo Err_cmdOpen_Click

    Dim stDocName As String
    Dim stLinkCriteria As String
     stDocName = "frmClasses"
    DoCmd.OpenForm stDocName, , , stLinkCriteria

Exit_cmdOpen_Click:
    Exit Sub
```

```
Err_cmdOpen_Click:
    MsgBox Err.Description
    Resume Exit_cmdOpen_Click

End Sub
```

The first line sets up the error handler. The second two lines define variables for the arguments of the OpenForm method. The next line sets the stDocName variable equal to the name of the form, frmClasses. Notice that the second variable is not assigned.

16

> **Caution**   If you didn't create frmClasses in the tasks above and used frmClassesFinal to examine the results, you must change the name of the form to frmClassesFinal for stDocName.

The next line is the line that opens the form. The DoCmd object has an OpenForm method to automate the accessing of forms. Its syntax is

```
DoCmd.OpenForm formname[, view][, filtername][, wherecondition]
➥[, datamode][, windowmode][, openargs]
```

The syntax includes the DoCmd object, followed by OpenForm, which is followed in turn by its arguments. The first argument, formname, is the form's name that's displayed in the Database window. This must be a string variable or a string inside quotations. It is required. The next argument, view, is the view type. This enables you to open the form in Form View, Datasheet View, or Design View. If this is omitted, it is defaulted to Form view. The next argument, filtername, enables you specify a saved filter to apply as you open the form. The wherecondition argument, is a WHERE clause to control what records are displayed. It is where you can apply SQL to control the form. Both of these arguments are optional. The datamode argument can indicate what type of access is allowed to the records. The window mode argument enables you to control the behavior of the window and the last argument allows you to pass information to the form as it opens. All these are optional.

In the case of the code generated by the wizard, all the arguments use the default or they aren't used, except for the form name and the WHERE condition. The form name is required and the WHERE condition variable is currently empty.

The rest of the code is the error handler. If an error occurs, it is displayed in a message box and the procedure is exited.

To take advantage of the WHERE condition argument, all you have to do is assign a value to stLinkCriteria.

Task: Restricting the Forms Records with the WHERE Condition

1. Click at the end of the `stDocName = "frmClass"` line and press Enter.

2. Enter the following code:

   ```
   stLinkCriteria = "[DepartmentID] =" & Me!frmDepartment
   ```

3. Save the form and close the Visual Basic Editor.

4. Click the View button on the toolbar to display the form in Form view. Notice that the Math department is the default.

5. Click the Open Classes button. Notice that the frmClasses form opens, but it is displaying 32 records instead of 104.

6. Close the frmClasses form.

7. Click the View button to return to the Design mode.

The form now passes on information as it opens the form. This means that the users will have to go through fewer records to find the ones they want.

> **Caution**
>
> If you clicked on the Look-Up combo box on frmClasses, you would notice that it still lists all the records. You need to add some VBA code to adjust its contents when you display the form.
>
> Another option is to disable the combo box if a WHERE condition is used. This can be accomplished with the Form_Open event. This is illustrated in the finished version of frmClasses, frmClassesFinal:
>
> ```
> Private Sub Form_Open(Cancel as Integer)
>     If Me.FilterOn = True Then Me.Combo27.Enabled = False
> End Sub
> ```

Creating Custom Menus and Toolbars

This lesson focuses on getting more from your forms. You have looked at how to build a form by using more than one table and how to provide some quick look-up functions and automation. For all the forms you have worked with, a lot of functionality is provided for record management. Most of it is provided from the menu and from the toolbar.

When you create a form, there is a standard form menu and toolbar to provide access to those record management functions. This menu provides the complete list of functions available when you are working with a form. The toolbar is a subset of those functions to give quick access to the ones you use the most. If a feature isn't available, it is disabled.

When you are creating your forms, you might not want to display all the functions. Some forms only need a subset of features. For example, the frmSelectDepartment form doesn't have a recordset. There isn't any record management needed. It only facilitates the access to the frmClasses.

Limiting what appears on a menu and toolbar—making fewer choices visible—will make menus and toolbars easier to use. There will also be fewer chances for mistakes when you are accessing a menu or using a toolbar.

16

Examining the Standard Form View Menu and Toolbar

When you open frmSelectDepartment, you have the standard menu, the Form View, and Formatting toolbar open. Much of this functionality isn't needed in the day-to-day use of this form.

The File menu has the options to access other databases, get external data, save the form, print, modify settings, and exit the application. It is not necessary or desirable to make all these choices available to all users. Eliminating many of these options from the File menu will also keep you from making inadvertent changes.

All the features on the Edit menu are for maintaining and managing records. As I said earlier, there are no records here to maintain and manage. The View menu allows the user to change the way they are looking at the form. In most cases, this is not needed during day-to-day operations.

The Insert Format and Records menus are disabled because there are no records attached to this form. They are adding visual clutter to the screen for the frmSelectDepartment form.

The Tools menu offers many of the database-maintenance features. Again, this menu's features are not often needed from this form. The Window menu provides window-management tools. These are also not needed with this form.

Displaying the last menu, the Help menu, is always a good idea. All users should be able to get to help from everywhere.

Two toolbars display when you open this form. The first is the Form View toolbar. This toolbar provides quick access to many of the record maintenance and management features mentioned above as unnecessary for this form.

The second toolbar is the Formatting toolbar. This toolbar is for setting up the appearance of a form. After the form is built, this will not be used often because the form isn't likely to change frequently.

Creating Custom Menus

To create a custom menu, first you need to determine what features will be needed when you and your users are working with the form or report. This will help you determine the contents of the new menu.

With frmSelectDepartment, very few features are needed. You would want to include a File menu because most applications have that menu. It doesn't need all the features usually listed. You probably only need a Close choice to close the form and the Exit feature to close Access entirely. You wouldn't need any of the other menus except Help because this form doesn't work with records.

After you have determined what is needed, you can begin creating the menu. You do not want to modify the standard menu because this is used by all forms that do not have a custom menu and toolbar—you might accidentally eliminate features you need in another form.

You need to start by creating a command bar. The process for creating command bars is the same as it is for all the Office applications.

Task: Creating a New Menu

1. Open frmSelectDepartment in Form View because you want to be able to see the standard menu as a model.

2. Right-click in the toolbar area or select View, Toolbars. Customize to display the Customize dialog (see Figure 16.33).

FIGURE 16.33

The Customize dialog enables you to manage toolbars and menus, add functions, or change options.

3. Select New to display the New Toolbar dialog (see Figure 16.34).

4. Enter `mnuSelectDepartment` as the Toolbar Name.

5. Click OK to create the new Toolbar (see Figure 16.35).

▼ 6. Select the Properties button to display the Toolbar Properties (see Figure 16.36).

▼   7. Select Menu Bar as the Type and click Close.

         8. Drag the new menu bar up to under the Form View menu.

FIGURE 16.34

*The New Toolbar dia-
log enables you to
name a new toolbar or
menu.*

FIGURE 16.35

*Whether you want to
create a menu or a
toolbar, it starts as a
toolbar.*

FIGURE 16.36

*The Toolbar
Properties window
enables you to change
the toolbar into a
menu.*

▲

The menu bar is now ready to receive commands. When you are creating a menu bar,
you will always start by creating a toolbar first. The difference between a toolbar and a
menu bar is the Type.

After you set the type in the Toolbar Properties window, you have a menu bar. The toolbar properties can also determine the toolbar or menu. They can be used to change the
name of the toolbar or menu. They can also determine if it can be docked to the side of
the window.

There are also check boxes to determine the menu bar's behavior. Show on Toolbar
Menu is for toolbars only. Because you are going to set up the menu bar that appears
when the form opens, you do not have to include this setting.

Allow Customizing determines whether a user can add functions to the menu bar. Depending on whether you are the only user, you may want to leave this setting on or turn it off. Allow Resizing and Allow Moving determine if the position and dimensions of the menu bar can be changed. Allow Showing/Hiding determines whether the menu bar can be turned off. In most cases, you won't allow that to happen.

After the properties are set, you are ready to build the menu.

Building the Menu

After the menu is created, you need to add commands to it by using the Customize dialog. The second tab is the Commands tab, which gives you a selection of command categories to select from. You can pick a category and view its selection of commands.

After you have located a command you need on your menu, you will point and drag it to its location on the menu. In the planning process for the menu and toolbar for this form, you determined that you needed a File menu with Close and Exit, a View menu with a command to open the form frmClasses without a WHERE condition, and the Help menu.

The first item on the menu is the custom File menu. When you are working with a menu bar, there is a special command to create a new menu. After the item is added to the menu you have to set its properties.

Task: Adding the Custom File Menu

1. Scroll through the list of categories until you locate New Menu and click on it.

2. Point to its only command, New Menu, and drag it to the menu bar.

3. Right-click on the New Menu button on the menu bar.

4. Select Properties to open its Properties window (see Figure 16.37).

FIGURE 16.37

The Menu Control Properties window determines the appearance and behavior of the item on the menu.

5. Select the Caption property and enter &File.

6. Click Close.

7. Select File from the Categories list.

8. Point to Close and drag it on top of the File command.

9. Notice that the menu drops down. Drag it to the first position on that menu and release the mouse button.

10. Scroll down in the Commands list until you locate Exit.

11. Drag Exit to the File menu and drop it under Close. Notice that there isn't a dividing line between these two items.

12. Right-click on Exit and Select Begin a Group. Notice that you now have a dividing line (see Figure 16.38).

16

FIGURE 16.38

The custom File menu is complete, with its dividing line.

File menu with dividing line

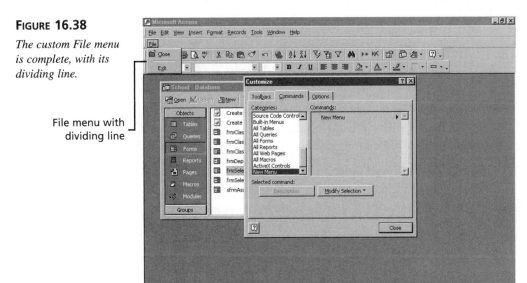

The Menu Control Properties window enables you to set the look and operation of the menu command. In the case of the File menu, except for creating the menu itself, you are using stock commands. There are no changes that need to be made to the properties because you are duplicating this command from a regular menu.

As your menus and toolbars become more complex, you will spend more time setting the command properties. In addition to the Caption property, you have a Shortcut Text property. This enables you to indicate the shortcut key combination that is referenced in the Autokeys macro for custom features.

The Screen Tip property allows you to determine what is displayed in the screen tip balloon when the command is pointed to. The On Action enables you to indicate the macro or function to be executed when a custom command is clicked.

The Style property indicates its appearance on the menu or toolbar. Help File and Help File ID are used to indicate the custom help file and topic for the command, if you are creating a custom help file.

The Parameter property enables you to store a text string that can be passed to a function that is executed with the On Action property. The Tag property is another string property that can be used by any custom functions. Begin a Group is also available from this dialog.

The File menu is complete. You are now ready to add a menu to view frmClasses without any criteria.

Adding a Custom View Menu

The frmSelectDepartment form allows the user to select a department and view the frmClasses form with only those records that are specific to that department. With the option group, you do not have the ability to see all the records.

In Day 19, "Working with VBA," you will see how to correct this problem with the use of VBA; but for now, you might want to add a View menu to provide access to the form without criteria. This involves adding the form to the menu directly.

Task: Adding a Custom View Menu

1. Scroll through the list of categories until you locate New Menu and click on it.
2. Point to the menu's only command, New Menu, and drag it to the menu bar.
3. Right-click on the New Menu item on the menu bar to display the shortcut menu.
4. Select Name, enter &View, and press Enter.
5. Select All Forms from the Categories list.
6. Drag frmClasses and place it as the first item on the new View menu.
7. Right-click on the frmClasses command and select Properties.
8. Enter &View Classes… as the caption.
9. Enter Open Classes for All Departments.

▼ 10. Click Close.

11. Click View, and notice the new View Classes choice, as shown in Figure 16.39.

The completed View menu

FIGURE 16.39

The View menu is now complete.

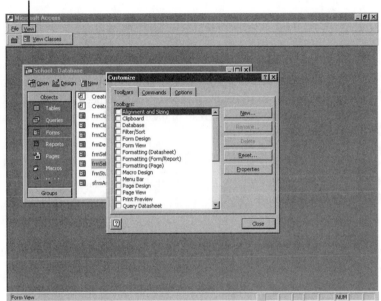

16

Adding the Standard Help Menu

The last element the menu needs is the standard Help menu. If you are not providing a custom help file, you will want to add the standard help menu. Maintaining help access throughout your database can be a big help to your user.

Task: Adding the Standard Help Menu to Your Menu Bar

1. Select the Built-In Menus category from the Categories list.

2. Scroll down in the Commands list to locate Help. Drag Help to the right of your View menu on the menu bar.

3. Select the Toolbars tab in the Customize dialog.

▲ 4. Click on the check box next to mnuSelectDepartment to uncheck it.

Your menu is now complete; its structure is compact, and it is turned off. The last step when creating a new menu is to turn it off. You do not want the menu up all the time. It needs to be visible only when the form is open. You will complete that step last. Now you have to create a corresponding toolbar.

Creating Custom Toolbars

You have created a menu that reduces the access to the record management commands, but you haven't taken care of the toolbars. The full Form toolbar will be shown when you view the form in Form view. It shows many of the features you eliminated on your custom menu. To solve this problem, you also need to create an abbreviated toolbar. The process is very similar to creating the menu. You will create the toolbar and then place the needed commands on it.

Task: Creating a Toolbar to Match Your Custom Menu

1. Select New to display the New Toolbar dialog.
2. Enter tlbSelectDepartment as the Toolbar Name.
3. Click OK to create the new toolbar.

After the toolbar is created, you can place the necessary buttons on it. You may want to drag it up under the other toolbars to dock it.

Building the Toolbar

The toolbar is now created and it is docked to the upper edge of the window, but it doesn't have any commands. When you want to add commands to the toolbar the process is the same as adding commands to the menu. You locate the command you want on the toolbar from the Categories list, and then you drag it to the toolbar. If you want a dividing line, you can set the Begin a Group property.

A toolbar normally adds support for the menu. The Form View toolbar gives quicker access to some of the most frequently used functions. When you create a smaller menu structure, you may want to add all the commands in your abbreviated menu. In this case, you would want to include the close Command and the Help command. Everything else can be omitted.

Task: Building the tlbSelectDepartment Toolbar

1. Select Commands from the Customize dialog.
2. Select File from the Categories list.
3. Drag the Close command to the new toolbar.
4. Select Window and Help from the Categories list.
5. Drag the Microsoft Access Help command to the new toolbar.

▼   6. Right-click on the help icon and select Begin a Group.

7. Select the Toolbars tab in the Customize dialog.

8. Click the checkbox next to tlbSelectDepartment to turn it off.

▲   9. Select Close to close the Customize dialog.

The toolbar is now complete and turned off. You are now ready to make it the toolbar for the form.

Selecting Menus and Toolbars for a Form

After the menu and toolbar are built, you need to set them up as the menu and toolbar for the form. This is done with properties. There are four properties that control menu and toolbar display for a form.

The Menu Bar property enables you to indicate what menu you want to display. The Toolbar property allows you to determine what toolbar is displayed when the form is opened. The Shortcut Menu property lets you determine whether you want to allow the user to right-click on the form to see a menu. The Shortcut Menu Bar property allows you to select a custom menu bar to serve as the shortcut menu.

When you right-click on the form, you get a shortcut menu (see Figure 16.40) that has many of the commands that are on the toolbar to speed up access to those functions. In the case of this form, you do not need any of those commands.

FIGURE 16.40

The form's shortcut menu is designed to provide quick access to some of the commands offered on the menu and toolbar.

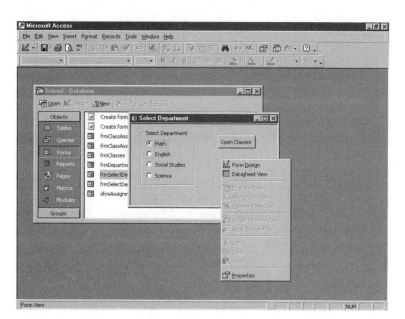

Task: Setting Up frmSelectDepartment's Menu and Toolbar

1. Click the View button from the toolbar to switch to the Design view.

2. Open the Properties window if needed, and select the Other tab.

3. Select the Menu Bar property.

4. Click on the drop-down arrow to display the custom menus available. Select menuSelectDepartment from the list.

5. Select the Toolbar property.

6. Click on the drop-down arrow to display the custom toolbars. Select tlbSelectDepartment from the list.

7. Set the Shortcut Menu property to No.

8. Save the form.

9. Click the View button on the toolbar to display the form in Form view.

The form is now displayed with only the custom menu and toolbar displayed. If you right-click on the form, nothing is displayed. You have now made it easier to locate the needed functions, and you have made it more difficult to alter the design of the form.

Summary

Today's lesson introduced some of the advanced techniques for form design. You learned that you can display data from multiple tables in one form, but there are some problems with this approach.

You explored several options that give you the ability to view the data from several tables without the disadvantages of using a query as the record source for a form. You learned how to incorporate data from more than one table with a subform. You also learned how to use combo and list boxes to display information from a look-up table.

You also took another look at VBA. You got to experiment with the Wizard to add functionality to your form. You also got to modify some VBA to dynamically filter the record source for a form.

The last topic covered in this section was how to add custom menus and toolbars to a form. These techniques can be used for forms or reports.

Q&A

Q Can I use more than one subform in a form?

A Yes, you can have more than one subform in a form. You can nest subforms up to three deep.

Q How do I add a shortcut key to a command on my menu?

A If you want to add a shortcut key to a custom menu item, you need to create an AutoKeys macro indicating the keystroke combination and the code you want to execute. For additional information, please see Day 7, "Automating Your Access App: A Macro Primer."

Q Could I use a list instead of an option group in frmSelectDepartment?

A Yes, you can. The VBA will be different and you can also eliminate the need for the menu item to open the form with classes for all departments. This is covered in Day 19, "Working with VBA."

16

Workshop

The Workshop helps you solidify the skills you learned in this lesson. Answers to the quiz questions appear in Appendix A, "Answers."

Quiz

1. What is the biggest disadvantage of using forms based on multiple tables?

2. What is the benefit of using a subform?

3. Why should you create custom menus and toolbars for your forms and reports?

Exercises

1. Modify frmStudents so that the Student ID is not the first field activated in the form. (Hint: Set the tab order.)

2. Create a subform to integrate with frmStudents to display their classes.

3. Create a custom menu and toolbar for frmClasses.

DAY 17

Developing Professional-Quality Reports

In Day 12, "Developing Reports with Graphics and Expressions," you started to explore different methods for improving the appearance and performance of your reports. This lesson builds on those skills to create more professional reports. Today, you'll learn the following:

- Exploring advanced report properties
- Formatting sections
- Creating special first and last page headers and footers
- Developing parameter reports
- Handling the Null (no data) report event
- Creating crosstab reports
- Publishing your reports on the Web

To follow along with today's lesson, you'll need the sample database, Classes.mdb, from the CD. You'll find the database and reports in \Day17\.

Classes.mdb uses the same scenario as Day 12, but this database manages the classes and student assignments for a high school. The name of the file is different from the Day 12 file in case you are storing all of the files in one location. You will need to copy it to another location before you can save the work you do in this lesson.

Exploring Advanced Report Properties

In addition to those properties explored in Day 12, there are some other properties that you might be able to take advantage of to create more polished reports. They can be used to affect the contents of the report as well as its appearance.

Using the Filter and Filter On Properties

The first two properties you might want to experiment with are the Filter and Filter On properties. These properties give you the ability to eliminate records from the contents of a report.

When you are working with queries, you have the ability to create a WHERE clause to eliminate records from the recordset. When you build a report, you can base it on a query. If you want to adjust the contents, you can adjust the WHERE clause of the query. In Day 15, "Examining Special-Use Queries," you learned that you could create a parameter query to ask you what records you wanted to work with.

When you were looking at forms in Day 5, "Creating Simple Forms for Data Access," you got a chance to look at filtering records. Creating a filter is like creating a temporary WHERE clause. You can specify what records you are going to work with.

The Filter and Filter On data properties give you an opportunity to set a temporary WHERE clause for the report and turn it on or off as needed. The Filter property is used to create the WHERE clause for the report. It is a text property that specifies the expression to use to limit the records returned. The Filter On property is used to turn the Filter property on and off.

This means that you can leave the query alone and adjust the report as needed. This also gives you a great deal of flexibility when you start expanding the functionality of the database with Visual Basic for Applications.

Task: Setting the Filter and Filter On Properties

▲ TASK

1. Launch Microsoft Access 2000 and open the Classes.mdb database.

2. Select the Report tab.

3. Open rptClassPhoneList in Design mode.

4. Select File, Save As and save the report as rptClassPhoneListModified.

5. Click the View button on the toolbar to preview the report. Notice that the records begin with the Sophomores, which have the Year field set to 1.

6. Click the Properties button from the toolbar to display the Properties window, if it isn't already showing.

7. Verify that the Report is the selected object and select the Data tab.

8. Select the Filter property and enter Year=3 as the Filter string, as shown in Figure 17.1.

17

FIGURE 17.1

The Filter property is a WHERE *clause without the* WHERE *keyword.*

9. Select the Filter On property and set it to Yes.

10. Click the View button on the toolbar to see the report in Preview, as shown in Figure 17.2.

FIGURE 17.2

The records for the sophomores or juniors are not displayed in this report because of the filter.

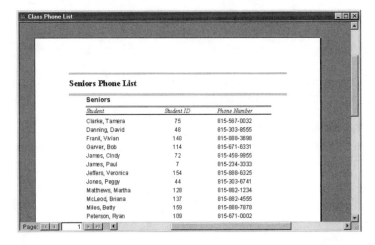

▼   11. Select the View button on the toolbar to get back to Design mode.

     12. Set the Filter On property back to No and preview the report again. Notice that you
         can again view the report with all of the classes displayed.

▲   13. Click the View button on the toolbar to return to the Design mode.

By setting the Filter property and then toggling the Filter On property between Yes and
No, you can have one report serving two purposes. This is great when you have a report
in which you sometimes need to see all the records, and at other times you only need a
specific subset of records.

In reality, you will probably want to be able to set the filter to each class and print it.
This takes a little more work and you will get to see how to accomplish this task later in
this lesson, when you explore parameter reports.

Note	When you are going to use the Filter property to control what records are used, you have to remember that you are creating a WHERE clause. You will notice that you set Year=3. You did not set it to Year="Seniors". The display of the word *Seniors* is completed with the Choose function, using the Year field. You still had to know that a senior is represented with the number 3.

If you are working with other data types, you also have to make sure that
you build the expression correctly. For instance, if you wanted to display
only those students with the last name Garver, you would have to remember
to surround the name with quotation marks. The Filter property would be
set as follows:

```
LastName="Garver"
```

If you are working with dates, you would also need to format those correctly. A date must be surrounded by pound (#) signs in a WHERE clause. For
example, if the Birthdate field were included in this query, it would be formatted as

```
Birthdate = #10/2/82#
```

As an extra benefit, you can also use the Filter On property with a text box and the IIF
function to set the title for the report.

Task: Using the Filter On Property to Create a Dynamic Title for a Report

TASK

1. Select the Class Phone List label and delete it.

2. Add a new text box in the report header and delete its attached label.

3. Set the following Format properties:

Property	Setting
Left	0"
Top	.1667"
Width	4"
Height	.3"
Font Name	Times New Roman
Font Size	18
Font Weight	Bold

4. Select the Data tab and set the Control Source property to

   `=IIF(=FilterOn = True, "Seniors Phone List", "Class Phone List")`

5. Try setting the Filter On property to Yes and No, previewing the report with each setting to see the title change.

6. Make sure the Filter On property is set to No.

7. Save the report.

Using the Order By and Order By On Properties

The filtering properties allow you to temporarily override the recordset settings for a report. The Order By and Order By On properties allow you to control the sort order of a report in the same way. The Order By property allows you to indicate a field, or group of fields, to sort your report by, and Order By On allows you to turn the Order By settings on and off as needed. Let's start by examining the different methods that can be used to sort your report.

When you create a query, you have the opportunity to set a Sort order in the Query with the ORDER BY clause. The rptClassPhoneListModified report is based on the qryClassPhoneList query. If you open this query in Design mode, you will see that the Sort row uses ascending order under the Year, LastName, and FirstName fields, as shown in Figure 17.3.

FIGURE 17.3

The Sort row allows you to determine how the recordset will be sorted.

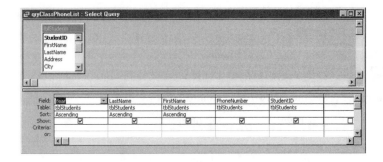

This means that the recordset will be sorted by Year, and then by LastName, and then by FirstName, as needed. When the report is created, Year will also be used to group the records together, but the sorting by LastName and FirstName is ignored. The report doesn't look at the underlying recordset for a sort order.

The first method for setting a sort order for a report is to use the Sorting and Grouping window for the report. If you use the Report Wizard to create a report, it prompts you as to whether you want any groups or any sorting. It then will place those settings in the Sorting and Grouping window for the report, as shown in Figure 17.4.

FIGURE 17.4

These are settings to group the records by Year and sort on LastName and FirstName.

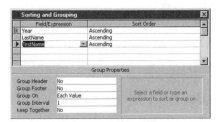

The last method is to use the Order By and Order By On properties. Doing so will allow you to control the sort order dynamically, but will have no effect if you have any sort order specified in the Sorting and Grouping window. If you have a field or fields specified to be used for grouping that is fine, but you can't just have a field for sorting specified.

The report we're using as an example has duplicate sort settings in the query and in the Sorting and Grouping window. What you need to do is clear out the LastName and FirstName settings, and then indicate your choices using the properties.

After you clear out the settings, the first step is to indicate what fields you want to use for sorting. This is done by typing the name of the field in the Order By property. If you want to use more than one field, you can separate them with commas. For instance, to duplicate what is already set in the Sorting and Grouping window, you would type LastName, FirstName.

After you have indicated the fields, you can turn them on by setting the Order By On property to Yes. It can be turned off simply by selecting No. It operates exactly like the Filter On property.

Task: Setting the Sort Order by Using the Order By and Order By On Properties

1. Select the Sorting and Grouping icon on the toolbar to display the Sorting and Grouping window if it isn't already visible.

2. Point to the LastName field selection button in the window, and drag down to the FirstName field to highlight the two fields.

3. Press the Delete key to delete these fields.

4. Select the Yes button in the confirmation window to confirm that you want to remove the sort by these two fields.

5. Close the Sorting and Grouping window.

6. Open the Properties window and select the Data tab if it isn't already showing.

7. Select the Order By property and type `LastName,FirstName`.

8. Press Enter and set the Order By On property to Yes.

9. Preview the report and notice that the report is now sorted by last name and then first name.

10. Click the View button to return to the design mode and set the Order By On property to No.

11. Preview the report and notice that the report is back to sorting by how they are entered in the table.

The Order By and Order By On properties allow you to apply a different order dynamically. The important thing to remember is that if these properties do not seem to be working, you need to check your Sorting and Grouping window because these properties cannot override those settings.

Using the Page Header and Page Footer Properties

The next two properties do not affect the contents of a report, but they give you some additional control over the appearance of a report. The report's Page Header and Page Footer properties allow you to determine when the page header and page footer, respectively, will print.

TASK

17

The report header and report footer sections will print only at the beginning and ending of the report as a whole. The page header and footer can print on every page, or they can be skipped if the report header, report footer, or both the report header and footer are printing on a page. These properties give you the flexibility to create a report header to print on the first page, and a smaller page header to print on the following pages. The same is true with the report footer and page footer.

In the rptClassPhoneList, there is a title in the report header in a larger font size than the rest of the text. The page header contains nothing at this point. Most of the time, the page header is a location to store the field titles, but this is located in the group header. When you preview the report, the first page looks fine. You can identify the report and the group and fields you are looking at.

As you can see in Figure 17.5, the presentation of the second page could be improved. The report header isn't displayed because it is the second page and currently the field names aren't displayed. The readers might find that they are turning back to page 1 to determine what they are looking at. This will slow them down and probably irritate them.

FIGURE 17.5

The second page of the report doesn't provide any information about the data you are look-ing at.

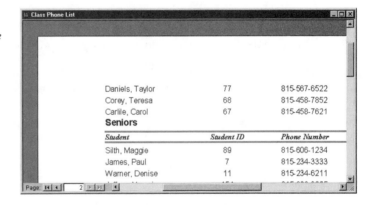

To minimize the time it takes for the reader to view the data in a report, you can create a custom page header and then select not to display it when the report header is displayed.

Task: Creating a Custom Page Header

1. Select the Format tab in the Properties window.

2. Set the Page Header property to Not with Rpt Hdr.

3. Point to the divider between the page header and year header and drag the year header down to increase the height of the page header to make room for some information.

4. Click on the Text Box control in the Toolbox.

▼ 5. Click in the page header to create a text box and delete its label.

6. Move the text box to the left of the page header.

7. Set its Control Source property to use the same expression as the text box in the report header.

```
=IIF(=FilterOn = True, "Seniors Phone List", "Class Phone List")
```

8. Click on one of the gray lines in the report header and copy it to the Clipboard.

9. Select the page header section and paste in the line from the Clipboard.

10. Move the gray line to the bottom of the page header.

11. Preview the report and look at the second page to view the new header, as shown in Figure 17.6.

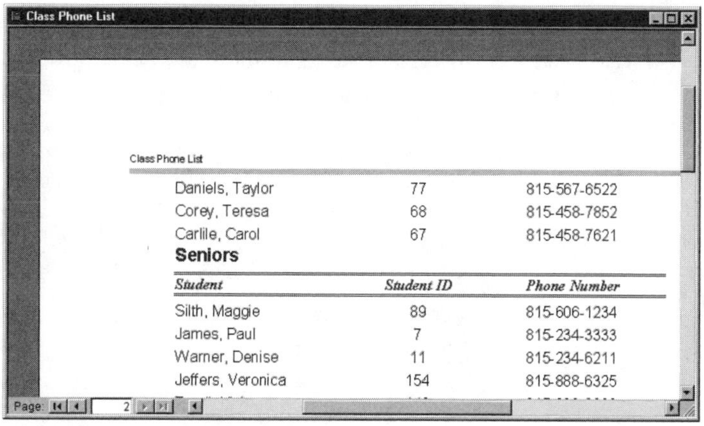

FIGURE 17.6

The page header now has a text box to repeat the report header information in smaller proportions.

▲ 12. Save and close the report.

Notice you do not see the page header on the first page and now you have more information about the report on the second page. If you hadn't set the Page Header property, you would see the page header under the report header.

This is still not a complete solution. You still do not know what fields you are viewing on the second page. You could have copied all of the field titles from the Year group header and pasted them into the page header, but another approach will be introduced later in "Formatting Sections." You will also get a chance to get some sophisticated results using report headers and footers in the section "Creating Special First and Last Page Headers and Footers," later in this lesson.

Using the Text Box's Hide Duplicates Property

The last property discussed in this section is the text box's Hide Duplicates property. Although it is not a report property that affects the look of the report as a whole, it can be used to create a special effect in your reports.

There are times when you need to add a grouping to a text box to get like data together and identify the group, but you do not want to have a line dedicated to listing the grouped field as you have seen in rptClassPhoneListModified. The Hide Duplicates property may be an answer.

If you preview the rptClassPhoneListAlternate, you will see this property in action. The year is displayed as the first column of the report with all of that year listed. You will notice that you only see the word *Sophomore* once.

If you open the report in Design mode, you will see how this was done (see Figure 17.7). The Year header is empty, and the field titles have been moved to the page header. The Page Header property has been left as the default to display on all pages.

FIGURE 17.7

The Hide Duplicates property allows you to create a more streamlined report.

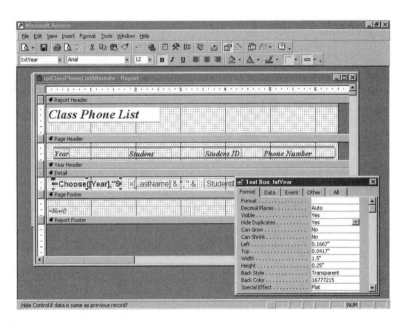

The text box that displays the Choose expression for the year, txtYear, has the Hide Duplicates property set to Yes. This means that for the record displayed, if the contents of this text box match the contents of the previous record, the information will not print.

If you have a lot of groups, this might save you a lot of space that would have to be allocated to a header. With some data, it might also make it easier to skim to locate a group of information.

Formatting Sections

As you have been exploring ways to improve your report performance and appearance, very little attention has been given to formatting sections. In this section, you'll learn about some of the properties that can improve the appearance of individual sections.

Using the Repeat Section Property

In the previous section, you looked at the Page Header and Page Footer properties to create a smaller page header to print on all pages, except the first page that has a report header for rptclassPhoneListModified. When you completed that process, your report was still missing the field labels.

One method for correcting this problem is to take the field labels and copy them to the page header. This identifies the fields, but it might still create some problems for the reader. If the user is reading the report, putting it down, and picking it up again, he would have to remember what group he was reading.

You can alleviate this problem by leaving the field labels where they are, and setting the Repeat Section property for the Year group header. This property is new in Microsoft Access 2000. It not only displays the labels, but also identifies the group.

Task: Using the Repeat Section Property to Display Field Titles on Every Page

1. Open the rptClassPhoneListModified report in Design mode.

2. Select the Year header section.

3. Open the Properties window and select the Format tab if it isn't already showing.

4. Select the Repeat Section property and set it to Yes.

5. Preview the second page of the report (see Figure 17.8).

6. Return to the Design mode.

FIGURE 17.8

*The report now shows
the Year header on
every page.*

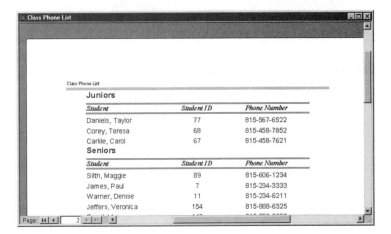

The Repeat Section property provides a quick method to display all the information about the records displayed at the top of the page. You might still not like the fact that only three records from the junior class are displayed on the second page. That can be fixed with the next set of properties.

Using the Keep Together and Grp Keep Together Properties

When you are working with smaller groups of information, you might not like to have the groups split up among pages. You've learned to use the Repeat Section property to show the group header at the top of the page if the section is continuing, but this solves only part of the problem.

The Keep Together and Grp Keep Together properties allow you to control where a section or a group will break. The Keep Together properties for sections and groups serve a similar purpose to widow and orphan control in Microsoft Word.

When Microsoft Access 2000 attempts to print a section or a group and Keep Together has been turned on, Access will determine whether it can fit the specified contents on the page. If not, it will move to the next page to print the contents. If the section or group is too large to fit on a page, Access will start on a new page and then continue on the next page.

You set the Keep Together property different for a section than for a group. To set the Keep Together property for a section, you can use the Properties window. You can select the Format tab and select the Keep Together property. It can be turned on by selecting Yes or turned off by selecting No. In the rptClassPhoneList, none of the sections is large enough to cause any problems for printing on a page, with the exception of the Detail section that holds the record data. In the next topic, when you are talking about creating special first and last page headers, Keep Together for a section will be more important.

The Detail section is best controlled by setting the Keep Together property for the group. When you want to set the Keep Together property for a group, you use the Keep Together setting in the Sorting and Grouping window.

In the Sorting and Grouping window, you can view all the properties for a group. The last property in this window is the Keep Together property. It is different from the Keep Together property for the sections because there are different settings for the behavior of the group.

Keep Together is set to No as the default. That gives you the appearance you currently see in this report. The second Year group starts on the first page, even though there isn't enough room for the whole group.

The second setting is Whole Group (see Figure 17.9). This choice means that Microsoft Access 2000 will attempt to fit the group header, all of the records, and the group footer on the same page.

FIGURE 17.9

The Keep Together group property gives you control over how a group will be broken across pages.

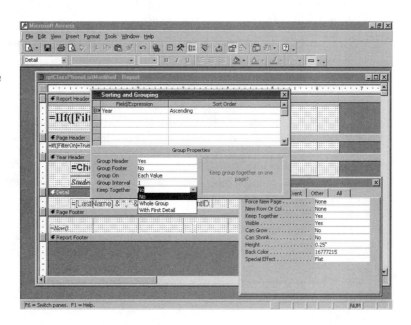

The last choice is With First Detail. If you choose it, Microsoft Access 2000 will place the group header and the first record on the same page. This means that you will not end up with the group header appearing at the bottom of a page, without any records.

For the Year group, set Keep Together to Whole Group and preview the results, shown in Figure 17.10. This creates a three-page report with each year starting on a separate page.

FIGURE 17.10

The Keep Together property starts each small group on a page of its own.

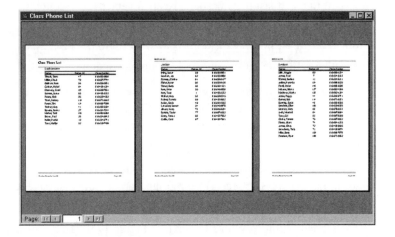

The last property setting is the Grp Keep Together property. This property is a report property, and controls how the Keep Together property for groups will be handled in a multiple-column report.

When you preview rptBirthdays, it is a three-column report with the data displayed down the column, and then going to the top of the next column. The data is grouped by month, and the group's Keep Together property is set to Whole Group.

In this case, the Keep Together property isn't doing as good a job as you would like because all of the data will fit on one page. If you look at the bottom of the first column and the top of the second column, you'll notice that May is split between the columns.

If you change the report's Grp Keep Together property from Per Page to Per Column, the report will look more the way you want it to. If you set the Grp Keep Together property to Per Column, all of the month of May will move to the second column (see Figure 17.11).

FIGURE 17.11

The Grp Keep Together property controls the behavior of a group's Keep Together property when the report has more than one column.

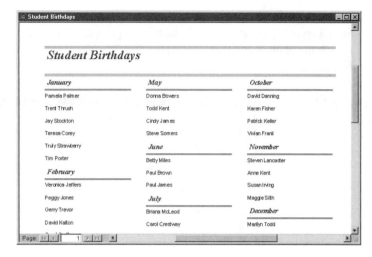

Using the New Row or Col Property

Another property that might be useful for formatting your reports is the New Row or Col property. This property allows you to force a break between sections. In a multiple-column report, you can force a row or column break, depending on which column layout was chosen for the report.

If you preview the rptClassList report, you will notice that it is a two-column report. The students are broken down by classes, and the report prints to the bottom of the first column and then continues in the second (see Figure 17.12).

FIGURE 17.12

This is a basic two-column report.

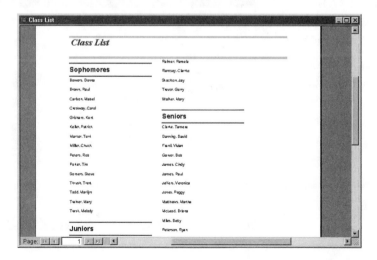

If you set the Keep Together property for the Year group to Whole Group and the Grp Keep Together property to Per Column, you get a cleaner breakdown between the classes as with the phone list report (see Figure 17.13). This pushes the seniors information to the second page.

FIGURE 17.13

The report now has a separate column for each class.

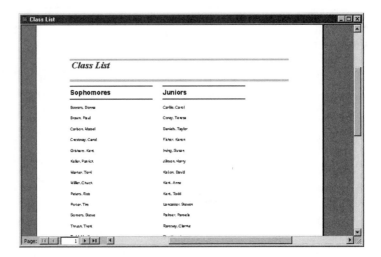

If you want a different look, you can work with the New Row or Col property. If you select the Year Header and set the New Row or Col property to After Section, you create a header displayed to the left, as shown in Figure 17.14.

FIGURE 17.14

The New Row or Col property allows you to create an offset group header from the Year group header.

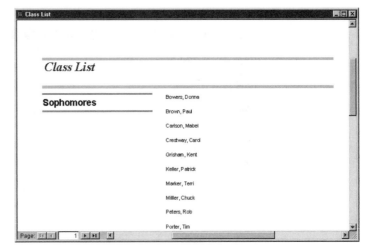

With this type of section formatting, you might want to adjust the placement of the Name field to line it up with the top of the Class text box. You might also want to change the line formatting above and below the Class text box. On Day 19, "Working with VBA," when you learn about Visual Basic for Applications, you will see a possible solution for formatting this style of report.

Using the Force New Page Property

The New Row and Col property allows you to force a new row or column for a section. The Force New Page property gives you the same control for page breaks.

This property is often used to create a separate cover page out of the Report Header section.

Task: Creating a Separate Cover Page with the Report Header

1. Open the rptClassPhoneListModified report in Design mode.
2. Open the Properties window and select the Format tab, if it isn't already selected.
3. Select the Report Header section.
4. Select the Force New Page property and set it to After Section. The result is the Report Header on a page by itself, with each class on a separate page (see Figure 17.15).

FIGURE 17.15

The Force New Page property can help you create a separate cover page.

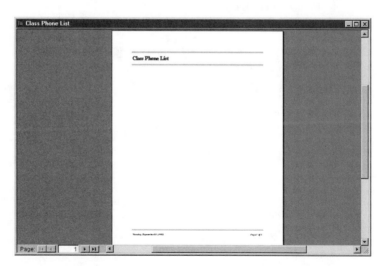

You might also want to set the Page Footer property not to print with Rpt Header. This will give the report a cleaner appearance.

You can force a page break before a section, after a section, or before and after a section. The default is None, not to force a page break at all. You'll do more with this property when you create special first and last page headers and footers, later in this lesson.

Using the Can Shrink and Can Grow Properties

The last two section properties we'll discuss are the Can Shrink and Can Grow properties. These allow you to control what will happen if the objects placed in a section are smaller or larger than originally designed. These are especially useful when incorporating subreports or OLE objects.

In Day 12, you created a report card. This report, rpt1999SecondQtrGrades, uses information from the tblStudents table, as well as a subreport, to get the students' progress from a query. It is designed so that two report cards fit on each page. It would be helpful if you could control whether a section could grow or shrink.

Task: Fixing the Report Card with the Can Grow Property

1. Open the rpt1999SecondQtrGrades report in Design mode.
2. Open the Properties window and select the Format tab, if it isn't already selected.
3. Preview the report and notice that there is room in the subreport for several more classes.
4. Return to Design mode.
5. Select the Detail section.
6. Notice that the Can Grow property is set to Yes and the Can Shrink property is set to No as a default.
7. Set the Can Grow property to No.
8. Select the subreport.
9. Notice that it has the same two properties with the same settings.
10. Set the Can Grow property to No.

11. Save and close the report.

If additional classes are added for a student, and a student has too many classes to display in the allotted space, the additional classes would be truncated. You'll learn more about how to fix this sort of problem in the next section.

Creating Special First and Last Page Headers and Footers

We have explored the advanced properties for the reports as well as the properties for the sections, and you have seen some possible formatting combinations for reporting. In the past with database reporting tools, the readers of the reports often wanted special formatting to duplicate what they could produce manually in a word processor.

They wanted a special cover page with their logo, letters of introduction or a special summary. They often overlooked how much work went into word processing to get those effects when making their demands.

You can create some "word processing" effects with your Microsoft Access 2000 reports and the ability to integrate Microsoft Word documents. In this section, you will explore how to create a custom cover page with a welcome letter, and how to follow a report with an explanation of the information.

For this topic, you are going to create a course catalog (see Figure 17.16) for the school for the 3rd and 4th quarters. It will have a custom cover, an introduction letter, a departments list, and the classes. It will be followed by an explanation that informs the students to contact the department chairs with any questions. You are going to start with the rpt19992ndSemClasses report.

FIGURE 17.16

The report header has been modified to be used as a cover page.

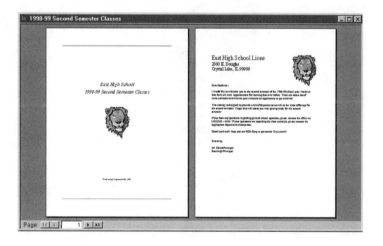

Creating a Special Report Header

When you preview this report, you will notice that it is similar to the reports that you have looked at already. The report header is used to create a title on the first page of the report, with nothing being done with the report footer. You might also notice that the page header has more in it than the other pages, and some additional formatting to make the start of each remaining page line up a little better with the first page.

 When you have completed all the work in this topic, you will have a formal cover page with additional material before the detail section and after it to explain the contents of this document. To save some time, rpt19992ndSemClasses has already been created. Open it in Design mode and save it as rpt19992ndSemClassesModified.

In the previous topic, you experimented with the Force New Page property. It can be set to force a new page before or after a section. That is the first step in creating a custom report header. By setting the Force New Page property to After Section, you will force the detail information to the next page. You will also want to set the report's Page Footer property to Not with Rpt Hdr to eliminate the date and page number from the bottom of the cover page. The result would display the lines and text of the report header on a page by itself (see Figure 17.17).

FIGURE 17.17

The report header now prints on a page by itself.

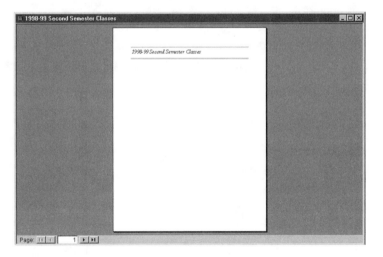

The cover page is created, but it is very basic and bland. After the cover page is created, you can dress it up using some of the other techniques you have learned. The page is like a blank canvas ready for embellishment.

When you are viewing the report header in Design mode, it has its Height property set at .7917". This setting leaves little room for embellishment. You will want to adjust the Height property to better represent the actual page margins. Just like with the left and right margins, you subtracted the Left and Right Margin settings from the Page Setup to get the Width property. You need to do a similar thing here.

The top and bottom margins are set at 1" as well, so the height can be adjusted up to 9". In Design mode, you now can see how much space you have. You might have to use the scrollbars to actually see the end of the space. Now you can add your visual effects.

Task: Embellishing Your Cover Page

1. Switch back to Design view.
2. Open the Properties window with the Format tab displayed if it isn't already.
3. Set the Picture property to display the lion clip art image located in the \Program Files\Common Files\Microsoft Shared\ClipArt\cagcat50 folder. The file is an01124_.wmf.
4. Leave the rest of the properties for the picture the same, except set the Picture Pages property to First Page.
5. Select the second line and set the Top property to 8.9".
6. Copy the label to the Clipboard and paste it into the report header.
7. Change the caption of the first label to East High School.
8. Move both labels down to above the lion image.
9. Set the labels' Width property to 6.5.
10. Set the labels' Text Align property to Center.
11. Add a text box below the lion image and delete its attached label.
12. Set the text box's Control Source property to =Now( ) to display the date.
13. Set the text box's Format property to Long Date.
14. Set the text box's Width to 6.5" and its Text Align property to Center.
15. Click the View button to preview the report. The cover page with its embellishments is complete (see Figure 17.18).

FIGURE 17.18

The report header has been dressed up to attract the eye.

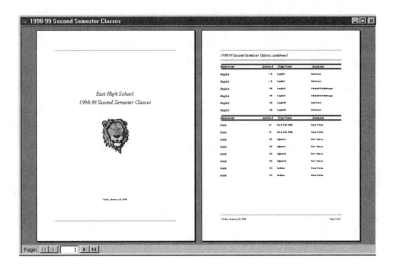

The key to adding polish to the cover page is to expand the height of the header to the dimensions of the page less the top and bottom margins. You can also employ more calculations to place the controls on the page.

Linking to a Word Processing File

Creating a decorative cover is only part of what you want to add to this report. The second page of this report needs to be a welcome letter. You could create this letter manually by adding labels and entering the text for each paragraph.

This method is very tedious and time-consuming. Creating the labels is only part of the process; you have to space them equally, making sure you have appropriate whitespace in between, and then you might have problems when the text changes.

If the text is created in Microsoft Word and then integrated into your report, you can save a great deal of time and aggravation. To make this lesson a bit easier, the letter has already been created.

Task: Adding the Welcome Letter

1. Scroll down so that you can see the 9″ mark in the report header.
2. Select the Page Break tool from the Toolbox and click at the 9″ mark.
3. Drag the page header border down to make some more room in the report header.
4. Select the Unbound object from the Toolbox and click below the page break you just created at the 9.5″ mark. This will open the Insert Object dialog.

▼ 5. Click the Create from File option button.

6. Click the Browse button to open the Browse dialog.

7. Using this dialog, locate the letter, Welcome to 2nd Semester, and click OK.

8. Click the Link Check box to establish the link to the file and click OK.

9. Set the object's Border Style to Transparent to get rid of the line around the letter.

10. Preview the second page of the report to view this letter (see Figure 17.19).

FIGURE 17.19

The report header now has a letter as the second page.

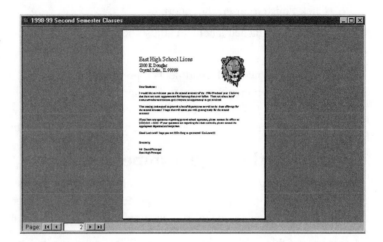

▲

Using an outside source for text like Microsoft Word makes changes easy. If the principal doesn't like the wording, it can be changed simply by changing the Microsoft Word file. This can be a great time saver, especially if you are developing a system for someone else.

Adding a Standalone Subreport

In Day 12, you added a subreport to the report cards that was linked to the main report. It is not required that the subreport be linked to the main report. Here you want to display the Departments report as a reference page.

The process is similar to adding a linked report, but you do not have to worry about establishing the link.

Task: Adding the Department List

1. Move the page header border down to create some more space in the report header.

2. Place a page break below the letter.

3. Select the SubForm/SubReport tool and click below the page break.

4. Select Use an Existing Report or Form, select rptDepartments, and click Next.

5. Select None from the list to establish a link, and click Next.

6. Click Finish to insert the report.

7. Delete the attached label and adjust the width of the subreport and main report as needed.

The report now shows the Departments report as the third page. This report is now designed to support a regular printer. If your printer does duplexing, you can add two page breaks instead of one to get the letter and the Departments report to print on odd pages. You would also need to add a page break following the subreport.

Modifying the Page Numbering

Another formatting trick that might be useful in this type of report is the ability to adjust what page number is displayed in the page footer. In some reports, you do not want to count the cover page as a page. You want the second page to be labeled as the first page.

In the case of this report, there will be no visible page numbering until the reader gets to page 4. If you do not want to count the cover page, the first number to display is 3. That can be accomplished by modifying the page numbering text box Control Source as follows:

```
="Page " & [Page]-1 & " of " & [Pages]-1
```

Creating a Special Report Footer

Next, let's create a custom footer. If you want the footer to reinforce who to contact for further information, you could again rely on labels. You would add the labels, add the text, and then work to get them aligned perfectly.

Again, this is tedious. You might find that creating the text in Microsoft Word is faster. You do not have to use the Unbound Object Frame tool to integrate the information. You can use the Clipboard. To illustrate this technique, the text has already been created in a Microsoft Word document.

Task: Copying Information from Microsoft Word

1. Open the Class Summary document in Microsoft Word and copy the text to the Clipboard.

2. Select the report footer and paste the information from the Clipboard.

3. Adjust the placement and spacing as needed.

4. Preview the last page of the report (see Figure 17.20).

FIGURE 17.20

The report footer shows the pasted text.

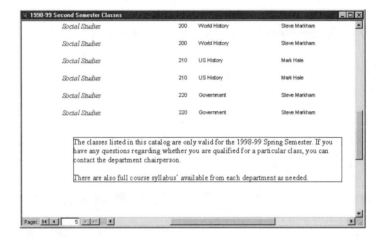

With these changes, the report is complete. These techniques allow you to add many of the word processing features to a report that can be generated automatically as needed without additional work on the part of the user.

Developing Parameter Reports

When you were working with the rptClassPhoneList report, you used the Filter and the Filter On properties to display only the seniors in the list. This is great if you only need to work with one subgroup of the records, but there are three classes.

NEW TERM In Day 15, you learned that it is possible to create a parameter query. Instead of specifying a criteria expression, you could prompt the user for the field value you wanted to use, thus creating a *parameter report*.

This technique can assist you in developing an all-purpose report with user-defined criteria. The same technique can also allow your users to customize other aspects of the report.

| **Caution** | Given that there are only three classes, a parameter query is a good choice to make it easier to only work with one class. If there were more choices or the numbers representing those choices weren't so easy to remember, it might be better to use a form to get that information.

Getting information from a form was illustrated on Day 16, "Implementing Advanced Form Concepts." The same technique could be used except you would use the OpenReport method instead of the OpenForm method. |

Task: Setting Up a Parameter Report

1. Select the query tab from the Database window.

2. Open the qryClassPhoneList query in Design mode.

3. Save the query as qryPromptPhoneList.

4. Select the criteria row of the Year field.

5. Type [What Year?] as shown in Figure 17.21.

6. Save and close the query.

FIGURE 17.21

The parameter has been added for the Year field.

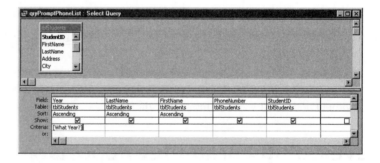

Task: Setting a Query as the Record Source

1. Select the Report tab from the Database window.

2. Open the rptPhoneListwithPrompt report in Design mode.

3. Save the report as rptPhoneListwithPromptModified.

4. Set the report's Record Source to qryPromptPhoneList.

5. Save and close the query.

6. Click the View button on the toolbar to test the report.

7. When prompted for the Year, enter 2.

8. View the report and notice that the report is now dynamic. It will display only the students who have the Year entered at the prompt (see Figure 17.22).

FIGURE 17.22

The report is now one page and it only displays the Year=2 (Junior) records.

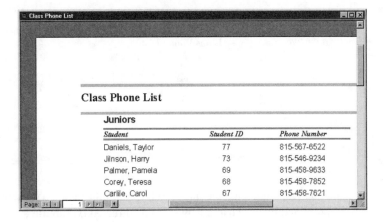

There is still a problem with the report. When you originally designed this report, you were working with filters. You used the IIF statement to create a dynamic title.

The IIF expression determined whether the Filter On property was true, and displayed one of two titles. That won't work with the new structure of this report. You want to have a dynamic title for the report. You will need to use a report parameter, and you will need to have the text box in the page header look at the title for the needed information.

Task: Adding a Dynamic Title

1. Click the View button to return to Design mode.

2. Select the txtTitle text box.

3. Open the Properties window and select the Data tab if needed.

4. Set the Control Source property to =[What title do you want for your report?].

5. Select the txtSubtitle text box in the page header.

6. Set the text box's Control Source property to =[txtTitle].

7. Click the View button on the toolbar to preview the results.

8. When prompted for the Year, enter 2.

9. When prompted for the title, enter Lions Phone List.

10. View the report. It now has a user-defined title displaying on the first page and in the page header (see Figure 17.23).

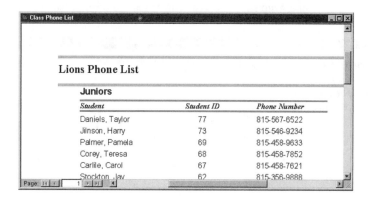

FIGURE 17.23

The report now displays only the Junior records with a custom title.

If you had just duplicated the question for both txtTitle and txtSubtitle, you would have been prompted twice. That is why you just directed txtSubtitle to look at txtTitle.

Handling the Null (No Data) Report Event

Next, we are going to explore what you do to prevent problems when the recordset used as the report's Record Source property is empty. For example, say you attempt to preview the Class Phone List report. When prompted for the year, you type a 4 instead of 1, 2, or 3, and you get an empty report. You will also see errors in which expressions were used to manipulate the display of fields.

With shorter reports, displaying an empty report will not greatly tax the patience of the user or the system, but it will be a source of irritation. With larger reports, the time required to display nothing will be more significant. What you want to do is not waste any time trying to display a report with no data in it.

When you were introduced to Visual Basic for Applications in Day 13, "Introducing VBA," you learned that all objects in Microsoft Access 2000 have events that affect them. With Visual Basic for Applications, you can add code to respond to the different events.

As you provide more dynamic features to your reporting, there will be a greater chance that a user will type the wrong thing when prompted. This will create a recordset with no records in it. When this happens, the report's NoData event will be executed.

The NoData event gives you a location at which to add Visual Basic for Applications code to deal with the problem before too much time elapses. The simplest solution for this problem is to communicate the problem to the user and then close the report.

Task: Creating a NoData Event Procedure

▼ TASK

1. Display the rptPhoneListwithPromptModified report in Design view.
2. Select the report.
3. Display the Properties window, with the Events tab displayed.
4. Select the On No Data property.
5. Select [Event Procedure] from its drop-down list and select the Build button to create the event and display it in the Visual Basic Editor.
6. Access creates the Private Sub procedure Report_NoData(), as shown in Figure 17.24.

FIGURE 17.24

The NoData() event is created and displayed in the Visual Basic editor.

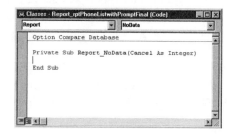

▲

Like all event procedures, NoData is local to this report. It has parentheses to store any arguments needed by the event procedure. With the NoData event, there is a built-in argument called Cancel.

The Cancel argument is the key to eliminating this waste of time. The Cancel argument allows you to decide whether to display or to print an empty report. If you do nothing in this event other than set the Cancel argument to True, you will save a great deal of time and resources. However, if that is all you put in this event, you might baffle your user. What he will see is that he has attempted to open the report and answered the prompts, but then nothing happens. He won't know that he has made a mistake. He will start by blaming Microsoft Access 2000 and you.

When you make a mistake in most applications, a message box opens, indicating a problem. With Visual Basic for Applications, you can communicate using this same vehicle by using the MsgBox() statement.

If you add the following two lines of code to the NoData() event, you will successfully dealt with the no data problem:

```
Msgbox "There are no records that match your criteria."
Cancel = True
```

You can then click the Save button on the toolbar and close the Microsoft Visual Basic Editor to return to your report. When you attempt to preview the report, enter a 4 for the Year and any title you want. After entering the prompt information, your message box will be displayed (see Figure 17.25)

FIGURE 17.25

The message box just communicates what is happening with the report before it closes.

When you click OK in the message box, the report will not be displayed. This will reduce the amount of time the user spends waiting for a report to display, especially because it wouldn't have any information in it anyway.

 Note

> The MsgBox() statement can be used as a statement or a function. For additional information, see Day 18, "Examining VBA."

Creating Crosstab Reports

In Day 15, you got to work with a crosstab query to compare your data in a spreadsheet-type design. The problem with creating a report based on a crosstab query is that the columns might not stay constant, but the columns displayed in a report need to remain constant.

NEW TERM You can create a crosstab report. A crosstab report is one that is based on a crosstab query. This is a two-step process: You first have to create the crosstab query and lock its columns, and then you create your report using the normal methods for creating reports. If you don't lock the columns in your crosstab query, you will need to use VBA to create your report, which can be time consuming and tedious.

For this example, you are going to work with a grade comparison by class. The base query and the crosstab query have been created for you already. If you open the qryGradeCountCrossTab query, you will see that each class is on a line by itself, with the grades as the column headings. You will also notice that there are no D grades (see Figure 17.26).

What you want is to show the column for D grades, regardless of whether there are any at the time you view the query. This requires a change to the crosstab query design.

FIGURE 17.26

As you can see in this query, there are currently no posted D grades.

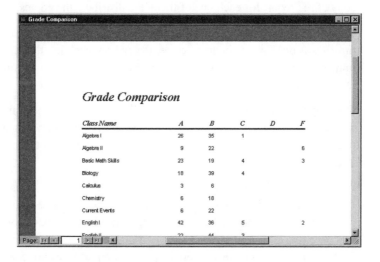

Creating Constant Column Headings

▼ TASK

1. Click the View button on the toolbar to go to the Design mode.

2. Save the query as qryGradeCountCrossTabModified.

3. Click on the background of the table pane.

4. Open the Properties window.

5. Select the Column Headings property.

6. Type "A","B","C","D","F" and press Enter.

7. Click the View button to display the query results. Notice that you now have a column for D grades, although there is nothing listed in it at the current time (see Figure 17.27).

17

FIGURE 17.27

The crosstab query now has a column for D grades, although there are none currently.

This is the way to lock in the columns or to sort them in a unique order. Now you can use any method you want to create your report.

Task: Using the Report Wizard to Create a Crosstab Report

1. Close the crosstab query.
2. Select the Reports tab from the Database window.
3. Click the New button to open the New Report window.
4. Select Report Wizard, select qrygradeCountCrossTabModified, and click Next.
5. Select all fields and click Next.
6. Do not select any grouping and click Next.
7. Choose to sort by ClassName and click Next.
8. Select a tabular layout, portrait orientation and click Next.
9. Select the Corporate Style and click Next.
10. Enter Grade Comparison for the title and click Finish.

You now have a report that will display the crosstab data and not have any problems if data is missing. If your crosstab query's columns cannot be specified in this manner, you might want to consider exporting to Microsoft Excel 2000.

Publishing Your Report on the Web

In the past, printing a report was the only method for sharing database information. In many cases, if you needed a group of people to see your information, you would print a copy of the report for each one of them and distribute the copies.

This approach wasted resources and time, and many times the report was outdated by the time it was distributed. In many cases, the person receiving the report would not have an immediate need for the information, and would require another copy when he or she was ready to receive the information.

One way to overcome this problem is to allow those with a need for the information to have access to the database. This requires each person who needs access to the information to develop a basic knowledge of working with Microsoft Access and to have access to the database.

Another approach is to take advantage of Data Access Pages. This method, introduced in Day 8, "Data Access Pages," provides access to live database information. If a person doesn't need access to the live data, but does need reports based on static information, you have two alternatives. You can export your report to be accessed from the Web using HTML, or you can create a report snapshot. A report snapshot can be accessed with or without the Web.

Exporting a Report to HTML

One method for sharing a report without printing it is to export it to HTML. After you have exported it, you can create a link to the report from any other Web page. This provides access to the information without wasting time and resources. It also means that when the information is needed, the information will be the most current version of the report.

Task: Exporting Your Roster Report to HTML

1. Select Reports from the Object list.

2. Select rptRoster from the list.

3. Select File, Export to open the Export As dialog (see Figure 17.28).

FIGURE 17.28

The Export As dialog allows you to specify a filename and a format for the report.

17

4. Enter a new filename, such as Roster, if desired.

5. Select HTML Document from the Save As Type list.

6. Click Save to open the HTML Output Options dialog (see Figure 17.29).

FIGURE 17.29

The HTML Output Options dialog allows you to control the formatting of the report as an HTML document.

7. Select an HTML template if desired, and click OK.

▲ 8. Your report is saved in HTML format.

The HTML report can be viewed with any Web browser. If you open the folder you set as the destination of the report (see Figure 17.30), you will see that a new HTML file has been created for each page of the report. With longer reports, the number of files created can be quite large.

FIGURE 17.30

The roster was four pages long, so only four files are created.

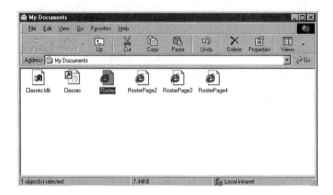

Double-click on the first file, and it will open in your default Web browser (see Figure 17.31). The results may not be what you expected from this report: The information is exported, but most of the formatting is lost. The roster in report form took advantage of page layout techniques such as extra spacing, columns and graphics such as the border and the lion mascot. All that is stripped out during the export except for the columns.

FIGURE 17.31

There is some loss of formatting when the report is exported to HTML.

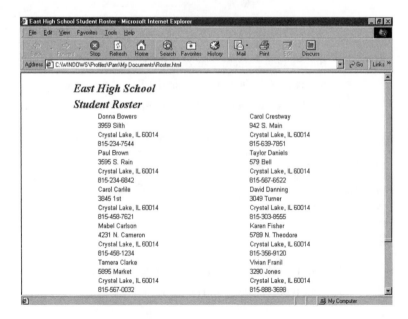

One positive aspect of the export is that it automatically adds the HTML codes to facilitate navigation between the files. It adds links to the First, Previous, Next, and Last pages at the bottom of the page (see Figure 17.32).

FIGURE 17.32

The links are added automatically.

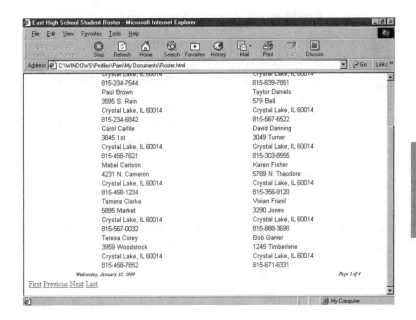

> **Tip**
>
> The ability to export to a HTML format can also be accomplished while the report is open. When you open the report, you can select File, Export to access the dialog. Once the dialog is open, the steps are the same.

Exporting a Report to a Snapshot

NEW TERM The loss of formatting and the file for each page might discourage you from exporting to the HTML format. With Microsoft Access 2000, you have another alternative. Microsoft has added a new export format. You can export your report as a report *snapshot*, which produces the report in one file that retains its formatting.

After the snapshot is created, it can be viewed using the Snapshot Viewer. This viewer is automatically installed when you install Microsoft Access 2000. If the person who needs this report won't have Microsoft Access loaded on her system, she can obtain the Snapshot Viewer from the Microsoft Access Developer's Web site.

If the user will have Internet Explorer 3.0 and higher, downloading the Snapshot Viewer isn't necessary. The Snapshot Viewer is bundled with Internet Explorer 3.0 and higher. This means that you can include a link to a report snapshot on a Web page.

Task: Creating a Report Snapshot

1. Select rptDepartments as your report.

2. Select File, Export to open the Export dialog.

3. Enter a new filename, such as Departments, if desired.

4. Select Snapshot Format from the Save As Type list.

5. Select AutoStart to view the snapshot after it is created if desired. If you selected AutoStart, the Snapshot Viewer will open with the report in view (see Figure 17.33). This displays the report with its formatting, and provides navigation buttons at the bottom of the window, similar to those found in the report window in Microsoft Access.

FIGURE 17.33

The Snapshot Viewer allows you to view the report without accessing the database.

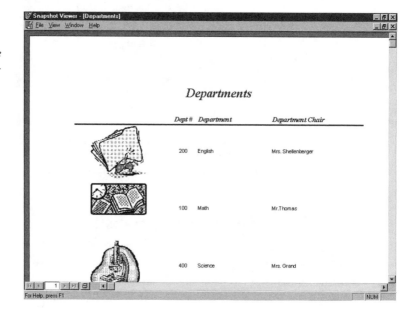

6. Click Save.

Summary

In this lesson, you had an opportunity to explore different methods for enhancing and sharing your reports. The first area you explored was the ability to use properties to control the contents and order of a report.

You also explored how to use the Page Header and Page Footer properties to change the appearance of the pages. You discovered that you can control the printing of sections with the Repeat Section and Keep Together properties. You also experimented with the New Row Col, Force New Page, Can Shrink, and Can Grow properties.

You also can create a special header and footer for the report. This can be done with the report header and report footer sections. If needed, you can also integrate files from other applications, such as a Microsoft Word document.

You also got a chance to vary the contents of the report with a parameter report. This can change the data, as well as elements of the standard report text. You also created a report to compare data using a crosstab report.

The last section gave you a chance to see two different methods for sharing reports electronically without the reader having access to the database. You can export it directly to HTML or use a report snapshot.

Q&A

Q Can I include an Excel workbook in my report header?

A Yes, you can include an Excel workbook in your report. Any application that allows you to create an OLE link can be included.

Q Are you limited to a specific number of pages in a report?

A Your report can't exceed 65,536 pages.

Q What is wrong if someone can't view a report snapshot using Internet Explorer?

A The user doesn't have the Snapshot Viewer installed on his system.

Q Can you automate the creation of HTML pages and report snapshots?

A Yes, you can use the `OutputTo()` method with Visual Basic for Applications to automate the creation of HTML pages and report snapshots.

Workshop

The Workshop contains questions and exercises to help you reinforce the material covered today. The answers appear in Appendix A, "Answers."

Quiz

1. What does the Filter property represent?
2. Why might you use a report header or report footer?
3. Why is the ability to link in other files important?
4. What is the advantage of a parameter report?

Exercises

1. Create a cover page for rptRoster.
2. Convert the rptMailingLabels report into a parameter report by creating a query and basing the parameter on gender.
3. Export the field trip eligibility report to a snapshot.

DAY 18

Examining VBA

In Day 13, you were introduced to Visual Basic for Applications (VBA). This lesson focuses on the foundation of the VBA language so you can begin automating your work. Today, you will learn the following:

- The purpose of VBA
- Objects
- Program flow and loops
- Statements and functions
- Error handling

To follow along with today's lesson, you'll need the sample database, Events.mdb, from the CD-ROM that accompanies this book. You'll find the database in \Day18\. Events.mdb manages the event scheduling for a conference center. Before you can use it, you will need to copy it to another location so you can save your work in this lesson.

Reviewing the Purpose of VBA

When you create a word processing document like a letter or a memo, the document is accessed for a short period of time. After you start the letter or the memo, it might take you a few minutes to several hours to get it to the printer or email.

When you work with Microsoft Access, what you create has a longer life span. You are looking at and storing the data for a longer period of time. As you work with Microsoft Access, you will find that you create forms and reports to meet specific information needs. You might also find that after you have created a form or report, you will use it frequently. That is where you will find uses for Visual Basic for Applications (VBA). When you find yourself completing the same task again and again, you start thinking about automation and how you can speed up the completion of that task.

You are now thinking like a developer whether you realize it or not. At this point, you are two persons in one: the developer and the user. It might help you automate better if you think of these two perspectives separately.

When you add forms and reports to your database, you are creating a database system. The forms and reports are the beginning of your interface.

Beginning with Day 13, "Introducing VBA," you started exploring possible uses for VBA. The key to successfully implementing VBA in your database system is having a foundation of knowledge about VBA, so that you can recognize where and how you can automate with it. This lesson is designed to give you that foundation in VBA. You will learn how you manage objects, how to control the path of your code and take advantage of the language, and how to tackle problems that will crop up during your code's execution.

The focus of this lesson is not to teach you everything there is to know about VBA, it is to give you an overview of VBA's structure. You will also learn how to track down specific information about a component.

Learning About Objects

When you develop your system using VBA, you are using an *object-oriented language*. This means that you are going to manage your objects.

NEW TERM   In VBA, an *object* is any component you create or manage. For the most part, objects are easy to spot. A form is an object, each section in the form is an object, and a control on the form is an object. There are also some objects that you do not create, but you take advantage of. The screen is an object, as is your printer.

When you work with VBA, you develop VBA code to control these objects. You work with properties, program for events, and take advantage of methods.

Understanding Properties

New Term As you have been creating your tables, queries, forms, and reports, you have been setting properties. A *property* is an attribute that controls the appearance or behavior of an object. There are three types of properties: design, run time, and read-only properties.

Design properties are the ones you have been working with the most in the previous lessons. Design properties are those properties that can be set up when the object is not in use. Design properties are those properties that are displayed in the Properties windows, like the Form Properties window (see Figure 18.1).

FIGURE 18.1

The Properties window will display all the properties available at design time.

You have set many design properties as you have worked with Microsoft Access in the earlier lessons. When you changed a Caption property for a label or changed the Control Source property for a text box, you were setting a design property. In most cases, these properties can also be set with VBA code.

The second type of property you have worked with is the run time property. This type of property can only be accessed when the object is active. In Day 16, "Implementing Advanced Form Concepts," you experimented with combo boxes and you used the Combo Box Wizard to generate a combo box to assist with looking up records on the form.

In the Events database, there is a lookup combo box located on the frmEvents form. This combo box uses runtime properties to display a record:

```
Private Sub Combo33_AfterUpdate()
    ' Find the record that matches the control.
    Me.RecordsetClone.FindFirst "[EventID] = " & Me![Combo33]
    Me.Bookmark = Me.RecordsetClone.Bookmark
End Sub
```

18

The RecordsetClone and Bookmark properties are both runtime properties. There cannot be a RecordsetClone until the form is displayed in Form view because the form doesn't have a recordset until then. The Bookmark property is the placeholder in a recordset. Again, you do not have a placeholder until the form get its recordset.

The last type of property is the read-only property. Some properties are available just to provide information. They cannot be modified directly. For example, the Count property can tell you how many forms are in your database or how many controls are on a form; you can't set the property to change that number, but you can access it to get information.

To reference a property in your code, you must identify the property you want to work with. You do that by specifying the object, followed by a period, followed by the name of the property, as shown in the following line:

`Object.property`

When you are setting properties in the Properties window, the properties are listed, followed by an entry area for the setting. When you want to change properties with code, you might have to make an adjustment to the name of the property.

Property names do not have spaces when you are referencing them in your code. If you are referring to a property that is displayed in the Properties window, and it is displayed with a space, just omit the space. For example, if you are trying to refer to the `BackColor` property for a section on a form, the reference would be

`Detail.BackColor`

If you want to assign a value to a property, you must set up an expression. The first part of the expression identifies the property and the second part is the value you want to assign.

You must make sure the value you are assigning matches the data type of the property. For example, if you wanted to change the caption of the label on a report, you would change the Caption property. The Caption property is a string property, so the value must be surrounded by quotation marks:

`lblTitle.Caption = "Access Quick Start Attendance"`

Understanding Events

NEW TERM   Objects can also have events. An *event* is an action that is triggered by a user or the system. When you are creating your interface, you will determine what user or system actions you will respond to when a form or report is displayed.

In the code sample for the frmEvents form's combo box, the user would have selected an event from the combo box. This would trigger the AfterUpdate event for the combo box. When the selection was made, the code repositioned the bookmark to display the record that matches the selection.

Another event that you have worked with in some of the previous lessons is the Click event. The Click event has been illustrated with the Command Button control. In frmEvents, there is a command button to display the attendance report for the selected event. Its Click event, shown here, displays the report in Preview:

```
Private Sub cmdAttendance_Click()
On Error GoTo Err_cmdAttendance_Click

    Dim stDocName As String, stCriteria as String

    stDocName = "rptEventAttendance"
    stCriteria = "[EventID] = " & Me!EventID
    DoCmd.OpenReport stDocName, acPreview,,stCriteria

Exit_cmdAttendance_Click:
    Exit Sub

Err_cmdAttendance_Click:
    MsgBox Err.Description
    Resume Exit_cmdAttendance_Click

End Sub
```

18

The Command Button Wizard generated the button and created the Click event for the command button. By adding VBA code to the Click event for this button, you are determining what action is taken. The events you are concerned with are those for your interface. To make it easier to identify what events are available for an object, there is a corresponding event property shown in the Properties window.

You can use the Event tab in the Properties window (see Figure 18.2) to review what events are available for an object. You still must determine the object you want to add code for and which event you want to use. Sometimes the choice of an event is an easy one, as in the example of the command button. The Click event is triggered when a user clicks a mouse button or presses the Enter key when the button has the focus or is the default button on the form.

FIGURE 18.2

The Event tab in Properties window will display the event properties for the available events.

There are other times when the choice is not as easy. In the frmAttendees form, the user can select an event to attend through a subform. As the form stands, the combo box for the events displays only those events with available spaces, but it doesn't take care of updating the Available Spaces field in the tblEvents table. This could lead to some data problems down the line. It is a perfect use for VBA. If you were going to add code to update tblEvents, you could use several events.

One choice is to use an event for the subform object. A subform object has two events. One of them is the On Exit event. You could add your code to this event, but there is a problem. The On Exit event is only triggered when the focus moves to another control on the form. It is possible to move to another record without leaving the subform.

A second choice is to use the events associated with the combo box on the subform. You could use the combo box's AfterUpdate event like the lookup combo shown above. This would be closer to updating the event record as the attendee is assigned to that class. But if you pressed the Esc key to cancel the insertion of this new record, you would have updated the Available Spaces field without really assigning anyone to the slot.

A better solution is to work with the events for the record on the subform. This means working with the form events. When you sign up an attendee for a class, you actually trigger several events during the process. As you make your first selection, you are triggering the insert events. As you move from the combo box to the Date field, you are triggering the focus events, LostFocus and GotFocus. As you type in the other controls, you are triggering the change event as well as the key events, KeyDown, KeyUp, and KeyPress.

You must make sure the record is updated in the tblRegistration table before you modify the tblEvents table. That means you need to wait until the record is updated, but you have two choices.

The BeforeUpdate event is triggered before the record is updated, and the AfterUpdate event is triggered after the record is updated. The BeforeUpdate event is great when you have to validate information entered before updating the record like checking to make sure the user has entered an existing state. In this example, it is the AfterUpdate event for the subform because you want that record saved before you change the record in tblEvents.

This use for VBA also brings up another coding need. What must happen when an attendee withdraws from an event? The process of determining what code is needed for the tblEvents update and deletion is discussed as you work through this lesson. The code needed to update of the tblEvents data will be constructed in Day 19, "Working with VBA."

NEW TERM Part of what causes problems with deciding which event to use is the number of events and the sequence of execution, known as the *order of events*. If you place code in one event and it doesn't perform as expected, it might mean that another event takes precedence over the one you chose.

As you develop VBA code in your system, you will find it easier to make the choice as to where your code should go. You can also learn more about the order of events through help. If you search for `order of events` using the Office Assistant or the Answer Wizard, you will be able to learn more about the order of events.

When you want to create an event, you can use a control wizard or set the event property from the Properties window to [Event Procedure] and click the Build button, or right-click on the object and select Build Event. Or you can create the event in the Visual Basic Editor directly. When you create an event with any of these methods, VBA will create the correct syntax, including any arguments.

Understanding Methods

NEW TERM In addition to properties and methods, objects can also have methods. A *method* is an action that affects an object. In the code example for displaying the report shown above, the `OpenReport` method is used. The syntax for a method is the following:

```
object.method argumentlist
```

A method is very similar to a statement or function, which will be reviewed later in this lesson. It is something you will add to a procedure to take action. In the case of `OpenReport`, the method is going to open the specified report in the selected mode:

```
DoCmd.OpenReport stDocName, acPreview,,stCriteria
```

Now you think about `OpenReport` and say it is affecting the behavior of the report, but when you examine the code, you notice that the name of the report is not the object. The object is `DoCmd`. The name of the report is actually represented by a variable, stDocName, as the first argument. The `DoCmd` object is a special object. It is a part of VBA to give you access to many of the Access actions that are also accessible from macros. You will spend a lot of time working with this object and its methods.

18

Understanding Object Models

Objects, with their properties, events, and methods, seem a bit confusing when you start working with them, but they will become easier in time. When you are attempting to automate your actions in Microsoft Access or one of the other Office applications, the process is the same. You will be working with that specific application's objects, which have their own properties, events, and methods.

NEW TERM Each Microsoft application has an *object model*, which organizes the individual objects into a hierarchy. The object models for each product cut down the learning process for automation. After you have learned the core elements of VBA presented in this lesson, you can begin automating in the other Office applications by learning their object hierarchies.

NEW TERM When you create a control on a form or report, it is a control object. There are normally many controls on a form or report. These objects are part of the control collection. A *collection* is a group of similar objects. Every form or report is a member of the form or report collection. By using these collections, you can keep track of an object and where it fits into the system.

When you are working with Microsoft Access, there isn't just one object model to work with. The Access object model allows you to manipulate the Microsoft Access objects, and data access models allow you to manipulate the data directly.

Examining the Access Object Model

The Access object model is designed to give you control over the application itself and the objects contained in the database you create. As mentioned above, the objects are grouped together to create collections and those collections are grouped under a central object.

The Application object is the central control for Microsoft Access with VBA. The Access object model is quite extensive. The full model is shown in Figure 18.3.

Note Don't let this chart of the model scare you away from working with VBA! Most of what you are going to need is located under five of the objects and collections. You have already used one of the objects to automate your work: the OpenReport method for the DoCmd object.

FIGURE 18.3

The Microsoft Access object model gives you control over the Microsoft Access environment.

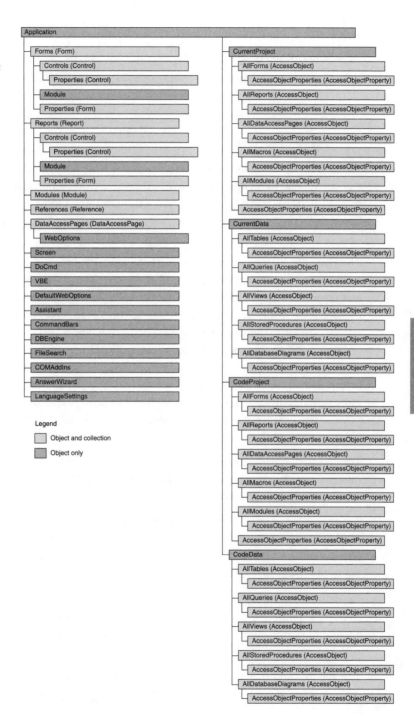

There are five objects and collections that you will work with the most:

- The DoCmd object
- The Forms collection
- The Reports collection
- The Screen object
- The Assistant object

The object you are going to work with the most is the DoCmd object, which has methods that correspond to many of the macro actions like OpenReport. Most of the code created by the Control Wizards use the DoCmd's methods. The OpenForm, OpenReport, and Close methods are the most popular. They provide most of your navigation in your database system.

The Forms and Reports collections store the forms and reports that are a part of your database system. You can use these collections to control the appearance of the forms and reports in the system. You may use the collections to reference a property like the Caption for a report to change its title bar to reflect the report contents or use one of the events to modify data in another table. The Screen object allows you to add flexibility to your code and change the screen appearance. The Screen object gives you control of what is currently displayed on the screen. You can change your mouse pointer for the screen to indicate different states of the system. You can also use it to make your code more generic. Instead of using an exact name to reference an object that has the focus, you can use the screen's ActiveForm, ActiveReport, or even ActiveControl to use in a query or to take other actions.

The Assistant object lets you add your own Assistant functions. If you are creating an interface for others to use, you might want to provide step-by-step instructions. With the Assistant object, you can control its behavior as well.

The remaining objects on the left side of the chart allow you to control other functions of Access. In the beginning, you will not be using these objects very often. They support advanced development like the creation of custom wizards and client server systems linking to Microsoft SQL Server. This is accomplished with a special Access file.

In addition to creating a database, you can also create an Access project. It allows you to store your interface elements in one database and the data in another source. It can be another Microsoft Access database or a third-party source, such as SQL Server. Working with projects and SQL Server is not in the scope of this book.

The key to working with VBA and the model is not to panic. Remember that with VBA, you are going to work with objects. You can set their properties, create event procedures to execute when triggered, and take advantage of their methods. Each object is a part of the overall model. It might be a part of a collection of similar objects. The last thing to remember is that help is always close at hand. Every aspect of the object model is fully documented in the help file. You can search for the name of an object and get help.

Examining the Data Object Models

With Microsoft Access, the Microsoft Access object model is not the end of the VBA picture. Microsoft Access has interface components as well as data, and they are handled separately.

When Access was first released, its automation capability was not as great as expected. With each version, it has been improved. The language elements for accessing your data directly with VBA have seen the greatest improvement as well as changes.

Initially, Microsoft Access had the Data Access Object (DAO) model. This was designed to give you access to the data directly without using an interface object. This worked fine, but many people were trying to use Microsoft Access to get to data stored in another source. Also, the DAO model was not fast enough for many tasks. To make this process easier, the Remote Data Object (RDO) model was added to Microsoft Access. This allowed you to develop code that could directly access data stored in an Object Linking and Embedding database (OLE DB).

As the need for remote access grew and more people started developing Microsoft Access applications using this approach, there were more comments, questions, and requests to make the access better, and more importantly, faster. In Microsoft Access 2000, the ActiveX Data Objects (ADO) are introduced.

The goal of ADO is to provide one model for all of your direct data access needs, regardless of what format the data is stored in or where it is stored. When you need to access data directly, you will want to use ADO. You will use this model to update the tblEvents table when an attendee registers for an event. This model is designed to give you access to your data, regardless of where it is stored. It has objects and collections just like the Microsoft Access model, as detailed in the following list:

- The Connection object lets you establish a link to the data.
- The Command object stores specific commands like SQL statements to execute in the server environment.
- The Parameter object lets you manage parameters for SQL statements.
- The Recordset object is the object you are going to use the most. This object allows you to manipulate your data directly.
- There are also Field, Error, and Property objects to manipulate the data object directly.

18

This new model is considered the best approach for accessing data directly because it is faster and offers greater flexibility. This is especially true if you store your data in an outside source.

Do	Don't
DO watch for ADO in the help topics to make sure you are using the ADO object model.	**DON'T** use DAO or RDO for new development. It is not as efficient, and it might not be upgraded with future releases. The DAO and RDO models are still available for backward compatibility.

Learning About Program Flow and Loops

In addition to working with objects, you will also need to learn how to control the flow of your code. Often you need to add VBA because you need to evaluate a condition with several different sets of steps that can be taken based on the results.

To control the program flow, you will rely on one of the program flow statements or loops. Each of these is discussed in the following sections.

Examining the `If...Then...Else` Statement

The first method for controlling the program flow is to use conditional logic. Conditional logic allows you to execute a group of statements based on the value of an expression. The `If...Then...Else` statement is the first method for condition testing.

The `If...Then...Else` statement is very flexible. It allows you to test one condition and execute one statement, test one condition and execute a group of statements, or test one condition and execute one group of statements if the expression is true and another group if the expression is false. The `If...Then...Else` statement also supports the testing of multiple conditions.

If you want to test one condition and execute one statement, you can use this single-line syntax:

```
If condition Then [statements] [Else elsestatements]
```

This structure begins with the `If` keyword, followed by the expression you want to test. You can test a variable value, property, or field by using the same structure as the expression created in Day 14, "Understanding SQL."

> **Note**
>
> As you examine difference statements and functions, you will have specific items that are required in the syntax. These are frequently referred to as *keywords*. They are components of statements and functions.

The expression to test is followed by the Then keyword and the statement you want to execute. If you need to execute more than one statement, the structure must grow to more than one line:

```
If condition Then
    [statements]
End If
```

In this case, the statement is listed below the If line with one line for each statement. The last line of this test will be the End If statement to indicate the end of the conditional block.

If you need to test one condition and take different actions based on whether the expression is true or false, you must use the expanded structure. The following structure is also used if you need to test more than one condition:

```
If condition Then
    [statements]
[ElseIf condition-n Then
    [elseifstatements] ...
[Else]
    [elsestatements]]
End If
```

The first line of the If..Then...Else code block is the same as above. It is the *condition* test. The statements that follow are those that are executed if the condition is true. If you have more than one condition to test, those statements will be followed by the ElseIf line.

The ElseIf keyword indicates that there is another condition to test. This will be followed by the statements to execute if that condition is true. These statements can be followed by an Else line if all of the conditions are false. The last line is the End If line to indicate the end of the condition block.

You will find this statement to be very valuable for simple tests. In frmEvents, you can add new events. As you create a new record, you have to enter the Event, EventTypeID, Status, and Location.

Suppose that if the EventTypeID is Seminar, the event is one day in duration, and 9 times out of 10 the event begins at 9:00 a.m. and ends at 5:00 p.m. If the event is a workshop, the event is one day, and only lasts until 12:00 p.m. You could add code for the AfterUpdate event for the Start Date to speed up the data entry (see Listing 18.1).

LISTING 18.1 THE CONDITIONAL TESTING OF THE START DATE FIELD FOR frmEVENTS

```
Private Sub StartDate_AfterUpdate()
    If Me!EventTypeID = 2 Then      'Seminar
        Me!EndDate = Me!StartDate
        Me!StartTime = #9:00:00 AM#
        Me!EndTime = #5:00:00 PM#
    ElseIf Me!EventTypeID = 3 Then      'Workshop
        Me!EndDate = Me!StartDate
        Me!StartTime = #9:00:00 AM#
        Me!EndTime = #12:00:00 PM#
    End If
End Sub
```

This test begins by testing the EventTypeID field to see whether it is equal to 2, which is a seminar. If it is true, the code sets the EndDate, StartTime, and EndTime fields. In this case, there is a second expression to test—if it equals 3, the event is a Workshop. This sets the same field values, but the EndTime is different.

Do	Don't
DO add comments at the end of the If line to indicate what a value means when working with foreign keys.	DON'T forget to use indented formatting with condition testing. Indenting all your code by one tab stop will help you define the beginning and ending of a procedure. Indenting the statements one tab stop further will help determine the beginning and end of the conditional block.

The If structure gives you the ability to execute actions only if your conditions are met. This example is good for illustrating how to use the If...Then...Else statement, but when you get to testing one expression with different values, there is an alternative. You can use the Select Case statement.

Examining the Select Case Statement

When you begin testing more than one condition in an If...Then...Else statement, the code can become a little difficult to read and maintain. If you are testing one entity with multiple values, you can use the Select Case statement.

The `Select Case` statement is cleaner in its layout and easier to maintain for this type of testing. In reality, the EventTypeID has three possible values: Class, Seminar, or Workshop. The `If...Then...Else` statement can be converted into a `Select Case` structure very easily. The syntax is as follows:

```
Select Case testexpression
[Case expressionlist-n
    [statements-n]] ...
[Case Else
    [elsestatements]]
End Select
```

You begin with the `Select Case` keywords, followed by `test expression`. This is not like the condition used in the `If...Then...Else` statement. It is only the item you want to test, such as `Me!EventTypeID`.

Each possible value is assigned its own clause. Each clause begins with the `Case` keyword followed by one of the possible values. This line is followed by the statements you want to execute for the value.

If there is a possibility that the contents of the test expression will not meet any of the cases, you should have a `Case Else` clause to determine what to do. The last line is the `End Select` to indicate the end of the condition block.

In frmEvents, a `Select Case` is perfect for testing EventTypeID because there are three possible values. If you open the `AfterUpdate` event for the StartDate field in frmEvents, the `If...Then...Else` code has been commented out, leaving the `Select Case` structure shown in Listing 18.2 to do the work.

18

LISTING 18.2   THE CONDITIONAL TESTING OF THE START DATE FIELD FOR FRMEVENTS USING `Select Case`

```
Select Case Me!EventTypeID
    Case 1     'Class
        Me!StartTime = #9:00:00 AM#
    Case 2     'Seminar
        Me!EndDate = Me!StartDate
        Me!StartTime = #9:00:00 AM#
        Me!EndTime = #5:00:00 PM#
    Case 3     'Workshop
        Me!EndDate = Me!StartDate
        Me!StartTime = #9:00:00 AM#
        Me!EndTime = #12:00:00 PM#
End Select
```

Notice that the test expression is just the field Me!StartDate. Each possible value has its own `Case` clause. In this case, there isn't a `Case Else` because if there is another value, you do not know what to fill in. The field will be left blank and the user can enter the data.

Tip

> Notice that the caption for the Confirmed field has an access key indicated with the C underlined so that if all of the date and time fields are automatically completed, you do not have to tab through them. You can just press Alt+C.

Examining the `Do...Loop` Statement

The `If...Then...Else` and the `Select Case` statements allow you to execute statements based on the results of a test. The `Do...Loop` statement is designed to allow you to execute a group of statements multiple times based on the value of an expression.

`Do...Loop` can execute a group of statements until it is manually terminated, it can execute a group of statements until a condition is met, and it can execute a group of statements while a condition is true. The last two variations can also be set up to execute the group of statements at least once.

The first `Do...Loop` structure is the variation that will execute until it is manually terminated with code. The syntax is shown in the following code:

```
Do
     [statements]
     [Exit Do]
     [statements]
Loop
```

The first line is the `Do` keyword to begin the loop. That is followed by the statements to execute. Somewhere within the statements must be an `Exit Do` line. This exits the loop and is normally part of a condition test. The last line is the `Loop` keyword to indicate the end of the repeating block.

In most cases, you want to repeat a group of statements based on the value of an expression. The last two loops allow you to test an expression as part of the loop.

If you want to execute a group of actions until a condition is true, use `Do...Until...Loop`. This tests the condition, and until it is true, continues looping through the statements. If you want to test a condition while a condition is true, you will use `Do...While...Loop`. This loop repeats the statements as long as the condition stays true.

Both forms of the `Do...Loop` allow you determine whether the statements are executed at least once. It is determined by the placement of the condition test. Because of this, there are two syntaxes for the `Do...Loop`.

If you want to test the condition before you execute any code you use the following syntax:

```
Do [{While ¦ Until} condition]
    [statements]
    [Exit Do]
    [statements]
Loop
```

You begin with the `Do` keyword followed by the `While` or `Until` keyword, depending on how you want to test the condition. This is followed by the `condition` expression. The statements to execute are on lines by themselves, and the last line is the `Loop` keyword. With this syntax, if the condition is false with the `While` keyword or if the condition is True with the `Until` keyword, the statements will not execute.

If you want to execute the code at least once, you will test the condition at the bottom of the loop with the following syntax:

```
Do
    [statements]
    [Exit Do]
    [statements]
Loop [{While ¦ Until} condition]
```

The structure starts with the `Do` keyword, followed by the statements to execute on lines by themselves. This is followed by the `Loop` keyword. Depending on what type of condition testing you are using, this is followed by the `While` or `Until` keyword and the condition to test.

The statements will execute at least once. They will be repeated depending on the results of the condition test at the bottom of the loop.

Regardless of which loop you use, or whether you test at the top or bottom of the loop, there must be statements that affect the value of the condition. Otherwise, you have an endless loop that will hang your system.

The `Do...Loop` is very useful for making sure a user completes a step before going on to the next one. It is also useful for working with data directly. You can cycle through the records of a recordset using a `Do...Loop`. You will get to see a `Do...Loop` in action later in this lesson.

18

Examining the `While...Wend` Loop

Another condition testing loop is the `While...Wend` loop. It is like the `Do...While` loop that checks the to see whether the condition is true at the top of the loop. The following code shows its syntax:

```
While condition
    [statements]
Wend
```

You begin with the `While` keyword, followed by `condition`. The statements are on the following lines. The last line is the `Wend` keyword to indicate the end of the repeated block.

The `While...Wend` is identical to the `Do...While...Loop` except that it is not as structured or flexible. It tests only at the beginning of the loop; there is no way to execute the statements once.

 Note

> The `While...Wend` structure is included as part of VBA because VBA has its roots with the old BASIC language. This is for backward compatibility. You will probably use the `Do...While...Loop` instead.

Examining the `For...Next` Loop

The next loop is the `For...Next` loop. This loop doesn't repeat a group of statements based on a condition test. It repeats a group of statements a set number of times. The syntax is the following:

```
For counter = start To end [Step step]
    [statements]
    [Exit For]
    [statements]
Next [counter]
```

The first word is the `For` keyword. This is followed by a variable to act as a counter. This is followed by the equal sign. The number at which to begin the count is next, followed by the `To` keyword and the last number of the count.

You can indicate how you want to count with the `Step` keyword and the step value. If you want to count by fives or count backward that can be done.

The statements to execute are next. If for some reason you need to end the repeat in this loop early, you can include the `Exit For` statement. The last line of the loop is the `Next` counter line. This increments or decrements the count depending on the step.

The `For...Next` loop is great for repeating a printing operation. It can also be used for record processing or manipulating object in Microsoft Access. The `For...Each...Next` loop is better for manipulating objects in Microsoft Access.

Examining the `For...Each...Next` Loop

The `For...Each...Next` loop is good for manipulating objects because it is specifically designed to work with object collections. If you want to modify a property for every form in your system, using the `For...Each...Next` loop will allow you to cycle through the collection of objects quickly. The syntax is as follows:

```
For Each element In group
    [statements]
    [Exit For]
    [statements]
Next [element]
```

The syntax begins with the `For Each` keywords. This is followed by the element that you want to manipulate. That element is followed by the `In` keyword and the group, which is the collection you are working with.

This is followed by the statements to repeat. The last line is the `Next` keyword followed by the elements. The elements and groups can work with arrays or collections.

Examining the `With...End...With` Statement

When you are working with the `For...Each...Next` statement, you are normally working with objects. If you need to set several properties or elements in an array, you might want to use the `With...End...With` structure. This cuts down on the typing as well as the time to execute because you only have to specify the object once. The syntax follows:

```
With object
    [statements]
End With
```

The `With` statement allows you to specify the object once and change several things at the same time. You begin with the `With` keyword, followed by the object you are working with.

The statements to modify the object are on lines by themselves. The structure of these lines is different. You will omit the name of the object and begin with the period. It is followed by the name of the property, the equal sign, and the value you want to assign.

This will be put to good use with in Day 19. You will work with database objects and collections.

18

Examining the `GoTo` Statement

The next statement is the `GoTo` statement. You might be saying this is a carryover from older versions of BASIC and you would be correct. When BASIC was introduced, this was the only way to control the flow of the program.

With VBA, that is no longer the case. Events and other conditional and loop structures give you more possibilities. This doesn't mean that there isn't a use for the `GoTo` statement. The `GoTo` statement is recommended for use when you write error-handling routines. Because the language has changed to forgo line numbers, the structure of the `GoTo` statement has changed as well. The syntax is as follows:

```
GoTo line
```

The `GoTo` keyword is first followed by the line indicator. Because you do not have line numbers in VBA, you have to indicate a line label. A line label is an unique user-defined keyword somewhere else in your code. You can see an example in the `cmdAttendance_Click` event on the frmEvents form. The error handling indicates that if a problem occurs, go to the line label `Err_cmdAttendance_Click`.

A line label does have some special naming and formatting requirements. A line label is another object inside your system. It must follow all the naming rules and one extra rule: It must be followed by a colon. A line label cannot be placed just anywhere. It must be flush with the left margin. That means it will be even with the `Sub` and `End Sub` statements. If you forget to do either one of these things—use a colon or set it flush left—it will not be recognized as a line label. The `GoTo` statement and line labels are explored further in the section "Learning About Debugging and Error-Handling," later in this lesson.

Examining the `Call` Statement

The last statement to be covered in this section is another method for controlling the program flow. In Day 16, you learned that there were three types of procedures. There are event procedures that are triggered by user and system events. There are functions that can be placed in an expression to return a value, and subprocedures that could only be called from other VBA code.

With subprocedures, you place the name of the procedure on a line by itself, with any arguments following it separated by commas. This is functional in VBA, but many developers prefer to take a more formal approach to make their code more readable and easier to maintain. If you take this approach, the syntax is as follows:

```
Call procedurename (arguments)
```

The Call keyword is first, followed by the name of the procedure. If there are any arguments for this procedure, you must surround them by parentheses.

Learning About Statements and Functions

In addition to using objects with their properties, events, and methods, and program flow statements, you will also need to perform specific actions. You will work with two additional types of language elements in your VBA code: statements and functions.

NEW TERM A *statement* is a code action that will execute. It is designed to take action and then it is finished. You have seen many statements as you have examined the conditional and loop structures.

Statements execute and then the code moves on. Statements do not return a value. The general syntax is the statement followed by any arguments. An example of a statement is the Beep statement.

The Beep statement allows you to provide an audio signal that something is finished or wrong. It generates the generic computer beep. (It is not fancy; it will not play WAV files.)

Another example of a statement is the MsgBox statement used in the cmdAttendance_Click event for the frmEvents form. As part of the error handling, if an error occurs, the MsgBox statement displays a message. The MsgBox statement is unique because it has two forms. It can be either accessed as a statement or as a function. You will use the statement when you want to give information to the user and do not need information back. The function allows you to give and get information from the user with command buttons. The function is covered in the "Examining the MsgBox Statement and Function" section.

NEW TERM A *function* is designed to be placed in an expression and return a value. You used many of the built-in functions in earlier lessons to create expressions in queries, forms, and reports.

An example of a function is the UCase function. In earlier lessons, you used the UCase function to change the appearance of text in reports, but it can also be used to modify the data directly as it is entered. If you open frmAttendees, you will see it has a State field.

In Day 17, "Developing Professional-Quality Reports," you used the UCase function in a text box to force the display of the state abbreviation in uppercase letters. If the UCase function is used in a procedure, you can change the data and not worry about formatting it later. In the State_AfterUpdate event, the State contents are changed before the record is saved with the following single line of code:

18

```
Me!State = UCase(Me!State)
```

As you type in a lowercase State abbreviation and move to the next field, the lowercase letters will change automatically. That will save a lot of time when you are formatting reports or preparing data to export to Word or Excel.

Examining the MsgBox Statement and Function

You will frequently use the MsgBox statement and function as you create your code. They provide one of the primary means for communicating information to your user.

The MsgBox statement and function can be used to notify a user that something is not right. They can also be used to confirm a user's actions. MsgBox can be used as a statement if you need to notify the user of something like the completion of a process or an error. This syntax is as follows:

```
MsgBox prompt[, buttons] [, title] [, helpfile, context]
```

If the user must make a decision based on the information you give him in the message box, you will use the function. The syntax is the same, except for parentheses around the arguments:

```
variable = MsgBox(prompt[, buttons] [, title] [, helpfile, context])
```

The first item is the MsgBox keyword. That is followed by the prompt and the text of the message to be displayed.

The prompt is followed by the buttons argument, which allows you to control the appearance of the message box as it is displayed. The buttons argument can contain several components.

You can indicate what buttons are needed in the dialog, what icon is displayed next to the message, what button is the default, and how the message box will function in Microsoft Access and across the environment. You can specify all of these components with one argument because you will add the values of your choices together to get the argument.

The first choice is to determine what icon you want displayed in the message box. If you do not indicate an icon, none will be displayed. You can choose from the four standard message icons by entering the appropriate constant (see Table 18.1).

TABLE 18.1 MESSAGE BOX ICON CONSTANTS

Constant	Value	Description
vbCritical	16	Display Critical Message icon.
vbQuestion	32	Display Warning Query icon.
vbExclamation	48	Display Warning Message icon.
vbInformation	64	Display Information Message icon.

The choice you make will set the tone for the message. For example, if the message is just informing the user that the process is complete, it is not a good idea to use the vbCritical icon, which is normally reserved for system failures.

The second choice you have to make is to determine which buttons are needed. If you are using the MsgBox statement, this question is easy, you need only the OK button because you aren't tracking what is clicked anyway. If the user must make a decision, you will need to give him possible answers. You can select one of the button constants shown in Table 18.2.

TABLE 18.2 MsgBox BUTTON CONSTANTS

Constant	Value	Description
vbOKOnly	0	Display OK button only (Default).
vbOKCancel	1	Display OK and Cancel buttons.
vbAbortRetryIgnore	2	Display Abort, Retry, and Ignore buttons.
vbYesNoCancel	3	Display Yes, No, and Cancel buttons.
vbYesNo	4	Display Yes and No buttons.
vbRetryCancel	5	Display Retry and Cancel buttons.

18

You can also determine what button is used as the default button when the message box is displayed. This can be very important if you are trying to communicate that data is about to be modified or deleted. You would not want the acceptance choice to be the default because if the user types quickly, he might hit the Enter key without realizing what he said yes to. You can select one of the default button choices from Table 18.3.

TABLE 18.3 MESSAGE BOX DEFAULT BUTTON CONSTANTS

Constant	Value	Description
vbDefaultButton1	0	First button is default.
vbDefaultButton2	256	Second button is default.
vbDefaultButton3	512	Third button is default.
vbDefaultButton4	768	Fourth button is default.

The last button setting is how the message box will relate to the system. When dialogs are displayed with applications, they do not allow you to do anything else with the system until the dialog question is resolved. This eliminates mistakes. This is known as being *application modal*. Some dialogs go one step beyond that, and do not allow you to do anything else on your computer until the question is resolved. This is *system modal*. You can use the modal constants listed in Table 18.4 to determine how important the message is to the operations on the computer.

TABLE 18.4 MESSAGE BOX MODAL CONSTANTS

Constant	Value	Description
VbApplicationModal	0	Application modal; the user must respond to the message box before continuing work in your system.
VbSystemModal	4096	System modal; the user cannot use any functions on the computer until the message box is closed.

There are also settings for Help access and appearance of the text to accommodate foreign languages. For more information, please refer to Help.

Two message boxes are used in frmEvents. The first is the MsgBox statement, and the second is an example of the MsgBox function in which a response is needed. With the MsgBox statement, none of the arguments are used except the prompt Err.Decription.

```
MsgBox Err.Description
```

This is part of the error-handling routine. It displays the error that was generated and nothing more. It doesn't need a response from the user other than to click the OK button to close the message box.

Another example is in the Form_BeforeUpdate event procedure. In many database systems, the system confirms any changes that are made before accepting them. By default, Microsoft Access accepts all changes when the focus moves to another record.

This event has code added to stop before accepting changes to confirm. It uses a MsgBox function to get that confirmation, as shown in Listing 18.3.

LISTING 18.3 THE MsgBox FUNCTION USED TO CONFIRM CHANGES

```
Private Sub Form_BeforeUpdate(Cancel As Integer)
    ' Test Added to determine whether the user really wants
    ' to save his or her changes.
    If Me.Dirty = True Then
        Dim strMessage As String, strTitle As String
        Dim lResponse As Long
        strMessage = "You have changed this event.Save changes?"
        strTitle = "Event Change"
        lResponse = MsgBox(strMessage, vbYesNo + vbQuestion, strTitle)
        If lResponse = vbNo Then
            Cancel = True
            Me.Undo
        End If
    End If
End Sub
```

In the first line after the comment lines in Listing 18.3, an If...Then...Else structure tests the Dirty property to determine whether the data has changed. If it has, the second two lines define three variables for the confirmation.

The next two lines set values for two of those variables. The strMessage variable holds the prompt for the MsgBox function. The strTitle variable holds the title for the MsgBox function.

The next line sets up the expression to display the message box and store the button selected in lResponse. The next four lines test the button pressed to determine whether the No button was selected. Notice that a constant for the button value is used. As outlined in Table 18.5, all the buttons have constants to make your code more readable.

TABLE 18.5 MESSAGE BOX RETURN CONSTANTS

Constant	Value
vbOK	1
vbCancel	2
vbAbort	3
vbRetry	4
vbIgnore	5
vbYes	6
vbNo	7

18

If the No button was selected and the vbNo value of 7 was returned, the Cancel argument is set to true to cancel the action in progress, and the Undo method for the form is executed to roll back any changes made to the record. Notice that the form name isn't spelled out. If you are referring to the form or report you are coding for, you can use the Me keyword. The last line is the End If line because if no changes were made to the record, this process will not be executed. To try out this new message box, you can make some changes to one of the events.

Task: Viewing the MsgBox Function in Action

1. Open frmEvents in Form view.

2. Change the event name to An Access Quick Start for Developers.

3. Move to the next record to trigger this event and view the message box shown in Figure 18.4.

FIGURE 18.4

The message box for the change of data.

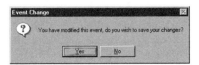

4. Click the No button in the message box.

5. Notice the original title for the event is back and you are not looking at the second record, as shown in Figure 18.5.

FIGURE 18.5

The original event title is intact and you didn't move to the second record.

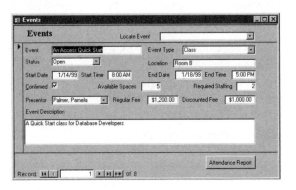

Examining the InputBox Function

Another function you might find useful is the InputBox function. If you need a quick answer from a user, you can take advantage of this built-in function. It displays a dialog asking a question, and then you can take the answer and use it in your system.

A good use for the InputBox function was illustrated in Day 17. In that lesson, you worked with a parameter in a report to add a custom title to a report. This worked quite well unless you forgot to enter a title. In that case, you had a report with no title.

With the InputBox function and VBA, you can get the benefit of a custom title with the backup of a default title.

Task: Giving a Report a Custom Title with the InputBox Function

1. Select the Reports tab from the Database window.
2. Double-click on rptEventAttendanceforInputBox to open it and display the input dialog (see Figure 18.6).

FIGURE 18.6

The InputBox *function displays this type of dialog.*

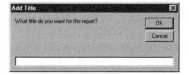

3. Enter Attendance for All Events in the dialog and click OK.
4. Notice the title matches what you typed in (see Figure 18.7).

FIGURE 18.7

The report shows the custom title.

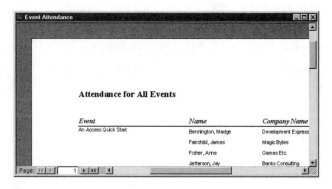

▲   5. Close the report and repeat these steps, except step 3, to view the default title.

When you use the InputBox function inside a user-defined function, you can eliminate the error of a report without a title. As you take a look at how this was accomplished, you will see that this code is written with variables to make it functional in any report.

Task: Viewing the `TitleSelection()` Code

1. Click the View button to view this report in Design mode.

2. Notice that the title isn't a label, but is a text box with the ControlSource property set to a function called `TitleSelection`. It sends one argument, which is the default title (see Figure 18.8).

FIGURE 18.8

The title of this report is a text box using a function instead of a label.

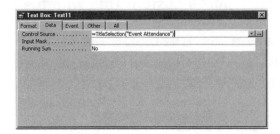

3. Click the Code button on the toolbar to display the Visual Basic Editor.

4. Scroll to view the function `TitleSelection`.

The `TitleSelection` function is not one of the built-in event procedures. It is a general function that can act as a control source. General functions and procedures will be discussed in more detail in Day 19. The TitleSelection function (as shown in Listing 18.4) is designed to evaluate whether the user entered a title.

LISTING 18.4 THE InputBox FUNCTION TO CUSTOMIZE A REPORT TITLE

```
Public Function TitleSelection(strDefault As String) As String
    Dim strInput As String
    strInput = InputBox("What title do you want for this report?",
    ➥"Add Title")
    If Len(strInput) > 0 Then
        TitleSelection = strInput
    Else
        TitleSelection = strDefault
    End If
End Function
```

The first line is the function declaration. This declaration statement establishes this procedure as a function indicating `strDefault` is a string argument that must be sent to the function and it will return a string value. The second line declares a variable to assign the results of the `InputBox` function.

The third line sets the variable strInput equal to the InputBox function. The next five lines are an If...Then...Else block to test whether anything was entered in the InputBox. It uses the Len function to test the length of the string.

If the length is greater than 0, the code assigns the variable to the function; otherwise, it uses the default string passed to the argument from where it was called.

The InputBox function gives you a method for getting information from a user without creating a form. The syntax is shown in the following code line:

```
InputBox(prompt[, title] [, default] [, xpos] [, ypos]
➡[, helpfile, context])
```

This syntax begins with the InputBox keyword. That is followed by the prompt argument, which is the text asking for the information. The title argument indicates what should be on the title bar. These were the only two arguments used in the sample code.

You can also set a default argument. For the title, you could duplicate the Event Attendance and have it displayed in the entry area of the input box. Providing a default title may save the users some typing because they may only need to modify the default.

The xpos and ypos arguments allow you to control the position of the input box. Although not useful with this example, xpos and ypos can be used to make sure that the input box doesn't cover information needed to answer the prompt. If these are omitted, the input box will be centered on the screen.

The helpfile argument indicates what help file to use if the user wants help. The con-text argument indicates what topic to use.

The InputBox function provides a quick way to solicit information from a user. If you need more than one answer, you can use more than one InputBox function. If you need several answers, you might want to use a form instead to avoid the visual confusion of one input box replaced with another, and another, and so on.

Learning About Debugging and Error Handling

As you are developing your system, you will learn more about VBA and Microsoft Access. As with learning anything new, the learning process involves trial and error. To get your finished system, you will have to correct any errors that are created. Three types of errors will occur when you are programming: syntax errors, runtime errors, and logic errors.

18

Examining the Types of Errors

The first type of error is a syntax error, which is technically a typographical error. You might sometimes type in a line of code and make a mistake. The Visual Basic Editor does several things to help you avoid these types of problem:

- You can turn on Auto Quick Info. This will provide a syntax guide as you type a statement or function, as shown in Figure 18.9. If you were entering the `InputBox` function, as soon as you typed `InputBox(`, the quick info would display.

FIGURE 18.9

Auto Quick Info provides hints as to the syntax of a function or statement.

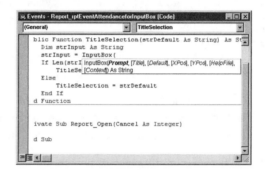

- You also can turn on Auto Syntax Check. This will validate each line of code as it is entered. If a line has a syntax problem, it will be displayed in red and a message box will be displayed, letting you know what type of mistake was made.

The second type of error is a runtime error. This type of error will stop the execution of your code. A runtime error can also be a typographical problem. You might be trying to open a form, but the name referenced isn't correct. Or you might be trying to access a file on a floppy and there isn't a floppy in the drive.

The last type of error is a logic error. This type of error is trickier than the first two because it will seem to execute properly, but it will not generate the expected results. This can often happen with calculations or when you are using conditional logic. Just including the incorrect operator in an expression can generate a logic error.

As a developer, you want to eliminate as many errors as possible. There are errors that cannot be eliminated, such as the failure of the user to place a floppy in the disk drive. When you can't eliminate an error, you need to build a mechanism for handling it.

Tracking down errors is a crucial part of developing your system. To track down errors is known as *debugging*, and to add code to deal with errors that cannot be eliminated is known as *error handling*. The last two sections will give you an overview of the techniques you can use to debug and add error handling to your code.

Examining the Debugging Process

The syntax-checking tools mentioned in the preceding section will locate and allow you to fix the syntax errors. For runtime and logic errors, you will have to rely on testing your system to make sure it does what you expect.

When you locate a problem, you are going to track down its source. The Visual Basic Editor has several tools to assist with this process.

To illustrate these tools, let's examine frmEventsforDebugging, which is an altered version of frmEvents. It has a logic problem in the BeforeUpdate event that will verify whether the user wants to save any changes made. Before you begin looking at the debugging tools, you need to see the problem.

Task: Examining the Logic Problem

1. Double-click on frmEventsforDebugging to open it.

2. Change the event title to Access Quick Start.

3. Move to the next record.

4. Click the No button in the message box to decline the option to save your changes.

5. Notice that you are looking at record 2 instead of record 1.

6. Move to the first record.

7. Notice that your event name took effect.

The test of the message box selection isn't functioning. If you switch to the Design view and open the code window, you can see the problem as shown in Listing 18.5.

LISTING 18.5 THE ERROR IN THE Form_BeforeUpdate EVENT

```
Private Sub Form_BeforeUpdate(Cancel As Integer)
    ' Test Added to determine whether the user really wants
    ' to save his or her changes.
    If Me.Dirty = True Then
        Dim strMessage As String, strTitle As String
        Dim lResponse As Long
        strMessage = "You changed this event. Save changes?"
        strTitle = "Event Change"
        lReponse = MsgBox(strMessage, vbYesNo + vbQuestion, strTitle)
        If lResponse = vbNo Then
            Cancel = True
            Me.Undo
        End If
    End If
End Sub
```

To make it easier for you to concentrate on the debugging tools, I'll tell you that the error is in the `MsgBox` line, and it sets the `lReponse` variable. That doesn't match the variable declared or tested in the `If` block, which is testing `lResponse` instead of `lReponse`. When the variable is tested, it has no value, so the code will never execute.

> **Tip**
>
> This problem could have been avoided entirely if the Require Variable Declaration option had been set. Unfortunately, this option is not set by default. This option places the `Option Explicit` statement in all modules. In that case, if a variable is added to your code that hasn't been explicitly declared, you will get a message. It is additional syntax checking for your code.

With runtime errors, you know very quickly when something isn't working. Microsoft Access will display the Microsoft Visual Basic error dialog. It will tell you what went wrong and give you an opportunity to end the run of the code or debug (see Figure 18.10).

FIGURE 18.10

The Microsoft Visual Basic error message gives you an opportunity to end the code or debug.

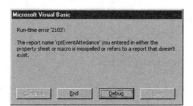

With logic errors, the process is not as straightforward. Because these types of errors will not stop the execution of your code, you must check the performance carefully. In this case, you had to notice that you weren't looking at record 2, and that the change was accepted in record 1.

What you must do is stop the execution of the code yourself. Then you can walk through debugging the code. There are several tools to assist you in determining what the problem is.

Adding a Breakpoint

NEW TERM The first thing you need to do is stop the code so you can watch as it executes. In older forms of BASIC, you would have added the `Stop` statement to your code. This approach still works, but there is a better method. You can set a breakpoint. A *breakpoint* is a line of code that is highlighted for evaluation. Visual Basic will stop the run of the code before executing the line.

Rather than adding the Stop statement line of code, you can select any executing line of code and make it a breakpoint. This eliminates the need to go back later and remove the Stop statement lines and possibly make more errors.

In this case, you know that the problem is with the test of the variable returned by the message box, so you might want to set the If lResponse = vbNo line as a breakpoint.

It is very easy to set a breakpoint. You simply point in the gray bar to left of the code and click. An alternative method is to place the cursor in the line you want to set as a breakpoint and select Debug, Toggle Breakpoint. The line will be highlighted and a dot will be placed next to it in the gray bar, as shown in Figure 18.11.

FIGURE 18.11

The breakpoint is highlighted and a dot is placed in the gray bar.

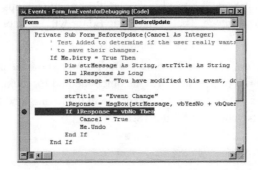

Using the Breakpoint

After the breakpoint is in place, you are ready to test your code. You will need to switch back to Access and switch to Form view.

Task: Using the Breakpoint to Test the Code

1. Press Alt+F11 to switch to Access and click the View button on the toolbar.

2. Change the event title to Access Quick Start for Developers.

3. Move to the next record.

4. Click the No button in the message box to avoid saving your changes.

5. Notice that instead of moving to the second record, the Visual Basic Editor has displayed with the breakpoint code activated (see Figure 18.12).

▼ TASK

18

FIGURE 18.12

The breakpoint has forced a halt to the code execution.

▲

When code is executing and it hits a breakpoint, the execution stops and the code enters what is known as *Break mode*. The Visual Basic Editor will be displayed with the line of code activated.

After the code is halted, you can do some exploring. You know the problem has something to do with the test of the variable. One quick method for looking at a variable is to point to it with mouse. If you point to lResponse in the highlighted line, you will get a balloon displaying its value (see Figure 18.13).

FIGURE 18.13

By pointing to variables and properties in your code, you can see their current value.

When you point to the variable, you see that its current value is 0. Because you selected No in the message box, the current value should be 7. If you point at lReponse on the line above, you will see that it is equal to 7.

In this simple block of code, with only one variable to worry about, it is easy to locate the problem. With more complex code, it might not be as easy. That is where some of the other tools might come in handy.

Examining the Locals Window

When you are in Break mode, the Locals window might make examining variables easier. It displays all the active data elements in one location (see Figure 18.14).

FIGURE 18.14

The Locals window displays all the data elements in one location.

Working with Break Mode

When you are debugging your code, you might not be able to see the problem as quickly as you can with this misspelled variable. Break mode suspends the execution of the code and allows you to try different methods for resolving the problem.

When you are in Break mode, you can set up any of the debugging tools, you can end the run of the code, continue to execute the code, or step through the code. Three buttons on the toolbar allow you to perform part of those tasks (see Figure 18.15).

FIGURE 18.15

The Run, Break, and Reset buttons allow you to control what happens when you are in Break mode.

18

The toolbar doesn't give you the ability to step through your code. To step through your code, you must select Debug, Step Into or press F8. If you press F8 now, you will see that the End If line is highlighted. The code skipped the Cancel operation entirely.

You can click the Reset button to halt the execution of the code entirely. Notice that the Locals window is clear. It is only active when you are in Break mode.

The breakpoint stopped the code execution, but the problem is higher in the code. To eliminate a breakpoint, you can click in the gray bar to remove it or select Debug, Clear All Breakpoints. Click next to If Me.Dirty = True Then to make it the breakpoint. This shifts the break of the code higher in the procedure, to allow you to walk through the code from the start of execution.

Adding a Watch Variable

NEW TERM   Pointing to variables or searching the Locals window might take a lot of time, depending on the complexity of your code. When you have many variables, you might want to set up a watch variable. A *watch variable* is a reference to a variable you want to track.

Task: Setting a Watch Variable and Testing the Code

1. Select Debug, Add Watch to view the Add Watch dialog (see Figure 18.16).

FIGURE 18.16

The Add Watch dialog allows you to set up a watch expression.

2. Type lResponse as the expression.
3. Make sure the watch type is Watch Expression and click OK.
4. Notice that the Watches window opens and the variable is set (see Figure 18.17).

FIGURE 18.17

The Watches window only displays those expression you set up instead of everything, as in the Locals window.

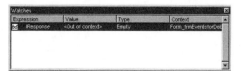

5. Switch back to Microsoft Access.
6. Notice the change is still there. Because you halted the execution, the change hasn't been accepted yet.
7. Move to the next record.
8. Notice the Visual Basic Editor is displayed with the breakpoint highlighted.
9. Press F8 and notice that the strMessage line is highlighted and is about to be executed. (The code skips declarations because declarations do not execute.)
10. Press F8 and notice that strMessage has a value in the Locals window.
11. Press F8 again, and the message box is displayed.
12. Click the No button in the message box.
13. Notice that lResponse still doesn't have a value, and click End to halt the execution of the code.

▼ 14. Select Debug, Clear All Breakpoints.

15. Select Debug, Edit Watches to open the Edit Watch dialog.

▲ 16. Click Delete to get rid of the watch expression.

The last three steps clear out the debugging settings. If you want, you can correct the spelling of lReponse to lResponse, switch to Microsoft Access, and move to the next record to see the corrected process.

You can set up watch expressions to break the code execution so that you don't have to use breakpoints. You can also set the code to break when an expression changes or when an expression is true. This feature is very useful because it eliminates the search for the variable name to set breakpoints above it or setting one breakpoint and using the Step Into command to execute each line individually. The Visual Basic Editor gives you a great deal of control over the execution of the code.

The key to good debugging is to verify each procedure as it is created. That way you are clear on exactly what is supposed to happen. For larger systems, the development process benefits from documenting what the code is supposed to do and formal testing.

Understanding the Error-Handling Process

18

Testing your code to make sure it operates as expected is only part of the job of creating good code. You also have to anticipate problems that might crop up as you or someone else uses your system.

You can't prevent some types of errors, such as a user trying to access a file that doesn't exist or attempting to access a floppy when there isn't one on the drive or a network drive when the network is not available.

NEW TERM As you write your code, you cannot eliminate the possibility that these things will happen, but you do have to write code that provides a mechanism for dealing with the problems. This process is known as *error handling*.

When you have used the Control Wizard to create code, the wizard has added some generic error handling to deal with any errors. This is to avoid displaying the Microsoft Visual Basic error message, in which the user can select Debug and view the code. As you create error handlers, you might want to add specific code to deal with specific problems.

NEW TERM When you create an error handler, there are several components. You have to initialize the error trap. An *error trap* is a line of code indicating that you want to handle the errors in your code rather than let Access handle them automatically. The next step is to develop code to deal with the error, and finally you have to determine how to proceed after the error is taken care of.

To give you a chance to create an error handler, you are going to look at an error that cannot be avoided by good coding. In Day 17, you looked at how to conserve resources by adding code to prevent a user from printing or previewing a report that doesn't have any data. This was accomplished using the NoData event.

This code takes care of the problem, unless you are attempting to automate the access to a report that uses this technique. If you open the frmEventsforErrorHandling form and look at the code for displaying the attendance report, you will see that it is the basic code without any of the error handling that is normally added by the Control Wizard:

```
Private Sub cmdAttendance_Click()
    Dim stDocName As String
    stDocName = "rptEventAttendanceforErrorHandling"
    DoCmd.OpenReport stDocName, acPreview
End Sub
```

It defines the variable for the report name. It assigns it a value and uses the OpenReport method to display it in Preview. When you actually run this code, it doesn't exactly perform as you would like, it notifies you of the problem twice.

Task: Viewing the No Data Problem

1. Switch back to Microsoft Access.

2. Click the View button to switch to Form view.

3. Move to the last record.

4. Click the Attendance Report button, and you will get the message box from the NoData event (see Figure 18.18).

FIGURE **18.18**

The NoData *event noti-*
fies you that there are
no attendees for this
event.

 5. Click OK.

After you click OK, you should be looking at the form, but the Microsoft Visual Basic debug message (see Figure 18.19) is displayed instead. It indicates that error 2501, The OpenReport action was canceled, has occurred.

FIGURE 18.19

The Microsoft Visual Basic debug message is displayed.

You are being notified that the Cancel argument was set for the report. This is basically notifying you that no data for this report exists twice. It is also opening up the possibility that someone will attempt to debug the code. There is no need to debug because the report was cancelled to avoid displaying an empty report.

What you must do is add error handling. To add error handling, click the Debug button to display the code and click the End button to halt the execution.

Initializing the Error Trap

The first step is to initialize the error handler to trap the errors. To begin trapping errors in your code, you use the On Error statement. The syntax is as follows:

```
On Error [GoTo line | Resume Next | GoTo 0]
```

The line begins with the On Error keywords, which set up the error trapping. It is followed with one of the three choices. These choices determine what happens when an error occurs:

- The most common choice is the GoTo line. This indicates that when an error occurs, you want the code to begin executing at a line label.
- The second choice is Resume Next. This indicates that you are going to handle the possible errors immediately after the line that created the error.
- The last choice is GoTo 0. This will allow you to disable error handling if needed. This also allows you to create several error-handling routines for different components of your code.

The On Error line must be placed above the code that could generate the error. In this case, that is the OpenReport line, but you can put it at the beginning of this procedure.

Task: Initializing Error Handling

1. Place the insertion point in front of the Dim keyword.
2. Type On Error GoTo ErrPreview and press Enter.

This has enabled the error trap and indicated that you want to execute the code under the line label ErrPreview. Now you have to build your error handler.

18

TASK

Setting Up the Error Handler

The first step in building an error handler is to separate the code that you want to execute every time from the code to execute if there is a problem. When you use the GoTo line, you must place an Exit Sub statement after the code. Then you need to add your line label for the error handler.

Task: Establishing the Error Handler

1. Place the insertion point after the OpenReport line and press Enter to get a blank line.

2. Type Exit Sub and press Enter.

3. Press Shift+Tab to remove the indent.

4. Type ErrPreview: and press Enter.

5. Press Tab to indent your code.

Building the Error Handler

After the error handler is set up, you need to determine what error occurred. This is done using the Error object, which stores the information about the error. It has two properties you will use in most cases: The Number property is the error number that has occurred, and the Description object is the text describing the error number.

In many cases, a Select Case structure works best for error handling. For different operations, you might need to check for specific errors, like 2501, and you might have to tackle what happens with a generic error.

You also must have a plan of action for dealing with the error. In most cases, you will display a message. Other times, you need to take specific steps to resolve the problem.

After you have resolved the problem, you are going to need to determine how to proceed. You have several choices. You can use the Resume statement to pick up with the line that created the problem and try again. You can use the Resume Next statement to pick up execution on the line below the one that generated the error, or you can exit the procedure.

In this case, error 2501 doesn't need any processing. You just need to exit the procedure. For all other errors, you need to display the error in a message box and then exit the procedure. You need to add the lines of code shown in Listing 18.6, beginning on the line below the line label.

LISTING 18.6 THE Select Case STATEMENT FOR ERROR HANDLING

```
Select Case Err.Number
    Case 2501    'OpenReport or OpenForm Cancelled
        Exit Sub
    Case Else
        Dim strMessage As String, strTitle As String
        strMessage = "Error " & Err.Number & ", " & Err.Description &
        ➥ " has occurred."
        strTitle = "Unexpected Error"
        MsgBox strMessage, vbInformation + vbOKOnly, strTitle
        Exit Sub
End Select
```

Now you can test your error handler to make sure that the double error messages aren't displayed.

Task: Testing the Error-Handling Code

1. Switch back to Microsoft Access.

2. Select the View button to switch to Form view if necessary.

3. Move to the last record and click the Attendance report button.

 4. Click OK to close the message box.

You can now look at the record without clicking any additional buttons. The process for dealing with this error from a user perspective is much cleaner and you or someone else will be less likely to modify your code by accident.

Summary

Today's lesson introduced some of the general VBA language components. You learned that the basis for most of the code you create will take advantage of objects within each application. You learned that these objects are manipulated by controlling their properties, adding code to their events, and using their methods.

You also learned that you can control the flow of your code though program flow and loop statements. You also learned about general statements and functions that allow you to modify data, communicate with users, and get information from them as well.

You also learned how to take care of errors that will crop up as you develop your code. You learned how to track errors down using the debugging tools, as well as how to add code to deal with errors that cannot be eliminated with error handling.

18

Q&A

Q How can I find out more about objects?

A To get information about an object or a collection, you can use the online Help. By entering the name of the object in the Index search, you can pull up a topic that will describe the object and provide links to all of the properties, methods, and events.

Q Can I have one error handler for my entire system?

A Yes, you can have one error handler for the entire system, but you will still need to use the technique displayed here to initialize the error handler. The code under the line label would provide the access to this general error handler.

Workshop

The Workshop helps you solidify the skills you learned in this lesson. Answers to the quiz questions appear in Appendix A, "Answers."

Quiz

1. In what case is the `Select Case` statement the best approach to test a value?

2. What is the advantage to adding error handling?

DAY 19

Working with VBA

Beginning with Day 13, "Introducing VBA," you have had a chance to see a few of the things that are possible with Visual Basic for Applications (VBA) to automate your work. This lesson is designed to give you some additional ideas regarding the power of VBA. Today, you will learn the following:

- How to use VBA to manipulate objects
- How to use VBA to automate data entry
- How to use VBA to work with data directly
- How to use VBA to modify the database
- How to create switchboards

Each section focuses on a different category of automation. This lesson is not designed to give you a complete reference of the actions, statements, and functions available. For additional information, you can refer to the online help.

| Note | If you want an additional resource for more information about using Visual Basic for Applications, see *Special Edition Using Visual Basic for Applications* (Que Publishing), which provides a foundation in VBA as well as an introduction to using VBA with each of the Office applications. |

To follow along with today's lesson, you'll need the sample database, Events19.mdb, from the CD-ROM that accompanies this book. You'll find the database and reports in \Day19\.

Events19.mdb is a copy of the database used on Day 18, "Examining VBA." It is used in this lesson to demonstrate how to track event scheduling for a conference center. It will be used as a foundation for the database interface built in this lesson. You will get a chance to see some of what VBA can do for you in your database.

Using VBA to Manipulate Objects

The first area in which you are going to begin implementing VBA is the manipulation of the other Microsoft Access objects, and this is one of the areas you have already worked with. You have experimented with opening queries and reports in Day 13, opening forms, moving to records in forms, and cleaning up data in Day 16, "Implementing Advanced Form Concepts," dealing with no data for a report in Day 17, "Developing Professional-Quality Reports," and confirming changes in Day 18.

In this section, you are going to see four additional tasks that you can automate. You are going to see how to control the size of a window, cancel the open operation of a form, place some graphic effects in a report, and how to check for duplicate information with VBA.

Controlling Window Size with VBA

When you are working with Microsoft Access objects, they are confined within the Microsoft Access window. If you open a form like frmEvents and maximize it, it takes up the entire workspace. You cannot see the database window or anything else you have open. If you close the form, you will notice the database window is also maximized.

Although none of the forms in this database requires a maximized display, you might need to maximize one form when it is displayed and return it to its appropriate size as it closes so the rest of the forms display in a window. You might also want to change the size or placement of a control as you maximize or resize a window to improve the visual appearance or provide additional space to enter information.

> **Note**
>
> When you maximize a form, you might want to remove all other windows from view so there are fewer distractions for the user. Another reason might be that you want to be able to display more information.

As an example, assume that when frmAttendees opens, you want to maximize it and resize the subform to fill the rest of the space. This would allow you to see more events attended by the person. This requires the modification of three of the form's events.

The first event that needs to change is the Activate event. The Activate event is triggered when the form gets the focus. You are going to use the Maximize method for the DoCmd object to accomplish this task.

Task: Maximizing a Form Automatically

1. Open frmAttendees in Design mode.

2. Save the form as frmAttendeesModified.

3. Open the Properties window for the form and select the Event tab.

4. Scroll down the list and set On Activate to [Event Procedure]. Click the Build button to launch the Visual Basic Editor.

5. Press Tab and add this line of code:

```
DoCmd.Maximize
```

The next step is to add code to the Deactivate event to reverse the process and restore the form to its original size. This is also done with the DoCmd object, but with the Restore method.

Task: Restoring a Form's Size Automatically

1. Select Deactivate from the Procedure list in the code window.

2. Press Tab and add this line of code:

```
DoCmd.Restore
```

3. Switch back to Access. Save and close the form.

4. Open the form and notice that the form automatically maximizes (see Figure 19.1).

5. Close the form and notice that the Database window is not maximized (see Figure 19.2).

19

FIGURE 19.1

The form automatically maximizes to fill the workspace.

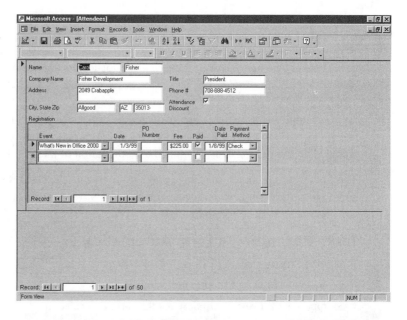

FIGURE 19.2

The form restores to a window as it deactivates, and no other windows are affected.

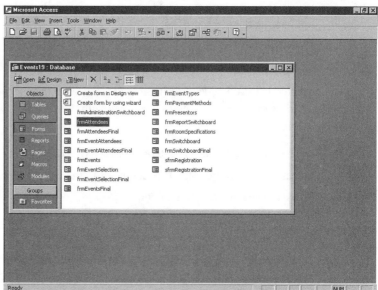

If you want to increase the size of the subform as the form is maximized or if it is resized manually, you can accomplish that with VBA. To accomplish this task, you use the Resize event, which is triggered when the form is resized manually, maximized, minimized, or restored.

In the Resize event, you are going to change the height of the subform. If you only wanted to accommodate the maximized size, you could experiment with different measurements; but this wouldn't account for the fact the user can manually restore the window and then resize it to whatever dimension he wants. To allow the user free rein to resize, you must base the size on the size of the form. The form has an InsideHeight property. You can use this property and subtract the Top property to get the correct measurement.

Task: Adjusting the Height of the Subform

TASK ▼

1. Open frmAttendeesModified in Design mode.

2. Open the Properties window for the form and select the Event tab.

3. Scroll down the list and set On Resize to [Event Procedure]. Click the Build button to launch the Visual Basic Editor.

4. Press Tab and add this line of code:

```
sfrmRegistration.Height = Me.InsideHeight - sfrmRegistration.Top
```

5. Switch back to Microsoft Access. Save and close the form.

6. Open the form and notice the change in size of the subform (see Figure 19.3)

FIGURE 19.3

The form automatically maximizes to fill the workspace, and the subform is larger.

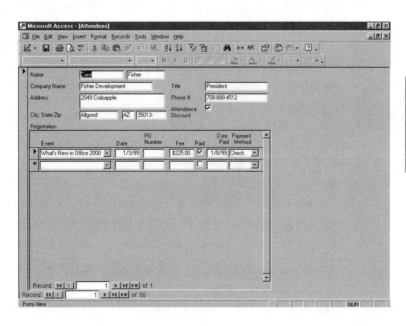

19

▼ 7. Manually restore the window.

▼ 8. Resize the window by dragging the border to a new position. Notice the subform changes as you drag the border.

▲ 9. Close the form.

Setting up your forms to have controls resize or reposition based on the size of the form is a great way of responding to how a user wants to work with your form. It is very useful when you are working with subforms. If you are considering this type of enhancement to your forms, you also must consider the time you spend on development. To automatically maximize and resize a control like a subform takes very little effort because there are three lines of code, but repositioning controls is different. If you are going to reposition controls based on the size of a form, you will have to use the form's InsideHeight and InsideWidth properties and then determine a position for each control. It will not only take some experimentation to get the right placement, but it will also slow the display of a form.

Canceling the Open Operation of a Form

In Day 17, you added code to your report for its NoData event to prevent the display of the report. This eliminated the time used to display an empty report. Forms do not have a NoData event like reports, but you can test to see whether there are any records and force the close of a form.

When a form opens, the Open event is triggered. One of the first tasks completed by the form is to build its recordset. You can access that recordset to determine whether there are any records before the form is displayed by using its RecordsetClone property.

If the RecordCount property is zero, you can set the Open event's Cancel argument to True to close the form and display a message with the message box statement. You also must use some error handling in the event that called the form to deal with the fact that the OpenForm method was cancelled.

In the sample database, the frmEvents form can open the Attendance report. You are going to add the functionality to open the frmEventAttendees form. You are also going to create the code to test to make sure there are no records.

Task: Adding the Test for Records to frmEventAttendees

1. Open frmEventAttendees in Design mode and save it as frmEventAttendeesModified.

2. Open the Properties window for the form and select the Event tab.

3. Set the On Open property to [Event Procedure] and click the Build button.

4. Add the following lines of code:

```
If Me.RecordSetClone.RecordCount = 0 Then
    Cancel = True
    MsgBox "There are no attendees for this event.",
    ➥vbInformation, "No Matching Records"
End If
```

5. Switch back to Microsoft Access. Save and close the form.

That completes the code for the test for records, now you must add the code to open the form with a criteria based on the selected event in frmEvents. It is very similar to the code created to open the report.

Task: Creating the Code for the New Button

1. Open frmEvents in Design mode and save it as frmEventsModified.

2. Right-click the Attendees View button and click Build Event.

3. Add the following lines of code to the cmdAttendeesForm_Click event:

```
On Error GoTo ErrView
Dim stDocName As String, stCriteria As String
stDocName = "frmEventAttendeesModified"
stCriteria = "[EventID] = " & Me!EventID
DoCmd.OpenForm stDocName, acNormal, , stCriteria
Exit Sub
ErrView:
Select Case Err.Number
    Case 2501    'OpenReport or OpenForm Cancelled
        Exit Sub
    Case Else
        Dim strMessage As String, strTitle As String
        strMessage = "Error " & Err.Number & ", " &
        ➥Err.Description & " has occurred."
        strTitle = "Unexpected Error"
        MsgBox strMessage, vbInformation + vbOKOnly,
        ➥strTitle
Exit Sub
End Select
```

4. Switch back to Microsoft Access and click the View button to switch to Form view.

5. Click the Attendees View button and notice that the form opens with information.

6. Close the form.

7. Move to the last record.

8. Click the Attendees View button and notice that you get the message box instead of the form (see Figure 19.4).

TASK

19

Figure 19.4

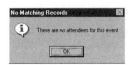

*There are no attendees
for the last event, so
you see this message
instead of the form.*

This code is similar to the code created in Day 18 to solve the problem when the NoData event cancels the opening of the report, and the OpenReport method was generating the error 2501. The same error is generated if a form's opening is cancelled.

The first line of code initializes the error handling. The next line sets up the variables for the OpenForm method. The next line specifies the form to open and the fourth line sets up the Where clause for the OpenForm method. The fifth line is the OpenForm method to open the form, followed by the Exit Sub statement to stop the execution before the error-handling code.

The remaining lines are identical to those shown in Day 17 because the error generated is the same. Because you added code to frmEventAttendees, you need to exit the sub procedure only if error 2501 is received. All other errors will be displayed in a message box and the procedure will be exited.

Adding Formatting to a Report with VBA

So far in this book, when you have created reports, you have often added visual effects by adding lines to the sections. You have added these lines by using the Line tool. There is also a rectangle control to allow you to place a box around information. Both of these controls have a disadvantage: They can only be used within a section, not for a whole page.

If you want a page border or a vertical line on the page, you must rely on VBA. With VBA, you can draw graphic objects directly on a form or report. You have the Line, Circle, and PSet methods to place graphics on the report.

If you open rptEventSummary (see Figure 19.5), you might decide that a vertical line extending from the bottom of the graphic sets the right tone for this report. You would have to add code to the report to place the line.

When you are adding code to a report, you must place the code in one of the report's events. There are the Format and Print events for each section, but you want to work with the report as a whole, so you must use the Page event, which is triggered after the formatting of a page, but before the printing of that page.

FIGURE 19.5

The graphic offers a spot for a natural vertical line beginning below the bottom edge of the graphic.

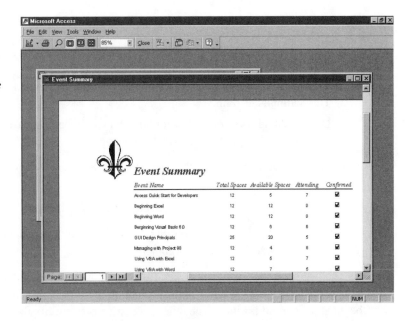

After you determine where to place your code, you must determine the placement of the line. Internally the report keeps track of how the report is measured. Five properties control the measurements of the report:

- ScaleMode—This sets the measurement type. You can use inches, centimeters, millimeters, points, pixels, or characters; the default is twips.

> **Note**
>
> A *twip* is a measurement you can use in VBA. A twip is 1/20 point. It gives you the greatest degree of control over object placement because there are 72 points in an inch, which means that there are 1,440 twips in an inch.

- ScaleTop and ScaleLeft—These indicate the vertical and horizontal coordinate for the drawing area. This is useful if you want to create standard graphing coordinates to allow placement of lines above and below zero on a chart.
- ScaleHeight and ScaleWidth—These indicate the size of the drawing area for the report.

For the purpose of this report, you do not need to adjust the ScaleLeft, ScaleTop, ScaleHeight, or ScaleWidth properties. You will also leave ScaleMode alone to get an idea of working with twips.

19

There are also three drawing properties to control how you draw on the form or report:

- DrawMode determines how lines are drawn. By default, the black pen is used, which is just a regular line.

- DrawStyle allows you to select a line style. By default, this is set to a solid line. This setting is also fine.

- DrawWidth allows you to control how thick the line is, measured in pixels. This will be useful to get a larger line for this report.

To draw the actual line, you use the `Line` method. It can be used to draw a line or a rectangle. The syntax is

```
object.Line [[Step](x1, y1)] ñ [Step](x2, y2)[, [color][, B[F]]]
```

You specify the object you want to draw on, followed by a period and the `Line` keyword. This can be followed with a `Step` argument.

As you begin to place drawings on the form or report, you will move the cursor position. This is tracked by the CurrentX and CurrentY properties. If you specify a step, it will begin at the current position. The other alternative is to specify the x and y position to begin with. This is followed by a hyphen and the step or the x,y coordinates at which to stop drawing.

That information can be followed with a color argument, specified using a fixed color setting or using the `RGB` color function. If it is followed by a B, a rectangle will be drawn; if the B is followed by an F, it will be a filled shape. To get these coordinates, you will have to do some math and some experimentation. For this example, the legwork has already been completed for you.

Task: Adding a Line to the Page

1. Open rptEventSummary in Design mode.

2. Save the report as rptEventSummaryModified.

3. Open the Properties window and select the Event tab.

4. Set the On Page property to [Event Procedure] and click the Build button.

5. Add the following two lines of code:
   ```
   Me.DrawWidth = 12
   Me.Line (669, 1600) - (669, Me.ScaleHeight)
   ```

6. Switch back to Microsoft Access and save the report.

7. Click the View button on the toolbar to preview the report. Notice that the line is below the emblem and runs to the end of the page margin (see Figure 19.6).

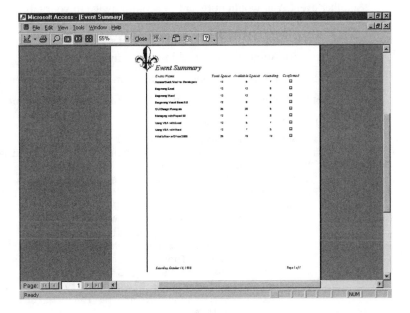

FIGURE 19.6

The line uses a fixed setting for the top of the line and uses the ScaleHeight property to draw until the margin of the page.

It takes some experimentation because the emblem is placed on the page with the Picture property. This means that the bottom point of the emblem doesn't exactly line up with a mark on the ruler. You would have had to guess at the closest point and then adjust to get it exact.

This same technique can be used to create a border around the page. You might want to experiment with some of the line borders in Microsoft Word to find a style you like and try to duplicate it with the line commands. If you like the thick and thin line combination, you might want to try the following:

```
Me.DrawWidth = 10
Me.Line (0,0) - (Me.ScaleWidth, Me.ScaleHeight),,B
Me.DrawWidth = 4
Me.Line (100,100) - (Me.ScaleWidth-115, Me.ScaleHeight-115),,B
```

This places a double border around the page. You can try out a report with this border in rptBoxExample.

Checking for Duplicate Information on a Form with VBA

Another idea for using VBA in your database is to use it to make sure a record doesn't exist before creating a new record. A potential attendee for an event might call in and be

19

asked whether he has attended an event before and answer no, but he really has attended another event. You would not want to add him twice to your table.

Task: Implementing Data Validation

1. Open frmAttendeesModified in Design mode.

2. Open the Properties window for the form and select the Event tab if needed.

3. Set the BeforeUpdate property to [Event Procedure] and click the Build button.

4. Enter the following code:

```
'The BeforeUpdate event allows you to test to see
'if a record exists before inserting it a second time.
If Me.NewRecord = True Then
    Dim strWhere As String, strMessage As String
    strWhere = "AttendeeLastName = '" & Me!AttendeeLastName & "'"
    Me.RecordsetClone.MoveFirst
    Me.RecordsetClone.FindFirst strWhere
    Do Until Me.RecordsetClone.NoMatch
        If Me.RecordsetClone!CompanyName = Me!CompanyName Then
            strMessage = "There is already an attendee matching "
            strMessage = strMessage &
            ➥"this information. Please verify and try again."
            MsgBox strMessage, vbInformation, "Matching Record"
            Cancel = True
            DoCmd.DoMenuItem acFormBar, acEditMenu, acUndo
            Me.Bookmark = Me.RecordsetClone.Bookmark
            Exit Sub
        End If
        Me.RecordsetClone.FindNext strWhere
    Loop
End If
```

5. Switch back to Microsoft Access.

6. Save the form.

7. Click the View button to switch to the Form view.

8. Click the New Record button.

9. Type Carol as the attendee first name and press Tab.

10. Type Fisher as the attendee last name and press Tab.

11. Type Fisher Development as the company name.

12. Click the Previous Record button to trigger the BeforeUpdate event. Notice the message box is displayed, indicating a duplicate record (see Figure 19.7), and click OK.

▼

FIGURE 19.7

The message box is displayed because a matching record was found.

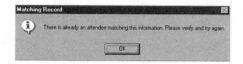

13. Notice that you are looking at the Fisher Development record that had the matching information.

14. Click the Last Record button and notice that the information you entered is gone. That record was cancelled.

When you first look at duplicate checking, you might be tempted to use the BeforeInsert event. The BeforeInsert event is triggered as a new record is created. This occurs when the first character is typed for a new record. Unfortunately, you do not have enough information at that point to make any identification.

The BeforeUpdate event has the same benefit because it has the Cancel argument, which allows you to roll back the operation. Its benefit is that it will not occur until the user has completed his entry. That way you have enough information to complete the verification. Let's examine the code to complete this verification.

To check for a duplicate information, you must search through the existing records to locate a match. You want to complete this only if this is a new record. To accomplish this, you are going to use the If structure.

The first line entered sets up that If structure. It uses the NewRecord property to determine whether this is an inserted record. If NewRecord is True, the check will begin.

The next line defines two variables. strWhere is a string to hold the criteria to look for. strMessage is for the message box if a duplicate is found. The next line sets the strWhere equal to an expression to test the last name of the attendee against the recordset.

The next line sets up the test. When you want to check for duplicates, you use the RecordsetClone property to gain access to the records. This line uses the MoveFirst method to get to the beginning of the recordset represented by the RecordsetClone property.

The fourth line inside the If structure uses the FindFirst method to take the criteria and see whether it exists in the recordset. Because there might be more people with the same last name, the next line sets up a Do Until loop to allow you to continue searching if a

19

match is not found for the rest of the test. It uses the NoMatch property. If you are using the `Find` method, the NoMatch property will be set to True if you reach the end of the recordset without a match.

After a record matching the last name is located, that is not enough for verification. You are going to have to compare at least one other field. To minimize the amount of coding, only the company name is used. You might want to include the first name, telephone number, or address as well.

To complete the verification, another `If` structure is used. It tests the CompanyName of the found record in the RecordsetClone against the CompanyName of the current record on the form. If there is a match, the next three lines set up the message and display the message box.

The next line sets the `Cancel` argument to True. This will cancel the update of the record. The next line uses the DoCmd object to access the `DoMenuItem` method. This allows you to access menu commands from code. Here you are undoing all of the data entered in the new record.

The next line uses the Bookmark properties of the recordsets. The Bookmark property is the pointer to the current record in a recordset. The recordset for the form is still pointing to this new record. The recordset represented by the RecordsetClone property is pointing to the matching record. This line of code points the form to the matching record by changing its Bookmark to the Bookmark of the RecordsetClone.

If a match is found, there is no need to continue searching. The bookmark line is followed by `Exit Sub` to end the execution of this event. This is followed by the closing of the `If` structure to check CompanyName.

If a match was not found for CompanyName, the next line uses the `FindNext` method to continue the search. This is followed by the close of the `Do Until` loop. This will force the code to repeat. It will test to see whether the NoMatch property is True, and then continue executing or drop to the close of the `If` for the LastName test and the `End Sub` line to stop the execution of the event.

The cornerstone of this test is the checking of the last name, followed by a check of at least one field. If you have called to order something over the phone, you have seen this in action. The representative will ask for your last name and first name. The representative will normally come back with your address as verification and then you can continue ordering.

Using VBA to Automate Data Entry

The second area where you may want to use VBA is to automate data entry to minimize the time spent on creating new records. This was first illustrated in Day 18. You used VBA to complete the beginning time, ending date, and ending time of an event based on the type of event and the beginning date. This saved the user the entry of three fields if she used your default for the type of event.

This code was placed in the start date's AfterUpdate event because the information needed to make the entries was geared off the type of event as well as the start date. The start date was entered last if the user was using the Tab key to navigate. The rest was placed in a Select Case structure to complete the fields, as shown in Listing 19.1.

LISTING 19.1 THE START DATE'S AfterUpdate EVENT TO ENTER DATA AUTOMATICALLY

```
Private Sub StartDate_AfterUpdate()
    Select Case Me!EventTypeID
        Case 1  'Class
            Me!StartTime = #9:00:00 AM#
        Case 2  'Seminar
            Me!EndDate = Me!StartDate
            Me!StartTime = #9:00:00 AM#
            Me!EndTime = #5:00:00 PM#
        Case 3  'Workshop
            Me!EndDate = Me!StartDate
            Me!StartTime = #9:00:00 AM#
            Me!EndTime = #12:00:00 PM#
    End Select
End Sub
```

19

If StartDate was entered without EventTypeID, nothing was entered. It is essentially a Case Else and none of the fields would be updated.

This does a lot to save the user time on inputting data, but you can make it even better. If there are some standard rates for classes, seminars, and workshops, you could fill in the default fees. As with the dates and times, you cannot use the Default property for these fields because they are dependent on what type of event is scheduled.

This fill-in operation also has one more twist. Three fields are needed for this operation. The EventTypeID and the StartDate are already being tested and used to fill in data. The EndDate is the field that makes this more of a challenge.

The EndDate can be filled in automatically with the VBA code in the StartDate_AfterUpdate event or it can be completed manually. This means that this fill in might be triggered from two different places. When you have to execute the same code from multiple places, you will want to create a general procedure. That way you can call it from both the StartDate_AfterUpdate event and the EndDate_AfterUpdate event.

Determining the Parameters for the Fill In

The first step is to determine the parameters for the fee fill in. You have three types of events: class, seminar, and workshop. The seminar and the workshop are both one-day or partial-day events that do not require an elaborate calculation for the fee. You could use a flat fee for each, such as $200 for workshops and $400 for seminars.

The classes are more of a challenge because they are multiple days. You could have a flat fee, but having the same default amount for a 5-day class and a 3-day class wouldn't be practical. Here you might want to find out how many days of class there are and then set a day rate, such as $250.

For all the events, you must also calculate a discounted fee. This could be a straight percentage, like 15% off, but you might want it to be cleaner. You might want to round to the greater dollar amount to avoid keeping track of cents.

Creating the General Functions

Because two events need to calculate the fees, you are going to want to create general functions to perform these calculations. You can create a general function or procedure in any module, but because the procedure is only needed on this form, you might want to keep it within this form's module.

Do	Don't
DO isolate actions that need to be used in several places in a general procedure. This makes it easier to update because you must change the code in one place once instead of in several.	DON'T create a separate module for every general procedure. If the procedure is only used by a form or report, place the procedure in its module to make it easier to track. When a procedure will be used by more than one form or report, create a module for it.

To create general procedures, you must create the general framework for the procedure. You must declare any arguments that are needed inside the argument's parentheses. You can indicate what type of value a function will return.

This is a very important step because if you do not declare what type of value will be returned, Access will default to returning a Variant value. As discussed previously, this can take up a lot more memory than is warranted for what needs to be returned.

For these calculations, you are going to create two functions: `CalculateFee` and `CalculateDiscount`. Both of these functions will be used to fill fields in the tblEvents table. Both RegularFee and DiscountFee are Currency fields. You can create both functions to return Currency values.

After these steps are completed, you add your code and then you can call these functions from the two events. The first step is to create the framework. You can create a general procedure using a dialog or by typing it. You will get to see both approaches in action.

Task: Creating the `CalculateFee` Function

1. Select View, Code or click the Code button from the toolbar to display the Visual Basic Editor.

2. Select Insert Procedure to open the Add Procedure dialog (see Figure 19.8).

FIGURE 19.8

The Add Procedure dialog automates the creation of general procedures.

3. Type `CalculateFee` as the name.

4. Select Function as the type.

5. Select Private as the scope and click OK to create the framework for the function (see Figure 19.9).

6. Access builds the `Private Function` and `End Function` lines for you and places the cursor on the line in between them.

7. Click after the parentheses on the first line and add the following code to the line:

`As Currency`

8. Move back to the second line and press the Tab key to indent the code.

FIGURE 19.9

The framework for the function is built for you.

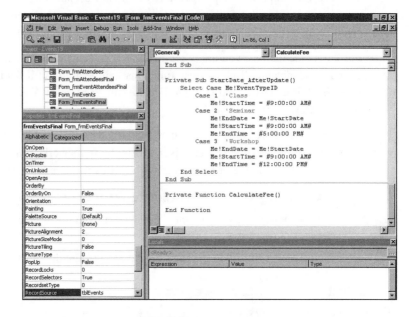

9. Add the following lines of code:

```
Select Case Me!EventTypeID
    Case 1  'Class
        Dim lDays As Long
        lDays = DateDiff("d", Me!StartDate, Me!EndDate) + 1
        CalculateFee = lDays * 250
    Case 2  'Seminar
        CalculateFee = 400
    Case 3  'Workshop
        CalculateFee = 200
End Select
```

This Select Case structure is again testing the value of the EventTypeID to fill in the values. For seminars and workshops, the code is very simple. You take the function name and set it to the fixed value for that type. With classes, the code is a bit more complicated. Here you must set up a variable to determine how many days the class is in session. This is accomplished with the DateDiff function. This function takes two dates and can calculate how many intervals are between them. The syntax is

```
DateDiff(interval, date1, date2[, firstdayofweek[, firstweekofyear]])
```

The DateDiff function begins with the keyword. It has five arguments. The first is the interval. In this case, "d" was used to indicate you want to know how many days in between. The second and third arguments are the two dates to compare. In this case, you are using the StartDate and EndDate fields.

The last two arguments allow you to change the default comparison parameters. You can indicate a different first day of the week instead of Sunday, and a different first day of the year other than January 1. With this function, you have to add 1 because it doesn't count the last date in the number returned.

The second function required is the `CalculateDiscount` function. It takes 15% of the RegularFee value and rounds up to the nearest dollar.

For `CalculateFee`, you used the Add Procedure dialog to create the framework for the procedure. The other method is to type the framework from scratch.

Task: Creating the `CalculateDiscount` Function

1. Press Ctrl+End to get to the bottom of the module and press Enter to add a blank line.

2. Type the following line and press Enter:

   ```
   Private Function CalculateDiscount () as Currency
   ```

3. Access moves you to the next line and adds the `End Function` line below.

4. Press the Tab key to indent the code.

5. Add the following code:

   ```
   Dim curAmount As Currency
   curAmount = Me!RegularFee * 0.85
   If curAmount - Int(curAmount) > 0 Then
       CalculateDiscount = Int(curAmount) + 1
   Else
       CalculateDiscount = curAmount
   End If
   ```

This code sets up a variable to allow you to manipulate the RegularFee field. It multiplies the RegularFee field by 85%, and then takes that number and subtracts the integer portion of the number using the `Int` function. If that value is greater than zero, there are cents. If there are cents, the `If` structure returns the integer portion plus one to round up. Otherwise, the curAmount variable is returned.

Calling the General Function from the Events

Now that the functions are created, you need to put them to use in the `AfterUpdate` events for both dates. You will need to verify that the fields have data in them before calling the functions to make sure that the functions will work correctly.

To begin, you need to modify the code for the `StartDate_AfterUpdate` event. This code uses `Select Case` to test the EventTypeID field and fill in values. Here the `Class` case doesn't provide all of the information needed for the fill in, so you need to add only four lines of code.

19

Task: Calling the Functions from the `AfterUpdate` Events

1. Scroll up in the code window to locate the `StartDate_AfterUpdate` event.

2. Modify the code so that it matches the following (note that the modified code appears in boldface):

```
Private Sub StartDate_AfterUpdate()
    Select Case Me!EventTypeID
        Case 1  'Class
            Me!StartTime = #9:00:00 AM#
        Case 2  'Seminar
            Me!EndDate = Me!StartDate
            Me!StartTime = #9:00:00 AM#
            Me!EndTime = #5:00:00 PM#
            Me!RegularFee = CalculateFee()
            Me!DiscountedFee = CalculateDiscount()
        Case 3  'Workshop
            Me!EndDate = Me!StartDate
            Me!StartTime = #9:00:00 AM#
            Me!EndTime = #12:00:00 PM#
            Me!RegularFee = CalculateFee()
            Me!DiscountedFee = CalculateDiscount()
    End Select
End Sub
```

The two lines of code that set the RegularFee and DiscountedFee fields to the results of the functions are added to the Seminar and Workshop cases only. You cannot add those lines to the `Class` case because you do not know how many days the class will be, so it is not completing the EndDate field.

Task: Adding Code to the `AfterUpdate` Event for the EndDate Field

1. Select EndDate from the Object list in the Code window.

2. Select `AfterUpdate` from the procedure list.

3. Press Tab to indent the code.

4. Add the following lines of code:

```
Me!RegularFee = CalculateFee()
Me!DiscountedFee = CalculateDiscount()
```

This code completes the code needed to add the fill in for the fee fields. When you have completed adding code for a specific function, you will want to test it.

Task: Testing the `CalculateFee` and `CalculateDiscount` Code

1. Switch back to Microsoft Access.

2. Save the form.

3. Click the View button from the toolbar to switch to the Form view.

4. Click the Add Record button.

5. Type `Beginning PowerPoint` for the event and press Tab.

6. Select Seminar and press Tab.

7. Select Open as the status and press Tab.

8. Select Room C as the location.

9. Type `3/4/99` as the StartDate and press Tab.

10. Notice that the remainder of the date and time fields are completed, as well as the fees.

11. Click the Add New record button.

12. Type `Access for Developers` for the event and press Tab.

13. Select Class and press Tab.

14. Select Open as the status and press Tab.

15. Select Room C as the Location.

16. Type `3/5/99` as the StartDate and press Tab.

17. Notice that the EndDate and EndTime, as well as the fees, are not completed and press Tab.

18. Type `3/8/99` as the EndDate and press Tab.

▲ 19. Notice that the fees have been filled in.

This code completes the job of minimizing the time it takes to enter data for a new record, but it has a flaw. If you have created a record previously and you are going into the record to change only the dates, the code will wipe out the dates and fee field data to reset them to the default. You could solve this problem two ways.

The first method for solving this problem is the easier of the two. It involves testing the NewRecord property used in the earlier example. By placing the following line of code at the beginning of the `AfterUpdate` events, you can preserve the data:

```
If Me.NewRecord = True then Exit Sub
```

19

The second method takes a bit longer to implement. You could add `If` statements to test each field before setting it. You could use the `IsNull` function to test to see whether there is information in the field prior to setting it. The code for the `StartDate_AfterUpdate` event would look like Listing 19.2.

LISTING 19.2 THE MODIFIED `AfterUpdate` EVENT TO CHECK FOR COMPLETED DATA

```
Private Sub StartDate_AfterUpdate()
    Select Case Me!EventTypeID
        Case 1  'Class
            If IsNull(Me!StartTime) then Me!StartTime = #9:00:00 AM#
        Case 2  'Seminar
            If IsNull(Me!Enddate) then Me!EndDate = Me!StartDate
            If IsNull(Me!StartTime) then Me!StartTime = #9:00:00 AM#
            If IsNull(Me!EndTime) then Me!EndTime = #5:00:00 PM#
            If IsNull(Me!RegularFee) then Me!RegularFee = CalculateFee()
            If IsNull(Me!DiscountedFee) Then
            ➥Me!DiscountedFee = CalculateDiscount()
        Case 3  'Workshop
            If IsNull(Me!Enddate) then Me!EndDate = Me!StartDate
            If IsNull(Me!StartTime) then Me!StartTime = #9:00:00 AM#
            If IsNull(Me!EndTime) then Me!EndTime = #12:00:00 PM#
            If IsNull(Me!RegularFee) then Me!RegularFee = CalculateFee()
            If IsNull(Me!DiscountedFee) Then
            ➥Me!DiscountedFee = CalculateDiscount()
    End Select
End Sub
```

Using VBA to Work with Data Directly

In addition to manipulating Microsoft Access objects and automating data entry with VBA, you can access the data directly to populate controls, as well as update a dataset based on information from another table. In this section, you will see three examples of how to access and manipulate data directly.

The first example will illustrate how to automate data entry using data from another table. The second example will illustrate how to use VBA to get data from a table and merge it with a fixed entry to populate a combo box. The last example will illustrate how to update information in another table based on actions taken in a form using VBA.

Automating Data Entry by Using Another Table

In the previous section, you looked at how to fill in fields based on the entries in fields on the same form with VBA. In frmAttendeesModified, you worked with controlling the window's appearance. However, there wasn't anything you could do to automate data entry on the main form.

On the subform, you could assist the user with completing one field. The fee for the event could be filled in when an event was selected. The problem is that the source of the fee information is in the tblEvents table, which is not part of the recordset for the subform. Also, setting the AttendanceDiscount field must be taken into account.

NEW TERM The first method for accessing data from another table when you are working with a form is to use one of the built-in functions. *Domain aggregate functions* are specifically designed to retrieve information from a record or from a group of records, or to retrieve statistical information about the group as a whole.

In this case, you need the fee information about an event as it is selected from the drop-down combo box. The domain aggregate function that will return a value from a record is the DLookup function, which allows you to set a criterion and retrieve one field value. The syntax is

```
DLookup(expr, domain[, criteria])
```

The syntax begins with the DLookup keyword and expects three arguments. The first argument is expr, which is the field value you want to return. The second argument is domain; this is the recordset you want to look in, and can be a table, query, or SQL statement. The last argument is criteria, the criteria that you want to use to locate the records.

For this example, call this function from the AfterUpdate event for the combo box for the EventID field on the subform. You will also need to take into account whether the attendee has a discount using the Attendance Discount field on the main form. So you will have two forms of DLookup, based on the Attendance Discount field in an If structure.

Task: Adding the Fill-In Capability for the Fee Field

1. Open the frmAttendeesModified form in Design mode.
2. Select the EventID combo box on the subform.
3. Right-click and select Properties to display the Properties window. Select the Event tab if needed.

4. Set the AfterUpdate property to [Event Procedure] and click the Build button.

5. Add the following lines of code:

```
If Me.Parent!AttendanceDiscount = True Then
    Me!RegistrationFee = DLookup("[DiscountedFee]",
    ➥"tblEvents", "[EventID] = " & Me.EventID)
Else
    Me!RegistrationFee = DLookup("[RegularFee]",
    ➥"tblEvents", "[EventID] = " & Me.EventID)
End If
```

6. Switch back to Microsoft Access and save the form and subform.

7. Click the View button from the toolbar to switch to Form view to test your work.

8. For the first record, select Beginning Excel as a new event. Notice that $400 is filled in for the fee.

9. Enter a date of 1/4/99, paid as Yes, 1/4/99 as the date paid, and a payment method of Cash.

The code tests the AttendanceDiscount field on the main form with the If statement. The AttendanceDiscount field is referenced through the Parent property for the subform, and then the DiscountedFee or RegularFee is retrieved, based on that field.

The domain aggregate functions are very useful. You can retrieve a value with DLookup as well as get statistics like counts and sums. Depending on the size of the domain, these functions can be quite a drain on resources.

Populating a Combo Box by Using a Table and VBA

Another method for accessing data directly from a recordset is to use VBA and the ActiveX Data Object (ADO) model. This allows you to create a recordset and work with each record separately.

In Day 16, you created a form with option buttons to allow you to select a department to base a report on. This worked fine, but it was somewhat limiting. If you added a new department, you had to modify the form to show a new department. Also, you were restricted to using one of the departments. You could not select all of the departments for the report. Using this approach to create a similar form to select events wouldn't be practical because you are constantly adding new events.

A better approach is to create combo boxes or list boxes to allow you to select all the events or to select an event. This could have the list based on the table, but you still need a way to add the All choice, which is where VBA and ADO come into play.

When you need to combine a static value, such as All, with a recordset to populate a list, you have to create a special function with built-in arguments. These arguments are automatically fed to the function from the list or combo box control.

To create this type of selection form, you first need to set up the visual display of the form. It is best to turn off the Control Wizard while you are designing this form because you do not want it to populate the list control automatically, or it might resemble the frmEventSelection form.

You are now ready to create the VBA to populate this form. The first step is to access the Visual Basic Editor. You can do this by selecting View, Code or by clicking the Code button on the toolbar. Access creates a Form_Load event by default. You can delete this event's three lines of code.

Before you can begin creating the function to populate the list box, you have to set up your database to access ADO. To minimize the size of the Microsoft Access application and the other Office applications, many of the tools you access with VBA are stored in type libraries. If you want to access an object in one of these libraries, you need to reference that library.

Task: Setting Up the Reference for the ActiveX Data Object Model

1. Select Tools, References to open the References dialog (see Figure 19.10).

2. Scroll to locate Microsoft ActiveX Data Object Library 2.0 and select it.

3. Click OK to close the dialog and accept your selection.

19

FIGURE 19.10

The References dialog allows you to gain access to objects in other applications and libraries.

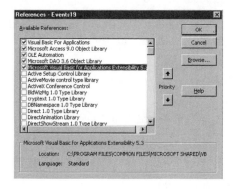

Now that you have established the access to the ADO library, you can create the function to populate the list control. When you want to populate a list or combo box control with VBA, the function can be named whatever you like, but it has specific arguments because when a form opens with a list or combo box, it goes through several steps to set up that control. The names of the arguments aren't fixed, but they must be a specific data type and order.

The function you create will provide information for Access as it goes through the steps to set up the combo box. Now to build the function, move to the bottom of the module and enter the code in Listing 19.3.

LISTING 19.3 THE mvarSelectionBuild FUNCTION TO POPULATE A LIST BOX

```
Private Function mvarSelectionBuild(fld As Control, id As Variant,
➥row As Variant, _col As Variant, code As Variant) As Variant
'    This will place the All choice at the top of the list
    Static rsEvent As ADODB.Recordset
    Select Case code
        Case acLBInitialize
            Set rsEvent = New ADODB.Recordset
            rsEvent.Open "qryEventSelectionBuild",
            ➥CurrentProject.Connection, adOpenStatic, adLockReadOnly
            mvarSelectionBuild = True
        Case acLBOpen
            mvarSelectionBuild = Timer    'Generate unique ID for control.
        Case acLBGetRowCount
            mvarSelectionBuild = rsEvent.RecordCount + 1
Case acLBGetColumnCount
            mvarSelectionBuild = 3
        Case acLBGetColumnWidth
            mvarSelectionBuild = True        'Forces use of default width.
        Case acLBGetValue
            If row = 0 Then
                Select Case col
                    Case 0
                        mvarSelectionBuild = 0
                    Case 1
                        mvarSelectionBuild = "All"
                    Case 2
                        mvarSelectionBuild = Null
                End Select
            Else
                rsEvent.MoveFirst
                rsEvent.Move row - 1
                mvarSelectionBuild = rsEvent(col)
            End If
        Case acLBGetFormat
```

```
            Case acLBClose
            Case acLBEnd
                    rsEvent.Close
        End Select
End Function
```

The first line of this function declares the function and sets up its arguments. It is a private function because it is only used by this form and will not be used anywhere else in the application.

The name of this function is `mvarSelectionBuild`. When you create general functions, there are naming conventions for those as well. `m` indicates the function is restricted to the module. `var` indicates the function returns a Variant data type, and `SelectionBuild` gives it a unique identifier.

Inside the parentheses, five arguments are declared. These are the arguments that will automatically be passed to this function from the list box as it is set up when the form is loaded into memory.

`mvarSelectionBuild` is expecting a control argument called `fld` as well as an `id` variant argument to identify the list or combo box. The function is expecting `row` and `col` variant arguments to identify what row and column are being set up. It also expects a Variant argument called `code` to indicate what pass of the set up is occurring.

The next line is a descriptive comment, followed by a variable declaration. When you want to work with records directly using ADO, you must create a recordset. To store that recordset, you use a special type of variable; rather than a string or some other data type variable, this is an object variable.

With the ActiveX Data Model, you need to create a recordset object to store the records defined by a table or query. Because you created the reference to the ActiveX Data Object 2.0 Library, you can declare the variable as the specific type of object from the library. In this case, it is `ADODB.Recordset`.

In this case, you are going to use this recordset during several passes through the function. To minimize the processing time, the recordset is declared as a static variable so that it will hold its value after it is created in memory.

The next part of the function sets up a `Select Case` structure. As the list is set up on the form, this function will be called several times. Each time it is called it will be passed the code argument. This indicates what part of the setup process is occurring. The `Select Case` structure tests the value of the `code` argument. It is evaluated against specific built-in constants.

19

The first `Case` clause tests whether the code matches the built-in constant `acLBInitialize`. This is the first pass and it initializes the control. During the initialization pass, the recordset is established with

```
Set rsEvent = New ADODB.Recordset
rsEvent.Open "qryEventSelectionBuild",
➥CurrentProject.Connection, adOpenStatic, adLockReadOnly
```

With ADO, the first step is to assign a value to the object variable. When you are working with object variables, the assignment is slightly different from a data variable. You need to start with the `Set` keyword, followed by the name of the variable, `rsEvent`. You have the equal sign, and then you build the rest of the expression. You need to create a new recordset, so you will use the `New` keyword followed by the type of object.

After the variable is established, you need to populate it with data. This is done with the `Open` method. The variable name followed by a period and the keyword `Open` indicates what you are trying to do. The `Open` method has up to seven arguments. If you were accessing data from an outside source, you would use most of them. Because you are working in Access, it isn't as complicated.

The first argument is the name of the table or query that defines the contents of the recordset. In this case, it is a query, qryEventsSelectionBuild. It has the three fields needed to place the information in the control.

The next argument is the active connection argument. Microsoft Access allows you to work with data from inside Access or from another source. If you were accessing data from another source, the active connection argument would have all the information to locate that data. Because you are using data from this database, you can use some properties. Here you are using the CurrentProject object and its connection property.

The CursorType argument allows you to indicate what type of recordset you need. In this case, you need to open it as a static recordset so you can get the RecordCount property. The next argument indicates what type of access is required. Here the user will not be making any changes, so it is opened as a read-only recordset.

The last argument is not used in this case. The Options argument provides some additional options to give you better control over your connection to remote data. The next line just sets the name of the function to `True` to indicate that it was completed successfully.

After the control is initialized, it is opened. Here you set the name of the function equal to `Timer` to have the system generate its unique identifier. The next case is to get the number of rows for the list.

```
mvarSelectionBuild = rsEvent.RecordCount + 1
```

This one line of code uses the RecordCount property to get the number of rows. You have to add 1 to this number because you are adding the All selection at the top of the list and there must be a row allocated for it.

The next Case clause, for acLBGetColumnCount, gets the number of columns. This is done by setting the function equal to a fixed number, in this case, 3—one for the EventID, the second for the name, and the last for the date.

The next Case clause, acLBGetColumnWidth, gets the column width. By setting this to True, you indicate that you want it to look at the property settings for the control.

The acLBGetValue case is the one that actually gets the information into the control. This represents a good number of passes through the function. It gets the row and col each time the function is used.

An If structure is created to determine whether this is the first row. If the mvarSelectionBuild function is populating the first row, the All choice is created. It uses a Select Case structure for the col argument to put the correct values in the correct columns. If it is the first column, column 0, you create a dummy EventID of 0. If it is column 1, you are creating the All text. The last column gets no value because the date isn't relevant in this case.

The Else clause of the row If structure uses the data from the recordset. Here it uses the MoveFirst method to get to the top of the recordset. It then uses the Move method with the row - 1 argument to move to the correct record. It then sets the name of the function equal to the recordset variable using the col argument as an index value to indicate which column in the recordset.

There are three additional cases: one to allow you to change the format of the data, one to execute code when the control is closed, and when the process is ended, the acLBEnd case. In this case, you are closing the recordset.

This is the code needed to set up a function to populate a list or combo box, but you are not finished. Now that the function is complete, you need to set up the properties for the list to use this function. You need to switch back to Microsoft Access and select the list box for this next step.

The first step is to set up the data properties. Row Source Type indicates how the control is populated. It has a drop-down list to select Table, Query, Value List, or Field List. In this case, you cannot use any of the choices. Here you need to type in the name of the function without its trailing parentheses.

The other data property that must be set is the Bound Column. You want to use the EventID to open the report, so you need to set it equal to 1.

19

You can also set the default property to 0. When you work with a combo box or a list on a form with a record source, the combo box or list will display the contents of its bound field. If the field isn't bound to a field or has no data, the control will show no selection. By setting the default property to 0, All Events is the default selection.

You also must set two of the format properties. The Column Count needs to be set to 3 to match the code, and the Column Widths need to be entered because the code is going to look at the property for the widths. Again, this might take some trial and error as you set up your own data.

You are now ready to use the list box, but you are not populating this list just to view events. You will want to view the attendance report based on the user's selection. This requires that you add code to the Attendance button.

Task: Adding Code to the Attendance Button

1. Right-click the Attendance button and select Build Event.
2. Select Code Builder from the Choose Build dialog.
3. Access creates a foundation for the button's Click event and places the insertion point in the correct location.
4. Add the following code:

```
Private Sub cmdReport_Click()
    On Error GoTo ReportErr
    Dim strWhere As String
    If lstEvents = 0 Then
        strWhere = ""
    Else
        strWhere = "[EventID] = " & lstEvents
    End If
    DoCmd.OpenReport "rptAttendanceSelection",
➥acViewPreview, , strWhere
    Exit Sub
ReportErr:
    Select Case Err.Number
        Case 2501
            Exit Sub
        Case Else
            Dim strMessage As String, strTitle As String
            strMessage = "Error " & Err.Number & ", " & _
➥Err.Description & _"has occurred."
            strTitle = "Unexpected Error"
            MsgBox strMessage, vbInformation, strTitle
    End Select
End Sub
```

This code is similar to the code used to open the report in earlier examples. The only difference is in how the strWhere variable is set up. Here an If structure evaluates the lstEvents control. If it is 0, which is All, strWhere is set to an empty string. Otherwise, it is set to the selected EventID.

In the If test, you are also seeing a shortcut for creating code. All objects have what is called a default property. The Value property is the default property for the list control. If you want to work with the default property, you can omit the name of the property and it will process faster.

Now you are ready to test the form.

Task: Testing the Form

◄ TASK

1. Switch back to Microsoft Access.

2. Save the form.

3. Select the View button on the toolbar to switch to Form view. Notice that the list is filled and that All is at the top of the list (see Figure 19.11).

FIGURE 19.11

The list is using the function to get its values.

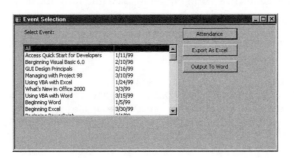

4. Select All and click the Attendance button. Notice that you are seeing all the events' attendance.

5. Close the Preview window.

6. Select an event and click the Attendance button. Notice that the where clause has restricted the report to that event.

▲ 7. Close the preview window and close the form.

Updating Information Directly

Another use for VBA and ADO is to update data directly. Earlier you made some changes to the frmAttendees form and saved it as frmAttendeesModified to work with objects on the form and the form itself. It has a need for this type of coding as well.

19

When the user makes a event choice in the subform, it takes care of setting up the attendee, but it doesn't automatically take care of the status of the event. As attendees are added or dropped from an event, you would like to automatically increment or decrement the attendees count as well as close the class when it is full.

This can be accomplished using events for the record of the subform as well as ADO to access the recordset for events. When an attendee is added to an event, you can add code to the AfterUpdate event to decrement the count of available spaces in tblEvents. As an event is deleted for an attendee, you can use the Delete event to increment the count.

Both events should test to see whether additional space is available and update the Status field. You will also need to take care of the event combo box on the subform to make sure it has the latest information for the next assignment.

Task: Implementing tblEvents Table Maintenance

1. Open frmAttendeesModified in Design view.

2. Select the subform to activate it.

3. Click the subform's Form button to make the form the active object.

4. Open the Properties window and select the Event tab.

5. Set the AfterUpdate event to [Event Procedure] and click the Build button.

6. Add the following code:

```
Private Sub Form_AfterUpdate()
    Dim rsDecrement As ADODB.Recordset, strWhere As String
    Set rsDecrement = New ADODB.Recordset
    rsDecrement.Open "tblEvents", CurrentProject.Connection,
    ➥adOpenDynamic, adLockOptimistic
    strWhere = "EventID = " & Me!EventID
    rsDecrement.Find strWhere, , adSearchForward
    rsDecrement!AvailableSpaces = rsDecrement!AvailableSpaces-1
    If rsDecrement!AvailableSpaces = 0 Then
    ➥rsDecrement!Status = "Closed"
    rsDecrement.Update
    rsDecrement.Close
    Set rsDecrement = Nothing
    Me!EventID.Requery
End Sub
```

7. Select Delete from the Procedures list in the code window.

8. Add the following code:

```
Private Sub Form_Delete(Cancel As Integer)
    Dim rsIncrement As ADODB.Recordset, strWhere As String
    Set rsIncrement = New ADODB.Recordset
    rsIncrement.Open "tblEvents", CurrentProject.Connection,
    ➥adOpenDynamic, adLockOptimistic
```

▼

```
        strWhere = "EventID = " & Me!EventID
        rsIncrement.Find strWhere, , adSearchForward
        rsIncrement!AvailableSpaces = rsIncrement!AvailableSpaces+1
        rsIncrement.Update
        rsIncrement.Close
        Set rsIncrement = Nothing
        Me!EventID.Requery
    End Sub
```

9. Switch back to Microsoft Access and save the form.

10. Switch to the Database window and open the frmEventsModified form. Notice how many available spaces there are for the Access Quick Start for Developers class.

11. Close the form.

12. Select the frmAttendeeModified form.

13. Click the View button on the toolbar to switch to the Form view.

14. For the first attendee, select the Access Quick Start for Developers class as a new event and enter any data. Make sure you press Enter to save the record.

15. Open frmEvents again and notice the change in the Available Spaces field.

16. Close the form.

17. Select the frmAttendeesModified form and delete the class for the first attendee.

18. Open the frmEvents form and notice that the Access quick Start for Developers is back at the original number of available spaces.

19. Close both forms.

The code for the AfterUpdate and Delete events is very similar. It uses VBA and ADO to create a recordset to look for the matching record and edit the data.

The first line declares the ADODB.Recordset variable, as well as strWhere to hold the search string. The next line sets that variable equal to a new ADODB.Recordset, just like the previous example.

The third line opens the recordset, pointing it to the tblEvents table. This line is different from the previous use because you want to edit the data. Here it is opened as a dynamic recordset that can be edited, and the locking is set to optimistic locking. This will lock the record when it is edited so no one else can edit the record while this procedure updates it.

The fourth line sets up the search string using the EventID from the subform. The fifth line uses the ADO Find method to locate the correct record. The Find method allows you to search through a recordset. It has the following syntax:

```
object.Find criteria skiprows, searchdirection, start
```

You begin with the name of the recordset, followed by a period and the Find keyword. This is followed by the search criteria. In this case, you are sending it strWhere. The skiprows argument is optional. It allows you to indicate how many rows to skip before beginning your search. You do not need this argument in this case.

The searchdirection argument allows you to search up or down in the recordset from the current position. Because the recordset is declared and set up each time you run this code, this argument is not required, but you indicated that it should search forward in the recordset.

The last argument is the start argument. This allows you to indicate that you want to begin searching at the current position in the recordset. Again because this recordset is being established each time, this argument isn't needed.

The sixth line of code sets the value of the AvailableSpaces field equal to itself, subtracting one with the AfterUpdate and adding one with the Delete to alter the number of spaces, depending on whether you are adding or deleting the attendee from the event.

The next line tests to see what the number is and changes the Status if necessary. After the field values are set, you are not done with the increment or decrement of the record. You need to specify the Update method to save those values.

After the record is saved, you can close the recordset with the Close method and then set the variable to Nothing to free up memory.

The last line of code takes care of the combo box on the subform. It is looking at the tblEvents table to get the list of available events. The Requery method retrieves the recordset supporting this combo, so that if the status of an event changed with this record, that change is reflected in the combo box list of available events.

Using VBA to Modify the Database

In the previous section, you learned how powerful VBA could be for manipulating records directly. It also gives you a great deal of control over the database itself. You can create objects, modify objects and their properties, and delete objects. In this section, you will see how to create a query to select records, use that query, and then delete it to free up space in the database.

To become familiar with the concepts involved in modifying objects with VBA, you are going to add the code to export to Excel from the frmEventSelection form. You will create a query to hold the SQL required to get the selected records, export the recordset to an Excel file, and delete the query when you are finished.

Understanding the Tools

When you want to modify specific objects in your database using VBA, you use two object models. If you are going to make a change to one of the interface objects—such as a form, report, or module—you use the Microsoft Access Object Model. It has collections for forms, reports, modules, and other interface components to allow you to work with an object and its properties.

If you want to modify a table or query, you use SQL, as discussed in Day 15, "Examining Special-Use Queries," you can use the Data Access Object (DAO) model; or you can use the ActiveX Data Object Extensions (ADOX) for Data Definition Language and Security.

In Day 18 and earlier in this lesson, ADO was introduced as the preferred method for accessing and manipulating data. It offers greater flexibility and speed, especially when you are going to access data from an outside source. ADOX is the ADO library that allows you create and modify ADO objects. Using the ADO and ADOX models is the recommended approach.

Adding the ADOX Reference

To minimize the size of the Microsoft Access application, you learned that the ADO functionality was stored in a library. The same is true for ADOX. Before you can create your VBA code, you must set up a reference to the ADOX library as well.

Task: Setting Up the ADOX Reference

1. Open the frmEventSelectionModified form in Design mode.
2. Right-click the Export as Excel button and click Build Event. The Visual Basic Editor opens, with your insertion point in the `cmdExport_Click` event.
3. Click Tools, References to open the References dialog.
4. Locate and select the check box for Microsoft ADO Ext. 2.1 for DDL and Security. (For the sample database, it should already be selected.)
5. Click OK. Now the library and its objects are available for use in your code.

19

Adding the Code for Exporting

In the frmEventSelection form, you added code for the general function that populated the list box. You also added code to the Attendance command button to use the selected choice to build a `WHERE` clause to be used by the `OpenReport` method to open the Attendance report with only those records selected.

For the cmdExport code, the process isn't as simple. To export a recordset, you are going to use DoCmd's `TransferSpreadsheet` method. Unlike the `OpenReport` or `OpenForm` methods, `TransferSpreadsheet` doesn't have a `WHERE` clause argument. To accomplish the same selection access, you must create a query with a `WHERE` clause and then export that query. After the export, you must get rid of the query because next time, you will want a different selection.

To accomplish this goal, you are going to create code to tackle all these tasks. This is the longest event procedure you have created in this book. You can choose to enter the code from scratch using the code in Listing 19.4, or you can skip the typing and open frmEventSelectionFinal to examine the code already entered.

Note

To make analyzing the code easier, there are comments in the code to indicate what each block of code does, and these comments have a line number at the right. VBA doesn't use line numbers to keep track of the code; the line numbers in the comments are there only to help with the code description in the book.

You do not have to add line numbers to your code. If you are trying to reference a line of code in the Visual Basic Editor as you are working, you can use the Standard toolbar, which has a line and column indicator. The number in the line and column indicator represents the line number from the top of the module. The line numbers in the comments indicate the number of lines from the top of this procedure.

LISTING 19.4 THE cmdExport_Click EVENT PROCEDURE

```
Private Sub cmdExport_Click()
'   Set Error Trap                               (Line 2)
    On Error GoTo ExportErr

'   Get Where Clause                             (Line 5)
    Dim strWhere As String, strSQL As String
    If lstEvents = 0 Then
        strWhere = ";"
    Else
        strWhere = "WHERE [tblEvents.EventID] = " & lstEvents & ";"
    End If

'   Defines ADO Extensions for                   (Line 13)
'   Data Definition Language Variables (ADOX)
    Dim catXLSExport As New ADOX.Catalog
    Dim cmdXLSExport As New ADODB.Command
```

```
'    Open the Catalog for query creation                (Line 18)
     catXLSExport.ActiveConnection = CurrentProject.Connection

'    Create the command representing the view (query).   (Line 21)
     strSQL = "SELECT tblEvents.EventID, tblEvents.EventName, "
     strSQL = strSQL & "tblEvents.StartDate, tblEvents.EndDate, "
     strSQL = strSQL & "tblAttendees.AttendeeLastName, "
     strSQL = strSQL & "tblAttendees.AttendeeFirstName "
     strSQL = strSQL & "FROM tblAttendees INNER JOIN (tblEvents "
     strSQL = strSQL & "INNER JOIN tblRegistration ON "
     strSQL = strSQL & "tblEvents.EventID = "
     strSQL = strSQL & "tblRegistration.EventID) ON "
     strSQL = strSQL & "tblAttendees.AttendeeID = "
     strSQL = strSQL & "tblRegistration.AttendeeID "
     strSQL = strSQL & strWhere
     cmdXLSExport.CommandText = strSQL

'    Get File Name                                       (Line 35)
     Dim strName As String
     Dim strPrompt As String, strInputTitle As String, strDefault As String
     Dim strMessage As String, strTitle As String, lOptions As Long
     strPrompt = "Enter the path and file name."
     strInputTitle = "Export to File"
     strDefault = "C:\My Documents\Attendees.XLS"
     strName = InputBox(strPrompt, strInputTitle, strDefault)
     If Len(strName) > 0 Then
         Dim strExists As String
         strExists = Dir(strName)
         If strExists <> "" Then
             strMessage = "The file exists. Export cancelled."
             strTitle = "Export Error"
             lOptions = vbInformation + vbOKOnly
             MsgBox strMessage, lOptions, strTitle
             Exit Sub
         End If
     Else
         strMessage = "You need to provide a file name."
         strTitle = "Export Error"
         lOptions = vbInformation + vbOKOnly
         MsgBox strMessage, lOptions, strTitle
         Exit Sub
     End If

'    Create the new View and Export                      (Line 61)
     catXLSExport.Views.Append "qryAttendeesExport", cmdXLSExport
     DoCmd.TransferSpreadsheet acExport, _
       acSpreadsheetTypeExcel9, "qryAttendeesExport", strName, True

'    Delete View (Query)                                 (Line 66)
```

continues

19

LISTING 19.4   CONTINUED

```
        catXLSExport.Views.Delete "qryAttendeesExport"
        Exit Sub

'    Error Handling                                    (Line 70)
    ExportErr:
        Select Case Err.Number
            Case -2147217816
                catXLSExport.Views.Delete "qryAttendeesExport"
                Resume
            Case Else
                strMessage = "Error " & Err.Number & ", " & Err.Description
                ➥& " The Export has been cancelled."
                strTitle = "Unexpected Error"
                MsgBox strMessage, vbInformation, strTitle
        End Select
    End Sub
```

Examining the `cmdExport_Click` Procedure

The `cmdExport_Click` procedure accomplishes several tasks to complete the export. There are some general setup steps, and then you must create the SQL statement and assign it. The next step is to get a filename to use for the export. After you have the information, you must create the query, export the recordset, and then delete it. This last step provides error handling in case something goes wrong.

Examining the General Setup

The first thing you needed to do with this procedure is enable error handling by setting your error trap with lines 2 and 3. This process has several areas where error handling is necessary. You are creating a new object, you will need to make sure that it doesn't already exist, and you are creating a file.

The next step is to get the information from the form. Lines 5–12 are identical to the lines used to open the report except for lines 8 and 10. If the user has selected an event, you must build the WHERE clause. With OpenReport, this string was used for the WHERE clause argument.

In this case, you are going to concatenate it with the rest of an SQL statement for the query object. This requires the WHERE keyword and the punctuation. Line 8 stores the semicolon because in this case, there isn't a WHERE clause and you just need to indicate the end of the SQL statement. Line 10 stores the WHERE clause with the WHERE keyword at the beginning and the semicolon at the end.

Lines 13–17 set up the object variables to create and build the query. catXLSExport is going to represent an ADOX Catalog object. The catalog is the object that stores all the collections and objects in ADOX. cmdXLSExport is the object variable to create the ADO Command object to store the SQL statement that needs to be created.

Lines 18–19 indicate what catalog will be used. In this case, you are working with one database and the assignment is easy. The ActiveConnection property is assigned to `CurrentProject.Connection`.

The Connection property for a database stores the information for how to get at the data. The Application object from the Microsoft Access Object model has a CurrentProject property to provide an easy mechanism for referencing the current database. This one line retrieves that information and makes it accessible for the Catalog object.

Building the SQL Statement and Assigning It

Lines 21–34 build the SQL statement and assign it to the command object. Creating SQL statements for your VBA code can be quite time consuming. You might want to use the QBE window and create the query in Design view. Then you can switch to SQL view and copy it to the Clipboard. After it is on the Clipboard, you can paste it into your VBA procedure. After it is pasted, you will have to format it for use in VBA.

For a SQL statement to be used in VBA it is treated as a string. In most cases, it's easiest to manage if you assign it to a string variable like strSQL. In this example, the SQL line is split between lines 22–31. It is not required to split it between lines, but it does make it easier to read (see Figure 19.12).

If you assigned the SQL statement to the variable on one line, it would be impossible to read. If a line is too long to be conveniently viewed in the window, you can often use the Visual Basic line continuation character. You can press a space and then type an underscore (_), press Enter, and continue entering your statement. This technique doesn't work when assigning a long string to a variable. The line continuation character can be used between statement or function arguments and between expression components, but it can't be placed in the middle of a string.

You can assign string values to variables by enclosing the text in quotation marks. Anything between the quotation marks isn't compiled by Visual Basic. The line continuation character is treated as text. This leaves the approach used in this example as your only tool. Here the SQL statement is broken up in readable substrings, and they are concatenated to the strSQL string.

Line 32 takes the strSQL string and concatenates the strWhere string to the end. Line 33 assigns the entire string to the CommandText property to the Command object variable. It is ready to use to create the query.

19

FIGURE 19.12

The use of several assignment lines eliminates scrolling.

Getting a Filename

For this operation, you must have a filename for the export of the query's recordset. You could have added a filename to the code, or you could prompt the user for a filename. Lines 35–60 use the `InputBox` function to get a filename from the user.

Lines 36–38 declare the variables that will be used to store data for this process. Lines 39–41 assign string values to variables to use as arguments for the `InputBox`. Line 42 uses the `InputBox` function to get a filename with a path from the user and store that name in a string variable, `strName`.

After you have a filename, you might think you are ready to export, but that isn't the case. The `TransferSpreadsheet` method is used to export later in this code. If the file exists, it will not complete the export. It also will not send back an error.

Lines 43–59 have an `If...Then...Else` structure to test the filename given. The `Len` function is used to see if a string was entered. If one was given, it has to be tested to see if the file exists.

Lines 44–45 set up a string variable called `strExists`. The `Dir` function is used to see whether the file exists. If it does, the `strExists` will be set to the filename found, which is `strName`.

Lines 46–52 show an `If` structure that tests whether `strExists` is not an empty string. If the filename doesn't exist, the `Dir` function returns an empty string and no action is required. If the file exists, lines 47–50 create and display a message box, letting the user know the filename is being used. Line 51 just exits the procedure to give the user a chance to start over.

Lines 53–59 are the `Else` clause for the string test for the name received from the `InputBox` function. If the string returned is empty, the `MsgBox` statement is used to let the user know and exit the procedure. Then he can start over.

Tip

> The `InputBox` function is not the best way to accomplish this task. The code to teat to see weather a file exists is only the tip of the iceburg for checks needed for file management. The block of code doesn't deal with bad path, inability to create a file, or a missing drive. All these conditions are possible and cause the error handling code to be executed. In this case, the result would be the same, a message box would be disabled, and the user could try again.
>
> Another method for getting a filename is to open the Windows save As dialog. Using the Windows standard dialog is discussed in Day 21, "Developer Considerations."

Creating, Exporting, and Deleting a Query

After you have a filename, you can begin creating the query and exporting the file with lines 61–65. Line 62 creates the query. With ADOX, the Catalog object has five collections to allow you to create and manage database objects:

- Tables—Stores the definition for the table objects in the database.
- Groups—Stores the user group information if you are using security..
- Users—Stores the user information if you are using security..
- Procedures—Stores the information about commands. Stored procedures are similar to action queries in an outside source..
- Views—Stores information about any views like an Access Select query..

For this export, the `Append` method is used to add a view to the catalog's View collection using the command (SQL statement) `cmdXLSExport`. After the view is created, the `TransferSpreadsheet` for the `DoCmd` object is used to export to the file.

19

> **Note** For additional information about using ADOX, please refer to online help
> (www.microsoft.com).

TransferSpreadsheet is used to export and import from a spreadsheet application. It
can handle other formats in addition to Excel. Its syntax is

```
DoCmd.TransferSpreadsheet transfertype, _
     spreadsheettype, tablename, filename, includefieldnames, range
```

This method has six arguments. You must indicate the transfer type, which is whether
you are importing or exporting. The spreadsheet type argument indicates the format.
tablename indicates the table or query, and *filename* is the name of the file.

includefieldnames and *range* allow you to determine whether you are using the elements. *range* can't be used during and export, and it is omitted from this code example.

Line 67 uses the Delete method for the catalog object to remove the created view. This
cleans up the database for the next use of this procedure.

> **Tip** If you create a view with this process and don't delete it, you will not see it
> in the Query list in the Database window.

Handling Errors

Beginning with line 70, the rest of the code handles any errors that might arise as the
code executes. The first Case clause handles error number -2147217816. This error can
occur when line 62 is executed. If you attempt to append a view with the same name as
an existing query, you will get this error. Line 74 uses the Delete method to get rid of
the view and uses the Resume statement to try the line of code again. This is followed by
a Case Else to display any other errors in a message box. After the error is displayed,
the procedure is exited and the user can try again.

Creating Switchboards

Throughout this lesson, you have been expanding your knowledge of how to let
Microsoft Access do more work for you. As your use of Microsoft Access grows, you
will begin to have many objects to support your work or you might be allowing others to
work with your database.

NEW TERM When your database grows, you might decide to make it easier to get to the objects you use the most. This makes it more of an application. One way to make Microsoft Access easier to use is to add a switchboard. A *switchboard* is a form with command buttons that launches other objects for you, so that you do not have to locate the object manually using the Database window. This is especially nice if you are letting others use your database who are not as familiar with Microsoft Access.

You must determine what needs to be accessed from a switchboard. This database isn't very large, but as you can see, it could be quite confusing to select the correct form to work with events or attendees if you were looking in the Database window (see Figure 19.13). There are forms named frmAttendees, frmEventAttendees, frmEvents, and frmEventSelection. Without a specific form name, the user might have to open all the forms to find the one needed.

FIGURE 19.13

The Forms list in the Database window has many choices for the user.

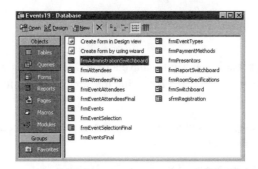

This database contains the forms for managing attendees and events as well as those for maintaining the smaller supporting tables. The Forms list also doesn't show the reports that you might want to access.

19

If your database is large, you can also have several switchboards for subareas of the database. For this database, there are two subswitchboards: frmAdministrationSwitchboard and frmReportSwitchboard.

When you decide to add a switchboard to your database, the first step is to design the visual appearance. You can be as creative as you want. You can add graphics, change colors, or add any formatting that you want. Although you might want to consider this carefully because graphics will take up memory and cause the form to load slower.

The Microsoft Access Database Wizard can create complete database applications for some purposes. It creates very elaborate switchboards. To save some time, the visual appearance has been created for you in frmSwitchboard. Go ahead and open it in Design mode.

Here the graphics are minimal. The clip art image used in the report example earlier is used with a title. Then the command buttons are added. The Microsoft Access Database Wizard doesn't use the command buttons by themselves. The switchboards created by the Database Wizards have smaller buttons with the Caption property cleared and use a label. This technique has been used here (see Figure 19.14).

FIGURE 19.14

This switchboard is simpler than those created by the Database Wizard.

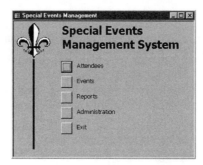

For this main switchboard, you want to have a button for working with attendees, managing events, accessing reports, and accessing the administration forms. You also have an Exit button.

After the visual display is complete and all your controls are named, you are ready to automate the accessing of objects.

Task: Adding Functionality to a Switchboard

1. Save the form as frmSwitchboardModified.

2. Right-click the Attendees command button.

3. Select Build Event and Code Builder, and then click OK to open the Visual Basic Editor and create the Click event.

4. Add the following code:

```
Private Sub cmdAttendees_Click()
    On Error GoTo ErrAttendees
    Dim stDocName As String
    stDocName = "frmAttendeesFinal"
    DoCmd.OpenForm stDocName, acNormal
    Exit Sub
ErrAttendees:
    Select Case Err.Number
        Case 2501    'OpenReport or OpenForm Cancelled
            Exit Sub
        Case Else
            Dim strMessage As String, strTitle As String
            strMessage = "Error " & Err.Number & ", " &
```

▼

```
                        ➥Err.Description & " has occurred."
                        strTitle = "Unexpected Error"
                        MsgBox strMessage, vbInformation + vbOKOnly,
                        ➥strTitle
                        Exit Sub
            End Select
    End Sub
```

5. Select cmdEvents from the Object list and add the following code:

```
    Private Sub cmdEvents_Click()
        On Error GoTo ErrEvents
        Dim stDocName As String
        stDocName = "frmEventsFinal"
        DoCmd.OpenForm stDocName, acNormal
        Exit Sub
    ErrEvents:
        Select Case Err.Number
            Case 2501    'OpenReport or OpenForm Cancelled
                Exit Sub
            Case Else
                Dim strMessage As String, strTitle As String
                strMessage = "Error " & Err.Number & ", " &
                ➥Err.Description & " has occurred."
                strTitle = "Unexpected Error"
                MsgBox strMessage, vbInformation + vbOKOnly,
                ➥strTitle
                Exit Sub
        End Select
    End Sub
```

6. Select cmdReports from the Object list and add the following code:

```
    Private Sub cmdReports_Click()
        On Error GoTo ErrReports
        Dim stDocName As String
        stDocName = "frmReportSwitchboard"
        DoCmd.OpenForm stDocName, acNormal
        Exit Sub
    ErrReports:
        Select Case Err.Number
            Case 2501    'OpenReport or OpenForm Cancelled
                Exit Sub
            Case Else
                Dim strMessage As String, strTitle As String
                strMessage = "Error " & Err.Number & ", " &
                ➥Err.Description & " has occurred."
                strTitle = "Unexpected Error"
                MsgBox strMessage, vbInformation + vbOKOnly,
                ➥strTitle
                Exit Sub
        End Select
    End Sub
```

▼

19

7. Select cmdAdministration from the Object list and add the following code:

```
Private Sub cmdAdministration_Click()
    On Error GoTo ErrAdmin
    Dim stDocName As String
    stDocName = "frmAdministrationSwitchboard"
    DoCmd.OpenForm stDocName, acNormal
    Exit Sub
ErrAdmin:
    Select Case Err.Number
        Case 2501    'OpenReport or OpenForm Cancelled
            Exit Sub
        Case Else
            Dim strMessage As String, strTitle As String
            strMessage = "Error " & Err.Number & ", " & _
            Err.Description & " has occurred."
            strTitle = "Unexpected Error"
            MsgBox strMessage, vbInformation + vbOKOnly, _
            strTitle
            Exit Sub
    End Select
End Sub
```

8. Select cmdExit from the Object list and add the following code:

```
Private Sub cmdExit_Click()
    DoCmd.Quit acQuitSaveAll
End Sub
```

9. Switch back to Microsoft Access and save the form.

The switchboard is now complete. You should recognize the code used for most of these buttons: It is the code to open a form with no WHERE condition. It just opens the form with all the records, if there are any.

The code for all the buttons except the Exit button is identical except for the form to be accessed. The first line initializes the error handler. The second and third line set up the form variable and assign it the name of the form. The next line uses the OpenForm method for the DoCmd object to display the form. This is followed by the Exit Sub and the error handling code.

Tip

If you have many buttons that only open another form with no criteria, you could have created a general procedure to open forms and then called that from each button's Click event. In most cases, your processing involves more complex actions.

The cmdExit button is different. It provides a mechanism for closing the database and exiting Access in one action. This is not necessary because this function is on the window as well as on the menu, but it is nice and minimizes movement for the user if he is pointing to the form.

It uses the `Quit` method for the `DoCmd` object. It saves all of the objects that have changes as it exits. The syntax is

```
DoCmd.Quit saveargument
```

The `DoCmd` object is followed by a period and the `Quit` keyword. This is followed by an argument to indicate what should happen to any objects that have been changed. The `acQuitSaveAll` argument saves all objects as it exits. You can prompt the user to save any objects with the `acQuitPrompt` constant or you can discard any changes with the `acQuitSaveNone` constant.

This finishes the switchboard form. It can now be used as a method for accessing other objects in this database. In Day 21, you will learn how to hide the Database window as it opens and to display a form automatically to further avoid confusion.

Summary

Today's lesson introduced some of the uses for VBA in your database. You learned several techniques for automating your work and accessing the database.

The first section introduced some additional techniques for manipulating Microsoft Access objects. You learned how to cancel the opening of a form if there is no data, similar to the technique for reports. You learned how to control the appearance of a report with VBA. You also learned how to validate data before accepting a record with VBA.

The second section worked on automating data entry. Here you looked at adding VBA to look at several other fields on the form and to add a value to a field.

You also got to experiment with manipulating data directly. You learned how to use an aggregate function to retrieve information about data, as well as to update data in another table based on entries on a form. You also created a more sophisticated combo box, as well as automated data entry based on the contents of an outside table.

You then took a look at modifying the database itself. You got a chance to create a query, manipulate it, and delete it with VBA. Last but not least, you developed a form to make it easier to access other objects in your database.

19

Q&A

Q Can I use VBA to validate data based on other tables?

A Yes, you can. If you want to validate data based on the contents of a recordset, you have to set up the recordset and then create your logic to test your expression. Most of the time, this code will be in a BeforeUpdate event because it has the Cancel argument. If you do not validate, you can set the Cancel argument equal to True to cancel the operation.

Q Can I create tables with VBA?

A Yes, you can create tables with a technique similar to that used to create the query.

Q Can I open any object from a switchboard?

A Yes, you can. You need to use the appropriate DoCmd method.

Workshop

The Workshop helps you solidify the skills you learned in this lesson. Answers to the quiz questions appear in Appendix A, "Answers."

Quiz

1. What event is used to test whether the form has data since there isn't a NoData event?

2. Why can't you use the BeforeInsert event to check for duplicate records?

3. Why might you need more than one switchboard for a database?

Exercises

1. Create an Attendee selection form based on state and display the Attendee Call list. (Hint: This will be similar to the frmEventSelection form.)

2. Add code to the Location combo box on frmEvents to retrieve the Capacity from the tblRooms table and place the value in the AvailableSpaces field on the form. (Hint: To see an example, look at code for the Event combo box on the registration subform to fill in the fee information.)

3. Add code for the Output to Word button on the frmEventSelection form to create a query, export the recordset to Word, and delete it. (Hint: This is identical to the Export button except it uses the OutputTo method.)

WEEK 3

Day 20

Understanding Access Security

In many cases, you started developing in Microsoft Access for yourself. As time goes on, you find that others need access to your system. With the forms, reports, and automation through Visual Basic for Application (VBA), your system is becoming more user friendly. You must make sure that everyone has access to the information they need without running the risk that they can damage the database or access restricted information. Today, you learn about the following:

- Understanding the structure of Access security
- Setting a database password
- Using user-level security
- Managing passwords
- Using the Security Wizard
- Closing security holes with MDE and ADE

To follow along with today's lesson, you'll need the sample database Security.mdb from the CD that accompanies this book. You'll find the database in \Day20\.

Security.mdb is a copy of the database used in Day 16, "Implementing Advanced Form Concepts," which tracks students and classes. It is used in this lesson to demonstrate how to use the Security Wizard and look at restricting the appearance of the system with VBA. For the rest of the chapter, you will be creating databases with security from scratch.

Understanding the Structure of Access Security

When you create a database system, you might want to prevent unauthorized access to that system. To protect your system, you can use several approaches. You can set a database password, build user-level security into the database, and save your database as an MDE or ADE file. (MDE and ADE files are compiled versions of your database or project.)

The key to selecting the correct approach or combination of approaches to security is determining what type of protection is needed. You will need to take a look at several factors.

First, you must determine who needs access to the database. If you are developing a database for your own use, no one else needs access, and you just need a way to keep others from opening the system. This can be accomplished with a database password.

Second, if more than one person needs access, you need to determine whether everyone's access needs are the same. If more than one person will be using the database, you have to evaluate what each person is going to be doing with the system.

You, as the developer, will need full access to make system changes. If someone is going to be viewing and entering data only, he does not need to be able to change objects. Eliminating the possibility that he could accidentally make changes to objects will be important. This can be especially important if the system deals with sensitive data.

In earlier lessons, you looked at a sales management database to track orders. If this system was expanded to track the sales of individual sales representatives, it might include some human resources information, like compensation rates. This would be considered sensitive because you probably wouldn't want the salespeople to know each other's compensation rates. This would require limiting their access to that information.

When more than one person needs access and with various levels, you need to use user-level security. This gives you control over different groups of users as well as individual users.

The last type of protection to consider is protecting your design and code. If you are concerned about people having access to your code, you might want to protect your code from theft, which will require the creation of an MDE or an ADE file.

Setting a Database Password

If you are the only one who needs access to your database, or if all the users who need access can have total access to your database, you can use a database password. It is the simplest method for protecting a database. In this section, you will learn how to set, use, and delete a database password. You will also take a look at the advantages and disadvantages of using a database password.

Setting the Password

It is easy to set up a database password. With the database open, select Tools, Security, Set Database Password. Access will prompt for a password and verification and you are finished.

Caution

It is a good idea to create a backup of your database before you set the password and write the password down to store it in a safe place. After you set the password, you can't access the system without it.

By creating a backup of the database before you add the password, you protect against typing errors as you set the password. After setting the password, you can close and re-open the database to test it. If your attempt to re-open it fails, you can restore the backup and set it again.

By storing the password in a safe place, you protect against errors in the future. Later if you forget the password, you can look it up.

20

Task: Setting a Database Password

1. Launch Access if it isn't already open.
2. Select Blank Access Database from the Create New Database Using group in the Microsoft Access opening dialog and click OK.
3. Type `Password Test` as the filename, and click Create.
4. Close the default table that is created for you.

5. Select Tools, Security, Set Database Password to open the Set Database Password dialog (see Figure 20.1).

FIGURE 20.1

The Set Database Password dialog gives you a chance to enter and verify the password.

6. Type `Protect` as the password and press Tab.

 7. Type `Protect` to verify and press Enter.

At this point, you have created a database password. It has been stored in your database file and is now ready to use when you open the database.

When you are setting your database password, you must follow these rules. You can use between 1 and 20 characters as a password. The password can contain any letters, numbers, or special characters, excluding the null character. A password is case sensitive, so remember that an uppercase *A* will be treated differently than a lowercase *a*.

There are also some guidelines to keep in mind. The whole purpose for setting a password is to make it harder for someone who doesn't belong in your database to get access to it. That means you want to make the password hard to guess. You should avoid common names. Don't use your name, the name of a family member, a pet's name, a birth date, a Social Security number, the name of your organization, or any other password that could easily be guessed. You might want to consider using letter and number combinations and using strange case settings such as Am14u or pC98DeVa. The key is to make it hard work to break into your database.

Using the Password

After the database password is set, you will be prompted each time you open the database for this password. You will not be able to open the file if you enter the wrong password.

Task: Trying Out Your New Password

1. Close the PasswordTest.mdb file.

2. Open the PasswordTest.mdb file to display the Password Required dialog (see Figure 20.2).

3. Type `Protect` and press Enter to open the database.

FIGURE 20.2

The Password Required dialog gives you a chance to enter the password.

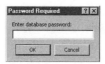

If you type the password incorrectly, Access does not open the database, but gives you an error message after you press Enter. Access then prompts you for the password again in case you made a typing mistake.

Deleting the Password

If you set a password, and later determine that one isn't necessary or that you need to move to user-level security, you can delete it.

Task: Deleting Your Database Password

1. Open the database for exclusive use and enter the password.

2. Select Tools, Security, Unset Database Password to display the Unset Database Password dialog (see Figure 20.3).

Note

When you need to open the database for exclusive use, this means that no one else is in the database at the time and it will prevent others from opening it while you have it open.

To open a database for exclusive use, select File, Open and select your database. Instead of clicking the Open button, click its drop-down arrow to display the menu and select Open Exclusive.

FIGURE 20.3

The Unset Database Password dialog gives you a chance to remove the password.

20

3. Enter the password and click OK.

Examining the Advantages and Disadvantages of a Database Password

Unfortunately, there are many more disadvantages to setting a database password than there are advantages. The one clear-cut advantage is the time required to turn this feature on and the planning and maintenance required.

Adding a database password requires no planning outside of thinking up a password. It can be applied to an existing database without any special steps. It is also very fast because you open one dialog after the database is open, enter the password twice, click OK, and you are finished. These advantages must be weighed against these disadvantages.

The first disadvantage of using a database password is the fact that the password is stored in the database file. That means it is very vulnerable to computer hackers. A good hacker with some good utilities can hack into the file and locate the password. It is highly recommended that you use encryption to offset this risk.

The second disadvantage is connected with the first. If a database will serve as a source for a link from another database, the password is stored as part of the link. The first time the user makes the connection to this linked database it will prompt for the password. After that it will rely on the password in the link unless it changes.

The third disadvantage is that after a person logs in to the database with a password, she has complete access. The user can modify the data, but she can also make any changes to your interface objects like forms, reports, or code. Because database passwords cannot provide user-level security, you cannot have various levels of security.

It is possible to hide more sensitive objects by altering their properties. This is not 100% effective because if a user turns on the option to view all hidden objects, he sees everything.

The fourth disadvantage is you cannot use database passwords with replication. When you replicate the database, you are creating multiple copies of the data. These copies need to be synchronized to make sure the data matches. This cannot happen if there is a database password.

Using User-Level Security

The second type of security is user-level security. This method of securing your database offers a greater level of control over the access to your data than does using a database password.

NEW TERM   With user-level security, you create a workgroup information file. The *workgroup information file* stores the information concerning user-level security. It will store the user groups, the individual users, their permissions, and their passwords to access specific objects.

Whether you realize it or not, you have been using a workgroup information file. When you begin working with Microsoft Access, you use the default workgroup information file, System.mdw. The file is in place, but it is not activated. Until this point, you have been acting as the administrator with full access to all objects.

If you want to use user-level security for your database system, you will need to create a new workgroup and set user groups and users. Although it is possible to set up security later with the Security Wizard, it is better if this is the first step in your development. The following are the general steps for setting up user security; each of these steps is covered in greater detail in the following sections:

1. Create a new workgroup.
2. Activate security.
3. Create a new administrator.
4. Log in as the new administrator.
5. Remove permissions for the default administrator.
6. Set up your user groups.
7. Set up the users.
8. Establish permissions for new objects.

 As you complete these steps, there is some information that you will need to remember in case you need to re-create the security file. You might find the Excel template Database Security Tracking.xlt, located in the \Day 20\ directory on the CD, to be very helpful for tracking this information.

Creating a Workgroup

When you are beginning to create your database system, it is easiest if you create the security first. This will eliminate a lot of re-setting of permissions later. The first step is to create a new workgroup information file or workgroup.

To create a new workgroup, you need to have Microsoft Access 2000 closed. To create a new workgroup, you are going to use the Microsoft Access Workgroup Administrator. When Microsoft Office is installed, this is one of the applications that is not set up on the Programs menu. You will need to hunt this application down.

20

Task: Running the Microsoft Access Workgroup Administrator from Windows Explorer

1. Select Start, Programs, Windows Explorer to launch the application.
2. Open the folder that contains your Microsoft Office files.
3. Locate the MS Access Workgroup Administrator shortcut and double-click to launch the Workgroup Administrator (see Figure 20.4).

FIGURE 20.4

The Workgroup Administrator allows you to create a new workgroup or join an existing one.

    4. Close the Windows Explorer.

If you will be managing several databases with different workgroups, you might want to consider copying this shortcut to the Start menu for easier access. This will enable you to access the Workgroup Administrator to join a group quicker.

After the Workgroup Administrator is open, you can create a new workgroup, join an existing workgroup, or exit the application. This is where that Microsoft Excel template might be useful for recording the information that will need to be tracked.

You want to create a new workgroup for your new database. You have to provide some information to uniquely identify the new file. You will specify a name for the owner, an organization name, and a workgroup ID.

Because the name and organization are often easy to guess if someone is trying to break into your security, the workgroup ID will act like a password. You can create a workgroup ID between 4 and 20 characters.

Note

It is best to follow the same rules as you would for passwords. You can use between 4 and 20 characters, using any combination of letters, numerals, and special characters. Remember to avoid common words that can be guessed and that the password is case sensitive.

You will be prompted to enter a filename as well as confirm all of this information.

Task: Creating a New Workgroup

1. Click Create to display the Workgroup Owner Information dialog (see Figure 20.5).

2. Type your name in the Name text box and press Tab.

3. Type `Special Events Inc.` in the Organization text box and press Tab.

4. Type SEI99Secwid (or any other password) in the Workgroup ID text box, press Enter, and Access will display the Workgroup Information File dialog (see Figure 20.6).

FIGURE 20.5

The Workgroup Owner Information dialog is used to uniquely identify the workgroup.

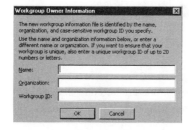

FIGURE 20.6

The Workgroup Information File dialog gives you an opportunity to specify a filename.

5. Click the Browse button to locate the folder where you copied the rest of the files for this lesson.

6. Type SEISec in the File name text box and press Enter.

7. Click the OK button to accept this filename and display the Confirm Workgroup Information dialog (see Figure 20.7).

FIGURE 20.7

The Confirm Workgroup Information dialog is great for double checking the information.

20

8. Either write this information down or double check it with the information you already entered into the Microsoft Excel template because you will not see the workgroup ID displayed again.

▼ 9. Click OK to confirm your entries. Access will display a message that your workgroup has been created (see Figure 20.8).

FIGURE 20.8

The message confirms the file was created.

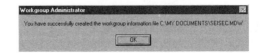

▲ 10. Click OK.

Access now shows that the workgroup is created and that you have joined the workgroup. You are now ready to create your database and activate the security. You can exit the Workgroup Administrator.

Activating Security

After you have created the workgroup, you need to create your database and activate security. As mentioned above, you have been using security since you first started working with Microsoft Access. It just wasn't active. You have been logging in as the Admin user. To activate security, you need to create a password for the Admin account.

Task: Activating Security

1. Launch Microsoft Access 2000.

2. Select Blank Access Database from the Create New Database Using group and click OK.

3. Type SEI System in the File name text box and browse to the folder where you copied the rest of the files for this lesson.

4. Click Create to create the database.

5. Close the default table that opens.

6. Select Tools, Security, User and Group Accounts to open the User and Group Accounts dialog.

7. Select the Change Logon Password tab (see Figure 20.9).

8. Press Tab to move to the New Password text box because there is no Old Password.

9. Type SEIAdmin as the password and press Tab.

▼ 10. Type SEIAdmin to verify and click OK.

FIGURE 20.9

The User and Group Accounts dialog allows you to create new users and groups as well as change passwords.

This activates the security system. When you are selecting a password, you want to make it difficult for someone to guess what it is, so again follow the rules and guidelines for passwords. After you set the password, you are ready to create a special administrator for your database.

Creating an Administrator

After you activate security, take the time to set up a special administrator for your database. Throughout this lesson, it has been stressed that you want to make it hard for someone to guess your security information.

If you were to create all of your objects using the Admin user account, it would be easy for someone to get access to your system because *Admin* is one of the first guesses a hacker will make. For the same reason, the word *password* wouldn't be a very good password.

When you create your new administrator account, you will assign it a name and a personal ID number (PID). The PID is like a PIN for an ATM machine. It is four digits. Again, try to avoid numbers that will be easy to guess, such as 1234 or 9876.

After the new user is created, you will need to make sure that it has full access to your system. This means that it must be part of the Admins group. By default, you have two groups created: the Admins group provides full access, and a User group that should have less access. This is discussed further in the "Setting Up Permissions" section.

Task: Creating a New Administrator

1. Select Tools, Security, User and Group Accounts to open the User and Group Accounts dialog (see Figure 20.10).

2. Click New to open the New User/Group dialog (see Figure 20.11).

20

FIGURE 20.10

The User and Group Accounts dialog Users tab is used to create new users like the new administrator.

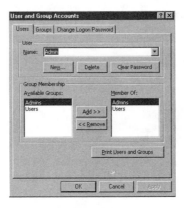

FIGURE 20.11

The New User/Group dialog allows you to name your user or group and assign it a PID to uniquely identify it.

3. Type SEIAdmin in the Name text box and press Tab.

4. Type 6416 in the Personal ID text box and press Enter.

5. Notice the account is now created and you are ready to set up its group membership.

6. Select Admins from the Available Groups category and click Add to make SEIAdmin part of the Admins group.

 7. Click OK.

After the administrator is created, the rest of the work you have to do should be done as SEIAdmin to make it the owner of the database. That means you need to close Microsoft Access and reopen it. This will kick off the logon process.

Logging In as the New Administrator

After you have activated security, you will see the logon prompt every time you open Microsoft Access when you are a member of that workgroup. When you want to modify the structure of the database, you want to log in as the administrator so you have full access to the database and all of the objects.

Task: Logging In as the New Administrator

1. Close Microsoft Access.

2. Select Start, Programs, Microsoft Access.

3. Select SEI Systems from the Open Existing File group and click OK to display the Logon dialog (see Figure 20.12).

FIGURE 20.12

When security is active, the Logon dialog will be displayed when you attempt to open any database.

 4. Type SEIAdmin in the Name text box and press Enter.

You didn't need to tab and enter a password because you haven't created one yet. If you are the only person who has access to the system while you are building it, you don't need to assign a password until you are ready for others to use the system.

If you are not the only person who has access to the system, you should complete the steps for setting a password in the "Activating Security" section immediately. In any case, you will need to set a password before anyone else gets access to the system. It is too easy for someone to log in as the administrator if no password is assigned because the last user to log on is remembered and your user account will be shown in the Logon dialog.

The next step is to finish setting up security. You need to disable the original Admin account and set up user groups and accounts.

Disabling the Default Administrator

After you are logged in as the new administrator, make sure the default administrator cannot be used as the administrator. That means removing it from the Admins group.

Task: Disabling the Admin Account

1. Select Tools, Security, User and Group Accounts to open the User and Group Accounts dialog.

2. Select Admin from the User Name drop-down, if needed.

3. Select Admins from the Member Of column and click Remove.

4. Click OK to close the dialog.

The Admin user account is now not a member of the Admins group. You could have selected Apply to accept the change and left the dialog open because you are going to be setting up your groups and users next.

20

Caution

The previous paragraph mentions that Admins no longer has the permissions of the Admins group. You need to complete all the steps for setting up security before it is truly disabled because the Users and Admins groups have identical permissions on all new objects except the database itself by default.

This means that all users have complete access to the database and its objects. This won't change until you set up permissions.

Setting Up User Groups and Users

The next step to setting up security is to establish any user groups or user accounts that will be needed for a new system. This is where some planning will save you a lot of time later.

In a discussion concerning what type of security you need for your database, one of the topics involved would be the need for several levels of access. If all you are going to need is an administrator to make changes to the objects of a system and a level for those who are going to enter and modify data, this step can be skipped.

When you have completed setting permissions and making changes to the system, you will use the Clear Password button for the Admin user. It will no longer prompt for that user to log on. It will open the database using the Admin account with those permissions. The users will never have to remember a user account name or password.

The one drawback to this approach is that if you need to make any changes to the system, you will have some extra steps. You will have to open the database, set a password, exit the database, open the database logging on as the new administrator, make any changes, open the User and Group Accounts dialog and clear the password for the Admin account, and close the database.

This approach is great if all the users need the same type of access, but it won't work if there are various levels of access. To get a better idea of this security need, take a look at a scenario for events management.

If you and several others will use the database, it might be very simple. You would need to have an administrator to modify the system and manage the security for the database. Everyone else would only be using the system to enter data. Then a single user or user accounts are needed. That would fit with the method of removing the password to prevent the logon prompt, but if you have an intermediate level you need another approach.

Let's assume that not all users can add events, only the events manager can add events because that requires scheduling and marketing approval. Let's also assume that the Marketing department needs special access as well. You always need to know who is logging in. That requires more than the Admins and Users groups; it requires a Management group as well.

Now that you know you need a new group, you must determine what user accounts you need. Currently, you have your new administrator account set up, as well as the old Admin account. When you move to various levels of access, you are better off avoiding the Admin account and setting up separate user accounts to minimize confusion.

Setting up separate user accounts also allows simultaneous use of the database by more than one user. With everyone using the Admin account, only one person could access the database with this user account at a time. It also makes tracking use easier.

For this scenario, assume that you need Mgmt and Mrkt groups, and that there is an events manager, named Kathy Brooks, who needs an account for KBrooks. Also, the marketing manger, Andrew Martin, needs an account. There are also two people entering attendees, Tom Williams and Deanna Cole, who will need accounts for TWilliams and DCole. To minimize the time involved with this process, it is a good idea to set up the groups and then set up the users.

For Kathy Brooks, the events manager, and Andrew Martin, the marketing manager, some more access is needed. There needs to be a managers group and a marketing group to support this.

Task: Setting Up a New Group

1. Select Tools, Security, User and Group Accounts to open the User and Group Accounts dialog.
2. Select the Groups tab (see Figure 20.13).

FIGURE 20.13

The Groups tab allows you to manage the groups that are a part of this workgroup.

20

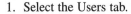

   3. Click New to open the New User/Group dialog.

   4. Type `Mgmt` in the Name text box and press Tab.

   5. Type `2345` in the Personal ID text box and press Enter.

   6. Type `Mrkt` in the Name text box and press Tab.

   7. Type `9000` in the Personal ID text box and press Enter.

After the groups are created, they can be assigned to a user. Now you need to create the individual user accounts.

Task: Setting Up Individual User Accounts

   1. Select the Users tab.

   2. Click the New button to open the New User/Group dialog.

   3. Type `KBrooks` in the Name text box and press Tab.

   4. Type `3456` in the Personal ID text box and press Enter.

   5. Notice that KBrooks is now a user account as part of the Users group by default.

   6. Select Mgmt from the Available Groups category and click Add.

   7. Click the New button to open the New User/Group dialog.

   8. Type `AMartin` in the Name text box and press Tab.

   9. Type `1456` in the Personal ID text box and press Enter.

  10. Select Mrkt from the Available Groups and click Add.

  11. Click the New button to open the New User/Group dialog.

  12. Type `TWilliams` in the Name text box and press Tab.

  13. Type `4567` in the Personal ID text box and press Enter.

  14. Click the New button to open the New User/Group dialog.

  15. Type `DCole` in the Name text box and press Tab.

  16. Type `5678` in the Personal ID text box and press Enter.

The new users are now created. When you create a new user, the user account begins with a blank password. The first time the user accesses the system, he will need to set a password. You will need to repeat this process every time you add new users to your system.

Deleting User Groups and Users

As groups and users no longer need access to the database, you will want to eliminate their group and user accounts. You also complete this process by using the User and Group Accounts dialog.

Task: Deleting the Mrkt Group

1. Select Tools, Security, User and Group Accounts to open the User and Group Accounts dialog.

2. Select the Groups tab.

3. Select Mrkt from the Name drop-down list.

4. Click the Delete button.

5. Notice that Access asks you to confirm the deletion because you cannot undo this action. You will need to re-create it with the same PID number, as shown in Figure 20.14.

FIGURE 20.14

Microsoft Access gives you the opportunity to confirm the deletion because this action cannot be undone.

 6. Click Yes to confirm the deletion.

The group has now been eliminated. If you attempt to delete the Admins or Users groups, you will not be able to. Access will inform you that it cannot complete the action. For any users who were members of the deleted group, the group has been deleted from their list.

Deleting a user account is very similar to deleting a group. It is also an action that cannot be undone, so it will have to be confirmed as well.

Task: Deleting a User Account

1. Select the Users tab.

2. Select AMartin from the User Name drop-down list.

3. Click the Delete button.

4. Click Yes in the confirmation dialog (see Figure 20.15).

 5. Click OK.

The user AMartin has now been deleted. If you need to get that user back, you will need to repeat the steps necessary to create a new user with the same PID number you used the first time.

20

FIGURE 20.15

This dialog confirms the deletion of a user account.

If you attempt to delete the Admins account or your administrator account, you will be prevented from doing so. Those accounts cannot be deleted.

Setting Up Permissions

Setting up the user groups and the user accounts is only part of the process of securing the database from unauthorized access and inadvertent changes. The next step is to assign permissions to the groups and user accounts.

Permissions are attributes that determine what type of access a user has for specific objects. When you work with user-level security, there are two types of permissions. You can assign permissions explicitly or implicitly. To assign permissions explicitly, you assign specific permissions to a user account. This doesn't affect any other user.

When you assign permissions implicitly, rather than assigning permissions to a user account, you establish permissions for a user group.

When you assign permissions, you set up permissions for a group or user account for any new objects, as well as any existing objects. That is why it is easier to begin by setting up your security before you create any objects in your database. Then you can set permissions for the new objects, and as you create objects they will automatically get those default permissions.

To set permissions, you must have the Administer permission or be the owner of the object. You can also set permissions if you are a member of the Admins group. You must also understand the different permissions that are available.

Understanding the Types of Permissions

When you are setting up your security, permissions are available for different types of objects in the database, but not for modules. Protecting modules is tackled differently.

Protecting modules is covered in the section "Closing Security Holes with MDE and ADE." For the database and the other objects, there are nine different types of permissions available:

- Open/Run—This permission applies to the database, forms, reports, and macros. If this permission is granted, the user can open the object and run any VBA procedures for the object. The user can also run macros.

- Open Exclusive—This applies to the database only. If this permission is set, the account or group can open the database and prevent others from opening it while they are in the database. This is very useful when you are making changes to the system. If other users happen to be logged in when the user attempts to open the database exclusive, they will get a message that they need to get the other users logged out and attempt the operation again.

- Read Design—This allows the user or group to open up objects in Design view. The user can look at the objects, properties, and code. The user will be able to make changes, but she will not be able to save the objects.

- Modify Design—This allows the user to make and save changes to objects as well as to delete the objects.

- Administer—This permission allows the user or group to set a database password and change the start up properties. For other objects, the user or group has full access, including the ability to assign permissions.

- Read Data—This permission allows the user to view the data and not make changes.

- Update Data—This permission allows the user to view and change the data.

- Insert Data—This permission allows the user to add new records.

- Delete Data—This permission allows the user to delete records.

Some of the permissions are linked, so when you set one, it automatically activates others. An example is Modify Design. If you select this permission, Read Design is automatically selected. This is to save you some time. If you want to be able to change a design, you must be able to read it.

Another factor of permissions is that for every object there is an owner. If a user or group is the owner of an object, that will override the permission settings. They will be able to

20

change the object, delete it, or change permissions for other users and groups. This allows other users to customize how they use the database. For example, if a user wants to see who has attended a specific seminar, the user can create his or her own query. When that query is no longer needed, the user can delete it.

Setting Permissions

When you set up a new workgroup and set up your user groups and accounts, all groups and users have the same permissions. You need to determine what permissions are needed for each group and account. After you have made the determination, you must set these permissions.

Setting up security first will make this task easier because you will have to set the permissions for new objects, and then each object created will receive those permissions. If you need to add security to an existing database, a better approach is to use the Security Wizard, which is discussed later in this lesson. It can save you a lot of time because it does much of the work for you.

 Tip

> If you must modify permissions to a group of objects, you can select more than one by clicking on the first one and Ctrl+clicking on the remainder.

When you are going to set up permissions, it is best to complete the group permissions first because doing so might enable you to avoid setting permissions for individual users. You might be asking why you created a Mgmt group instead of just modifying the permissions of KBrooks. Having a group will make it easier to give a new user the same permissions without having to set each permission for each object exactly like KBrooks.

If Kathy Brooks is promoted or fired, or the organization determines that the assistant manager can also approve events, it will speed up access for the new person. You have only to delete or add a user, assign her to the Mgmt group, and you are finished.

The first step is to reduce the permissions of the Users group so its members do not have the full access of the Admins group. They shouldn't be able to open the database exclusively and lock out other users, administer the database or modify any designs. Whether you want to grant them the View Design permission might depend on what types of actions they are going to take with the database. If they are going to perform mail merge with Microsoft Word, it might be helpful to be able to see the field types.

Task: Assigning Permissions to the Users Group

1. Select Tools, Security, User and Group Permissions to open the User and Group Permissions dialog (see Figure 20.16).

2. Select Groups to display the groups in the list.

3. Select users from the User/Group Name list.

FIGURE 20.16

The User and Group Permissions dialog is used to set permissions and change ownership.

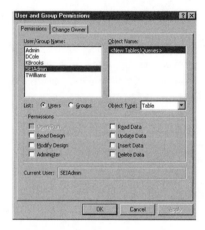

4. Select Database from the Object Type list.

5. Click on Open Exclusive and Administer to remove the permissions.

6. Click Apply to accept the changes and avoid being prompted to save the changes.

7. Select Table from the Object Type list and notice it is for tables and queries.

8. Click on Modify Design to remove this permission, and click Apply.

9. Select Form from the Object Type list.

10. Click on Read Design, Modify Design, and Administer to remove those permissions, and click Apply.

11. Select Report from the Object Type list.

12. Click on Read Design, Modify Design, and Administer to remove those permissions, and click Apply.

13. Select Macro from the Object Type list.

14. Click on Read Design, Modify Design, and Administer to remove those permissions, and click Apply.

15. Click OK.

20

You have set the permissions for the Users group. You would need to repeat these steps for the Mgmt group. In this example, the Mgmt group was added to restrict who can add events. Adding events will add records to the event table using a form. To restrict the access of general users to create new events, you would have to wait until the table and/or form was created. After the individual objects were created, you would remove the Update Data, Insert Data, and Delete Data permissions for those objects.

Examining the Advantages and Disadvantages of Using User-Level Security

The disadvantage of using user-level security is the time required to set up and maintain user-level security. It is much slower than setting a database password, but this disadvantage is outweighed by the significant advantages.

With user-level security, you have greater control over the access of the database. It is not all or nothing. If more than one person is going to access the database, you can control his access on an object basis. It also makes it easier to maintain a multi-user environment. With VBA, you can also change the appearance of the objects based on who the user is. For more information, this is illustrated in Day 21, "Developer Considerations."

Managing Passwords

Throughout this lesson, passwords have been the key to protecting a database. As with all passwords, keeping them secret is crucial. When you have completed the database, you might want to consider what guidelines you want to provide to the other users regarding passwords.

Note

> Throughout this lesson, the concept of creating good passwords has been stressed again and again. The reason this concept has been repeated is because it is the cornerstone to your security.
>
> If you set up a user-level security system and one of the users who is a member of the Admin group sets a bad password, someone who attempts to guess the user's password and succeeds has complete access to your system. They could delete data or destroy your interface. Everyone must follow the password guidelines to make it a well-secured system.

You will need to tell the other users that the passwords can be between 1 and 20 characters and that passwords are case-sensitive. Further, you might want to pass on the guidelines for passwords to make them harder for others to guess.

You might also want to let them know not to give their passwords to others, and to try to avoid letting people see over their shoulder as they log on. This is somewhat protected because what is typed is hidden with asterisks, but if a person can see what keys are pressed that benefit might be neutralized.

You must tell users to change their password the first time they log on. You might also want to recommend that they change their password every so many days. Regardless, they will need to follow the steps provided in the "Activating Security" section to change their password.

Using the Security Wizard

So far this lesson has dealt with setting up security from scratch before you begin your development. Unfortunately, many databases begin as single-user databases in which security is normally not an initial concern. As the database grows, more people need access and then you need security.

In those cases, you have many existing objects to add security to, and you created those systems with the default workgroup, but you need a special workgroup for this database. Microsoft Access provides a Security Wizard to assist with creating a workgroup and adding an existing database to that workgroup.

 To give you an example of using the Security Wizard, you are going to run it on the existing Security database provided on the CD. To begin, you need to switch back to the default workgroup.

 Note When you use the Security Wizard, it cannot import the Visual Basic references to other object libraries, and it will not import your toolbars and menus. These will have to be re-created.

Task: Joining the Default Workgroup

1. Exit Microsoft Access.

2. Select Start, Programs, Windows Explorer to launch the application.

3. Open the folder that contains the Microsoft Office files.

4. Locate the WorkGroupAdminShortcut file and double-click it to launch the Workgroup Administrator.

5. Close the Windows Explorer.

 6. Click Join.

20

7. Click the Browse button and use the dialog to locate and select the System.mdw file, which should be in the Office folder.

8. Click OK.

9. Click OK in the message box.

10. Select Exit.

11. Launch Microsoft Access and open the Security.mdb database from the folder you copied it to.

This is a copy of the students and classes database used in earlier lessons. You are now ready to run the Security Wizard.

Task: Running the Security Wizard

1. Select Tools, Security, User Level Security Wizard to launch the wizard (see Figure 20.17).

2. Access informs you that it will create a new workgroup file as well as create a new copy of the database.

3. Click Next to display the workgroup information file settings (see Figure 20.18).

FIGURE 20.17

The first step for the wizard is to determine whether you are using a workgroup already and to prompt whether you want to modify the workgroup you are working with or to create a new one.

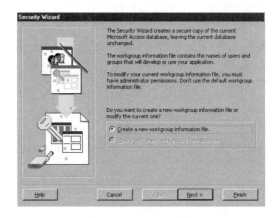

4. Use the default filename given or use the Browse button to select a new folder and filename. You can type a new WID or use the default provided.

5. Type in your name as the Your Name entry and type East High School in the Company text box.

6. Select I Want to Create a Shortcut to Open My Secured Database.

▼ 7. Click Next to display the object selection (see Figure 20.19).

FIGURE 20.18

This Security Wizard dialog prompts for the workgroup information.

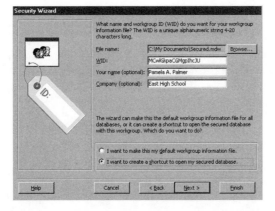

FIGURE 20.19

This Security Wizard dialog allows you to determine which objects to protect.

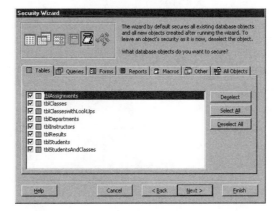

8. Notice as you click on the tabs that all existing objects are selected for securing, until the Other tab.

9. Click on the Other tab and select the Select All button.

10. Click the Next button to display the VBA project password choice (see Figure 20.20).

11. Type `SEIAdmin` as the password and select Next to display the group creation choices (see Figure 20.21).

12. Select Full Data Users and write down the name and Group ID.

13. Select Full Permissions and write down the name and Group ID.

▼ 14. Select Next to display the Users group permissions selection (see Figure 20.22).

20

FIGURE 20.20

This Security Wizard dialog sets a VB password.

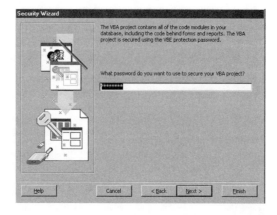

FIGURE 20.21

This Security Wizard dialog allows you to create your groups.

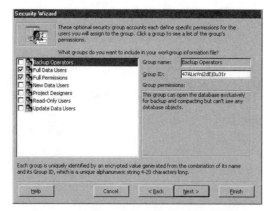

FIGURE 20.22

This Security Wizard dialog sets up permissions for the Users group.

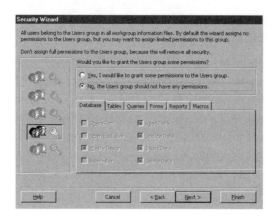

▼   15. Notice that the default is to give the Users group no permissions, and click Next to display the user set up (see Figure 20.23).

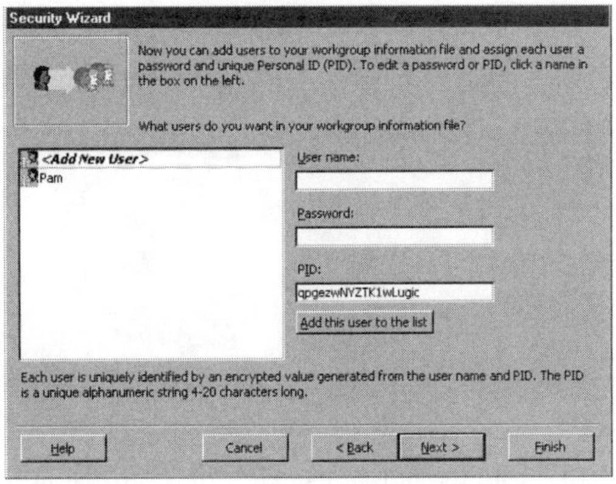

FIGURE 20.23

This Security Wizard dialog allows you to set up user accounts.

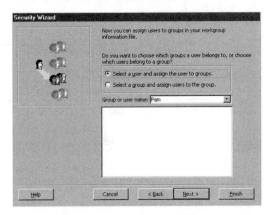

16. Type EHSAdmin in the User Name text box and EHSAdmin in the Password text box.

17. Select Add This User to the List.

18. Click on Add New User from the list to create as many users as needed and click Next to assign users to groups (see Figure 20.24).

FIGURE 20.24

This Security Wizard dialog assigns groups to users.

20

19. Select the Select a Group and Assign Users to the Group option.

20. Select the Admins group and select EHSAdmin.

21. Repeat for all of your groups.

▼   22. Click Next to display the database name entry (see Figure 20.25).

FIGURE 20.25

This final Security Wizard dialog allows you to give a new database name.

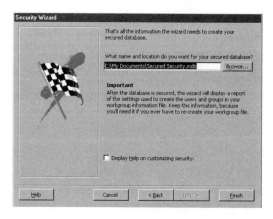

23. Select Finish to create the new files. After the conversion is complete, a report is displayed (see Figure 20.26).

FIGURE 20.26

The report serves as a record of your settings in case you need to re-create the security for the database.

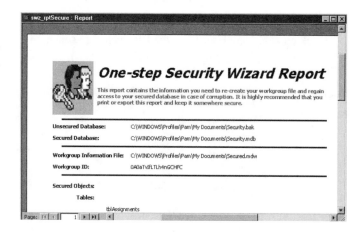

24. Print or export the report to store in a secure location in case the security becomes corrupted and it needs to be re-created.

From this point, you can use the new shortcut to open the database with its security. If you need to make any changes to security after you run the wizard, you can make them manually using the techniques in this lesson or re-run the wizard with the new database open.

Closing Security Holes with MDE and ADE

As you used the Security Wizard, it asked whether you wanted to set a VB project password. You can set a VB project password to protect your code from modification, but it still allows the code to be viewed and copied.

You might want to protect the VBA code from even being viewed and copied. This can prevent the users from attempting to create a form or report using your code, and then later coming to you for help if it doesn't work. Protecting your code is even more important if you are selling your databases. It is economically sound to protect your intellectual property.

To eliminate the possibility of the user having any access to your code, you can create an MDE from your Access database or an ADE file from your Access project. Both provide the same benefits.

When you create your database, you will create a standard MDB file, or if you are working with an Access project, you will create an ADP file. You will add all of the tables, queries, forms, reports, macros, and modules needed to create your interface. You will design and test your system to make sure it is working as expected. Then you will create the MDE or ADE file using the Tools, Database Utilities menu.

When you create the MDE or ADE file, Microsoft Access will compile all of the interface objects, remove the source code, and compact the file. This protects the interface from unauthorized access. The user will be able to open and run forms, reports, macros, and code, but she will not be able to look at the design or its underlying code. As an added benefit, the compiled file is smaller. It is optimized, so it will take up less space and will use less memory.

The user will be able to use all of the objects, but she won't be able to make modifications. The user will not be able to add, delete, or modify the objects or references. The user cannot rename objects, nor can she import or export objects to another database to borrow your design.

There are some rules that you need to follow if you are going to use an MDE or ADE file. The first rule is you need to save the original file that was used to create the MDE or ADE. If you need to make any changes to the database, you will make the changes to the original and then create the MDE or ADE file again.

Because you cannot change the MDE or ADE file, you should consider placing the tables in a separate database and creating a link to that database. Then you can overlay the new MDE or ADE file and not have to be concerned with losing data. For additional information on linking to another database, please refer to Day 21, "Developer Considerations."

20

If you are using replication on a database and you want to make it into an MDE file, it cannot happen directly. You must remove the database from replication, and then you will make the file and add it to replication.

If you set up code passwords, you must remove them. If your code cannot be accessed, it cannot be compiled. After you have created the MDE or ADE file, the passwords aren't needed because the code is removed.

As stated earlier, it is possible to borrow functionality from other applications that support VBA by setting up references. If you establish references for any other Microsoft Access databases, they must also be saved as MDE or ADE to be used.

When a new version of Microsoft Access becomes available, it will not automatically convert MDE and ADE files. You will have to convert the MDE and ADP source files and then re-make the MDE or ADE files.

With these guidelines, you are ready to create the MDE file.

Task: Making an MDE from the Security.MDB File

1. Select Tools, Database Utilities, Make MDE File to open the Database to Save as MDE dialog (see Figure 20.27).

2. Click Browse and select the Security.MDB file.

3. Click the Make MDE button to display the Save MDE As dialog (see Figure 20.28).

FIGURE 20.27

The Database to Save as MDE dialog allows you to select the file to use as the source.

4. Enter a new filename if desired, and click Save.

FIGURE 20.28

The Save MDE As dialog allows you to provide a name for the MDE file.

Access will compile the database, remove the code, and compact to the new filename. It is now ready to copy to where the users are looking, and it is ready to run. If you open the new Security.MDE file, you will notice that the Design and New buttons are disabled for forms, reports, macros, and modules.

Summary

Today's lesson introduced some of the methods for protecting your database. If you only need to keep people from opening the database, setting a database password will probably handle your security needs.

If you need various levels of access for your users, you will need to move to user-level security, which allows you to control security on an object basis by setting up groups, users, and permissions.

The last form of security discussed was protecting your interface objects from inadvertent access and theft. This can be done by creating an MDE or ADE file. The objects are compiled, the code is removed, and the new file is compacted. As an extra benefit, the code should run faster and take up less space in memory and on the drive.

20

Q&A

Q Can I use user-level security with MDE and ADE files?

A Yes, you can. You would set up the MDB or ADP file with its security and then create the MDE or ADE file.

Q Can I make it easier for users to set passwords without the User and Group Accounts dialog?

A Yes, you can create a form to get the password and a verification word. Test to see that they match and create the password with VBA.

Q Can I change my interface based on who is logged in?

A Yes, you can. You will need to use the User function to see who is logged in. For more information, please refer to Day 21, "Developer Considerations."

Workshop

The Workshop helps you solidify the skills you learned in this lesson. Answers to the quiz questions appear in Appendix A, "Answers."

Quiz

1. What is the length of a workgroup ID?
2. Why do you always have to set up permissions when you create a new workgroup?
3. What is the benefit of using a database password?

Exercises

1. Add a new group for Accounting to SEI Security.
2. Add a new user named Mary Campbell to SEI Security.
3. Create an MDE from the Events database from Day 19, "Working with VBA."

DAY 21

Developer Considerations

When you begin to consider allowing others to work with your database, you must determine what kind of access is needed, where you are going to store the data, and how to get assistance to users when they are accessing your system. Today's lesson covers the following topics:

- Examining multiuser considerations
- Using external data sources
- Accessing the Win32 API
- Adding help to your applications
- Setting the database startup properties

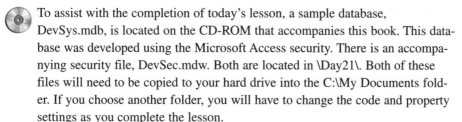 To assist with the completion of today's lesson, a sample database, DevSys.mdb, is located on the CD-ROM that accompanies this book. This database was developed using the Microsoft Access security. There is an accompanying security file, DevSec.mdw. Both are located in \Day21\. Both of these files will need to be copied to your hard drive into the C:\My Documents folder. If you choose another folder, you will have to change the code and property settings as you complete the lesson.

The sample database is a copy of the database used in Day 19, "Working with VBA." It tracks event scheduling for a conference center. It will be used as a foundation for completing the application started in previous sections.

Examining Multiuser Considerations

As you have completed the previous lessons, you have been working toward building a database application. Creating an application can speed up your access to your data and the forms and reports you have created. On Day 20, "Understanding Access Security," you started to explore ways to secure your database. This step becomes necessary as you want to allow other users to have access to your system. Because you want to allow other users to have access to your database, you must take a little more time planning your database in addition to determining your security strategy. You must also determine your database storage and access needs, the structure of your system, and record locking. Each of these is examined today.

It is best that you consider these items before you begin creating your database. If you have created a database and others begin to need access, it is not a tragedy. You can always go back and add multiuser access. It just takes more work than if you think of these issues before you begin.

Determining Your Database Needs

When you are developing a system to support more than one user, you must think in terms of growth. There is a good chance the amount of data stored in the system will increase. You will also be increasing the number of people accessing the system at once. You also must take into account that more people using a system will increase the administration demands on you. All these areas will affect how you structure the database, and you must carefully consider them before you make any decisions. Each of these areas is examined in greater detail today.

Determining the Amount of Data

One of the first things you must consider is the amount of data that the system will need to process and store. This can be a determining factor as to where you store your data. When you work with Microsoft Access, keep in mind that a Microsoft Access file cannot exceed 2GB in size. If you have both the interface and the tables stored in the same file, this limit also includes the temporary space accumulated as you run queries and use VBA to create recordsets. At a minimum, you must establish a regular schedule for compacting your database.

It is OK if you are close to the 2GB limit; Microsoft Access allows you to access data stored in an external source. That means you can have a file for the data and a file for the interface objects. You can even go so far as to place each table in a separate Microsoft Access file. This does mean that no one individual table can exceed 1GB.

If your data needs are going to exceed this limit, you must consider another storage medium. Microsoft Access enables you to access many external sources. For example, you could place your data in Microsoft SQL Server, which is a client/server database. Its size limitation provides greater flexibility. The file size cannot exceed 1TB. Using Microsoft SQL Server is not without some drawbacks. You will have to learn how to manage your data with SQL Server and you will have some additional administration duties.

You also have access to other database formats through *Open Database Connectivity* (ODBC). If you are already storing your data in another format, like DB2 or Oracle, and you have the appropriate driver, you can access the data from Microsoft Access.

 Note   If you are not sure about the amount of data, or this is a small database that is outgrowing the storage capability of Microsoft Access, you aren't stuck with your choice. As your database grows, you can export it to another source for storage. Also, the Upsizing Wizard is available under Tools, Database Utilities to help you move to Microsoft SQL Server.

Determining the Number of Users

After you have analyzed your data storage needs, you must look at how many users will need access to your database system. This question is not as easy as the data storage question. Although the limit for concurrent users is 255, that number can be smaller. Here you must look at the type of access the users need as well as how many users will be accessing the data at one time.

Another factor in this decision is your hardware. The method the users will use to access the data, the speed of their machines and your server, as well as the operating systems being used can be factors in this decision. The type of user interaction is also important. If you have a group of users who are only inserting new records, their use of the system is dramatically different from many users who must look up information and user queries.

Again, if you are not sure of the answers to these questions, Microsoft Access is very forgiving. With the ability to move to another storage medium and still use Microsoft Access for your interface, you can adapt as the usage changes.

21

Determining the Type of Support Available

Another factor in the decision-making process is what types of support are going to be needed for this system. If you will be the only one supporting this system, keeping it in Microsoft Access might be beneficial because you understand the techniques to maintain the system. If you use Microsoft SQL Server as the data storage, you must consider the time required to maintain the Microsoft SQL Server environment. If you are developing for a company that already has a team administering Microsoft SQL Server, this might not be an issue at all.

Determining Your Database Structure

The reason you were gathering information about the amount of data, the number of users, and their use needs is that you must determine the structure of your database. When you were the only person accessing your system, keeping everything in one file on your machine was an effective means for maintaining the system. As more people use the system, this will have to change.

When you design your system, you are going to choose between these structures. You might decide to move the database to your network and have everyone share the same file. A second approach is to replicate the database so everyone has his or her own copy. A third approach is to use the Internet for access. A last approach is to divide the interface from the data; you place the data and security file on the network, and everyone gets his or her own copy of the interface.

Sharing the System

If you developed a database for your own use, you will most likely move it to the network so everyone can use the same file initially. The benefit of this approach is that it is quick to implement. After you set up your choice for securing the database, you use the Windows Explorer to copy it to the network. You then notify everyone where the database is, and you are in business.

The problem with this approach is that everyone is using the same file. Depending on the number of users, and whether they are using it at the same time, the response time will dramatically increase. It might take so long to get a response that using the database will lose its benefit.

Replicating the Database

NEW TERM   The second approach supported by Microsoft Access is *replication*. Replication is the process of making special copies of the database, called replicas. Each user has his own copy of the database. The users will have the access you give them in the security setup process, but everyone will be working independently. The benefit of this approach is the response time for each user. Because each user is working with a separate copy on his or her machine, no one has to wait for anyone else.

This approach isn't for all systems because there are some drawbacks. It is ideal for users who only need to look up information, for users who spend most of their time inserting new information, and for users who will deal with only a subset of the records rather than use all of them. An example is a remote sales team. Each salesperson has his own client list, and the salesperson looks up prices and inserts new orders. The crossover between affected records will be minimal or none.

The drawbacks include a time lapse to get a complete picture of all the data and the additional administration required. To use this approach, you will have to create the replicas and distribute them to the users. As soon as the first user makes a change, no one has a complete picture of the data, including you. Your master database will not show the change made in user 1's replica.

This is where the administration will increase. You will have to determine how often you must update your master database to get back to a clear picture. Also, you will have to develop a schedule to get the replicas back from the users. When you get the database replicas back, you will use the replication tools to integrate all the changes made by everyone. If more than one user makes a change to the same record, you will have to resolve any conflicts between those changes.

In a best-case scenario, the users could upload their replicas each evening and use VBA to integrate the changes. You will still have to reconcile problems and get the database back to the users so they can continue to work. It will require some down time for the users in which they cannot make changes to their replica.

Using the Internet

The third possibility is to use the Internet. If the users only need to see data, you could publish your reports on the Internet to let them browse through a report or even print a copy. If they need to interact with the data, you could use one of the new Data Access Pages. Both of these approaches might be a possibility for you.

For additional information on publishing your reports for the Internet, please refer to Day 17, "Developing Professional-Quality Reports." For more information on creating and using Data Access Pages, please refer to Day 8, "Data Access Pages."

Splitting the Database

The last approach is to separate the data from the interface in two separate files. You place the data and the security file on the network and place a copy of the database with the interface on each user's machine. This approach has many advantages and is the most popular structure for multiuser development. The first benefit is the ability to grow. With the data in a separate file, you have more room to add new data. If you outgrow Microsoft Access for your data storage, you can migrate to the new source and establish a link from the interface. Often this can be done with no change to your interface.

The second benefit is the response time for the users. Because the processing is occurring on their machines, the loss of speed because of someone else's actions will not affect each user as much.

The third benefit is for the developer. You can make modifications to the system without disrupting everyone's work. The users can continue working with the data with the existing system. When you implement a change, you can distribute a new copy of the interface to overlay the old one on their machines easily. The overlay of a new interface might take some additional coding to make this seamless to the user. To make this easier for you if you already have a database, a Database Splitter Wizard is located under Tools, Database Utilities to assist with the process of splitting a database.

 Tip

> You might not see the Database Splitter Wizard when you first click the Tools, Database Utilities menu. This menu doesn't show all the options initially to make it easier to locate the commands you use the most. You might need to click the down arrow on the menu to display all the menu items before you can select the Database Splitter Wizard.

This approach will get additional coverage later in this lesson. You are going to manually walk through the process of splitting a database, as well as take a look at Microsoft's code for making it seamless for the user.

Determining a Record-Locking Strategy

After you have selected a structure, you must determine how you are going to protect against attempted concurrent changes to the data. You are going to determine what type of record locking is required for your system.

You can set up record locking on a form or query basis by using the Record Locks property. You can also set the default for this property for new forms and queries with your options. When you are using VBA and ADO to create recordsets, record locking is controlled by one of the arguments for the Open method.

There are three settings for record locking. You can choose for No Locks, All Records, or Edited Records. Each of these will have an impact on response time and user access. The default set up by Microsoft Access is No Locks. The No Locks setting provides the quickest response time as you navigate and make changes because there is no tracking or reporting of edits. That means if someone opens a form or query and begins to make changes to a record, no other user will know that those changes are in progress. Additional users can access the same record and begin to make their changes simultaneously. The last user to update the record wins; that user's version of the record is the one available for others to use in the future.

The second setting is to use All Records. This means no one can access a recordset after a user begins editing a record. If a user opens a form or query and begins to edit a record, no one else will be able to open the form or query. The user will get a message box (see Figure 21.1) informing him that he cannot lock the underlying table. If a user is already in a form or query and he attempts to make a change, his changes will not register in the table. This has the benefit of preventing concurrent edits, but it can also prevent users from even viewing information. It is great when you are making global changes to the table, such as with an action query.

FIGURE 21.1

Using an All Records setting for the Record Locks property will prevent other users from accessing the records.

The last setting is one you will probably want to use most of the time. You can set the Record Locks property to Edited Record. This will allow other users to view other records and even the record being changed, but it will not allow others to make changes to the record with an edit in progress.

If a user has edited a record and another user accesses that record, the record selector will display the international not symbol (see Figure 21.2). This will indicate that an edit is in progress. If the user misses that indicator and attempts to change a field, the change will not register. This allows access to all the other records, as well as viewing privileges for the record being changed, without creating confusion by not knowing when a change is taking place.

The Edited Record setting is great for protecting against concurrent changes, but there is some overhead associated with it. You might have noticed that when you have a database open, a new file is created in the same folder as the database. The new file has the same name as the database, but it has an .LDB extension. An LDB file is a temporary file that stores the record-locking information.

21

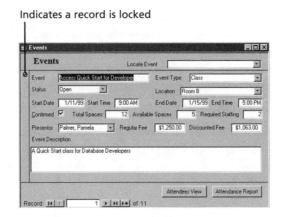

Indicates a record is locked

FIGURE 21.2

Using the Edited Record setting for the Record Locks property will prevent other users from editing a record that is already being edited.

The overhead associated with this setting is to update this temporary file. As you begin editing a record, this file must be updated to lock that record or all the records, depending on the Record Locks property. As you navigate between records, this file must be checked to determine whether the record is locked to know what type of access you are going to have.

Regardless of the overhead, you will still want to use this setting most of the time to protect against concurrent edits. The Edited Record setting has been improved with this release of Microsoft Access. This setting used to lock more than the record being edited. It used page locking, and locked the surrounding 2KB. Now you have a choice. You can lock the surrounding page, which is now 4KB, or you can lock the specific record. This can be set up with your options.

Ideally, you make these record-locking decisions before you begin developing a new database. That way you can set up your defaults for all the new objects you create. To set up your default record locking strategy, complete the following task.

Task: Setting the Default Record-Locking Method

TASK

1. With a database open, select Tools, Options.

2. Select the Advanced tab (see Figure 21.3).

3. Select Shared as the Default Open Mode.

4. Select the Default Record Locking setting of your choice.

 5. Select the Open Databases Using Record-Level Locking check box if you want.

For those objects you have already created before changing your options, you will have to open the object, open the Properties window, and manually change the Record Locks property. It is under the general properties for queries, and under the Data tab for forms and reports.

FIGURE 21.3

The Advanced tab for the Options dialog lets you set up your defaults.

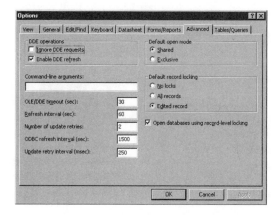

Splitting a Database

After you have made the decisions regarding multiuser access, implement them and begin developing your system, or get your existing database ready to use these decisions. If you can make these decisions before you do any development, you are better off because they will take less time to implement. The most common approach is to have the data separate from the system and use linking to provide the access. You will use the Edited Record setting for most forms and queries for your system to protect against concurrent changes. If you are starting a new system, you will need to complete the following:

1. Set up your workgroup information file using the Workgroup Administrator, as explained in Day 20.
2. Launch Microsoft Access.
3. Create a database file for the data.
4. Set up your default options as described earlier.
5. Create your tables.
6. Close the data database.
7. Create a database for your interface.
8. Create a link to your tables.
9. Begin your development.

Unfortunately, you might not have the opportunity to begin from scratch. You might already have an existing system. In that case, the process is a little more complicated. For the rest of this section, you will walk through splitting your existing system and getting it

21

ready to have more than one user accessing the system at one time. To save some time, it is assumed that you have already completed the steps in Day 20 to implement user-level security.

Do	**DON'T**
DO remember to back up your system before attempting to split it into two databases.	**DON'T** forget to give the files unique descriptive names so you can tell the data file from the system and security files. This will assist with the distribution of the system to your users.

Joining the Workgroup

To complete the rest of this section, you must have copied the files from the CD. You will need to join the workgroup with the security for the sample file. To do so, complete the following task.

Task: Joining the DevSys Workgroup

1. Select Start, Programs, Windows Explorer to launch the application.
2. Open the folder that contains the Microsoft Office files.
3. Locate the MS Access WorkGroup Administrator shortcut file and double-click to launch the Workgroup Administrator.
4. Close the Windows Explorer.
5. Click the Join button to open the Workgroup Information File dialog.
6. Click the Browse button to locate the DevSec.MDW file.
7. Click OK after the file is displayed in this dialog, and click OK to confirm that you have joined the workgroup.
8. Click Exit to close the Workgroup Administrator.

Getting Ready to Create a Data Database

After you have joined the workgroup, you must get a new database and set your default options. To do so, complete the steps in the following task.

Task: Creating a Database to Store the Tables

1. Launch Microsoft Access.
2. Select Create New Database Using Blank Access Database from the initial dialog box.

▼

3. Name the database DevData.mdb and place it in the same folder as the security and system files.

4. Enter `DevAdmin` as the Name in the Logon dialog box and press Enter because there isn't a password at this time.

5. Select Tools, Options, and then select the Advanced tab.

6. Select Shared as the Default Open Mode, and select Edited Record as the Default Record Locking.

7. Make sure the Open Database Using Record-Level Locking check box is selected. Click OK.

8. Close the database that will store the tables. You will move the tables from the original database in a little bit.

▲

9. Open DevSys.mdb.

Setting the Record-Locking Properties

When you have an existing database, you might have to adjust the record-locking properties of your existing objects. This must be done with the Record Locks property for each object. The first question you must ask is, "Will the user be accessing the object directly?" In the case of many queries, the answer is no. With reports, the data isn't being modified, so record locking is not an issue.

With the forms, you might need to make a judgement call. With frmAdministrationSwitchboard, frmEventSelection, frmReportSwitchboard, and frmSwitchboard, record locking is not an issue because they do not have record sources. With all the others, you will need to adjust the Record Locks property. To set the property, complete the following task.

Task: Setting Record Locking for Existing Objects

1. Open frmAttendees in Design mode.

2. Open the Properties window and select the Data tab.

3. Select Edited Record for the Record Locks property.

4. Save and close the form.

5. Repeat steps 1–4 for frmEventAttendees, frmEvents, frmEventTypes, frmPaymentMethods, frmPresenters, frmRoomSpecifications, and sfrmRegistration.

▲

6. Close DevSys.mdb.

21

If the majority of the forms must be changed, you might consider using the `For...Each...Next` statement introduced in Day 18. You can use VBA to go through the

Forms collections, modify the property, and then manually reset the few forms that do not need to change. Depending on the number of objects that need to change, this might save you quite a bit of time.

Using External Data Sources

Now you have two databases, but you have not transferred the tables from one to the other. Microsoft Access is very supportive of sharing information, both between databases and to and from outside sources. You can import database objects from an Access database or other format, export data from an Access database to an Access database or other format, as well as create a link to another database source.

When you are splitting a database, you use the Import function to move the tables from the system database to the data database. Then you open the system database and create a link to the data database. In this section, you will also see how to get data from an outside source. In this case, you will use an Excel spreadsheet.

Moving the Tables from the System Database

After the database is created and the options are set, you are ready to move the tables from the original database. You do not need to have the record locking set for the interface objects. You could have saved the steps for opening and closing the databases by reversing this step with the record-locking step.

Microsoft Access is very supportive of copying objects from other databases, as well as using data from an external source. For this step, you are going to use the Import command. At this stage, you will need to make sure no one else is in the system database because you will be removing the data temporarily. If anyone is accessing the tables, you will get a message informing you that you cannot delete a table because it is in use.

Importing the Tables

The first step is to get the tables from the system database into your new data database. To import the tables from DevSys.mdb into DevData.mdb, complete the following task.

Task: Moving the Tables into the Data Database

▼ TASK

1. Open DevData.mdb.
2. Select File, Get External Data, Import to open the file browser.
3. Select DevSys.mdb from the correct folder.
4. Select Import to open the Import Objects dialog (see Figure 21.4).
5. Select the Tables tab if needed.
6. Click the Select All button.

▼

▼
FIGURE 21.4

The Import Objects dialog lets you select the objects to import.

▲   7. Click the OK button to begin the import process.

Depending on the number of tables, this process might take a few minutes. After it is complete, you are ready to remove the tables from the system database.

Removing the Tables from the System Database

Now the tables are in two locations. You want to remove them from the system database so that you can create a link to the new database. To remove the tables from the system database, work through the following task.

Task: Deleting the Tables from the System Database

1. Close DevData.mdb.
2. Open DevSys.mdb.
3. Select the first table and press the Delete key.
4. Click Yes to confirm the deletion in the message box (see Figure 21.5).

FIGURE 21.5

Select Yes to confirm the deletion.

5. If there is a relationship between the table you are deleting and other tables, you will have to select Yes to delete the relationships in the message box (see Figure 21.6).

FIGURE 21.6

You will also have to delete any relationships.

21

▲   6. Repeat steps 1 through 4 for the remaining tables.

After the tables are deleted, you must create a link to them.

Creating a Link to the New Database

Now the tables exist in DevData.mdb only. If you attempt to open any queries, forms, or reports in DevSys.mdb, you will get an error message (see Figure 21.7). You are now going to link to DevData.mdb.

FIGURE 21.7

You will get an error message if you try to open objects dependent on the tables.

To create a link to the tables in DevData.mdb, complete the following task.

Task: Creating a Link to the DevData Tables

1. Select File, Get External Data, Link Tables to open the link file browser.

2. Select DevData.mdb from the correct folder and select Link to open the Link Tables dialog (see Figure 21.8).

3. Notice that the only tab is Tables. You cannot link to other objects.

FIGURE 21.8

The Link Tables dialog allows you to select the tables for which to create a link.

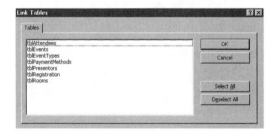

4. Click the Select All button to select all the tables.

 5. Click OK to link the tables.

After a few moments, the tables will be displayed on the Tables list in the Database window for DevSys.mdb. Their icons will be displayed differently—there will be an arrow next to them (see Figure 21.9). This indicates that this is a link instead of a local table.

FIGURE 21.9

A linked table shows a table icon with an arrow next to it to distinguish it from local tables.

Now that the tables are linked, your queries, forms, and reports will be fine. If you open any of them, you will not get an error message. You will see the query, form, or report displayed with its data.

If you attempt to open a linked table in Design mode, Microsoft Access prevents you from making some changes. If you select a table and select the Design button, you will see a message box informing you that you can't make all changes because the table is linked (see Figure 21.10).

FIGURE 21.10

Linked tables have some restrictions if you try to modify their design from another database.

If you select Yes in this message box, you can still view the table structure but you cannot change certain properties, such as Name. Another factor is that the connection to the table is controlled by a property. If you open the Table Properties window, you will see that the description indicates the full path for the database that contains the table (see Figure 21.11).

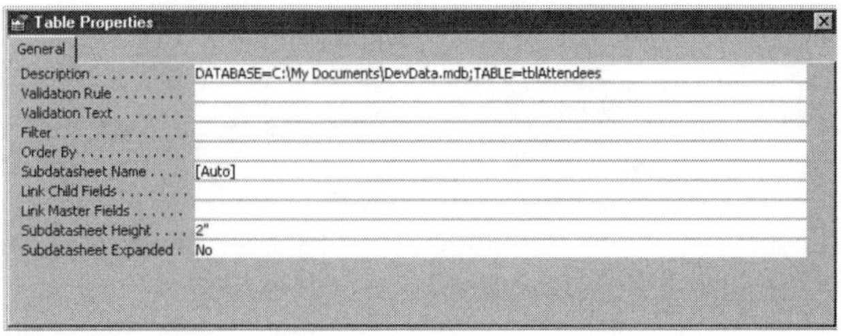

FIGURE 21.11

Linked tables are also dependent on the name and location of the source database. If that information changes, the tables must be relinked.

21

If the database is renamed or moved, this link will be invalid. This information is also stored in the Connect property for the table. If many users access the system, having them relink to the tables might create confusion and support problems. Later today, in "Accessing the Win32 API," you will see how to automate relinking tables.

Accessing Data from an Outside Source

In addition to importing Access objects and creating links to Access tables, you can also work with other formats. You can import from and export to outside sources including other databases, text files, and spreadsheets. You can also create links to other database formats, such as Microsoft SQL Server.

When you are importing from an outside source, Microsoft Access offers as much assistance as possible through the Import Wizard. To give you a chance to see it in action, you are going to walk through importing a Microsoft Excel worksheet. If someone sent a worksheet of attendees to be integrated with your list, you could save yourself the time entering data by using the Import function. To import a Microsoft Excel worksheet, complete the following task.

Task: Import an Excel Worksheet

1. Select File, Get External Data, Import to open the Import file browser.

2. Select Microsoft Excel as the File Type.

3. Select Students from the file list.

4. Select Import to open the Import Spreadsheet Wizard (see Figure 21.12).

FIGURE 21.12

The Import Spreadsheet Wizard will assist you with matching the data to fields in your table.

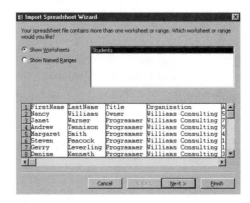

5. If necessary, select the Students worksheet from the list, and click Next to display the column headings selection screen (see Figure 21.13).

FIGURE 21.13

If the spreadsheet has column headings, you can indicate that here.

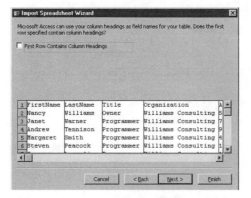

6. Make sure that First Row Contains Column Headings is selected and click Next to determine where to import the data (see Figure 21.14).

FIGURE 21.14

You can choose to import into an existing table or create a new one.

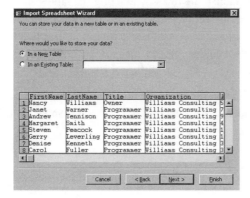

7. Select In an Existing Table, and select tblAttendees. Click Next to change any attributes about the spreadsheet data (see Figure 21.15).

8. Click Finish to complete the import.

9. Click OK to close the message box indicating the import is complete.

10. Open tblAttendees to see the new data at the bottom of the table.

For importing all kinds of data, there are wizards to assist you with matching your structures with the data being imported. You can also create new tables and then integrate the data with existing tables using an append query to give you a greater level of control over the data. The key is not to waste your time re-entering data that already exists in another format. In most cases, you can import it with very little trouble.

21

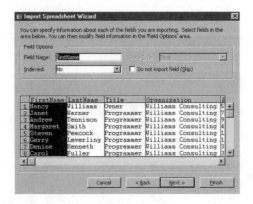

Accessing the Win32 API

In the previous section, you created links to the tables in the new database. If the location of the database changes or if the database is renamed, the links will not be valid. The user will have to re-establish the links by deleting the tables and relinking them. This can be confusing and annoying for a user with less experience than you received when you created the links in the first place. You knew what file you were looking for and what tables were needed. Re-establishing the links might send the user on a file hunt all over his system and the network with very little guidance.

You might consider automating the process with VBA. To accomplish this task, you are going to use VBA and take advantage of the Windows Application Programming Interface (API).

Understanding the API

One of the benefits of working with the Windows environment from a user perspective is that after you learn how to do something like close a window, operate a menu, or use a dialog, that knowledge can be used in other applications because all application use the same techniques for those functions. This minimizes the learning curve as you pick up new applications. This is not a coincidence. Whether you are developing a system using Microsoft Access and Visual Basic for Applications or using another language like Visual Basic or C++, you are taking advantage of general Windows routines or procedures. These procedures are known as the Windows API. They control the appearance of windows, the behavior of menus and controls, and specific general processes like file browsing.

When you are using Microsoft Access and VBA, you are taking advantage of the API. It is using the API, but its use is hidden from you because the use is built into the objects you are working with, such as the forms to create windows.

Most of what you need to accomplish in your system can be taken care of by using the Microsoft Access objects and their properties, methods, and events. When VBA was developed, Microsoft recognized that there might be times when you need to have more direct contact with the API; therefore, the capability to call API functions directly was included. There are many API functions, but many of them are not needed in Microsoft Access because of the Microsoft Access objects.

One good use for the API is to assist with the process of dynamically linking to the tables when you split the database. You should check to make sure the links are valid as the user launches the database. If they are, there isn't a problem. The user can begin working. If the connection isn't valid, you should indicate a problem to the user and provide a mechanism for her to locate the file so you can use VBA to re-establish the links. When most users want to locate a file, they are used to using the File Open dialog or what is commonly referred to as a file browser.

Using the standard File Open dialog isn't a part of Microsoft Access. This is a time when you might want to access the Windows API directly. After the user locates the file, you can use that information to re-establish the connections.

Using the API

Taking advantage of one of the API functions is a two-step process. The first step is to declare the function in your code and define any variables, constants, or user-defined types needed for the function. The second step is to call the function in your VBA code to activate it and get the action or information required.

The Windows API is the generic programming interface for Windows. It is designed to be accessed from many languages. With VBA and Visual Basic, much of the functionality is hidden with the use of objects, properties, methods, and events; there is often very little need to access the API directly. With C++, the need is greater because programmers control the behavior of objects directly.

Because of this difference, the Windows API syntax is much more like C++ than VBA. This might make using the API a little difficult for you. To assist you with using the API, the Office Developer's Edition has a Windows API Viewer and an associated help file to provide information on the functions, syntax, and argument requirements for the API.

Declaring an API Function

The first step is to declare the function. This must be done in the General Declarations section of a module. The function must have the following syntax:

```
Declare Function functionname Lib libraryname, [Alias aliasname]
➥(argumentlist) as Type
```

21

The function begins with the Declare keyword to indicate the intention to use an outside function. This is followed by the Function or Sub keyword to indicate what type of procedure you are accessing. The majority of procedures are functions.

This is followed by the name of the function. The next word is the Lib keyword. The procedures are not stored as separate files on the computer; they are bundled together and stored in libraries, which are files on the computer. Lib is followed by the name of the file inside quotations. You will not include a path because the libraries are registered and Windows knows where they are.

In some cases, the library name might be followed by the Alias keyword and an alias name in quotations. This combination is included because C++ and VBA have different rules for naming procedures. This allows you to have a name for the function that meets the VBA rules, and then to use the alias to indicate its true name. The help file provided is very useful because it includes the Declare statements, and you will want to use them when calling them from VBA.

This is followed by the list of arguments inside parentheses. If it is a function, you will also include the As keyword and the data type that will be returned. This is another area that might cause some problems because the C++ data types are different from VBA. Again, the help file is useful because it will provide the VBA compatible data type.

 Caution

> The most common difference between C++ data types and VBA data types is the String type. C++ stores strings with a null terminator. To send a VBA string to an API call, you must add the null character to the string. This is illustrated in the dynamic linking example with the modDynamicLinks module.

This declaration is followed with the variable, constant, and user-defined types required by the function. The help file will also include those for you to copy and paste.

Using an API Function

After the function is declared, you can use it as you would any of the built-in functions or one of your user-defined functions. You will set up a variable with a matching data type to the function and then set up an expression:

```
Dim strFileName as String
strFileName = functionname(argumentlist)
```

Using an API Function to Locate DevData.mdb

To retrieve the location of the data file, you use two API functions: GetOpenFileName and GetSaveFileName. They open and control the standard File Open and File Save dialogs. In previous releases of Microsoft Access, Microsoft included an example of dynamic linking with the Solutions database. With greater emphasis on using SQL Server, this sample database wasn't included.

To illustrate dynamic linking with an Access database, a revised version of the dynamic linking module from the Solutions database has been included in DevSys.MDB. You are going to open it and examine the code that makes this work. Then you will add code to call the function to the frmSwitchboard form.

The modDynamicLinks module has many lines of code to control the dynamic linking process, which is why you are examining this code instead of typing it. In addition, within the general declarations section, there are 12 functions. Each is discussed separately below.

Examining the General Declarations

When you open this module in the Visual Basic Editor, the first thing you see is the general declarations. This has the variable and constants needed for this task as well as the API function declarations as shown in Listing 21.1.

LISTING 21.1 THE MODDYNAMICLINK GENERAL DECLARATIONS

```
Option Explicit
Option Compare Database

'    Declaration of API Functions
Declare Function GetOpenFileName Lib "comdlg32.dll" Alias _
    "GetOpenFileNameA" (pOpenfilename As OPENFILENAME) As Boolean
Declare Function GetSaveFileName Lib "comdlg32.dll" Alias _
    "GetSaveFileNameA" (pOpenfilename As OPENFILENAME) As Boolean

'    Type Declaration for the GetOpenFileName and GetSaveFileName.
Type MSA_OPENFILENAME
    strFilter As String        'Used for the File Type Dropdown
    ' Created with MSA_CreateFilterString()
    ' Default = All Files, *.*
    lngFilterIndex As Long    'Initial filter to display
    ' Default = 1
    strInitialDir As String   'Initial directory to open in.
    ' Default = Current working directory.
    strInitialFile As String 'Default file name
```

continues

21

LISTING 21.1   CONTINUED

```
        ' Default = ""
        strDialogTitle As String
        strDefaultExtension As String
        ' Default = System Values (Open File, Save File).
        lngFlags As Long 'Flags (see constant list) to be used.
        ' Default = no flags.
        strFullPathReturned As String ' Full path of file picked.
        ' If a nonexistent file is entered,
        ' only the text in the "File Name" box is returned.
        strFileNameReturned As String ' File name of file picked.
        intFileOffset As Integer
        ' Offset in full path (strFullPathReturned) where the file name
        ' (strFileNameReturned) begins.
        intFileExtension As Integer
        ' Offset in (strFullPathReturned) where the extension begins.
End Type

Const ALLFILES = "All Files"

Type OPENFILENAME
        lStructSize As Long
        hwndOwner As Long
        hInstance As Long
        lpstrFilter As String
        lpstrCustomFilter As Long
        nMaxCustrFilter As Long
        nFilterIndex As Long
        lpstrFile As String
        nMaxFile As Long
        lpstrFileTitle As String
        nMaxFileTitle As Long
        lpstrInitialDir As String
        lpstrTitle As String
        Flags As Long
        nFileOffset As Integer
        nFileExtension As Integer
        lpstrDefExt As String
        lCustrData As Long
        lpfnHook As Long
        lpTemplateName As Long
End Type

'    Constants for GetOpenFileName and GetSaveFileName
Const OFN_ALLOWMULTISELECT = &H200
Const OFN_CREATEPROMPT = &H2000
Const OFN_EXPLORER = &H80000
Const OFN_FILEMUSTEXIST = &H1000
Const OFN_HIDEREADONLY = &H4
Const OFN_NOCHANGEDIR = &H8
```

```
Const OFN_NODEREFERENCELINKS = &H100000
Const OFN_NONETWORKBUTTON = &H20000
Const OFN_NOREADONLYRETURN = &H8000
Const OFN_NOVALIDATE = &H100
Const OFN_OVERWRITEPROMPT = &H2
Const OFN_PATHMUSTEXIST = &H800
Const OFN_READONLY = &H1
Const OFN_SHOWHELP = &H10


'   Constants for Application Specific Information
Const strDATABASE As String = "Events Management"
Const strFILE As String = "DevData.MDB"
Const strPATH As String = "C:\My Documents\"
Const strTable As String = "tblEventTypes"
```

The Option Explicit and Option Compare Database lines set up the variable declaration and sorting options for this module. These two lines are inserted automatically based on your option settings.

The next five lines are the API function declarations. You have the declarations for both the File Open and the File Save As. In this example, you are only going to call on the GetOpenFileName dialog. Notice that both functions use an alias because both functions have two versions to support different development languages. They also expect an argument for a user-defined type.

As introduced in Day 18, a user-defined type allows you to create a variable data type combining several variables. The next 26 lines declare that user-defined type.

For MSA_OPENFILENAME, the individual variables provide information to set the options for the dialogs. You can control the file type list as well as set a default. You can set a default directory and add a dialog title or default save extension. You also can control a flags variable to set up the dialog's behavior by adding settings from the supporting constants list, which is defined lower in the declarations.

strFullPathReturned, strFileNameReturned, intFileOffset, and intFileExtension are the variables that store the filename information after one is selected.

The ALLFILES constant is used to create a filter. This is followed by another type declaration that looks similar to the one above.

As discussed earlier, the Windows API is designed to be used from any development environment. Unfortunately, the functions are biased for use by C because they were developed with C. In VBA, some data types are stored differently from C. This means that they must be translated for use in C and by the API function calls. This second type is to assist with translation.

21

The next 15 lines are the constants for the `flags` variables. For this specific use of the dialogs, the flag settings aren't needed. In the original Microsoft Solutions database, the complete declarations were provided so that you could write your own functions using these API calls.

In Day 19, you used VBA to automate the export of data to Excel and Word. The filenames used were hard coded into the procedures; you could use the `GetSaveFileName` function to allow the user to select the filename. In that case, you might need some of these settings. Each is defined in Table 21.1. You could use more than one of these settings by adding them together.

TABLE 21.1 FLAG CONSTANTS

Flag	Purpose
OFN_ALLOWMULTISELECT	Supports the selection of more than one file at a time.
OFN_CREATEPROMPT	Supports the creation of a new file if the filename entered in the File Open dialog doesn't exist.
OFN_EXPLORER	Supports the use of Microsoft Windows Explorer.
OFN_FILEMUSTEXIST	Forces the file to exist.
OFN_HIDEREADONLY	Hides any file with the Read Only property set.
OFN_NOCHANGEDIR	Prevents the user from changing directories.
OFN_NODEREFERENCELINKS	Prevents the use of links.
OFN_NONETWORKBUTTON	Eliminates access to network drives.
OFN_NOREADONLYRETURN	Eliminates the return of read-only filenames.
OFN_NOVALIDATE	Turns off file validation.
OFN_OVERWRITEPROMPT	Prompts that a filename entered will overwrite an existing file.
OFN_PATHMUSTEXIST	Tests a path entered to make sure it exists.
OFN_READONLY	Forces the file to be opened read-only.
OFN_SHOWHELP	Accesss standard dialog help.

The last five lines are the most important for you in the declarations. They were not part of Microsoft's example. If you are creating several database applications, you will want to add dynamic linking to all of them. Rather than creating this module from scratch, you can copy it into your database. After it is copied, you can change these four constants so you can tailor its performance to the current database. The `strDATABASE` constant is the one to give the system title. You also must add the default filename for `strFILE` and default path for the application. Don't forget to add the trailing backslash for the path.

The last constant is strTABLE. It must have the name of the smallest table and is used to test the connection.

Examining the CheckLinks Function

The first step for a dynamic linking process is to see whether the current connection specified for the tables is valid. With the modDynamicLinks module, this is accomplished with the CheckLinks function shown in Listing 21.2.

LISTING 21.2 THE CheckLinks FUNCTION

```
Public Function CheckLinks() As Boolean
'    Check links to the database used for data storage.
'    It returns True if links are OK.

'    Attempt to create a recordset with a linked table
     Dim rsTestSet As ADODB.Recordset
     On Error Resume Next
     Set rsTestSet = New ADODB.Recordset
     rsTestSet.Open strTable, CurrentProject.Connection,
     ➥adOpenStatic, adLockOptimistic
     If Err.Number = 0 Then
         CheckLinks = True
     Else
         CheckLinks = False
     End If
End Function
```

The CheckLinks function returns True if the links are valid. This is tested using ADO. A variable called rsTestSet is declared as an ADODB recordset. Error handling is established and the variable is created as a new recordset. The Open method is used to set up the link to the table specified with the strTABLE constant.

If the connection isn't valid, the Open method generates an error. The CheckLinks function uses the Resume Next statement to handle the errors as they happen in the same path as the code. If the Number property for the Err object is 0, no error occurred and CheckLinks is set to True, otherwise it is set to False.

Reviewing the RelinkTables Function

If the CheckLinks function is set to False, the table connections must be reset. This is accomplished with the RelinkTables function shown in Listing 21.3.

21

LISTING 21.3 THE RelinkTables FUNCTION

```
Public Function RelinkTables() As Boolean
'    Tries to refresh the links to the database.
'    Returns True if successful.

'    Defines variables needed for path location and error handling.
     Dim strAccessDirectory As String
     Dim strSearchPath As String
     Dim strFileName As String
     Dim intError As Integer
     Dim strError As String

'    Defines Constants                                     Line 12
     Const conMaxTables = 8
     Const conNonExistentTable = 3011
     Const conNotDatabase = 3078
     Const conDatabaseNotFound = 3024
     Const conAccessDenied = 3051
     Const conReadOnlyDatabase = 3027

'    Get directory where MSAccess.exe is located.      Line 20
     strAccessDirectory = SysCmd(acSysCmdAccessDir)

'    Test Default Directory                            Line 23
     If Dir(strPATH) <> "" Then
         strSearchPath = strPATH
     Else
         strSearchPath = strAccessDirectory
     End If

'    Look for the database.                            Line 30
     If (Dir(strSearchPath & strFILE) <> "") Then
         strFileName = strSearchPath & strFILE
     Else
         ' Can't find the database, so display the Open dialog box.
         Dim strMsg As String
         strMsg = "Can't verify table connections, "
         strMsg = strMsg & "Please locate the " & strFILE & "."
         MsgBox strMsg, vbExclamation, strDATABASE
         strFileName = FindDatabase(strSearchPath)
         If strFileName = "" Then
             strError = "Sorry, you must locate the " & strFILE
             strError = strError & " to open " & strDATABASE & "."
             GoTo ErrLinkFailed
         End If
     End If

'    Fix the links.                                    Line 47
     If RefreshLinks(strFileName) Then
```

```
        RelinkTables = True
        Exit Function
    Else
        Select Case Err.Number
            Case conNonExistentTable, conNotDatabase
                strError = "File '" & strFileName & _
                    "' does not contain the required tables."
            Case conDatabaseNotFound
                strError = "You can't run " & strDATABASE & _
                    " until you locate the database."
            Case conAccessDenied
                strError = "Couldn't open " & strFileName & _
                    " because it's read-only or located on
                    ➡a read-only share."
            Case conReadOnlyDatabase
              strError = "Can't relink tables because " & strDATABASE & _
                    " is read-only or is located on a read-only share."
            Case Else
                strError = Err.Description
        End Select
    End If
ErrLinkFailed:
    MsgBox strError, vbCritical, strDATABASE
    RelinkTables = False
End Function
```

The first 19 lines declare the variables and constants required to relink the tables and track any errors. Lines 20–21 retrieve the path for Access. This is accomplished with the SysCmd method. This method can be used to retrieve information about Access as well as manipulate the status bar and add a custom progress meter.

After retrieving the Access directory, the constant strPATH is tested to see whether it exists. This is accomplished with the Dir method. This tests the constant and, if it is valid, assigns the value to the srtSearchPath variable to be used with the File Open dialog as the default folder. If it isn't valid, the path for Access will be used as the start-up path for the dialog.

After the path is set, the function tests to see whether the database is located in that folder. If that file is located the strSearchPath and strFILE are concatenated and stored as strFileName.

If the file isn't located a message box is used to indicate it can't be found and the FindDatabase function is called to access the File Open dialog. That function assigns a value to strFileName. Beginning on line 40, an If statement is used to test the filename. If it is empty, no file was selected by the user, and it uses the GoTo statement to move to error handling.

21

Line 47 is the first line of the process to relink the tables. It tests the results of a function called RefreshLinks with the filename. If this function returns a True value, the RelinkTables function is set to True and the function is finished. If the RefreshLinks function returns a False value, the Err object is tested to set the strError variable to display in a message box.

The error codes are represented with the constants defined. It tackles a problem with a missing table, missing database, or attribute settings for a table, file, or drive.

The ErrLinkFailed: label is the end of the problem solving. It displays the message and sets the function to False.

Examining the FindDatabase Function

Line 39 of the RelinkTables function calls the FindDatabase function if the default database name couldn't be found in the folder. This function controls the file find operation, as shown in Listing 21.4.

LISTING 21.4 THE FindDatabase FUNCTION

```
Function FindDatabase(strSearchPath) As String
'    Displays the Open dialog box to locate the database.
'    It returns the full path.
     Dim msaof As MSA_OPENFILENAME
'    Set options for the dialog box.
     msaof.strDialogTitle = "Where Is " & strDATABASE & "?"
     msaof.strInitialDir = strSearchPath
     msaof.strFilter = MSA_CreateFilterString("Databases", "*.mdb")
'    Call the Open dialog routine.
     MSA_GetOpenFileName msaof
'    Return the path and file name.
     FindDatabase = Trim(msaof.strFullPathReturned)
End Function
```

The FindDatabase function begins by declaring a variable using the user-defined type required by the API functions. Then various elements of this variable are assigned values. The dialog title is provided as well as the search path.

The strFilter element can't be assigned as simply. It calls on the MSA_CreateFilterString function to create the File Type list. After these elements are assigned values, the MSA_GetOpenFileName function is called. It is the function that uses the API call.

After a filename is selected, it is assigned to the strFullPathElement of the msaof variable. The excess space is removed from it, and it is returned by the FindDatabase function.

Examining the `MSA_CreateFilterString` Function

This function (see Listing 21.5) is called from the `FindDatabase` function to build the filter string that supports the File Type drop-down list in the dialog. This expects two strings for each type; the name as well as the generic extension. In this case, it is passed `Databases` and `*.MDB` from the `FindDatabase` function.

LISTING 21.5 THE MSA_CreateFilterString FUNCTION

```
Function MSA_CreateFilterString(ParamArray varFilt() As Variant) _
    As String
'   Creates a filter string from the passed in arguments.
'   Returns "" if no arguments are passed in.
'   Expects an even number of arguments (filter name, extension),
'   but if an odd number is passed in, it appends "*.*".
    Dim strFilter As String
    Dim intRet As Integer
    Dim intNum As Integer

    intNum = UBound(varFilt)
    If (intNum <> -1) Then
        For intRet = 0 To intNum
            strFilter = strFilter & varFilt(intRet) & vbNullChar
        Next
        If intNum Mod 2 = 0 Then
            strFilter = strFilter & "*.*" & vbNullChar
        End If
        strFilter = strFilter & vbNullChar
    Else
        strFilter = ""
    End If
    MSA_CreateFilterString = strFilter
End Function
```

Those values are represented in the function as `varFilt`. It looks different than other arguments you have created because an array is needed to hold multiple values. To accommodate the use of this function for more than one purpose, it uses the `ParamArray` keyword to indicate that it is a dynamic array. This doesn't restrict the function to a set number of types.

This function is going to take all those values and concatenate them into one string. It also tackles the possibility that an uneven number of elements were received. It declares three variables: `strFilter` to the temporary filter string, `intRet` for loop processing, and `intNum` for the number of elements received. Then the processing can begin. The `intNum` variable is assigned a value by using the `UBounds` function to get the upper bounds of the `varFilt` array to process the items. If items are passed to this function, a value will be retrieved. If no items are passed to this function the `UBounds` function will return –1.

21

An If statement is used to test intNum, and if it isn't equal to -1, then the intNum is used in the For...Next loop to concatenate the strings. vbNullChar is used to terminate the entry.

intNum is then tested with the Mod operator to divide the intNum by 2 to see if it is an even number. If it isn't, it adds the *.* string to make sure there is an even number.

If intNum was equal to -1, the strFilter variable is set to an empty string. The last step is to set the name of the function to the value of strFilter.

Calling the GetFileName Function

After the filter is constructed by FindDatabase, the MSA_OpenFileName function (shown in Listing 21.6) is called to display the Open dialog. In modDynamicLinks, two functions use the Windows API function GetOpenFileName. MSA_OpenFileName is the one used for dynamic linking because you can send in an initial directory, filters, and other settings.

LISTING 21.6   THE MSA_GetOpenFileName FUNCTION

```
Private Function MSA_GetOpenFileName(msaof As MSA_OPENFILENAME) _
    As Integer
'   Opens the Open dialog.
    Dim of As OPENFILENAME
    Dim intRet As Integer
    MSAOF_to_OF msaof, of
    intRet = GetOpenFileName(of)
    If intRet Then
        OF_to_MSAOF of, msaof
    End If
    MSA_GetOpenFileName = intRet
End Function
```

The second version of this function is called MSA_SimpleGetOpenFileName, which accesses the Open dialog with default options. Although they aren't needed for dynamic linking, there are also MSA_GetSaveFileName and MSA_SimpeGetSaveFileName functions. These can be used to create files.

In MSA_GetOpenFileName, it is a little bit more complex than calling the API function. You must prepare the arguments before you send them. In this function, it is receiving msaof as an MSA_OPENFILENAME type. Then two variables are declared. The of variable is declared as an OPENFILENAME type to support the storage of the arguments required by the GetOpenFileName function. With Microsoft's example for dynamic linking, the prefix MSA was used to indicate data stored in Microsoft Access format. The second variable declared is intRet. The GetOpenFileName API function returns an Integer value. It is set to -1, which is True if the function was successful.

The next line calls the MSA_to_OF subprocedure to perform the conversion. Line 7 is the one that actually calls the function. It sets the variable intRet equal to the GetOpenFileName function sending it the of variable, which is the variable storing the data in a format that will be recognized by the function.

Lines 8–10 test intRet to make sure that the function was successful. If it was successful, the OF_to_MSA subprocedure is called to convert the of variable back to a format that VBA can use. The last step is to set the function equal to the value of intRet.

Converting Data

To handle the fact that the String data type for VBA doesn't match the String for the API, this module has MSA_to_OF and OF_to_MSA to convert the values back and forth. It also assigns values to some of the other elements of the user-defined types.

MSA_to_OF (see Listing 21.7) takes the Microsoft Access strings and converts it to the format expected by the GetOpenFileName function. It also initializes some of the other elements required.

LISTING 21.7 THE MSA_to_OF SUBPROCEDURE

```
Private Sub MSAOF_to_OF(msaof As MSA_OPENFILENAME, of As OPENFILENAME)
'    This sub converts from the Access String to an Win32 String.
     Dim strFILE As String * 512
'    Initialize some parts of the structure.
     of.hwndOwner = Application.hWndAccessApp
     of.hInstance = 0
     of.lpstrCustomFilter = 0
     of.nMaxCustrFilter = 0
     of.lpfnHook = 0
     of.lpTemplateName = 0
     of.lCustrData = 0
     If msaof.strFilter = "" Then
         of.lpstrFilter = MSA_CreateFilterString(ALLFILES)
     Else
         of.lpstrFilter = msaof.strFilter
     End If
     of.nFilterIndex = msaof.lngFilterIndex
     of.lpstrFile = msaof.strInitialFile _
         & String(512 - Len(msaof.strInitialFile), 0)
     of.nMaxFile = 511
     of.lpstrFileTitle = String(512, 0)
     of.nMaxFileTitle = 511
     of.lpstrTitle = msaof.strDialogTitle
     of.lpstrInitialDir = msaof.strInitialDir
     of.lpstrDefExt = msaof.strDefaultExtension
```

21

continues

LISTING 21.7   CONTINUED

```
        of.Flags = msaof.lngFlags
        of.lStructSize = Len(of)
End Sub
```

The subprocedure received both the msaof and the of variables as arguments from the function that initiated the call. It declares a fixed-length string variable to store the file-name while processing. It is declared as a fixed-length string because it has the asterisk followed by the 512 value. The asterisk indicates that it is fixed-length and it is followed by any number to indicate the number of characters.

Lines 4–11 initialize some of the elements of the of variable that are needed. Line 4 identifies the system for the function. Every window on the system is identified by its hWnd property. When calling many of the API functions, you will have to identify your application for the function. The Application object has the hWndAccessApp property that stores that identifier.

Lines 12–14 reconcile the filter. An If statement is used to test to see whether strFilter from the msaof has anything in it. If it doesn't, the MSA_CreateFilterString function is called to create one single type of all files. If it isn't an empty string it is assigned to the corresponding element in the of variable. If it isn't an empty string, the file types were already created and converted.

Lines 15–25 translate the MSAOPENFILENAME to OPENFILENAME types. Most are direct assignments because they are numbers or the conversion is already complete. The lpstrFile is different; it's assigned the value of the strInitialFile concatenated with the results of the String function. The String function returns a string of repeated characters for a specific length. In this case, the length of the strInitialFile variable is calculated with the Len function and it is subtracted from 512, which is the fixed length of the string. It is filled with the null character.

After the function is called, the information must be converted back into the Microsoft Access format. The OF_to_MSA subprocedure (see Listing 21.8) takes care of this task.

LISTING 21.8   THE OF_to_MSA SUBPROCEDURE

```
Private Sub OF_to_MSOF(of As OPENFILENAME, msaof As MSA_OPENFILENAME)
'    Converts from the Win32 String to an Access String.
    msaof.strFullPathReturned = Left(of.lpstrFile, InStr(of.lpstrFile, _
        vbNullChar) - 1)
    msaof.strFileNameReturned = of.lpstrFileTitle
    msaof.intFileOffset = of.nFileOffset
    msaof.intFileExtension = of.nFileExtension
End Sub
```

The `GetOpenFileName` API function sets some of the elements of the user-defined type as files are selected. The `strFullPathReturned` stores the name and path of the database file selected. It is set to the corresponding value without the null characters at the end. This is accomplished with the `Left` function, which returns a specific number of characters from a string. It uses the `InStr` function to locate the first null character and subtract one from it to get the furthest character to the right in the string that has a valid character.

After all the processing required to get a filename, the process returns to the `RelinkTables` function to proceed with the `RefreshLinks` function.

Examining the `RefreshLinks` Function

The `RefreshLinks` function (see Listing 21.9) re-establishes the connection to the tables in the located file. The original function used the Data Access Object model to re-establish the table links, but Microsoft now recommends using ADO. It receives the `strFileName` variable as an argument with the new name for the database.

LISTING 21.9   THE `RefreshLinks` FUNCTION

```
Private Function RefreshLinks(strFileName As String) As Boolean
'    Refresh links to the supplied database. Return True if successful.
    On Error GoTo ErrRefresh
    Dim cat As New ADOX.Catalog, tbl As ADOX.Table
    Dim lTables As Long, lCount As Long
    Set cat.ActiveConnection = CurrentProject.Connection
    lTables = cat.Tables.Count
    For lCount = 1 To lTables - 1
        Set tbl = cat.Tables(lCount)
        If tbl.Type = "LINK" Then
            tbl.Properties(6).Value = strFileName
        End If
    Next lCount
    RefreshLinks = True          ' Relinking complete.
    Exit Function
ErrRefresh:
    RefreshLinks = False
End Function
```

On line 3, the error handling is initialized. Lines 4–5 declare variables for a catalog, a table, a long variable for the number of tables in the catalog's `Table` collection, and a long variable to serve as a counter for the `For Next` loop.

Line 6 assigns a value for the catalog. It sets its `ActiveConnection` property equal to the `Connection` property for the `CurrentProject` object.

21

Line 7 assigns a value for `lTables`. It takes the `Count` property of the Tables collection to determine how many tables will need to be checked.

Line 8 sets up the `For...Next` loop to examine each table separately using `lCount`. Line 9 sets up the table variable to point to the table in the `Tables` collection with the corresponding index.

Line 9 sets up an `If` statement to test the table's `Type` property to determine whether it needs to be relinked. The `Table` object has a set of properties and collections to control its behavior. The `Type` property is a string property that stores information about its role in the database. In the Help file, three types are listed, but if you are using linked tables, the `LINK` value is a fourth choice.

If the type of table is linked, the filename that was chosen with the File Open dialog must be added as the connection string. This is also a little more complex than it might look. When you are working with a table stored in an outside source, you will have to work with its Properties collection to access provider-specific properties. In the Help file, these properties aren't defined because they are different with each database. If you are linking to tables in an Access database there are 10 properties that you can access. Each property has a Name, Type, Value and Attributes properties.

For this process, the seventh property has an index of 6 and it is the Link Data Source property. To correct the connection, this property is set to the value of `strFileName`. If no error occurs in this process, the `RefreshLinks` function returns a value of `False`, which will generate an error message for the user.

Activating the Dynamic Linking

`modDynamicLinks` is part of this database, but it is currently not being used. You must call these functions. In Day 19, you learned about the concept of adding a central form to act as a manager for the database—a switchboard.

The frmSwitchboard form is a perfect object to test the links to the table because it doesn't have an underlying table. Later in this lesson, you will set up the database startup options to automatically load this form to further automate the process.

To test the tables, it is best to complete this task when the form is loaded into memory. This is accomplished with the `Form Load` event. The following code must be added to the `Form_Load` event for frmSwitchboard:

```
Private Sub Form_Load()
    On Error GoTo LoadErr
    If CheckLinks() = False Then
        If RelinkTables() = False Then
            DoCmd.Close acForm, "frmSwitchboardFinal"
```

```
            DoCmd.Quit acQuitSaveAll
        End If
    End If
    Exit Sub
LoadErr:
    MsgBox Err.Description, vbCritical, "Database Load Failure"
End Sub
```

To make the code for dynamic linking easier to integrate into any database, very little of the processing is accomplished with this form. The second line initializes error handling with its corresponding line label at the end of the procedure.

Line 3 has an `If` statement to test the results of the `CheckLinks` function. If it is `False`, the tables must be relinked. This is accomplished with a nested `If` statement to call the `RelinkTables` function. If it is set to `False`, it means the relink failed. If that is the case, the `Close` method is used to close the form and the `Quit` method is used to exit Access.

Viewing the Results

Now all the code is in place to take care of dynamically linking the database tables. Here you will get to see a missing file relink and the default file relink.

Task: Viewing Dynamic Linking in Action

1. Save all your work and close Access.
2. Change the name of DevData.MDB to DevData1.MDB.
3. Launch Access and open DevSys.MDB; log on as DevAdmin with no password.
4. Double-click frmSwitchboard.
5. Notice that Access doesn't display the form immediately. It displays an error message indicating the problem with the table connections (see Figure 21.16).

FIGURE 21.16

The error message about the table connections is displayed.

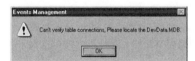

6. Click OK to close the message and display the File Open dialog (see Figure 21.17).
7. Notice that the dialog is displaying the default directory C:\My Documents.
8. Select the file DevData1.MDB and click Open. Notice that the switchboard is now displayed.
9. Select the Tables list from the Database window and select tblAttendees.

21

FIGURE 21.17

The File Open dialog is opened with the settings specified with your code.

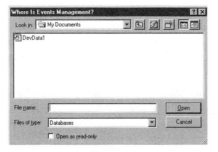

10. Click the Design button and click Yes in the message box notifying you that the table is linked.

11. Open the Properties window and notice the string that is shown as the description. Notice that the DevData1.MDB file is listed as the Database.

12. Close the table window and exit Access.

13. Change the name of the database back to DevData.MDB, which is the default specified in the code.

14. Launch Access and open DevSys.MDB; log on as DevAdmin with no password.

15. Open the frmSwitchboard form.

16. Notice that you were not prompted to find the file.

17. Open tblAttendees in Design mode. Notice that the Description now points to DevData.MDB.

Relinking is now automated for your user. The only thing users have to know is the location of the database. With the browser, they can search for it as needed, and typos are minimized because they can select rather than type. This process is further automated in the "Setting the Database Startup Properties" section in this lesson. You learn how to automatically open frmSwitchboard when you open the database.

Adding Help to Your Applications

As you begin learning a new product, you appreciate any guidance that is available to assist you with understanding the application and its functions. You might take a class or purchase a book, but you also rely on resources within the application.

When you are designing your system, give some thought to what types of assistance you are going to provide. Creating an application that gets the user started faster, with forms that are designed to speed up data entry and access, is only part of providing assistance.

Most applications provide some type of online assistance. Microsoft Access has three mechanisms for a user to get help. The first is the status bar (see Figure 21.18). At the bottom of the window, a line provides information regarding what the user is looking at.

FIGURE 21.18

The status bar provides information about the user's actions.

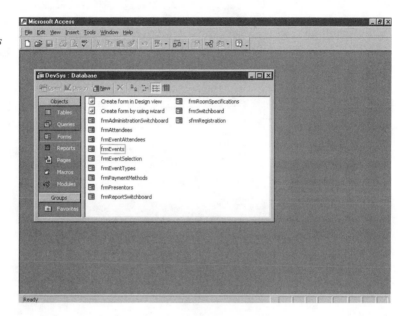

The Database window indicates that the application is ready for the user to select an object or action. You can control what information is displayed on the status bar. In many cases, you also can get a control tip by pointing to an object (see Figure 21.19).

The second type of help is used in Microsoft Office to provide a more interactive form of help. It is known as the Office Assistant (see Figure 21.20).

The assistant is customizable. You can pick an assistant, such as Clippit or the Genius. It will pop up when it sees you doing something that it can assist with or when you want to ask a question. It is one method of providing instructions for using one of your objects.

The last type of assistance normally provided by an application is a help system. The user can select Help and another window will open and give him a choice of topics, or it will automatically open to a context-specific topic (see Figure 21.21). You probably have been taking advantage of this feature in many applications. You learned how valuable it could be with the Visual Basic Editor.

21

FIGURE **21.19**

A control tip is visible when you point to a toolbar button or control.

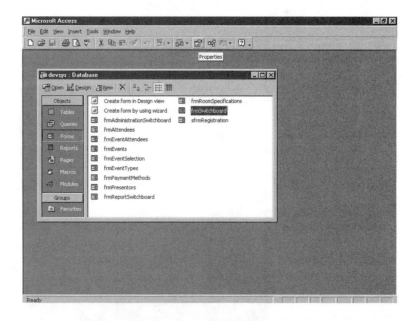

FIGURE **21.20**

The Office Assistant provides more interactive support.

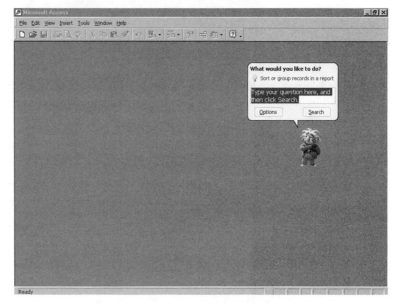

FIGURE 21.21

The Help window provides information about a particular function of an application.

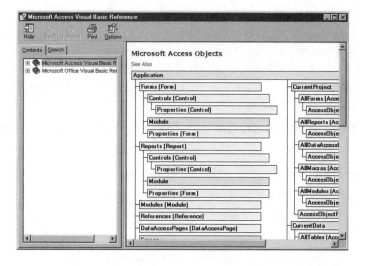

When you are designing your application, you can include all, some, or none of these help tools to assist the user working with your application. You might find they are well worth the effort. The help tools could dramatically cut down on the number of questions you receive about how to work with your database system. Each method is covered in greater detail in the following sections.

Adding Status Bar Text or a Control Tip

Adding text to the status bar or adding a control tip can be the easiest method for providing help for your users. They are both added with property settings: the Status Bar Text and Control Tip properties, respectively. You can add up to 255 characters of instructions for your user. You can add status bar text globally for a field by setting this property for the field in a table, or you can add text to individual controls in a form. To add status bar text to a field for all forms, complete the following task.

Task: Adding Status Bar Text for tblEvents

1. Select the Tables tab in the Database window.
2. Select tblEvents and open it in Design mode.
3. Select Yes to indicate that you understand that it is attached.
4. Notice that you do not see a property for status bar text.
5. Click in the Description column for EventName.
6. Type Enter the Official Name of the Event and press Enter.

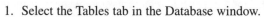

7. Save the table and close it.

21

If you create new forms based on this table, you will get Enter the Official Name of the Event as the default status bar text. It will not affect forms that were created prior to the change. There are times when you need to add status bar text to a form that is already created or is not based on a table. Then you need to use the Properties window for the form. This is also required to set a control tip. To add the Status Bar Text and Control Tip Text properties to a control on a form, complete the following task.

Task: Adding Status Bar Text for frmSwitchboard

1. Select the Forms tab in the Database window.

2. Open frmSwitchboard in Design mode.

3. Select the Attendees command button and open the Properties window.

4. Select the Other tab.

5. Select Status Bar Text.

6. Type Opens the Attendees Form and press Enter.

7. Select Control Tip Text, type Attendees Form, and press Enter.

8. Save the form.

9. Click the View button to switch to Form view.

10. Notice that Attendees is the selected button and the status bar text is displayed.

11. Point to the button until the control tip text is displayed.

 12. Close the form.

When you are designing your application, these small touches can assist the user with very little effort. As with most of the topics in this lesson, it is best to think of them as you create each object to minimize the time spent going back and adding these property settings after the form is created.

Programming the Office Assistant

As you started working with Office 2000, you probably met the Office Assistant. The Office Assistant is a help tool designed to provide a more interactive help. It might have greeted you the first time you launched one of the applications. The assistant is an animated figure that responds to your requests for help when it is active. By default, it is set to respond as ClipIt, an animated paper clip (see Figure 21.22).

With VBA, you can control the appearance as well as the behavior of the Office Assistant. There are properties and methods to set all the options as well as select an assistant. You can also display information using the assistant. This is accomplished using a balloon object.

FIGURE 21.22

The assistant provides help in an interactive manner.

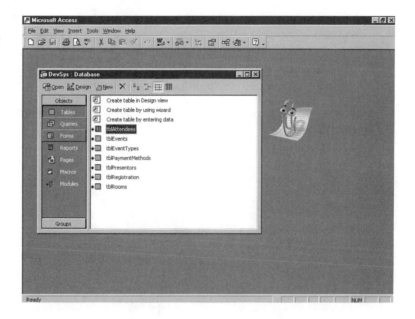

To get an idea of how to manipulate the Office Assistant, you are going to add the Office Assistant to frmRoomSpecifications. To work with the Office Assistant, you need to gain access to the assistant, verify that it is enabled, display it, access its options, and add code to communicate with the user with balloons.

Before you can begin to use the Office Assistant in your application, you must reference it in the Visual Basic Editor. This process is identical to accessing the ADO or ADOX libraries.

Task: Setting the Reference for the Office Library

1. Open frmRoomSpecification in Design view and open the Properties window.
2. Select the On Open property and click the Build button.
3. Select Code Builder in the dialog and click OK.
4. Select Tools, References to display the References - DevSys dialog.
5. Select Microsoft Office 9.0 Object Library from the list and click OK.

After you set the reference to the library, you can add code to control the Office Assistant. The Office object library has an Assistant object with properties and methods to control its appearance and behavior. The Assistant object has a property to represent the text area that is displayed by the assistant. This is called a *balloon*. The first step is to control its display.

21

In this case, you want to take advantage of the Office Assistant when the frmRoomSpecifications form is open. You are going to want to make sure that it is displayed and ready for use when the form opens and reset it back to the way it was before you opened the form as it closes. You must add some module-level variables as well as two events to the frmRoomSpecifications form.

The first step is to add the module-level variables to the top of this module. There are five variables:

```
Private MyAssistant As Assistant
Private MyBalloon As Balloon
Private bEnabled As Boolean
Private strOriginalAssistant As String
Private bOriginalState As Boolean
```

The MyAssistant variable is declared as an Assistant object. MyBalloon is declared as a Balloon object to manage the text. The remaining three variables store information about the state of the Assistant object when this form is opened.

The assistant is one of the features that might not be used by all users. The assistant does slow some processes down and may be disabled by a more experienced user. A new user is probably very grateful for its assistance. The three variables, bEnabled, strOriginalAssistant, and bOriginalState store the original settings of the assistant before you make any changes.

As the form opens, you are going to want to set up the assistant and as the form closes, you will want to reset any assistant options you changed. This is accomplished by adding the following Form_Open and Form_Close events (see Listing 21.10).

LISTING 21.10 THE FRMROOMSPECIFICATIONS Open AND Close EVENTS

```
Private Sub Form_Open(Cancel As Integer)
    Set MyAssistant = Assistant
    If MyAssistant.Visible = True Then
        bOriginalState = True
    Else
        bOriginalState = False
        If MyAssistant.On = True Then
            bEnabled = True
            MyAssistant.Visible = True
        Else
            bEnabled = False
            MyAssistant.On = True
            MyAssistant.Visible = False
            strOriginalAssistant = MyAssistant.FileName
            MyAssistant.FileName = _
                "c:\Program Files\Microsoft Office\Office\genius.acs"
            MyAssistant.Animation = msoAnimationAppear
```

```
            MyAssistant.Visible = True
        End If
    End If
End Sub

Private Sub Form_Close()
    If bOriginalState = True Then
        Exit Sub
    Else
If bEnabled = False Then
            If MyAssistant.FileName <> strOriginalAssistant Then
                MyAssistant.FileName = strOriginalAssistant
            End If
            MyAssistant.On = False
        End If
    End If
End Sub
```

As the form opens, the Form_Open event is executed. This event must test the status of the Office Assistant and get it ready for use. The second line sets up the Assistant object for use. It takes the MyAssistant variable and assigns it to represent the assistant with the Assistant keyword. There is only one assistant on the system.

Now you are ready to set it up for use. The Assistant object has properties to represent all the Assistant options displayed in its Options dialog (see Figure 21.23). It also has a property to determine whether it is in view and which assistant has been chosen.

FIGURE 21.23

The assistant options control its behavior.

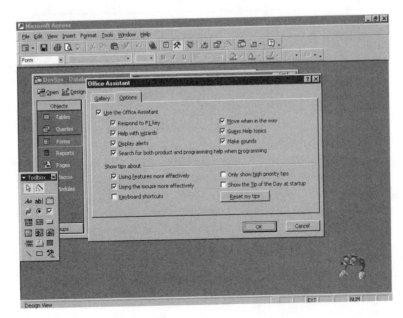

21

Line 3 sets up the If structure to test the assistant's Visible property. This indicates whether the assistant is currently in use. If it is set to True, the assistant is already launched and running. Line 4 stores this setting in bOriginalState so it can be used when the form closes.

If the Visible property is set to False, the user wasn't using the assistant, which means you are going to have to set it up with code. Line 6 preserves the Visible setting.

If the assistant isn't visible, the next step is to determine whether the user has disabled the assistant. This is accomplished by testing the On property. Lines 7–17 set up the assistant for use.

Line 7 tests to see whether the assistant is enabled, but is just not visible at this moment. If that is true, the bEnabled variable is set to True to preserve that state for closing the form and the assistant is made visible. If the assistant isn't enabled, you have more work to do with your code. Line 12 turns on the assistant by setting the On property to True. Line 13 sets the Visible property to False. This line wouldn't be necessary if all you wanted to do was activate the assistant with the current settings because enabling the assistant makes it visible automatically. In this case, you are going to customize the assistant before you display it.

The FileName property stores the filename and its path for the assistant. The current file-name is stored in the variable and then set to the Genius Assistant file. You can choose from any assistant loaded on the system.

> **Caution**
>
> Not all the assistant files are loaded with the default installation of Microsoft Office. For this example, please verify that this file is located on your hard drive and in this default location. Make any changes that are needed. In a real application, you would want to add error handling to test the location and file. You would want to suspend any actions for the assistant in that case.

The next line sets the Animation property for the assistant. The Animation property enables you to select the actions performed by the assistant. In this case, the Animation property is set to msoAnnimationAppear. This is a constant that represents the arrival of the assistant; there are 35 constants representing various actions. Experiment with the different constant settings to see which actions meet your needs. After the animation is selected, the assistant is made visible.

The assistant is now ready for use. The `Form_Close` event has code to reset the assistant settings as the form closes. The second line of the `Form_Close` event tests the value of the `bOriginalState` variable. This stored the original setting of the `Visible` property. If it is `True`, there is nothing to reset because you made no changes to the assistant if it was already in use.

If `bOriginalState` is `False`, you might have made changes. The `Else` clause tests to see whether `bEnabled` equals `False`. If it does, it resets the filename using the variable and disables the assistant with the `On` property.

Manipulating the Office Assistant

Displaying the assistant is only part of the work required to get the most from this feature. Displaying it is cute, but hardly functional. The next step is to add messages for the user. You add messages by creating balloon objects and displaying them in response to user actions. Each balloon you create can have a heading, leader text, labels, and button combinations. You have to set these up with properties. For example, you want to remind the user of what makes a good room title when they create a new record. You can add a `BeforeInsert` event (see Listing 21.11).

LISTING 21.11 CREATING A BALLOON

```
Private Sub Form_BeforeInsert(Cancel As Integer)
    Set MyBalloon = MyAssistant.NewBalloon
    MyAssistant.Animation = msoAnimationThinking
    With MyBalloon
        .Heading = "Room "
        .Text = "It will appear on the Event Schedule. It should:"
        .Labels(1).Text = "Be descriptive"
        .Labels(2).Text = "Match the room nameplate"
        .Labels(3).Text = "Indicate a building as needed."
    End With
    MyBalloon.Animation = msoAnimationGestureRight
    MyBalloon.Show
End Sub
```

Line 2 sets the variable `MyBalloon` equal to the `NewBalloon` property for the `MyAssistant` object. The `Animation` property is used to display a thinking pose. The `With` structure is used to set the balloon properties.

The `Heading` property is the title of the balloon. The `Text` property is the descriptive text in the balloon. If you want to have a list, you will set the `Text` property for the Labels collection for the balloon. You can have up to five labels in a balloon. You reference them by their index number. Notice that they begin with 1 instead of 0 like most collections.

21

Under the `End With`, the `Animation` property is used again to change the pose of the assistant. Notice it is a gesture to the right (the assistant's right, not yours). This time it is for the balloon instead of the assistant. It will be displayed only when the balloon is visible. This is followed by the line to display the balloon with the `Show` method.

As the user types the first character in the Room field the balloon is displayed. If she clicks one of the labels or the OK button or types another character, the balloon will be closed.

Another method for using the assistant is in lieu of a message box. You can display messages and get responses to take action with VBA. For example, if a record changes, you could prompt the user to print a new event schedule using the following `AfterUpdate` event (see Listing 21.12).

LISTING 21.12   USING THE ASSISTANT LIKE A MESSAGE BOX

```
Private Sub Form_AfterUpdate()
    Dim lReturn As Long
    Set MyBalloon = MyAssistant.NewBalloon
    MyAssistant.Animation = msoAnimationThinking
    With MyBalloon
        .Heading = "Event Schedule"
        .Text = "Do you want to print a new event schedule?"
        .Icon = msoIconAlert
        .Button = msoButtonSetYesNo
    End With
    MyBalloon.Animation = msoAnimationGestureRight
    lReturn = MyBalloon.Show
    If lReturn = -3 Then
        DoCmd.OpenReport "rptEventSchedule", acViewPreview
    End If
End Sub
```

The second line declares a variable to store the button clicked in the balloon. `Set` statement indicates a new balloon. Line 4 adds some animation while the balloon is set up. The `With` structure again sets the properties for the balloon. The Labels collection settings are dropped and replaced with two new properties.

The `Icon` property enables you to control the graphic displayed in the balloon to indicate urgency. It is like one of the options for the `Msgbox` function. There are predefined constants for your selections.

The `Button` property determines what buttons are displayed at the bottom of the balloon. Here the user can select Yes or No. There are also predefined constants for all the selections.

There is another animation setting followed by the Show method. This time it isn't just shown, it is placed as part of an equation to populate lReturn with the code for the button selected.

The lReturn variable is then tested with an If statement. If it returns -3, the OpenReport method is used to preview the report. Notice that the code returned doesn't match the code returned by MsgBox. There are more choices, so there are more codes. Again, you will have to experiment with different settings to see what works best for you.

After you have added this code, you are ready to test it. You will need to save your work and close the frmRoomSpecifications form.

Task: Viewing Assistant Balloons in Action

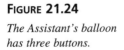

1. Open the frmRoomSpecifications form.
2. Click the Add Record button.
3. Type R and notice the balloon is displayed and the assistant completes his gesture and rests (see Figure 21.24).

FIGURE 21.24

The Assistant's balloon has three buttons.

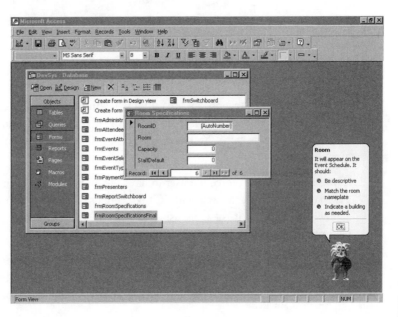

4. Type Room F and press Tab.
5. Enter 25 as the Capacity and 4 as the Staff Default.
6. Click the First Record button and view the new balloon, as shown in Figure 21.25.

FIGURE 21.25

The assistant can act as a message box.

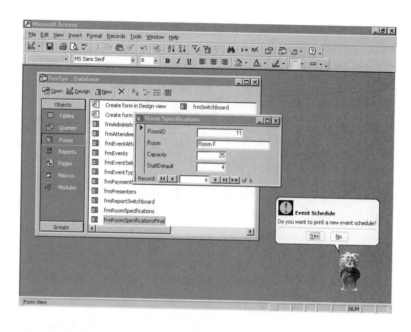

7. Click Yes and view the preview of the report.

8. Close the report and the form.

These examples of the assistant are only the beginning of what it can do for you. You can change the style of the balloon to provide a method for a user to indicate a choice with the BalloonType property. You have a wide selection of animation actions as well as button selections.

If you aren't going to force the user to have the assistant on, you might need to test the Visible property for the assistant. If it is True, use the assistant balloons to communicate with the user. If it is False, use a message box. It takes more time to write the code, but your database will look more professional.

You can also use VBA to link the assistant to a Help file. It can serve as a filter for the Answer Wizard in the help application. It is one area that you will want to spend some time experimenting with to find out what property settings work best for your application.

Creating a Help File

The last type of help you can create for your users is a help file that can be accessed from the menu, using F1 or integrated with Office Assistant. This is an approach that most Windows applications use. A table of contents provides a list of the topics available.

There are cross-references between topics to get to related information, and the file can be searched by keyword or by using a full text search.

This type of assistance involves more work than using the Status Bar Text and Control Tip Text properties. It also can be more time consuming that using the assistant. It is not something you want to undertake lightly. With an online help file, you are creating an online document.

In Windows, you have been used to seeing the table of contents index and search in one window and a separate window opening for the information. This was created using a utility called the Help Workshop. With Office 2000, you are using a different type of help: HTML Help.

Creating a help file requires five steps and a good plan. The topics must be created. A table of contents and index must be constructed, and the help project must be created, and these files need to be compiled into a help file. The last step is to integrate the help file into your database system.

In larger organizations, different people are dedicated to these tasks. If you are going to develop the help system alone, you will have to take on different roles. The first role is that of the writer. You will have to create the topics for the various aspects of your system. This involves not only writing the material, but adding special formatting to create the functionality within the Help utility. You will also draft the table of contents.

The second role is to manage the compile of the document into the help file. This requires two sets of skills. You must know how to create the instructions to compile the file. You will also need to test and resolve any conflicts. This will require the same skills as the writer to correct any problems in the document.

The last role is that of a developer. You will need to be able to indicate what help file your system will use. You will also need to indicate which topic to display when help is selected from a form or report. This is done by setting the Help File and Help Context ID properties. You can also add a custom Help menu and access through the Office Assistant with a custom control and VBA.

Examining a Standard Help File

To get an idea of some typical elements in a help file, look at the Microsoft Access help file. To open help, select Help, Contents to open the Help window (see Figure 21.26).

The help file opens in a separate window. It is a separate utility that is a part of Windows. When it opens, it is a two-paned window. The left pane is the Contents pane, which is a tabbed pane that shows a list of the information in the file. When you see a book icon, you can double-click it to expand it. If you see a document icon, you can double-click it to display a topic.

21

FIGURE 21.26

The Help window is used to display online information.

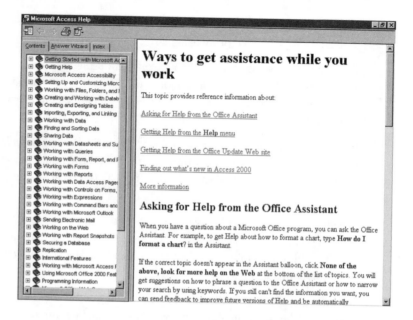

The second tab is the Answer Wizard tab, which allows the user to type a word or phrase and search the entire text of the file to see whether there is a topic that matches. There might also be an Index tab that allows a keyword search based on a predefined list.

The right pane displays the topic information. The topic pane includes text. It might include graphics or other objects, like video or audio clips. It might also include links to other information. The topic pane can include a cross-reference called a *jump* (see Figure 21.27). A jump is shown in another color and underlined. It can be clicked on and it will move to the referenced topic.

The topic pane can also include a *pop-up* (see Figure 21.28). A pop-up is shown in another color and underlined, or it can be an icon. It can also be clicked on. It will not load another topic, but it will display information in a smaller pop-up area over the topic.

You will have to determine what is needed for your system. This involves analyzing your system and outlining your document. It involves the writer and the developer so the plan will be coordinated.

FIGURE 21.27

*A jump leads to
another topic.*

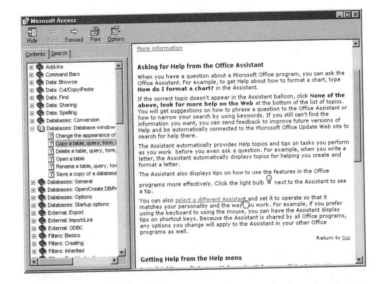

FIGURE 21.28

*A pop-up is often used
for definitions.*

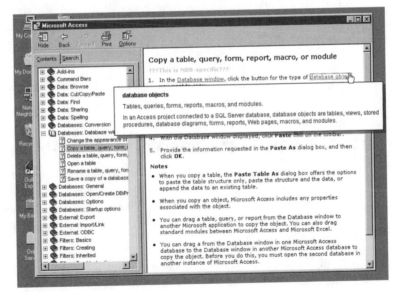

21

Planning the Help File

When you are designing your help file, you must take care of help for those objects you create. You do not have to re-create the help contents for the Access functionality. For example, you would have to create a topic for the frmSwitchboard form, but you would not have to write a topic for using Edit, Find.

The Help window can be used like a book. The user can browse through the help file to learn more about the system. He can also use it to look up answers. You must determine what topics are required, as well as what codes will be needed for that topic to provide the access required by the user.

The role of planning might take both the writer and the developer because the work might be occurring at the same time. You might want to consider using Microsoft Excel to track the topics and the related information during the planning phase.

When the planning is complete, you are ready to create the help file. To create a help file, you need a special utility. The Microsoft Office Developer's Edition ships with the HTML Help Workshop. It creates and tracks all element of your help project. The HTML Help Workshop also ships with an ActiveX control to link help into your database or any VBA project. It also ships with a help file outlining the details and tools required to create your own help file.

For complex applications, a help file can be a real asset. It can answer many of the user's questions without troubling you with a phone call.

Setting the Database Startup Properties

This lesson has focused on making it easier for a less-experienced user to work with your system. You used VBA to make it easier to move from form to form and report. You added API calls to get information from Windows and looked at how to add help, but at this point, the user still has to locate the starting point for the application from the Database window.

You might want to consider eliminating this step by setting your database's startup properties. If you select Tools, Startup it will open the Startup dialog (see Figure 21.29).

Here you can specify many settings to curb the actions of the user and keep him from getting into trouble. At a minimum, you will want to set the Application Title and the Display Form/Page settings. There are many settings to choose from, as shown in Table 21.2.

FIGURE 21.29

The Startup properties give you an opportunity to set up how your database opens and behaves.

TABLE 21.2   THE DATABASE STARTUP SETTINGS

Setting	Description
Application Title	Sets the text you want on the main title bar.
Display Form/Page	Sets the form or page to display when the database opens.
Application Icon	Sets a special icon for the database.
Displays Database Window	Sets whether the Database window opens hidden.
Display Status Bar	Determines whether a status bar is visible.
Menu Bar	Sets a default menu bar to use in all windows unless otherwise noted.
Shortcut Menu Bar	Sets a default shortcut menu bar for the database.
Allow Full Menus	Controls how much of the full menus are displayed when used.
Allow Default Shortcut Menus	Controls whether shortcut menus are available globally.
Allow Built-In Toolbars	Determines whether the default toolbars are available.
Allow Toolbar/Menu Changes	Determines whether the user can customize the system.
Advanced	
Allow Viewing of Code After Error	Determines whether the user can get to the Visual Basic Editor if permissions allow it.
Use Special Access Keys	Determines whether many shortcut keys are disabled.

These settings give you a great deal of control over the database. At a minimum, you should avoid confusion by displaying your switchboard and hiding the database window. To change the settings for this system's settings, work through the following task.

▼ TASK

Task: Setting the Startup Properties for DevSys

1. Select Application Title and enter Events Management.
2. Select frmSwitchboard as the Display Form/Page.

21

▼   3. Deselect the Display Database Window check box.

     4. Click OK.

     5. Close the database and reopen it. Notice that the Database window doesn't display,
▲   and the switchboard is open and ready for the user to make a selection.

| Tip | If you need the Database window, press the F11 key. |

After you set up an icon for your database on a user's desktop, it will be very hard for
her not to get started correctly with your system. With a little care and planning, you can
minimize the amount of time you spend answering simple questions with your system.

Summary

Today's lesson introduced some of the things you must consider when you are going to
develop for a multiuser environment. The key to a successful implementation is planning. Considering your data needs, users and their types of use, and available support is
going to have an impact on your system and its performance. All these areas will affect
your system's structure. You can just place the database on your network, replicate the
system and give everyone a copy, use the Internet, or split the data from the system
objects. This is by far the most common approach because of its flexibility.

After those decisions are made, you must determine what type of protection you are
going to provide when the records are edited. You are going to determine your record-
locking strategy. For better or for worse, the default setting is no locks, which offers no
protection. You will probably want to go with locking the record being edited.

To give you a chance to implement a database for multiuser access, you walked through
splitting the database. Then you had an opportunity to deal with dynamically connecting
to the data using an API call. The API can dramatically increase your ability to control
the environment.

After splitting the database, you looked at how to reduce the need for support for your
users. This was accomplished by implementing help. You could use some simple property settings or create a complete help file. You could also add the tutorial approach with
an Office Assistant.

Last but not least, you looked at how to simplify the start of your system by setting the database startup properties, including loading a form automatically. You also hid the Database window to avoid confusing the user with too many open windows at the same time.

Q&A

Q Where can I get more information about the Windows API?

A Detailed information is provided with the Office Developer's Kit, as well as through the Microsoft Web site.

Q Can I add other types of files to my help file other than graphics and video clips?

A Yes, it will support files with applications with OLE support, but the application must be resident on the user's computer.

Q Can I change the Office Assistant?

A Yes, you can. The type of assistant is controlled with properties, but you might want to think twice. If someone is using a particular assistant, he is probably attached to it.

Workshop

The Workshop contains questions and exercises to help you reinforce the material covered today. The answers appear in Appendix A, "Answers."

Quiz

1. What are the benefits of splitting the system from the data in a multiuser environment?
2. What is the biggest disadvantage of splitting the database?
3. Why is help a valuable asset with multiuser systems?

21

WEEK 3

In Review

This week, you've worked to increase your knowledge of the
skills needed to develop full-featured database applications
with Access 2000. You have learned how to get more from
SQL as well as improve the appearance and performance of
your forms. You have also explored the fundamentals of
VBA, which is a powerful resource for automating tasks in
Access 2000. In Day 20 and Day 21, you received an introduction to some of the issues you must address when developing a database for more than one user, including securing
the database, updating the system, and providing help.

15

16

17

18

19

20

21

Appendix A

Answers

Day 1, "Understanding Relational Database Concepts"

1. Foreign key.

2. Information. Data would be the voting records themselves.

3. Disagree. The type of data model Access uses has no bearing on the need to backup.

4. No, that's what the repair/compact utility does.

Day 2, "From Idea to Project"

1. Forms. Reports.

2. No. It will open in form view (data view).

3. Yes, by clicking on the Run toolbar button.

4. Visual Basic for Applications (VBA).

5. In tables.

6. Fields.

7. No. A record can contain many different data types.

Day 3, "Exploring the Data Foundations— The Table"

1. No. The idea of a primary key is that no two records can have the same key value.

2. Yes, but there's no practical reason for this to occur.

3. Only to the extent to have identical fields for linking.

4. Use the Tools-Relationships window and drag to link the common fields.

5. First.

Day 4, "Using Queries for Data Retrieval"

1. Click the filter by form button on the toolbar when in datasheet view.

2. Records where the criterion field is greater than 100.

3. Nothing. There can be no record where the surname is both Cassel and Palmer.

4. The one leftmost in design view.

5. Specifies the fields to link two or more database objects.

6. Yes. Uncheck the Show box for the fields you don't wish to display.

Day 5, "Creating Simple Forms for Data Access"

1. The large black square at the upper left of the control or its label.

2. Highlight it then press the Del key or choose Edit-Delete [Cut] from the main menu.

3. Locate its hot spot for sizing and then dragging it to its new size. There are also height and width properties for any control in the Properties list box.

4. Yes.

5. No.

6. This is a trick question. There are no differences.

Day 6, "Generating Basic Reports"

1. This is a trick question. There is no way to control the AutoReport wizard.
2. No differences. The procedures are the same.
3. Keeps a group on a page if possible.
4. The number of pages in the entire report.
5. Puts one space between the fields Name and LastName.

Day 7, "Automating Your Access Apps: A Macro Primer"

1. Action Arguments.
2. No, only the macro saved name.
3. No.
4. The field City does not equal New York.
5. Yes, and similar date tests are very common as macro conditions.

Day 8, "Data Access Pages"

1. The bound object (a table or query), the Page object within the Access database container, and an HTML file linked to the database.
2. Yes. In the Data Link Properties dialog box there are properties to set the source to SQL Server and the connection to such a database.
3. In the toolbox, drag the Hotspot control to the Page. Specify an image and a site to link to. That's it.

Day 9, "Refining Your Tables"

1. Yes. For the data in a table, edit the hyperlink (f2) and note the address has two parts the second surrounded by #'s. Edit the part to the left of the #'s to be the label you wish to use. If you use the Insert, Hyperlink dialog box, just fill in the text box with the label you prefer.
2. No, only the two cities Madrid or London.
3. No, you can change from the default by entering a phrase as the Validation Text property.
4. Restrict data entry to any but Denver.

Day 10, "Designing Customized Forms"

1. No, you must change them individually.

2. Yes. You can mix and match most of these properties.

3. Yes, but you must set the form's Allow Design Changes to All. This property is on the Other tab.

4. You need to change the Colors property on the Settings tab of the Display Properties dialog box in Windows itself (not Access). If you don't have more colors available, you need to change your driver or your display adapter.

5. Yes. Select the various objects you wish to alter the properties for. The Properties list box will change to read Multiple Selection in its title bar. Changes made to any property will affect all objects selected.

Day 11, "Sorting Data with Queries and Joins"

1. Using sequential numbers that are formatted into either a date or time format for display.

2. No. You can create your own functions by programming them using VBA.

3. `Datediff()`

4. It switches (trades) table or query data for values specified in the Switch function.

Day 12, "Developing Reports with Graphics and Expressions"

1. The Image control is best to display a graphic in a fixed location because you have control over the placement of the graphic.

2. The Size Mode property determines what happens to the image as the control's size is adjusted. Clip will maintain the original size of the image, Stretch will adjust the graphic to fill the control without regard to maintaining the proportions, and Zoom will size the image maintaining its aspect ratio.

3. The `Switch` function allows you to set up several expressions, each with a separate value to be displayed depending on the results of the evaluation.

A

4. If the Same as Detail check box is selected, you must adjust your Width property to create a report with multiple columns. If it is not selected, you can create Report and Page Headers/Footers of the width of the page and add controls to the Detail and Group Header/Footer sections within the confines of the smaller column width.

Day 13, "Introducing VBA"

1. Assigning a name for a control as it is created by the Control Wizard or as you create it manually, will make your code easier to read.

2. A module is a storage location for code. It can be attached to a form or report, or it can be a standalone object to be shared by more than one form or report in your application. It can also be shared across applications.

3. Most of the time, you will execute code based on a user or system action. This means that most of the time you will create event procedures.

4. Variables provide a temporary storage location in memory for data. They are a great way to transfer a value from one control to another, evaluate an expression, and share information between objects.

Day 14, "Understanding SQL"

1. SQL is valuable in working with databases because of performance issues. If you only need to find a small number of fields meeting a specific criterion, it is more efficient to create a query that retrieves only what is needed. That way you are not retrieving all the fields and all the records.

   SQL also provides a method for combining information from more than one table. This can minimize the use of lookup functions in reports and forms.

2. When you build the expression in Design view, you type a name for the expression followed by a colon and the expression you want to use. If you are typing the expression in the SELECT clause, you type the expression followed by the AS keyword and the name you want to call the expression.

3. The begin date used as a test value must be surrounded by pound symbols.

4. It allows you to retrieve a range of values between two values, but it acts like a greater-than and less-than combination. It will not display values equal to either of the specified values.

Day 15, "Examining Special-Use Queries"

1. It is quite common to select the destination table for the new records instead of the source table when selecting the tables in the Show table dialog.

2. There is a possibility of a typographical error.

3. A form allows you to set multiple criteria without several prompt windows.

Day 16, "Implementing Advanced Form Concepts"

1. It is too easy to modify data from a supporting table that affects all the records related to that table.

2. A subform enables you to combine information from more than one table without combining the data. This division makes it easier to group data for access and viewing.

3. If you are creating a form to automate actions in your database, you are attempting to minimize the time spent working with the data.

   The creation of a custom menu or toolbar also minimizes the time spent working with the form and report. You will spend less time wading through all the commands for the ones you need.

   A side benefit to creating custom forms and reports is that it is less likely you will inadvertently change the design of a form or report if the View button isn't so accessible.

Day 17, "Developing Professional-Quality Reports"

1. The Filter property allows you to create the criteria for the report. It is similar to creating a WHERE clause for a SQL statement without the WHERE keyword.

2. If you need to have some introductory or summary material on the first and last page of the report that differs from the page header and page footer.

3. If you are putting together a larger report and there is information that is static and not related to the database information or is created by someone else, linking allows that information to be compiled and formatted outside of Microsoft Access.

4. It allows the user of report to change the criteria and text elements without modifying the design of a report.

Day 18, "Examining VBA"

1. `Select Case` is best for testing one variable that can have several different values. If you use `If...Then...Else`, the code can be very difficult to read. `Select Case` makes it easy to determine what the value of the variable is.

2. It eliminates the possibility that you will edit your code unintentionally. It also make problems that occur seem less intimidating.

Day 19, "Working with VBA"

1. The `Open` event can be used because the recordset is already built, but there is a `Cancel` argument to allow you to close the form.

2. It is triggered as you enter the first character of the new record. With only one character for the record, you don't have enough data to compare to existing records.

3. To minimize the number of options viewed at a time to minimize confusion.

Day 20, "Understanding Access Security"

1. A workgroup ID needs to be between 4 and 20 characters.

2. The Users group has full permissions to begin with, and you usually don't really want the users to have full permissions.

3. A database password is a quick method for setting security.

Day 21, "Developer Considerations"

1. It increases the response speed of the system because everyone has their own copy of the system. It also makes it easier to upgrade the system because you do not have to worry about migrating data or closing the system down for an upgrade.

2. If the data moves, the links to the tables must be re-established, but that is not an issue if you use dynamic linking.

3. It minimizes the number of support issues that you have to resolve as the developer of the system.

INDEX

Symbols

& (ampersand), 187, 329, 472

' (apostrophe), 486

* (asterisk), 301, 328, 404

* (asterisk) wildcard, 107, 129-130

[ ] (brackets), 138, 377

, (comma), 375

/ (divisor) operand, 301

" " (double quotation marks), 187

... (ellipsis), 218

= (equal) operator, 398

= (equal sign), 187, 219, 325, 329, 333

= (equal sign) button, 333

! (exclamation point/bang), 114, 473-474

@;"Empty" Format property, 97

@@@-@@@@ Format property, 97

< Format property, 97

> Format property, 96-97

> (greater than) operator, 398

>= (greater than or equal to) operator, 398

> (greater than sign), 132, 333

< (less than) operator, 398

<= (less than or equal to) operator, 398

< (less than sign), 132

- (minus sign), 94

* (multiplication symbol), 328

< > (not equal) operator, 398

number/pound sign, 68, 396, 404

( ) (parentheses), 364

. (period), 375, 473-474

+ (plus sign), 90, 94

* (product) operand, 301

? (question mark), 404

? (question mark) wildcard, 130

; (semicolon), 386

_ (underscore), 621

3D effects, 276

A

abstract data, 16

acccessing menu commands, 596

accepting data (tables), 73

access
  code, 366
  restricting, 366, 632-633
  user, 445

Access
  applications
    adding code, 355
    creating, 311
  customizing, 39
  exiting, 629

X-Z

The Authoritative Encyclopedia of Computing

Resource Centers
Books & Software
Personal Bookshelf
WWW Yellow Pages
Online Learning
Special Offers
▶ *Choose the online ebooks
that you can view from your
personal workspace on our site.*
Site Search
Industry News

About MCP   Site Map   Product Support

Turn to the *Authoritative* Encyclopedia of Computing

You'll find over 150 full text books online, hundreds of shareware/freeware applications, online computing classes and 10 computing resource centers full of expert advice from the editors and publishers of:

- Adobe Press
- BradyGAMES
- Cisco Press
- Hayden Books
- Lycos Press
- New Riders

- Que
- Que Education & Training
- Sams Publishing
- Waite Group Press
- Ziff-Davis Press

The Authoritative Encyclopedia of Computing

Get the best information and learn about latest developments in:

- Design
- Graphics and Multimedia
- Enterprise Computing and DBMS
- General Internet Information
- Operating Systems
- Networking and Hardware
- PC and Video Gaming
- Productivity Applications
- Programming
- Web Programming and Administration
- Web Publishing

When you're looking for computing information, consult the authority. The Authoritative Encyclopedia of Computing at mcp.com.

SAMS
Teach Yourself
in 21 Days

Microsoft Office 2000
Laurie Ulrich
ISBN: 0-672-31448-7
$29.99/$44.95

Sams Teach Yourself in 21 Days *teaches you all the skills you need to master the basics and then moves on to the more advanced features and concepts. This series is designed for the way you learn. Go chapter by chapter through the step-by-step lessons or just choose those lessons that interest you the most.*

Other Sams Teach Yourself in 21 Days Titles

Microsoft SQL Server 7.0
Richard Waymire and Rick Sawtell
ISBN: 0-672-31290-5
$39.99/$59.95

Microsoft Windows NT Server 4
Peter Davis
ISBN: 0-672-31555-6
$29.99/$44.95

Microsoft Small Business Server 4.5
Harry Brelsford
ISBN: 0-672-31513-0
$29.99/$44.95

Microsoft Exchange Server 5.5
Jason Vanvalkenburgh
ISBN: 0-672-31525-4
$29.99/$44.95

Microsoft Visual Basic 6
Greg Perry
ISBN: 0-672-31310-3
$29.99/$44.95

Database Programming with Visual Basic
Smith and Amundsen
ISBN: 0-672-31308-1
$45.00/$67.95

SQL, Second Edition
Stephens, Plew, Morgan, and Perkins
ISBN: 0-672-31110-0
$39.99/$59.95

Internet Programming with Visual Basic 6
Peter Aitken
ISBN: 0-672-31459-2
$29.99/44.95

Microsoft Excel 2000 Programming
Matthew Harris
ISBN: 0-672-31543-2
$29.99/$44.95

Microsoft FrontPage 2000
Denise Tyler
ISBN: 0-672-31499-1
$39.99/$59.95

SAMS

www.samspublishing.com

All prices are subject to change.

Other Related Titles

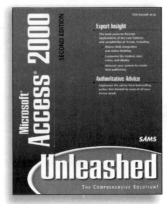

Microsoft Access 2000 Unleashed
Forte, Howe, and Ralston
ISBN: 0-672-31291-3
$39.99/$59.95

Visual Basic Applications for Office 2000 Unleashed
Paul McFedries
ISBN: 0-672-31567-X
$39.99/$59.95

Microsoft SQL Server 7 Unleashed
Greg Mable et. al.
ISBN: 0-672-31227-1
$49.99/$74.95

Sams Teach Yourself Microsoft Publisher 2000 in 24 Hours
Ned Snell
ISBN: 0-672-31572-6
$19.99/$29.95

Sams Teach Yourself Microsoft Outlook 2000 in 24 Hours
Herb Tyson
ISBN: 0-672-31449-5
$19.99/$29.95

Sams Teach Yourself Microsoft Word 2000 in 10 Minutes
Peter Aitken
ISBN: 0-672-31441-X
$12.99/$19.95

Microsoft Visual Basic 6 Unleashed
Rob Thayer
ISBN: 0-672-31309-X
$39.99/$59.95

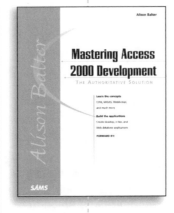

Alison Balter's Mastering Microsoft Access 2000 Development
Alison Balter
ISBN: 0-672-31484-3
$49.99/$74.95

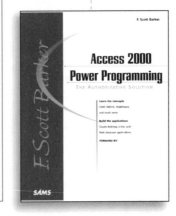

F. Scott Barker's Microsoft Access 2000 Power Programming
F. Scott Barker
ISBN: 0-672-31506-8
$49.99/$74.95

SAMS

www.samspublishing.com

All prices are subject to change.

Get **FREE** books and more...when you register this book online for our Personal Bookshelf Program

http://register.samspublishing.com/

SAMS

 Register online and you can sign up for our *FREE Personal Bookshelf Program*...unlimited access to the electronic version of more than 200 complete computer books — immediately! That means you'll have 100,000 pages of valuable information onscreen, at your fingertips!

 Plus, you can access product support, including complimentary downloads, technical support files, book-focused links, companion Web sites, author sites, and more!

 And, don't miss out on the opportunity to sign up for a *FREE subscription to a weekly e-mail newsletter* to help you stay current with news, announcements, sample book chapters and special events including sweepstakes, contests, and various product giveaways.

 We value your comments! Best of all, the entire registration process takes only a few minutes to complete...so go online and get the greatest value going—absolutely FREE!

Don't Miss Out On This Great Opportunity!

Sams®is a brand of Macmillan Computer Publishing USA—for more information, visit: *www.mcp.com*

Copyright ©1999 Macmillan Computer Publishing USA

What's on the CD

The companion CD-ROM contains the source code used in the book, graphics, and Access-related shareware products.

Windows 95 Installation Instructions

1. Insert the CD-ROM disc into your CD-ROM drive.
2. From the Windows 95 desktop, double-click the My Computer icon.
3. Double-click the icon representing your CD-ROM drive.
4. Double-click the icon titled START.EXE to run the CD-ROM interface.

 If Windows 95 is installed on your computer, and you have the AutoPlay feature enabled, the START.EXE program starts automatically whenever you insert the disc into your CD-ROM drive.

Windows NT Installation Instructions

1. Insert the CD-ROM disc into your CD-ROM drive.
2. From File Manager or Program Manager, choose Run from the File menu.
3. Type <drive>\START.EXE and press Enter, where <drive> corresponds to the drive letter of your CD-ROM. For example, if your CD-ROM is drive D:, type D:\START.EXE and press Enter. This will run the CD-ROM interface.